£2·20

AN ANTHOLOGY OF WORLD POETRY

An
Anthology of World Poetry

Edited by MARK VAN DOREN

In English Translations by
CHAUCER, SWINBURNE, DOWSON, SYMONS
ROSSETTI, WALEY, HERRICK, POPE
FRANCIS THOMPSON
AND OTHERS

Cassell and Company Ltd
LONDON, TORONTO, MELBOURNE
AND SYDNEY

First published in 1929

Printed in Great Britain

PREFACE

THE scope of this anthology is so wide—
in time from the thirty-fifth century B.C.
to the twentieth century A.D. and in space
from China and Japan around through India,
Persia, Arabia, Palestine, Egypt, Greece, and
Rome to Europe and America—that there is
no poet in human history who might not
have found a place in it had he ever fallen
into the hands of a becoming translator.
Not all the poets, of course, are here. The
book, big as it is, would have been still bigger
had I found more material exactly suited to
my purpose, which was to provide a collection
revealing those riches of the world's poetry
thus far gathered into readable English.

For my purpose was not to " represent "
these various poetical literatures. My experience with previous collections which have
attempted to do such a thing for " The Poets
and Poetry of Europe," " The Poets and
Poetry of Greece and Rome," and so on has
convinced me that nothing is deadlier than
a compilation designed with reference to the
originals alone. This is an anthology of the
world's best poetry in the best English I
could unearth, and when I found no good
English at all I left the poet out. Pindar,

for instance, is absent from these pages not
because I was unwilling to accept his great
reputation but because I discovered no
English version of him which made him
seem great—or even, for that matter, readable. Hence also some apparent oddities in
the proportions observed, certain minor poets
receiving, it would seem, more than their due
of space at the expense of ampler figures let
off with very little. I simply went by what
I found, preferring, if I had to be repre-
sentative at all, to represent the present state
of English translation in these cases, and
considering that there might be some interest
in the fact that a minor Frenchman, say, had
been given more attention in our language
than a major Persian or Russian.

Homer is not here because I decided to
exclude parts of long narrative poems, and
indeed never—though I broke the rule in a
few inconspicuous instances—to offer abridg-
ments. Virgil, Dante, Firdawsí, and Kalidasa
appear only through their shorter works ; and
Goethe, like the Greek tragic dramatists, is
represented in his masterpiece solely by lyrics
which may be said to stand alone. I might
add at this point that I have confined myself
to translations in verse. Much good work
has been done in prose, but for various
reasons I disregarded it.

If the book does after all fairly represent the

poetry of the world, and I am sanguine enough to think that it does on a scale not hitherto attempted, the credit goes to a race of translators which runs back at least as far as Chaucer. The index including their names at the end of the volume is almost a list of the best British and American poets, and indeed an interesting comparison might be made between that index and the succession of names to be found under the last three headings in the table of contents, where it will be seen that I have assembled, in order to make good my title, an anthology of original poems in the English language.

That this comparison should be extended to the poetry itself I do not suggest, since I am as much convinced as anybody that translation does not give us what creation gives. Yet I finish the anthology in the faith that it spreads a rich and beautiful feast, and in doing so I must yield to the temptation to point out some of the better and longer things —some of them hitherto not generally accessible—that are here provided. FitzGerald's Omar Khayyám and the Song of Songs take their places as a matter of course ; but Lafcadio Hearn's "The River of Heaven" from the Manyō Shū, E. Powys Mathers' "Black Marigolds" from Bilhana, Lady Anne Blunt's and Wilfrid Scawen Blunt's Ode from Imr El Kais, Robert Hillyer's twenty-seven prayers from the Egyptian Book of the Dead, Thomas Stanley's "Vigil of Venus," and Rossetti's New Life from Dante were not matters of course, and I should be happy if this volume helped to make them as widely known as they deserve to be. I am further tempted to speak of certain famous English poems which will introduce themselves to some readers now for the first time, perhaps, as translations. But I will resist that temptation and leave the pleasure of discovery to those readers.

I trust the volume will be easy to use. Towards that end I have made the table of contents complete and have supplied full indexes. The arrangement is by countries, or rather by languages, and within each section the order of poets is chronological, the name of the translator being given at the end of each poem. Occasionally I have prefixed a note to a poet's work in its proper place, not so much to give information about that poet as to suggest his quality and to make him stand out. Further than that there is no apparatus. The poetry is expected to speak for itself. The things which might be said about all these poets are so numerous, and sometimes so difficult to say, that no one, I like to think, could have said them in the space available.

Horace, Catullus, Heine, Hafiz, Sappho, and others are each rendered by various—

perhaps too various—hands. There would have been an advantage in presenting a single poet through a single translator, but on the whole I preferred variety, and I found the comparison of methods an engaging game. As usual, too, I was interested only in what seemed to me the best versions, and was content to take them from as many sources as might be.

I have much courteous assistance to acknowledge in another place, but wish to make particular mention now of the kindness of William Ellery Leonard, Max Eastman, and Allen Tate in giving me unpublished material for my collection. To Ludwig Lewisohn, E. Powys Mathers, Robert Hillyer, Jethro Bithell, Howard Mumford Jones, Ezra Pound, Havelock Ellis, and Louis Untermeyer I am indebted for generous and helpful letters. And to Mr. Albert Boni I am under greater obligations than I can well state. The book was his idea long ago; with it in mind he had collected an extensive library which was put entirely at my disposal; and throughout the labour of compilation he was an invaluable adviser.

MARK VAN DOREN.

New York, 1928.

ACKNOWLEDGMENTS

THE editor and publishers herewith render thanks to the following individuals for permission to use their poems and translations:

Hilda Aldington ("H. D."), Mary Austin, John Bailey, Henry Adams Bellows, Jethro Bithell, G. K. Chesterton, Padraic Colum, C. Fillingham Coxwell, L. Cranmer-Byng, Walter de la Mare, Babette Deutsch and Avrahm Yarmolinsky, John Dos Passos, Max Eastman, Havelock Ellis, William Dudley Foulke, Robert Frost, H. W. Garrod, H. J. C. Grierson, G. B. Grundy, Robert Hillyer, Aldous Huxley, Douglas Hyde, A. V. Williams Jackson, Robinson Jeffers, Howard Mumford Jones, Margaret Jourdain, Richard Le Gallienne, Jessie Lemont, William Ellery Leonard, Ludwig Lewisohn, Vachel Lindsay, Edward Marsh, E. Powys Mathers, P. E. Matheson, Paul Elmer More, Margarete Münsterberg, R. A. Nicholson, Seumas O'Sullivan, Ezra Pound, Curtis Hidden Page, Edwin Arlington Robinson, W. H. D. Rouse, George William Russell ("A. E."), Arthur W. Ryder, Maurice Samuel, Carl Sandburg, George Santayana, Joseph T. Shipley, Constance Lindsay Skinner, Dulcie L. Smith, Herbert J. Spinden, James Stephens, Marie Syrkin, Wilfrid Thorley, Louis Untermeyer, Arthur Waley, Charles Whibley, and F. A. Wright;

And to the following publishers, agents, or individuals holding copyright in the poems specified for permission to reprint:

George Allen & Unwin, Ltd., for J. M. Synge's "Prelude" and "In Kerry," from his *Poems*; Gilbert Murray's translation from *Hippolytus*.

The American Scandinavian Foundation, for Henry Adams Bellows' translation of "Voluspo" from *The Poetic Edda*, and for Robert Hillyer's translation of "There is a Charming Land" from *A Book of Danish Verse*.

D. Appleton & Company, for Margarete Münsterberg's poems from *A Harvest of German Verse*.

John Bailey, for permission to use his translation of Carducci's *Primo Vere*.

George Bell & Sons, Ltd., for translations from Charles Stuart Calverley's *Collected Poems*; Richard Garnett's translation from Heine.

Ernest Benn, Ltd., for W. B. Yeats's "To an Isle in the Water" and "When you are Old"; verse from Frank Nicholson's *Old German Love Songs*; translations from the Irish, by Douglas Hyde.

Jethro Bithell, for permission to use his translations from *The Minnesingers*.

ACKNOWLEDGMENTS

A. & C. Black, Ltd., for translations by John Addington Symonds from *Studies in the Greek Poets.*

Basil Blackwell, for translations by E. Powys Mathers, from *Sung to Shuyar, The Garden of Bright Waters,* and *Black Marigolds;* A. J. Butler's translation of Erinna, from *Amaranth and Asphodel.*

Wilfrid Scawen Blunt's executors, for "Imr-el-Kais," from *The Seven Golden Odes of Pagan Arabia.*

Horatio F. Brown's Trust, for verses from John Addington Symonds's *Wine, Women, and Song.*

Burns, Oates & Washbourne, Ltd., for Francis Thompson's "A Sunset" and "Heard on the Mountains," from his *Collected Works;* G. K. Chesterton's "Happy who like Ulysses," from *Poems;* Alice Meynell's "I go by Road" and "The Shepherdess."

Jonathan Cape, Ltd., for James Joyce's "I hear an Army," from *Chamber Music;* W. H. Davies's "Leisure."

Chatto and Windus, for George MacDonald's translation of Uhland's "In a Lonely Garden Walking." Permission to include this has also been kindly accorded by the executors of the late George MacDonald.

Constable & Co., Ltd., for Arthur Waley's translations from Chinese, from 170 *Chinese Poems;* translations from Helen Waddell's *Lyrics from the Chinese;* Lafcadio Hearn's "River of Heaven"; two poems by George Santayana; George Meredith's "Beauty Roh-traut" (also by permission of Charles Scribners' Sons, New York).

J. M. Dent & Sons, Ltd., for Romesh Dutt's "Indra," from *Indian Poetry;* Arthur W. Ryder's translations from *Kalidasa;* W. E. Leonard's translations from the Latin, from *Lucretius.*

P. J. & A. E. Dobell, for James Thomson's translations from Heine.

Havelock Ellis, for permission to use his translations from the Spanish.

Faber & Gwyer, Ltd., for T. S. Eliot's verses.

Richard S. Garnett, for kind permission to include various poems by the late Richard Garnett.

George G. Harrap & Co., Ltd., for translations from the French by Wilfrid Thorley, from *A Bouquet from France.*

Harper & Brothers, for Natalie Curtis's translations from *The Indians' Book.*

William Heinemann, Ltd., for Gertrude Bell's verses from *Poems from the Divan of Hafiz;* Lorna de' Lucchi's translations from Alfieri and Leopardi, from *An Anthology of Italian Poems;* translations by Sir Edmund Gosse, from *The Collected Poems of Edmund Gosse;* Wilfrid Thorley's "Sound of the Horn," from *Fleur de Lys;* poems by A. C. Swinburne.

Kegan Paul, Trench, Trübner & Co., Ltd., for Sir Edwin Arnold's

"Hymn to Vishnu," from *Indian Poetry*; C. F. Coxwell's "The Peasant and the Sheep," from *Kriloff's Fables*.

John Lane, the Bodley Head, Ltd., for "Non sum qualis eram," "Vitæ summa brevis," and two translations from Paul Verlaine, from *The Poems of Ernest Dowson*; translations by Richard Garnett, from *Dante, Petrarch, Camoens*, for the inclusion of which poems Mr. R. S. Garnett has kindly given his permission; "The Doves," from Katharine Tynan Hinkson's *Miracle Plays*; translations by Babette Deutsch, from *Modern Russian Poetry*; Romilda Rendel's translations from Leopardi and Carducci, from *An Anthology of Italian Lyrics*.

Mrs. Walter Leaf, for permission to use Walter Leaf's *Idyll of the Rose*.

Longmans, Green & Co., Ltd., for Andrew Lang's translations from Greek and French, published in *Poems*.

Macmillan & Co., Ltd., for Thomas Hardy's verses from *Collected Poems*; "A Mountain Wind" and "Immortality," from *Collected Poems* of "A. E."; James Stephens's "Deirdre" and "The Daisies"; W. E. Henley's translations from the French; Wilfrid Scawen Blunt's "Camel-Rider" and "Days of our Youth" in his *From the Arabic*; Matthew Arnold's "An Horatian Echo"; Vachel Lindsay's "Eagle that is Forgotten," from *Collected Poems*; William Butler Yeats's "The Cold Heaven," from *Early Poems*, for the inclusion of which Mr. Yeats's permission has also been given; Padraic Colum's "River-mates" and "A Drover," permission for this has also been granted by the Macmillan Company of New York.

John Masefield, for permission to use two translations from the Spanish and his "Sonnet" from *Lollingdon Downs*.

Methuen & Co., Ltd., Rudyard Kipling's "Recessional," for the inclusion of which Mr. Kipling also gave his kind consent.

John Murray, for translations from the Italian by John Addington Symonds, from *Italian Byways, Renaissance in Italy*, and *Sonnets of Michelangelo*; L. Cranmer-Byng's translations, from *Odes of Confucius*; Allen Upward's "The Pear-tree"; Dulcie Lawrence Smith's translation from *Mutamid*, the last three authors appearing in the *Wisdom of the East* series.

Moira O'Neill, for permission to reprint "Corrymeela" from her *Songs of the Glens of Antrim*.

Open Court Company, for W. E. Leonard's translation from Æsop.

Seumas O'Sullivan, for permission to include his poems and translations.

Oxford University Press, for W. H. Fyfe's translation of "Sleep," from "Statius"; H. W. Garrod's "Love and Death," Catullus, from the *Oxford Book of Latin Verse*; Frederick York Powell's translation of

ACKNOWLEDGMENTS

Maeterlinck's "Last Word" and Paul Fort's "Ballade"; H. A. R. Gibb's "Cordova" from *Arabic Literature*; John Todhunter's translations, from *Heine's Book of Songs*; Austin Dobson's translation from the French, from *Collected Poems*; W. D. Foulke's "Petrarch," from *Some Love Songs of Petrarch*; P. E. Matheson's "The Road," and "A Night in a Village," from *Holy Russia*; Arthur Waley's translation from the Japanese, from *Japanese Poetry*.

Cecil Palmer, for verses translated from Greek and Latin by E. A. Robinson.

James B. Pinker & Sons, for Aldous Huxley's "L'Après-Midi d'un Faune" and "First Philosopher's Song"; Walter de la Mare's "Farewell"; Robert Graves's "Lost Love."

The Richards Press, Ltd., for Walter Leaf's "Lion over the Tomb of Leonidas," from *Little Poems from the Greek*.

George Routledge and Sons, Ltd., for F. A. Wright's "Ah, woe is me," "Hylas," and "Winter at Tomi" in Broadway Translations of *Mirror of Venus* and *Lover's Handbook*.

Walter Scott Publishing Co., Ltd. (in liquidation), for William Morris's translations of Volsunga Sagas, from Camelot Classics; translations from French and German by William Toynbee, Elizabeth Craigmyle, and Kate F. Kroeker, in Canterbury Poets.

Martin Secker, Ltd., for Emily Dickinson's "Success" and "A Wounded Deer leaps Highest," from *Complete Poems*; James Elroy Flecker's "Don Juan in Hell," and "Pannyra of the Golden Heel," from *Collected Poems*; Lord Alfred Douglas's "Le Balcon" and "Harmonie du Soir," from *Collected Poems*; Edna St. Vincent Millay's "Sonnet," from *The Harp Weaver and Other Poems*.

Arthur Symons, who courteously allowed many verses of his to be included.

Talbot Press, Ltd., Dublin, for "The Spark," from *The Complete Poetical Works of Joseph Mary Plunkett*; "John-John," and a translation of Padraic Pearse's "Ideal" from *The Complete Poetical Works of Thomas MacDonagh*.

Truslove and Hanson, fort ranlations from the French, from Margaret Jourdain's *Poems*.

University Press, Cambridge, for verses from R. A. Nicholson's *Translations of Eastern Poetry and Prose*, and other volumes; T. R. Glover's translation of Ausonius, from *Life and Letters in the Fourth Century*.

Charles Whibley, for permission to use his translations from the Greek.

Williams and Norgate, Ltd., translations from Sir Charles Lyall's *Ancient Arabian Poetry*.

TABLE OF SECTIONS

CONTENTS

CHINESE

CONTENTS

CONTENTS

CONTENTS

CONTENTS

CONTENTS

EGYPTIAN

CONTENTS

GREEK

CONTENTS

CONTENTS

CONTENTS

CONTENTS

CONTENTS

CONTENTS

CONTENTS

CONTENTS

CONTENTS

CONTENTS

CONTENTS

CONTENTS

CONTENTS

CONTENTS

CONTENTS

CONTENTS

CONTENTS

CONTENTS

CONTENTS

CONTENTS

CONTENTS

CONTENTS

CONTENTS

CONTENTS

CONTENTS

CONTENTS

CONTENTS

CONTENTS

CONTENTS

CONTENTS

CONTENTS

CONTENTS

CONTENTS

CHINESE

FROM THE SHI KING, OR BOOK OF ODES

Compiled c. 500 B.C.

THE Shi King was compiled by Confucius from earlier collections which had been long existent. It was through the Odes that Confucius taught his own generation to understand the manners and customs and simple feelings of the men of old. These are the natural songs that float upward from the happy valleys and down the sedge-strewn banks of the wandering K'e. They are naïve and bright as on their birthday, with that most precious quality of truth and unconscious art which never lets them tarnish or fade.—L. CRANMER-BYNG.

The Morning Glory

THE morning glory climbs above my head,
Pale flowers of white and purple, blue and red.
     I am disquieted.

Down in the withered grasses something stirred;
I thought it was his footfall that I heard.
     Then a grasshopper chirred.

I climbed the hill just as the new moon showed,
I saw him coming on the southern road.
     My heart lays down its load.

Helen Waddell

How Goes the Night?

HOW goes the night?
Midnight has still to come.
Down in the court the torch is blazing bright;
I hear far off the throbbing of the drum.

How goes the night?
The night is not yet gone.
I hear the trumpets blowing on the height;
The torch is paling in the coming dawn.

How goes the night?
The night is past and done.
The torch is smoking in the morning light,
The dragon banner floating in the sun.

Helen Waddell

Under the Pondweed

UNDER the pondweed do the great fish go,
In the green darkness where the rushes grow.
    The King is in Hao.

Under the pondweed do the great fish lie;
Down in Hao the sunny hours go by.
    The King holds revelry.

Under the pondweed do the great fish sleep;
The dragon-flies are drowsy in the heat.
    The King is drinking deep.

Helen Waddell

I Wait my Lord

THE gourd has still its bitter leaves,
And deep the crossing at the ford.
    I wait my lord.

The ford is brimming to its banks;
The pheasant cries upon her mate.
    My lord is late.

The boatman still keeps beckoning,
And others reach their journey's end.
I wait my friend.

Helen Waddell

The Pear-tree

THIS shade-bestowing pear-tree, thou
Hurt not, nor lay its leafage low;
Beneath it slept the Duke of Shaou.

This shade-bestowing pear-tree, thou
Hurt not, nor break one leafy bough;
Beneath it stayed the Duke of Shaou.

This shade-bestowing pear-tree, thou
Hurt not, nor bend one leafy bough;
Beneath it paused the Duke of Shaou.

Allen Upward

Maytime

DEEP in the grass there lies a dead gazelle,
The tall white grass enwraps her where she fell.
With sweet thoughts natural to spring,
A pretty girl goes wandering
With lover that would lead astray.

The little dwarf oaks hide a leafy dell,
Far in the wilds there lies a dead gazelle;
The tall white grass enwraps her where she fell,
And beauty, like a gem, doth fling
Bright radiance through the blinds of spring.
"Ah, gently! do not disarray
My kerchief! gently, pray!
Nor make the watch-dog bark
Under my lattice dark."

L. Cranmer-Byng

You Will Die

YOU have coats and robes,
But you do not trail them;
You have chariots and horses,
But you do not ride them.
By and by you will die,
And another will enjoy them.

You have courtyards and halls,
But they are not sprinkled and swept;
You have bells and drums,
But they are not struck.
By and by you will die,
And another will possess them.

You have wine and food;
Why not play daily on your lute,
That you may enjoy yourself now
And lengthen your days ?
By and by you will die,
And another will take your place.

H. A. Giles

Woman

A CLEVER man builds a city,
A clever woman lays one low;
With all her qualifications, that clever woman
Is but an ill-omened bird.
A woman with a long tongue
Is a flight of steps leading to calamity;
For disorder does not come from heaven,
But is brought about by women.
Among those who cannot be trained or taught
Are women and eunuchs.

H. A. Giles

ANONYMOUS

C. 124 B.C.

Fighting South of the Castle

THEY fought south of the Castle,
They died north of the wall.
They died in the moors and were not buried.
Their flesh was the food of crows.
" Tell the crows we are not afraid;
We have died in the moors and cannot be buried.
Crows, how can our bodies escape you ? "
The waters flowed deep
And the rushes in the pool were dark.
The riders fought and were slain:
Their horses wander neighing.
By the bridge there was a house.
Was it south, was it north ?
The harvest was never gathered.
How can we give you your offerings ?
You served your Prince faithfully,
Though all in vain.
I think of you, faithful soldiers;
Your service shall not be forgotten,
For in the morning you went out to battle
And at night you did not return.

Arthur Waley

ANONYMOUS

1st century B.C.

Old and New

SHE went up the mountain to pluck wild herbs;
She came down the mountain and met her former
    husband.
She knelt down and asked her former husband
" What do you find your new wife like ? "

" My new wife, although her talk is clever,
Cannot charm me as my old wife could.
In beauty of face there is not much to choose,
But in usefulness they are not at all alike.
My new wife comes in from the road to meet me;
My old wife always came down from her tower.
My new wife is clever at embroidering silk;
My old wife was good at plain sewing.
Of silk embroidery one can do an inch a day;
Of plain sewing, more than five feet.
Putting her silks by the side of your sewing,
I see that the new will not compare with the old."

Arthur Waley

ANONYMOUS

1st century ?

Old Poem

COLD, cold the year draws to its end,
The crickets and grasshoppers make a doleful
chirping.
The chill wind ceases its violence.
My wandering love has no coat to cover him.
He gave his embroidered furs to the Lady of Lo,
But from me his bedfellow he is quite estranged.
Sleeping alone in the depth of the long night
In a dream I thought I saw the light of his face.
My dear one thought of our old joys together,
He came in his chariot and gave me the front reins.
I wanted so to prolong our play and laughter,
To hold his hand and go back with him in his coach.
But, when he had come he would not stay long
Nor stop to go with me to the Inner Chamber.
Truly without the falcon's wings to carry me
How can I rival the flying wind's swiftness ?
I go and lean at the gate and think of my grief,
My falling tears wet the double gates.

Arthur Waley

TSO SSŪ

3rd century

The Scholar in the Narrow Street

FLAP, flap, the captive bird in the cage
Beating its wings against the four corners.
Depressed, depressed the scholar in the narrow street:
Clasping a shadow, he dwells in an empty house.
When he goes out, there is nowhere for him to go:
Bunches and brambles block up his path.
He composes a memorial, but it is rejected and un‹
read,
He is left stranded, like a fish in a dry pond.
Without—he has not a single farthing of salary:
Within—there is not a peck of grain in his larder.
His relations upbraid him for his lack of success:
His friends and callers daily decrease in number.
Su Ch'in used to go preaching in the North
And Li Ssū sent a memorandum to the West.
I once hoped to pluck the fruits of life:
But now alas, they are all withered and dry.
Though one drinks at a river, one cannot drink
more than a bellyful ;
Enough is good, but there is no use in satiety.
The bird in a forest can perch but on one bough,
And this should be the wise man's pattern.

Arthur Waley

FU HSÜAN

Died 278

A Gentle Wind

A GENTLE wind fans the calm night:
A bright moon shines on the high tower.
A voice whispers, but no one answers when I call:
A shadow stirs, but no one comes when I beckon.

The kitchen-man brings in a dish of lentils:
Wine is there, but I do not fill my cup.
Contentment with poverty is Fortune's best gift:
Riches and Honour are the handmaids of Disaster.
Though gold and gems by the world are sought and
prized,
To me they seem no more than weeds or chaff.

Arthur Waley

CHAN FANG-SHENG

4th century

Sailing Homeward

CLIFFS that rise a thousand feet
Without a break,
Lake that stretches a hundred miles
Without a wave,
Sands that are white through all the year,
Without a stain,
Pine-tree woods, winter and summer
Ever-green,
Streams that for ever flow and flow
Without a pause,
Trees that for twenty thousand years
Your vows have kept,
You have suddenly healed the pain of a traveller's
heart,
And moved his brush to write a new song.

Arthur Waley

T'AO CH'IEN

365–427

I Built My Hut

I BUILT my hut in a zone of human habitation,
Yet near me there sounds no noise of horse or coach.
Would you know how that is possible ?
A heart that is distant creates a wilderness round it.

I pluck chrysanthemums under the eastern hedge,
Then gaze long at the distant summer hills.
The mountain air is fresh at the dusk of day:
The flying birds two by two return.
In these things there lies a deep meaning;
Yet when we would express it, words suddenly fail us.

Arthur Waley

Shady, Shady

SHADY, shady the wood in front of the Hall:
At midsummer full of calm shadows.
The south wind follows summer's train:
With its eddying puffs it blows open my coat.
I am free from ties and can live a life of retirement.
When I rise from sleep, I play with books and harp.
The lettuce in the garden still grows moist:
Of last year's grain there is always plenty left.
Self-support should maintain strict limits:
More than enough is not what I want.
I grind millet and make good wine:
When the wine is heated, I pour it out for myself.
My little children are playing at my side,
Learning to talk, they babble unformed sounds.
These things have made me happy again
And I forget my lost cap of office.
Distant, distant I gaze at the white clouds:
With a deep yearning I think of the Sages of Antiquity.

Arthur Waley

EMPEROR CH'IEN WĒN-TI

6th century

Lo-Yang

A BEAUTIFUL place is the town of Lo-yang :
The big streets are full of spring light.
The lads go driving out with harps in their hands:
The mulberry girls go out to the fields with their
baskets.

Golden whips glint at the horses' flanks,
Gauze sleeves brush the green boughs.
Racing dawn, the carriages come home,—
And the girls with their high baskets full of fruit.

Arthur Waley

LI T'AI,PO

701–762

IT is permitted to very few to live in the hearts of their countrymen as Li T'ai,po has lived in the hearts of the Chinese. There is no doubt at all that in Li T'ai,po we have one of the world's greatest lyrists.— FLORENCE AYSCOUGH.

In the Mountains on a Summer Day

GENTLY I stir a white feather fan,
With open shirt sitting in a green wood.
I take off my cap and hang it on a jutting stone;
A wind from the pine,tree trickles on my bare head.

Arthur Waley

TU FU

712–770

*ENGLISH writers on Chinese literature are fond of announcing that Li T'ai,po is China's greatest poet ; the Chinese themselves, however, award this place to Tu Fu. We may put it that Li T'ai,po was the people's poet, and Tu Fu the poet of scholars.—*ARTHUR WALEY.

The Emperor

ON a throne of new gold the Son of the Sky
is sitting among his Mandarins. He shines
with jewels and is like a sun surrounded by stars.

The Mandarins speak gravely of grave things;
but the Emperor's thought has flown out by
the open window.

In her pavilion of porcelain the Empress is
sitting among her women. She is like a bright
flower among leaves.

She dreams that her beloved stays too long
at council, and wearily she moves her fan.

A breathing of perfumed air kisses the face
of the Emperor.

" My beloved moves her fan, and sends me a
perfume from her lips."

Towards the pavilion of porcelain walks the
Emperor, shining with his jewels ; and leaves his
grave Mandarins to look at each other in
Silence.

E. Powys Mathers

PO CHÜI

772–846

THERE is a story that he was in the habit of reading his poems to
an old peasant woman and altering any expression which she could
not understand. The poems of his contemporaries were mere elegant
diversions which enabled the scholar to display his erudition, or the
literary juggler his dexterity. No poet in the world can ever have
enjoyed greater contemporary popularity than Po.—ARTHUR WALEY.

Rejoicing at the Arrival of Ch'en Hsiung

WHEN the yellow bird's note was almost stopped ;
And half formed the green plum's fruit ;
Sitting and grieving that spring things were over,
I rose and entered the Eastern Garden's gate.

I carried my cup and was dully drinking alone:
Suddenly I heard a knocking sound at the door.
Dwelling secluded, I was glad that someone had
    come;
How much the more, when I saw it was Ch'en
    Hsiung !
At ease and leisure,—all day we talked;
Crowding and jostling, the feelings of many years,
How great a thing is a single cup of wine !
For it makes us tell the story of our whole lives.

Arthur Waley

On Being Sixty

BETWEEN thirty and forty, one is distracted by the
    Five Lusts;
Between seventy and eighty, one is a prey to a
    hundred diseases.
But from fifty to sixty one is free from all ills;
Calm and still—the heart enjoys rest.
I have put behind me Love and Greed; I have done
    with Profit and Fame;
I am still short of illness and decay and far from de-
    crepit age.
Strength of limb I still possess to seek the rivers and
    hills;
Still my heart has spirit enough to listen to flutes and
    strings.
At leisure I open new wine and taste several cups;
Drunken I recall old poems and sing a whole volume.
Meng-te has asked for a poem and herewith I exhort
    him
Not to complain of three-score, "the time of
    obedient ears."

Arthur Waley

Remembering Golden Bells

RUINED and ill,—a man of two score;
    Pretty and guileless,—a girl of three.
Not a boy,—but still better than nothing:
To soothe one's feeling,—from time to time a kiss!
There came a day,—they suddenly took her from me;
Her soul's shadow wandered I know not where.
And when I remember how just at the time she died
She lisped strange sounds, beginning to learn to talk,
Then I know that the ties of flesh and blood
Only bind us to a load of grief and sorrow.
At last, by thinking of the time before she was born,
By thought and reason I drove the pain away.
Since my heart forgot her, many days have passed
And three times winter has changed to spring.
This morning, for a little, the old grief came back,
Because, in the road, I met her foster-nurse.

Arthur Waley

YUAN CHĒN

779–831

The Pitcher

I DREAMT I climbed to a high, high plain;
    And on the plain I found a deep well.
My throat was dry with climbing and I longed to drink,
And my eyes were eager to look into the cool shaft.
I walked round it; I looked right down;
I saw my image mirrored on the face of the pool.
An earthen pitcher was sinking into the black depths;
There was no rope to pull it to the well-head.
I was strangely troubled lest the pitcher should be lost,
And started wildly running to look for help.
From village to village I scoured that high plain;
The men were gone: the dogs leapt at my throat.

I came back and walked weeping round the well;
Faster and faster the blinding tears flowed—
Till my own sobbing suddenly woke me up;
My room was silent, no one in the house stirred;
The flame of my candle flickered with a green smoke;
The tears I had shed in the candle-light.
A bell sounded ; I knew it was the midnight-chime;
I sat up in bed and tried to arrange my thoughts:
The plain in my dream was the graveyard at
  Ch'ang-an,
Those hundred acres of untilled land.
The soil heavy and the mounds heaped high ;
And the dead below them laid in deep troughs.
Deep are the troughs, yet sometimes dead men
Find their way to the world above the grave.
And to-night my love who died long ago
Came into my dream as the pitcher sunk in the well.
That was why the tears suddenly streamed from my
  eyes,
Streamed from my eyes and fell on the collar of my
  dress.

Arthur Waley

OU-YANG HSIU

11th century

The Cicada

IN the summer of the first year of Chia-yu (A.D. 1056)
there was a great flood. By order of the Emperor I
went to the Wine Spring Temple to pray for fine
weather, when I heard a cicada singing. Upon which
subject I wrote this poem :

Hushed was the courtyard of the temple;
Solemn stood I, gazing
At the bright roofs and gables,
The glorious summits of that towering shrine.

Untroubled were my thoughts, intently prayed
My fasting soul, for every wandering sense
Was gathered to its home.
Unmoved I watched the motions of the world,
Saw deep into the nature of ten thousand things.
Suddenly the rain was over, no wind stirred
The morning-calm; round all the sky
Was cloudless blue, and the last thunder rolled.
Then we, to strew sweet-scented herbs upon the floor,
Drew near the coloured cloister, by whose side
Some old trees grew amid the grass
Of the deserted court.   Here was a thing that cried
Upon a tree-top, sucking the shrill wind
To wail it back in a long whistling note—
That clasping in its arms
A tapering twig perpetually sighed,
Now shrill as flute, now soft as mandolin;
Sometimes a piercing cry
Choked at its very uttering, sometimes a cold tune
Dwindled to silence, then suddenly flowed again,
A single note, wandering in strange keys,
An air, yet fraught
With undertone of hidden harmony.
" What creature can this be ? "   " Cicada is its
        name."
" Are you not he, cicada,
Of whom I have heard tell you can transform
Your body, magically moulding it
To new estate ?   Are you not he who, born
Upon the dung-heap, coveted the sky,
The clean and open air ;
Found wings to mount the wind, yet skyward sailing
Upon a leafy tree-top checked your flight,
Pleased with its trim retreat ?   Are you not he
Who with the dew for drink, the wind for food,
Grows never old nor languid ; who with looped
        locks

Frames womanish beauty?
Again your voice, cicada!
Not grave; not gay; part Lydian,
Part Dorian your tune that, suddenly begun,
Suddenly ceases.
Long since have I marvelled
How of ten thousand creatures there is not one
But has its tune; how as each season takes its turn
A hundred new birds sing, each weather wakes
A hundred insects from their sleep.
Now lisp the mango-birds
Like pretty children, prattling at their play.
As shuttle at the sounding loom
The tireless cricket creaks. Beautiful the flexions
Of tongue and trilling throat, how valiantly
They spend themselves to do it!
And even the croakers of the pond,
When they get rain to fill
Their miry, parching puddles, while they sip
New rivulets and browse the soppy earth,
Sing through the live-long night. And like enough
May frogs be passionate; but oh, what seeks
The silent worm in song?
These and a thousand others, little and great,
Too many to name them all,
Myriads of creatures—each after its own shape and
    skin,
Hold at their season ceaseless tournament of song;
But swiftly, swiftly
Their days run out, time transmutes them, and there
    is silence,
Desert-silence where they sang.

                    "Alas, philosophy has taught
That the transcending mind in its strange, level
    world
Seeks not kinds, contraries, classes or degrees.

And if of living things
Man once seemed best, what has he but a knack
Of facile speech, what but a plausible scheme
Of signs and ciphers that perpetuate
His thoughts and phrases ?   And on these expends
His brooding wits, consumes his vital breath;
One droning out the extremity of his woe,
Another to the wide world publishing
His nobleness of heart !

                " Thus, though he shares
The brief span of all creatures, yet his song
A hundred ages echoes after him.
But you, cicada,
What know you of this ?   Only for yourself
You make your music. . . ."
            So was I pondering, comparing,
Setting difference by difference, gain by gain,
When suddenly the clouds came back and overhead
The storm blazed and crashed, spilling huge drops
Out of the rumbling sky. . . .
                  And silent now
Was the cicada's voice.

                        Arthur Waley

JAPANESE

FROM THE MANYŌ-SHŪ

Compiled 8th century

JAPANESE poetry, as an art, may be said to begin with the Manyo Shu (" Ten-thousand Leaves Collection "). The chief poets of the Manyo were Kakinomoto no Hitomaro and Yamabe no Akahito.— ARTHUR WALEY.

Princess Daihaku

7th century

HOW will you manage
To cross alone
The autumn mountain
Which was so hard to get across
Even when we went the two of us together ?

Hioki No Ko-Okima

7th century

ON the shore of Nawa
The smoke of the saltburners,
When evening comes,
Failing to get across,
Trails over the mountain.

Hitomaro

c. 700

I

O BOY cutting grass
On that hill,
Do not cut like that !
Just as it is
I want it to be grass for the honourable horse
Of my Lord who is going to deign to come.

2

On the moor of Kasuga
The rising of smoke is visible.
The women surely
Must have plucked lettuces on the spring
    moor and must be boiling them.

3

For my Sister's sake
In plucking with my hand
The plum-blossom of the top branch
I have got wet
With the dew of the lower boughs!

4

May the men who are born
From my time onwards
Never, never meet
With a path of love-making
Such as mine has been!

The Priest Hakutsu

c. 704

O PINE-TREE standing
    At the side of the stone house,
When I look at you,
It is like seeing face to face
The men of old time.

Yakamochi

d. 785

1

WHEN evening comes
I will leave the door open beforehand and then wait
For him who said he would come
To meet me in my dreams.

2

By way of pretext
I said " I will go
And look at
The condition of the bamboo fence ";
But it was really to see you !

The Lady of Sakanoye
8th century

1

THE dress that my Brother has put on is thin,
O wind from Sao,
Do not blow hard
Till he reaches home.

2

My heart, thinking
" How beautiful he is "
Is like a swift river
Which though one dams it and dams it,
Will still break through.

3

Unknown love
Is as bitter a thing
As the maiden-lily
Which grows in the thickets
Of the summer moor.

Anonymous

SHALL we make love
Indoors
On this night when the moon has begun to shine
Over the rushes
Of Inami Moor ?

Arthur Waley

The River of Heaven

HE is coming, my long-desired lord, whom I have been waiting to meet here, on the banks of the River of Heaven. . . . The moment of loosening my girdle is nigh.

Over the Rapids of the Everlasting Heaven, floating in his boat, my lord will doubtless deign to come to me this very night.

Though winds and clouds to either bank may freely come or go, between myself and my far-away spouse no message whatever may pass.

To the opposite bank one might easily fling a pebble; yet, being separated from him by the River of Heaven, alas! to hope for a meeting (except in autumn) is utterly useless.

From the day that the autumn wind began to blow (I kept saying to myself), "Ah! when shall we meet?"— but now my beloved, for whom I waited and longed, has come indeed!

Though the waters of the River of Heaven have not greatly risen (yet, to cross) this near stream and to wait upon my lord and lover remains impossible.

Though she is so near that the waving of her (long) sleeves can be distinctly seen, yet there is no way to cross the stream before the season of autumn.

When we were separated, I had seen her for a moment only,—and dimly as one sees a flying midge; now I must vainly long for her as before, until time of our next meeting!

Methinks that Hikoboshi must be rowing his boat to meet his wife,—for a mist (as of oar-spray) is rising over the course of the Heavenly Stream.

While awaiting my lord on the misty shore of the River of Heaven, the skirts of my robe have somehow become wet.

On the River of Heaven, at the place of the august ferry, the sound of the water has become loud: perhaps my long-awaited lord will soon be coming in his boat.

As Tanabata (slumbers) with her long sleeves rolled up, until the reddening of the dawn, do not, O storks of the river-shallows, awaken her by your cries.

(She sees that) a mist is spreading across the River of Heaven. . . . " To-day, to-day," she thinks, " my long-awaited lord will probably come over in his boat."

By the ferry of Yasu, on the River of Heaven, the boat is floating : I pray you tell my beloved that I stand here and wait.

Though I (being a Star-god) can pass freely to and fro through the great sky,—yet to cross over the River of Heaven, for your sake, was weary work indeed !

From the august Age of the God-of-Eight-Thousand-Spears, she had been my spouse in secret only; yet now, because of my constant longing for her, our relation has become known to man.

From the time when heaven and earth were parted she has been my own wife:—yet, to be with her, I must always wait till autumn.

With my beloved, of the ruddy-tinted cheeks, this night indeed will I descend into the bed of the River of Heaven, to sleep on a pillow of stone.

When I see the water-grasses of the River of Heaven bend in the autumn wind (I think to myself): " The time for our meeting seems to have come."

When I feel in my heart a sudden longing for my husband, then on the River of Heaven the sound of the rowing of the night-boat is heard, and the plash of the oars resounds.

In the night when I am reposing with my (now) far-away spouse, having exchanged jewel-pillows with her, let not the cock crow, even though the day should dawn.

Though for a myriad ages we should remain hand in hand and face to face, our exceeding love could never come to an end. (Why then would Heaven deem it necessary to part us ?)

The white cloth which Tanabata has woven for my sake, in that dwelling of hers, is now, I think, being made into a robe for me.

Though she be far-away, and hidden from me by five hundred layers of white cloud, still shall I turn my gaze each night toward the dwelling-place of my younger sister (wife).

When autumn comes, and the river-mists spread over the Heavenly Stream, I turn toward the river (and long); and the nights of my longing are many !

But once in the whole year, and only upon the seventh night (of the seventh month), to meet the beloved person—and lo ! the day has dawned before our mutual love could express (or " satisfy ") itself !

The love-longing of one whole year having ended to-night, every day from to-morrow I must again pine for him as before.

Hikoboshi and Tanabata-tsumé are to meet each other to-night;—ye waves of the River of Heaven, take heed that ye do not rise !

Oh ! that white cloud driven by the autumn-wind— can it be the heavenly hire of Tanabata-tsumé ?

Because he is my not-often-to-be-met-beloved, hasten to row the boat across the River of Heaven ere the night be advanced.

Late in the night, a mist spreads over the River of Heaven; and the sound of the oar of Hikoboshi is heard.

On the River of Heaven a sound of plashing can be distinctly heard: is it the sound of the rippling made by Hikoboshi quickly rowing his boat?

Perhaps this evening shower is but the spray (flung down) from the oar of Hikoboshi, rowing his boat in haste.

From to-morrow alas! after having put my jewel-bed in order, no longer reposing with my lord, I must sleep alone!

The wind having risen, the waves of the river have become high;—this night cross over in a row-boat, I pray thee, before the hour be late!

Even though the waves of the River of Heaven run high, I must row over quickly, before it becomes late in the night.

Long ago I finished weaving the material; and, this evening, having finished sewing the garment for him— (why must) I still wait for my lord?

Is it that the current of the River of Heaven (has become too) rapid? The jet-black night advances— and Hikoboshi has not come!

Oh, ferryman, make speed across the stream!—my lord is not one who can come and go twice in a year!

On the very day that the autumn-wind began to blow, I set out for the shallows of the River of Heaven;—I pray you, tell my lord that I am waiting here still!

Methinks Tanabata must be coming in her boat; for a cloud is even now passing across the clear face of the moon.

Lafcadio Hearn

FROM THE KOKIN SHŪ

Compiled 9th century

Ono No Takamura

802–852

DID I ever think
That decaying
In the loneliness of a barbarian land
I should become a shore-hunter
Tugging at the ropes of fishermen ?

Ono No Komachi

834–880

A THING which fades
With no outward sign—
Is the flower
Of the heart of man
In this world !

Ono No Yoshiki

d. 902

MY love
Is like the grasses
Hidden in the deep mountain:
Though its abundance increases,
There is none that knows.

Anonymous

1

O CUCKOO,
Because the villages where you sing
Are so many,
I am estranged from you, even
In the midst of my love !

2

Hoping all the time
That we should meet
In my dreams,—
I spent the whole night
Without being able to sleep.

3

When the dawn comes
With the flicker flicker
Of sunrise
How sad the helping each other to
       put on our clothes !

4

If only, when one heard
That Old Age was coming
One could bolt the door,
Answer " not at home "
And refuse to meet him !

Arthur Waley

FROM THE SHŪI SHŪ
Compiled 10th century

Hitomaro
c. 700

W HEN,
Halting in front of it, I look
At the reflection which is in the depths
Of my clear mirror,

It gives me the impression of meeting
An unknown old gentleman.

Nakatsukasa

c. 900

IF it were not for the voice
Of the nightingale,
How would the mountain/village
Where the snow is still unmelted
Know the spring ?

Minamoto No Shigeyuki

d. 1000

WINTER has at last come
Unmistakably, even to my cottage
In the land of Tsu,
Which lies hidden
Among the rush/leaves.

Arthur Waley

SAIGYO HŌSHI

1118–1190

Seven Poems

1

IN my boat that goes
Over manifold salt/ways
Towards the open sea
Faintly I hear
The cry of the first wild/goose.

2

Mingling my prayer
With the clang of the bell
Which woke me from my dreams,
Lo, ten times I have recited the
Honourable Name.

3

Since I am convinced
That Reality is in no way
Real,
How am I to admit
That dreams are dreams?

4

Startled
By a single scream
Of the crane which is reposing
On the surface of the swamp,
All the other birds are crying.

5

Those ships which left
Side by side
The same harbour
Towards an unknown destination
Have rowed away from one another!

6

Like those boats which are returning
Across the open sea of Ashiya
Where the waves run high,
I think that I too shall pass
Scatheless through the storms of life.

7

Although I do not know
At all whether anything
Honourable deigns to be there,
Yet in extreme awe
My tears well forth.

Arthur Waley

FUJIWARA IETAKA

1158-1237

Old Scent of the Plum-tree

REMEMBERING what passed
Under the scent of the plum-tree,
I asked the plum-tree for tidings
Of that other.
Alas . . . the cold moon of spring. . . .
E. Powys Mathers

FROM THE HYAKU-NIN-ISSHU

13th century

Princess Shoku

I WOULD that even now
My thread of life were broken—
So should my secret vow
Remain unspoken.

Lady Horikawa

HOW can one e'er be sure
If true love will endure?
My thoughts this morning are
As tangled as my hair.

Fujiwara No Michinobu

THE day will soon be gone,
And night come back, I know . . .
Yet how I hate the dawn
That bids me go.

Lady Sanuki

LIKE a great rock, far out at sea,
  Submerged at even the lowest tide,
Unseen, unknown of man—my sleeve
  Is never for a moment dried.

Curtis Hidden Page

BASHŌ

Seven Poems

1644–1694

I

QUICK-FALLING dew,
Ah, let me cleanse in you
  This wretched life.

2

The roadside thistle eager
To see the travellers pass,
Was eaten by the passing ass!

3

Friend sparrow, do not eat, I pray
The little buzzing flies that play
  Among my flowers.

4

A lonely pond in age-old stillness sleeps . . .
  Apart, unstirred by sound or motion . . . till
Suddenly into it a lithe frog leaps.

5

Old battle-field, fresh with Spring flowers again—
  All that is left of the dream
Of twice ten thousand warriors slain.

6

Old men, white-haired, beside the ancestral graves,
  All of the household now
Stand lonesome, leaning on their staves.

7

O cricket, from your cheery cry
  No one could ever guess
How quickly you must die.

Curtis Hidden Page

SANSKRIT

FROM THE RIGVEDA

THE Rigveda consists of 1,028 hymns, comprising over ten thousand verses. The hymns are generally simple, and betray a childlike and simple faith in the gods, to whom sacrifices are offered and libations of the Soma juice are poured, and who are asked for increase of progeny, cattle, and wealth, and implored to help the Aryans in their still doubtful struggle against the black aborigines of the Punjab.—ROMESH DUTT.

Indra, the Supreme God

HIGHEST of Immortals bright,
God of gods by lofty might,
He, before whose prowess high
Tremble earth and upper sky,
He is,—mortals, hear my verse,—
Indra, Lord of Universe !

He, who fixed the staggering earth,
Shaped the mountains at their birth,
Sky's blue vault held up and bent,
Measured out the firmament,
He is,—listen to my verse,—
Indra, Lord of Universe !

He, who quelled the cloud-fiend's might,
Rolled the seven great rivers bright,
Pierced the caverns of the gloom,
Conquered bright kine from its womb,
Lit the lightning's fire of old,
He is Indra, warrior bold !

He, who shaped with cunning hand
Wonders of the sea and land,

Quelled the Aryans' impious foe,
Doomed the Dasa to his woe,
Robbed the bandit in his hold,
He is Indra, hunter bold !

Have you, doubting, questioned me,—
Where is Indra, who is He ?
Mortals, in your impious thought
Have you whispered—He is not !
Jealous God ! In vengeance dire
He can smite ye in his ire !

But his ceaseless mercies seek
High and lowly, strong and weak,
Priest who chants his sacred lays,
Worshipper who sings his praise,
Him who on the altar's flame
Pours libations to his name !

His the kine and steeds of war,
Village home and battle-car ;
His right arm uplifts the sun,
Opes the ruddy gates of dawn ;
His red bolt the dark cloud rends,
Grateful showers for mortals sends !

Hosts advancing to the fray
Cry to him on battle's day;
And the strong man shouts his fame,
And the lowly lisps his name;
Warrior-chief on battle-car
Prays to Indra, God of War !

We but triumph by his blade,
Nations court his friendly aid ;
Moveless hills that heavenward tower
Tremble at his mighty power;
And the world so vast and broad
Images the mighty God !

Swift his weapons, red and dire,
To the impious speak his ire ;
And his favours never rain
On the boastful and the vain;
And his red right hand can smite
Godless Dasas in the fight !

For he slew Sambara bold,
Sheltered in his mountain hold,
In the fortieth autumn/tide;
Slew the dragon in his pride,
Vritra, rain/withholding cloud,
Titan of the inky shroud !

Seven bright rays bedeck his bow,
Seven great rivers from him flow;
Thunder/armed, quick to ire,
He, in vengeance swift and dire,
Laid the proud Rauhina low,
Heaven/aspiring impious foe !

Earth and sky confess his sway,
Trembling hills obeisance pay;
Wielder of the bolt of heaven,
Be to him libations given;—
He accepts this Soma wine,
Listens to this lay of mine !

Brew the Soma fresh and fair,
Pour libations rich and rare,
For he blesses when we pray,
Helps the singer of his lay;—
He accepts this Soma wine,
Listens to this lay of mine !

Mighty Indra, strong and true,
Hymns to thee and gifts are due,
And our priests libations pour
For thy blessings' endless store;

Speak to us,—for thou art near,—
Let our brave sons know no fear !

Romesh Dutt

Pushan, God of Pasture

PUSHAN, God of golden day,
Shorten thou the shepherd's way,
Vanquish every foe and stranger,
Free our path from every danger;
Cloud-born Pushan, ever more,
Lead us as you led before !

Smite the wild wolf, fierce and vile,
Lurking in the dark defile,
Smite the robber and the thief,
Stealing forth to take our life;
Cloud-born Pushan, ever more,
Lead us as you led before!

Chase him, Pushan, in thy wrath,
Who infests the lonely path,
Robber with his ruthless heart,
Slayer with his secret dart;
Child of clouds, for ever more,
Lead us as you led before !

Trample with thy heavy tread
On the darksome man of dread,
On the low and lying knave,
Smooth-tongued double-dealing slave;
Child of clouds, for ever more,
Lead us as you led before !

Thou dost pathless forests know,
Thou canst quell the secret foe,
Thou didst lead our fathers right,
Wonder-worker, orb of light;

Grant from thy unfailing store
Wealth and blessings ever more !

Thou hast treasures manifold,
Glittering weapons, arms of gold;
Foremost of the Sons of Light,
Shepherds' God and Leader bright,
Grant from thy unfailing store
Wealth and blessings ever more !

Lead us through the dark defile
Past pursuers dread and vile,
Lead us over pleasant ways
Sheltered by thy saving grace,
Lead us o'er this trackless shore,
And we follow ever more !

Where the grass is rich and green,
And the pasture's beauteous sheen,
And the meadow's soft and sweet,
Lead us, safe from scorching heat,
Blessings on thy servants pour,
And we follow ever more !

Fill our hearts with hope and courage,
Fill our homes with food and forage,
Save us from a cruel fate,
Feed us and invigorate;
We are suppliants at thy door,
And we follow ever more !

Heart and voice we lift in praise,
Chant our hymns and pious lays,
From the Bright One, good and gracious,
Ask for food and pasture spacious;
Shepherds' God ! befriend the poor,
And we follow ever more !

Romesh Dutt

FROM THE PANCHATANTRA

2nd century B.C., *et seq.*

Kings

IN sensuous coil
    And heartless toil,
In sinuous course
And armoured force,
In savage harms
That yield to charms—
In all these things
Are the snakes like kings.

Uneven, rough,
And high enough—
Yet low folk roam
Their flanks as home,
And wild things haunt
Them, hungry, gaunt—
In all these things
Are hills like kings.

The things that claw, and the things that gore
    Are unreliable things;
And so is a man with a sword in his hand,
    And rivers, and women, and kings.

Arthur W. Ryder

The Penalty of Virtue

THE fruit-tree's branch by very wealth
    Of fruit is bended low;
The peacock's feathered pride compels
    A sluggish gait and slow;

The blooded horse that wins his race,
Must like a cow be led:
The good in goodness often find
    An enemy to dread.

Where Jumna's waves roll blue
With sands of sapphire hue,
Black serpents have their lair;
And who would hunt them there,
But that a jewel's bright star
From each hood gleams afar?
By virtue rising, all
By that same virtue fall.

The man of virtue commonly
    Is hateful to the king,
While riches to the scamps and fools
    Habitually cling:
The ancient chant " By virtue great
    Is man " has run to seed;
The world takes rare and little note
    Of any plucky deed.

                            Arthur W. Ryder

True Friendship

'TIS hard to find in life
    A friend, a bow, a wife,
    Strong, supple to endure,
    In stock and sinew pure,
    In time of danger sure.

False friends are common.   Yes, but where
True nature links a friendly pair,
The blessing is as rich as rare.

To bitter ends
You trust true friends,
Not wife nor mother,
Not son nor brother.

No long experience alloys
True friendship's sweet and supple joys;
No evil men can steal the treasure;
'Tis death, death only, sets a measure.

Arthur W. Ryder

Fool and False

WITH the shrewd and upright man
    Seek a friendship rare;
Exercise with shrewd and false
    Superheedful care;
Pity for the upright fool
    Find within your heart;
If a man be fool and false,
    Shun him from the start.

Arthur W. Ryder

Poverty

A BEGGAR to the graveyard hied
And there " Friend corpse, arise," he cried;
" One moment lift my heavy weight
Of poverty ; for I of late
Grow weary, and desire instead
Your comfort; you are good and dead."
The corpse was silent.   He was sure
'Twas better to be dead than poor.

Arthur W. Ryder

AMAROU

1st century ?

The Drunken Rose

HAS not the night been as a drunken rose
Without a witness ? And the girl of bloom
Has given up all.   What little cries of joy !
What wanton words repeated !
But white dawn shows the rose and green pet bird,
The mighty talker and awake all night.
Hark ! The old woman comes; he will tell all.
What shall she, fluttering ?   Snap small rubies off
From the bright ear-rings, facets sharp as steel;
These with the seed-pulp of the passion-fruit,
His sweet prepared breakfast, mingle featly . . .
So, busy jargoner, silent for ever more.

E. Powys Mathers

KALIDASA

c. 500

RARELY *has a man walked the earth who observed the phenomena of living nature as accurately as he. His nature was one of singular balance, equally at home in a splendid court and on a lonely mountain. For something like fifteen hundred years Kalidasa has been more widely read in India than any other author who wrote in Sanskrit.*—ARTHUR W. RYDER.

The Seasons

SUMMER

PITILESS heat from heaven pours
    By day, but nights are cool;
Continual bathing gently lowers
    The water in the pool;
The evening brings a charming peace:
    For summer-time is here,
When love that never knows surcease
    Is less imperious, dear.

Yet love can never fall asleep;
　For he is waked to-day
By songs that all their sweetness keep
　And lutes that softly play,
By fans with sandal-water wet
　That bring us drowsy rest,
By strings of pearls that gently fret
　Full many a lovely breast.

The sunbeams like the fires are hot
　That on the altar wake;
The enmity is quite forgot
　Of peacock and of snake;
The peacock spares his ancient foe,
　For pluck and hunger fail;
He hides his burning head below
　The shadow of his tail.

Beneath the garland of the rays
　That leave no corner cool,
The water vanishes in haze
　And leaves a muddy pool;
The cobra does not hunt for food
　Nor heed the frog at all
Who finds beneath the serpent's hood
　A sheltering parasol.

Dear maiden of the graceful song,
　To you may summer's power
Bring moonbeams clear and garlands long
　And breath of trumpet-flower,
Bring lakes that countless lilies dot,
　Refreshing water-sprays,
Sweet friends at evening, and a spot
　Cool after burning days.

The Rains

The rain advances like a king
    In awful majesty;
Hear, dearest, how his thunders ring
    Like royal drums, and see
His lightning-banners wave; a cloud
    For elephant he rides,
And finds his welcome from the crowd
    Of lovers and of brides.

The clouds, a mighty army, march
    With drumlike thundering
And stretch upon the rainbow's arch
    The lightning's flashing string;
The cruel arrows of the rain
    Smite them who live, apart
From whom they love, with stinging pain,
    And pierce them to the heart.

The forest seems to show its glee
    In flowering nipa plants;
In waving twigs of many a tree
    Wind-swept, it seems to dance;
Its ketak-blossom's opening sheath
    Is like a smile put on
To greet the rain's reviving breath,
    Now pain and heat are gone.

To you, dear, may the cloudy time
    Bring all that you desire,
Bring every pleasure, perfect, prime,
    To set a bride on fire;
May rain whereby life wakes and shines
    Where there is power of life,
The unchanging friend of clinging vines,
    Shower blessings on my wife.

AUTUMN

The autumn comes, a maiden fair
  In slenderness and grace,
With nodding rice-stems in her hair
  And lilies in her face.
In flowers of grasses she is clad;
  And as she moves along,
Birds greet her with their cooing glad
  Like bracelets' tinkling song.

A diadem adorns the night
  Of multitudinous stars;
Her silken robe is white moonlight,
  Set free from cloudy bars;
And on her face (the radiant moon)
  Bewitching smiles are shown:
She seems a slender maid, who soon
  Will be a woman grown.

Over the rice-fields, laden plants
  Are shivering to the breeze;
While in his brisk caresses dance
  The blossom-burdened trees;
He ruffles every lily-pond
  Where blossoms kiss and part,
And stirs with lover's fancies fond
  The young man's eager heart.

WINTER

The bloom of tenderer flowers is past
  And lilies droop forlorn,
For winter-time is come at last,
  Rich with its ripened corn;
Yet for the wealth of blossoms lost
  Some hardier flowers appear
That bid defiance to the frost
  Of sterner days, my dear.

The vines, remembering summer, shiver
  In frosty winds, and gain
A fuller life from mere endeavour
  To live through all that pain;
Yet in the struggle and acquist
  They run as pale and wan
As lonely women who have missed
  Known love, now lost and gone.

Then may these winter days show forth
  To you each known delight,
Bring all that women count as worth
  Pure happiness and bright;
While villages, with bustling cry,
  Bring home the ripened corn,
And herons wheel through wintry sky,
  Forget sad thoughts forlorn.

EARLY SPRING

Now, dearest, lend a heedful ear,
  And listen while I sing
Delights to every maiden dear,
  The charms of early spring:
When the earth is dotted with the heaps
  Of corn, when heron scream
Is rare but sweet, when passion leaps
  And paints a livelier dream;

When all must cheerfully applaud
  A blazing open fire;
Or if they needs must go abroad,
  The sun is their desire;
When every body hopes to find
  The frosty chill allayed
By garments warm, a window blind
  Shut, and a sweet young maid.

Then may the days of early spring
    For you be rich and full
With love's proud, soft philandering
    And many a dandy-pull,
With sweetest rice and sugar-cane:
    And may you float above
The absent grieving and the pain
    Of separated love.

SPRING

A stalwart soldier comes, the spring,
    Who bears the bow of Love;
And on that bow, the lustrous string
    Is made of bees, that move
With malice as they speed the shaft
    Of blossoming mango-flower
At us, dear, who have never laughed
    At love, nor scorned his power.

Their blossom-burden weights the trees;
    The winds in fragrance move;
The lakes are bright with lotuses,
    The women bright with love;
The days are soft, the evenings clear
    And charming; everything
That moves and lives and blossoms, dear,
    Is sweeter in the spring.

The groves are beautifully bright
    For many and many a mile
With jasmine-flowers that are as white
    As loving woman's smile:
The resolution of a saint
    Might well be tried by this;
Far more, young hearts that fancies paint
    With dreams of loving bliss.

Arthur W. Ryder

BHARTRIHARI

c. 500

IN short verses the Hindus excel. Their mastery of form, their play of fancy, their depth and tenderness of feeling, are all exquisite. Of the many who wrote such verses, the greatest is Bhartrihari.—ARTHUR W. RYDER.

Time

TIME is the root of all this earth;
  These creatures, who from Time had birth,
    Within his bosom at the end
Shall sleep; Time hath nor enemy nor friend.

  All we in one long caravan
  Are journeying since the world began;
    We know not whither, but we know
Time guideth at the front, and all must go.

  Like as the wind upon the field
  Bows every herb, and all must yield,
    So we beneath Time's passing breath
Bow each in turn,—why tears for birth or death ?

Paul Elmer More

Peace

COURAGE, my Soul ! now to the silent wood
  Alone we wander, there to seek our food
    In the wild fruits, and woo our dreamless sleep
      On soft boughs gathered deep.

  There loud authority in folly bold,
  And tongues that stammer with disease of gold,
    And murmur of the windy world shall cease,
      Nor echo through our peace.

Paul Elmer More

BILHANA

11th century

Black Marigolds

(*A free interpretation of the Chauraspanchasika*)

EVEN now
My thought is all of this gold-tinted king's daughter
With garlands tissue and golden buds,
Smoke tangles of her hair, and sleeping or waking
Feet trembling in love, full of pale languor;
My thought is clinging as to a lost learning
Slipped down out of the minds of men,
Labouring to bring her back into my soul.

Even now
If I see in my soul the citron-breasted fair one
Still gold-tinted, her face like our night stars,
Drawing unto her; her body beaten about with flame,
Wounded by the flaring spear of love,
My first of all by reason of her fresh years,
Then is my heart buried alive in snow.

Even now
If my girl with lotus eyes came to me again
Weary with the dear weight of young love,
Again I would give her to these starved twins of arms
And from her mouth drink down the heavy wine,
As a reeling pirate bee in fluttered ease
Steals up the honey from the nenuphar.

Even now
I bring her back, ah, wearied out with love
So that her slim feet could not bear her up;
Curved falls of her hair down on her white cheeks;
In the confusion of her coloured vests
Speaking that guarded giving up, and her scented
        arms
Lay like cool bindweed over against my neck.

Even now
I bring her back to me in her quick shame,
Hiding her bright face at the point of day:
Making her grave eyes move in watered stars,
For love's great sleeplessness wandering all night,
Seeming to sail gently, as that pink bird,
Down the water of love in a harvest of lotus.

Even now
If I saw her lying all wide eyes
And with collyrium the indent of her cheek
Lengthened to the bright ear and her pale side
So suffering the fever of my distance,
Then would my love for her be ropes of flowers, and
        night
A black-haired lover on the breasts of day.

Even now
I see the heavy startled hair of this reed-flute player
Who curved her poppy lips to love dances,
Having a youth's face madding like the moon
Lying at her full; limbs ever moving a little in love,
Too slight, too delicate, tired with the small burden
Of bearing love ever on white feet.

Even now
She is present to me on her beds,
Balmed with the exhalation of a flattering musk,
Rich with the curly essence of santal;
Girl with eyes dazing as the seeded-wine,
Showing as a pair of gentle nut-hatches
Kissing each other with their bills, each hidden
By turns within a little grasping mouth.

Even now
She swims back in the crowning hour of love
All red with wine her lips have given to drink,
Soft round the mouth with camphor and faint blue

Tinted upon the lips, her slight body,
Her great live eyes, the colourings of herself
A clear perfection; sighs of musk outstealing
And powdered wood spice heavy of Cashmir.

Even now
I see her; fair face blond like gold
Rich with small lights, and tinted shadows surprised
Over and over all of her ; with glittering eyes
All bright for love but very love-weary,
As it were the conjuring disk of the moon when Rahu
    ceases
With his dark stumbling-block to hide her rays.

Even now
She is art-magically present to my soul
And that one word of strange heart's ease, good-bye,
That in the night, in loth moving to go,
And bending over to a golden mouth,
I said softly to the turned away
Tenderly tired hair of this king's daughter.

Even now
My eyes that hurry to see no more are painting,
    painting
Faces of my lost girl. O golden rings,
That tap against cheeks of small magnolia leaves,
O whitest so soft parchment where
My poor divorced lips have written excellent
Stanzas of kisses, and will write no more.

Even now
Death sends me the flickering of powdery lids
Over wild eyes and the pity of her slim body
All broken up with the weariness of joy ;
The little red flowers of her breasts to be my comfort
Moving above scarves, and for my sorrow
Wet crimson lips that once I marked as mine.

Even now
By a cool noise of waters in the spring
The asoka with young flowers that feign her fingers
And bud in red; and in the green vest pearls kissing
As it were rose leaves in the gardens of God; the
    shining at night
Of white cheeks in the dark; smiles from light
    thoughts within,
And her walking as of a swan: these trouble me.

Even now
The pleased intimacy of rough love
Upon the patient glory of her form
Racks me with memory; and her bright dress
As it were yellow flame, which the white hand
Shamefastly gathers in her rising haste,
The slender grace of her departing feet.

Even now
When all my heavy heart is broken up
I seem to see my prison walls breaking
And then a light, and in that light a girl,
Her fingers busied about her hair, her cool white arms
Faint rosy at the elbows, raised in the sunlight,
And temperate eyes that wander far away.

Even now
I seem to see my prison walls come close,
Built up of darkness, and against that darkness
A girl no taller than my breast and very tired,
Leaning upon the bed and smiling, feeding
A little bird and lying slender as ash-trees,
Sleepily aware as I told of the green
Grapes and the small bright-coloured river flowers.

Even now
I see her, as I used, in her white palace
Under black torches throwing cool red light,
Woven with many flowers and tearing the dark.

I see her rising, showing all her face
Defiant timidly, saying clearly:
Now I shall go to sleep, good-night, my ladies.

Even now
Though I am so far separate, a flight of birds
Swinging from side to side over the valley trees,
Passing my prison with their calling and crying,
Bring me to see my girl. For very bird-like
Is her song singing, and the state of a swan
In her light walking, like the shaken wings
Of a black eagle falls her nightly hair.

Even now
I know my princess was happy. I see her stand
Touching her breasts with all her flower-soft fingers,
Looking askance at me with smiling eyes.
There is a god that arms him with a flower
And she was stricken deep. Here, oh die here.
Kiss me and I shall be purer than quick rivers.

Even now
They chatter her weakness through the two bazaars
Who was so strong to love me. And small men
That buy and sell for silver being slaves
Crinkle the fat about their eyes; and yet
No Prince of the Cities of the Sea has taken her,
Leading to his grim bed. Little lonely one,
You clung to me as a garment clings; my girl.

Even now
Only one dawn shall rise for me. The stars
Revolve to-morrow's night and I not heed.
One brief cold watch beside an empty heart
And that is all. This night she rests not well;
Oh, sleep; for there is heaviness for all the world
Except for the death-lighted heart of me.

Even now
My sole concern the slipping of her vests,
Her little breasts the life beyond this life.
One night of disarray in her green hems,
Her golden cloths, outweighs the order of earth,
Making of none effect the tides of the sea.
I have seen her enter the temple meekly and there
    seem
The flag of flowers that veils the very god.

Even now
I mind the coming and talking of wise men from
    towers
Where they had thought away their youth.   And I,
    listening,
Found not the salt of the whispers of my girl,
Murmur of confused colours, as we lay near sleep;
Little wise words and little witty words,
Wanton as water, honeyed with eagerness.

Even now
I call to mind her weariness in the morning
Close lying in my arms, and tiredly smiling
At my disjointed prayer for her small sake.
Now in my morning the weariness of death
Sends me to sleep.   Had I made coffins
I might have lived singing to three score.

Even now
The woodcutter and the fisherman turn home,
With on his axe the moon and in his dripping net
Caught yellow moonlight.   The purple flame of fire
Calls them to love and sleep.   From the hot town
The maker of scant songs for bread wanders
To lie under the clematis with his girl.
The moon shines on her breasts, and I must die.

Even now
I have a need to make up prayers, to speak
My last consideration of the world
To the great thirteen gods, to make my balance
Ere the soul journeys on.   I kneel and say:
Father of Light.   Leave we it burning still
That I may look at you.   *Mother of the Stars,*
Give me your feet to kiss; I love you, dear.

Even now
I seem to see the face of my lost girl
With frightened eyes, like a wood wanderer,
In travail with sorrowful waters, unwept tears
Labouring to be born and fall; when white face
        turned
And little ears caught at the far murmur,
The pleased snarling of the tumult of dogs
When I was buried away down the white road.

Even now
When slow rose-yellow moons looked out at night
To guard the sheaves of harvest and mark down
The peach's fall, how calm she was and love worthy.
Glass-coloured starlight falling as thin as dew
Was wont to find us at the spirit's starving time
Slow straying in the orchard paths with love.

Even now
Love is a god and Rati the dark his bride;
But once I found their child and she was fairer,
That could so shine.   And we were each to each
Wonderful and a presence not yet felt
In any dream.   I knew the sunset earth
But as a red gold ring to bear my emerald
Within the little summer of my youth.

Even now
I marvel at the bravery of love,
She, whose two feet might be held in one hand
And all her body on a shield of the guards,
Lashed like a gold panther taken in a pit
Tearfully valiant, when I too was taken;
Bearding her black-beard father in his wrath,
Striking the soldiers with white impotent hands.

Even now
I mind that I loved cypress and roses, dear,
The great blue mountains and the small grey hills,
The sounding of the sea.   Upon a day
I saw strange eyes and hands like butterflies;
For me at morning larks flew from the thyme
And children came to bathe in little streams.

Even now
Sleep left me all these nights for your white bed
And I am sure you sistered lay with sleep
After much weeping.   Piteous little love,
Death is in the garden, time runs down,
The year that simple and unexalted ran till now
Ferments in winy autumn, and I must die.

Even now
I mind our going, full of bewilderment
As who should walk from sleep into great light,
Along the running of the winter river,
A dying sun on the cool hurrying tide
No more by green rushes delayed in dalliance,
With a clear purpose in his flower-flecked length
Informed, to reach Nirvana and the sea.

Even now
I love long black eyes that caress like silk,
Ever and ever sad and laughing eyes,
Whose lids make such sweet shadow when they close

It seems another beautiful look of hers.
I love a fresh mouth, ah, a scented mouth,
And curving hair, subtle as a smoke,
And light fingers, and laughter of green gems.

Even now
I mind asking: Where love and how love Rati's
    priestesses?
You can tell me of their washings at moon-down
And if that warm basin have silver borders.
Is it so that when they comb their hair
Their fingers, being purple-stained, show
Like coral branches in the black sea of their hair?

Even now
I remember that you made answer very softly,
We being one soul, your hand on my hair,
The burning memory rounding your near lips:
I have seen the priestesses of Rati make love at moon-
    fall
And then in a carpeted hall with a bright gold lamp
Lie down carelessly anywhere to sleep.

Even now
I have no surety that she is not Mahadevi
Rose red of Siva, or Kapagata
The wilful ripe Companion of the King,
Or Krishna's own Lakshmi, the violet-haired.
I am not certain but that dark Brahma
In his high secret purposes
Has sent my soft girl down to make the three worlds
    mad
With capering about her scented feet.

Even now
Call not the master painters from all the world,
Their thin black boards, their rose and green and
    grey,
Their ashes of lapis ultramarine,

Their earth of shadows the umber.   Laughing at art
Sunlight upon the body of my bride,
For painting not nor any eyes for ever.
Oh warm tears on the body of my bride.

Even now
 I mind when the red crowds were passed and it was
          raining
How glad those two that shared the rain with me;
For they talked happily with rich young voices
And at the storm's increase, closer and with content,
Each to the body of the other held
As there were no more severance for ever.

Even now
The stainless fair appearance of the moon
Rolls her gold beauty over an autumn sky
And the stiff anchorite forgets to pray;
How much the sooner I, if her wild mouth
Tasting of the taste of manna came to mine
And kept my soul at balance above a kiss.

Even now
Her mouth carelessly scented as with lotus dust
Is water of love to the great heat of love,
A tirtha very holy, a lover's lake
Utterly sacred.   Might I go down to it
But one more time, then should I find a way
To hold my lake for ever and ever more
Sobbing out my life beside the waters.

Even now
I mind that the time of the falling of blossoms started
          my dream
Into a wild life, into my girl;
Then was the essence of her beauty spilled
Down on my days so that it fades not,
Fails not, subtle and fresh, in perfuming
That day, and the days, and this the latest day.

Even now
She with young limbs as smooth as flower pollen,
Whose swaying body is laved in the cool
Waters of languor, this dear bright-coloured bird,
Walks not, changes not, advances not
Her weary station by the black lake
Of Gone Forever, in whose fountain vase
Balance the water-lilies of my thought.

Even now
Spread we our nets beyond the farthest rims
So surely that they take the feet of dawn
Before you wake and after you are sleeping
Catch up the visible and invisible stars
And web the ports the strongest dreamer dreamed,
Yet is it all one, Vidya, yet it is nothing.

Even now
The night is full of silver straws of rain,
And I will send my soul to see your body
This last poor time. I stand beside our bed;
Your shadowed head lies leaving a bright space
Upon the pillow empty, your sorrowful arm
Holds from your side and clasps not anything.
There is no covering upon you.

Even now
I think your feet seek mine to comfort them.
There is some dream about you even now
Which I'll not hear at waking. Weep not at dawn,
Though day brings wearily your daily loss
And all the light is hateful. Now is it time
To bring my soul away.

Even now
I mind that I went round with men and women,
And underneath their brows, deep in their eyes,
I saw their souls, which go slipping aside

In swarms before the pleasure of my mind;
The world was like a flight of birds, shadow or flame
Which I saw pass above the engraven hills.
Yet was there never one like to my woman.

Even now
Death I take up as consolation.
Nay, were I free as the condor with his wings
Or old kings throned on violet ivory,
Night would not come without beds of green floss
And never a bed without my bright darling.
It is most fit that you strike now, black guards,
And let this fountain out before the dawn.

Even now
I know that I have savoured the hot taste of life
Lifting green cups and gold at the great feast.
Just for a small and a forgotten time
I have had full in my eyes from off my girl
The whitest pouring of eternal light.
The heavy knife.   As to a gala day.

E. Powys Mathers

JAYADEVA

12th century

From the Gītā Gōvinda

HYMN TO VISHNU

O THOU that held'st the blessed Veda dry
    When all things else beneath the floods were
    hurled;
Strong Fish-God ! Ark of Men ! *Jai !* Hari, *jai !*
    Hail, Keshav, hail; thou Master of the world !

The round world rested on thy spacious nape;
    Upon thy neck, like a mere mole, it stood:
O thou, that took'st for us the Tortoise-shape,
    Hail, Keshav, hail ! Ruler of wave and wood !

The world upon thy curving tusk sate sure,
  Like the Moon's dark disk in her crescent pale;
O thou who didst for us assume the Boar,
  Immortal Conqueror ! hail, Keshav, hail !

When thou thy Giant Foe didst seize and rend,
  Fierce, fearful, long, and sharp were fang and nail ;
Thou who the Lion and the Man didst blend,
  Lord of the Universe, hail, Narsingh, hail !

Wonderful Dwarf !—who with a threefold stride
  Cheated King Bali—where thy footsteps fall
Men's sins, O Wamuna ! are set aside :
  O Keshav, hail ! thou Help and Hope of all !

The sins of this sad earth thou didst assail,
  The anguish of its creatures thou didst heal;
Freed are we from all terrors by thy toil:
  Hail, Purshuram, hail ! Lord of the biting steel !

To thee the fell Ten-Headed yielded life.
  Thou in dread battle laid'st the monster low !
Ah, Rama ! dear to Gods and men that strife;
  We praise thee, Master of the matchless bow !

With clouds for garments glorious thou dost fare,
  Veiling thy dazzling majesty and might,
As when Jamuna saw thee with the share,
  A peasant—yet the King of Day and Night.

Merciful-hearted ! when thou camest as Boodh—
  Albeit 'twas written in the Scriptures so—
Thou bad'st our altars to be no more imbrued
  With blood of victims: Keshav ! bending low—

We praise thee, Wielder of the sweeping sword,
  Brilliant as curving comets in the gloom,
Whose edge shall smite the fierce barbarian horde;
  Hail to thee, Keshav ! hail, and hear, and come,

And fill this song of Jayadev with thee,
   And make it wise to teach, strong to redeem,
And sweet to living souls.   Thou Mystery !
   Thou Light of Life ! Thou Dawn beyond the
     dream !

Fish ! that didst outswim the flood ;
Tortoise ! whereon earth hath stood;
Boar ! who with thy tusk held'st high
The world, that mortals might not die;
Lion ! who hast giants torn;
Dwarf ! who laugh'dst a king to scorn;
Sole Subduer of the Dreaded !
Slayer of the many-headed !
Mighty Ploughman ! Teacher tender !
Of thine own the sure Defender !
Under all thy ten disguises
Endless praise to thee arises.

                    Sir Edwin Arnold

ARABIAN

FROM THE MU'ALLAQÁT

Compiled 8th century

IMR EL KAIS

THE ancient poetry of Arabia, immediately before the advent of Mohammed, is the most delightful wild flower of literature the Eastern world can show. The " Seven Golden Odes," or the " Seven Suspended Poems," have come to be considered the classic poems, and have obtained for their authors a special position as the most famous singers of Pagan Arabia.—WILFRID SCAWEN BLUNT.

6th century

Ode

WEEP, ah weep love's losing, love's with its dwelling⸗
  place set where the hills divide Dakhúli and
Háumali.
Túdiha and Mikrat ! There the hearth⸗stones of her
  stand where the South and North winds cross⸗weave
  the sand⸗furrows.
See the white⸗doe droppings strewn by the wind on
  them, black on her floor forsaken, fine⸗grain of pep⸗
  percorns.
Here it was I watched her, lading her load⸗camels,
  stood by these thorn⸗trees weeping tears as of colo⸗
  cynth.
Here my twin friends waited, called to me camel⸗borne:
  Man ! not of grief thou diest. Take thy pain patiently.
Not though tears assuage thee, deem it beseemeth thee
  thus for mute stones to wail thee, all thy foes wit⸗
  nesses.
What though fortune flout thee ! Thus Om Howéyrith
  did, thus did thy Om Rebábi, fooled thee in Másali.
O, where these two tented, sweet was the breath of them,
  sweet as of musk their fragrance, sweet as gáranfoli.

Mourned I for them long days, wept for the love of
them, tears on my bosom raining, tears on my sword-
handle.
Yes, was I unvanquished. Had I not happiness, I at
their hands in Dáret, Dáret of Júljuli?

O that day of all days! Slew I my milch-camel, feasted
the maidens gaily,—well did they load for me!
Piled they high the meat-strings. All day they pelted
me, pelted themselves with fatness, fringes of camel-
meat.
Climbed I to her howdah, sat with Onéyzata, while at
my raid she chided: Man! must I walk afoot?
Swayed the howdah wildly, she and I close in it: There!
my beast's back is galled now. Slave of Grief, down
with thee.
Answered I: Nay, sweet heart, loosen the rein of him.
Think not to stay my kisses. Here will I harvest them.
Grieve not for thy camel. Grudge not my croup-
riding. Give me—and thee—to taste things sweeter
than clove-apples,
Kisses on thy white teeth, teeth, nay the pure petals,
even and clean and close-set, wreathing a camomile.
Wooed have I thy equals, maidens and wedded ones.
Her, the nursling's mother, did I not win to her?
What though he wailed loudly, babe of the amulets,
turned she not half towards him, half of her clasped
to me?
Woe is me, the hard heart! How did she mock at me,
high on the sand-hill sitting, vowing to leave and go!
Fátima, nay my own love, though thou wouldst break
with me, still be thou kind awhile now, leave me not
utterly.
Clean art thou mistaken. Love is my malady. Ask me
the thing thou choosest. Straight will I execute.
If so be thou findest aught in thy lover wrong, cast
from thy back my garments, moult thee my finery.

Woe is me, the hard heart ! When did tears trouble
   thee save for my soul's worse wounding, stricken and
   near to die ?

Fair too was that other, she the veil-hidden one, howdahed
   how close, how guarded ! Yet did she welcome me.

Passed I twixt her tent-ropes,—what though her near-
   of-kin lay in the dark to slay me, blood-shedders all
   of them.

Came I at the mid-night, hour when the Pleiades showed
   as the links of seed-pearls binding the sky's girdle.

Stealing in, I stood there. She had cast off from her
   every robe but one robe, all but her night-garment.

Tenderly she scolded : What is this stratagem ? Speak,
   on thine oath, thou mad one. Stark is thy lunacy.

Passed we out together, while she drew after us on our
   twin track to hide it, wise, her embroideries,

Fled beyond the camp-lines. There in security dark in
   the sand we lay down far from the prying eyes.

By her plaits I wooed her, drew her face near to me, won
   to her waist how frail-lined, hers of the ankle-rings.

Fair-faced she—no redness-noble of countenance, smooth
   as of glass her bosom, bare with its necklaces.

Thus are pearls yet virgin, seen through the dark water,
   clear in the sea-depths gleaming, pure, inaccessible.

Coyly she withdraws her, shows us a cheek, a lip, she a
   gazelle of Wújra,—yearling the fawn with her.

Roe-like her throat slender, white as an áriel's, sleek to
   thy lips up-lifted,—pearls are its ornament.

On her shoulders fallen thick lie the locks of her, dark
   as the dark date-clusters hung from the palm-branches.

See the side-plaits pendent, high on the brows of her,
   tressed in a knot, the caught ones fast with the fallen
   ones.

Slim her waist,—a well-cord scarce has its slenderness.
   Smooth are her legs as reed-stems stripped at a water-
   head.

The morn through she sleepeth, muck/stream in indo/
lence, hardly at noon hath risen, girded her day
dresses.

Soft her touch,—her fingers fluted as water/worms, sleek
as the snakes of Thobya, tooth/sticks of Ishali.

Lighteneth she night's darkness, ay, as an evening lamp
hung for a sign of guidance lone on a hermitage.

Who but shall desire her, seeing her standing thus, half
in her childhood's short frock, half in her woman's
robe !

Strip thee of youth's fooling, thou in thy manhood's
prime.   Yet to her love be faithful,—hold it a robe
to thee.

Many tongues have spoken, warned me of craft in love.
Yet they have failed an answer,—all were thine
enemies.

Dim the frear night broodeth,—veil upon veil let down,
dark as a mad sea raging, tempting the heart of me.

Spake I to Night stoutly, while he, a slow camel, dragged
with his hind/feet halting,—gone the forehand of him.

Night ! I cried, thou snail Night, when wilt thou turn
to day ? When ? Though in sooth day's dawning
worse were than thou to me.

Sluggard Night, what stays thee ? Chained hang the
stars of thee fast to the rocks with hempen ropes set
unmoveable.

Water/skins of some folk—ay, with the thong of them
laid on my nága's wither—borne have I joyfully,

Crossed how lone the rain/ways, bare as an ass/belly;
near me the wolf, starved gamester, howled to his
progeny.

Cried I: Wolf, thou wailest.   Surely these lives of ours,
thine and my own, go empty, robbed of prosperity.

All we won we leave here.   Whoso shall follow us, seed
in our corn/track casting, reap shall he barrenness.

Rode I forth at day-dawn—birds in their nests asleep—
  stout on my steed, the sleek-coat, him the game-
  vanquisher.
Lo, he chargeth, turneth,—gone is he—all in one, like
  to a rock stream-trundled, hurled from its eminence.
Red-bay he,—his loin-cloth chafing the ribs of him.
  Shifts as a rain-stream smoothing stones in a river-bed.
Hard is he,—he snorteth loud in the pride of him, fierce
  as a full pot boiling, bubbling beneath the lid.

Straineth he how stoutly, while, as spent fishes swim,
  tied to his track the fleet ones plough his steps wearily.
See, in scorn he casteth youth from the back of him,
  leaveth the horseman cloakless, naked the hard-ride.
As a sling-stone hand-whirled, so is the might of him,
  loosed from the string that held it, hurled from the
  spliced ribbon.
Lean his flanks, gazelle-like, legs as the ostrich's; he like
  a strong wolf trotteth; lithe as a fox-cub he.
Stout his frame; behind him, look, you shall note of him
  full-filled the hind-leg gap, tail with no twist in it.
Polished, hard his quarters, smooth, as the pounding-
  stone used for a bridegroom's spices, grind-slab of
  colocynth.
As the henna juice lies dyed on a beard grown hoar, so on
  his neck the blood-stains mark the game downridden.
Rushed we on the roe-herd. Sudden, as maids at play
  circling in skirts low-training, forth leaped the does
  of it.
Flashing fled they, jewels, shells set alternately on a
  young gallant's neck-string, his the high-pedigreed.
Yet he gained their leaders, far while behind him lay
  bunched in a knot the hindmost, ere they fled scatter-
  wise.
'Twixt the cow and bull herds held he in wrath his road;
  made he of both his booty,—sweatless the neck of him.

All that day we roasted, seethed the sweet meat of them,
row upon row in cauldrons, firelighters all of us.

Nathless home at night-fall, he in the fore-front still.
Where is the eye shall bind him ?   How shall it follow
him ?

The night through he watcheth, scorneth him down to
lay, close, while I sleep, still saddled, bridled by side
of me.

Friend, thou seest the lightning. Mark where it
wavereth, gleameth like fingers twisted, clasped in
the cloud-rivers.

Like a lamp new-lighted, so is the flash of it, trimmed
by a hermit nightly pouring oil-sesame.

Stood I long a watcher, twin-friends how dear with me,
till in Othéyb it faded, ended in Dáriji.

By its path we judged it: rain over Káttan is; far in
Sitár it falleth, streameth in Yáthoboli.

Gathereth gross the flood-head dammed in Kutéyfati.
Woe to the trees, the branched ones ! Woe the
kanáhboli !

El Kanaan hath known it, quailed from the lash of it.
Down from their lairs it driveth hot-foot the ibexes.

Known it too hath Téyma ; standeth no palm of her
there, nor no house low-founded,—none but her rock-
buildings.

Stricken stood Thabira whelmed by the rush of it, like
an old chief robe-folded, bowed in his striped mantle.

Nay, but he Mujéymir, tall-peaked at dawn of day,
showed like a spinster's distaff tossed on the flood-
water.

Cloud-wrecked lay the valley piled with the load of it,
high as in sacks the Yemámi heapeth his corn-
measures.

Seemed it then the song-birds, wine-drunk at sun-rising,
loud through the valley shouted, maddened with
spiceries,

While the wild beast corpses, grouped like great bulbs
up-torn, cumbered the hollow places, drowned in the
night-trouble.

> *Translated by Lady Anne Blunt and done into English*
> *verse by Wilfrid Scawen Blunt*

IBN KOLTHÚM

6th century

Pour us Wine

RISE and hold up the curved glass,
And pour us wine of the morning, of El Andar.

Pour wine for us, whose golden colour
Is like a water stream kissing flowers of saffron.

Pour us wine to make us generous
And carelessly happy in the old way.

Pour us wine that gives the miser
A sumptuous generosity and disregard.

O Oum-Amr, you have prevented me from the cup
When it should have been moving to the right;
And yet the one of us three that you would not serve
Is not the least worthy.

How many cups have I not emptied at Balbek,
And emptied at Damas and emptied at Cacerin !

More cups ! more cups ! for death will have his day;
His are we and he ours.

By herself she is fearless
And gives her arms to the air,
The limbs of a long camel that has not borne.

She gives the air her breasts,
Unfingered ivory.

She gives the air her long self and her curved self,
And hips so round and heavy that they are tired.

All these noble abundances of girlhood
Make the doors divinely narrow and myself insane.

Columns of marble and ivory in the old way,
And anklets chinking in gold and musical bracelets.

Without her I am a she-camel that has lost,
And howls in the sand at night.

Without her I am as sad as an old mother
Hearing of the death of her many sons.

E. Powys Mathers

FROM THE MUFADDALIYAT

Compiled 8th century

ALQAMAH

6th century

His Camel

SO leave her, and cast care from thy heart with a sturdy
mount—a camel that ambles tireless, carrying riders
twain;

To Harith, the generous Lord, I drive her unsparing on,
with pantings that shake her breast and throb through
her ribs and flanks:

A fleet runner whose flesh over sides and where neck
meets hump has banished beneath noon-tide's hot
breath and the onward press;

And yet after night's long toil the dawn breaks and finds
her fresh as antelope, young and strong, that flees from
the hunter's pack:

They crouched by the *artà*-brake, the hunters, and
thought to win a safe prey: but she escaped their
shafts and pursuing hounds.

So travels my beast, and makes her object a man far off,
and little by little gains the way to his bounteous hand.

Yet, thou wast her labour's end—God keep thee from
curse, O King!—and through all the Desert's same-
ness sped she, beset with fears.

Towards thee the Pole-stars led, and there where men's
feet had passed a track plain to see that wound by
cairns over ridges scarred.

There bodies of beasts outworn lay thickly along the
road, their bones gleaming white, their hides all
shrivelled and hard and dry.

I bring her to drink the dregs of cisterns all mire and
draff; and if she mislikes it, all the choice is to journey
on.

Sir Charles Lyall

AL-ASWAD SON OF YA'FUR

6th century

Old Age

IF now thou seest me a wreck, worn out and minished
of sight, and all my limbs without strength to bear
my body along,

And I am deaf to the calls of love and lightness of youth,
and follow wisdom in meekness, my steps easy to
guide—

Time was I went every night, hair combed, to sellers of
wine, and squandered lightly my wealth, compliant,
easy of mood.

Yea, once I played, and enjoyed the sweetest flavour of
youth, my wine the first of the grape, mingled with
purest of rain—

Wine bought from one with a twang in his speech, and
rings in his ears, a belt girt round him: he brought it
forth for good silver coin.

A boy deals it to our guests, girt up, two pearls in his
ears, his fingers ruddy, as though stained deep with
mulberry juice,

And women white like the moon or statues stately to see,
that softly carry around great cups filled full with the
wine—

White women, dainty, that shoot the hearts of men with
their eyes, fair as a nest full of ostrich eggs betwixt
rock and sand.

Kind words they speak, and their limbs are soft and
smooth to the touch, their faces bright, and their
hearts to lovers gentle and mild.

Low speech they murmur, in tones that bear no secrets
abroad: they gain their ends without toil, and need
no shouting to win.

Sir Charles Lyall

SALĀMAH SON OF JANDAL

6th century

Gone is Youth

GONE is Youth, gone with praise—Youth full of
marvellous things ! gone and that is a race wherein
none may overtake.

Fled is it swiftly, and this hoary Eld comes on its track—
ah, would that the galloping steeds could reach it and
bring it back !

Gone is fair Youth, that time whose gains are fullness
of praise: in it was delight for us: no delight is left
for the old !

Yea, two days were good—the day of assemblies and
moots of the tribe, and the day of journeying through
light and darkness to fall on our foes—

The day we pushed on our steeds homewards the way
they had gone, with hoofs chipped, jaded and worn
by onset again and again;

And the galloping steeds came home with streaks
of blood on their breasts, as though their necks
were the stones where victims in Rajab are slain;

Yea, each one fleet, when the sweat soaks through the
saddle-pad clear of skin, smooth cheeked, bright of
hair, a galloper tireless of pace.

Not thin his forelock, nor humped his nose, no weakling
of limb: preferred is he in the dealing of milk, well
nurtured at home.

Each leg apart in its gallop seems to stream with a rush
of speed as though from a bucket of water poured o'er
the field.

Up starts he briskly, as starts a shepherd who in his
sleep has left his flock to a wolf to harry, and wakes
in alarm.

His withers rise to a neck far reaching upwards, below
a breast blood-stained, like a stone on which red
saffron is ground.

He races the wild asses, brown, green-lipped with the
grass: a thousand drop off behind him, easily wins
he unspurred.

To how many wretches have these by God's will brought
wealth and ease ! how many rich have they spoiled
and stript of all luxury !

With such as these do men enter battle with confident
heart in spite of spear-play: with such, hard pressed,
secure in their flight.

Of late Ma'add thought to do us hurt: but cooled was
their wrath before our spears, and the stroke of
swords not meant but to bruise:

Yea, swords of proof, and the spear-heads furbished
bright, set on shafts hard-grained, not hollow, with
knots to bind together their length;

Their heads gained glitter from hands of men that fight
in the van—no mongrels they, dark of hue, no
slinkers puny of build !

The clip made even their shafts, and straight they carry
the steel: no crooked stem canst thou see, but polished well-fitted spears;

Blue steel their points, red and straight their slender
Indian stems: atop they bear after fight the heads of
chieftains slain.

Our men, when battle is joined, ply briskly, skilled in
the play, lances like ropes at the well, where many
drawers combine.

Both armies led from Ma'add, the men from Upland
and Plain, both feel the pain of our spears, and cannot hide it with lies.

For me, I find that the Sons of Sa'd shine before all ;
with warriors first in the fight like firebrands kindled
to blaze;

Tamim the stock they uphold in wealth of glory and
fame:—whoso bears credit among mankind, he owes
it to race.

A people they, when a year of famine presses, their tents
bring strength to starvelings, and rest to wandering
sons of the Wild.

When bites Calamity, sharp-toothed, cruel, patience is
theirs to bear unflinching, and countless men to stand
for the lost.

When wind blows chill from the North, we pitch our
tents in the dales where drought has left in their
bottoms stumps and brushes to burn:

Their paddocks hoary with frost, their brook-beds
trampled and bare, their wallowing-grounds naught
but dust, rainless, all greenery gone.

When one comes calling to us for help and succour in
need, clear is our answer to him—forth start we
straight in his cause;

Swiftly we saddle the camels strong and eager to go,
and quick we set on our short-haired steeds the gear
for the road.

Men say—" Their beasts are kept tethered close to where
they are fed: though scant the milk of their camels,
spared is it ever for them."

So stand we, great in men's eyes: our ladies ne'er turn
aside whenso they travel from Khatt to upland lava
plains.

Sir Charles Lyall

KHANSÁ

Tears

7th century

TEARS, ere thy death, for many a one I shed,
But thine are all my tears since thou art dead.
To comforters I lend my ear apart,
While pain sits ever closer to my heart.

R. A. Nicholson

TA' ABBATA SHARRA

Ever Watchful

7th century

NOR exults he nor complains he; silent bears whate'er
befalls him,
Much desiring, much attempting; far the wanderings
of his venture.
In one desert noon beholds him; evening finds him
in another;
As the wild ass lone he crosses o'er the jagged and
headlong ridges.
Swifter than the wind unpausing, onward yet, nor
rest nor slackness,
Wild the howling gusts outspeeded in the distance
moan and falter,
Light the slumber on his eyelids, yet too heavy all
he deems it;
Ever watchful for the moment when to draw the
bitter faulchion;
When to plunge it in the heart,blood of the many,
mustered foemen.

W. G. Palgrave

OMAR BEN ABI RABI'A

d. 720

The Damsel

AH for the throes of a heart sorely wounded !
Ah for the eyes that have smit me with madness !
Gently she moved in the calmness of beauty,
Moved as the bough to the light breeze of morning,
Dazzled my eyes as they gazed, till before me
All was a mist and confusion of figures.
Ne'er had I sought her, and ne'er had she sought me;
Fated the love, and the hour, and the meeting !
There I beheld her, as she and her damsels
Paced 'twixt the temple and outer enclosure:
Damsels the fairest, the loveliest, the gentlest,
Passing like slow-wending heifers at evening,
Ever surrounding with courtly observance
Her whom they honour, the peerless of women.
Then to a handmaid, the youngest, she whispered:
" 'Omar is near; let us mar his devotions.
Cross on his path that he needs may observe us;
Give him a signal, my sister, demurely."
" Signals I gave, but he marked not or heeded,"
Answered the damsel, and hasted to meet me.
Ah for that night by the vale of the sand-hills !
Ah for the dawn when in silence we parted !
He who the morn may awake to her kisses
Drinks from the cup of the blessed in heaven !

W. G. Palgrave

FROM THE HAMÂSAH

Compiled 9th century

HITTÂN, SON OF AL‑MU’ ALLÀ OF TAYYI

His Children

FORTUNE has brought me down—her wonted way—
    from station great and high to low estate;
Fortune has rent away my plenteous store;
    of all my wealth honour alone is left.
Fortune has turned my joy to tears; how oft
    did Fortune make me laugh with what she gave !
But for these girls, the *kata's* downy brood,
    unkindly thrust from door to door as hard—
Far would I roam and wide to seek my bread
    in Earth that has no end of breadth and length.
Nay, but our children in our midst, what else
    but our hearts are they, walking on the ground ?
If but the breeze blow harsh on one of them,
    mine eye says no to slumber all night long.

Sir Charles Lyall

ABU ’L’ALÁ AL‑MA’ ARRÎ

973–1057

Aweary am I

AWEARY am I of living in town and village—
And oh, to be camped alone in a desert region,
Revived by the scent of lavender when I hunger
And scooping into my palm, if I thirst, well‑water !
Meseemeth, the Days are dromedaries lean and jaded
That bear on their backs humanity travelling on‑
    ward;
They shrink not in dread from any portentous night‑
    mare,

Nor quail at the noise of shouting and rush of panic,
But journey along for ever with those they carry,
Until at the last they kneel by the dug-out houses.
No need, when in earth the maid rests covered over,
No need for her locks of hair to be loosed and plaited;
The young man parts from her, and his tears are
flowing—
Even thus do the favours flow of disgustful Fortune.

R. A. Nicholson

IBN ZAYDŪN

1003–1071

Cordova

STILL round thy towers descends the fertile rain !
Still sing the doves in every leafy den !
Cordova, fairest home of gallant men,
Where youth my childhood's trinkets snapped in
twain
And noble sires begat me noble, free !

Happy those days, with purer pleasures blest,
Those winding vales we roamed with boyish zest,
White-throated, raven-haired, all mirth and jest.
Chide not the trailing robes, the silken vest,
The reckless pride of youth—no wantons we.

Say to an age whose joys long since are fled,
Its traces by the lapse of nights now faint and
mouldered
(Softly the breeze its evening fragrance shed !
Bright shone its stars o'er the night-traveller's head !):
"Farewell from one whose love still burns for
thee ! "

H. A. R. Gibb

MU'TAMID, KING OF SEVILLE

1040–1095

FOR though his sun of power went down so long ago that the West has forgotten the colours of his glory, and though the kingdom for which he gave his blood and his children and the years of his life now bows to other rulers, another faith, yet among a beauty-loving race he still preserves—by reason of those lines which wars have not scattered nor Time effaced—a gentle eminence.—DULCIE L. SMITH.

The Fountain

THE sea hath tempered it; the mighty sun
Polished the blade,
And from the limpid sheath the sword leaps forth;
Man hath not made
A better in Damascus—though for slaughter
Hath steel somewhat advantage over water.

Thy Garden

MY thoughts are as a garden-plot, that knows
No rain but of thy giving, and no rose
Except thy name. I dedicate it thine,
My garden, full of fruits in harvest time.

Tears of the World

WEEP for me, friends, for now that I am hence,
Lo, in Time's dust the footprints of my pride !
Lament, strong lions of my great defence,
Shed tears, my young gazelles and dewy-eyed !
Look ye, the cold stars even in the height
Weep, and the clouds lift not their mournful night.

Weep, Wahid, weep, and Zahi with the towers,
Weep ye for him that shall not come again.

All waters of the earth, all dew and showers
   Have tears for Mu'tamid, and the summer rain
That once strewed pearls upon him, is become
A sea-wave full of sand and sound and foam.

Woo not the World

WOO not the world too rashly, for behold,
   Beneath the painted silk and broidering,
   It is a faithless and inconstant thing.
(Listen to me, Mu'tamid, growing old.)

And we—that dreamed youth's blade would never
   rust,
   Hoped wells from the mirage, roses from the
   sand—
The riddle of the world shall understand
And put on wisdom with the robe of dust.

                 Dulcie L. Smith

IBN AL-ARABI

                1165–1240

Ode

WHO can support the anguish of love?
   Who can drain the bitter draught of destiny?

     I said in my grief,
     In my burning passion:
     " O would that he who caused my sickness
     Had tended me when I was sick ! "

     He passed by the house door,
     Mocking, hiding himself;
     Veiling his head,
     And turning away.

His veiling did me no hurt;
I was only hurt by his having turned away from me.

                R. A. Nicholson

Ode

THEY journeyed,
When the darkness of night
Had let down her curtain;
And I said to her:
" Pity a passionate lover,
Outcast and distraught,
Whom desires eagerly encompass,
And at whom
Speeding arrows are aimed
Wheresoever he bends his course."

She displayed her teeth
And lightning flashed,
And I knew not
Which of the twain rent the gloom.
And I said:
" Is it not enough for him
That I am in his heart,
And that he beholds me at every moment ?
Is it not enough ? "

R. A. Nicholson

FROM THE THOUSAND AND ONE NIGHTS

13th century ?

Dates

WE grow to the sound of the wind
Playing his flutes in our hair,

Palm-tree daughters,
Brown-flesh Bedouin,
Fed with light
By our gold father;

We are loved of the free-tented,
The sons of space, the hall-forgetters,
The wide-handed, the bright-sworded
Masters of horses.

Who has rested in the shade of our palms
Shall hear us murmur ever above his sleep.

The Song of the Narcissus

MY beauty is not wine to me,
For I have eyes of languor,
And balance like music
And am nobly born.

I consider the flowers,
I talk with the flowers in moonlight.
My beauty gives me a throne among them,
Yet I am a slave.

I am a slave,
The cincture of obedience,
The good servant
Who stands with a straight body
And bowed head.

I bare my neck,
I abide in my pure tent
Pitched on an emerald column;
My robe is gold and silver.

My modesty will excuse the wantoning of my eyes
As I hang my head above the waters.

Psalm of Battle

GOD is praise and glory;
Therefore glory and praise be unto Him
Who led me by the hand in stony places,
Who gave me a treasure of gold and a throne of gold
And set a sword of victory in my hand !

He covered the earth with the shadow of my king-
    dom,
And fed me when I was a stranger
Among strange peoples;
When I was lowly He accounted me
And He has bound my brow about with triumph.

His enemies fled before my face like cattle;
The Lord breathed upon them and they were not !
Not with the ferment of a generous wine
But with death's evil grape
He has sent them drunken into the darkness.

We died, we died in the battle,
But He has set us upon happy grass
Beside an eternal river of scented honey.

Haroun's Favourite Song

AN early dew woos the half-opened flowers,
Wind of the south, dear child,
Close clings about their stalks for drunken hours;
    And yet your eyes, dear child,
Cool pools which rise, dear child,
    High in the mountains of my soul,
    These, these
The lips have drunken whole;
And yet your mouth, dear child,
        Your mouth, dear child, is envied of the bees.

The Sleeper

SLEEPER, the palm-trees drink the breathless noon,
A golden bee sucks at a fainting rose,
Your lips smile in their sleep.   Oh, do not move.

Sleeper, oh, do not move the gilded gauze
Which lies about your gold, or you will scare
The sun's gold fire which leaps within your crystal.

Sleeper, oh, do not move; your breasts in sleep,
Allah, they dip and fall like waves at sea;
Your breasts are snow, I breathe them like sea foam,
I taste them like white salt.   They dip and fall.

Sleeper, they dip and fall.   The smiling stream
Stifles its laugh, the gold bee on the lea
Dies of much love and rosy drunkenness,
My eyes burn the red grapes upon your breasts.

Sleeper, oh, let them burn, let my heart's flower,
Fed on the rose and santal of your flesh,
Burst like a poppy in this solitude,
In this cool silence.

Laments

Abu Nowas for the Barmacides

SINCE earth has put you away, O sons of Barmak,
The roads of morning twilight and evening twilight
Are empty.   My heart is empty, O sons of Barmak.

The Wazir Dandan for Prince Sharkan

WISE to have gone so early to reward,
        Child of the sword;
    Wise with a single new-bathed eagle's flight
        To have touched the white
    Wild roses spread for feet in paradise.

Ah, my son, wise
Soon to have drained the new and bitter cup
Which, once drunk up,
Leads straightway to an old immortal wine
Pressed from God's vine.

Her Rival for Aziza

I PASSED a tomb among green shades
Where seven anemones with down-dropped heads
Wept tears of dew upon the stone beneath.
I questioned underneath my breath
Who the poor dead might be
And a voice answered me. . . .
So now I pray that Allah may be moved
To drop sleep on her eyes because she loved.
She will not care though lovers do not come
To wipe the dust from off a lover's tomb,
She will not care for anything.   But I please
To plant some more dew-wet anemones
    That they may weep.

Haroun Al-Rachid for Heart's-Life

CHILD, who went gathering the flowers of death,
My heart's not I, I cannot teach my heart;
It cries when I forget.
It has not learnt my art
To forget lips when scented with their breath
Or the red cup, when I am drunken yet.

Tumadir Al-Khansa for her Brother

WEEP ! Weep ! Weep !
    These tears are for my brother.
    Henceforth that veil which lies between us,
    That recent earth,
    Shall not be lifted again.

You have gone down to the bitter water
Which all must taste,
And you went pure, saying:
" Life is a buzz of hornets about a lance point."

But my heart remembers, O son of my father and
mother,
I wither like summer grass,
I shut myself in the tent of consternation.

He is dead, who was the buckler of our tribe
And the foundation of our house,
He has departed in calamity.

He is dead, who was the lighthouse of courageous
men,
Who was for the brave
As fires lighted upon the mountains.

He is dead, who rode costly horses,
Shining in his garments.
The hero of the long shoulder-belt is dead,
The young man of valiance and beauty breathes
no more;
The right hand of generosity is withered,
And the beardless king of our tribe shall breathe
no more.

He shall be cold beneath his rock.

Say to his mare Alwa
That she must weep
As she runs riderless for ever. . . .

When the red millstone ground the flowers of youth,
You shattered a thousand horses against the squad-
rons;
High on the groaning flanks of Alwa
You lifted the bright skirts of your silver mail.

You made the lances live,
You shook their beams,
You quenched their beams in red,
O tiger of the double panoply.

White women wandered with disordered veils
And you saved them in the morning.
Your captives were as troops of antelopes
Whose beauty troubles the first drops of rain. . . .

How effortless were your rhymes of combat
Chanted in tumult, O my brother !
They pierced like lances,
They live among our hearts for ever.

Let the stars go out,
Let the sun withdraw his rays,
He was our star and sun.

Who now will gather in the strangers at dusk
When the sad North whistles with her winds ?
You have laid down and left in the dust, O wanderers,
Him who nourished you with his flocks
And bared his sword for your salvation.
You set him low in the terrible house
Among a few stakes planted,
You threw down boughs of salamah upon him.
He lies among the tombs of our fathers,
Where the days and the years shall pass over him
As they have passed over our fathers.
Your loss is a great distress to me,
Child of the Solamides,
I shall be glad no more. . . .

While you have tears, O daughters of the Solamides,
Weep ! Weep ! Weep !

INSCRIPTIONS AT THE CITY OF BRASS

1

ENTER and learn the story of the rulers:
They rested a little in the shadow of my towers
And then they passed.
They were dispersed like those shadows
When the sun goes down;
They were driven like straws
Before the wind of death.

2

THE drunkenness of youth has passed like a fever,
And yet I saw many things,
Seeing my glory in the days of my glory.
The feet of my war-horse
Drummed upon the cities of the world,
I sacked great towns like a hot wind
And fell like thunder upon far lands.
The kings of the earth were dragged behind my
chariot
And the people of the earth behind my laws;
But now
The drunkenness of youth has passed like a fever,
Like foam upon sand.
Death took me in a net:
My armies warred against him in vain,
My courtiers flattered him in vain.
Listen, O wayfarer, to the words of my death,
For they were not the words of my life:
Save up your soul
And taste the beautiful wine of peace,
For to-morrow the earth shall answer:
He is with me,
My jealous breast holds him for ever.

3

ABOUT this table
Sat many hawk-eyed kings
With many one-eyed kings
To bear them company;
But now all sit in the dark and none are able,
None are able to see.

4

IN the name of the Eternal,
In the name of the Master of Strength,
In the name of Him who moves not !
Wayfarer in this place,
Look not upon the glass of appearance,
For a breath may shatter it
And illusion is a pit for the feet of men.
I speak of my power:
I had ten thousand horses
Groomed by captive kings ;
I had a thousand virgins of royal blood
To serve my pleasure,
And a thousand excellent virgins
With moon-coloured breasts,
Chosen from all the world.
They brought forth little princes in my chambers
And the little princes were as brave as lions.
I had peculiar treasures,
And the West and the East were two heads
Bowing before me.
I thought my power eternal
And the days of my life
Fixed surely in the years;
But a whisper came to me
From Him who dies not.
I called my captains and my strong riders,
Thousands upon thousands

With swords and lances;
I called my tributary kings together
And those who were proud rulers under me.
I opened the boxes of my treasure to them, saying:
" Take hills of gold, mountains of silver,
And give me one more day upon the earth."
But they stood silent,
Looking upon the ground;
So that I died
And death came to sit upon my throne.
I was Kush bin Shadad bin Ad,
Surnamed the Great.

5

O SONS of men,
You add the future to the future
But your sum is spoiled
By the grey cypher of death.
There is a Master
Who breathes upon armies,
Building a narrow and dark house for kings.
These wake above their dust
In a black commonwealth.

6

O SONS of men,
Why do you put your hands before your eyes
And play in this road as if for ever,
Which is a short passing to another place ?
Where are the kings
Whose loins jetted empires,
Where are the very strong men,
Masters of Irak ?
Where are the lords of Ispahan,
O sons of men ?

7

O SONS of men,
  You see a stranger upon the road,
  You call to him and he does not stop.
He is your life
Walking towards time,
  Hurrying to meet the kings of India and China,
  Hurrying to greet the sultans of Sina and Nubia,
  Who were blown over the mountain crest
By a certain breath,
Even as he.

8

O SONS of men,
  Lean death perches upon your shoulder
Looking down into your cup of wine,
Looking down on the breasts of your lady.
You are caught in the web of the world
And the spider Nothing waits behind it.
Where are the men with towering hopes ?
They have changed places with owls,
Owls who lived in tombs
And now inhabit a palace.

                                    E. Powys Mathers

FROM THE ARABIC

I

THE CAMEL-RIDER

THERE is no thing in all the world but love,
  No jubilant thing of sun or shade worth one sad tear.
  Why dost thou ask my lips to fashion songs
  Other than this, my song of love to thee ?

See where I lie and pluck the thorns of grief,
Dust on my head and fire, as one who mourns his slain.
Are they not slain, my treasures of dear peace ?
This their red burial is, sand heaped on sand.

Here came I in the morning of my joys.
Before the dawn was born, through the dark downs
    I rode.
The low stars led me on as with a voice,
Stars of the scorpion's tail in the deep South.

Sighing I came, and scattering wide the sand.
No need had I to urge her speed with hand or heel,
The creature I bestrode. She knew my haste,
And knew the road I sought, the road to thee.

Jangling her bells aloud in wantonness,
And sighing soft, she too, her sighs to my soul's sighs.
Behind us the wind followed thick with scents
Of incense blossoms and the dews of night.

The thorn trees caught at us with their crook'd hands;
The hills in blackness hemmed us in and hid the road;
The spectres of the desert howled and warned;
I heeded nothing of their words of woe.

Thus till the dawn I sped in my desire,
Breasting the ridges, slope on slope, till morning broke;
And lo ! the sun revealed to me no sign,
And lo ! the day was widowed of my hope.

Where are the tents of pleasure and dear love,
Set in the Vale of Thyme, where winds in Spring are
    fain ?
The highways of the valley, where they stood
Strong in their flocks, are there. But where are they ?

The plain was dumb, as emptied of all voice;
No bleat of herds, no camels roaring far below
Told of their presence in the pastures void,
Of the waste places which had been their homes.

I climbed down from my watch-tower of the rocks,
To where the tamarisks grow, and the dwarf palms,
    alarmed.
I called them with my voice, as the deer calls,
Whose young the wolves have hunted from their place.

I sought them in the foldings of the hill,
In the deep hollows shut with rocks, where no winds
    blow.
I sought their footsteps under the tall cliffs,
Shut from the storms, where the first lambs are born.

The tamarisk boughs had blossomed in the night,
And the white broom which bees had found, the wild
    bees' brood.
But no dear signal told me of their life,
No spray was torn in all that world of flowers.

Where are the tents of pleasure and dear love,
For which my soul took ease for its delight in Spring,
The black tents of her people beautiful
Beyond the beauty of the sons of kings?

The wind of war has swept them from their place,
Scattering them wide as quails, whom the hawk's hate
    pursues;
The terror of the sword importunate
Was at their backs, nor spared them as they flew.

The summer wind has passed upon their fields;
The rain has purged their hearth-stones, and made
    smooth their floors;
Low in the valley lie their broken spears,
And the white bones which are their tale forlorn.

Where are the sons of Saba in the South,
The men of mirth and pride to whom my songs
    were sung,
The kinsmen of her soul who is my soul,
The brethren of her beauty whom I love?

She mounted her tall camel in the waste,
Loading it high for flight with her most precious things;
She went forth weeping in the wilderness,
Alone with fear on that far night of ill.

She fled mistrusting, as the wild roe flees,
Turning her eyes behind her, while fear fled before;
No other refuge knew she than her speed,
And the black land that lies where night is born.

Under what canopy of sulphurous heaven,
Dark with the thunderclouds unloosing their mad
    tongues,
Didst thou lie down aweary of thy burden,
In that dread place of silence thou hadst won?

Close to what shelter of what naked rocks,
Carved with what names of terror of what kings of old,
Near to what monstrous shapes unmerciful,
Watching thy death, didst thou give up thy soul?

Or dost thou live by some forgotten well,
Waiting thy day of ransom to return and smile,
As the birds come when Spring is in the heaven,
And dost thou watch me near while I am blind?

Blind in my tears, because I only weep,
Kindling my soul to fire because I mourn my slain,
My kindred slain, and thee, and my dear peace,
Making their burial thus, sand heaped on sand.

For see, there nothing is in all the world
But only love worth any strife or song or tear.
Ask me not then to sing or fashion songs
Other than this, my song of love to thee.

II

THE DAYS OF OUR YOUTH

THESE are the days of our youth, our days of glory
and honour.
Pleasure begotten of strength is ours, the sword in
our hand.
Wisdom bends to our will, we lead captivity captive.
Kings of our lives and love, receiving gifts from
men.

Why do I speak of wisdom ?   The prize is not for
the wisest.
Reason, the dull ox, ploughs a soil which no joy
shall reap.
Folly is fleeter far 'neath the heel of the fearless rider,
Folly the bare-backed steed we bestride, the steed
of the plains.

Mine is a lofty ambition, as wide as the world I covet.
Vast is the empire I claim for thee, thou spouse of
my soul.
Show me new lands to win, and, by God in heaven,
I swear it:
These shall be mine and thine to-night for all
time to hold.

Time is our slave and Fortune's.   We need not years
for fruition.
Here in our hands behold a key which unlocks the
world.
Each new day is a life.   For us there is no to-morrow.
Love no yesterday knows nor we, but to-day is ours.

See, what a wealth I bring thee, what treasure of
myrrh and spices !
Every kingdom of Earth have I sacked to procure
thee gold.

All the knowledge that fools have learned at the feet
of women,
  All that the wise have been taught in tears for
  thy sake I know.

Give thyself up to Love.   There is naught divine but
madness.
  Give thyself up to me Love's priest in his inmost
  shrine.
Shut thy eyes on the world, sublime in thy abnegation.
  Only the wise who have bowed their will shall
  receive the prize.

Shut thy eyes on the light.   I have nobler dreams to
read thee,
  Here in the shades of this darkened room, than the
  sun can show.
Is there not light in my eyes to-night more light than the
dreamlight ?
  See it breaks in streams on thy face; it illumes thy soul.

Let me persuade thy weakness.   I see thee here with my
reason.
  Let me convince thee of love with thy lips till thou
  cease to think.
Let me enfold thee with words more sweet than the
prayers of angels,
  Speaking thus with my hand on thy heart till it
  cease to beat.

Let me assuage thy grief with laughter, thy fear with
kisses.
  Let me cajole thy doubts with surprise, thy pride
  with tears.
Let me outshame the shame of thy face, outblush thy
blushes.
  Let me teach thee what Love can dare and yet
  dream no shame.

Let me uncover thy bosom and prove to thee its glory.
Let me preach to thee of thyself the live night long.
Let me chant new hymns to thy praise as I kneel
and worship,
Rising still like a god from my knees from eve till
morn.

Let me discourse of love with my hands and lips and
bosom.
Let me explain with my limbs the joy that a soul can
feel.
Let me unveil to thy bodily sense thy god incarnate
Taking flesh in a visible form for thy body's need.

Lo, on the mount of Love, the holiest place of holies,
Incense and prayer and the people's shout and the
fires have risen.
Love descends on the feast. He mounts the pyre in
silence,
Victim and priest and god in one, to thy dreams
revealed.

There, the rite is accomplished. Whatever Love
knows thou knowest.
Sudden the victim staggers and falls. In the dust it
lies.
See the hot blood flows for thy sake, it o'erflows the altar.
Dost thou not feel it stream in thy veins? It still
lives in thee.

These are the days of our youth, the days of our
dominion.
All the rest is a dream of death and a doubtful
thing.
Here we at least have lived, for love is all life's
wisdom,
Joy of joys for an hour to-day; then away, farewell!

Wilfrid Scawen Blunt

PERSIAN

ZOROASTER

7th century B.C. ?

From the Sacred Book

THIS I ask Thee—tell it to me truly, Lord !
Who the Sire was, Father first of Holiness ?
Who the pathway for the sun and stars ordained ?
Who, through whom is't moon doth wax and wane
    again ?
This and much else do I long, O God, to know.

This I ask Thee—tell it to me truly, Lord !
Who set firmly earth below, and kept the sky
Sure from falling ?   Who the streams and trees did
    make ?
Who their swiftness to the winds and clouds hath
    yoked ?
Who, O Mazda, was the Founder of Good Thought ?

This I ask Thee—tell it to me truly, Lord !
Who, benignant, made the darkness and the light ?
Who, benignant, sleep and waking did create ?
Who the morning, noon, and evening did decree
As reminders to the wise, of duty's call ?

A. V. Williams Jackson

FIRDAWSÍ

935–1025

Alas for Youth

MUCH have I laboured, much read o'er
Of Arabic and Persian lore,
    Collecting tales unknown and known;
    Now two-and-sixty years are flown.

Regret, and deeper woe of sin,
'Tis all that youth has ended in,
And I with mournful thoughts rehearse
Bu Táhir Khusrawáni's verse:
" I mind me of my youth and sigh,
Alas for youth, for youth gone by ! "

R. A. Nicholson

OMAR KHAYYÁM

d. 1123

*A*ND *this, I think, especially distinguishes Omar from all other
Persian poets: That, whereas with them the Poet is lost in his Song,
the Man in Allegory and Abstraction ; we seem to have the Man—
the* Bonhomme—*Omar himself, with all his humours and passions, as
frankly before us as if we were really at Table with him, after the Wine
had gone round.*—EDWARD FITZGERALD.

Rubaiyat

A WAKE ! for Morning in the Bowl of Night
Has flung the Stone that puts the Stars to Flight :
   And lo ! the Hunter of the East has caught
The Sultan's turret in a noose of light.

Dreaming when Dawn's Left Hand was in the Sky,
I heard a Voice within the Tavern cry,
   " Awake, my little ones, and fill the Cup
Before Life's Liquor in its Cup be dry."

And as the Cock crew, those who stood before
The Tavern shouted—" Open then the Door !
   You know how little while we have to stay,
And, once departed, may return no more."

Now the New Year reviving old Desires,
The thoughtful Soul to Solitude retires,
   Where the WHITE HAND OF MOSES on the Bough
Puts out, and Jesus from the Ground suspires.

Iram indeed is gone with all his Rose,
And Jamshyd's Seven-ringed Cup where no one knows;
　　But still the Vine her ancient Ruby yields,
And still a Garden by the Water blows.

And David's lips are lockt; but in divine
High-piping Pehlevì, with " Wine ! Wine ! Wine !
　　Red Wine ! "—the Nightingale cries to the Rose
That yellow cheek of hers to incarnadine.

Come, fill the Cup, and in the fire of Spring
Your Winter garment of Repentance fling:
　　The Bird of Time has but a little way
To fly—and Lo ! the Bird is on the Wing.

And look—a thousand blossoms with the Day
Woke—and a thousand scattered into Clay:
　　And this first Summer Month that brings the Rose
Shall take Jamshyd and Kaikobad away.

But come with old Khayyám and leave the Lot
Of Kaikobad and Kaikhosru forgot:
　　Let Rustum lay about him as he will,
Or Hatim Tai cry Supper—heed them not.

With me along the strip of Herbage strown
That just divides the desert from the sown,
　　Where name of Slave and Sultán is forgot—
And pity Sultan Mahmúd on his Throne !

Here with a Loaf of Bread beneath the Bough,
A Flask of Wine, a Book of Verse—and Thou
　　Beside me singing in the wilderness—
And Wilderness is Paradise enow.

" How sweet is mortal Sovranty "—think some:
Others—" How blest the Paradise to come ! "
　　Ah, take the Cash in hand and waive the Rest;
Oh, the brave Music of a *distant* drum !

Look to the Rose that blows about us—" Lo,
Laughing," she says, " into the world I blow,
  At once the silken tassel of my Purse
Tear, and its Treasure on the Garden throw."

The Worldly Hope men set their Hearts upon
Turns Ashes—or it prospers ; and anon,
  Like Snow upon the Desert's dusty Face,
Lighting a little hour or two—is gone.

And those who husbanded the Golden Grain,
And those who flung it to the winds like Rain,
  Alike to no such aureate Earth are turned
As, buried once, Men want dug up again.

Think, in this battered Caravanserai
Whose doorways are alternate Night and Day,
  How Sultán after Sultán with his Pomp
Abode his Hour or two, and went his way.

They say the Lion and the Lizard keep
The Courts where Jamshyd gloried and drank deep:
  And Bahrám, that great Hunter—the Wild Ass
Stamps o'er his Head, and he lies fast asleep.

I sometimes think that never blows so red
The Rose as where some buried Cæsar bled;
  That every Hyacinth the Garden wears
Dropt in her Lap from some once lovely Head.

And this delightful Herb whose tender Green
Fledges the River's Lip on which we lean—
  Ah, lean upon it lightly ! for who knows
From what once lovely Lip it springs unseen !

Ah, my Beloved, fill the Cup that clears
To-DAY of past Regrets and future Fears—
  To-morrow !—Why, To-morrow I may be
Myself with Yesterday's Seven thousand Years.

For some we loved, the loveliest and the best
That Time and Fate of all their vintage prest,
  Have drunk their Cup a Round or two before,
And one by one crept silently to rest,

And we, that now make merry in the Room
They left, and Summer dresses in new bloom,
  Ourselves must we beneath the Couch of Earth
Descend—ourselves to make a Couch—for whom?

Ah, make the most of what we yet may spend,
Before we too into the Dust descend;
  Dust into Dust, and under Dust to lie,
Sans Wine, sans Song, sans Singer, and—sans End.

Alike for those who for TO∕DAY prepare,
And those that after a TO∕MORROW stare,
  A Muezzin from the Tower of Darkness cries,
" Fools ! your Reward is neither Here nor There ! "

Why, all the Saints and Sages who discussed
Of the Two Worlds so learnedly, are thrust
  Like foolish Prophets forth; their Words to Scorn
Are scattered, and their Mouths are stopt with Dust.

Oh, come with old Khayyám, and leave the wise
To talk; one thing is certain, that Life flies;
  One thing is certain, and the rest is lies;
The Flower that once has blown for ever dies.

Myself when young did eagerly frequent
Doctor and Saint, and heard great argument
  About it and about: but evermore
Came out by the same door as in I went.

With them the seed of Wisdom did I sow,
And with mine own hand laboured it to grow;
  And this was all the Harvest that I reaped—
" I came like Water, and like Wind I go."

Into this Universe, and *Why* not knowing
Nor *Whence*, like Water willy-nilly flowing;
   And out of it, as Wind along the Waste,
I know not *Whither*, willy-nilly blowing.

What, without asking, hither hurried *Whence?*
And, without asking, *Whither* hurried hence?
   Another and another Cup to drown
The Memory of this Impertinence.

Up from Earth's Centre through the Seventh Gate
I rose, and on the Throne of Saturn sate,
   And many a Knot unravel'd by the Road;
But not the knot of Human Death and Fate.

There was a Door to which I found no Key;
There was a Veil past which I could not see:
   Some little talk awhile of ME and THEE
There seemed—and then no more of THEE and ME.

Then to the rolling Heaven itself I cried,
Asking, " What Lamp had Destiny to guide
   Her little Children stumbling in the Dark? "
And—" A blind Understanding! " Heaven replied.

Then to the earthen Bowl did I adjourn
My Lip the secret Well of Life to learn:
   And Lip to Lip it murmured—" while you live
Drink!—for once dead you never shall return."

I think the Vessel, that with fugitive
Articulation answered, once did live,
   And merry-make; and the cold Lip I kissed,
How many Kisses might it take—and give!

For in the Market-place, one Dusk of Day,
I watched the Potter thumping his wet Clay:
   And with its all obliterated Tongue
It murmured—" Gently, Brother, gently, pray! "

Ah, fill the Cup;—what boots it to repeat
How Time is slipping underneath our feet:
    Unborn To/morrow and dead YESTERDAY
Why fret about them if to/day be sweet !

One Moment in Annihilation's waste,
One Moment of the Well of Life to taste—
    The Stars are setting and the Caravan
Starts for the Dawn of Nothing—Oh, make haste !

How long, how long, in definite pursuit
Of This and That endeavour and dispute ?
    Better be merry with the fruitful Grape
Than sadden after none, or bitter, Fruit.

You know, my Friends, how long since in my House
For a new Marriage I did make Carouse:
    Divorced old barren Reason from my Bed,
And took the Daughter of the Vine to Spouse.

For " Is " and " Is/NOT " though *with* Rule and Line,
And " UP/AND/DOWN " *without*, I could define,
    I yet in all I only cared to know,
Was never deep in anything but—Wine.

And lately, by the Tavern Door agape,
Came stealing through the Dusk an Angel Shape
    Bearing a Vessel on his Shoulder; and
He bid me taste of it; and 'twas—the Grape !

The Grape that can with Logic absolute
The Two/and/Seventy jarring Sects confute:
    The subtle Alchemist that in a trice
Life's leaden metal into Gold transmute:

The mighty Mahmúd, the victorious Lord,
That all the misbelieving and black Horde
    Of Fears and Sorrows that infest the Soul
Scatters and slays with his enchanted Sword.

But leave the wise to wrangle, and with me
The Quarrel of the Universe let be:
  And, in some corner of the Hubbub couched,
Make Game of that which makes as much of Thee.

For in and out, above, about, below,
'Tis nothing but a Magic Shadow-show,
  Played in a Box whose Candle is the Sun,
Round which we Phantom Figures come and go.

And if the Wine you drink, the Lip you press,
End in the Nothing all Things end in—Yes—
  Then fancy while Thou art, Thou art but what
Thou shalt be—Nothing—Thou shalt not be less.

While the Rose blows along the River Brink,
With old Khayyám the Ruby Vintage drink:
  And when the Angel with his darker Draught
Draws up to Thee—take that, and do not shrink.

'Tis all a Chequer-board of Nights and Days
Where Destiny with Men for Pieces plays;
  Hither and thither moves, and mates, and slays,
And one by one back in the Closet lays.

The Ball no question makes of Ayes and Noes,
But Right or Left as strikes the Player goes;
  And He that tossed Thee down into the Field,
He knows about it all—HE knows—HE knows !

The Moving Finger writes; and, having writ,
Moves on: nor all thy Piety nor Wit
  Shall lure it back to cancel half a Line,
Nor all thy Tears wash out a Word of it.

And that inverted Bowl we call the Sky,
Whereunder crawling cooped we live and die,
  Lift not thy hands to *It* for help—for It
Rolls impotently on as Thou or I.

With Earth's first Clay They did the Last Man's knead,
And there of the Last Harvest sowed the Seed:
　　Yes, the first Morning of Creation wrote
What the Last Dawn of Reckoning shall read.

I tell thee this—When, started from the Goal,
Over the shoulders of the flaming Foal
　　Of Heaven Parwín and Mushtara they flung,
In my predestined Plot of Dust and Soul

The Vine had struck a fibre: which about
If clings my Being—let the Sufí flout;
　　Of my Base metal may be filed a Key,
That shall unlock the Door he howls without.

And this I know: whether the one True Light
Kindle to Love, or Wrath consume me quite,
　　One Glimpse of It within the Tavern caught
Better than in the Temple lost outright.

Oh Thou, who didst with Pitfall and with Gin
Beset the Road I was to wander in,
　　Thou wilt not with Predestination round
Enmesh me, and impute my Fall to Sin?

Oh Thou, who Man of baser Earth didst make,
And who with Eden didst devise the Snake:
　　For all the Sin wherewith the Face of Man
Is blackened, Man's forgiveness give—and take!

　　*　　*　　*　　*　　*　　*　　*　　*

Listen again. One Evening at the Close
Of Ramazan, ere the better Moon arose,
　　In that old Potter's Shop I stood alone
With the clay Population round in Rows.

And, strange to tell, among the Earthen Lot
Some could articulate, while others not:
　　And suddenly one more impatient cried—
" Who *is* the Potter, pray, and who the Pot ? "

Then said another—" Surely not in vain
My substance of the common Earth was ta'en,
   That He who subtly wrought me to the shape,
Should stamp me back to common Earth again."

Another said—" Why, ne'er a peevish Boy
Would break the Bowl from which he drank in joy;
   Shall He that made the Vessel in pure Love
And Fancy, in an after Rage destroy ! "

None answered this : but after silence spake
Some Vessel of a more ungainly Make:
   " They sneer at me for leaning all awry:
What ! did the Hand then of the Potter shake ? "

Said one—" Folks of a surly Tapster tell,
And daub his Visage with the Smoke of Hell;
   They talk of some strict Testing of us—Pish !
He's a good fellow, and 'twill all be well."

Then said another with a long-drawn Sigh,
" My Clay with long Oblivion is gone dry:
   But, fill me with the old familiar Juice,
Methinks I might recover by and by."

So while the Vessels one by one were speaking,
One spied the little Crescent all were seeking:
   And then they jogged each other, " Brother !
     Brother !
Hark for the Porter's shoulder-knot a-creaking ! "

Ah, with the Grape my fading Life provide,
And wash my Body whence the Life has died,
   And in a winding-sheet of Vine-leaf wrapt
So bury me by some sweet Garden-side,

That even my buried Ashes such a snare
Of Perfume shall fling up into the Air
   As not a True Believer passing by
But shall be overtaken unaware.

Indeed the Idols I have loved so long
Have done my credit in Men's Eyes much wrong:
  Have drowned my Honour in a shallow Cup,
And sold my Reputation for a Song.

Indeed, indeed, Repentance oft before
I swore—but was I sober when I swore?
  And then and then came Spring, and Rose-in-hand
My thread-bare Penitence apieces tore.

And much as Wine has played the Infidel,
And robbed me of my Robe of Honour—Well,
  I often wonder what the Vintners buy
One half so precious as the Goods they sell.

Alas, that Spring should vanish with the Rose!
That Youth's sweet-scented manuscript should close!
  The Nightingale that in the branches sang,
Ah whence, and whither flown again, who knows!

Ah, Love! could you and I with Fate conspire
To grasp this sorry Scheme of Things entire,
  Would not we shatter it to bits—and then
Re-mould it nearer to the Heart's Desire!

*   *   *   *   *   *   *   *

Ah, Moon of my Delight who know'st no wane,
The Moon of Heaven is rising once again:
  How oft hereafter rising shall she look
Through this same Garden after me—in vain!

And when Thyself with shining Foot shall pass
Among the Guests Star-scattered on the Grass,
  And in thy joyous Errand reach the spot
Where I made One—turn down an empty Glass!

                                   Edward FitzGerald

JALĀLU'DDĪN RŪMĪ

1207–1273

A Beauty that all Night Long

A BEAUTY that all night long teaches love-tricks to
   Venus and the moon,
Whose two eyes by their witchery seal up the two
   eyes of heaven.
Look to your hearts! I, whate'er betide, O Moslems,
Am so mingled with him that no heart is mingled
   with me.
I was born of his love at the first, I gave him my
   heart at the last;
When the fruit springs from the bough, on that
   bough it hangs.
The tip of his curl is saying, " Ho ! betake thee to
   rope-dancing."
The cheek of this candle is saying, " Where is a
   moth that it may burn ? "
For the sake of dancing on that rope, O heart,
   make haste, become a hoop;
Cast thyself on the flame, when his candle is lit.
Thou wilt never more endure without the flame,
   when thou hast known the rapture of burning;
If the water of life should come to thee, it would
   not stir thee from the flame.

R. A. Nicholson

SA'DI

d. 1291

From the Gulistan

SADI'S favourite mode is a simplicity and tenderness of heart, a delicacy of feeling and judgment, and that exquisitely natural vein in which he relates his many apologues and parables with a sort of sen= tentious and epigrammatic turn.—JAMES ROSS.

HE HATH NO PARALLEL

SHOULD any ask me on His form to dwell,
Helpless I say,—" He hath no parallel."
The lovers by the loved one all are slain,
No voice can answer from the dead again.

THE GIFT OF SPEECH

NOW, while thou hast the wondrous power of word,
Let every thought in shining grace appear;
To=morrow, when Death's messenger is here,
He will constrain thee to depart unheard.

ON THE DECEPTION OF APPEARANCES

THE man that never will declare his thought
Conceals a soul of honour or of sin.
Dost think yon silent jungle holdeth naught?
Perchance a lurking tiger sleeps therein.

FRIENDSHIP

HE is no friend who in thine hour of pride
Brags of his love and calls himself thy kin.
He is a friend who hales his fellow in,
And clangs the door upon the wolf outside.

TAKE THE CRUST

MY precious life I spent considering
What I should eat in summer, wear in spring.
Vile belly ! take the crust ! 'tis nobler food
Than all the capons plucked in servitude.

MESNEVI

IF livelihood by knowledge were endowed,
None would be poorer than the brainless crowd;
Yet fortune on the fool bestows the prize,
And leaves but themes for wonder to the wise.

The luck of wealth dependeth not on skill,
But only on the aid of Heaven's will:
So it has happened since the world began—
The witless ape outstrips the learned man;
A poet dies of hunger, grief, and cold;
A fool among the ruins findeth gold.

LOVE'S LAST RESOURCE

SINCE naught avails, let me arise and leave,
Though down the way of swords I wounded crawl;
Perchance I shall attain to touch her sleeve,
And surely on her threshold dying fall.

ALAS !

SHE, who could neither rest nor sleep
Ere round her she had scattered hyacinths and roses,
Now with the roses of her face death-strewn reposes,
And o'er her tomb wild brambles creep.

L. Cranmer-Byng

COURAGE

WHOEVER hath washed his hands of living
Utters his mind without misgiving.

In straits which no escape afford
The hand takes hold of the edge of the sword.

HELP

VEX no man's secret soul—if that can be—
 The path of life hath far too many a thorn !
Help whom thou may'st—for surely unto thee
 Sharp need of help will e'er the end be borne.

THE SOOTHSAYER

WHAT could he know of sky and stars or heaven's
 all-hidden life,
Who did not see in his own house the knave that
 kissed his wife ?

WEALTH

HE that owns wealth, in mountain, wold, or waste,
Plays master—pitches tent at his own taste;
 Whilst he who lacks that which the world commends
 Must pace a stranger, e'en in his own lands.

Sir Edwin Arnold

From the Bustan

THE DANCER

I HEARD how, to the beat of some quick tune,
There rose and danced a Damsel like the moon,
 Flower-mouthed and Pâri-faced; and all around her
Neck-stretching Lovers gathered close; but, soon

A flickering lamp-flame caught her skirt, and set
Fire to the flying gauze. Fear did beget
 Trouble in that light heart ! She cried amain.
Quoth one among her worshippers, "Why fret,

Tulip of Love ? Th' extinguished fire hath burned
Only one leaf of thee; but I am turned
 To ashes—leaf and stalk, and flower and root—
By lamp-flash of thine eyes ! "—" Ah, Soul concerned

Solely with self ! "—she answered, laughing low,
" If thou wert Lover thou hadst not said so.
Who speaks of the Belov'd's woe as not his
Speaks infidelity, true Lovers know ! "

THE GREAT PHYSICIAN

A TUMULT in a Syrian town had place:
They seized an old man there of wit and grace;
Still in my ear lingers his noble saying,
When, fettered fast, they smote him in the face.

Quotha: " If of all Sultans the Sultán
Gives not the word for plunder, who else can ?
Who, save upon His bidding, would be bold
To do such deeds ? Therefore I hold the man

That wrongs me not mine enemy but friend;
God hath appointed him unto this end !
If there fall scorn or honour, gifts or shackles,
'Tis God—not Zayd or Omar—who doth send."

Right, Sheykh ! no griefs the wise heart will annoy;
The Great Physician sharp drugs doth employ !
A sick man's not more skilful than his Hâkim;
Take what the Friend gives as a bliss and joy.

Sir Edwin Arnold

Ode

UNTIL thine hands clasp girdlewise the waist of the
Belov'd,
Thou ne'er wilt kiss to heart's desire the mouth of
the Belov'd.
Know'st thou what is the life of him the sword of
Love hath slain ?
To bite an apple from the orchard cheek of the
Belov'd.
Khusrau and Shirin's mighty love is rased and
washed away

By tide of turmoil swelling high 'twixt me and the
    Belov'd.
The champion whom in far war's field no paynim
    arrow slew,
His blood was shed by bow-like fair eyebrow of the
    Belov'd.
Gone is mine heart, mine eye weeps blood; and if my
    faint soul lives,
'Tis only that I may bestow its life on the Belov'd.
Aye, one day I will fling myself beneath his Arab's hoof,
Unless disdain and pride pull in the rein of the Belov'd.
Howbeit in this quest, alas, I never win to joy,
It may be that my name will pass the lips of the Belov'd.
Sith life must once be yielded up, whatever fate befall,
Most sweet to die in Love's abode at the door of the
    Belov'd !
Surely will I then bear with me this passion to the grave,
And from the grave arise and ask the way to the Belov'd.
All men cry out against the hand of hated enemy,
But Sa'di cried against the unloving heart of the Belov'd.

R. A. Nicholson

HAFIZ

d. 1389

HAFIZ *is the prince of Persian poets, and in his extraordinary gifts adds to some of the attributes of Pindar, Anacreon, Horace, and Burns the insight of a mystic.*—RALPH WALDO EMERSON.

A Persian Song of Hafiz

SWEET maid, if thou wouldst charm my sight,
    And bid these arms thy neck enfold;
    That rosy cheek, that lily hand,
    Would give thy poet more delight
    Than all Bocara's vaunted gold,
    Than all the gems of Samarcand.

Boy, let yon liquid ruby flow,
And bid thy pensive heart be glad,
Whate'er the frowning zealots say:
Tell them, their Eden cannot show
A stream so clear as Rocnabad,
A bow'r so sweet as Mosellay.

Oh ! when these fair perfidious maids,
Whose eyes our secret haunts infest,
Their dear destructive charms display,
Each glance my tender heart invades,
And robs my wounded soul of rest,
As Tartars seize their destined prey.

In vain with love our bosoms glow:
Can all our tears, can all our sighs,
New lustre to those charms impart ?
Can cheeks, where living roses blow,
Where Nature spreads her richest dyes,
Require the borrowed gloss of art ?

Speak not of fate:—ah ! change the theme,
And talk of odours, talk of wine,
Talk of the flow'rs that round us bloom:
'Tis all a cloud, 'tis all a dream;
To love and joy thy thoughts confine,
Nor hope to pierce the sacred gloom.

Beauty has such resistless pow'r,
That ev'n the chaste Egyptian dame
Sighed for the blooming Hebrew boy:
For her how fatal was the hour
When to the banks of Nilus came
A youth so lovely and so coy !

But ah ! sweet maid, my counsel hear
(Youth should attend when those advise
Whom long experience renders sage):

While music charms the ravished ear,
While sparkling cups delight our eyes,
Be gay, and scorn the frowns of age.

What cruel answer have I heard ?
And yet, by Heav'n, I love thee still !
Can aught be cruel from thy lips ?
Yet say, how fell that bitter word
From lips which streams of sweetness fill,
Which naught but drops of honey sip ?

Go boldly forth, my simple lay,
Whose accents flow with artless ease,
Like orient pearls at random strung;
Thy notes are sweet, the damsels say,
But oh, far sweeter, if they please
The Nymph for whom these notes are sung.

Sir William Jones

Odes

I

SAKI, for God's love, come and fill my glass;
　　Wine for a breaking heart, O, Saki, bring !
　For this strange love which seemed at first, alas !
　　So simple and so innocent a thing,
　How difficult, how difficult it is !
　　　Because the night-wind kissed the scented curl
　　　On the white brow of a capricious girl,
　And, passing, gave me half the stolen kiss,
　　Who would have thought one's heart could bleed
　　　　and break
　For such a very little thing as this ?
　　Wine, Saki, wine—red wine, for pity's sake !

O Saki, would to God that I might die !
   Would that this moment I might hear the bell
      That bids the traveller for the road prepare,
  Be the next stopping-place or heaven or hell !
Strange caravan of death—no fears have I
   Of the dark journey, gladly would I dare
The fearful river and the whirling pools;
   Ah ! they that dwell upon the other side,
      What know they of the burdens that we bear ?
With lit-up happy faces having died,
      What know they of Love's bitter mystery,
      The love that makes so sad a fool of me ?
A fool of HAFIZ !—yea, a fool of fools.

                Richard Le Gallienne

2

COMRADES, the morning breaks, the sun is up;
   Over her pearly shoulder the shy dawn
   Winds the soft floating mists of silver lawn;
Comrades, the morning cup ! the morning cup !

With dew the tulip's cheek is dappled grey,
   And from the ground sweet smells of morning rise,
   The breeze blows softly out of Paradise;
Drink to the morning of another day !

The red rose sits upon her emerald throne,
   The glittering grass about her feet is spread;
   Wine, Saki, bright as fire, as rubies red !
Comrades, the morning cup, ere morn be flown !

What ! they have shut the wine-house up again !
   On such a morning closed the tavern door !
   Great Opener of Doors, Thee we implore,
Open it for us, for we knock in vain.

It is a wonderful and wicked thing
  They at this season should the tavern close;
  Drink shall we none the less—under the rose;
The Water of Life runs from this little spring.

Sikandar's mirror is this magic cup;
  In it the whole round world reflected lies;
  'Tis filled with pictures for anointed eyes;
'Tis the World's wisdom thou art drinking up.

Under the red rose drinking the red wine,
  In a red dawn, and kissing her red lips,
  No honey-bee from such a flower sips—
No emperor lives such a life as mine.

Once more, O HAFIZ, dawns the morning cup,
  Another day in which to seek her face!
  Patience! the day will come, in some strange place,
When thy strong hands her veil at last lift up.

Richard Le Gallienne

3

THE rose is not the rose unless thou see;
  Without good wine, spring is not spring for me.

Without thy tulip cheek, the gracious air
Of gardens and of meadows is not fair.

Thy rosy limbs, unless I may embrace,
Lose for my longing eyes full half their grace;

Nor does thy scarlet mouth with honey drip
Unless I taste its honey, lip to lip.

Vainly the cypress in the zephyr sways,
Unless the nightingale be there to praise.

Nothing the mind imagines can be fair,
Except the picture that it makes of her.

Surely good wine is good, and green the end
Of gardens old—but not without the Friend.

HAFIZ, the metal of thy soul is base:
Stamp not upon it the Beloved's face.

Richard Le Gallienne

4

A GRIEVOUS folly shames my sixtieth year—
   My white head is in love with a green maid;
     I kept my heart a secret, but at last
I am betrayed.
Like a mere child I walked into the snare;
   My foolish heart followed my foolish eyes;
     And yet, when I was young—in ages past—
I was so wise.

If only she who can such wonders do
   Could from my cheeks time's calumny erase,
   And change the colour of my snow-white
      locks—
   Give a young face
To my young heart, and make my old eyes new,
   Bidding my outside tell the inward truth !
     O 'tis a shallow wit wherewith time mocks
An old man's youth !

Ah ! it was always so with us who sing !
   Children of fancy, we are in the power
     Of any dream, and at the bidding we
   Of a mere flower;
Yet HAFIZ, though full many a foolish thing
   Ensnared thy heart with wonder, never thou
     Wert wont imagination's slave to be
As thou art now.

Richard Le Gallienne

5

WHERE is my ruined life, and where the fame
    Of noble deeds?
Look on my long·drawn road, and whence it came,
    And where it leads!

Can drunkenness be linked to piety
    And good repute?
Where is the preacher's holy monody,
    Where is the lute?

From monkish cell and lying garb released,
    Oh heart of mine,
Where is the Tavern fane, the Tavern priest,
    Where is the wine?

Past days of meeting, let the memory
    Of you be sweet!
Where are those glances fled, and where for me
    Reproaches meet?

His friend's bright face warms not the enemy
    When love is done—
Where is the extinguished lamp that made night
    day,
    Where is the sun?

Balm to mine eyes the dust, my head I bow
    Upon thy stair.
Where shall I go, where from thy presence? thou
    Art everywhere.

Look not upon the dimple of her chin,
    Danger lurks there!
Where wilt thou hide, oh trembling heart, fleeing in
    Such mad haste—where?

To steadfastness and patience, friend, ask not
    If Hafiz keep—
Patience and steadfastness I have forgot,
    And where is sleep ?
            Gertrude Lowthian Bell

6

THE jewel of the secret treasury
Is still the same as once it was ; the seal
Upon Love's treasure casket, and the key,
Are still what thieves can neither break nor steal;
Still among lovers loyalty is found,
And therefore faithful eyes still strew the ground
With the same pearls that mine once strewed for thee.

Question the wandering winds and thou shalt know
That from the dusk until the dawn doth break,
My consolation is that still they blow
The perfume of thy curls across my cheek.
A dart from thy bent brows has wounded me—
Ah, come ! my heart still waiteth helplessly,
Has waited ever, till thou heal its pain.

If seekers after rubies there were none,
Still to the dark mines where the gems had lain
Would pierce, as he was wont, the radiant sun,
Setting the stones ablaze.   Would'st hide the stain
Of my heart's blood ?   Blood-red the ruby glows
(And whence it came my wounded bosom knows)
Upon thy lips to show what thou hast done.

Let not thy curls waylay my pilgrim soul,
As robbers use, and plunder me no more !
Years join dead years, but thine extortionate rule
Is still the same, merciless as before.

Sing, Hafiz, sing again of eyes that weep !
For still the fountain of our tears is deep
As once it was, and still with tears is full.

Gertrude Lowthian Bell

7

WIND from the east, oh Lapwing of the day,
I send thee to my Lady, though the way
Is far to Saba, where I bid thee fly;
Lest in the dust thy tameless wings should lie,
Broken with grief, I send thee to thy nest,
Fidelity.

Or far or near there is no halting-place
Upon Love's road—absent, I see thy face,
And in thine ear my wind-blown greetings sound,
North winds and east waft them where they are
bound,
Each morn and eve convoys of greeting fair
I send to thee.

Unto mine eyes a stranger, thou that art
A comrade ever-present to my heart,
What whispered prayers and what full meed of
praise
I send to thee.

Lest Sorrow's army waste thy heart's domain,
I send my life to bring thee peace again,
Dear life thy ransom !   From thy singers learn
How one that longs for thee may weep and burn;
Sonnets and broken words, sweet notes and songs
I send to thee.

Give me the cup ! a voice rings in mine ears
Crying: " Bear patiently the bitter years !
For all thine ills, I send thee heavenly grace.
God the Creator mirrored in thy face
Thine eyes shall see, God's image in the glass
      I send to thee.

" Hafiz, thy praise alone my comrades sing;
Hasten to us, thou that art sorrowing !
A robe of honour and a harnessed steed
      I send to thee."

          Gertrude Lowthian Bell

8

LADY that hast my heart within thy hand,
Thou heed'st me not ; and if thou turn thine ear
Unto the wise, thou shalt not understand—
Behold the fault is thine, our words were clear.
For all the tumult in my drunken brain
Praise God, who trieth not His slave in vain;
Nor this world nor the next shall make me fear !

My weary heart eternal silence keeps—
I know not who has slipped into my heart;
Though I am silent, one within me weeps.
My soul shall rend the painted veil apart.
Where art thou, Minstrel ! touch thy saddest strings
Till, clothed in music such as sorrow sings,
My mournful story from thy zither sweeps.

Lo, not at any time I lent mine ear
To hearken to the glories of the earth;
Only thy beauty to mine eyes was dear.
Sleep has forsaken me, and from the birth
Of night till day I weave bright dreams of thee;
Drunk with a hundred nights of revelry,
Where is the tavern that sets forth such cheer !

My heart, sad hermit, stains the cloister floor
With drops of blood, the sweat of anguish dire;
Ah, wash me clean, and o'er my body pour
Love's generous wine ! the worshippers of fire
Have bowed them down and magnified my name,
For in my heart there burns a living flame,
Transpiercing Death's impenetrable door.

What instrument through last night's silence rang ?
My life into his lay the minstrel wove,
And filled my brain with the sweet song he sang.
It was the proclamation of thy love
That shook the strings of Life's most secret lyre,
And still my breast heaves with last night's desire,
For countless echoes from that music sprang.

And ever since the time that Hafiz heard
His Lady's voice, as from a rocky hill
Reverberates the softly spoken word,
So echoes of desire his bosom fill.

Gertrude Lowthian Bell

9

I CEASE not from desire till my desire
Is satisfied; or let my mouth attain
My love's red mouth, or let my soul expire,
Sighed from those lips that sought her lips in vain.
Others may find another love as fair;
Upon her threshold I have laid my head,
The dust shall cover me, still lying there,
When from my body life and love have fled.

My soul is on my lips ready to fly,
But grief beats in my heart and will not cease,
Because not once, not once before I die,
Will her sweet lips give all my longing peace.

My breath is narrowed down to one long sigh
For a red mouth that burns my thoughts like fire:
When will that mouth draw near and make reply
To one whose life is straitened with desire ?

When I am dead, open my grave and see
The cloud of smoke that rises round thy feet:
In my dead heart the fire still burns for thee;
Yea, the smoke rises from my winding-sheet !
Ah, come, Beloved ! for the meadows wait
Thy coming, and the thorn bears flowers instead
Of thorns, the cypress fruit, and desolate
Bare winter from before thy steps has fled.

Hoping within some garden ground to find
A red rose soft and sweet as thy soft cheek,
Through every meadow blows the western wind,
Through every garden he is fain to seek.
Reveal thy face ! that the whole world may be
Bewildered by thy radiant loveliness;
The cry of man and woman comes to thee,
Open thy lips and comfort their distress !

Each curling lock of thy luxuriant hair
Breaks into barbèd hooks to catch my heart,
My broken heart is wounded everywhere
With countless wounds from which the red drops start.
Yet when sad lovers meet and tell their sighs,
Not without praise shall Hafiz' name be said,
Not without tears, in those pale companies
Where joy has been forgot and hope has fled.

Gertrude Lowthian Bell

10

THE days of Spring are here ! the eglantine,
The rose, the tulip from the dust have risen—
And thou, why liest thou beneath the dust ?

Like the full clouds of Spring, these eyes of mine
Shall scatter tears upon the grave thy prison,
Till thou too from the earth thine head shalt thrust.

Gertrude Lowthian Bell

11

I HAVE borne the anguish of love, which ask me not
    to describe:
I have tasted the poison of absence, which ask me not
    to relate.

Far through the world have I roved, and at length I
    have chosen
A sweet creature (a ravisher of hearts), whose name
    ask me not to disclose.

The flowing of my tears bedews her footsteps
In such a manner as ask me not to utter.

On yesternight from her own mouth with my own
    ears I heard
Such words as pray ask me not to repeat.

Why dost thou bite thy lip at me? What dost thou
    not hint (*that I may have told*)?
I have devoured a lip like a ruby: but whose, ask me
    not to mention.

Absent from thee, and the sole tenant of my cottage,
I have endured such tortures, as ask me not to
    enumerate.

Thus am I, HAFIZ, arrived at extremity in the ways
    of Love,
Which, alas! ask me not to explain.

John Hindley

12

I SAID to heaven that glowed above,
O hide yon sun-filled zone,
Hide all the stars you boast;
For, in the world of love
And estimation true,
The heaped-up harvest of the moon
Is worth one barley-corn at most,
The Pleiads' sheaf but two.

If my darling should depart,
And search the skies for prouder friends,
God forbid my angry heart
In other love should seek amends.

When the blue horizon's hoop
Me a little pinches here,
Instant to my grave I stoop,
And go find thee in the sphere.

Ralph Waldo Emerson

13

OFT have I said, I say it once more,
I, a wanderer, do not stray from myself.
I am a kind of parrot; the mirror is holden to me;
What the Eternal says, I stammering say again.
Give me what you will; I eat thistles as roses,
And according to my food I grow and I give.
Scorn me not, but know I have the pearl,
And am only seeking one to receive it.

Ralph Waldo Emerson

HEBREW

FROM THE OLD TESTAMENT

10th–1st centuries B.C.

The Song of Deborah and Barak

—JUDGES V.

PRAISE ye the Lord for the avenging of Israel, when the people willingly offered themselves.

Hear, O ye kings; give ear, O ye princes; I, even I, will sing unto the Lord; I will sing praise to the Lord God of Israel.

Lord, when thou wentest out of Seir, when thou marchedst out of the field of Edom, the earth trembled, and the heavens dropped, the clouds also dropped water.

The mountains melted from before the Lord, even that Sinai from before the Lord God of Israel.

In the days of Shamgar the son of Anath, in the days of Jael, the highways were unoccupied, and the travellers walked through byways.

The inhabitants of the villages ceased, they ceased in Israel, until that I Deborah arose, that I arose a mother in Israel.

They chose new gods; then was war in the gates: was there a shield or spear seen among forty thousand in Israel?

My heart is toward the governors of Israel, that offered themselves willingly among the people. Bless ye the Lord.

Speak, ye that ride on white asses, ye that sit in judgment, and walk by the way.

They that are delivered from the noise of archers in the places of drawing water, there shall they rehearse the righteous acts of the Lord, even the righteous acts toward the inhabitants of his villages in Israel: then shall the people of the Lord go down to the gates.

Awake, awake, Deborah: awake, awake, utter a song: arise, Barak, and lead thy captivity captive, thou son of Abinoam.

Then he made him that remaineth have dominion over the nobles among the people: the Lord made me have dominion over the mighty.

Out of Ephraim was there a root of them against Amalek; after thee, Benjamin, among thy people; out of Machir came down governors, and out of Zebulun they that handle the pen of the writer.

And the princes of Issachar were with Deborah; even Issachar, and also Barak: he was sent on foot into the valley. For the divisions of Reuben there were great thoughts of heart.

Why abodest thou among the sheepfolds, to hear the bleatings of the flocks? For the divisions of Reuben there were great searchings of heart.

Gilead abode beyond Jordan: and why did Dan remain in ships? Asher continued on the seashore, and abode in his breaches.

Zebulun and Naphtali were a people that jeoparded their lives unto the death in the high places of the field.

The kings came and fought; then fought the kings of Canaan in Taanach by the waters of Megiddo; they took no gain of money.

They fought from heaven; the stars in their courses fought against Sisera.

The river of Kishon swept them away, that ancient river, the river Kishon. O my soul, thou hast trodden down strength.

Then were the horsehoofs broken by the means of the prancings, the prancings of their mighty ones.

Curse ye Meroz, said the angel of the Lord, curse ye

bitterly the inhabitants thereof; because they came not to the help of the Lord, to the help of the Lord against the mighty.

Blessed above women shall Jael the wife of Heber the Kenite be, blessed shall she be above women in the tent.

He asked water, and she gave him milk; she brought forth butter in a lordly dish.

She put her hand to the nail, and her right hand to the workmen's hammer; and with the hammer she smote Sisera, she smote off his head, when she had pierced and stricken through his temples.

At her feet he bowed, he fell, he lay down: at her feet he bowed, he fell: where he bowed, there he fell down dead.

The mother of Sisera looked out at a window, and cried through the lattice, Why is his chariot so long in coming? why tarry the wheels of his chariots?

Her wise ladies answered her, yea, she returned answer to herself,

Have they not sped? have they not divided the prey; to every man a damsel or two; to Sisera a prey of divers colours, a prey of divers colours of needlework, of divers colours of needlework on both sides, meet for the necks of them that take the spoil?

So let all thine enemies perish, O Lord: but let them that love him be as the sun when he goeth forth in his might.

Hannah's Song of Thanksgiving
—I SAMUEL ii.

MY heart rejoiceth in the Lord, mine horn is exalted in the Lord: my mouth is enlarged over mine enemies; because I rejoice in thy salvation.

There is none holy as the Lord: for there is none beside thee: neither is there any rock like our God.

Talk no more so exceeding proudly; let not arrogancy come out of your mouth: for the Lord is a God of knowledge, and by him actions are weighed.

The bows of the mighty men are broken, and they that stumbled are girded with strength.

They that were full have hired out themselves for bread; and they that were hungry ceased: so that the barren hath born seven; and she that hath many children is waxed feeble.

The Lord killeth, and maketh alive: he bringeth down to the grave, and bringeth up.

The Lord maketh poor, and maketh rich: he bringeth low, and lifteth up.

He raiseth up the poor out of the dust, and lifteth up the beggar from the dunghill, to set them among princes, and to make them inherit the throne of glory: for the pillars of the earth are the Lord's and he hath set the world upon them.

He will keep the feet of his saints, and the wicked shall be silent in darkness; for by strength shall no man prevail.

The adversaries of the Lord shall be broken to pieces; out of heaven shall he thunder upon them: the Lord shall judge the ends of the earth; and he shall give strength unto his king, and exalt the horn of his anointed.

David's Lament for Saul and Jonathan

—2 Samuel i.

THE beauty of Israel is slain upon thy high places: how are the mighty fallen !

Tell it not in Gath, publish it not in the streets of Askelon; lest the daughters of the Philistines rejoice, lest the daughters of the uncircumcised triumph.

Ye mountains of Gilboa, let there be no dew, neither let there be rain upon you, nor fields of offerings: for there the shield of the mighty is vilely cast away, the shield of Saul, as though he had not been anointed with oil.

From the blood of the slain, from the fat of the mighty, the bow of Jonathan turned not back, and the sword of Saul returned not empty.

Saul and Jonathan were lovely and pleasant in their lives, and in their death they were not divided: they were swifter than eagles, they were stronger than lions.

Ye daughters of Israel, weep over Saul, who clothed you in scarlet, with other delights, who put on ornaments of gold upon your apparel.

How are the mighty fallen in the midst of the battle ! O Jonathan, thou wast slain in thine high places.

I am distressed for thee, my brother Jonathan: very pleasant hast thou been unto me: thy love to me was wonderful, passing the love of women.

How are the mighty fallen, and the weapons of war perished !

The Book of Psalms

PSALM I

BLESSED is the man that walketh not in the counsel of the ungodly, nor standeth in the way of sinners, nor sitteth in the seat of the scornful:

But his delight is in the law of the Lord; and in his law doth he meditate day and night.

And he shall be like a tree planted by the rivers of water, that bringeth forth his fruit in his season; his leaf also shall not wither; and whatsoever he doeth shall prosper.

The ungodly are not so; but are like the chaff which the wind driveth away.

Therefore the ungodly shall not stand in the judgment, nor sinners in the congregation of the righteous.

For the Lord knoweth the way of the righteous: but
the way of the ungodly shall perish.

PSALM 8

O LORD our Lord, how excellent is thy name in all
the earth! who hast set thy glory above the heavens.

Out of the mouth of babes and sucklings hast thou
ordained strength because of thine enemies, that thou
mightest still the enemy and the avenger.

When I consider thy heavens, the work of thy fingers,
the moon and the stars, which thou hast ordained;

What is man, that thou art mindful of him? and the
son of man, that thou visitest him?

For thou hast made him a little lower than the angels,
and hast crowned him with glory and honour.

Thou madest him to have dominion over the works
of thy hands; thou hast put all things under his feet:

All sheep and oxen, yea, and the beasts of the field;

The fowl of the air, and the fish of the sea, and
whatsoever passeth through the paths of the seas.

O Lord our Lord, how excellent is thy name in all
the earth!

PSALM 19

THE heavens declare the glory of God; and the firmament sheweth his handywork.

Day unto day uttereth speech, and night unto night
sheweth knowledge.

There is no speech nor language where their voice
is not heard.

Their line is gone out through all the earth, and their
words to the end of the world. In them hath he set a
tabernacle for the sun,

Which is as a bridegroom coming out of his chamber, and rejoiceth as a strong man to run a race.

His going forth is from the end of the heaven, and his circuit unto the ends of it: and there is nothing hid from the heat thereof.

The law of the Lord is perfect, converting the soul: the testimony of the Lord is sure, making wise the simple.

The statutes of the Lord are right, rejoicing the heart: the commandment of the Lord is pure, enlightening the eyes.

The fear of the Lord is clean, enduring for ever: the judgments of the Lord are true and righteous altogether.

More to be desired are they than gold, yea, than much fine gold: sweeter also than honey and the honeycomb.

Moreover by them is thy servant warned: and in keeping of them there is great reward.

Who can understand his errors? cleanse thou me from secret faults.

Keep back thy servant also from presumptuous sins; let them not have dominion over me: then shall I be upright, and I shall be innocent from the great transgression.

Let the words of my mouth, and the meditation of my heart, be acceptable in thy sight, O Lord, my strength, and my redeemer.

PSALM 23

THE Lord is my shepherd; I shall not want.

He maketh me to lie down in green pastures: he leadeth me beside the still waters.

He restoreth my soul: he leadeth me in the paths of righteousness for his name's sake.

Yea, though I walk through the valley of the shadow of death, I will fear no evil: for thou art with me; thy rod and thy staff they comfort me.

Thou preparest a table before me in the presence of mine enemies; thou anointest my head with oil; my cup runneth over.

Surely goodness and mercy shall follow me all the days of my life: and I will dwell in the house of the Lord for ever.

PSALM 24

THE earth is the Lord's, and the fullness thereof; the world, and they that dwell therein.

For he hath founded it upon the seas, and established it upon the floods.

Who shall ascend into the hill of the Lord ? or who shall stand in his holy place ?

He that hath clean hands, and a pure heart; who hath not lifted up his soul unto vanity, nor sworn deceitfully.

He shall receive the blessing from the Lord, and righteousness from the God of his salvation.

This is the generation of them that seek him, that seek thy face, O Jacob.

Lift up your heads, O ye gates; and be ye lift up, ye everlasting doors; and the King of glory shall come in.

Who is this King of glory ? The Lord strong and mighty, the Lord mighty in battle.

Lift up your heads, O ye gates; even lift them up, ye everlasting doors; and the King of glory shall come in.

Who is this King of glory ? The Lord of hosts, he is the King of glory.

PSALM 29

GIVE unto the Lord, O ye mighty, give unto the Lord glory and strength.

Give unto the Lord the glory due unto his name ; worship the Lord in the beauty of holiness.

The voice of the Lord is upon the waters: the God of glory thundereth: the Lord is upon many waters.

The voice of the Lord is powerful; the voice of the Lord is full of majesty.

The voice of the Lord breaketh the cedars; yea, the Lord breaketh the cedars of Lebanon.

He maketh them also to skip like a calf; Lebanon and Sirion like a young unicorn.

The voice of the Lord divideth the flames of fire.

The voice of the Lord shaketh the wilderness; the Lord shaketh the wilderness of Kadesh.

The voice of the Lord maketh the hinds to calve, and discovereth the forests: and in his temple doth every one speak of his glory.

The Lord sitteth upon the flood; yea, the Lord sitteth King for ever.

The Lord will give strength unto his people; the Lord will bless his people with peace.

PSALM 42

AS the hart panteth after the water brooks, so panteth my soul after thee, O God.

My soul thirsteth for God, for the living God: when shall I come and appear before God?

My tears have been my meat day and night, while they continually say unto me, Where is thy God?

When I remember these things, I pour out my soul in me: for I had gone with the multitude, I went with them to the house of God, with the voice of joy and praise, with a multitude that kept holyday.

Why art thou cast down, O my soul? and why art thou disquieted in me? hope thou in God: for I shall yet praise him for the help of his countenance.

O my God, my soul is cast down within me: therefore will I remember thee from the land of Jordan, and of the Hermonites, from the hill Mizar.

Deep calleth unto deep at the noise of thy water-spouts: all thy waves and thy billows are gone over me.

Yet the Lord will command his lovingkindness in the daytime, and in the night his song shall be with me, and my prayer unto the God of my life.

I will say unto God my rock, Why hast thou forgotten me? why go I mourning because of the oppression of the enemy?

As with a sword in my bones, mine enemies reproach me; while they say daily unto me, Where is thy God?

Why art thou cast down, O my soul? and why art thou disquieted within me? hope thou in God: for I shall yet praise him, who is the health of my countenance, and my God.

PSALM 46

GOD is our refuge and strength, a very present help in trouble.

Therefore will not we fear, though the earth be removed, and though the mountains be carried into the midst of the sea;

Though the waters thereof roar and be troubled, though the mountains shake with the swelling thereof.

There is a river, the streams whereof shall make glad the city of God, the holy place of the tabernacles of the most High.

God is in the midst of her; she shall not be moved: God shall help her, and that right early.

The heathen raged, the kingdoms were moved: he uttered his voice, the earth melted.

The Lord of hosts is with us; the God of Jacob is our refuge.

Come, behold the works of the Lord, what desolations he hath made in the earth.

He maketh wars to cease unto the end of the earth; he breaketh the bow, and cutteth the spear in sunder; he burneth the chariot in the fire.

Be still, and know that I am God: I will be exalted among the heathen, I will be exalted in the earth.

The Lord of hosts is with us; the God of Jacob is our refuge.

PSALM 55

GIVE ear to my prayer, O God; and hide not thyself from my supplication.

Attend unto me, and hear me: I mourn in my complaint, and make a noise;

Because of the voice of the enemy, because of the oppression of the wicked: for they cast iniquity upon me, and in wrath they hate me.

My heart is sore pained within me: and the terrors of death are fallen upon me.

Fearfulness and trembling are come upon me, and horror hath overwhelmed me.

And I said, Oh that I had wings like a dove! for then would I fly away, and be at rest.

Lo, then would I wander far off, and remain in the wilderness.

I would hasten my escape from the windy storm and tempest.

Destroy, O Lord, and divide their tongues: for I have seen violence and strife in the city.

Day and night they go about it upon the walls thereof: mischief also and sorrow are in the midst of it.

Wickedness is in the midst thereof: deceit and guile depart not from her streets.

For it was not an enemy that reproached me; then I could have borne it: neither was it he that hated me that did magnify himself against me; then I would have hid myself from him:

But it was thou, a man mine equal, my guide, and mine acquaintance.

We took sweet counsel together, and walked unto the house of God in company.

Let death seize upon them, and let them go down quick into hell: for wickedness is in their dwellings, and among them.

As for me, I will call upon God; and the Lord shall save me.

Evening, and morning, and at noon, will I pray, and cry aloud: and he shall hear my voice.

He hath delivered my soul in peace from the battle that was against me: for there were many with me.

God shall hear, and afflict them, even he that abideth of old. Because they have no changes, therefore they fear not God.

He hath put forth his hands against such as be at peace with him: he hath broken his covenant.

The words of his mouth were smoother than butter, but war was in his heart: his words were softer than oil, yet were they drawn swords.

Cast thy burden upon the Lord, and he shall sustain thee: he shall never suffer the righteous to be moved.

But thou, O God, shalt bring them down into the pit of destruction: bloody and deceitful men shall not live out half their days; but I will trust in thee.

PSALM 77

I CRIED unto God with my voice, even unto God with my voice; and he gave ear unto me.

In the day of my trouble I sought the Lord: my sore ran in the night, and ceased not: my soul refused to be comforted.

I remembered God, and was troubled: I complained, and my spirit was overwhelmed.

Thou holdest mine eyes waking: I am so troubled that I cannot speak.

I have considered the days of old, the years of ancient times.

I call to remembrance my song in the night: I commune with mine own heart: and my spirit made diligent search.

Will the Lord cast off for ever? and will he be favourable no more?

Is his mercy clean gone for ever? doth his promise fail for evermore?

Hath God forgotten to be gracious? hath he in anger shut up his tender mercies?

And I said, This is my infirmity: but I will remember the years of the right hand of the most High.

I will remember the works of the Lord: surely I will remember thy wonders of old.

I will meditate also of all thy work, and talk of thy doings.

Thy way, O God, is in the sanctuary: who is so great a God as our God?

Thou art the God that doest wonders; thou hast declared thy strength among the people.

Thou hast with thine arm redeemed thy people, the sons of Jacob and Joseph.

The waters saw thee, O God, the waters saw thee; they were afraid: the depths also were troubled.

The clouds poured out water: the skies sent out a sound: thine arrows also went abroad.

The voice of thy thunder was in the heaven: the lightnings lightened the world: the earth trembled and shook.

Thy way is in the sea, and thy path in the great waters, and thy footsteps are not known.

Thou leddest thy people like a flock by the hand of Moses and Aaron.

PSALM 90

LORD, thou hast been our dwelling-place in all generations.

Before the mountains were brought forth, or ever thou hadst formed the earth and the world, even from everlasting to everlasting, thou art God.

Thou turnest man to destruction; and sayest, Return, ye children of men.

For a thousand years in thy sight are but as yesterday when it is past, and as a watch in the night.

Thou carriest them away as with a flood; they are as a sleep: in the morning they are like grass which groweth up.

In the morning it flourisheth, and groweth up; in the evening it is cut down, and withereth.

For we are consumed by thine anger, and by thy wrath are we troubled.

Thou hast set our iniquities before thee, our secret sins in the light of thy countenance.

For all our days are passed away in thy wrath: we spend our years as a tale that is told.

The days of our years are threescore years and ten: and if by reason of strength they be fourscore years, yet is their strength labour and sorrow: for it is soon cut off, and we fly away.

Who knoweth the power of thine anger? even according to thy fear, so is thy wrath.

So teach us to number our days, that we may apply our hearts unto wisdom.

Return, O Lord, how long? and let it repent thee concerning thy servants.

O satisfy us early with thy mercy; that we may rejoice and be glad all our days.

Make us glad according to the days wherein thou hast afflicted us, and the years wherein we have seen evil.

Let thy work appear unto thy servants, and thy glory unto their children.

And let the beauty of the Lord our God be upon us: and establish thou the work of our hands upon us; yea, the work of our hands establish thou it.

PSALM 91

HE that dwelleth in the secret place of the most High shall abide under the shadow of the Almighty.

I will say of the Lord, He is my refuge and my fortress: my God; in him will I trust.

Surely he shall deliver thee from the snare of the fowler, and from the noisome pestilence.

He shall cover thee with his feathers, and under his wings shalt thou trust: his truth shall be thy shield and buckler.

Thou shalt not be afraid for the terror by night; nor for the arrow that flieth by day;

Nor for the pestilence that walketh in darkness; nor for the destruction that wasteth at noonday.

A thousand shall fall at thy side, and ten thousand at thy right hand; but it shall not come nigh thee.

Only with thine eyes shalt thou behold and see the reward of the wicked.

Because thou hast made the Lord, which is my refuge, even the most High, thy habitation;

There shall no evil befall thee, neither shall any plague come nigh thy dwelling.

For he shall give his angels charge over thee, to keep thee in all thy ways.

They shall bear thee up in their hands, lest thou dash thy foot against a stone.

Thou shalt tread upon the lion and adder: the young lion and the dragon shalt thou trample under feet.

Because he hath set his love upon me, therefore will I deliver him: I will set him on high, because he hath known my name.

He shall call upon me, and I will answer him: I will be with him in trouble; I will deliver him, and honour him.

With long life will I satisfy him, and shew him my salvation.

PSALM 95

O COME, let us sing unto the Lord: let us make a joyful noise to the rock of our salvation.

Let us come before his presence with thanksgiving, and make a joyful noise unto him with psalms.

For the Lord is a great God, and a great King above all gods.

In his hand are the deep places of the earth: the strength of the hills is his also.

The sea is his, and he made it: and his hands formed the dry land.

O come, let us worship and bow down: let us kneel before the Lord our maker.

For he is our God; and we are the people of his pasture, and the sheep of his hand. To-day if ye will hear his voice,

Harden not your heart, as in the provocation, and as in the day of temptation in the wilderness:

When your fathers tempted me, proved me, and saw my work.

Forty years long was I grieved with this generation, and said, It is a people that do err in their heart, and they have not known my ways:

Unto whom I swear in my wrath that they should not enter into my rest.

PSALM 103

B LESS the Lord, O my soul: and all that is within me, bless his holy name.

Bless the Lord, O my soul, and forget not all his benefits:

Who forgiveth all thine iniquities; who healeth all thy diseases;

Who redeemeth thy life from destruction; who crowneth thee with lovingkindness and tender mercies;

Who satisfieth thy mouth with good things; so that thy youth is renewed like the eagle's.

The Lord executeth righteousness and judgment for all that are oppressed.

He made known his ways unto Moses, his acts unto the children of Israel.

The Lord is merciful and gracious, slow to anger, and plenteous in mercy.

He will not always chide: neither will he keep his anger for ever.

He hath not dealt with us after our sins, nor rewarded us according to our iniquities.

For as the heaven is high above the earth, so great is his mercy toward them that fear him.

As far as the east is from the west, so far hath he removed our transgressions from us.

Like as a father pitieth his children, so the Lord pitieth them that fear him.

For he knoweth our frame; he remembereth that we are dust.

As for man, his days are as grass: as a flower of the field, so he flourisheth.

For the wind passeth over it, and it is gone; and the place thereof shall know it no more.

But the mercy of the Lord is from everlasting to everlasting upon them that fear him, and his righteousness unto children's children;

To such as keep his covenant, and to those that remember his commandments to do them.

The Lord hath prepared his throne in the heavens; and his kingdom ruleth over all.

Bless the Lord, ye his angels, that excel in strength, that do his commandments, hearkening unto the voice of his word.

Bless ye the Lord, all ye his hosts; ye ministers of his, that do his pleasure.

Bless the Lord, all his works, in all places of his dominion: bless the Lord, O my soul.

PSALM 121

I WILL lift up mine eyes unto the hills, from whence cometh my help.

My help cometh from the Lord, which made heaven and earth.

He will not suffer thy foot to be moved: he that keepeth thee will not slumber.

Behold, he that keepeth Israel shall neither slumber nor sleep.

The Lord is thy keeper: the Lord is thy shade upon thy right hand.

The sun shall not smite thee by day, nor the moon by night.

The Lord shall preserve thee from all evil: he shall preserve thy soul.

The Lord shall preserve thy going out and thy coming in from this time forth, and even for evermore.

PSALM 133

BEHOLD, how good and how pleasant it is for brethren to dwell together in unity!

It is like the precious ointment upon the head, that ran down upon the beard, even Aaron's beard: that went down to the skirts of his garments;

As the dew of Hermon, and as the dew that descended upon the mountains of Zion: for there the Lord commanded the blessing, even life for evermore.

PSALM 136

O GIVE thanks unto the Lord; for he is good; for his mercy endureth for ever.

O give thanks unto the God of gods: for his mercy endureth for ever.

O give thanks to the Lord of lords: for his mercy endureth for ever.

To him who alone doeth great wonders: for his mercy endureth for ever.

To him that by wisdom made the heavens: for his mercy endureth for ever.

To him that stretched out the earth above the waters: for his mercy endureth for ever.

To him that made great lights: for his mercy endureth for ever:

The sun to rule by day: for his mercy endureth for ever:

The moon and stars to rule by night: for his mercy endureth for ever.

To him that smote Egypt in their firstborn: for his mercy endureth for ever:

And brought out Israel from among them: for his mercy endureth for ever:

With a strong hand, and with a stretched-out arm: for his mercy endureth for ever.

To him which divided the Red Sea into parts: for his mercy endureth for ever:

And made Israel to pass through the midst of it: for his mercy endureth for ever:

But overthrew Pharaoh and his host in the Red Sea; for his mercy endureth for ever.

To him which led his people through the wilderness: for his mercy endureth for ever.

To him which smote great kings: for his mercy endureth for ever:

And slew famous kings: for his mercy endureth for ever:

Sihon king of the Amorites: for his mercy endureth for ever:

And Og the king of Bashan: for his mercy endureth for ever:

And gave their land for an heritage: for his mercy endureth for ever:

Even an heritage unto Israel his servant: for his mercy endureth for ever.

Who remembered us in our low estate: for his mercy endureth for ever:

And hath redeemed us from our enemies: for his mercy endureth for ever.

Who giveth food to all flesh: for his mercy endureth for ever.

O give thanks unto the God of heaven: for his mercy endureth for ever.

PSALM 137

BY the rivers of Babylon, there we sat down; yea, we wept, when we remembered Zion.

We hanged our harps upon the willows in the midst thereof.

For there they that carried us away captive required of us a song; and they that wasted us required of us mirth, saying, Sing us one of the songs of Zion.

How shall we sing the Lord's song in a strange land?

If I forget thee, O Jerusalem, let my right hand forget her cunning.

If I do not remember thee, let my tongue cleave to the roof of my mouth: if I prefer not Jerusalem above my chief joy.

Remember, O Lord, the children of Edom in the day of Jerusalem; who said, Rase it, rase it, even to the foundation thereof.

O daughter of Babylon, who art to be destroyed: happy shall he be that rewardeth thee as thou hast served us.

Happy shall he be that taketh and dasheth thy little ones against the stones.

The Book of Job

Job's Curse

LET the day perish wherein I was born, and the night in which it was said, There is a man-child conceived.

Let that day be darkness; let not God regard it from above, neither let the light shine upon it.

Let darkness and the shadow of death stain it; let a cloud dwell upon it; let the blackness of the day terrify it.

As for that night, let darkness seize upon it; let it not be joined unto the days of the year, let it not come into the number of the months.

Lo, let that night be solitary, let no joyful voice come therein.

Let them curse it that curse the day, who are ready to raise up their mourning.

Let the stars of the twilight thereof be dark; let it look for light, but have none; neither let it see the dawning of the day:

Because it shut not up the doors of my mother's womb, nor hid sorrow from mine eyes.

Why died I not from the womb ? why did I not give up the ghost when I came out of the belly ?

Why did the knees prevent me ? or why the breasts that I should suck ?

For now should I have lain still and been quiet, I should have slept: then had I been at rest,

With kings and counsellors of the earth, which built desolate places for themselves;

Or with princes that had gold, who filled their houses with silver:

Or as an hidden untimely birth I had not been; as infants which never saw light.

There the wicked cease from troubling; and there the weary be at rest.

There the prisoners rest together; they hear not the voice of the oppressor.

The small and great are there; and the servant is free from his master.

Wherefore is light given to him that is in misery, and life unto the bitter in soul;

Which long for death, but it cometh not; and dig for it more than for hid treasures;

Which rejoice exceedingly, and are glad, when they can find the grave?

Why is light given to a man whose way is hid, and whom God hath hedged in?

For my sighing cometh before I eat, and my roarings are poured out like the waters.

For the thing which I greatly feared is come upon me, and that which I was afraid of is come unto me.

I was not in safety, neither had I rest, neither was I quiet; yet trouble came.

Job's Entreaty

MAN that is born of a woman is of few days, and full of trouble.

He cometh forth like a flower, and is cut down: he fleeth also as a shadow, and continueth not.

And dost thou open thine eyes upon such an one, and bringest me into judgment with thee?

Who can bring a clean thing out of an unclean? not one.

Seeing his days are determined, the number of his months are with thee, thou hast appointed his bounds that he cannot pass;

Turn from him, that he may rest, till he shall accomplish, as an hireling, his day.

For there is hope of a tree, if it be cut down, that it will sprout again, and that the tender branch thereof will not cease.

Though the root thereof wax old in the earth, and the stock thereof die in the ground;

Yet through the scent of water it will bud, and bring forth boughs like a plant.

But man dieth, and wasteth away: yea, man giveth up the ghost, and where is he?

As the waters fail from the sea, and the flood decayeth and drieth up:

So man lieth down, and riseth not: till the heavens be no more, they shall not awake, nor be raised out of their sleep.

O that thou wouldest hide me in the grave, that thou wouldest keep me secret, until thy wrath be past, that thou wouldest appoint me a set time, and remember me!

If a man die, shall he live again? all the days of my appointed time will I wait, till my change come.

Thou shalt call, and I will answer thee: thou wilt have a desire to the work of thine hands.

For now thou numberest my steps: dost thou not watch over my sin?

My transgression is sealed up in a bag, and thou sewest up mine iniquity.

And surely the mountain falling cometh to nought, and the rock is removed out of his place.

The waters wear the stones: thou washest away the things which grow out of the dust of the earth: and thou destroyest the hope of man.

Thou prevailest for ever against him, and he passeth: thou changest his countenance, and sendest him away.

His sons come to honour, and he knoweth it not; and they are brought low, but he perceiveth it not of them.

But his flesh upon him shall have pain, and his soul within him shall mourn.

Then the Lord answered

WHO is this that darkeneth counsel by words without knowledge ?

Gird up now thy loins like a man; for I will demand of thee, and answer thou me.

Where wast thou when I laid the foundations of the earth ? declare, if thou hast understanding.

Who hath laid the measures thereof, if thou knowest ? or who hath stretched the line upon it ?

Whereupon are the foundations thereof fastened ? or who laid the corner-stone thereof,

When the morning stars sang together, and all the sons of God shouted for joy ?

Or who shut up the sea with doors, when it brake forth, as if it had issued out of the womb ?

When I made the cloud the garment thereof, and thick darkness a swaddling band for it,

And brake up for it my decreed place, and set bars and doors,

And said, Hitherto shalt thou come, but no further: and here shall thy proud waves be stayed ?

Hast thou commanded the morning since thy days; and caused the dayspring to know his place;

That it might take hold of the ends of the earth, that the wicked might be shaken out of it ?

It is turned as clay to the seal; and they stand as a garment.

And from the wicked their light is withholden, and the high arm shall be broken.

Hast thou entered into the springs of the sea ? or hast thou walked in the search of the depth ?

Have the gates of death been opened unto thee ? or hast thou seen the doors of the shadow of death ?

Hast thou perceived the breadth of the earth? declare if thou knowest it all.

Where is the way where light dwelleth ? and as for darkness, where is the place thereof,

That thou shouldest take it to the bound thereof, and that thou shouldest know the paths to the house thereof ?

Knowest thou it, because thou wast then born ? or because the number of thy days is great ?

Hast thou entered into the treasures of the snow ? or hast thou seen the treasures of the hail,

Which I have reserved against the time of trouble, against the day of battle and war ?

By what way is the light parted, which scattereth the east wind upon the earth ?

Who hath divided a water-course for the overflowing of waters, or a way for the lightning of thunder;

To cause it to rain on the earth, where no man is; on the wilderness, wherein there is no man;

To satisfy the desolate and waste ground; and to cause the bud of the tender herb to spring forth ?

Hath the rain a father ? or who hath begotten the drops of dew ?

Out of whose womb came the ice ? and the hoary frost of heaven, who hath gendered it ?

The waters are hid as with a stone, and the face of the deep is frozen.

Canst thou bind the sweet influences of Pleiades, or loose the bands of Orion ?

Canst thou bring forth Mazzaroth in his season ? or canst thou guide Arcturus with his sons ?

Knowest thou the ordinances of heaven? canst thou
set the dominion thereof in the earth?

Canst thou lift up thy voice to the clouds, that abundance of waters may cover thee?

Canst thou send lightnings, that they may go, and
say unto thee, Here we are?

Who hath put wisdom in the inward parts? or who
hath given understanding to the heart?

Who can number the clouds in wisdom? or who can
stay the bottles of heaven,

When the dust groweth into hardness, and the clods
cleave fast together?

Wilt thou hunt the prey for the lion? or fill the
appetite of the young lions,

When they couch in their dens, and abide in the
covert to lie in wait?

Who provideth for the raven his food? when his
young ones cry unto God, they wander for lack of meat.

KNOWEST thou the time when the wild goats of the
rock bring forth? or canst thou mark when the
hinds do calve?

Canst thou number the months that they fulfil? or
knowest thou the time when they bring forth?

They bow themselves, they bring forth their young
ones, they cast out their sorrows.

Their young ones are in good liking, they grow up
with corn; they go forth, and return not unto them.

Who hath sent out the wild ass free? or who hath
loosed the bands of the wild ass?

Whose house I have made the wilderness, and the
barren land his dwellings.

He scorneth the multitude of the city, neither regardeth he the crying of the driver.

The range of the mountains is his pasture, and he
searcheth after every green thing.

Will the unicorn be willing to serve thee, or abide by thy crib?

Canst thou bind the unicorn with his band in the furrow? or will he harrow the valleys after thee?

Wilt thou trust him, because his strength is great? or wilt thou leave thy labour to him?

Wilt thou believe him, that he will bring home thy seed, and gather it into thy barn?

Gavest thou the goodly wings unto the peacocks? or wings and feathers unto the ostrich?

Which leaveth her eggs in the earth, and warmeth them in dust,

And forgetteth that the foot may crush them, or that the wild beast may break them.

She is hardened against her young ones, as though they were not hers: her labour is in vain without fear:

Because God hath deprived her of wisdom, neither hath he imparted to her understanding.

What time she lifteth up herself on high, she scorneth the horse and his rider.

Hast thou given the horse strength? hast thou clothed his neck with thunder?

Canst thou make him afraid as a grasshopper? the glory of his nostrils is terrible.

He paweth in the valley, and rejoiceth in his strength: he goeth on to meet the armed men.

He mocketh at fear, and is not affrighted; neither turneth he back from the sword.

The quiver rattleth against him, the glittering spear and the shield.

He swalloweth the ground with fierceness and rage: neither believeth he that it is the sound of the trumpet.

He saith among the trumpets, Ha, ha! and he smelleth the battle afar off, the thunder of the captains, and the shouting.

Doth the hawk fly by thy wisdom, and stretch her wings toward the south?

Doth the eagle mount up at thy command, and make her nest on high?

She dwelleth and abideth on the rock, upon the crag of the rock, and the strong place.

From thence she seeketh the prey, and her eyes behold afar off.

Her young ones also suck up blood: and where the slain are, there is she.

Out of the Whirlwind

GIRD up thy loins now like a man: I will demand of thee, and declare thou unto me.

Wilt thou also disannul my judgment? wilt thou condemn me, that thou mayest be righteous?

Hast thou an arm like God? or canst thou thunder with a voice like him?

Deck thyself now with majesty and excellency; and array thyself with glory and beauty.

Cast abroad the rage of thy wrath: and behold every one that is proud, and abase him.

Look on every one that is proud, and bring him low; and tread down the wicked in their place.

Hide them in the dust together; and bind their faces in secret.

Then will I also confess unto thee that thine own right hand can save thee.

Behold now behemoth, which I made with thee ; he eateth grass as an ox.

Lo now, his strength is in his loins, and his force is in the navel of his belly.

He moveth his tail like a cedar: the sinews of his stones are wrapped together.

His bones are as strong pieces of brass; his bones are like bars of iron.

He is the chief of the ways of God: he that made him can make his sword to approach unto him.

Surely the mountains bring him forth food, where all the beasts of the field play.

He lieth under the shady trees, in the covert of the reed, and fens.

The shady trees cover him with their shadow; the willows of the brook compass him about.

Behold he drinketh up a river, and hasteth not: he trusteth that he can draw up Jordan into his mouth.

He taketh it with his eyes: his nose pierceth through snares.

CANST thou draw out leviathan with an hook? or his tongue with a cord which thou lettest down?

Canst thou put an hook into his nose? or bore his jaw through with a thorn?

Will he make many supplications unto thee? will he speak soft words unto thee?

Will he make a covenant with thee? wilt thou take him for a servant for ever?

Wilt thou play with him as with a bird? or wilt thou bind him for thy maidens?

Shall the companions make a banquet of him? shall they part him among the merchants?

Canst thou fill his skin with barbed irons? or his head with fish spears?

Lay thine hand upon him, remember the battle, do no more.

Behold, the hope of him is in vain: shall not one be cast down even at the sight of him?

None is so fierce that dare stir him up: who then is able to stand before me?

Who hath prevented me, that I should repay him? whatsoever is under the whole heaven is mine.

I will not conceal his parts, nor his power, nor his comely proportion.

Who can discover the face of his garment? or who can come to him with his double bridle?

Who can open the doors of his face? his teeth are terrible round about.

His scales are his pride, shut up together as with a close seal.

One is so near to another, that no air can come between them.

They are joined one to another, they stick together, that they cannot be sundered.

By his neesings a light doth shine, and his eyes are like the eyelids of the morning.

Out of his mouth go burning lamps, and sparks of fire leap out.

Out of his nostrils goeth smoke, as out of a seething pot or caldron.

His breath kindleth coals, and a flame goeth out of his mouth.

In his neck remaineth strength, and sorrow is turned into joy before him.

The flakes of his flesh are joined together: they are firm in themselves; they cannot be moved.

His heart is as firm as a stone; yea, as hard as a piece of the nether millstone.

When he raiseth up himself, the mighty are afraid; by reason of breakings they purify themselves.

The sword of him that layeth at him cannot hold: the spear, the dart, nor the habergeon.

He esteemeth iron as straw, and brass as rotten wood.

The arrow cannot make him flee: slingstones are turned with him into stubble.

Darts are counted as stubble: he laugheth at the shaking of a spear.

Sharp stones are under him: he spreadeth sharp-pointed things upon the mire.

He maketh the deep to boil like a pot: he maketh the sea like a pot of ointment.

He maketh a path to shine after him; one would think the deep to be hoary.

Upon earth there is not his like, who is made without fear.

He beholdeth all high things: he is a king over all the children of pride.

Ecclesiastes

CAST THY BREAD UPON THE WATERS

CAST thy bread upon the waters: for thou shalt find it after many days.

Give a portion to seven, and also to eight; for thou knowest not what evil shall be upon the earth.

If the clouds be full of rain, they empty themselves upon the earth: and if the tree fall toward the south, or toward the north, in the place where the tree falleth, there it shall be.

He that observeth the wind shall not sow; and he that regardeth the clouds shall not reap.

As thou knowest not what is the way of the spirit, nor how the bones do grow in the womb of her that is with child: even so thou knowest not the works of God who maketh all.

In the morning sow thy seed, and in the evening withhold not thine hand: for thou knowest not whether shall prosper, either this or that, or whether they both shall be alike good.

REMEMBER NOW THY CREATOR

REMEMBER now thy Creator in the days of thy youth, while the evil days come not, nor the years draw nigh, when thou shalt say, I have no pleasure in them;

While the sun, or the light, or the moon, or the stars, be not darkened, nor the clouds return after the rain:

In the day when the keepers of the house shall tremble, and the strong men shall bow themselves, and the grinders cease because they are few, and those that look out of the windows be darkened;

And the doors shall be shut in the streets, when the sound of the grinding is low, and he shall rise up at the voice of the bird, and all the daughters of music shall be brought low;

Also when they shall be afraid of that which is high, and fears shall be in the way, and the almond tree shall flourish, and the grasshopper shall be a burden, and desire shall fail: because man goeth to his long home, and the mourners go about the streets:

Or ever the silver cord be loosed, or the golden bowl be broken, or the pitcher be broken at the fountain, or the wheel broken at the cistern:

Then shall the dust return to the earth as it was ; and the spirit shall return unto God who gave it.

The Song of Songs

I

LET him kiss me with the kisses of his mouth: for thy love is better than wine.

Because of the savour of thy good ointments thy name is as ointment poured forth, therefore do the virgins love thee.

Draw me, we will run after thee: the king hath brought me into his chambers: we will be glad and rejoice in thee, we will remember thy love more than wine: the upright love thee.

I am black, but comely, O ye daughters of Jerusalem, as the tents of Kedar, as the curtains of Solomon.

Look not upon me, because I am black, because the sun hath looked upon me: my mother's children were angry with me; they made me the keeper of the vineyards; but mine own vineyard have I not kept.

Tell me, O thou whom my soul loveth, where thou feedest, where thou makest thy flock to rest at noon: for why should I be as one that turneth aside by the flocks of thy companions?

If thou know not, O thou fairest among women, go thy way forth by the footsteps of the flock, and feed thy kids beside the shepherds' tents.

I have compared thee, O my love, to a company of horses in Pharaoh's chariots.

Thy cheeks are comely with rows of jewels, thy neck with chains of gold.

We will make thee borders of gold with studs of silver.

While the king sitteth at his table, my spikenard sendeth forth the smell thereof.

A bundle of myrrh is my well-beloved unto me; he shall lie all night betwixt my breasts.

My beloved is unto me as a cluster of camphire in the vineyards of En-gedi.

Behold, thou art fair, my love; behold, thou art fair; thou hast doves' eyes.

Behold, thou art fair, my beloved, yea, pleasant: also our bed is green.

The beams of our house are cedar, and our rafters of fir.

2

I AM the rose of Sharon, and the lily of the valleys.

As the lily among thorns, so is my love among the daughters.

As the apple tree among the trees of the wood, so is my beloved among the sons. I sat down under his shadow with great delight, and his fruit was sweet to my taste.

He brought me to the banqueting house, and his banner over me was love.

Stay me with flagons, comfort me with apples: for I am sick of love.

His left hand is under my head, and his right hand doth embrace me.

I charge you, O ye daughters of Jerusalem, by the roes, and by the hinds of the field, that ye stir not up, nor awake my love, till he please.

The voice of my beloved ! behold, he cometh leaping upon the mountains, skipping upon the hills.

My beloved is like a roe or a young hart: behold, he standeth behind our wall, he looketh forth at the windows, shewing himself through the lattice.

My beloved spake, and said unto me, Rise up, my love, my fair one, and come away.

For, lo, the winter is past, the rain is over and gone;

The flowers appear on the earth; the time of the singing of birds is come, and the voice of the turtle is heard in our land;

The fig tree putteth forth her green figs, and the vines with the tender grape give a good smell. Arise, my love, my fair one, and come away.

O my dove, that art in the clefts of the rock, in the secret places of the stairs, let me see thy countenance, let me hear thy voice; for sweet is thy voice, and thy countenance is comely.

Take us the foxes, the little foxes, that spoil the vines: for our vines have tender grapes.

My beloved is mine, and I am his : he feedeth among the lilies.

Until the day break, and the shadows flee away, turn, my beloved, and be thou like a roe or a young hart upon the mountains of Bether.

3

BY night on my bed I sought him whom my soul loveth: I sought him, but I found him not.

I will rise now, and go about the city in the streets, and in the broad ways I will seek him whom my soul loveth: I sought him, but I found him not.

The watchmen that go about the city found me: to whom I said, Saw ye him whom my soul loveth?

It was but a little that I passed from them, but I found him whom my soul loveth: I held him, and would not let him go, until I had brought him into my mother's house, and into the chamber of her that conceived me.

I charge you, O ye daughters of Jerusalem, by the roes, and by the hinds of the field, that ye stir not up, nor wake my love, till he please.

Who is this that cometh out of the wilderness like pillars of smoke, perfumed with myrrh and frankincense, with all powders of the merchant?

Behold his bed, which is Solomon's; three score valiant men are about it, of the valiant of Israel.

They all hold swords, being expert in war: every man hath his sword upon his thigh because of fear in the night.

King Solomon made himself a chariot of the wood of Lebanon.

He made the pillars thereof of silver, the bottom thereof of gold, the covering of it of purple; the midst thereof being paved with love, for the daughters of Jerusalem.

Go forth, O ye daughters of Zion, and behold king Solomon with the crown wherewith his mother crowned him in the day of his espousals, and in the day of the gladness of his heart.

4

BEHOLD, thou art fair, my love; behold, thou art fair; thou hast doves' eyes within thy locks: thy hair is as a flock of goats, that appear from mount Gilead.

Thy teeth are like a flock of sheep that are even shorn, which came up from the washing; whereof every one bear twins, and none is barren among them.

Thy lips are like a thread of scarlet, and thy speech is comely: thy temples are like a piece of a pomegranate within thy locks.

Thy neck is like the tower of David, builded for an armoury, whereon there hang a thousand bucklers, all shields of mighty men.

Thy two breasts are like two young roes that are twins, which feed among the lilies.

Until the day break, and the shadows flee away, I will get me to the mountain of myrrh, and to the hill of frankincense.

Thou art all fair, my love; there is no spot in thee.

Come with me from Lebanon, my spouse, with me from Lebanon: look from the top of Amana, from the top of Shenir and Hermon, from the lions' dens, from the mountains of the leopards.

Thou hast ravished my heart, my sister, my spouse; thou hast ravished my heart with one of thine eyes, with one chain of thy neck.

How fair is thy love, my sister, my spouse! how much better is thy love than wine! and the smell of thine ointments than all spices!

Thy lips, O my spouse, drop as the honeycomb: honey and milk are under thy tongue; and the smell of thy garments is like the smell of Lebanon.

A garden enclosed is my sister, my spouse; a spring shut up, a fountain sealed.

Thy plants are an orchard of pomegranates, with pleasant fruits; camphire, with spikenard,

Spikenard and saffron; calamus and cinnamon, with all trees of frankincense; myrrh and aloes, with all the chief spices:

A fountain of gardens, a well of living waters, and streams from Lebanon.

Awake, O north wind; and come, thou south; blow upon my garden, that the spices thereof may flow out. Let my beloved come into his garden, and eat his pleasant fruits.

5

I AM come into my garden, my sister, my spouse: I have gathered my myrrh with my spice; I have eaten my honeycomb with my honey; I have drunk my wine with my milk: eat, O friends; drink, yea, drink abundantly, O beloved.

I sleep, but my heart waketh: it is the voice of my beloved that knocketh, saying, Open to me, my sister, my love, my dove, my undefiled: for my head is filled with dew, and my locks with the drops of the night.

I have put off my coat; how shall I put it on? I have washed my feet; how shall I defile them?

My beloved put in his hand by the hole of the door, and my bowels were moved for him.

I rose up to open to my beloved; and my hands dropped with myrrh, and my fingers with sweet-smelling myrrh, upon the handles of the lock.

I opened to my beloved; but my beloved had withdrawn himself, and was gone: my soul failed when he spake: I sought him, but I could not find him; I called him, but he gave me no answer.

The watchmen that went about the city found me, they smote me, they wounded me; the keepers of the walls took away my veil from me.

I charge you, O daughters of Jerusalem, if ye find my beloved, that ye tell him, that I am sick of love.

What is thy beloved more than another beloved, O thou fairest among women? what is thy beloved more than another beloved, that thou dost so charge us?

My beloved is white and ruddy, the chiefest among ten thousand.

His head is as the most fine gold; his locks are bushy, and black as a raven.

His eyes are as the eyes of doves by the rivers of waters, washed with milk, and fitly set.

His cheeks are as a bed of spices, as sweet flowers: his lips like lilies, dropping sweet-smelling myrrh.

His hands are as gold rings set with the beryl: his belly is as bright ivory overlaid with sapphires.

His legs are as pillars of marble, set upon sockets of fine gold: his countenance is as Lebanon, excellent as the cedars.

His mouth is most sweet: yea, he is altogether lovely. This is my beloved, and this is my friend, O daughters of Jerusalem.

6

WHITHER is thy beloved gone, O thou fairest among women? whither is thy beloved turned aside? that we may seek him with thee.

My beloved is gone down into his garden, to the beds of spices, to feed in the gardens, and to gather lilies.

I am my beloved's, and my beloved is mine: he feedeth among the lilies.

Thou art beautiful, O my love, as Tirzah, comely as Jerusalem, terrible as an army with banners.

Turn away thine eyes from me, for they have overcome me: thy hair is as a flock of goats that appear from Gilead.

Thy teeth are as a flock of sheep which go up from the washing, whereof every one beareth twins, and there is not one barren among them.

As a piece of a pomegranate are thy temples within thy locks.

There are threescore queens, and fourscore concubines, and virgins without number.

My dove, my undefiled is but one; she is the only one of her mother, she is the choice one of her that bare her. The daughters saw her, and blessed her; yea, the queens and the concubines, and they praised her.

Who is she that looketh forth as the morning, fair as the moon, clear as the sun, and terrible as an army with banners?

I went down into the garden of nuts to see the fruits of the valley, and to see whether the vine flourished, and the pomegranates budded.

Or ever I was aware, my soul made me like the chariots of Amminadib.

Return, return, O Shulamite; return, return, that we may look upon thee. What will ye see in the Shula mite? As it were the company of two armies.

7

HOW beautiful are thy feet with shoes, O prince's daughter! the joints of thy thighs are like jewels, the work of the hands of a cunning workman.

Thy navel is like a round goblet, which wanteth not liquor: thy belly is like an heap of wheat set about with lilies.

Thy two breasts are like two young roes that are twins.

Thy neck is as a tower of ivory; thine eyes like the fishpools in Heshbon, by the gate of Bathrabbim; thy nose is as the tower of Lebanon which looketh toward Damascus.

Thine head upon thee is like Carmel, and the hair of thine head like purple; the king is held in the galleries.

How fair and how pleasant art thou, O love, for delights!

This thy stature is like to a palm tree, and thy breasts to clusters of grapes.

I said, I will go up to the palm tree, I will take hold of the boughs thereof: now also thy breasts shall be as clusters of the vine, and the smell of thy nose like apples;

And the roof of thy mouth like the best wine for my beloved, that goeth down sweetly, causing the lips of those that are asleep to speak.

I am my beloved's, and his desire is toward me.

Come, my beloved, let us go forth into the field; let us lodge in the villages.

· Let us get up early to the vineyards; let us see if the vine flourish, whether the tender grape appear, and the pomegranates bud forth: there will I give thee my loves.

The mandrakes give a smell, and at our gates are all manner of pleasant fruits, new and old, which I have laid up for thee, O my beloved.

8

O THAT thou wert as my brother, that sucked the breasts of my mother! when I should find thee without, I would kiss thee; yea, I should not be despised.

I would lead thee, and bring thee into my mother's house, who would instruct me: I would cause thee to drink of spiced wine of the juice of my pomegranate.

His left hand should be under my head, and his right hand should embrace me.

I charge you, O daughters of Jerusalem, that ye stir not up, nor awake my love, until he please.

Who is this that cometh up from the wilderness, leaning upon her beloved? I raised thee up under the apple tree: there thy mother brought thee forth: there she brought thee forth that bare thee.

Set me as a seal upon thine heart, as a seal upon thine arm: for love is strong as death; jealousy is cruel as the grave: the coals thereof are coals of fire, which hath a most vehement flame.

Many waters cannot quench love, neither can the floods drown it: if a man would give all the substance of his house for love, it would utterly be contemned.

. We have a little sister, and she hath no breasts: what shall we do for our sister in the day when she shall be spoken for ?

If she be a wall, we will build upon her a palace of silver: and if she be a door, we will enclose her with boards of cedar.

I am a wall, and my breasts like towers: then was I in his eyes as one that found favour.

Solomon had a vineyard at Baalhamon; he let out the vineyard unto keepers; every one for the fruit thereof was to bring a thousand pieces of silver.

My vineyard, which is mine, is before me: thou, O Solomon, must have a thousand, and those that keep the fruit thereof two hundred.

Thou that dwellest in the gardens, the companions hearken to thy voice: cause me to hear it.

Make haste, my beloved, and be thou like to a roe or to a young hart upon the mountains of spices.

Isaiah

The Messiah

BEHOLD, a virgin shall conceive, and bear a son, and shall call his name Immanuel.

Butter and honey shall he eat, that he may know to refuse the evil, and choose the good.

For before the child shall know to refuse the evil, and choose the good, the land that thou abhorrest shall be forsaken of both her kings.

The Lord shall bring upon thee, and upon thy people, and upon thy father's house, days that have not come, from the day that Ephraim departed from Judah; even the king of Assyria.

And it shall come to pass in that day, that the Lord shall hiss for the fly that is in the uttermost part of the rivers of Egypt, and for the bee that is in the land of Assyria;

And they shall come, and shall rest all of them in the desolate valleys, and in the holes of the rocks, and upon all thorns, and upon all bushes.

In the same day shall the Lord shave with a razor that is hired, namely, by them beyond the river, by the king of Assyria, the head, and the hair of the feet: and it shall also consume the beard.

And it shall come to pass in that day, that a man shall nourish a young cow, and two sheep;

And it shall come to pass, for the abundance of milk that they shall give he shall eat butter: for butter and honey shall every one eat that is left in the land.

And it shall come to pass in that day, that every place shall be, where there were a thousand vines at a thousand silverlings, it shall even be for briers and thorns.

With arrows and with bows shall men come thither; because all the land shall become briers and thorns.

And on all hills that shall be digged with the mattock, there shall not come thither the fear of briers and thorns: but it shall be for the sending forth of oxen, and for the treading of lesser cattle.

The Rod of Jesse

AND there shall come forth a rod out of the stem of Jesse, and a Branch shall grow out of his roots:

And the spirit of the Lord shall rest upon him, the spirit of wisdom and understanding, the spirit of counsel and might, the spirit of knowledge and the fear of the Lord;

And shall make him of quick understanding in the fear of the Lord: and he shall not judge after the sight of his eyes, neither reprove after the hearing of his ears:

But with righteousness shall he judge the poor, and reprove with equity for the meek of the earth: and he shall smite the earth with the rod of his mouth, and with the breath of his lips shall he slay the wicked.

And righteousness shall be the girdle of his loins, and faithfulness the girdle of his reins.

The wolf also shall dwell with the lamb, and the leopard shall lie down with the kid; and the calf and the young lion and the fatling together; and a little child shall lead them.

And the cow and the bear shall feed; their young ones shall lie down together: and the lion shall eat straw like the ox.

And the sucking child shall play on the hole of the asp, and the weaned child shall put his hand on the cockatrice' den.

They shall not hurt nor destroy in all my holy mountain: for the earth shall be full of the knowledge of the Lord, as the waters cover the sea.

And in that day there shall be a root of Jesse, which shall stand for an ensign of the people; to it shall the Gentiles seek: and his rest shall be glorious.

WATCHMAN, WHAT OF THE NIGHT?

HE calleth to me out of Seir, Watchman, what of the night? Watchman, what of the night?

The watchman said, The morning cometh, and also the night: if ye will enquire, enquire ye: return, come.

In the forest in Arabia shall ye lodge, O ye travelling companies of Dedanim.

The inhabitants of the land of Tema brought water to him that was thirsty, they prevented with their bread him that fled.

For they fled from the swords, from the drawn sword, and from the bent bow, and from the grievousness of war.

Jeremiah

THE MISERY OF JERUSALEM

HOW doth the city sit solitary, that was full of people ! how is she become as a widow ! she that was great among the nations, and princess among the provinces, how is she become tributary !

She weepeth sore in the night, and her tears are on her cheeks: among all her lovers she hath none to comfort her: all her friends have dealt treacherously with her, they are become her enemies.

Judah is gone into captivity because of affliction, and because of great servitude: she dwelleth among the heathen, she findeth no rest: all her persecutors overtook her between the straits.

The ways of Zion do mourn, because none come to the solemn feasts: all her gates are desolate: her priests sigh, her virgins are afflicted, and she is in bitterness.

Her adversaries are the chief, her enemies prosper; for the Lord hath afflicted her for the multitude of her transgressions: her children are gone into captivity before the enemy.

And from the daughter of Zion all her beauty is departed: her princes are become like harts that find no pasture, and they are gone without strength before the pursuer.

Jerusalem remembered in the days of her affliction and of her miseries all her pleasant things that she had in the days of old, when her people fell into the hand of the enemy, and none did help her: the adversaries saw her, and did mock at her sabbaths.

Jerusalem hath grievously sinned; therefore she is removed: all that honoured her despise her, because they have seen her nakedness: yea, she sigheth, and turneth backward.

Her filthiness is in her skirts; she remembereth not her last end; therefore she came down wonderfully; she had no comforter. O Lord, behold my affliction: for the enemy hath magnified himself.

The adversary hath spread out his hand upon all her pleasant things: for she hath seen that the heathen entered into her sanctuary, whom thou didst command that they should not enter into thy congregation.

All her people sigh, they seek bread; they have given their pleasant things for meat to relieve the soul: see, O Lord, and consider; for I am become vile.

Is it nothing to you, all ye that pass by? behold, and see if there be any sorrow like unto my sorrow, which is done unto me, wherewith the Lord hath afflicted me in the day of his fierce anger.

From above hath he sent fire into my bones, and it prevaileth against them: he hath spread a net for my feet, he hath turned me back: he hath made me desolate and faint all the day.

The yoke of my transgressions is bound by his hand: they are wreathed, and come up upon my neck: he hath made my strength to fall: the Lord hath delivered me into their hands, from whom I am not able to rise up.

The Lord hath trodden under foot all my mighty men in the midst of me: he hath called an assembly against me to crush my young men: the Lord hath trodden the virgin, the daughter of Judah, as in a winepress.

For these things I weep; mine eye, mine eye runneth down with water, because the comforter that should relieve my soul is far from me: my children are desolate, because the enemy prevaileth.

Zion spreadeth forth her hands, and there is none to comfort her: the Lord hath commanded concerning Jacob, that his adversaries should be round about him: Jerusalem is as a menstruous woman among them.

The Lord is righteous; for I have rebelled against his commandment: hear, I pray you, all people, and behold my sorrow: my virgins and my young men are gone into captivity.

I called for my lovers, but they deceived me: my priests and mine elders gave up the ghost in the city, while they sought their meat to relieve their souls.

Behold, O Lord; for I am in distress: my bowels are troubled; mine heart is turned within me; for I have grievously rebelled: abroad the sword bereaveth, at home there is as death.

They have heard that I sigh: there is none to comfort me: all mine enemies have heard of my trouble; they are glad that thou hast done it; thou wilt bring the day that thou hast called, and they shall be like unto me.

Let all their wickedness come before thee; and do unto them as thou hast done unto me for all my transgressions: for my sighs are many, and my heart is faint.

Zechariah

Open Thy Doors, O Lebanon

OPEN thy doors, O Lebanon, that the fire may devour thy cedars.

Howl, fir tree; for the cedar is fallen; because the mighty are spoiled: howl, O ye oaks of Bashan; for the forest of the vintage is come down.

There is a voice of the howling of the shepherds; for their glory is spoiled: a voice of the roaring of young lions; for the pride of Jordan is spoiled.

Thus saith the Lord my God, Feed the flock of the slaughter;

Whose possessors slay them, and hold themselves not guilty: and they that sell them say, Blessed be the Lord; for I am rich: and their own shepherds pity them not.

For I will no more pity the inhabitants of the land, saith the Lord: but, lo, I will deliver the men every one into his neighbour's hand, and into the hand of his king: and they shall smite the land, and out of their hand I will not deliver them.

And I will feed the flock of slaughter, even you, O poor of the flock. And I took unto me two staves; the one I called Beauty, and the other I called Bands; and I fed the flock.

Three shepherds also I cut off in one month; and my soul loathed them, and their soul also abhorred me.

Then said I, I will not feed you: that that dieth, let it die; and that that is to be cut off, let it be cut off; and let the rest eat every one the flesh of another.

And I took my staff, even Beauty, and cut it asunder, that I might break my covenant which I had made with all the people.

And it was broken in that day: and so the poor of the flock that waited upon me knew that it was the word of the Lord.

And I said unto them, If ye think good, give me my price; and if not, forbear. So they weighed for my price thirty pieces of silver.

And the Lord said unto me, Cast it unto the potter: a goodly price that I was prised at of them. And I took the thirty pieces of silver and cast them to the potter in the house of the Lord.

Then I cut asunder mine other staff, even Bands, that I might break the brotherhood between Judah and Israel.

Authorised Version

SOLOMON IBN GABIROL

1021—1058

The Royal Crown

I

WONDERFUL are thy works, as my soul over=
whelmingly knoweth.

Thine, O Lord, are the greatness and the might, the
beauty and the triumph and the splendour.

Thine, O Lord, is the Kingdom, and Thou art
exalted as head over all.

Thine are the riches and honour. Thine the crea=
tures of the heights and depths.

They bear witness that they perish, while Thou
endurest.

Thine is the might in whose mystery our thoughts
can find no stay, so far art Thou beyond us. . . .

Thine is the lovingkindness that ruleth over all Thy
creatures, and the good treasured up for those who fear
Thee.

Thine are the mysteries that transcend understanding
and thought.

Thine is the existence from the shadow of whose
light every being was created,

Of which we say, in His shadow we live.

Thine are the two worlds between which Thou hast
set a boundary,

The first for deeds and the second for reward. . . .

II

THOU art One, the first of every number, and the
foundation of every structure.

Thou art One, and at the mystery of Thy Oneness
the wise of heart are struck dumb,

For they know not what it is.

Thou art One, and Thy Oneness can neither be in-
creased nor lessened,
It lacketh naught, nor doth aught remain over.
Thou art One, but not like a unit to be grasped or
counted,
For number and change cannot reach Thee.
Thou art not to be envisaged, nor to be figured thus
and thus. . . .

III

THOU existest, but hearing of ear cannot reach Thee,
nor vision of eye,
Nor shall the How have sway over Thee, nor the
Wherefore and Whence.
Thou existest, but for Thyself and for none other
with Thee.
Thou existest, and before Time began Thou wast,
And without place Thou didst abide.
Thou existest, and Thy secret is hidden and who shall
attain to it ?
" So deep, so deep, who can discover it ? "

IV

THOU livest, but not from any restricted season nor
from any known period.
Thou livest, but not through breath and soul, for
Thou art soul of the soul.
Thou livest, but not with the life of man, which is like
unto vanity and its end the moth and the worm.
Thou livest, and he who layeth hold of Thy secret
shall find eternal delight:
" He shall eat and live for ever."

V

THOU art great, and compared with Thy greatness
all greatness is humbled and all excess diminished.
Incalculably great is Thy being,
Superber than the starry heaven,

Beyond and above all grandeur,
" And exalted beyond all blessing and praise." . . .

VII

THOU art Light celestial, and the eyes of the pure
shall behold Thee,
But the clouds of sin shall veil Thee from the eyes
of the sinners.
Thou art Light, hidden in this world but to be revealed in the visible world on high. . . .

VIII

THOU art God, and all things formed are Thy servants
and worshippers.
Yet is not Thy glory diminished by reason of those
that worship aught beside Thee,
For the yearning of them all is to draw nigh Thee,
But they are like the blind,
Setting their faces forward on the King's highway,
Yet still wandering from the path.
One sinketh into the well of a pit,
And another falleth into a snare,
But all imagine they have reached their desire,
Albeit they have suffered in vain.
But Thy servants are those walking clear-eyed in the
straight path,
Turning neither to the right nor the left,
Till they come to the court of the King's palace.
Thou art God, by Thy Godhead sustaining all that
hath been formed,
And upholding in Thy Unity all creatures.
Thou art God and there is no distinction betwixt Thy
Godhead and Thy Unity, Thy pre-existence and Thy
existence,
For 'tis all one mystery,
And although the name of each be different,
" Yet they are all proceeding to one place."

IX

THOU art wise. And wisdom is the fount of life and from Thee it welleth,
And by the side of Thy wisdom all human knowledge turneth to folly.
Thou art wise, more ancient than all primal things,
And wisdom was the nursling at Thy side.
Thou art wise, and Thou hast not learnt from any beside Thee,
Nor acquired wisdom from any save Thyself.
Thou art wise, and from Thy wisdom Thou hast set apart Thy appointed purpose,
Like a craftsman and an artist,
To draw up the films of being from Nothingness
As light is drawn that darteth from the eye:
Without bucket from the fountain of light hath Thy workman drawn it up,
And without tool hath he wrought. . . .

XXIV

WHO shall understand the mysteries of Thy crea-
tions ? For Thou hast exalted above the ninth sphere the sphere of intelligence.
It is the Temple confronting us,
" The tenth that shall be sacred to the Lord."
It is the Sphere transcending height,
To which conception cannot reach,
And there stands the veiled palanquin of Thy glory.
From the silver of Truth hast Thou cast it,
And of the gold of Reason hast Thou wrought its arms,
And on a pillar of Righteousness set its cushions,
And from Thy power is its existence,
And from and toward Thee its yearning,
" And unto Thee shall be its desire."

Israel Zangwill

JUDAH HALEVI

1850—1140

Parting

IF parting be decreed for the two of us,
Stand yet a little while I gaze upon thy face. . . .

By the life of love, remember the days of thy longing,
As I remember the nights of thy delight.
As thine image passeth into my dreams,
So let me pass, I entreat thee, into thy dreams.
Between me and thee roar the waves of a sea of tears
And I cannot pass over unto thee.
But O, if thy steps should draw nigh to cross—
Then would its waters be divided at the touch of thy
foot.
Would that after my death unto mine ears should come
The sound of the golden bells upon thy skirts !
Or shouldst thou be asking how fareth thy beloved, I
from the depths of the tomb
Would ask of thy love and thy welfare.
Verily, to the shedding of mine heart's blood
There be two witnesses, thy cheeks and thy lips.
How sayest thou it is not true, since these be my wit-
nesses
For my blood, and that thine hands have shed it ?
Why desirest thou my death, whilst I but desire
To add years unto the years of thy life ?
Though thou dost rob my slumber in the night of my
longing,
Would I not give the sleep of mine eyes unto thy eye-
lids ? . . .
Yea, between the bitter and the sweet standeth my
heart—
The gall of parting, and the honey of thy kisses.

After thy words have beaten out my heart into thin
    plates,
Thine hands have cut it into shreds.
It is the likeness of rubies over pearls
What time I behold thy lips over thy teeth.
The sun is on thy face, and thou spreadest out the
    night
Over his radiance with the clouds of thy locks.
Fine silk and broidered work are the covering of thy
    body,
But grace and beauty are the covering of thine eyes.
The adornment of maidens is the work of human hands,
But thou—majesty and sweetness are thine adorn<
    ment. . . .
In the field of the daughters of delight, the sheaves of
    love
Make obeisance unto thy sheaf. . . .
I cannot hear thy voice, but I hear
Upon the secret places of my heart, the sound of thy
    steps.
On the day when thou wilt revive
The victims whom love for thee hath slain—on the
    day when thy dead shall live anew,
Then turn again to my soul to restore it to my body;
    for on the day
Of thy departure, when thou wentest forth, it went out
    after thee.

                    Nina Salaman

CHAIM NACHMAN BIALIK

                                  1873–

The Mathmid

THERE are abandoned corners of our Exile,
Remote, forgotten cities of Dispersion,
    Where still in secret burns our ancient light,
    Where God has saved a remnant from disaster.

There, brands that glimmer in a ruin of ashes,
Pent and unhappy souls maintain the vigil—
Spirits grown old beyond the count of time,
Grown old beyond the reckoning of days.
And when thou goest forth alone, at nightfall,
Wandering in one of these, the sacred cities,
When heaven above is quick with breaking stars,
And earth beneath with whispering spirit-winds—
Thine ear will catch the murmur of a voice,
Thine eye will catch the twinkle of a light
Set in a window, and a human form—
A shadow, like the shadow of death—beyond,
A shadow trembling, swaying back and forth,
A voice, an agony, that lifts and falls,
And comes toward thee upon the waves of silence.
Mark well the swaying shadow and the voice:
It is a *Mathmid* in his prison-house,
A prisoner, self-guarded, self-condemned,
Self-sacrificed to study of the Law. . . . .

Within these walls, within this prison-house,
Six years have passed above his swaying form:
Within these walls the child became the youth,
The youth became the man, fore-ripened swift,
And swift as these went, swifter yet were gone
The cheek's bloom and the lustre of his eyes.
Six years have passed since first he set his face
To the dark corner of the inner walls;
Six years since he has seen, for joyous sunlight,
Grey limestone, lizards and the webs of spiders;
Six years of hunger, years of sleeplessness,
Six years of wasting flesh and falling cheeks—
And all, to him, as if it had not been.
He knows that Jews have studied thus of old,
He knows the fame and glory they have won.

Since that dark corner has become his own,
No man, no living thing, has seen his coming,
No man, no living thing, has seen his going.
Not even the rising and the setting suns
Have witnessed his arrival, his return;
The morning-star, black midnight and the moon
Alone knew when he slept and when he rose:
Daylight has never looked upon his ways,
The mid-day sun has never burned his skin.
In the dimmest dawn, " before thou canst distinguish
A white thread from an azure, wolf from dog "—
(Thereby the Jew shall know, the Rabbis say,
The hour for morning-prayer is not yet come)—
In the dimmest dawn, while through the lifeless dark
Ten thousand times ten thousand stars yet shine,
Before the crowing of the cock disturbs
The burghers of the city, sleep-enfolded,
Yea, even before the most elect of faith
Rise to do honour to Creation's Lord:
In that hour, when the world in silence trembles
Before the new awakening of life,
Trembles as if she dreamed the last of dreams,
As if a wandering and secret thought
Made a light stirring in her folded wings—
In that hour from his stolen sleep he starts,
Dresses in darkness and to his corner runs.
Light are his footsteps on the garden path,
Only the winds have heard them passing by,
Only the stars have seen them running swift.

But there are moments when a playful wind
Out of the blue deep like the Tempter comes,
And with a loving hand his earlock fondles,
And whispers to him with dissolving sweetness.
And the boy's eyelids cling to one another,
As if they pleaded with him: " Brother, brother,
Have pity on the dark eyes under us;

And we are weary, for with thee we suffer:
A full day we have toiled, a summer day,
And half a summer night: it is enough.
Brother, return and sleep, and we with thee,
Too short thy sleep was to restore our strength. . . ."
But sudden starts the boy, draws his lean hand
Across his eyes, as if temptation sat
Upon his leaden lid: and clear and swift
His footsteps echo from the empty streets.

And then the wind that blows about the garden
Takes up the theme, and gentle is its voice:
" *Green is my cradle, child of happiness,*
Joy in my blossom, ere thine own be withered. . . ."
And left and right of him the flowers and grasses
Speak to him from their dreams, "*We too are sleeping.*"
Even the stars above him take on voices,
And wink: " *We sleep, although our eyes are open.*"
The drunken odours of a thousand flowers
Mount to his nostrils in resistless waves:
They break upon his eyes, his lips, his throat.
He bares his breast then to receive the wind,
And lifts his strengthless hands as if in prayer:
" *O dear wind, take me, carry me from here,*
And find a place for me where I may rest:
For here is only weariness and pain. . . ."
His raised hands bruise against the garden fence,
And tell him he has wandered from the path:
Swift he recalls his vows, recalls his corner,
And turns him from the Tempter's voice, and flees.

In the Yeshivah reigns a sacred silence
Which he, the sacred youth, is first to break;
For there, in the dark corner, wait for him—
Faithful companions since the day he came—
Three friends: his stand, his candle and his Talmud.
As if the moments could not move too swiftly

That lie between him and his trusted friends,
He hastens to his place and takes his stand,
And like a pillar stands from morn till night.
Still standing he will eat his midday crust,
Still standing he will half outwatch the night.
Granite is yielding clay compared with him—
A Jewish boy unto the Torah vowed.

" *Oi, omar Rabba, tonu rabonon,*
Thus Rabba speaks, and thus our teachers taught,"
(Backward and forward swaying he repeats,
With ceaseless singsong the undying words);
The dawn, the garden, the enchanted fields,
Are gone, are vanished like a driven cloud,
And earth and all her fullness are forgotten. . . .

Maurice Samuel

From "Songs of the People"

I

TWO steps from my garden rail
Sleeps my well beneath its pail:
  Every sabbath comes my love
  And I let him drink thereof.

All the world is sleeping now
Like the fruit beneath the bough.
  Father, mother, both are gone,
  And my heart wakes here alone.

And the pail awakes with me,
Dripping, dripping, drowsily:
  Drops of gold and crystal clear . . .
  And my love is drawing near.

Hist ! I think that something stirred;
Was it he, or but a bird ?
    Dearest friend, my lover dear,
    There is no one with me here.

By the trough we sit and speak,
Hand in hand and cheek to cheek;
    Hear this riddle: Can you tell
    Why the pitcher seeks the well ?

That you cannot answer, nor
What the pail is weeping for ?
    Morn to even, drop by drop,
    Fall its tears and cannot stop.

This then tell me, why my breast
Daylong, nightlong is oppressed.
    Spoke my mother truth in saying
    That your heart from me was straying ?

And my lover answered: See,
Enemies have slandered me.
    Ere another year be gone,
    We shall marry, foolish one.

On that golden day of days
Shall the summer be ablaze.
    Fruited branches overhead
    Shall in benediction spread.

Friend and kinsman, young and old
Shall be gathered to behold,
    And with music and with mirth
    They shall come to lead us forth.

And the bridal canopy
In this place shall lifted be.
    I shall slip a ring of gold
    On this finger that I hold,

And pronounce the blessing: " Thee
God makes consecrate to me."
And my enemies shall there
Burst with envy and despair.

Maurice Samuel

2

ON a hill there blooms a palm
'Twixt Tigris and Euphrates old,
And among the leafy branches
Sits the phœnix, bird of gold.

Bird of gold, go forth and find me
Him whose bride I am to be:
Search and circle till thou find him,
Bind him, bring him, bird, to me.

If thou hast no thread of scarlet,
Give him greeting without end:
Tell him, golden bird, my spirit
Languishes towards my friend.

Tell him: Now the garden blossoms,
Closed except to his command;
Mid the leaves the golden apple
Waits and trembles for his hand.

Tell him, nightly on my pillow
Wakes the longing without name,
And the whiteness of my body
Burns my couch as with a flame.

If he comes not, hear my secret:
All prepared my coffer stands;
Linen, silk, and twenty singlets
Wrought and knitted by these hands.

And the softest of all feathers
By my mother plucked and stored:
Through the nights she filled the cushions
For her daughter's bridal hoard.

And the bridal veil of silver
Waits to deck me when I marry:
Bride and dowry, both are ready—
Wherefore does the bridegroom tarry?

.   .   .   .

Seethe and whisper, magic potion:
Thus the phœnix makes reply:
" In the night to thy beloved
With my secret will I fly.

" In his dreams I give thy greeting,
In his dreams reveal thy face:
Lo ! upon a broomstick mounted
Unto thee he flies apace.

" And he comes and speaks: ' Behold me,
Oh, my joy, my hope, my pride:
Not with golden gifts or dowry,
But with love become my bride.

" ' Gold and silk I have aplenty—
Fire of youth and ringlets fine:
Both I give thee—swiftly, lightly,
Come to me, beloved mine.' "

.   .   .   .

When the night was dark above me
And the stars with clouds were stilled,
On his quest the phœnix vanished—
And his words are unfulfilled.

And at morn, at noon, at even,
Still I watch the clouds of fire:
" Clouds above me, answer, Wherefore
Comes he not, my heart's desire ? "

Maurice Samuel

The Dead ·of the Wilderness [1]

YONDER great shadow—that blot on the passionate
glare of the desert—
'Tis not an army of lions couched in the sun with
their young ones,
'Tis not the pride of the forests of Bashan uprooted
and fallen:
Those are the Dead of the Wilderness under the
sunlight recumbent.
Hard by their tents are they laid, like children of
Anak for stature,
Stretched on the desolate sands like numberless
lions in slumber;
Under the might of their limbs the floor of the
desert is hollowed.
Armed as for battle they sleep and clad in the
armour of giants;
Swords like crags at their heads and spears 'twixt
their shoulders protruding,
Bound to their girdle the quiver and firm in the sand
is the lance thrust.

Deep in the earth are their heads sunk, heavy with
tangles neglected,
Matted and monstrous and vast, and uncouth as the
mane of a lion;

[1] The subject of this poem is derived from a Talmudic legend
which says that the Jews who left Egypt did not die in the desert,
as the Bible tells, but were cast into slumber.—(Tr.)

Trembles a moment above them and breaks into
    circles of motion,
Suddenly chooses a body outstretched and over it
    stands and is moveless;
And the body beneath it is darkened and half of its
    neighbour.
Suddenly quivers the air as the pinions stupendous are
    folded.
Full with his weight like a meteor descending he falls
    on his victim—
One of the eagle-kings, crag-born, crooked of beak and
    of talon.
Over the breast of the sleeper a granite-like talon is
    lifted;
Yet but an instant and granite on granite will ring in
    the stillness;
And in that instant he pauses and stands with his
    talon uplifted,
Stilled and rebuked in his pride by the loftier pride of
    the sleeper;
Wondering stands, then unfolds the strength of his
    pinions and rises,
Beating great waves through the air and screaming in
    stretches of sunlight,
Scales untiring the measureless heights and is lost in
    the splendour.
Long, long after still flutters, held fast on the point of
    a lance-head,
One grey feather that fell unseen and unmarked was
    abandoned,
Flutters and strains at the lance-head and fluttering
    earthwards is wafted.
Silence returns to the desert and peace to the sleep of
    the heroes.

Sometimes when midday is hot and the desert swoons
    under the sunlight,

Slides from its fastness a serpent, vast as the beam of a
weaver,
Issues to warm on the sands the glistening rings of his
body.
Now he shrinks on himself, coils himself moveless and
breathless,
Languid with joy in the warmth and bathing in light
as in waters;
Now he wakes and uncoils and stretches his length in
the sunlight,
Opens the width of his jaws and his scales are like
network of lightnings,
Spangled and knitted in splendour, a lonely delight in
the desert.
Sudden he starts from his languor, leaps into rigid
attention,
Bends and unwinds on the sand, then swiftly he glides
from his station
Over the waste till he reaches the army of sleepers and
stands then,
Lifted one-third in the air, like a column of bright
hieroglyphics,
Raises his crown and outstretches his neck and his
eyeballs green sparkle.
Swaying he broods on the slumbering army from margin
to margin.
Vast is the soundless encampment and countless the
dead it encloses,
Numberless, numberless faces and foreheads exposed to
the heavens.

Then like a flash reawakens the hatred of dead generations,
Gleams in the start of his eyes like a brand that is
sudden uncovered.
Hatred instinctive and ancient runs through the shuddering body.

Trembling he lowers his head and darts with it hither
    and thither,
Hangs then suspended an instant and stares in the face
    of a sleeper.
Under their hoods are his eyeballs twin centres of
    hatred and fury;
Hissing he opens his jaws and the flash of his fangs
    is uncovered—
And in that instant he pauses, sinks on the coils of his
    body,
Stilled and rebuked in his rage by the bitterer rage of
    the sleeper,—
Sinks and uncircles his length and turns from the visage
    of granite,
Moves off, a rhythm of waves till his splendour is lost
    in the distance.
Silence returns to the desert and peace to the sleep of
    the heroes.

Moonlight descends on the waste and sleeps on the
    measureless broadness,
Lays on the desert a garment speckled with light and
    with shadow.
Pallid the wilderness league after league rolls from
    dimness to dimness.
Broad at the foot of the towering crags are their shadows
    recumbent,
Couched like dragons primeval, things from the dawn
    of creation.
Gathered in monstrous conspiracy under the cover of
    darkness—
They will arise ere the morning, return to the caverns
    they came from.
Mournful the moon from her loneliness looks on the
    mystery threefold—
Wilderness, midnight and monsters crept out from the
    dawn of creation.

Lapped is the desert in merciless dreams of its old
    desolation,
Wails in its dreams, and its wailing half-uttered is broken
    and stifled.

Sometimes a wandering lion, thewed as with roots of
    an oak tree,
Massive and certain of footstep comes down to the army
    and stands there,
Raises his head from his shoulders, heavy, magnifi-
    cent-crested.
Fitfully gleam the two eyeballs over the enemy army;
Vast is the army outspread and its vastness is utterly
    silent;
Dark is the sleep of the heroes, there is not an eyelid
    aflutter.
Shadows of lances, like thongs, are close on their bodies
    and bind them.
Moonlight is spilled on their faces and rims the black
    mass of their eyebrows.
Stonelike in wonder the lion stares at their slumbering
    power,
Till from his wonder awaking he shakes with his roaring
    the desert,
Startling the mountains and setting the flanks of the
    desert atremble.
Far pours the strength of his voice, and the crags in
    the distance give answer,
Hither and thither is rolled till it crumbles in fragments
    of thunder.
Then in a wailing responsive arises the cry of the jackals,
Mingles with howling of beasts till the night-time is
    hideous with voices—
This is the wail of the desert, a desperate protest and
    bitter,
Worn with the infinite vigil and weary with long desola-
    tion.

Still stands the lion, intent on the tumult his strength
    has awakened;
Silent he turns from the dead and is kingly again in
    his silence,
Turns and departs like a king and his eyes are like
    torches attendant,
Massive and certain of step departs and is lost in the
    darkness.
Long is the desert awake and its bitterness will not be
    silenced,
Long it moans for its ancient pain and the comfortless
    future.
Dawn returns and the desert is weary from moaning,
    and slumbers,
Slumbers and yet is awake, and shrinks from the day and
    its evil.
Slow dies the moon in her pallor and drops to the rim
    of the heavens;
Stealthy the shadows arise from under the crags, and
    they are not.
Gaunt stand the rocks to the morning and anger is
    written upon them;
Under the wrath of their looks the desert is timid and
    trembles,
Strains to answer with anger responsive and fails and
    is voiceless,
Stilled by the shattering sun. And silence returns as
    for ever.
Deep is the sleep of the heroes . . . and cycle succeeds
    unto cycle.

But there are moments when, tortured too long by the
    silence eternal,
Wild with unbearable sickness of æons, the desert up-
    rises,
Wakens and rages for vengeance against the inhuman
    Creator,

Raises a column of sand to ascend to the fastness of
heaven,
Once and for ever to meet Him and shatter the throne
of His glory,
Once for the torture eternal to loose the floods of its fury,
Sweep His whole world into darknes sand bring back
the kingdom of chaos. . . . .
Then the Creator is stirred, and His anger envelops
the heavens,
Like a great cover of iron, He bends them to blot out
the desert.
Red from the blast of His breath, the flame of His anger
outbreaking
Wraps the desert in fury and scatters its crags in a
furnace.
Stubborn and bitter the desert responds, and new furies
are loosened,
Rise from the bowels of Hell, and all earth is in fury
confounded.
Seized by the madness that spins like a vehement wheel
in the vastness
Tigers and lions, with manes uplifted and eyeballs
aglitter,
Join in the riot infernal, and howl with the voice of the
tempest,
Lifted and torn by the strength of the tempest like
gossamer insects.
And in that instant—
Wakes the terrible power that slumbered in chains,
Suddenly stirs and arises the old generation of heroes,
Mighty in battle: their eyes are like lightning, like
blades are their faces.
Then flies the hand to the sword.
Sixty myriads of voices—a thunder of heroes—awaken,
Crash through the tempest and tear asunder the rage
of the desert.

Round them in wildness and blindness:

And they cry

" We are the mighty !
The last generation of slaves and the first generation
of freemen !
Alone our hand in its strength
Tore from the pride of our shoulders the yoke of
bondage.
We lifted our heads to the heavens and behold their
broadness was narrow in the pride of our eyes,
So we turned to the desert, we said to the Wilderness:
' Mother ! '
Yea, on the tops of the crags, in the thickness of clouds,
With the eagles of heaven we drank from her fountains
of freedom.
And who is lord of us ?
Even now, though the God of vengeance has shut the
desert upon us,
A song of strength and revolt has reached us, and we
arise.
To arms ! To arms ! Form ranks ! Forward !
Forward into the heavens and the wrath thereof.
Behold us ! We will ascend
With the tempest !
Though the Lord has withdrawn His hand from us,
And the Ark stands moveless in its place,
Still we will ascend—alone !
Even under the eye of His wrath, daring the lightning
of His countenance,
We will carry with storm the citadels of the hills,
And face to face in combat encounter the armed foe !
Listen !
The storm, too, calls unto us—' Courage and daring ! '
To arms ! To arms ! Let the hills be shattered and the
mountains blasted into dust,
Or let our lifeless bodies be heaped in countless cairns.

Forward !
On to the hills ! ''

.   .   .   .   .

And in that instant the desert is wild with a fierce
    anger—
And who shall conquer it ?
In the storm goes up a terrible voice, a mingling of
    cries.
It must be surely
That the desert is bringing to birth a deed of evil,
A bitter thing, a cruel and a terrible. . . .

Passed is the tempest.   The desert is silent, and pure is
    the silence.
Bright is the broadness of heaven, and marvellous quiet
    beneath it.
Now from their terror awaking, the caravans trapped in
    the tempest
Rise from their crouching and call on their God and
    adore Him and praise Him.
Still in the sand are the sixty myriads of heroes aslumber.
Darkened their faces, for death has brought them to
    peace with their Maker.
No man knoweth the place of their slumber.   The crags
    of the desert,
Split by the strength of their rising, over them closed in
    their falling.
Sometimes a rider, in daring adventure his caravan
    leaving,
Spurs his horse ever onwards and enters the heart of
    the desert.
Strong is the heart of the rider, and swift is the horse to
    the spurring.
Riding he flings up his spear in the sunlight, and takes
    it descending,
Throws it and takes it again, and throws it again and
    pursues it;

Like to a river of lightning it flashes and dances before
      him.
Far in the distance a vision appears, and the horse is
      drawn onwards,
Mounts with its rider a hill the clouds overtopping—
      and sudden,
Quivering it pauses and looks, then bounds to the rear
      by its whole length.
Startled the rider uplifts his hand for a shadow and
      gazes. . . .
Stonelike he stands with his horse, and the terror of God
      is upon him.
Then leaps the horse in its strength and, turning,
      descends like an arrow. . . .
Fast spurs the rider and halts not until, with his caravan
      meeting,
Swift he dismounts and tells of the vision he saw in the
      stillness.
Marvelling listen the Arabs, and wonder is writ on their
      faces.
Then speaks the oldest amongst them, a patriarch sprung
      from the Prophet,
Answers the tale of the rider: " Blessed be Allah the
      True One;
For by the Beard of the Prophet, it was not a vision
      thou sawest.
Those are the Dead of the Wilderness thou hast dis-
      covered and gazed on.
This was the host of the Lord, a people of valour
      gigantic,
Older than man can remember—yea, of the first genera-
      tions,
Stubborn and strong was this people, stiff-necked as the
      crags of the desert,
Deaf to the word of their Prophet, and proud with the
      God of their fathers.

Therefore He cast sleep upon them, and sealed up their
  path with the mountains,
Laid His command on the wilderness for a memorial
  eternal. . . .
Allah protect true Believers from touching the hem of
  their garments.
Once did a son of the Faithful lay hand on a fringe and
  uplift it.
Withered his body became till the fringe was restored
  to the sleeper.
These are the sires of the race of the Book. . . ."
                              Then the speaker is silent,
Wordless the Arabs have heard, and they tremble and
  give praise to Allah.
Silent they walk at the side of their camels to weariness
  laden.
Long is the whiteness that gleams on their hoods to be
  seen in the distance.
Slow sway the camels their monstrous backs till they fail
  in the brightness,
Bearing away from the desert one more of its marvellous
  legends.
Stillness returns as of old. Desolate stretches the desert.

Maurice Samuel

YEHOASH

Solomon Bloomgarden

1870–

An Old Song

(Yiddish)

IN the blossom-land Japan
Somewhere thus an old song ran.

Said a warrior to a smith
" Hammer me a sword forthwith.

Make the blade
Light as wind on water laid.
Make it long
As the wheat at harvest song.
Supple, swift
As a snake, without rift,
Full of lightnings, thousand-eyed !
Smooth as silken cloth and thin
As the web that spiders spin.
And merciless as pain, and cold."

" On the hilt what shall be told ? "

" On the sword's hilt, my good man,"
Said the warrior of Japan,
" Trace for me
A running lake, a flock of sheep
And one who sings her child to sleep."

Marie Syrkin

EGYPTIAN

FROM THE BOOK OF THE DEAD

3500 B.C. *et seq.*

*B*OTH *external detail and central faith of the Egyptian religion are incorporated in the Chapters of Coming Forth by Day, commonly known as the Book of the Dead. About 3500* B.C., *when the first Chapter was set down by the scribes, many of the symbols were already so ancient that the men who wrote them were ignorant of their significance. Yet all were retained, because all were holy to the traditional-minded people of the Nile. . . . This race loved life and pleasure with a fierce intensity; all the sombre pomp of the ritual of the dead had as its object the prolongation of an existence too delightful to relinquish. It is erroneous to picture the early Egyptians as an austere, funereal people. . . . Their theology, their sacraments, and their conception of the after life are based on a single doctrine: eternal life manifested through eternal living forms.*—ROBERT HILLYER.

The Dead Man ariseth and singeth a Hymn to the Sun

*H*OMAGE to thee, O Ra, at thy tremendous rising !
Thou risest ! Thou shinest ! the heavens are rolled
aside !
Thou art the King of Gods, thou art the All-
comprising,
From thee we come, in thee are deified.

Thy priests go forth at dawn; they wash their hearts
with laughter;
Divine winds move in music across thy golden
strings.
At sunset they embrace thee, as every cloudy rafter
Flames with reflected colour from thy wings.

Thou sailest over the zenith, and thy heart rejoices;
Thy Morning Boat and Evening Boat with fair
winds meet together;

Before thy face the goddess Maat exalts her fateful
    Feather,
And at thy name the halls of Anu ring with voices.

O Thou Perfect ! Thou Eternal ! Thou Only One !
Great Hawk that fliest with the flying Sun !
Between the Turquoise Sycamores that risest, young for
    ever,
Thine image flashing on the bright celestial river.

Thy rays are on all faces; Thou art inscrutable.
Age after age thy life renews its eager prime.
Time whirls its dust beneath thee; thou art immutable,
Maker of Time, thyself beyond all Time.

Thou passest through the portals that close behind the
    night,
Gladdening the souls of them that lie in sorrow.
The True of Word, the Quiet Heart, arise to drink thy
    light;
Thou art To-day and Yesterday; Thou art To-morrow !

Homage to thee, O Ra, who wakest life from slumber !
Thou risest ! Thou shinest ! Thy radiant face appears !
Millions of years have passed,—we cannot count their
    number,—
Millions of years shall come. Thou art above the years !

He singeth a Hymn to Osiris, the Lord of Eternity

GLORY to Osiris, the Prince of Everlastingness,
  Who travelleth through all the million years into
    Eternity,
    Crowned with the North and South, the Lord of
      gods and men,
    Bearing the crook and whip of mercy and of power.

O King of Kings, O Prince of Princes, Lord of Lords,
Through thee the world is green again by virtue of
    thy Passion;
Thou leadest in thy train what has been and what
    shall be,
Thy heart shall rest content upon the hidden
    Mountain.

Thy body is of shining metal, and thy head is azure;
The colour of the turquoise plays about thee where thou
    goest.
All-pervading is thy body, radiant thy countenance,
As the fields and river valleys of the world hereafter.

Grant my spirit strength on earth, and triumph in
    eternity.
Grant me favourable winds to sail about thy Kingdom.
Grant me wings on which to rise and fly up like the
    phœnix.
Grant me welcome freely in the pylons of the gods.

In the House of Coolness, let thy bread be given to me,
The blessed food of them who rise from death with
    thee, Victorious,
And let there be a home for me amid the happy
    meadows
Where I may sow and reap those sunny fields of wheat
    and barley.

He asketh Absolution of God

O THOU who speedest Time's advancing wing,
Thou dweller in all mysteries of Life,
Thou guardian of every word I speak,—
Behold thou art ashamed of me, thy son;
Thy heart is full of sorrow and of shame,
For that my sins were grievous in the world,
And proud my wickedness and my transgression.

O be at peace with me, O be at peace !
And break the barriers that loom between us !
Let all my sins be washed away, and fall
Forgotten to the right and left of thee.
Yea, do away with all my wickedness,
And put away the shame that fills thy heart,
That thou and I henceforth may be at peace !

He holdeth fast to the Memory of his Identity

IN the Great House, and in the House of Fire,
On the dark night of counting all the years,
  On the dark night when months and years are num-
    bered,—
O let my name be given back to me !

When the Divine One on the Eastern Stairs
Shall cause me to sit down with him in peace,
And every god proclaims his name before me,—
Let me remember then the name I bore !

He approacheth the Hall of Judgment

O MY Heart, my Mother, my Heart, my Mother,
The seed of my being, my earthly existence,
  O stay with me still in the Hall of the Princes,
  In the presence of the God who keepeth the
    Balance.
  And when thou art weighed in the scale with the
    feather
  Of Truth, then render no judgment against me;
  Let not the Lords of the Trial cry before me:
  He hath wrought Evil and spoken Untruth !

And ye, divine Gods, cloud-enthroned with your
    sceptres,
At the weighing of words, speak me fair to Osiris.
Lift up my cause to the Forty-two Judges,
And let me not die yet again in Amentet.

Behold, O my Heart, if there be not a parting
Between us, our name shall be one with to-morrow,
Yea, Millions-of-Years is the name we have written,
Yea, Millions-of-Years, O my Mother, my Heart !

He is declared True of Word

THUS saith the great god Thoth,
    The judge of Right and Truth,
    Unto the Company of Gods
    Who sit before Osiris :

    " Now verily this heart
    Was weighed, and it is pure.
    No wickedness was found in him
    Whose heart withstood the Balance."

    And thus respond the gods
    Who sit before Osiris,
    " Thy words are true, let him come in
    And live in peace for ever.

    " Give him a house amid
    The everlasting Fields.
    Let not Oblivion devour
    The soul that is triumphant."

    Thus Horus, son of Isis,
    Saith to divine Osiris,
    " O Father, I have brought to thee
    This vindicated spirit.

"His deeds have been adjudged,
His heart weighed in the Balance;
Grant him thy cakes and ale, and grant
Him welcome in thy presence."

Thus saith the living soul,
"Behold, O Lord of lords,
Here to thy presence am I come,
Sinless before Osiris.

"Thou art the Beautiful,
The Prince of all the World,
Thee have I loved, O favour me,
And make me thy Beloved."

He cometh forth into the Day

I AM here, I have traversed the Tomb, I behold thee,
   Thou who art strong !
I have passed through the Underworld, gazed on Osiris,
   Scattered the night.

I have come, I have gazed on my Father, Osiris,
   I am his son.
I am the son who loveth his Father,
   I am beloved.

I have made me a path through the western horizon,
   Even as God.
I have followed his footsteps, and won through his
   magic
   Millions of years.

The Gate between Heaven and Earth standeth open,
   Glad is my path.
Hail, every god ! every soul ! out of darkness
   Shineth my light !

Like the Hawk I went in; I come forth like the Phœnix,
 Star of the dawn.
In the beautiful world by the bright Lake of Horus,
 Riseth the Day.

He biddeth Osiris to arise from the Dead

ARISE up on thy feet, O Quiet Heart!
 O Quiet Heart, thy body is made perfect.
Isis among the reeds beside the Nile
And in the dark papyrus swamps bewailed thee,
And sheltered Horus to avenge thy fate.
He hath come forth from secret habitations;
He hath warred mightily against thy foe,
And now he saileth in the boat of Sunrise.
Come forth, O Quiet Heart,—I have avenged thee.

He maketh himself One with Osiris

I AM the Prince in the Field,
 I am Osiris.
I am Horus and Ra,
 One with Osiris.

I was on guard at his door
 In his birth‹chamber.
I was brought forth at his birth;
 I am Osiris.

One with his heart and his strength,
 Ever renewing
 My youth with his youth in the place
 Whither he goeth.

Slaying his slayer, I too
  Rise out of darkness;
Thus I take vengeance myself,
  Working his vengeance.

All that is offered to him
  Decketh my altar.
He who hath risen from Death
  Beareth me with him.

He maketh himself One with the God Ra

I AM the Lord of Light, the self-begotten Youth,
First-born of life primeval, first Name from nameless
    matter.
I am the Prince of Years; my body is Eternity;
My form is Everlastingness that trampleth down the
    darkness.
Call me by name: the Master who dwelleth in the
    Vineyard,
The Boy who roameth through the town, the Young
    Man in the plain.
Call me by name: the Child who travelleth toward his
    Father,
The Child of Light who findeth his Father in the
    Evening.

He maketh himself One with the only God, whose Limbs are the Many Gods

O EVERLASTING Kingdom of the Sceptre,
  O Resting-place where Ra's bright boat is moored,
  O White Crown of the Form which is divine!
I come! I am the Child! I am the Child!

My hair is Nu, my face the disk of Ra,
My eyes are Hathor, and my neck is Isis;—
Each member of my body is a god,
My flesh and bones, the names of Living Gods.
Thoth shelters me, for always, day by day,
I come as Ra, I come as he whose name
Is yet unknown.   I come as Yesterday,
As Prophet of the million years to be
For nations and for peoples still untold.
I am the Child who marcheth down the road
Of Yesterday, To-day, and of To-morrow.
I am the One, the Only One, who goeth
For ever round his course through all horizons;
Whose moment is in your bodies, but whose forms
Rest in their temple, secret and unveiled;
Who holdeth you in his hand, but whom no hand
Can ever hold; who knoweth your name and season,
But whom you cannot know, nor any mortal;
For whom the days return in constant passing,
Moving in splendour toward the end of time.

Yea, I am He, and shall not die again;
Nor men, nor sainted dead, nor even gods
Shall drag me back from my immortal path !

He walketh by Day

I AM Yesterday, To-day and To-morrow,
The Divine Hidden Soul who created the gods,
And who feedeth the blessed.

I am Lord of the Risers from Death,
Whose Forms are the lamps in the House of the Dead,
Whose shrine is the Earth.

When the sky is illumined with crystal,
Then gladden my road and broaden my path
And clothe me in light.

Keep me safe from the Sleeper in Darkness,
When eventide closeth the eyes of the god
And the door by the wall.

In the dawn I have opened the Sycamore;
My Form is the form of all women and men,
My spirit is God.

He defendeth his Heart against the Destroyer

I AM the Pure, the True of Word, Triumphant,
I am the Prince in the Field: I am Osiris.
In his death-chamber I was born with him,
I died with him, and now I rise from death.
My heart hath been adjudged before Osiris,
And none shall carry it away from me.
Yea, this, my heart, hath wept before Osiris,
And supplicated in the Hall of Judgment.
And now I sit victorious in peace,
Upon the Mountain of Eternity.
Stretching my hand, I grasp the southern breeze,
Opening my nostrils, breathe the western wind;
A shining flame, I light the way for Him
Who Opens the portals of the Million Years.
I am the standard of young plants and flowers,
I am the Flower-bush that blooms for ever.

He establisheth his Triumph

HAIL, thou who shinest from the Moon
And walkest through the crowded night
Lifting high thy torch !

I also come, a Shining Soul
Standing firm upon my feet
Despite my shadowy foes.

Open wide the Gate of Death
For me who bear the Rod of Gold
Victorious through the Dark !

He entereth the House of the Goddess Hathor

I AM the pure traveller.
Behold thou me ! Behold thou me,
O Ahi of the threshold.
For lo, I too would follow
Hathor, who is Love.

He embarketh in the Boat of Ra

HAIL, thou Great God in thy Boat,
Let me be thy Sailor !
Grant me speech with mariners
Of Sunrise and of Sunset.
I have travelled to thy port,
O take me in Thy travels;
Make me of thy followers
Among the stars that sleep not.
I have touched no filthy thing,
Naught that is not holy;
Morning Boat and Evening Boat
Feed me from thine altar.
Of white barley is my bread,
And my ale, red barley;
Pure the heart that sings the hymn,
Safe from many travels.
Let me sail with thee, O Ra !
In thy Boat, O Traveller !

He commandeth a Fair Wind

OPEN to me !
    Who art thou ? and whither goest thou ?
What is thy name ?
    My name ? Lo, I am one of you.
For I am setting forth to the temple of the gods,
And I sail in a boat named the Assembler of Souls.

He knoweth the Souls of the West

HIGH on the Mountain of Sunrise where standeth
    the Temple of Sebek,
There lieth a serpent of flint and glistening plates
    of metal.
His name is The Dweller in Fire, and he is the foe
    of the Morning,
He stoppeth the Boat of Ra, and wrappeth the
    Boatman in slumber.
But he shall be held in restraint and the Boat of
    Ra sail onward,
Yea, I am the Man who restraineth the Serpent
    with mighty enchantment
And fettereth the foe of the Sunrise till Ra resume
    the horizon.
I, even I, have fettered him, and greeted the Souls
    of the West,
The Lord of the Mountain of Sunset, and Hathor,
    the Lady of Evening.

He knoweth the Souls of the East

I EVEN I know the Eastern Gate of Heaven,
Whence Ra shall come in the Golden Boat of the
    Morning,

Sailing before fair winds to the Port of Triumph.

I even I have hoisted the sails of the morning;
I have embarked with Ra by the Turquoise Sycamores,
And I am his sailor for ever in endless travels.

Mine eyes have gazed on the Fields of Peace, whose
  ramparts
Are girded with iron, whose harvest is bursting with
  plenty;
And there the Souls of the East are the deathless reapers.

I even I have seen the deathless Triumphant,
And the Morning Star who walks divinely among them.
The Fields of Peace have been given to me as my City.

He overcometh the Serpent of Evil in the Name of Ra

NOW get thee back, retreat, depart, O Serpent,
Or thou shalt drown deep in the Pool of Sky
In the slaughter place thy father hath ordained.
Behold, my spirit riseth even as Ra,
I am become the Soul of Ra the Terrible,
Yea I have issued from the House of Terror.
Now get thee back, depart; the arrows of Ra
Fly through the shadow; beaming darts of light
Flash at thy head and tear thy bones asunder,
As the roaring clouds lift up on the horizon
With gnashing fires to fetter thee dumb in death,
To fetter thy mouth that thy words be scattered in
  silence.
In the Halls of the Mighty I hear the voice of the
  Gods.
Hail! saith the old god Tem, make strong your
  faces,
O soldiers of Ra, that evil be driven before us.

And there crieth the voice of Seb : Hail ! all you Princes,
Make firm the seats of them who sail with the sun,
Now rise you up with your weapons and strike with
    lightning.
Hail ! saith Hathor the lovely; and loudly responding
The Company of Gods who go round the Pool of
    Turquoise:
Hail ! we will lift up the Mighty One over his foes.
Let praise be recited before him by you and by us !
O Ra ! Thou terrible Light ! the heavens are quaking
With the sound of gods on the march, and the Serpent
    dieth.

Now get thee back, retreat, depart, O thou Serpent !
Behold I am Ra of the Eastern and Western Skies !

He is Like the Lotus

I AM the pure lotus,
    Springing up in splendour
    Fed by the breath of Ra.

    Rising into sunlight,
    Out of soil and darkness,
    I blossom in the Field.

He is Like the Serpent Saka

I AM the Serpent, fat with years,
    Who dwelleth in remote domains,
    Who day by day dieth and is born,
    Even as I die and am born.

He prayeth for Ink and Palette that he may write

HAIL, aged God who lookest on thy Father,
And guardest hidden books of Thoth unopened !
Behold, I am a scribe, and I have copied
Each day the words of beautiful Osiris
Even as Thoth hath done.   O therefore grant me
Eternal use of these, my ink and palette;
And every day thou shalt receive my writings,
And thou shalt find that I have written truly.

He kindleth a Fire

THE Shining Eye of Horus cometh.
In peace it blazeth in the darkness.
And Ra is glad on the horizon
To see its flame consuming Evil.
Against the power of Set I kindle
Fire to shine with Ra, and follow
Adoring in his train for ever
Upon the hands of the Twin Sisters.

In peace the Eye of Horus liveth.

He singeth in the Underworld

PURE is the body on the Earth,
The Spirit in the Field ;
Pure are the praises from my mouth
Happy with two-fold joy.

The Serpent dieth in the place
Established by the gods.
Osiris liveth, and his throne
Is set upon the waters.

Thy beauties are a flowing stream
Resting the traveller,
A house of festival, where all
Adore their chosen gods.

Thy beauties are a columned court
With incense burned to Ra.
Thy face is brighter than the hall
Where shineth the full moon.

Thy hair is rippling like the hair
Of women from the East,
And blacker than the doors which guard
The midnight underworld.

Thy face is azure blue, and bright
As lapis lazuli;
The rays of Ra are on thy face.
Thy garments are of gold.

Thine eyebrows are twin goddesses
Who sit enthroned in peace,
And when thy nostrils breathe, the winds
Of heaven bend the grain.

Thine eyes look on the Mount of Dawn;
Thy hands are crystal pools;
Thy knees are sedges where the birds
Sing in their golden nest.

Thy feet are on the happy path;
O thou, the favoured one,
Thou bathest in the Lake of God,
And goest on thy way.

The Other World

HERE are cakes for thy body,
Cool water for thy throat,
Sweet breezes for thy nostrils,
And thou art satisfied.

No longer dost thou stumble
Upon thy chosen path,
From thy mind all evil
And darkness fall away.

Here by the river,
Drink and bathe thy limbs,
Or cast thy net, and surely
It shall be filled with fish.

The holy cow of Hapi
Shall give thee of her milk,
The ale of gods triumphant
Shall be thy daily draught.

White linen is thy tunic,
Thy sandals shine with gold;
Victorious thy weapons,
That death come not again.

Now upon the whirlwind
Thou followest thy Prince,
Now thou hast refreshment
Under the leafy tree.

Take wings to climb the zenith,
Or sleep in Fields of Peace;
By day the Sun shall keep thee,
By night the rising Star.

Adoration of the Disk by King Akhnaten and Princess Nefer Neferiu Aten

THY dawn, O Ra, opens the new horizon,
And every realm that thou hast made to live
Is conquered by thy love, as joyous Day
Follows thy footsteps in delightful peace.

And when thou settest, all the world is bleak;
Houses are tombs where blind men lie in death;
Only the lion and the serpent move
Through the black oven of the sightless night.

Dawn in the East again ! the lands awake,
And men leap from their slumber with a song;
They bathe their bodies, clothe them with fresh
  garments,
And lift their hands in happy adoration.

The cattle roam again across the fields;
Birds flutter in the marsh, and lift their wings
Also in adoration, and the flocks
Run with delight through all the pleasant meadows.

Both north and south along the dazzling river
Ships raise their sails and take their course before
  thee;
And in the ocean, all the deep-sea fish
Swim to the surface to drink in thy light.

For thou art all that lives, the seed of men,
The son within his mother's womb who knows
The comfort of thy presence near, the babe
To whom thou givest words and growing wisdom;

The chick within the egg, whose breath is thine,
Who runneth from its shell, chirping its joy,
And dancing on its small, unsteady legs
To greet the splendour of the rising sun.

Thy heart created all, this teeming earth,
Its people, herds, creatures that go afoot,
Creatures that fly in air, both land and sea,
Thou didst create them all within thy heart.

Men and their fates are thine, in all their stations,
Their many languages, their many colours,
All thine, and we who from the midst of peoples,
Thou madest different, Master of the Choice.

And lo, I find thee also in my heart,
I, Khu en Aten, find thee and adore.
O thou, whose dawn is life, whose setting, death,
In the great dawn, then lift up me, thy son.

Robert Hillyer

GREEK

HOMERIC HYMNS

7th century B.C. ?

Hymn to Earth the Mother of All

O UNIVERSAL Mother, who dost keep
From everlasting thy foundations deep,
Eldest of things, Great Earth, I sing of thee !
All shapes that have their dwelling in the sea,
All things that fly, or on the ground divine
Live, move, and there are nourished—these are
    thine;
These from thy wealth thou dost sustain; from thee
Fair babes are born, and fruits on every tree
Hang ripe and large, revered Divinity !

The life of mortal men beneath thy sway
Is held; thy power both gives and takes away !
Happy are they whom thy mild favours nourish;
All things unstinted round them grow and flourish;
For them, endures the life-sustaining field
Its load of harvest, and their cattle yield
Large increase, and their house with wealth is filled.
Such honoured dwell in cities fair and free,
The homes of lovely women, prosperously;
Their sons exult in youth's new budding gladness,
And their fresh daughters free from care and
    sadness,
With bloom-inwoven dance and happy song,
On the soft flowers the meadow-grass among,
Leap round them sporting—such delights by thee
Are given, rich Power, revered Divinity.

Mother of gods, thou wife of starry Heaven,
Farewell ! be thou propitious, and be given
A happy life for this brief melody,
Nor thou nor other songs shall unremembered be.

Percy Bysshe Shelley

Hymn to Selene

DAUGHTERS of Jove, whose voice is melody,
Muses, who know and rule all minstrelsy,
Sing the wide-wingèd Moon !   Around the earth,
From her immortal head in Heaven shot forth,
Far light is scattered—boundless glory springs;
Where'er she spreads her many-beaming wings
The lampless air glows round her golden crown.

But when the Moon divine from Heaven is gone
Under the sea, her beams within abide,
Till, bathing her bright limbs in Ocean's tide,
Clothing her form in garments glittering far,
And having yoked to her immortal car
The beam-invested steeds whose necks on high
Curve back, she drives to a remoter sky
A western Crescent, borne impetuously.
Then is made full the circle of her light,
And as she grows, her beams more bright and bright
Are poured from Heaven, where she is hovering
    then,
A wonder and a sign to mortal men.

The Son of Saturn with this glorious Power
Mingled in love and sleep—to whom she bore
Pandeia, a bright maid of beauty rare
Among the Gods, whose lives eternal are.

Hail Queen, great Moon, white-armed Divinity,
Fair-haired and favourable ! thus with thee

My song beginning, by its music sweet
Shall make immortal many a glorious feat
Of demigods, with lovely lips, so well
Which minstrels, servants of the Muses, tell.

Percy Bysshe Shelley

Hymn to Athena

I SING the glorious Power with azure eyes,
Athenian Pallas ! timeless, chaste, and wise,
Tritogenia, town-preserving maid,
Revered and mighty; from his awful head
Whom Jove brought forth, in warlike armour dressed,
Golden, all radiant ! wonder strange possessed
The everlasting Gods that Shape to see,
Shaking a javelin keen, impetuously
Rush from the crest of Ægis-bearing Jove;
Fearfully Heaven was shaken, and did move
Beneath the might of the Cerulean-eyed;
Earth dreadfully resounded, far and wide;
And, lifted from its depths, the sea swelled high
In purple billows, the tide suddenly
Stood still, and great Hyperion's son long time
Checked his swift steeds, till, where she stood sublime,
Pallas from her immortal shoulders threw
The arms divine; wise Jove rejoiced to view.
Child of the Ægis-bearer, hail to thee,
Nor thine nor others' praise shall unremembered be.

Percy Bysshe Shelley

Hymn to Castor and Pollux

YE wild-eyed Muses, sing the Twins of Jove,
Whom the fair-ankled Leda, mixt in love
With mighty Saturn's heaven-obscuring Child,
On Taygetus, that lofty mountain wild,

Brought forth in joy, mild Pollux void of blame,
And steed-subduing Castor, heirs of fame.
These are the Powers who earth-born mortals save
And ships, whose flight is swift along the wave,
When wintry tempests o'er the savage sea
Are raging, and the sailors tremblingly
Call on the twins of Jove with prayer and vow,
Gathered in fear upon the lofty prow,
And sacrificed with snow-white lambs—the wind
And the huge billow bursting close behind,
Even then beneath the weltering waters bear
The staggering ship—they suddenly appear,
On yellow wings rushing athwart the sky,
And lull the blasts in mute tranquillity,
And strew the waves on the white ocean's bed,
Fair omen of the voyage; from toil and dread
The sailors rest, rejoicing in the sight,
And plough the quiet sea in safe delight.

Percy Bysshe Shelley

ALCMAN

c. 680 B.C.

Fragment

THE mountain summits sleep, glens, cliffs, and caves
Are silent;—all the black earth's reptile brood,
The bees, the wild beasts of the mountain wood;
In depths beneath the dark red ocean's waves
Its monsters rest; whilst, wrapt in bower and spray,
Each bird is hush'd, that stretch'd its pinions to
the day.

Thomas Campbell

MIMNERMUS

620 B.C.

Youth and Age

AH! fair and lovely bloom the flowers of youth;
   On men and maids they beautifully smile:
But soon comes doleful eld, who, void of ruth,
   Indifferently afflicts the fair and vile;
Then cares wear out the heart: old eyes forlorn
   Scarce reck the very sunshine to behold—
Unloved by youths, of every maid the scorn—
   So hard a lot God lays upon the old.

J. A. Symonds

ALCÆUS

610 B.C.

Let Us Drink

WHY wait we for the torches' lights?
Now let us drink, while day invites,
In mighty flagons hither bring
The deep-red blood of many a vine,
That we may largely quaff, and sing
The praises of the god of wine,
The son of Jove and Semele,
Who gave the jocund wine to be
A sweet oblivion to our woes.
Fill, fill the goblet, one and two;
Let every brimmer, as it flows,
In sportive chase the last pursue.

John Herman Merivale

The Storm

JOVE descends in sleet and snow,
Howls the vexed and angry deep;
Every stream forgets to flow,
Bound in winter's icy sleep,

Ocean wave and forest hoar
To the blast responsive roar.

Drive the tempest from your door,
Blaze on blaze your hearthstone piling,
And unmeasured goblets pour
Brimful, high with nectar smiling.
Then, beneath your poet's head
Be a downy pillow spread.

John Herman Merivale

SAPPHO

610 B.C.

JUDGING even from the mutilated fragments fallen within our reach from the broken altar of her sacrifice of song, I for one have always agreed with all Grecian tradition in thinking Sappho to be beyond all question and comparison the very greatest poet that ever lived.— ALGERNON CHARLES SWINBURNE.

Ode to Aphrodite

DEATHLESS Aphrodite, throned in flowers,
Daughter of Zeus, O terrible enchantress,
With this sorrow, with this anguish, break my spirit,
Lady, no longer!

Hear anew the voice! O hear and listen!
Come, as in that island dawn thou camest,
Billowing in thy yokèd car to Sappho
Forth from thy father's

Golden house in pity! . . . I remember:
Fleet and fair thy sparrows drew thee, beating
Fast their wings above the dusky harvests,
Down the pale heavens,

Lighting anon! And thou, O blest and brightest,
Smiling with immortal eyelids, asked me:
"Maiden, what betideth thee? Or wherefore
Callest upon me?

" What is here the longing more than other,
Here in this mad heart ?   And who the lovely
One beloved thou wouldst lure to loving ?
    Sappho, who wrongs thee ?

" See, if now she flies, she soon must follow;
Yes, if spurning gifts, she soon must offer;
Yes, if loving not, she soon must love thee,
    Howso unwilling. . . ."

Come again to me !   O now !   Release me !
End the great pang !   And all my heart desireth
Now of fulfilment, fulfil !   O Aphrodite,
    Fight by my shoulder !
                William Ellery Leonard

Ode to Anactoria

PEER of the golden gods is he to Sappho,
He, the happy man who sits beside thee,
Heark'ning so divinely close thy lovely
    Speech and dear laughter.

This it was that made to flutter wildly
Heart of mine in bosom panting wildly ! . . .
Oh ! I need to see thee but a little,
    When, as at lightning,

Voice within me stumbles, tongue is broken,
Tingles all my flesh with subtle fire,
Ring my ears with waterfalls and thunders,
    Eyes are in midnight,

And a sweat bedews me like a shower,
Tremor hunts my body down and seizes,
Till, as one about to die, I linger
    Paler than grass is. . . .
                William Ellery Leonard

Farewell to Anactoria

NEVER the tramp of foot or horse,
Nor lusty cries from ships at sea,
Shall I call loveliest on the dark earth—
    My heart moves lovingly.

I say that what one loves is best—
The midnight fastness of the heart. . . .
Helen, you filched the beauty of men
    With unpitying art !

White Paris from Idean hills
For you the Trojan towers razed—
Who swiftly ploughed the black seas
    Had on your white arms gazed !

Oh, how loving from afar
Led you to grief, for in your mind
The present was too light, as ever
    Among fair womankind. . . .

So, Anactoria, you go away
With what calm carelessness of sorrow !
Your gleaming footstep and your grace,
    When comes another morrow,

Much would I rather then behold
Than Lydian cars or infantry.
I ask the lot of blessedness,
    Belovèd, in memory.

Allen Tate

Fragments

HESPERUS THE BRINGER

O HESPERUS, thou bringest all good things—
    Home to the weary, to the hungry cheer,
To the young bird the parent's brooding wings,
    The welcome stall to the o'erlaboured steer;

Whate'er of peace about our hearthstone clings,
   Whate'er our household gods protect of dear,
Are gathered round us by thy look of rest;
Thou bring'st the child too to its mother's breast.

                    Lord Byron

ONE GIRL

1

LIKE the sweet apple which reddens upon
   the topmost bough,
Atop on the topmost twig,—which the
   pluckers forgot, somehow,—
Forgot it not, nay, but got it not, for none
   could get it till now.

2

Like the wild hyacinth flower which on the
   hills is found,
Which the passing feet of the shepherds
   for ever tear and wound,
Until the purple blossom is trodden in the
   ground.

                    D. G. Rossetti

MOTHER, I CANNOT MIND MY WHEEL

MOTHER, I cannot mind my wheel;
   My fingers ache, my lips are dry;
Oh! if you felt the pain I feel!
   But oh, who ever felt as I!

              Walter Savage Landor

THE DUST OF TIMAS

THIS dust was Timas; and they say
   That almost on her wedding day
She found her bridal home to be
The dark house of Persephone.

And many maidens, knowing then
That she would not come back again,
Unbound their curls; and all in tears,
They cut them off with sharpened shears.

Edwin Arlington Robinson

ROUND ABOUT ME

ROUND about me hum the winds of autumn,
Cool between the apple boughs: and slumber,
Flowing from the quivering leaves to earthward,
Spreads as a river.

LOVE

LOVE, like a mountain-wind upon an oak,
Falling upon me, shakes me leaf and bough.

FULL MOON

OFF in the twilight hung the low full moon,
And all the women stood before it grave,
As round an altar. Thus at holy times
The Cretan damsels dance melodiously
With delicate feet about the sacrifice,
Trampling the tender bloom of the soft grass.

ALONE

THE moon and seven Pleiades have set;
It is the midnight now; the hours go by;
And still I'm lying in my bed alone.

FOR EVER DEAD

DEATH shall be death for ever unto thee,
Lady, with no remembrance of thy name
Then or thereafter; for thou gatherest not
The roses of Pieria, loving gold
Above the Muses. Even in Hades' House
Wander thou shalt unmarked, flitting forlorn
Among the shadowy, averted dead.

William Ellery Leonard

THEOGNIS

540 B.C.

Enjoyment

ENJOY your time, my soul ! another race
Shall shortly fill the world, and take your place
With their own hopes and fears, sorrow and mirth;
I shall be dust the while, and crumbled earth.
But think not of it. Drink the racy wine
Of rich Taygetus, pressed from the vine
Which Theotimus in the sunny glen
(Old Theotimus, loved of gods and men),
Planted and watered from a plenteous source,
Teaching the wayward stream a better course:
Drink it, and cheer your heart, and banish care,
A load of wine will lighten your despair.

John Hookham Frere

Hope

FOR human nature Hope remains alone
Of all the deities; the rest are flown.
Faith is departed; Truth and Honour dead;
And all the Graces too, my friends, are fled.
The scanty specimens of living worth,
Dwindled to nothing, and extinct on earth.
Yet whilst I live and view the light of heaven,
Since Hope remains and never has been driven
From the distracted world—the single scope
Of my devotion is to worship Hope.
When hecatombs are slain, and altars burn,
When all the deities adored in turn,
Let Hope be present; and with Hope, my friend,
Let every sacrifice commence and end.

Yes, Insolence, Injustice, every crime,
Rapine and Wrong, may prosper for a time;
Yet shall they travel on to swift decay,
Who tread the crooked path and hollow way.

John Hookham Frere

Poverty

FOR noble minds, the worst of miseries,
Worse than old age, or wearisome disease,
Is Poverty. From Poverty to flee,
From some tall precipice into the sea,
It were a fair escape to leap below!
In Poverty, dear Kyrnus, we forego
Freedom in word and deed, body and mind;
Action and thought are fetter'd and confin'd.
Let me then fly, dear Kyrnus, once again!
Wide as the limits of the land and main,
From these entanglements; with these in view,
Death is the lighter evil of the two.

John Hookham Frere

ANACREON AND ANACREONTICS

6th century B.C. *et seq.*

The Wounded Cupid

CUPID, as he lay among
Roses, by a bee was stung.
Whereupon in anger flying
To his mother, said, thus crying,
Help! O help! your boy's a-dying.
And why, my pretty lad? said she.
Then blubbering replièd he,
A wingèd snake has bitten me,
Which country people call a bee.

At which she smiled, then with her hairs
And kisses, drying up his tears,
Alas ! said she, my wag, if this
Such a pernicious torment is;
Come, tell me then how great's the smart
Of those thou woundest with thy dart !

Robert Herrick

The Cheat of Cupid

Or, The Ungentle Guest

ONE silent night of late,
    When every creature rested,
Came one unto my gate,
    And knocking, me molested.

Who's that, said I, beats there,
    And troubles thus the sleepy ?
Cast off, said he, all fear,
    And let not locks thus keep ye.

For I a boy am, who
    By moonless nights have swervèd;
And all with showers wet through,
    And e'en with cold half starvèd.

I pitiful arose,
    And soon a taper lighted,
And did myself disclose
    Unto the lad benighted.

I saw he had a bow,
    And wings too, which did shiver;
And looking down below,
    I spied he had a quiver.

I to my chimney's shine
    Brought him, as love professes,
And chafed his hands with mine,
    And dried his dropping tresses.

But when he felt him warmed,
    Let's try this bow of ours
And string, if they be harmed,
    Said he, with these late showers.

Forthwith his bow he bent,
    And wedded string and arrow,
And struck me that it went
    Quite through my heart and marrow.

Then laughing loud, he flew
    Away, and thus said, flying,
Adieu, mine host, adieu,
    I'll leave thy heart a-dying.

Robert Herrick

Love

I'LL sing of heroes and of kings,
In mighty numbers, mighty things.
Begin, my Muse !—but lo ! the strings
To my great song rebellious prove;
The strings will sound of naught but love.
—I broke them all, and put on new;
—'Tis this, or nothing, now will do.
" These, sure," said I, " will me obey;
These, sure, heroic notes will play."
Straight I began with thundering Jove
And all th' immortal powers; but Love,
Love smil'd; and from my enfeebled lyre
Came gentle airs, such as inspire
Melting love and soft desire.—

Farewell, then, heroes ! farewell, kings !
And mighty numbers, mighty things !
Love tunes my heart just to my strings.

Abraham Cowley

The Grasshopper

HAPPY insect ! what can be
In happiness compar'd to thee ?
Fed with nourishment divine,
The dewy morning's gentle wine !
Nature waits upon thee still,
And thy verdant cup does fill;
'Tis filled wherever thou dost tread,
Nature self's thy Ganymede.
Thou dost drink, and dance, and sing;
Happier than the happiest king !
All the fields which thou dost see,
All the plants belong to thee;
All that summer hours produce;
Fertile made with early juice.
Man for thee does sow and plough;
Farmer he, and landlord thou !
Thou dost innocently joy;
Nor does thy luxury destroy;
The shepherd gladly heareth thee,
More harmonious than he.
Thee country hinds with gladness hear,
Prophet of the ripen'd year !
Thee Phœbus loves, and does inspire;
Phœbus is himself thy sire.
To thee, of all things upon earth,
Life's no longer than thy mirth.
Happy insect, happy, thou
Dost neither age nor winter know;
But, when thou'st drunk, and danc'd and sung

Thy fill, the flowery leaves among
(Voluptuous and wise withal,
Epicurean animal !)—
Sated with thy summer feast,
Thou retir'st to endless rest.

Abraham Cowley

Age

OFT am I by the women told,
  " Poor Anacreon ! thou grow'st old;
Look ! how thy hairs are falling all;
Poor Anacreon, how they fall ! "—
Whether I grow old or no,
By the effects I do not know;
But this I know, without being told,
'Tis time to live, if I grow old;
'Tis time short pleasures now to take,
Of little life the best to make,
And manage wisely the last stake.

Abraham Cowley

The Epicure

UNDERNEATH this myrtle shade,
  On flowery beds supinely laid,
With odorous oils my head o'erflowing,
And around it roses growing,
What should I do but drink away
The heat and troubles of the day ?
In this more than kingly state,
Love himself shall on me wait.
Fill to me, Love; nay, fill it up;
And mingled cast into the cup
Wit, and mirth, and noble fires,
Vigorous health, and gay desires.

The wheel of life no less will stay
In a smooth than rugged way:
Since it equally doth flee,
Let the motion pleasant be.
Why do we precious ointments shower?
Nobler wines why do we pour?
Beauteous flowers why do we spread
Upon the monuments of the dead?
Nothing they but dust can show,
Or bones that hasten to be so.
Crown me with roses whilst I live,—
Now your wines and ointments give;
After death I nothing crave;
Let me alive my pleasures have!
All are Stoics in the grave.

Abraham Cowley

Beauty

HORNS to bulls wise Nature lends;
Horses she with hoofs defends;
Hares with nimble feet relieves;
Dreadful teeth to lions gives;
Fishes learn through streams to slide;
Birds through yielding air to glide;
Men with courage she supplies;
But to women these denies.
What then gives she? Beauty, this
Both their arms and armour is:
She, that can this weapon use,
Fire and sword with ease subdues.

Thomas Stanley

Roses

ROSES (Love's delight) let's join
To the red-cheek'd God of Wine;
Roses crown us, while we laugh,
And the juice of Autumn quaff!
Roses of all flowers the king,
Roses the fresh pride o' th' Spring,
Joy of every deity.
Love, when with the Graces he
For the ball himself disposes,
Crowns his golden hair with roses.
Circling then with these our brow,
We'll to Bacchus' temple go:
There some willing beauty lead,
And a youthful measure tread.

Thomas Stanley

The Combat

NOW will I a lover be;
Love himself commanded me.
Full at first of stubborn pride,
To submit my soul denied;
He his quiver takes and bow,
Bids defiance, forth I go,
Arm'd with spear and shield, we meet;
On he charges, I retreat:
Till perceiving in the fight
He had wasted every flight,
Into me, with fury hot,
Like a dart himself he shot,
And my cold heart melts; my shield
Useless, no defence could yield;
For what boots an outward screen
When, alas, the fight's within!

Thomas Stanley

The Swallow

CHATTERING swallow ! what shall we,
Shall we do to punish thee ?
Shall we clip thy wings, or cut
Tereus-like thy shrill tongue out ?
Who Rhodantha driv'st away
From my dreams by break of day.

Thomas Stanley

All Things Drink

FRUITFUL earth drinks up the rain;
Trees from earth drink that again;
The sea drinks the air, the sun
Drinks the sea, and him the moon.
Is it reason then, d'ye think,
I should thirst when all else drink ?

Thomas Stanley

The Picture

PAINTER, by unmatch'd desert
Master of the Rhodian art,
Come, my absent mistress take,
As I shall describe her : make
First her hair, as black as bright,
And if colours so much right
Can but do her, let it too
Smell of aromatic dew;
Underneath this shade, must thou
Draw her alabaster brow;
Her dark eyebrows so dispose
That they neither part nor close,
But by a divorce so slight
Be disjoin'd, may cheat the sight:
From her kindly killing eye
Make a flash of lightning fly,

Sparkling like Minerva's, yet
Like Cythera's mildly sweet:
Roses in milk swimming seek
For the pattern of her cheek:
In her lip such moving blisses,
As from all may challenge kisses;
Round about her neck (outvying
Parian stone) the Graces flying;
And o'er all her limbs at last
A loose purple mantle cast;
But so ordered that the eye
Some part naked may descry,
An essay by which the rest
That lies hidden, may be guess'd.
  So, to life th' hast come so near,
  All of her, but voice, is here.

Thomas Stanley

Spring

SEE the Spring herself discloses,
And the Graces gather roses;
See how the becalmèd seas
Now their swelling waves appease;
How the duck swims, how the crane
Comes from winter home again;
See how Titan's cheerful ray
Chaseth the dark clouds away;
Now in their new robes of green
Are the ploughman's labours seen:
Now the lusty teeming Earth
Springs each hour with a new birth;
Now the olive blooms: the vine
Now doth with plump pendants shine;
And with leaves and blossoms now
Freshly bourgeons every bough.

Thomas Stanley

Old I Am

OLD I am, yet can (I think)
Those that younger are out-drink;
When I dance no staff I take,
But a well-fill'd bottle shake:
He that doth in war delight,
Come, and with these arms let's fight;
Fill the cup, let loose a flood
Of the rich grape's luscious blood;
Old I am, and therefore may,
Like Silenus, drink and play.

Thomas Stanley

Youthful Age

YOUNG men dancing, and the old
Sporting I with joy behold;
But an old man gay and free
Dancing most I love to see;
Age and youth alike he shares,
For his heart belies his hairs.

Thomas Stanley

The Wish

NIOBE on Phrygian sands
Turn'd a weeping statue stands,
And the Pandionian Maid
In a swallow's wings array'd;
But a mirror I would be,
To be look'd on still by thee;
Or the gown wherein thou'rt drest,
That I might thy limbs invest;
Or a crystal spring, wherein
Thou might'st bathe thy purer skin;

Or sweet unguents, to anoint
And make supple every joint;
Or a knot, thy breast to deck;
Or a chain, to clasp thy neck;
Or thy shoe I wish to be,
That thou might'st but tread on me.

Thomas Stanley

The Cup

MAKE me a bowl, a mighty bowl,
Large as my capacious soul,
Vast as my thirst is.   Let it have
Depth enough to be my grave.
I mean the grave of all my care,
For I intend to bury't there.
Let it of silver fashioned be,
Worthy of wine ! worthy of me !
Worthy to adorn the spheres
As that bright Cup among the stars !

Yet draw no shapes of armour there,
No casque nor shield nor sword nor spear,
Nor wars of Thebes nor wars of Troy,
Nor any other martial toy.
For what do I vain armour prize,
Who mind not such rough exercise ?
But gentle sieges, softer wars,
Fights that cause no wounds or scars.
I'll have not battles on my plate,
Lest sight of them should brawls create,
Lest that provoke to quarrels too,
Which wine itself enough can do.

John Oldham

Anacreon's Dove

" LOVELY courier of the sky,
  Whence and whither dost thou fly ?
Scattering, as thy pinions play,
Liquid fragrance all the way.
Is it business ? Is it love ?
Tell me, tell me, gentle Dove."

" Soft Anacreon's vows I bear,
Vows to Myrtale the fair;
Graced with all that charms the heart,
Blushing nature, smiling art,
Venus, courted by an ode,
On the Bard her Dove bestow'd.
Vested with a master's right,
Now Anacreon rules my flight:
As the letters that you see,
Weighty charge consign'd to me:
Think not yet my service hard,
Joyless task without reward:
Smiling at my master's gates,
Freedom my return awaits:
But the liberal grant in vain
Tempts me to be wild again.
Can a prudent Dove decline
Blissful bondage such as mine ?
Over hills and fields to roam,
Fortune's guest without a home;
Under leaves to hide one's head,
Slightly shelter'd, coarsely fed;
Now my better lot bestows
Sweet repast, and soft repose;
Now the generous bowl I sip
As it leaves Anacreon's lip ;

Void of care, and free from dread
From his fingers snatch his bread,
Then with luscious plenty gay
Round his chambers dance and play;
Or, from wine as courage springs,
O'er his face expand my wings;
And, when feast and frolic tire,
Drop asleep upon his lyre.
This is all; be quick and go,
More than all thou can'st not know;
Let me now my pinions ply,—
I have chatter'd like a pye."

Samuel Johnson

SIMONIDES OF CEOS

480 B.C.

Thermopylæ

GO tell the Spartans, thou that passest by,
That here, obedient to their laws, we lie.

William Lisle Bowles

BACCHYLIDES

450 B.C.

Peace on Earth

TO mortal men Peace giveth these good things:
Wealth, and the flowers of honey-throated song;
   The flame that springs
On carven altars from fat sheep and kine,
Slain to the gods in heaven; and, all day long,
Games for glad youths, and flutes, and wreaths, and
   circling wine.

Then in the steely shield swart spiders weave
   Their web and dusky woof:
Rust to the pointed spear and sword doth cleave;
   The brazen trump sounds no alarms;
Nor is sleep harried from our eyes aloof,
But with sweet rest my bosom warms:
The streets are thronged with lovely men and young,
And hymns in praise of boys like flames to heaven
   are flung.

John Addington Symonds

SOPHOCLES

495–406 B.C.

WHO saw life steadily, and saw it whole.—MATTHEW ARNOLD.

Chorus from Ajax

FAIR Salamis, the billow's roar
   Wanders around thee yet;
And sailors gaze upon thy shore
   Firm in the Ocean set.
Thy son is in a foreign clime
   Where Ida feeds her countless flocks,
   Far from thy dear remembered rocks,
Worn by the waste of time,—
Comfortless, nameless, hopeless,—save
In the dark prospect of the yawning grave.
   And Ajax, in his deep distress
     Allied to our disgrace,
   Hath cherished in his loneliness
     The bosom friend's embrace.

Frenzy hath seized thy dearest son,
Who from thy shores in glory came
The first in valour and in fame;
The deeds that he hath done
Seem hostile all to hostile eyes;
The sons of Atreus see them and despise.

Woe to the mother, in her close of day,
Woe to her desolate heart, and temples grey,
When she shall hear
Her loved one's story whispered in her ear !
" Woe, woe ! " will be the cry,—
No quiet murmur like the tremulous wail
Of the lone bird, the querulous nightingale,—
But shrieks that fly
Piercing, and wild, and loud, shall mourn the tale;
And she will beat her breast, and rend her hair,
Scattering the silver locks that Time hath left her there.

Oh ! when the pride of Græcia's noblest race
Wanders, as now, in darkness and disgrace,
When Reason's day
Sets rayless—joyless—quenched in cold decay,
Better to die, and sleep
The never-waking sleep, than linger on,
And dare to live, when the soul's life is gone:
But thou shalt weep,
Thou wretched father, for thy dearest son,
Thy best beloved, by inward Furies torn,
The deepest, bitterest curse thine ancient house hath
borne !

Winthrop Mackworth Praed

EURIPIDES

480–406 B.C.

SAD Electra's poet.—MILTON.

Choruses from the Cyclops

LOVE SONG

ONE with eyes the fairest
  Cometh from his dwelling.
Someone loves thee, rarest,
  Bright beyond my telling.
In thy grace thou shinest
Like some nymph divinest,
In her caverns dewy:—
All delights pursue thee,
Soon pied flowers, sweet-breathing,
Shall thy head be wreathing.

CHORUS OF SATYRS, DRIVING THEIR GOATS

WHERE has he of race divine
  Wandered in the winding rocks?
Here the air is calm and fine
  For the father of the flocks;
Here the grass is soft and sweet,
And the river-eddies meet
In the trough beside the cave,
Bright as in their fountain wave.
Neither here, nor on the dew
  Of the lawny uplands feeding?
Oh, you come!—a stone at you
  Will I throw to mend your breeding;
Get along, you hornèd thing,
Wild, seditious, rambling!
An Iacchic melody
  To the golden Aphrodite

Will I lift, as erst did I
   Seeking her and her delight
With the Mænads, whose white feet
To the music glance and fleet.
Bacchus, O belovèd, where
Shaking wide thy yellow hair,
Wanderest thou alone, afar ?
   To the one-eyed Cyclops we,
Who by right thy servants are,
   Minister in misery,
In these wretched goat-skins clad,
   Far from thy delights and thee.
                    Percy Bysshe Shelley

Choruses from Hippolytus

O FOR THE WINGS OF A DOVE

COULD I take me to some cavern for mine hiding,
   In the hilltops where the Sun scarce hath trod;
Or a cloud make the home of mine abiding,
   As a bird among the bird-droves of God.
Could I wing me to my rest amid the roar
Of the deep Adriatic on the shore
Where the water of Eridanus is clear,
   And Phaeton's sad sisters by his grave
Weep into the river, and each tear
   Gleams a drop of amber, in the wave.

To the strand of the Daughters of the Sunset,
   The Apple-tree, the singing and the gold;
Where the mariner must stay him from his onset,
   And the red wave is tranquil as of old;
   Yea, beyond that pillar of the End
   That Atlas guardeth, would I wend;

Where a voice of living waters never ceaseth
In God's quiet garden by the sea,
And Earth, the ancient life-giver, increaseth
Joy among the meadows, like a tree.

Gilbert Murray

No More, O my Spirit

No more, O my spirit,
are we flawless,
we have seen evil undreamt:
I myself saw it:
the Greek, the most luminous,
the Athenian, the star-like,
banished through his father's hate
to a country far distant.

O sand dunes and sand-stretches
of the Athenian coast,
O mountain-thickets
where you climbed,
following the wild beasts,
with hounds, delicate of feet,
hunting with the dæmon, Artemis!

No more
will you mount your chariot,
yoked with horses of Enetas,
nor spur forward your steed
toward the stadium at Limnas,
and your chant, ever rapturous,
and the answering lyre-note,
shall cease in the king's house:
far in the forest depth
in the glades where she loves to rest,

Latona's child shall be crownless:
at your flight
the contest of the maidens will cease,
and their love-longing, comfortless.

And because of your fate,
I accept bitter hurt,
and weep:
ai, ai poor mother,
your birth-pangs were fruitless:
I am wroth with these spirits:
alas, Karites, never-separate,
why, why have you sent him forth,
the unfortunate, blameless,
from his palace,
from his own gates?

H. D.

Chorus from Iphigeneia in Aulis

AND Pergamos,
City of the Phrygians,
Ancient Troy
Will be given up to its fate.
They will mark the stone battlements
And the circle of them
With a bright stain.
They will cast out the dead—
A sight for Priam's queen to lament
And her frightened daughters.

And Helen, child of Zeus,
Will cry aloud for the mate
She has left in that Phrygian town.

May no child of mine,
Nor any child of my child
Ever fashion such a tale

As the Phrygians shall murmur,
As they stoop at their distaffs,
Whispering with Lydians,
Splendid with weight of gold—

" Helen has brought this.
They will tarnish our bright hair.
They will take us as captives
For Helen—born of Zeus
When he sought Leda with bird-wing
And touched her with bird-throat—
If men speak truth.

" But still we lament our state,
The desert of our wide courts,
Even if there is no truth
In the legends cut on ivory
Nor in the poets
Nor the songs."

H. D.

ARISTOPHANES

444–380 B.C.

*THE half divine humorist in whose incomparable genius the highest
qualities of Rabelais were fused and harmonised with the supremest
gifts of Shelley.*—ALGERNON CHARLES SWINBURNE.

Chorus of Birds

COME on then, ye dwellers by Nature in darkness,
    and like to the leaves' generations,
That are little of might, that are moulded of mire,
    unenduring and shadow-like nations,
Poor plumeless ephemerals, comfortless mortals, as
    visions of shadows fast fleeing
Lift up your mind unto us that are deathless, and
    dateless the date of our being;

Us, children of heaven; us, ageless for ay; us, all of
    whose thoughts are eternal:
That ye may from henceforth, having heard of us all
    things aright as to matters supernal,
Of the being of birds and beginning of Gods and of
    streams and the dark beyond reaching,
Trustfully knowing aright, in my name bid Prodicos
    pack with his preaching.
It was Chaos, and Night at the first, and the blackness of
    darkness, and Hell's broad border,
Earth was not, nor air, neither heaven; when in depths
    of the womb of the dark without order
First thing, first born of the black-plumed Night, was a
    wind-egg hatcht in her bosom,
Whence timely with seasons revolving again sweet Love
    burst out as a blossom,
Gold wings glittering forth of his back, like whirlwinds
    gustily turning.
He, after his wedlock with Chaos, whose wings are of
    darkness, in Hell broad burning,
For his nestlings begat him the race of us first and
    upraised us to light new-lighted.
And before this was not the race of the Gods, until all
    things by Love were united:
And of kind united in kind with communion of Nature
    the sky and the sea are
Brought forth and the earth and the race of the Gods
    everlasting and blest. So that we are
Far away the most ancient of all things blest! And
    that we·are of Love's generation
There are manifest manifold signs. We have wings and
    with us have the Loves habitation;
And manifold fair young folk that forswore love once,
    ere the bloom of them ended
Have the men pursued that pursued and desired them
    subdued by the help of us only befriended,

With such bait as a quail, a flamingo, a goose, or a
    cock's comb staring and splendid.
All best good things that befall men come from us birds,
    as is plain to all reason:
For first we proclaim and make known to them Spring
    and the Winter and Autumn in season;
Bid sow, when the crane starts clanging for Afric in
    shrill-voiced emigrant number
And calls to the pilot to hang up his rudder again for
    the season and slumber;
And then weave a cloak for Orestes the thief, lest he
    strip men of theirs if it freezes.
And again thereafter the kite reappearing announces a
    change in the breezes,
And that here is the season for shearing your sheep of
    their spring wool.   Then does the swallow
Give you notice to sell your greatcoat and provide
    something light for the heat that's to follow.
Thus are we as Ammon or Delphoi unto you, Dodona,
    nay Phoibus Apollo !
For, as first ye come all to get auguries of birds, even
    such is in all things your carriage,
Be the matter a matter of trade, or of earning your
    bread, or of any one's marriage.
And all things ye lay to the charge of a bird that belongs
    to discerning prediction.
Winged fame is a bird, as you reckon; you sneeze and
    the sign's as a bird for conviction.
All tokens are *birds* with you—sounds, too, and lackeys
    and donkeys.   Then must it not follow
That we are to you all as the manifest Godhead that
    speaks in prophetic Apollo ?

Algernon Charles Swinburne

THEOCRITUS

3rd century B.C.

THAT which distinguishes Theocritus from all other poets, both Greek and Latin, and which raises him even above Virgil in his Eclogues, is the inimitable tenderness of his passions, and the natural expression of them in words so becoming of a pastoral. A simplicity shines through all he writes : he shows his art and learning by disguising both.—JOHN DRYDEN.

IDYLL I

The Death of Daphnis

THYRSIS

SWEET are the whispers of yon pine that makes
Low music o'er the spring, and, Goatherd, sweet
Thy piping; second thou to Pan alone.
Is his the hornèd ram ? then thine the goat.
Is his the goat ? to thee shall fall the kid;
And toothsome is the flesh of unmilked kids.

GOATHERD

Shepherd, thy lay is as the noise of streams
Falling and falling ay from yon tall crag.
If for their meed the Muses claim the ewe,
Be thine the stall-fed lamb; or if they choose
The lamb, take thou the scarce less-valued ewe.

THYRSIS

Pray by the Nymphs, pray, Goatherd, seat thee here
Against this hill-slope in the tamarisk shade,
And pipe me somewhat, while I guard thy goats.

GOATHERD

I durst not, Shepherd, O I durst not pipe
At noontide; fearing Pan, who at that hour
Rests from the toils of hunting.   Harsh is he;

Wrath at his nostrils ay sits sentinel.
But, Thyrsis, thou canst sing of Daphnis' woes;
High is thy name for woodland minstrelsy:
Then rest we in the shadow of the elm
Fronting Priapus and the Fountain-nymphs.
There, where the oaks are and the Shepherd's seat,
Sing as thou sang'st erewhile, when matched with him
Of Libya, Chromis; and I'll give thee, first,
To milk, ay thrice, a goat—she suckles twins,
Yet ne'ertheless can fill two milkpails full;—
Next, a deep drinking-cup, with sweet wax scoured,
Two-handled, newly-carven, smacking yet
O' the chisel. Ivy reaches up and climbs
About its lip, gilt here and there with sprays
Of woodbine, that enwreathed about it flaunts
Her saffron fruitage. Framed therein appears
A damsel ('tis a miracle of art)
In robe and snood: and suitors at her side
With locks fair-flowing, on her right and left,
Battle with words, that fail to reach her heart.
She, laughing, glances now on this, flings now
Her chance regards on that: they, all for love
Wearied and eye-swoln, find their labour lost.
Carven elsewhere an ancient fisher stands
On the rough rocks: thereto the old man with pains
Drags his great casting-net, as one that toils
Full stoutly: every fibre of his frame
Seems fishing; so about the grey-beard's neck
(In might a youngster yet) the sinews swell.
Hard by the wave-beat sire a vineyard bends
Beneath its graceful load of burnished grapes;
A boy sits on the rude fence watching them.
Near him two foxes: down the rows of grapes
One ranging steals the ripest; one assails
With wiles the poor lad's scrip, to leave him soon
Stranded and supperless. He plaits meanwhile

With ears of corn a right fine cricket-trap,
And fits it on a rush: for vines, for scrip,
Little he cares, enamoured of his toy.
The cup is hung all round with lissom briar,
Triumph of Æolian art, a wondrous sight.
It was a ferryman's of Calydon:
A goat it cost me, and a great white cheese.
Ne'er yet my lips came near it, virgin still
It stands. And welcome to such boon art thou,
If for my sake thou'lt sing that lay of lays.
I jest not: lad, sing: no songs thou'lt own
In the dim land where all things are forgot.

THYRSIS

Begin, sweet Maids, begin the woodland song.
The voice of Thyrsis. Ætna's Thyrsis I.
Where were ye, Nymphs, oh where, while Daphnis
    pined ?
In fair Peneus' or in Pindus' glens ?
For great Anapus' stream was not your haunt,
Nor Ætna's cliff, nor Acis' sacred rill.
Begin, sweet Maids, begin the woodland song.
O'er him the wolves, the jackals howled o'er him;
The lion in the oak-copse mourned his death.
Begin, sweet Maids, begin the woodland song.
The kine and oxen stood around his feet,
The heifers and the calves wailed all for him.
Begin, sweet Maids, begin the woodland song.
First from the mountain Hermes came, and said,
" Daphnis, who frets thee ? Lad, whom lov'st thou so ? "
Begin, sweet Maids, begin the woodland song.
Came herdsmen, shepherds came, and goatherds came;
All asked what ailed the lad. Priapus came
And said, " Why pine, poor Daphnis ? while the maid
Foots it round every pool and every grove,
    (Begin, sweet Maids, begin the woodland song)

" O lack-love and perverse, in quest of thee;
Herdsman in name, but goatherd rightlier called.
With eyes that yearn the goatherd marks his kids
Run riot, for he fain would frisk as they:
  (*Begin, sweet Maids, begin the woodland song*)
" With eyes that yearn dost thou too mark the laugh
Of maidens, for thou may'st not share their glee."
Still naught the herdsman said: he drained alone
His bitter portion, till the fatal end.
  Begin, sweet Maids, begin the woodland song.
Came Aphrodite, smiles on her sweet face,
False smiles, for heavy was her heart, and spake:
" So, Daphnis, thou must try a fall with Love !
But stalwart Love hath won the fall of thee."
  Begin, sweet Maids, begin the woodland song.
Then " Ruthless Aphrodite," Daphnis said,
" Accursed Aphrodite, foe to man !
Say'st thou mine hour is come, my sun hath set ?
Dead as alive, shall Daphnis work Love woe."
  Begin, sweet Maids, begin the woodland song.
" Fly to Mount Ida, where the swain (men say)
And Aphrodite—to Anchises fly:
There are oak-forests; here but galingale,
And bees that make a music round the hives.
  Begin, sweet Maids, begin the woodland song.
" Adonis owed his bloom to tending flocks
And smiting hares, and bringing wild beasts down.
  Begin, sweet Maids, begin the woodland song.
" Face once more Diomed: tell him ' I have slain
The herdsman Daphnis ! now I challenge thee.'
  Begin, sweet Maids, begin the woodland song.
" Farewell, wolf, jackal, mountain-prisoned bear !
Ye'll see no more by grove or glade or glen
Your herdsman Daphnis ! Arethuse, farewell,
And the bright streams that pour down Thymbris' side.
  Begin, sweet Maids, begin the woodland song.

"I am that Daphnis, who lead here my kine,
Bring here to drink my oxen and my calves.
 Begin, sweet Maids, begin the woodland song.
"Pan, Pan, oh whether great Lyceum's crags
Thou haunt'st to-day, or mightier Mænalus,
Come to the Sicel isle ! Abandon now
Rhium and Helice, and the mountain-cairn
(That e'en gods cherish) of Lycaon's son !
 Forget, sweet Maids, forget your woodland song.
"Come, king of song, o'er this my pipe, compact
With wax and honey-breathing, arch thy lip:
For surely I am torn from life by Love.
 Forget, sweet Maids, forget your woodland song.
"From thicket now and thorn let violets spring.
Now let white lilies drape the juniper,
And pines grow figs, and nature all go wrong:
For Daphnis dies. Let deer pursue the hounds,
And mountain-owls outsing the nightingale.
 Forget, sweet Maids, forget your woodland song."

So spake he, and he never spoke again.
Fain Aphrodite would have raised his head;
But all his thread was spun. So down the stream
Went Daphnis: closed the waters o'er a head
Dear to the Nine, of nymphs not unbeloved.
 Now give me goat and cup; that I may milk
The one, and pour the other to the Muse.
Fare ye well, Muses, o'er and o'er farewell !
I'll sing strains lovelier yet in days to be.

GOATHERD

 Thyrsis, let honey and the honeycomb
Fill thy sweet mouth, and figs of Ægilus:
For ne'er cicala trilled so sweet a song.
Here is the cup; mark, friend, how sweet it smells:
The Hours, thou'lt say, have washed it in their well.

Hither, Cissætha ! Thou, go milk her ! Kids,
Be steady, or your pranks will rouse the ram.

Charles Stuart Calverley

IDYLL IV

The Herdsmen

BATTUS. Who owns these cattle, Corydon ? Philon∗
das ? Prythee say.

CORYDON. No, Ægon: and he gave them me to tend
while he's away.

BATTUS. Dost milk them in the gloaming, when none
is nigh to see ?

CORYDON. The old man brings the calves to suck,
and keeps an eye on me.

BATTUS. And to what region then hath flown the
cattle's rightful lord ?

CORYDON. Hast thou not heard ? With Milo he
vanished Elisward.

BATTUS. How ! was the wrestler's oil e'er yet so
much as seen by him ?

CORYDON. Men say he rivals Heracles in lustiness of
limb.

BATTUS. I'm Polydeuces' match (or so my mother
says) and more.

CORYDON. —So off he started; with a spade, and of
these ewes a score.

BATTUS. This Milo will be teaching wolves how they
should raven next.

CORYDON. —And by these bellowings his kine pro∗
claim how sore they're vexed.

BATTUS. Poor kine ! they've found their master a
sorry knave indeed.

CORYDON. They're poor enough, I grant you: they
have not heart to feed.

BATTUS. Look at that heifer! sure there's naught, save bare bones, left of her.

Pray, does she browse on dewdrops, as does the grass, hopper?

CORYDON. Not she, by heaven! She pastures now by Æsarus' glades,

And handfuls fair I pluck her there of young and green grass blades;

Now bounds about Latymnus, that gathering-place of shades.

BATTUS. That bull again, the red one, my word but he is lean!

I wish the Sybarite burghers ay may offer to the queen

Of heaven as pitiful a beast: those burghers are so mean!

CORYDON. Yet to the Salt Lake's edges I drive him, I can swear;

Up Physcus, up Neæthus' side—he lacks not victual there,

With dittany and endive and foxglove for his fare.

BATTUS. Well, well! I pity Ægon. His cattle, go they must

To rack and ruin, all because vain-glory was his lust.

The pipe that erst he fashioned is doubtless scored with rust?

CORYDON. Nay, by the Nymphs! That pipe he left to me, the self-same day

He made for Pisa: I am too a minstrel in my way:

Well the flute-part in *Pyrrhus* and in *Glauca* can I play.

I sing too *Here's to Croton* and *Zacynthus O 'tis fair*,

And *Eastward to Lacinium:*—the bruised Milo there

His single self ate eighty loaves; there also did he pull

Down from its mountain dwelling, by one hoof grasped, a bull,

And gave it Amaryllis: the maidens screamed with fright;

As for the owner of the bull he only laughed out-right.

BATTUS. Sweet Amaryllis! thou alone, though dead, art unforgot.

Dearer than thou, whose light is quenched, my very goats are not.

Oh for the all-unkindly fate that's fallen to my lot!

CORYDON. Cheer up, brave lad! to-morrow may ease thee of thy pain:

Ay for the living are there hopes, past hoping are the slain:

And now Zeus sends us sunshine, and now he sends us rain.

BATTUS. I'm better. Beat those young ones off! E'en now their teeth attack

That olive's shoots, the graceless brutes! back, with your white face, back!

CORYDON. Back to thy hill, Cymætha! Great Pan, how deaf thou art!

I shall be with thee presently, and in the end thou'lt smart.

I warn thee, keep thy distance. Look, up she creeps again!

Oh were my hare-crook in my hand, I'd give it to her then!

BATTUS. For heaven's sake, Corydon, look here! Just now a bramble-spike

Ran, there, into my instep—and oh how deep they strike,

Those lancewood-shafts! A murrain light on that calf, I say!

I got it gaping after her. Canst thou discern it, pray?

CORYDON. Aye, aye; and here I have it, safe in my finger-nails.

BATTUS. Eh! at how slight a matter how tall a warrior quails!

CORYDON. Ne'er range the hill-crest, Battus, all san-
dal-less and bare;
Because the thistle and the thorn lift ay their plumed
heads there.
BATTUS. —Say, Corydon, does that old man we wot
of (tell me please !)
Still haunt the dark-browed little girl whom once he used
to tease ?
CORYDON. Aye, my oor boy, that doth he: I saw
them yesterday
Down by the byre; and, trust me, loving enough were
they.
BATTUS. Well done, my veteran light-o'-love ! In
deeming thee mere man,
I wronged the sire: some Satyr he, or an uncouth-limbed
Pan.

Charles Stuart Calverley

Idyll XXI

The Fishermen

WANT quickens wit: Want's pupils needs must work,
O Diophantus: for the child of toil
Is grudged his very sleep by carking cares:
Or, if he taste the blessedness of night,
Thought for the morrow soon warns slumber off.
  Two ancient fishers once lay side by side
On piled-up sea-wrack in their wattled hut,
Its leafy wall their curtain. Near them lay
The weapons of their trade, basket and rod,
Hooks, weed-encumbered nets, and cords and oars,
And, propped on rollers, an infirm old boat.
Their pillow was a scanty mat, eked out
With caps and garments: such the ways and means,
Such the whole treasury of the fishermen.
They knew no luxuries: owned nor door nor dog;

Their craft their all, their mistress Poverty:
Their only neighbour Ocean, who for ay
Round their lorn hut came floating lazily.
   Ere the moon's chariot was in mid-career,
The fishers girt them for their customed toil,
And banished slumber from unwilling eyes,
And roused their dreamy intellects with speech:—

ASPHALION. They say that soon flit summer-nights
    away,
Because all lingering is the summer day:
Friend, it is false; for dream on dream have I
Dreamed, and the dawn still reddens not the sky.
How? am I wandering? or does night pass slow?

COMRADE. Asphalion, scout not the sweet summer so.
'Tis not that wilful seasons have gone wrong,
But care maims slumber, and the nights seem long.

A. Didst thou e'er study dreams? For visions fair
I saw last night; and fairly thou should'st share
The wealth I dream of, as the fish I catch.
Now, for sheer sense, I reckon few thy match;
And, for a vision, he whose motherwit
Is his sole tutor best interprets it.
And now we've time the matter to discuss:
For who could labour, lying here (like us)
Pillowed on leaves and neighboured by the deep,
Or sleeping amid thorns no easy sleep?
In rich men's halls the lamps are burning yet;
But fish come alway to the rich man's net.

C. To me the vision of the night relate;
Speak, and reveal the riddle to thy mate.

A. Last evening, as I plied my watery trade,
(Not on an o'erfull stomach—we had made

Betimes a meagre meal, as you can vouch)
I fell asleep; and lo ! I seemed to crouch
Among the boulders, and for fish to wait,
Still dangling, rod in hand, my vagrant bait.
A fat fellow caught it: (e'en in sleep I'm bound
To dream of fishing, as of crusts the hound:)
Fast clung he to the hooks; his blood outwelled;
Bent with his struggling was the rod I held:
I tugged and tugged: my efforts made me ache:
" How, with a line thus slight, this monster take ? "
Then gently, just to warn him he was caught,
I twitched him once; then slacked and then made taut
My line, for now he offered not to run;
A glance soon showed me all my task was done.
'Twas a gold fish, pure metal every inch,
That I had captured. I began to flinch:
" What if this beauty be the sea⁄king's joy,
Or azure Amphitrite's treasured toy ! "
With care I disengaged him—not to rip
With hasty hook the gilding from his lip:
And with a tow⁄line landed him, and swore
Never to set my foot on ocean more,
But with my gold live royally ashore.
So I awoke: and, comrade, lend me now
Thy wits, for I am troubled for my vow.

C. Ne'er quake: you're pledged to nothing, for no
    prize
You gained or gazed on. Dreams are naught but lies.
Yet may this dream bear fruit; if, wide⁄awake
And not in dreams, you'll fish the neighbouring lake.
Fish that are meat you'll there mayhap behold,
Not die of famine, amid dreams of gold.

Charles Stuart Calverley

Epigram II
The Flute of Daphnis

I AM the flute of Daphnis. On this wall,
He nailed his tribute to the great god Pan,
What time he grew from boyhood, shapely, tall,
And felt the first deep ardours of a man.
Thro' adult veins more swift the song,tide ran,—
A vernal stream whose swollen torrents call
For instant ease in utterance. Then began
That course of triumph reverenced by all.
Him the gods loved, and more than other men
Blest with the flower of beauty, and endowed
His soul of music with the strength of ten.
Now on a festal day I see the crowd
Look fondly at my resting,place, and when
I think whose lips have prest me, I am proud.

Epigram IV
A Sacred Grove

I KNOW a spot where Love delights to dream,
Because he finds his fancies happen true.
Within its fence no myrtle ever grew
That failed in wealth of flower; no sunny beam
Has used its vantage vainly. You might deem
Yourself a happy plant and blossom too,
Or be a bird and sing as thrushes do,
So sweet in that fair place doth nature seem.
A matted vine invests the rocks above,
And tries to kiss a runlet leaping through
With endless laughter. Hither at noon comes Love,
And woos the god who is not hard to woo,
Taking his answer from the nested dove
That ever hymneth skies for ever blue.

Epigram XI

The Epitaph of Eusthenes

A BARD is buried here, not strong, but sweet;
  A Teacher too, not great, but gently wise;
This modest stone (the burghers thought it meet)
May tell the world where so much virtue lies.
His happy skill it was in mart and street
To scan men's faces with a true surmise,
Follow the spirit to its inmost seat,
And read the soul reflected in the eyes.
No part had he in catholic renown,
Which none but god-inspired poets share;
Not his to trail the philosophic gown,
That only sages of the School may wear;
But his at least to fill an alien town
With friends, who make his tomb their loving care.

Epigram XVIII

The Monument of Cleita

H ERE Cleita sleeps.   You ask her life and race?
  Read on, and learn a simple tale and true.
A nurse she was from the far land of Thrace,
Who tended little Medëos while he grew
A healthy, happy child, and did imbue
His nascent mind with godliness and grace;
So fencing him from evil that he knew
No word of what is impious or base.
And when at length, her tale of years all told,
She came to lie in this reposeful spot,
Young Medëos, still a child, but sagely old,
Upreared this monument, that unforgot
The care beyond his recompense of gold
Might live a memory and perish not.

Epigram XXI
The Grave of Hipponax

HERE lies a bard, Hipponax—honoured name !
Sweet were the songs that won him endless praise,
And yet his life was sweeter than his lays.
Traveller, a question fronts thee: Canst thou claim
Kinship with such in conduct void of blame ?
If not, forbear this precinct; go thy ways;
Lest some bright watcher of the tomb should raise
A jealous hand to cover thee with shame.
But if thy soul is free from shade of guilt,
Or, having sinned, hath been at length forgiven,
To thee all rights of common kin belong;
Lay down thy weary limbs, and, if thou wilt,
Let slumber wrap them round, nor fear that Heaven
Will suffer any sprite to do thee wrong.

Edward Cracroft Lefroy

Idyll XI
The Cyclops

AND so an easier life our Cyclops drew,
The ancient Polyphemus, who in youth
Loved Galatea while the manhood grew
Adown his cheeks, and darkened round his mouth.
No jot he cared for apples, olives, roses;
Love made him mad; the whole world was neg,
lected,
The very sheep went backward to their closes
From out the fair green pastures, self,directed.
And singing Galatea, thus, he wore
The sunrise down along the weedy shore,
And pined alone, and felt the cruel wound
Beneath his heart, which Cypris' arrow bore,
With a deep pang: but, so, the cure was found;

And, sitting on a lofty rock, he cast
His eyes upon the sea, and sang at last:
" O whitest Galatea, can it be
  That thou shouldst spurn me off who love thee so ?
More white than curds, my girl, thou art to see,
More meek than lambs, more full of leaping glee
  Than kids, and brighter than the early glow
On grapes that swell to ripen,—sour like thee !
Thou comest to me with the fragrant sleep,
  And with the fragrant sleep thou goest from me;
  Thou fliest . . . fliest as a frightened sheep
Flies the grey wolf !—yet love did overcome me,
So long !—I loved thee, maiden, first of all,
  When down the hills (my mother fast beside thee)
I saw thee stray to pluck the summer⹒fall
  Of hyacinth⹒bells, and went myself to guide thee;
And since my eyes have seen thee, they can leave thee
  No more, from that day's light !   But thou . . . by
    Zeus,
Thou wilt not care for *that*, to let it grieve thee !
  I know thee, fair one, why thou springest loose
From my arm round thee.   Why ?   I tell thee, dear !
  One shaggy eyebrow draws its smudging road
Straight through my ample front, from ear to ear;
  One eye rolls underneath; and yawning, broad,
Flat nostrils feel the bulging lips too near.
Yet . . . ho, ho !—*I*,—whatever I appear,—
  Do feed a thousand oxen !   When I have done,
I milk the cows, and drink the milk that's best !
  I lack no cheese, while summer keeps the sun;
And after, in the cold, it's ready prest !
  And then, I know to sing, as there is none
Of all the Cyclops can, . . . a song of thee,
Sweet apple of my soul, on love's fair tree,
And of myself who love thee . . . till the West
Forgets the light, and all but I have rest.

I feed for thee, besides, eleven fair does,
  And all in fawn; and four tame whelps of bears.
Come to me, sweet ! thou shalt have all of those
  In change for love ! I will not halve the shares.
Leave the blue sea, with pure white arms extended
  To the dry shore; and, in my cave's recess,
Thou shalt be gladder for the noon-light ended;
  For here be laurels, spiral cypresses,
Dark ivy, and a vine whose leaves infold
  Most luscious grapes; and here is water cold,
The wooded Ætna pours down thro' the trees
From the white snows, which gods were scarce too bold
  To drink in turn with nectar. Who with these
  Would choose the salt wave of the lukewarm seas ?
Nay, look on me ! If I am hairy and rough,
  I have an oak's heart in me; there's a fire
In these grey ashes which burns hot enough;
  And, when I burn for *thee*, I grudge the pyre
No fuel . . . not my soul, nor this one eye,—
Most precious thing I have, because thereby
I see thee, fairest ! Out, alas ! I wish
My mother had borne me finnèd like a fish,
That I might plunge down in the ocean near thee,
  And kiss thy glittering hand between the weeds,
If still thy face were turned; and I would bear thee
  Each lily white, and poppy fair that bleeds
Its red heart down its leaves !—one gift, for hours
  Of summer,—one for winter; since to cheer thee,
I could not bring at once all kinds of flowers.
Even now, girl, now, I fain would learn to swim,
If stranger in a ship sailed nigh, I wis,
  That I may know how sweet a thing it is
  To live down with you in the deep and dim !
Come up, O Galatea, from the ocean,
  And, having come, forget again to go !
As I, who sing out here my heart's emotion,
  Could sit for ever. Come up from below !

Come, keep my flocks beside me, milk my kine;
   Come, press my cheese, distrain my whey and curd !
Ah, mother ! she alone . . . that mother of mine . . .
   Did wrong me sore ! I blame her ! Not a word
Of kindly intercession did she address
Thine ear with for my sake; and ne'ertheless
   She saw me wasting, wasting, day by day:
   Both head and feet were aching, I will say,
All sick for grief, as I myself was sick.
   O Cyclops, Cyclops ! whither hast thou sent
   Thy soul on fluttering wings ?   If thou wert bent
On turning bowls, or pulling green and thick
   The sprouts to give thy lambkins, thou wouldst make
      thee
   A wiser Cyclops than for what we take thee.
Milk dry the present ! Why pursue too quick
That future which is fugitive aright ?
Thy Galatea thou shalt haply find,
Or else a maiden fairer and more kind;
For many girls do call me thro' the night,
   And, as they call, do laugh out silvery.
   I, too, am something in the world, I see ! "

While thus the Cyclops love and lambs did fold,
Ease came with song, he could not buy with gold.

Elizabeth Barrett Browning

BION

3rd century B.C.

IDYLL I

Lament for Adonis

WAIL, wail, Ah for Adonis ! He is lost to us,
      lovely Adonis !
   Lost is lovely Adonis ! The Loves respond with
      lamenting.

Nay, no longer in robes of purple recline, Aphrodite:
Wake from thy sleep, sad queen, black-stoled, rain
  blows on thy bosom;
Cry to the listening world, *He is lost to s lovely*
  Adonis !
  Wail, wail, Ah for Adonis ! The Loves respond
  with lamenting.

Lovely Adonis is lying, sore hurt in his thigh, on the
  mountains,
Hurt in his thigh with the tusk, while grief consumes
  Aphrodite:
Slowly he drops toward death, and the black blood
  drips from his fair flesh,
Down from his snow-white skin; his eyes wax dull 'neath
  the eyelids,
Yea and the rose hath failed his lips, and around them
  the kisses
Die and wither, the kisses that Kupris will not re-
  linquish:
Still, though he lives no longer, a kiss consoles Aphro-
  dite;
But he knows not, Adonis, she kissed him while he was
  dying.
  Wail, wail, Ah for Adonis ! The Loves respond
  with lamenting.

Cruel, cruel the wound in the thigh that preys on
  Adonis:
But in her heart Cytherea hath yet worse wounds to
  afflict her.
Round him his dear hounds bay, they howl in their
  grief to the heavens;
Nymphs of the woodlands wail: but she, the Queen
  Aphrodite,
Loosing her locks to the air, roams far and wide through
  the forest,

Drowned in grief, dishevelled, unsandalled, and as she
   flies onward,
Briers stab at her feet and cull the blood of the goddess.
She with shrill lamentation thro' glen and thro' glade
   is carried,
Calling her Syrian lord, demanding him back, and de-
   manding.
But where he lies, dark blood wells up and encircles
   the navel;
Blood from the gushing thighs empurples the breast;
   and the snow-white
Flank that was once so fair, is now dyed red for Adonis.
   Wail, wail, Ah, Cytherea ! The Loves respond with
   lamenting.

She then hath lost her lord, and with him hath lost her
   celestial
Beauty; for fair was he, and fair, while he lived, Aphro-
   dite:
Now in his death her beauty hath died. *Ah, Ah,
   Cytherea !*
All the mountains lament, and the oaks moan, *Ah for
   Adonis !*
Streams as they murmur and flow complain of thy griefs,
   Aphrodite:
Yea and the springs on the hills, in the woods, weep
   tears for Adonis:
Flowers of the field for woe flush crimson red; and
   Cythêra,
Thorough the dells and the glens, shrills loud the dirge
   of her anguish:
Woe, woe, Ah, Cytherea ! He is lost to us, lovely Adonis !
Echo repeats the groan: *Lost, lost, is lovely Adonis !*
Kupris, who but bewailed thy pangs of a love over-
   whelming ?

She, when she saw, when she knew the unstanchable
   wound of Adonis,

When she beheld the red blood on his pale thigh's
  withering blossom,
Spreading her arms full wide, she moaned out: " Stay,
  my Adonis !
Stay, ill-fated Adonis ! that I once more may approach
  thee !
Clasp thee close to my breast, and these lips mingle with
  thy lips !
Rouse for a moment, Adonis, and kiss me again for the
  last time;
Kiss me as long as the kiss can live on the lips of a
  lover;
Till from thy inmost soul to my mouth and down to
  my marrow
Thy life-breath shall run, and I quaff the wine of thy
  philtre,
Draining the draught of thy love: that kiss will I
  treasure, Adonis,
E'en as it were thyself; since thou, ill-starred, art de-
  parting,
Fleeing me far, O Adonis, to Acheron faring, the sad
  realm
Ruled by a stern savage king: while I, the unhappy,
  the luckless,
I live; goddess am I, and I may not follow or find thee.
Persephone, take thou my lord, my lover; I know thee
Stronger far than myself: all fair things drift to thy
  dwelling.
I meanwhile am accursed, possessed with insatiable
  sorrow,
Weeping my dead, my Adonis who died, and am shaken
  and shattered.
Diest thou then, my desired ? and desire like a dream
  hath escaped me.
Widowed is now Cytherea; the Loves in her halls are
  abandoned;

Perished with thee is my girdle.   Ah, why wouldst thou
    hunt, over-bold one ?

Being so beautiful, why wast thou mad to fight with a
    wild beast ? ''

Thus then Kupris mourned; and the Loves respond with
    lamenting:

*Wail, wail, Ah for Adonis !   He is lost to us, lovely
    Adonis !*

Tears the Paphian shed, drop by drop for the drops of
    Adonis'

Blood; and on earth each drop, as it fell, grew into a
    blossom:

Roses sprang from the blood, and the tears gave birth
    to the wind-flower.

    Wail, wail, Ah, Cytherea !   He is lost to us, lovely
    Adonis !

    Wail, wail, Ah for Adonis !   He is lost to us, lovely
    Adonis !

Now in the oak-woods cease to lament for thy lord,
    Aphrodite.

No proper couch is this which the wild leaves strew for
    Adonis.

Let him thy own bed share, Cytherea, the corpse of
    Adonis;

E'en as a corpse he is fair, fair corpse as fallen aslumber.

Now lay him soft to sleep, sleep well in the wool of the
    bedclothes,

Where with thee through the night in holy dreams he
    commingled,

Stretched on a couch all gold, that yearns for him stark
    though he now be.

Shower on him garlands, flowers: all fair things died in
    his dying;

Yea, as he faded away, so shrivel and wither the
    blossoms.

Syrian spikenard scatter, anoint him with myrrh and
    with unguents:
Perish perfumes all, since he, thy perfume, is perished.
    Wail, wail, Ah for Adonis!   The Loves respond with
    lamenting.

Lapped in his purple robes is the delicate form of
    Adonis.
Round him weeping Loves complain and moan in their
    anguish,
Clipping their locks for Adonis: and one of them treads
    on his arrows,
One of them breaks his bow, and one sets heel on the
    quiver;
One hath loosed for Adonis the latchet of sandals, and
    some bring
Water to pour in an urn; one laves the wound in his
    white thigh;
One from behind with his wings keeps fanning dainty
    Adonis.
    Wail, wail, Ah for Adonis!   The Loves respond with
    lamenting.

Wail, wail, Ah, Cytherea! The Loves respond with
    lamenting.
Every torch at the doors hath been quenched by thy
    hand, Hymenæus;
Every bridal wreath hath been torn to shreds; and no
    longer,
Hymen, Hymen no more is the song, but a new song
    of sorrow,
Woe, woe! and *Ah for Adonis!* resounds in lieu of the
    bridesong.
This the Graces are shrilling, the son of Cinyras hymn-
    ing,
Lost is lovely Adonis! in loud antiphonal accents.

Woe, woe ! sharply repeat, far more than the praises of
    Paiôn,
Woe ! and *Ah for Adonis !* the Muses who wail for
    Adonis,
Chaunt their charms to Adonis.—But he lists not to
    their singing;
Not that he wills not to hear, but the Maiden doth not
    release him.
Cease from moans, Cytherea, to-day refrain from the
    death-songs:
Thou must lament him again, and again shed tears in a
    new year.

                     John Addington Symonds

A Dream of Venus

I DREAMT I saw great Venus by me stand,
Leading a nodding infant by the hand;
And that she said to me familiarly—
" Take Love, and teach him how to play to me."
She vanisht then.   And I, poor fool, must turn
To teach the boy, as if he wished to learn.
I taught him all the pastoral songs I knew
And used to sing; and I informed him, too,
How Pan found out the pipe, Pallas the flute,
Phœbus the lyre, and Mercury the lute.
But not a jot for all my words cared he,
But lo ! fell singing his love-songs to me;
And told me of the loves of gods and men,
And of his mother's doings; and so then
I forgot all I taught him for my part,
But what he taught me I learnt all by heart.

                         Leigh Hunt

MOSCHUS

3rd century B.C.

Lament for Bion

YE mountain valleys, pitifully groan !
Rivers and Dorian springs, for Bion weep !
Ye plants, drop tears; ye groves, lamenting moan !
Exhale your life, wan flowers; your blushes deep
In grief, anemones and roses, steep;
In whimpering murmurs, Hyacinth ! prolong
The sad, sad woe thy lettered petals keep;
Our minstrel sings no more his friends among—
Sicilian Muses ! now begin the doleful song.

Ye nightingales ! that mid thick leaves set loose
The gushing gurgle of your sorrow, tell
The fountains of Sicilian Arethuse
That Bion is no more—with Bion fell
The song—the music of the Dorian shell.
Ye swans of Strymon ! now your banks along
Your plaintive throats with melting dirges swell
For him, who sang like you the mournful song;
Discourse of Bion's death the Thracian nymphs among—

The Dorian Orpheus, tell them all, is dead.
His herds the song and darling herdsman miss,
And oaks, beneath whose shade he propt his head;
Oblivion's ditty now he sings for Dis;
The melancholy mountain silent is;
His pining cows no longer wish to feed,
But moan for him; Apollo wept, I wis,
For thee, sweet Bion ! and in mourning weed
The brotherhood of Fauns, and all the Satyr breed.

The tears by Naiads shed are brimful bourns;
Afflicted Pan thy stifled music rues;

Lorn Echo 'mid her rocks thy silence mourns,
Nor with her mimic tones thy voice renews;
The flowers their bloom, the trees their fruitage lose;
No more their milk the drooping ewes supply;
The bees to press their honey now refuse;
What need to gather it and lay it by,
When thy own honey-lip, my Bion ! thine is dry ?

Sicilian Muses ! lead the doleful chant;
Not so much near the shore the dolphin moans;
Nor so much wails within her rocky haunt
The nightingale; nor on their mountain thrones
The swallows utter such lugubrious tones;
Nor Cëyx such for faithful Halcyon,
Whose song the blue wave, where he perished, owns;
Nor in the valley, neighbour to the sun,
The funeral birds so wail their Memnon's tomb upon—

As these moan, wail, and weep for Bion dead,
The nightingales and swallows, whom he taught,
For him their elegiac sadness shed;
And all the birds contagious sorrow caught;
The sylvan realm was all with grief distraught.
Who, bold of heart, will play on Bion's reed,
Fresh from his lip, yet with his breathing fraught ?
For still among the reeds does Echo feed
On Bion's minstrelsy.   Pan only may succeed

To Bion's pipe; to him I make the gift;
But, lest he second seem, e'en Pan may fear
The pipe of Bion to his mouth to lift.
For thee sweet Galatea drops the tear,
And thy dear song regrets, which sitting near
She fondly listed; ever did she flee
The Cyclops and his songs—but ah ! more dear
Thy song and sight than her own native sea;
On the deserted sands the nymph without her fee

Now sits and weeps, or weeping tends thy herd.
Away with Bion all the muse-gifts flew—
The chirping kisses breathed at every word:
Around thy tomb the Loves their playmate rue;
Thee Cypris loved—more than the kiss she drew,
And breathed upon her dying paramour.
Most musical of rivers ! now renew
Thy plaintive murmurs; Meles ! now deplore
Another son of song—as thou didst wail of yore

That sweet, sweet mouth of dear Calliope;
The threne, 'tis said, thy waves for Homer spun,
With saddest music filled the refluent sea;
Now melting wail and weep another son !
Both loved of fountains; that of Helicon
Gave Melesigenes his pleasant draught;
But to his Arethuse did Bion run,
And from her urn the glowing rapture quaffed:
Thy elder glory sung how Helen bloomed and laughed;

On Thetis' mighty son his descant ran
And Menelaus; but our Bion chose
Not arms and tears to sing, but Love and Pan;
While browsed his herd, his gushing music rose;
He milked his kine; did pipes of reeds compose;
Taught how to kiss; and fondled in his breast
Young Love, and Cypris pleased.   For Bion flows
In every glorious land a grief confest;
Ascra for her own bard, wise Hesiod, less exprest;

Bœotian Hylæ mourned for Pindar less;
Teös regretted less her minstrel hoar,
And Mitylene her sweet poetess;
Nor for Alcæus Lesbos suffered more;
Nor lovely Paros so much did deplore
Her own Archilochus.   Breathing her fire
Into her sons of song, from shore to shore

For thee the pastoral Muse attunes her lyre
To woeful utterance of passionate desire.

Sicelidas, the famous Samian star,
And he with smiling eye and radiant face,
Cydonian Lycidas, renowned afar,
Lament thee; where quick Hales runs his race
Philetas wails; Theocritus, the grace
Of Syracuse, thee mourns; nor these among
Am I remiss Ausonian wreaths to place
Around thy tomb; to me doth it belong
To chant for thee, from whom I learnt the Dorian song;

Me with thy minstrel skill as proper heir—
Others thou didst endow with thine estate.
Alas ! alas ! when in a garden fair
Mallows, crisp dill, and parsley yield to fate,
These with another year regerminate;
But when of mortal life the bloom and crown,
The wise, the good, the valiant, and the great
Succumb to death, in hollow earth shut down,
We sleep, for ever sleep—for ever lie unknown.

Thus art thou squeezed, while frogs may croak at will;
I envy not their croak.   Thee poison slew—
How kept it in thy mouth its nature ill ?
If thou didst speak, what cruel wretch could brew
The draught ?   He did of course thy song eschew.
But Justice all o'ertakes.   My tears fast flow
For thee, my friend.   Could I, like Orpheus true,
Odysseus or Alcides, pass below
To gloomy Tartarus, how quickly would I go !

To see, and hear thee, haply, sing for Dis;
But in the nymph's ear warble evermore,
O dearest friend ! thy sweetest harmonies.
For whilom, on her own Etnëan shore,
She sang wild snatches of the Dorian lore.

Nor will thy singing unrewarded be;
Thee to thy mountain,haunts she will restore,
As she gave Orpheus his Eurydice.
Could I charm Dis with songs, I too would sing for thee.

George Chapman

IDYLL VI
Love's Lesson

PAN loved his neighbour Echo; Echo loved
A gamesome Satyr; he, by her unmoved,
Loved only Lyde; thus through Echo, Pan,
Lyde, and Satyr, Love his circle ran.
Thus all, while their true lovers' hearts they grieved,
Were scorned in turn, and what they gave received.
O all Love's scorners, learn this lesson true;
Be kind to Love, that he be kind to you.

Ernest Myers

IDYLL IX
The Craft of a Keeper of Sheep

WOULD that my father had taught me the craft of
a keeper of sheep,
For so in the shade of the elm,tree, or under the
rocks on the steep
Piping on reeds I had sat, and had lulled my sorrow
to sleep.

Ernest Myers

The Ocean

WHEN winds that move not its calm surface sweep
The azure sea, I love the land no more;
The smiles of the serene and tranquil deep
Tempt my unquiet mind.—But when the roar

Of Ocean's grey abyss resounds, and foam
Gathers upon the sea, and vast waves burst,
I turn from the drear aspect to the home
Of earth and its deep woods, where intersperst,
When winds blow loud, pines make sweet melody.
Whose house is some lone bark, whose toil the sea,
Whose prey the wondering fish, an evil lot
Has chosen.—But I my languid limbs will fling
Beneath the plane, where the brook's murmuring
Moves the calm spirit, but disturbs it not.

Percy Bysshe Shelley

Cupid turned Ploughman

IMITATED

HIS lamp, his bow, and quiver laid aside,
A rustic wallet o'er his shoulders tied,
Sly Cupid always on new mischiefs bent,
To the rich field and furrowed tillage went;
Like any ploughman toiled the little god,
His tune he whistled, and his wheat he sowed,
Then sat and laughed, and to the skies above
Raising his eye, he thus insulted Jove:
" Lay by your hail, your hurtful storms restrain
And as I bid you, let it shine or rain;
Else you again beneath my yoke shall bow,
Feel the sharp goad, or draw the servile plough;
What once Europa was, Nannette is now."

Matthew Prior

ÆSOP'S FABLES

3rd century B.C. ?

The Vine and the Goat

A GOAT was nibbling on a Vine,
On glossy leaves and tendrils fine:
" Why wilt thou rend me thus, alas—

And is there then no good in grass ?
But when the vintage comes, I'll be,
Thou bearded Goat, revenged on thee—
For at the altar 'twill be mine
To furnish to the priest the wine
Which he with pious lips and eyes
Shall pour o'er thee, thou sacrifice
To Dionysos, god of grapes."

The Shepherd-boy and the Wolf

A SHEPHERD-BOY beside a stream
" The Wolf, the Wolf," was wont to scream,
And when the Villagers appeared,
He'd laugh and call them silly-eared.
A Wolf at last came down the steep—
" The Wolf, the Wolf—my legs, my sheep ! "
The creature had a jolly feast,
Quite undisturbed, on boy and beast.

For none believes the liar, forsooth,
Even when the liar speaks the truth.

The Ass in the Lion's Skin

A N Ass put on a Lion's skin and went
About the forest with much merriment,
Scaring the foolish beasts by brooks and rocks,
Till at last he tried to scare the Fox.
But Reynard, hearing from beneath the mane
That raucous voice so petulant and vain,
Remarked, " O Ass, I too would run away,
But that I know your old familiar bray."

That's just the way with asses, just the way.

The Mountain in Labour

A MOUNTAIN was in great distress and loud
She roared and rumbled, till there rushed a crowd
Of peasants, kings, and princes, looking at her
And wondering what of all things was the matter,

When mid her pangs there issued from her side
A Mouse—who gave one little squeak and died.
The moral here is learnèd and occult—
The bigger fuss, the smaller the result.

The Swan and the Goose

A RICH man bought a Swan and Goose—
That for song, and this for use.
It chanced his simple-minded cook
One night the Swan for Goose mistook.
But in the dark about to chop
The Swan in two above the crop,
He heard the lyric note, and stayed
The action of the fatal blade.

And thus we see a proper tune
Is sometimes very opportune.

William Ellery Leonard

THE GREEK ANTHOLOGY

490 B.C.—1000 A.D.

T HE *Anthology may from some points of view be regarded as the
most valuable relic of antique literature which we possess. Com-
posed of several thousand short poems, written at different times and by
a multitude of authors, it is co-extensive with the whole current of Greek
history, from the splendid period of the Persian war to the decadence
of Christianised Byzantium. Perhaps, however, the true secret of their
charm is this : that in their couplets, after listening to the choric raptures
of triumphant public art, we turn aside to hear the private utterances,*

the harmoniously modulated whispers, of a multitude of Greek poets telling us their inmost thoughts and feelings. The unique melodies of Meleager, the chaste and exquisite delicacy of Callimachus, the clear, dry style of Straton, Plato's unearthly subtlety of phrase, Antipater's perfect polish, the good sense of Palladas, the fretful sweetness of Agathias, the purity of Simonides, the gravity of Poseidippus, the pointed grace of Philip, the few but mellow tones of Sappho and Erinna, the tenderness of Simmias, the biting wit of Lucillius, the sunny radiance of Theocritus— all these good things are ours in the Anthology. But beyond these perfumes of the poets known to fame is yet another. Over very many of the sweetest and the strongest of the epigrams is written the pathetic word ἀδέσποτον—"without a master." Hail to you, dead poets, unnamed, but dear to the Muses ! Surely with Pindar and Anacreon, with Sappho and with Sophocles, the bed of flowers is spread for you in those "black-petalled hollows of Pieria" where you bade Euripides farewell.—JOHN ADDINGTON SYMONDS.

AGATHIAS

Rhodanthe

WEEPING and wakeful all the night I lie,
    And with the dawn the grace of sleep is near,
But swallows flit about me with their cry,
    And banish drowsihead and bring the tear.
    Mine eyes must still be weeping, for the dear
Thought of Rhodanthe stirs in memory;
Ye chattering foes have done ! it was not I
    Who silenced Philomel : go, seek the sheer

Clefts of the hills, and wail for Itylus
    Or clamour from the hoopoe's craggy nest,
But let sweet sleep an hour abide with us,
    Perchance a dream may come, and we be blest,
A dream may take Rhodanthe piteous,
    And bring us to that haven of her breast.

Andrew Lang

Not Such your Burden

NOT such your burden, happy youths, as ours—
  Poor women‑children nurtured daintily—
For ye have comrades when ill‑fortune lours,
  To hearten you with talk and company;
And ye have games for solace, and may roam
  Along the streets and see the painters' shows.
But woe betide us if we stir from home—
  And there our thoughts are dull enough, God
    knows !

              William M. Hardinge

Plutarch

CHAERONEAN Plutarch, to thy deathless praise
Does martial Rome this grateful statue raise;
Because both Greece and she thy fame have shared,
(Their heroes written and their lives compared);
But thou thyself could'st never write thine own;
Their lives have parallels, but thine has none.

                  John Dryden

ANONYMOUS

Spirit of Plato

EAGLE ! why soarest thou above that tomb ?
  To what sublime and star‑ypaven home
    Floatest thou ?
  I am the image of swift Plato's spirit,
  Ascending heaven—Athens doth inherit
    His corpse below.

           Percy Bysshe Shelley

Epitaph on Achilles

THIS mound the Achæans reared—Achilles' tomb—
For terror to the Trojans yet to be,
Leans seaward, that his mighty spirit whom
Sea Thetis bore may hear its dirge of the sea.
William M. Hardinge

This Stone

THIS stone, beloved Sabinus, on thy grave
Memorial small of our great love shall be.
I still shall seek thee lost; from Lethe's wave,
Oh, drink not thou forgetfulness of me.
Goldwin Smith

Dion of Tarsus

DION of Tarsus, here I lie, who sixty years have seen.
I was not ever wed, and would my father had not
been !
Alma Strettell

Riches

POOR in my youth, and in life's later scenes
Rich to no end, I curse my natal hour,
Who naught enjoyed while young, denied the means:
And naught when old enjoy'd, denied the power.
William Cowper

Grapes

WHILE yet the grapes were green, thou didst refuse
me ;
When they were ripe, didst proudly pass me by;
But do not grudge me still a single cluster,
Now that the grapes are withering and dry.
Alma Strettell

The Tomb of Diogenes

" TELL me, good dog, whose tomb you guard so well."
" The Cynic's." " True; but who that Cynic tell."
" Diogenes, of fair Sinope's race."
" What ? He that in a tub was wont to dwell ? "
" Yes: but the stars are now his dwelling place."

John Addington Symonds

The Lion over the Tomb of Leonidas

OF beasts am I, of men was he most brave
Whose bones I guard, bestriding this his grave.

Walter Leaf

Not of Itself, but Thee

I SEND thee myrrh, not that thou mayest be
By it perfumed, but it perfumed by thee.

Richard Garnett

Nature's Travail

LONG Nature travailed, till at last she bore
Homer: then ceased from bearing evermore.

Goldwin Smith

ANTIPATER
Erinna

THOUGH short her strain nor sung with mighty
boast;
Yet there the power of song had dwelling room;
So lives her name for ever, nor lies lost
Beneath the shadow of the wings of gloom,

While birds of after days, in countless host,
   Slumber and fade forgotten in the tomb.
Better the swan's brief note than thousand cries
Of rooks in springtime blown about the skies.

A. J. Butler

Aristeides

ONE heifer and one fleecy sheep
   Were Aristeides' scanty store;
With this poor wealth he strove to keep
   Grim pinching hunger from his door.
Yet strove in vain; a wolf the one
   And labour pa ns the other slew,
And left the herdsman, all undone,
   His loss of livelihood to rue.
Poor wretch !   The thong, which lately bound .
   His wallet, round his neck he tied,
And near his cabin, where the sound
   No more was heard of lowing, died.

Charles Whibley

Pindar

AS the war-trumpet drowns the rustic flute,
   So when your lyre is heard all strings are mute:
Not vain the labour of those clustering bees
Who on your infant lips spread honey-dew;
Witness great Pan who hymned your melodies,
Pindar, forgetful of his pipes for you.

John Addington Symonds

Undying Thirst

THIS rudely sculptured porter-pot
   Denotes where sleeps a female sot;
   Who passed her life, good easy soul,
   In sweetly chirping o'er her bowl.

Not for her friends or children dear
She mourns, but only for her beer.
E'en in the very grave, they say,
She thirsts for drink to wet her clay;
And, faith, she thinks it very wrong
This jug should stand unfilled so long.

Robert Bland

ANYTES

A Shepherd's Gift

TO shaggy Pan, and all the Wood-Nymphs fair,
Fast by the rock this grateful offering stands,
A shepherd's gift—to those who gave him there
Rest, when he fainted in the sultry air;
And reached him sweetest water with their hands.

John William Burgon

ARCHIAS OF BYZANTIUM

Sea Dirge

CRUSHED by the waves upon the crag was I,
    Who still must hear these waves among the dead,
Breaking and brawling on the promontory,
    Sleepless; and sleepless is my weary head !
For me did strangers bury on the coast
    Within the hateful hearing of the deep,
Nor Death, that lulleth all, can lull my ghost,
    One sleepless soul among the souls that sleep !

Andrew Lang

ASCLEPIADES
Eumares

TUMULTUOUS sea, whose wrath and foam are spent
So nigh to Eumares' worn monument;
Spare if thou wilt and shatter if thou must,
For nothing shalt thou find but bones and dust.

Richard Garnett

CALLIMACHUS
Heraclitus

THEY told me, Heraclitus, they told me you were
dead,
They brought me bitter news to hear and bitter
tears to shed.
I wept as I remembered how often you and I
Had tired the sun with talking and sent him down
the sky.
And now that thou art lying, my dear old Carian
guest,
A handful of grey ashes, long, long ago at rest,
Still are thy pleasant voices, thy nightingales, awake;
For Death, he taketh all away, but them he cannot
take.

William Cory

Timon's Epitaph

HERE lie I, Timon; who, alive, all living men did hate:
Pass by, and curse thy fill; but pass and stay not here
thy gait.

William Shakespeare

His Son

BUT twelve short years you lived, my son,
    Just twelve short years, and then you died:
And now your life's brief course is run,
    This grave a father's hopes doth hide.

G. B. Grundy

Saon of Acanthus

HERE lapped in hallowed slumber Saon lies,
    Asleep, not dead ; a good man never dies.

J. A. Symonds

Sopolis

NOW would to God swift ships had ne'er been made !
    Then, Sopolis, we had not mourned thy shade—
Dear son of Diocleides seaward sent !
Now somewhere in deep seas thy corse is tost
Hither and thither—and for whom we lost
    We find thy name and empty monument.

William M. Hardinge

Crethis

FOR Crethis' store of tales and pleasant chat
    Oft sigh the Samian maidens, missing that
Which cheered their tasks, but she, beyond their call,
Sleeps here the sleep that must be slept by all.

Richard Garnett

CARPHYLLIDES

A Happy Man

WHEN these graven lines you see,
    Traveller, do not pity me;
    Though I be among the dead,
    Let no mournful word be said.

Children that I leave behind,
And their children, all were kind;
Near to them and to my wife,
I was happy all my life.

My three sons I married right,
And their sons I rocked at night;
Death nor sorrow ever brought
Cause for one unhappy thought.

Now, and with no need of tears,
Here they leave me, full of years,—
Leave me to my quiet rest
In the region of the blest.

Edwin Arlington Robinson

CRINAGORAS
Epitaph on an Infant

FULL oft of old the islands changed their name
And took new titles from some heir of fame;
Then dread not yet the wrath of Gods above,
But change your own and be " The Isles of Love ";
For Love's own name and shape the infant bore
Whom late we buried on yon sandy shore.
Break softly there, thou never-weary wave,
And, earth, lie lightly on his little grave.

John William Burgon

DIOTIMUS
Without the Herdsman

COVERED with snow, the herd, with none to guide,
Came to the stall adown the mountain side;
For, ah ! Therimachus beneath an oak
Slept the long sleep, from which he ne'er awoke,
Sent to his slumber by the lightning's stroke.

John William Burgon

ERINNA

Baucis

MY funeral-shaft, and marble shapes that dwell
Beside it, and sad urn, receptacle
Of all I am, salute who seek thy tomb,
If from my own, or other cities come;
And say to them, a bride I hither came,
Tenos my country, Baucis was my name.
Say also, this inscription for her friend
Erinna, handmaid of the Muses, penned.

Richard Garnett

ISIDORUS

On a Fowler

WITH reeds and bird-lime from the desert air
Eumelus gather'd free, though scanty, fare,
Nor lordly patron's hand he deign'd to kiss :
Thrice thirty years he lived, and to his heirs
His reeds bequeath'd, his bird-lime, and his snares.

William Cowper

LEONIDAS OF ALEXANDRIA

Menodotis

MENODOTIS'S portrait here is kept;
Most odd it is
How very like to all the world, except
Menodotis.

Richard Garnett

LEONIDAS OF TARENTUM
The Fisherman

THERIS the old, the waves that harvested,
    More keen than birds that labour in the sea,
With spear and net, by shore and rocky bed
    Not with the well-manned galley, laboured he;
Him not the Star of Storms, nor sudden sweep
    Of wind with all his years hath smitten and bent,
But in his hut of reeds he fell asleep,
    As fades a lamp when all the oil is spent:
This tomb nor wife nor children raised, but we
    His fellow-toilers, fishers of the sea.
                        Andrew Lang

The Spinning Woman

MORNING and evening, sleep she drove away,
    Old Platthis,—warding hunger from the door,
And still to wheel and distaff hummed her lay
    Hard by the gates of Eld, and bent and hoar;
Plying her loom until the dawn was grey,
    The long course of Athene did she tread:
With withered hand by withered knee she spun
    Sufficient for the loom of goodly thread,
Till all her work and all her days were done.
    And in her eightieth year she saw the wave
Of Acheron,—old Platthis,—kind and brave.
                        Andrew Lang

The Tomb of Crethon

I AM the tomb of Crethon; here you read
His name; himself is number'd with the dead;
    Who once had wealth not less than Gyges' gold;
    Who once was rich in stable, stall, and fold;

Who once was blest above all living men—
With lands, how narrow now, how ample then !
John Herman Merivale

Cleitagoras

SHEPHERDS that on this mountain ridge abide,
Tending your goats and fleecy flocks alway,
A little favour, but most grateful, pay
Cleitagoras, nor be the boon denied !
For sake of mother earth, and by the bride
Of Hades under earth, let sheep, I pray,
Bleat near me, and the shepherd softly play
From the scarred rock across the pasture wide.

Ah ! but, in early spring, cull meadowsweet,
Neighbour, and weave a garland for my tomb;
And with ewe's milk be the stone edge bedewed
When the lambs play about their mother's feet.
So shall you honour well the shades, from whom
Are thanks—and from the dead is gratitude.
William M. Hardinge

The Last Journey

WITH courage seek the kingdom of the dead;
The path before you lies,
It is not hard to find, nor tread;
No rocks to climb, no lanes to thread;
But broad, and straight, and even still,
And ever gently slopes down-hill;
You cannot miss it, though you shut your eyes.
Charles Merivale

LUCIANUS
Artificial Beauty

YOU give your cheeks a rosy stain,
  With washes dye your hair,
But paint and washes both are vain
  To give a youthful air.

Those wrinkles mock your daily toil;
  No labour will efface them;
You wear a mask of smoothest oil,
  Yet still with ease we trace them.

An art so fruitless then forsake,
  Which though you much excel in,
You never can contrive to make
  Old Hecuba young Helen.

William Cowper

LUCILLIUS
On an Old Woman

MYCILLA dyes her locks, 'tis said,
  But 'tis a foul aspersion;
She buys them black, they therefore need
  No subsequent immersion.

William Cowper

Treasure

THEY call thee rich; I deem thee poor;
  Since, if thou darest not use thy store,
But savest only for thine heirs,
  The treasure is not thine, but theirs.

William Cowper

MELEAGER

Upon a Maid that died the Day she was married

THAT morn which saw me made a bride,
The evening witnessed that I died.
Those holy lights, wherewith they guide
Unto the bed the bashful bride,
Served but as tapers, for to burn,
And light my relics to their urn.
This epitaph, which here you see,
Supplied the epithalamy.

Robert Herrick

O Gentle Ships

O GENTLE ships that skim the seas,
And cleave the strait where Hellè fell,
Catch in your sails the northern breeze,
And speed to Cos where she doth dwell,
My love, and see you greet her well !

And if she looks across the blue,
Speak, gentle ships, and tell her true—
" He comes, for Love hath brought him back,
No sailor, on the landward tack."

If thus, O gentle ships, ye do,
Then may ye win the fairest gales,
And swifter speed across the blue,
While Zeus breathes friendly on your sails.

Andrew Lang

Of his Death

AH! Love, my Master, hear me swear
By all the locks of Timo's hair,
By Demo, and that fragrant spell
Wherewith her body doth enchant
Such dreams as drowsy lovers haunt,
By Ilias' mirth delectable,
And by the lamp that sheds his light
On love and lovers all the night,
By those, ah Love, I swear that thou
Hast left me but one breath, and now
Upon my lips it fluttereth,
Yet *this* I'll yield, my latest breath,
Even this, oh Love, for thee to Death!

Andrew Lang

In the Spring

NOW the bright crocus flames, and now
    The slim narcissus takes the rain,
And, straying o'er the mountain's brow,
    The daffodillies bud again.
The thousand blossoms wax and wane
    On wold, and heath, and fragrant bough,
    But fairer than the flowers art thou
Than any growth of hill or plain.

Ye gardens cast your leafy crown,
That my love's feet may tread it down,
    Like lilies on the lilies set;
My Love, whose lips are softer far
Than drowsy poppy petals are,
    And sweeter than the violet!

Andrew Lang

Love at the Door

COLD blows the winter wind: 'tis Love,
    Whose sweet eyes swim with honeyed tears,
That bears me to thy doors, my love,
    Tossed by the storm of hopes and fears.

Cold blows the blast of aching Love;
    But be thou for my wandering sail,
Adrift upon these waves of love,
    Safe harbour from the whistling gale!

                    J. A. Symonds

The Little Love-god

I

A PLAGUE is Love, a plague! but yet
    what profit shall it prove
again and oft again to fret
and cry: *A plague is Love?*

The boy but laughs to hear such news;
    chid with a tongue let loose,
enjoys it; and if I abuse,
he thrives upon abuse.

O hither through the green wave sent,
    Cypris, I must admire
how thou from that moist element
hast brought to birth a fire!

II

LET him be sold, though still he sleep
    upon his mother's breast!
let him be sold! why should I keep
so turbulent a pest?

For wingéd he was born, he leers,
and sharply with his nails
he scratches, and amid his tears
oft laughs the while he wails.

Withal and further, glances keen
he plies, devoid of shame,
a ceaseless babbler, wild, nor e'en
to his own dear mother tame.

An utter monster: on that ground
sold he shall be to-day:
if any trader outward bound
would buy a boy, this way!

But see, in tears beseecheth he:
nay, thee no more I sell:
fear not, with my Zenophile
remain thou here to dwell.

Walter Headlam

Of Himself

TYRE brought me up, who born in thee had been,
Assyrian Athens, city Gadarene;
My name is Meleager, Eucrates
My sire, my skill with graceful strains to please;
My Syrian lineage do not discommend,
One world have all, one origin, one end;
Stricken in years, I yet can touch the string,
And this unto the tomb, my neighbour, sing;
Salute my garrulous old age, and be
Thine own what now thou honourest in me.

Richard Garnett

Lost Desire

LOVE brought by night a vision to my bed,
One that still wore the vesture of a child
But eighteen years of age—who sweetly smiled
Till of the lovely form false hopes were bred
  And keen embraces wild.
Ah ! for the lost desire that haunts me yet,
Till mine eyes fail in sleep that finds no more
That fleeting ghost !   Oh, lovelorn heart, give o'er—
Cease thy vain dreams of beauty's warmth—forget
  The face thou longest for !

     William M. Hardinge

Spring

NOW Winter's winds are banished from the sky,
Gay laughs the blushing face of flowery Spring:
Now lays the land her duskier raiment by
And dons her grass-green vest, for signal why
Young plants may choose themselves apparelling.

Now drinking tender dews of generous morn,
The meadows break into their summer smile,
The rose unfolds her leaves; and glad, the while,
In far-off hills the shepherd winds his horn,
And his white brede the goatherd's heart beguile.

Now sail the sailors over billowing seas
While careless Zephyr fills the canvas fair,
And singing crowds with dances debonair
Praise Dionysus for the grapes' increase—
The berried ivy twisted in their hair.

Forth from the rotting hide now bees are come—
Deft craftsmen working well and warily—
And in the hive they settle, while they ply
Fresh-flowing waxen store, with busy hum,
And small pierced cells for their sweet industry.

Now shrilleth clear each several bird his note,
The Halcyon charms the wave that knows no gale,
About our eaves the swallow tells her tale,
Along the river banks the swan, afloat,
And down the woodland glades the nightingale.

Now tendrils curl and earth bursts forth anew—
Now shepherd's pipe and fleecy flocks are gay—
Now sailors sail, and Bacchus gets his due—
Now wild birds chirp and bees their toil pursue—
Sing, poet, thou—and sing thy best for May !

William M. Hardinge

A Garland for Heliodora

I'LL frame, my Heliodora ! a garland for thy hair,
Which thou, in all thy beauty's pride, mayst not
disdain to wear;
For I with tender myrtles white violets will twine,
White violets, but not so pure as that pure breast of
thine;
With laughing lilies I will twine narcissus, and the
sweet
Crocus shall, in its yellow hue, with purple hyacinth
meet.
And I will twine with all the rest, and all the rest above,
Queen of them all, the red red rose, the flower which
lovers love.

Christopher North

NICIAS

The Fountain at the Tomb

STAY, weary traveller, stay !
   Beneath these boughs repose;
A step out of the way
   My little fountain flows.

And never quite forget
The monumental urn,
Which Simus here hath set
His buried child to mourn.

Charles Merivale

PALLADAS
Vanity of Vanities

NAKED to earth was I brought—naked to earth I
descend.
Why should I labour for naught, seeing how naked
the end?

William M. Hardinge

PAULUS SILENTIARIUS
No Matter

MY name, my country, what are they to thee?
What, whether proud or base my pedigree?
Perhaps I far surpassed all other men;
Perhaps I fell below them all. What then?
Suffice it, stranger, that thou seest a tomb.
Thou knowst its use. It hides—no matter whom.

William Cowper

United

HOW long must we two hide the burning gaze,
And look by stealth in one another's eyes?
Let us proclaim our love; and whoso stays
The sweet embrace that lulls all miseries—
The sword's our doctor: best that you and I
Should live together, or together die.

W. H. D. Rouse

PLATO

A Farewell

VENUS, take my votive glass,
Since I am not what I was:
What from this day I shall be,
Venus, let me ever see.

Matthew Prior

Morning and Evening Star

THOU wert the morning star among the living,
Ere thy fair light had fled;
Now, having died, thou art as Hesperus, giving
New splendour to the dead.

Percy Bysshe Shelley

On Alexis

" FAIR is Alexis " I no sooner said
When everyone his eyes that way convey'd.
My soul, as when some dog a bone we show
Who snatcheth it—lost we not Phædrus so ?

Thomas Stanley

On Archæanassa

TO Archæanassa, on whose furrow'd brow
Love sits in triumph, I my service vow.
If her declining graces shine so bright,
What flames felt you who saw her noon of light ?

Thomas Stanley

Love Sleeping

WITHIN the covert of a shady grove
We saw the little red-cheek'd god of Love:
He had nor bow nor quiver: these among
The neighbouring trees upon a bough were hung.
Upon a bank of tender rosebuds laid,
He smiling slept; bees with their noise invade
His rest, and on his lips their honey made.

Thomas Stanley

On a Seal

FIVE oxen, grazing in a flowery mead,
A jasper seal, done to the life, doth hold;
The little herd away long since had fled,
Were't not enclos'd within a pale of gold.

Thomas Stanley

Farewell

FAR from the deep roar of the Ægean main,
Here lie we in the midst of Media's plain.
Farewell, great Fatherland ! Farewell to thee,
Eubœa's neighbour, Athens ! Farewell, Sea !

Charles Whibley

POSIDIPPUS
Doricha

SO now the very bones of you are gone
Where they were dust and ashes long ago;
And there was the last ribbon you tied on
To bind your hair, and that is dust also;

And somewhere there is dust that was of old
A soft and scented garment that you wore—
The same that once till dawn did closely fold
You in with fair Charaxus, fair no more.

But Sappho, and the white leaves of her song,
Will make your name a word for all to learn,
And all to love thereafter, even while
It's but a name; and this will be as long
As there are distant ships that will return
Again to your Naucratis and the Nile.

Edwin Arlington Robinson

RUFINUS

The Lover's Posy

I SEND a garland to my love
Which with my own hands I wove:
Rose and lily here there be
Twined with cool anemone,
White narcissus, dewy wet,
And the purple violet.
Take and bind it on your brow,
Nor be proud, as you are now.
As the flowers bloom and fade,
So must you too, haughty maid.

W. H. D. Rouse

SIMMIAS OF THEBES

To Prote

THOU art not dead, my Prote ! thou art flown
To a far country better than our own;
Thy home is now an island of the blest;
There 'mid Elysian meadows take thy rest,

Or lightly trip along the flowery glade,
Rich with the asphodels that never fade !
Nor pain, nor cold, nor toil shall vex thee more,
Nor thirst, nor hunger on that happy shore;
Nor longings vain (now that blest life is won)
For such poor days as mortals here drag on;
To thee for ay a blameless life is given
In the pure light of ever-present Heaven.

J. A. Symonds

SIMONIDES

On Two Brothers

THIS earth Pythonax and his brother hides,
Who died before they reached youth's lovely prime.
The tomb their father built them; which abides
For ever, though they lived so short a time.

W. H. D. Rouse

LATIN

TITUS LUCRETIUS CARUS

95–52 B.C.

*THE distinguishing character of Lucretius (I mean of his soul and genius) is a certain kind of noble pride, and positive assertion of his opinions. . . . From this sublime and daring genius of his it must of necessity come to pass that his thoughts must be masculine, full of argumentation, and that sufficiently warm. From the same fiery temper proceeds the loftiness of his expressions, and the perpetual torrent of his verse, where the barrenness of his subject does not too much constrain the quickness of his fancy. . . . He was so much an atheist that he forgot sometimes to be a poet.—*JOHN DRYDEN.

Address to Venus

GREAT Venus, Queene of Beautie and of grace,
　　The joy of Gods and men, that under skie
　　Dost fayrest shine, and most adorne thy place;
　　That with thy smyling looke doest pacifie
　　The raging seas and makst the stormes to flie:
　　　Thee, Goddess, thee the winds, the clouds do
　　　　feare;
　　And when thou spredst thy mantle forth on hie
　　　The waters play, and pleasant lands appear,
And heavens laugh, and all the world shews joyous
　　cheare.

Then doth the dædale earth throw forth to thee
　　Out of her fruitfull lap abundant flowres;
And then all living wights, soone as they see
　　The Spring break forth out of his lusty bowres,
　　They all doe learne to play the Paramours;
　　　First doe the merry birds, thy pretty pages,
　　Privily priked with thy lustful powres,
　　　Chirpe loud to thee out of their leavy cages
And thee their mother call to coole their kindly
　　rages.

Then doe the salvage beasts begin to play
    Their pleasant friskes, and loath their wonted food;
The Lyons rore; the Tygres loudly bray;
    The raging Buls rebellow through the wood,
    And breaking forth dare tempt the deepest flood
        To come where thou doest draw them with desire.
    So all things else, that nourish vitall blood,
        Soone as with fury thou doest them inspire
In generation seeke to quench their inward fire.

So all the world by thee at first was made,
    And dayly yet thou doest the same prepayre:
Ne ought on earth that merry is and glad,
    Ne ought on earth that lovely is and fayre
    But thou the same for pleasure didst prepayre:
        Thou art the root of all that joyous is:
        Great God of men and women, queene of the air,
        Mother of laughter and welspring of blisse,
O graunt that of my love at last I may not misse!

                                            Edmund Spenser

Beyond Religion

WHILST human kind
    Throughout the lands lay miserably crushed
    Before all eyes beneath Religion—who
    Would show her head along the region skies,
    Glowering on mortals with her hideous face—
    A Greek it was who first opposing dared
    Raise mortal eyes that terror to withstand,
    Whom nor the fame of Gods nor lightning's stroke
    Nor threatening thunder of the ominous sky
    Abashed; but rather chafed to angry zest
    His dauntless heart to be the first to rend
    The crossbars at the gates of Nature old.
    And thus his will and hardy wisdom won;
    And forward thus he fared afar, beyond

The flaming ramparts of the world, until
He wandered the unmeasurable All.
Whence he to us, a conqueror, reports
What things can rise to being, what cannot,
And by what law to each its scope prescribed,
Its boundary stone that clings so deep in Time.
Wherefore religion now is under foot,
And us his victory now exalts to heaven.
    I know how hard it is in Latian verse
To tell the dark discoveries of the Greeks,
Chiefly because our pauper-speech must find
Strange terms to fit the strangeness of the thing;
Yet worth of thine and the expected joy
Of thy sweet friendship do persuade me on
To bear all toil and wake the clear nights through,
Seeking with what of words and what of song
I may at last most gloriously uncloud
For thee the light beyond, wherewith to view
The core of being at the centre hid.
And for the rest, summon to judgments true,
Unbusied ears and singleness of mind
Withdrawn from cares; lest these my gifts, arranged
For thee with eager service, thou disdain
Before thou comprehendest: since for thee
I prove the supreme law of Gods and sky,
And the primordial germs of things unfold,
Whence Nature all creates, and multiplies
And fosters all, and whither she resolves
Each in the end when each is overthrown.

                                    William Ellery Leonard

Against the Fear of Death

WHAT has this bugbear Death to frighten man,
If souls can die, as well as bodies can?
For, as before our birth we felt no pain,
When Punic arms infested land and main,

When heaven and earth were in confusion hurl'd
For the debated empire of the world,
Which awed with dreadful expectation lay,
Soon to be slaves, uncertain who should sway:
So, when our mortal frame shall be disjoin'd,
The lifeless lump uncoupled from the mind,
From sense of grief and pain we shall be free;
We shall not feel, because we shall not be.
Though earth in seas, and seas in heaven were lost,
We should not move, we only should be toss'd.
Nay, e'en suppose when we have suffered fate
The soul should feel in her divided state,
What's that to us ? for we are only we,
While souls and bodies in our frame agree.
Nay, though our atoms should revolve by chance,
And matter leap into the former dance;
Though time our life and motion could restore,
And make our bodies what they were before,
What gain to us would all this bustle bring ?
The new-made man would be another thing.
When once an interrupting pause is made,
That individual being is decay'd.
We, who are dead and gone, shall bear no part
In all the pleasures, nor shall feel the smart,
Which to that other mortal shall accrue,
Whom to our matter time shall mould anew.
For backward if you look on that long space
Of ages past, and view the changing face
Of matter, toss'd and variously combin'd
In sundry shapes, 'tis easy for the mind
From thence to infer, that seeds of things have been
In the same order as they now are seen:
Which yet our dark remembrance cannot trace,
Because a pause of life, a gaping space,
Has come betwixt, where memory lies dead,
And all the wandering motions from the sense are fled.

For whosoe'er shall in misfortunes live,
Must be, when those misfortunes shall arrive;
And since the man who is not, feels not woe,
(For death exempts him, and wards off the blow,
Which we, the living, only feel and bear,)
What is there left for us in death to fear ?
When once that pause of life has come between
'Tis just the same as we had never been.

John Dryden

CAIUS VALERIUS CATULLUS

87–57 B.C.

TENDEREST of Roman poets nineteen hundred years ago
TENNYSON.

My Sweetest Lesbia

MY sweetest Lesbia, let us live and love,
And though the sager sort our deeds reprove,
Let us not weigh them.   Heaven's great lamps do
    dive
Into their west, and straight again revive,
But, soon as once set is our little light,
Then must we sleep one ever-during night.

If all would lead their lives in love like me,
Then bloody swords and armour should not be;
No drum nor trumpet peaceful sleeps should move,
Unless alarm came from the camp of Love:
But fools do live and waste their little light,
And seek with pain their ever-during night.

When timely death my life and fortune ends,
Let not my hearse be vext with mourning friends,
But let all lovers rich in triumph come
And with sweet pastimes grace my happy tomb:

And, Lesbia, close up thou my little light,
And crown with love my ever/during night.

Thomas Campion

To Celia

KISS me, sweet : the wary lover
Can your favours keep, and cover,
When the common courting jay
All your bounties will betray.
Kiss again ! no creature comes;
Kiss, and score up wealthy sums
On my lips, thus hardly sundered,
While you breathe.   First give a hundred,
Then a thousand, then another
Hundred, then unto the other
Add a thousand, and so more;
Till you equal with the store
All the grass that Romney yields,
Or the sands in Chelsea fields,
Or the drops in silver Thames,
Or the stars that gild his streams
In the silent summer/nights,
When youths ply their stolen delights;
That the curious may not know
How to tell 'em as they flow,
And the envious when they find
What their number is, be pined.

Ben Jonson

The Death of Lesbia's Bird

PITY ! mourn in plaintive tone
The lovely starling dead and gone !
Pity mourns in plaintive tone
The lovely starling dead and gone.

Weep, ye Loves ! and Venus ! weep
The lovely starling fallen asleep !
Venus sees with tearful eyes—
In her lap the starling lies !
While the Loves all in a ring
Softly stroke the stiffened wing.

Samuel Taylor Coleridge

Lesbia Railing

LESBIA for ever on me rails.
To talk of me she never fails.
Now, hang me, but for all her art,
I find that I have gained her heart.
My proof is this: I plainly see
The case is just the same with me;
I curse her every hour sincerely,
Yet, hang me, but I love her dearly.

Jonathan Swift

True or False

NONE could ever say that she,
Lesbia ! was so loved by me.
Never all the world around
Faith so true as mine was found.
If no longer it endures
(Would it did !) the fault is yours.
I can never think again
Well of you: I try in vain.
But . . . be false . . . do what you will.—
Lesbia ! I must love you still.

Walter Savage Landor

Sappho

LIKE to a god he seems to me,
O more than god, if that may be,
The man who, seated next to thee,
 Gazes, and hears

Thy laugh of love that snatched away
My soul and sense: for on the day
I saw thee, lady, voice could say
 Not any word;

But tongue grew stark, and thro' my frame
Fed unforeseen a subtle flame,
And rang my ears, and eyes became
 Veiled, as in night.

William Ellery Leonard

Hymn to Diana

DIANA guardeth our estate,
Girls and boys immaculate:
Boys and maidens pure of stain,
Be Diana our refrain.

O Latonia, pledge of love
Glorious to most glorious Jove,
Near the Delian olive-tree
Latonia gave thy life to thee,

That thou shouldst be for ever queen
Of mountains and of forests green;
Of every deep glen's mystery;
Of all streams and their melody:

Women in travail ask their peace
From thee, our Lady of Release:
Thou art the Watcher of the Ways;
Thou art the Moon with borrowed rays;

And as thy full or waning tide
Marks how the monthly seasons glide,
Thou, Goddess, sendest wealth of store
To bless the farmer's thrifty floor !

Whatever name delights thine ear,
By that name be thou hallowed here;
And as of old be good to us,
The lineage of Romulus !

Richard Claverhouse Jebb

Sirmio

GEM of all isthmuses and isles that lie,
Fresh or salt water's children, in clear lake
Or ampler ocean: with what joy do I
Approach thee, Sirmio !   Oh ! am I awake,
Or dream that once again my eye beholds
Thee, and has looked its last on Thynian wolds ?
Sweetest of sweets to me that pastime seems,
When the mind drops her burden: when—the pain
Of travel past—our own cot we regain,
And nestle on the pillow of our dreams !
'Tis this one thought that cheers us as we roam.
Hail, O fair Sirmio !   Joy, thy lord is here !
Joy too, ye waters of the Garda Mere !
And ring out, all ye laughter-peals of home.

Charles Stuart Calverley

Love and Death

FRIEND, if the mute and shrouded dead
Are touched at all by tears,
By love long fled and friendship sped
And the unreturning years,

O then, to her that early died,
  O doubt not, bridegroom, to thy bride
Thy love is sweet and sweeteneth
  The very bitterness of death.

H. W. Garrod

To Varus

SUFFENUS, whom so well you know,
My Varus, as a wit and beau,
Of smart address and smirking smile,
Will write you verses by the mile.
You cannot meet with daintier fare
Than title-page and binding are;
But when you once begin to read
You find it sorry stuff indeed,
And you are ready to cry out
Upon this beau—" O what a lout ! "
No man on earth so proud as he
Of his own precious poetry,
Or knows such perfect bliss as when
He takes in hand that nibbled pen.
Have we not all some faults like these ?
Are we not all Suffenuses ?
In others the defect we find,
But cannot see our sack behind.

Walter Savage Landor

A Fib detected

VARUS, whom I chanced to meet
The other evening in the street,
Engaged me there, upon the spot,
To see a mistress he had got.
She seemed, as far as I can gather,
Lively and smart and handsome rather.

There, as we rested from our walk,
We entered into various talk—
As, how much might Bithynia bring?
And had I found it a good thing?
I answered, as it was the fact,
The province had been stript and sackt;
That there was nothing for the prætors,
And still less for us wretched creatures,
His poor companions and toad-eaters.
"At least," says she, "you bought some fellows
To bear your litter; for they tell us,
Our only good ones come from there."
I chose to give myself an air;
"Why, truly, with my poor estate,
The difference wasn't quite so great
Betwixt a province, good or bad,
That where a purchase could be had,
Eight lusty fellows, straight and tall,
I shouldn't find the wherewithal
To buy them." But it was a lie;
For not a single wretch had I—
No single cripple fit to bear
A broken bedstead or a chair.
She, like a strumpet, pert and knowing,
Said—"Dear Catullus, I am going
To worship at Serapis' shrine—
Do lend me, pray, those slaves of thine."
I answered—"It was idly said,—
They were a purchase Cinna made
(Caius Cinna, my good friend)—
It was the same thing in the end,
Whether a purchase or a loan—
I always used them as my own;
Only the phrase was inexact—
He bought them for himself in fact.
But you have caught the general vice

Of being too correct and nice,
Over-curious and precise;
And seizing with precipitation
The slight neglects of conversation."

John Hookham Frere

The Yacht

STRANGER, the bark you see before you says
That in old times and in her early days
She was a lively vessel that could make
The quickest voyages, and overtake
All her competitors with sail or oar;
And she defies the rude Illyrian shore,
And Rhodes with her proud harbour, and the seas
That intersect the scattered Cyclades,
And the Propontic and the Thracian coast,
(Bold as it is) to contradict her boast.
She calls to witness the dark Euxine sea
And mountains that had known her as a tree,
Before her transformation, when she stood
A native of the deep Cytorian wood,
Where all her ancestors had flourished long,
And, with their old traditionary song,
Had whispered her responses to the breeze,
And waked the chorus of her sister trees.
Amastris, from your haven forth she went,
You witnessed her first outset and descent,
Adventuring on an unknown element.
From thence she bore her master safe and free
From danger and alarm through many a sea;
Nor ever once was known to lag behind,
Foremost on every tack, with every wind.
At last, to this fair inland lake, she says
She came to pass the remnant of her days,
Leaving no debt due to the Deities
For vows preferred in danger on the seas:

Clear of incumbrance, therefore, and all other
Contentious claims, to Castor or his brother
As a free gift and offering she devotes
Herself, as long as she survives and floats.

John Hookham Frere

Acme and Septimius

WHILST on Septimius' panting breast
(Meaning nothing less than rest)
Acme lean'd her loving head,
Thus the pleas'd Septimius said.

My dearest Acme, if I be
Once alive, and love not thee
With a passion far above
All that e'er was callèd love,
In a Lybian desert may
I become some lion's prey,
Let him, Acme, let him tear
My breast, when Acme is not there.

The God of Love who stood to hear him,
(The God of Love was always near him)
Pleas'd and tickl'd with the sound,
Sneez'd aloud, and all around
The little Loves that waited by,
Bow'd and blest the augurie.

Acme enflam'd with what he said,
Rear'd her gently bending head,
And her purple mouth with joy
Stretching to the delicious boy,
Twice (twice could scarce suffice)
She kissed his drunken, rolling eyes.

My little Life, my All (said she)
So may we ever servants be

To this best God, and ne'er retain
Our hated liberty again,
So may thy passion last for me,
As I a passion have for thee,
Greater and fiercer much than can
Be conceiv'd by thee a man.
Into my marrow is it gone,
Fixed and settled in the bone,
It reigns not only in my heart,
But runs, like life, through ev'ry part.
She spoke; the God of Love aloud
Sneez'd again, and all the crowd
Of little loves that waited by,
Bow'd and blest the augurie.
This good omen thus from heaven
Like a happy signal given,
Their loves and lives (all four) embrace
And hand in hand run all the race.
To poor Septimius (who did now
Nothing else but Acme grow)
Acme's bosom was alone
The whole world's imperial throne,
And to faithful Acme's mind
Septimius was all human kind.

If the Gods would please to be
But advis'd for once by me,
I'd advise 'em when they spy
Any illustrious piety,
To reward her, if it be she;
To reward him, if it be he;
With such a husband, such a wife,
With Acme's and Septimius' life.

Abraham Cowley

PUBLIUS VERGILIUS MARO

70–19 B.C.

THOU that singest wheat and woodland,
tilth and vineyard, hive and horse and herd;
All the charm of all the Muses
often flowering in a lonely word.

TENNYSON.

ECLOGUE I

The Shepherd's Gratitude

MELIBŒUS.   Stretched in the shadow of the broad
beech, thou
Rehearsest, Tityrus, on the slender pipe
Thy woodland music.   We our fatherland
Are leaving, we must shun the fields we love:
While, Tityrus, thou, at ease amid the shade,
Bidd'st answering woods call Amaryllis "fair."

TITYRUS.   O Melibœus! 'Tis a god that made
For me this holiday: for god I'll ay
Account him; many a young lamb from my fold
Shall stain his altar.   Thanks to him, my kine
Range, as thou seest them: thanks to him, I play
What songs I list upon my shepherd's pipe.

M.   For me, I grudge thee not; I marvel much:
So sore a trouble is in all the land.
Lo! feeble *I* am driving hence my goats—
Nay *dragging*, Tityrus, one, and that with pain.
For, yearning here amidst the hazel-stems,
She left her twin kids—on the naked flint
She left them; and I lost my promised flock.
This evil, I remember, oftentimes
(Had not my wits been wandering) oaks foretold
By heaven's hand smitten: oft the wicked crow
Croaked the same message from the riften holm.
—Yet tell me, Tityrus, of this " God " of thine.

T.   The city men call *Rome* my folly deemed
Was e'en like this of ours, where week by week
We shepherds journey with our weanling flocks.
So whelp to dog, so kid (I knew) to dam
Was likest: and I judged great things by small.
But o'er all cities this so lifts her head,
As does o'er osiers lithe the cypress tree.

    M.   What made thee then so keen to look on Rome?

    T.   Freedom: who marked, at last, my helpless state:
Now that a whiter beard than that of yore
Fell from my razor; still she marked, and came
(All late) to help me—now that all my thought
Is Amaryllis, Galatea gone.
While Galatea's, I despaired, I own,
Of freedom, and of thrift.   Though from my farm
Full many a victim stept, though rich the cheese
Pressed for yon thankless city: still my hand
Returned not, heavy with brass pieces, home.

    M.   I wondered, Amaryllis, whence that woe,
And those appeals to heav'n: for whom the peach
Hung undisturbed upon the parent tree.
Tityrus was gone!   Why, Tityrus, pine and rill,
And all these copses, cried to thee, " Come home! "

    T.   What could I do?   I could not step from out
My bonds; nor meet, save there, with Pow'rs so kind.
There, Melibœus, I beheld that youth
For whom each year twelve days my altars smoke.
Thus answered he my yet unanswered prayer:
" Feed still, my lad, your kine, and yoke your bulls."

    M.   Happy old man!   Thy lands are yet thine own!
Lands broad enough for thee, although bare stones
And marsh choke every field with reedy mud.
Strange pastures shall not vex thy teeming ewes,
Nor neighbouring flocks shed o'er them rank disease.
Happy old man!   Here, by familiar streams
And holy springs, thou'lt catch the leafy cool.

Here, as of old, yon hedge, thy boundary line,
Its willow-buds a feast for Hybla's bees,
Shall with soft whisperings woo thee to thy sleep.
Here, 'neath the tall cliff, shall the vintager
Sing carols to the winds: while all the time
Thy pets, the stockdoves, and the turtles make
Incessantly their moan from aery elms.

    T.   Aye, and for this shall slim stags graze in air,
And ocean cast on shore the shrinking fish;
For this, each realm by either wandered o'er,
Parthians shall Arar drink, or Tigris Gauls;
Ere from this memory shall fade that face!

    M.   And we the while must thirst on Libya's sands,
O'er Scythia roam, and where the Cretan stems
The swift Oaxes; or, with Britons, live
Shut out from all the world. Shall I e'er see,
In far-off years, my fatherland? the turf
That roofs my meagre hut? see, wondering last,
Those few scant cornblades that are realms to me?
What! must rude soldiers hold these fallows trim?
That corn barbarians? See what comes of strife,
Poor people—where we sowed, what hands shall reap!
Now, Melibœus, pr'thee graft thy pears,
And range thy vines! Nay on, my she-goats, on,
Once happy flock! For never more must I,
Outstretched in some green hollow, watch you hang
From tufted crags, far up: no carols more
I'll sing: nor, shepherded by me, shall ye
Crop the tart willow and the clover-bloom.

    T.   Yet here, this one night, thou mayst rest with me,
Thy bed green branches. Chestnuts soft have I
And mealy apples, and our fill of cheese.
Already, see, the far-off chimneys smoke,
And deeper grow the shadows of the hills.

Charles Stuart Calverley

Eclogue IV

The Messiah

SICILIAN Muse, begin a loftier strain !
Tho' lowly shrubs, and trees that shade the plain,
Delight not all; Sicilian Muse, prepare
To make the vocal woods deserve a consul's care.
The last great age, foretold by sacred rhymes,
Renews its finished course: Saturnian times
Roll round again; and mighty years, begun
From their first orb, in radiant circles run.
The base degenerate iron offspring ends;
A golden progeny from heaven descends.
O chaste Lucina, speed the mother's pains,
And haste the glorious birth ! thy own Apollo reigns !
The lovely boy, with his auspicious face,
Shall Pollio's consulship and triumph grace;
Majestic months set out with him to their appointed
    race.
The father banished virtue shall restore,
And crimes shall threat the guilty world no more.
The son shall lead the life of gods, and be
By gods and heroes seen, and gods and heroes see.
The jarring nations he in peace shall bind,
And with paternal virtues rule mankind.
Unbidden Earth shall wreathing ivy bring,
And fragrant herbs (the promises of spring),
As her first offerings to her infant king.
The goats with strutting dugs shall homeward speed,
And lowing herds secure from lions feed.
His cradle shall with rising flowers be crowned:
The serpent's brood shall die; the sacred ground
Shall weeds and poisonous plants refuse to bear;
Each common bush shall Syrian roses wear.
But when heroic verse his youth shall raise,
And form it to hereditary praise,

Unlaboured harvests shall the fields adorn,
And clustered grapes shall blush on every thorn;
The knotted oaks shall showers of honey weep,
And thro' the matted grass the liquid gold shall creep.
Yet of old fraud some footsteps shall remain:
The merchant still shall plough the deep for gain;
Great cities shall with walls be compassed round,
And sharpened shares shall vex the fruitful ground;
Another Tiphys shall new seas explore;
Another Argo land the chiefs upon the Iberian shore;
Another Helen other wars create,
And great Achilles urge the Trojan fate.
But when to ripened manhood he shall grow,
The greedy sailor shall the seas forego;
No keel shall cut the waves for foreign ware,
For every soil shall every product bear.
The labouring hind his oxen shall disjoin;
No plough shall hurt the glebe, no pruning hook the
	vine;
Nor wool shall in dissembled colours shine.
But the luxurious father of the fold,
With native purple, or unborrowed gold,
Beneath his pompous fleece shall proudly sweat;
And under Tyrian robes the lamb shall bleat.
The Fates, when they this happy web have spun,
Shall bless the sacred clue, and bid it smoothly run.
Mature in years, to ready honours move,
O of celestial seed! O foster son of Jove!
See, labouring Nature calls thee to sustain
The nodding frame of heaven, and earth, and main!
See to their base restored, earth, seas, and air;
And joyful ages, from behind, in crowding ranks appear.
To sing thy praise, would Heaven my breath prolong,
Infusing spirits worthy such a song,
Not Thracian Orpheus should transcend my lays,
Nor Linus crowned with never-fading bays;

Tho' each his heavenly parent should inspire;
The Muse instruct the voice, and Phœbus tune the lyre.
Should Pan contend in verse, and thou my theme,
Arcadian judges should their god condemn.
Begin, auspicious boy, to cast about
Thy infant eyes, and, with a smile, thy mother single out:
Thy mother well deserves that short delight,
The nauseous qualms of ten long months and travail to
    requite.
Then smile: the frowning infant's doom is read;
No god shall crown the board, nor goddess bless the bed.

John Dryden

Eclogue VII

Corydon and Thyrsis

BENEATH a holm repaired two jolly swains
(Their sheep and goats together grazed the plains),
Both young Arcadians, both alike inspired
To sing, and answer as the song required.
Daphnis, as umpire, took the middle seat,
And fortune thither led my weary feet;
For, while I fenced my myrtles from the cold,
The father of my flock had wandered from the fold.
Of Daphnis I inquired: he, smiling, said:
" Dismiss your fear," and pointed where he fed;
" And, if no greater cares disturb your mind,
Sit here with us, in covert of the wind.
Your lowing heifers, of their own accord,
At watering time will seek the neighbouring ford.
Here wanton Mincius winds along the meads,
And shades his happy banks with bending reeds.
And see, from yon old oak that mates the skies,
How black the clouds of swarming bees arise."
What should I do ! Nor was Alcippe nigh,
Nor absent Phyllis could my care supply,

To house, and feed by hand my weaning lambs,
And drain the strutting udders of their dams.
Great was the strife betwixt the singing swains;
And I preferred my pleasure to my gains.
Alternate rhyme the ready champions chose:
These Corydon rehearsed, and Thyrsis those.

CORYDON.   Ye Muses, ever fair, and ever young,
Assist my numbers, and inspire my song.
With all my Codrus, O inspire my breast !
For Codrus, after Phœbus, sings the best.
Or, if my wishes have presum'd too high,
And stretched their bounds beyond mortality,
The praise of artful numbers I resign,
And hang my pipe upon the sacred pine.

THYRSIS.   Arcadian swains, your youthful poet crown
With ivy wreaths; tho' surly Codrus frown:
Of, if he blast my Muse with envious praise,
Then fence my brows with amulets of bays,
Lest his ill arts, or his malicious tongue,
Should poison, or bewitch my growing song.

C.   These branches of a stag, this tusky boar
(The first essay of arms untried before)
Young Micon offers, Delia, to thy shrine:
But speed his hunting with thy power divine;
Thy statue then of Parian stone shall stand;
Thy legs in buskins with a purple band.

T.   This bowl of milk, these cakes (our country
      fare),
For thee, Priapus, yearly we prepare,
Because a little garden is thy care;
But, if the falling lambs increase my fold,
Thy marble statue shall be turned to gold.

C.   Fair Galatea, with thy silver feet,
O, whiter than the swan, and more than Hybla sweet,

Tall as a poplar, taper as the bole,
Come, charm thy shepherd, and restore my soul !
Come, when my lated sheep at night return,
And crown the silent hours, and stop the rosy morn !

   T.   May I become as abject in thy sight
As seaweed on the shore, and black as night;
Rough as a bur; deformed like him who chaws
Sardinian herbage to contract his jaws;
Such and so monstrous let thy swain appear,
If one day's absence looks not like a year.
Hence from the field, for shame: the flock deserves
No better feeding while the shepherd starves.

   C.   Ye mossy springs, inviting easy sleep,
Ye trees, whose leafy shades those mossy fountains keep,
Defend my flock ! The summer heats are near,
And blossoms on the swelling vines appear.

   T.   With happy fires our cheerful hearth is crowned;
And firs for torches in the woods abound:
We fear not more the winds and wintry cold,
Than streams the banks, or wolves the bleating fold.

   C.   Our woods, with juniper and chestnuts crowned,
With falling fruits and berries paint the ground ;
And lavish Nature laughs, and strows her stores around :
But, if Alexis from our mountains fly,
Even running rivers leave their channels dry.

   T.   Parched are the plains, and frying is the field,
Nor withering vines their juicy vintage yield;
But, if returning Phyllis bless the plain,
The grass revives, the woods are green again,
And Jove descends in showers of kindly rain.

   C.   The poplar is by great Alcides worn;
The brows of Phœbus his own bays adorn;

The branching vine the jolly Bacchus loves;
The Cyprian queen delights in myrtle groves;
With hazel Phyllis crowns her flowing hair;
And, while she loves that common wreath to wear,
Nor bays, nor myrtle boughs, with hazel shall compare.

    T.   The towering ash is fairest in the woods;
In gardens pines, and poplars by the floods:
But, if my Lycidas will ease my pains,
And often visit our forsaken plains,
To him the towering ash shall yield in woods,
In gardens pines, and poplars by the floods.

    MELIBŒUS.   These rhymes I did to memory commend
When vanquished Thyrsis did in vain contend;
Since when 'tis Corydon among the swains,
Young Corydon without a rival reigns.

John Dryden

ECLOGUE IX
Lycidas and Mæris
LYCIDAS

HO, Mœris! whither on thy way so fast?
This leads to town.

MŒRIS

        O Lycidas, at last
The time is come I never thought to see,
(Strange revolution for my farm and me!)
When the grim captain in a surly tone
Cries out: "Pack up, ye rascals, and be gone."
Kick'd out, we set the best face on 't we could;
And these two kids, t'appease his angry mood,
I bear—of which the Furies give him good!

LYCIDAS

Your country friends were told another tale;
That, from the sloping mountain to the vale,
And dodder'd oak, and all the banks along,
Menalcas sav'd his fortune with a song.

MŒRIS

Such was the news, indeed; but songs and rhymes
Prevail as much in these hard iron times,
As would a plump of trembling fowl, that rise
Against an eagle sousing from the skies.
And, had not Phœbus warn'd me, by the croak
Of an old raven from a hollow oak,
To shun debate, Menalcas had been slain,
And Mœris not surviv'd him, to complain.

LYCIDAS

Now Heav'n defend !   Could barb'rous rage induce
The brutal son of Mars t' insult the sacred Muse !
Who then should sing the nymphs, or who rehearse
The waters gliding in a smoother verse !
Or Amaryllis praise—that heav'nly lay,
That shorten'd, as we went, our tedious way:
" O Tit'rus, tend my herd, and see them fed;
To morning pastures, evening waters, led;
And 'ware the Libyan ridgil's butting head."

MŒRIS

Or what unfinish'd he to Varus read;
" Thy name, O Varus, (if the kinder pow'rs
Preserve our plains, and shield the Mantuan tow'rs,
Obnoxious by Cremona's neighb'ring crime,)
The wings of swans, and stronger-pinion'd rhyme,
Shall raise aloft, and soaring bear above,
Th' immortal gift of gratitude to Jove."

LYCIDAS

Sing on, sing on; for I can ne'er be cloy'd:
So may thy swarms the baleful yew avoid;
So may thy cows their burden'd bags distend,
And trees to goats their willing branches bend.
Mean as I am, yet have the Muses made
Me free, a member of the tuneful trade:
At least the shepherds seem to like my lays;
But I discern their flattr'y from their praise:
I nor to Cinna's ears, nor Varus', dare aspire,
But gabble, like a goose, amidst the swan-like choir.

MŒRIS

'Tis what I have been conning in my mind;
Nor are they verses of a vulgar kind.
" Come, Galatea, come, the seas forsake:
What pleasures can the tides with their hoarse murmurs
        make ?
See, on the shore inhabits purple spring,
Where nightingales their love-sick ditty sing:
See, meads with purling streams, with flow'rs the ground,
The grottoes cool, with shady poplars crown'd;
And creeping vines on arbours weav'd around.
Come, then, and leave the waves' tumultuous roar;
Let the wild surges vainly beat the shore."

LYCIDAS

Or that sweet song I heard with such delight;
The same you sung alone one starry night:
The tune I still retain, but not the words.

MŒRIS

" Why, Daphnis, dost thou search in old records,
To know the seasons when the stars arise ?
See, Cæsar's lamp is lighted in the skies:

The star whose rays the blushing grapes adorn,
And swell the kindly ripening ears of corn.
Under this influence, graft the tender shoot:
Thy children's children shall enjoy the fruit."
The rest I have forgot; for cares and time
Change all things, and untune my soul to rhyme.
I could have once sung down a summer's sun;
But now the chime of poetry is done:
My voice grows hoarse; I feel the notes decay,
As if the wolves had seen me first to-day.
But these, and more than I to mind can bring,
Menalcas has not yet forgot to sing.

LYCIDAS

Thy faint excuses but inflame me more:
And now the waves roll silent to the shore;
Hush'd winds the topmost branches scarcely bend,
As if thy tuneful song they did attend:
Already we have half our way o'ercome;
Far off I can discern Bianor's tomb.
Here, where the labourer's hands have form'd a bow'r
Of wreathing trees, in singing waste an hour.
Rest here thy weary limbs; thy kids lay down:
We've day before us yet to reach the town;
Or if, ere night, the gath'ring clouds we fear,
A song will help the beating storm to bear.
And, that thou may'st not be too late abroad,
Sing, and I'll ease thy shoulders of thy load.

MŒRIS

Cease to request me; let us mind our way:
Another song requires another day.
When good Menalcas comes, if he rejoice,
And find a friend at court, I'll find a voice.

John Dryden

The Georgics

WHAT makes a plenteous harvest, when to turn
The fruitful soil, and when to sow the corn;
The care of sheep, of oxen, and of kine,
And how to raise on elms the teeming vine;
The birth and genius of the frugal bee,
I sing, Mæcenas, and I sing to thee.
    Ye deities, who fields and plains protect,
Who rule the seasons, and the year direct,
Bacchus and fostering Ceres, powers divine,
Who gave us corn for mast, for water, wine;
Ye Fauns, propitious to the rural swains,
Ye nymphs, that haunt the mountains and the plains,
Join in my work, and to my numbers bring
Your needful succour; for your gifts I sing.
And thou, whose trident struck the teeming earth,
And made a passage for the courser's birth;
And thou, for whom the Cæan shore sustains
Thy milky herds, that graze the flow'ry plains;
And thou, the shepherds' tutelary god,
Leave, for a while, O Pan, thy loved abode;
And, if Arcadian fleeces be thy care,
From fields and mountains to my song repair.
Inventor, Pallas, of the fattening oil,
Thou founder of the plough, and ploughman's toil;
And thou, whose hands the shroud-like cypress rear,
Come, all ye gods and goddesses, that wear
The rural honours, and increase the year:
You, who supply the ground with seeds of grain;
And you, who swell those seeds with kindly rain;
And chiefly thou, whose undetermined state
Is yet the business of the gods' debate,
Whether in after time to be declared
The patron of the world, and Rome's peculiar guard,

Or o'er the fruits and seasons to preside,
And the round circuit of the year to guide—
Powerful of blessings, which thou strewest around,
And with thy goddess-mother's myrtle crowned.
Or wilt thou, Cæsar, choose the watery reign,
To smooth the surges, and correct the main?
Then mariners, in storms, to thee shall pray;
Even utmost Thule shall thy power obey,
And Neptune shall resign the fasces of the sea. . . .
Be thou propitious, Cæsar! guide my course,
And to my bold endeavours add thy force:
Pity the poet's and the ploughman's cares;
Interest thy greatness in our mean affairs,
And use thyself betimes to hear and grant our prayers.

John Dryden

QUINTUS HORATIUS FLACCUS

65–8 B.C.

*T*HAT *which will distinguish his style from all other poets is the elegance of his words, and the numerousness of his verse; there is nothing so delicately turned in the Roman language. There appears in every part of his language a kind of noble and bold purity. There is a secret happiness attends his choice, which in Petronius is called* curiosa felicitas. *But the most distinguishing part of all his character seems to me to be his briskness, his jollity, and his good humour.*—JOHN DRYDEN.

To the Ship in which Virgil
sailed to Athens

(ODES, I, 3)

SO may the auspicious Queen of Love,
And the twin Stars (the seed of Jove),
And he who rules the raging wind,
To thee, O sacred ship, be kind,
And gentle breezes fill thy sails,
Supplying soft Etesian gales,
As thou, to whom the Muse commends
The best of poets and of friends,

Dost thy committed pledge restore,
And land him safely on the shore;
And save the better part of me
From perishing with him at sea.
Sure he, who first the passage tried,
In harden'd oak his heart did hide,
And ribs of iron arm'd his side !
Or his at least, in hollow wood
Who tempted first the briny flood;
Nor fear'd the winds' contending roar
Nor billows beating on the shore;
Nor Hyades portending rain;
Nor all the tyrants of the main.
What form of death could him affright
Who, unconcern'd, with steadfast sight,
Could view the surges mounting steep,
And monsters rolling in the deep ?
Could through the ranks of ruin go,
With storms above, and rocks below ?
In vain did Nature's wise command
Divide the waters from the land,
If daring ships, and men profane,
Invade the inviolable main;
The eternal fences overleap,
And pass at will the boundless deep.
No toil, no hardship can restrain
Ambitious man inured to pain;
The more confin'd, the more he tries,
And at forbidden quarry flies.
Thus bold Prometheus did aspire,
And stole from heaven the reed of fire:
A train of ills, a ghastly crew,
The robber's blazing track pursue;
Fierce Famine, with her meagre face,
And fevers of the fiery race,
In swarms the offending wretch surround,

All brooding on the blasted ground;
And limping Death, lash'd on by Fate,
Comes up to shorten half our date.
This made not Dedalus beware,
With borrow'd wings to sail in air:
To hell Alcides forced his way,
Plunged through the lake, and snatch'd the prey.
Nay, scarce the gods, or heavenly climes,
Are safe from our audacious crimes:
We reach at Jove's imperial crown,
And pull the unwilling thunder down.

John Dryden

To Thaliarchus
(ODES, I, 9)

BEHOLD yon mountain's hoary height,
    Made higher with new mounts of snow;
Again behold the winter's weight
    Oppress the labouring woods below:
And streams with icy fetters bound,
Benumb'd and cramp'd to solid ground.

With well-heap'd logs dissolve the cold,
    And feed the genial hearth with fires;
Produce the wine, that makes us bold,
    And sprightly wit and love inspires.
For what hereafter shall betide,
God, if 'tis worth his care, provide.

Let him alone, with what he made,
    To toss and turn the world below:
At his command the storms invade;
    The winds by his commission blow;
Till with a nod he bids them cease,
And then the calm returns, and all is peace.

To-morrow and her works defy,
 Lay hold upon the present hour,
And snatch the pleasures passing by,
 To put them out of Fortune's power.
Nor Love, nor Love's delights, disdain;
Whate'er thou gett'st to-day is gain.

Secure those golden, early joys,
 That youth, unsour'd by sorrow, bears,
Ere withering Time the taste destroys
 With sickness and unwieldy years.
For active sports, for pleasing rest,
This is the time to be possest;
The best is but in season best.

The appointed hour of promis'd bliss,
 The pleasing whisper in the dark,
The half-unwilling, willing kiss,
 The laugh that guides thee to the mark,
When the kind nymph would coyness feign,
And hides but to be found again:
These, these are joys the gods for youth ordain.

     John Dryden

To Mæcenas

(ODES, III, 29)

DESCENDED of an ancient line,
 That long the Tuscan sceptre sway'd,
Make haste to meet the generous wine,
 Whose piercing is for thee delay'd:
 The rosy wreath is ready made;
And artful hands prepare
The fragrant Syrian oil, that shall perfume thy hair.

When the wine sparkles from afar,
 And the well-natur'd friend cries, come away;

Make haste and leave thy business and thy care,
  No mortal interest can be worth thy stay.
Leave, for a while, thy costly country seat;
And, to be great indeed, forget
The nauseous pleasures of the great.
  Make haste and come:
Come and forsake thy cloying store;
Thy turret that surveys from high
  The smoke, and wealth, and noise of Rome,
And all the busy pageantry
That wise men scorn, and fools adore.
Come, give thy soul a loose, and taste the pleasures of
    the poor.
Sometimes 'tis grateful for the rich to try
A short vicissitude, and fit of poverty:
  A savoury dish, a homely treat,
  Where all is plain, where all is neat,
Without the stately spacious room,
The Persian carpet, or the Tyrian loom,
  Clear up the cloudy foreheads of the great.

The sun is in the Lion mounted high;
  The Syrian star barks from afar,
And with his sultry breath infects the sky;
The ground below is parch'd, the heavens above us fry.
  The shepherd drives his fainting flock
  Beneath the covert of a rock,
And seeks refreshing rivulets nigh:
The sylvans to their shades retire,
Those very shades and streams new shades and streams
    require,
And want a cooling breeze of wind to fan the raging fire.
  Thou, what befits the new Lord Mayor;
  And what the city factions dare,
  And what the Gallic arms will do,
  And what the quiver-bearing foe,
  Art anxiously inquisitive to know:

But God has wisely hid from human sight
  The dark decrees of future fate,
And sown their seeds in depths of night.
  He laughs at all the giddy turns of state,
  Where mortals search too soon, and fear too late.

Enjoy the present smiling hour,
And put it out of Fortune's power;
The tide of business, like the running stream,
  Is sometimes high and sometimes low,
  A quiet ebb or a tempestuous flow,
And always in extreme.
Now with a noiseless gentle course
  It keeps within the middle bed;
  Anon it lifts aloft its head,
And bears down all before it with impetuous force;
  And trunks of trees come rolling down,
  Sheep and their folds together drown:
Both house and homestead into seas are borne,
And rocks are from their old foundations torn,
And woods, made thin with winds, their scatter'd
    honours mourn.

Happy the man, and happy he alone,
He, who can call to/day his own:
He who, secure within, can say,
To/morrow do thy worst, for I have lived to/day.
Be fair or foul, or rain or shine,
The joys I have possess'd, in spite of fate, are mine.
Not Heaven itself upon the past has power,
But what has been, has been, and I have had my hour.

Fortune that with malicious joy
  Does man, her slave, oppress,
Proud of her office to destroy,
  Is seldom pleased to bless:
Still various, and inconstant still,
But with an inclination to be ill,

Promotes, degrades, delights in strife,
And makes a lottery of life.
  I can enjoy her while she is kind;
  But when she dances in the wind,
And shakes her wings, and will not stay,
I puff the prostitute away;
  The little or the much she gave, is quietly resign'd;
Content with poverty my soul I arm,
And Virtue, though in rags, will keep me warm.

          What is 't to me,
Who never sail in her unfaithful sea,
If storms arise, and clouds grow black;
If the mast split, and threaten wreck?
Then let the greedy merchant fear
  For his ill-gotten gain,
And pray to gods that will not hear
While the debating winds and billows bear
  His wealth unto the main.
For me, secure from Fortune's blows,
Secure of what I cannot lose,
In my small pinnace I can sail,
  Contemning all the blustering roar;
And running with a merry gale,
With friendly stars my safety seek
Within some little winding creek,
  And see the storm ashore.

John Dryden

Country Life

(Epode 2)

HOW happy in his low degree,
    How rich, in humble poverty, is he,
Who leads a quiet country life;
Discharg'd of business, void of strife,
    And from the griping scrivener free!

Thus, ere the seeds of vice were sown,
  Liv'd men in better ages born,
Who plough'd, with oxen of their own,
  Their small paternal field of corn.
Nor trumpets summon him to war,
  Nor drums disturb his morning sleep,
Nor knows he merchants' gainful care,
  Nor fears the dangers of the deep.
The clamours of contentious law,
  And court and state he wisely shuns,
Nor brib'd with hopes, nor dar'd with awe,
  To servile salutations runs;
But either to the clasping vine
  Does the supporting poplar wed,
Or with his pruning hook disjoin
  Unbearing branches from their head,
  And grafts more happy in their stead;
Or climbing to a hilly steep,
  He views his herds in vales afar,
Or shears his overburden'd sheep,
  Or mead for cooling drink prepares
  Or virgin honey in the jars,
Or, in the now declining year,
  When beauteous Autumn rears his head,
He joys to pull the ripen'd pear,
  And clust'ring grapes with purple spread.
Sometimes beneath an ancient oak,
  Or on the matted grass he lies:
No God of Sleep he need invoke;
  The stream, that o'er the pebbles flies,
  With gentle slumber crowns his eyes.
The wind, that whistles through the sprays,
  Maintains the concert of the song:
And hidden birds with native lays
  The golden sleep prolong.
But when the blast of winter blows,

And hoary frost invests the year,
Into the naked woods he goes,
   And seeks the tusky boar to rear,
   With well-mouth'd hounds and pointed spear !
Or spreads his subtle nets from sight,
   With twinkling glasses, to betray
The larks that in the meshes light,
   Or makes the fearful hare his prey.
Amidst his harmless, easy joys,
   No anxious care invades his health,
Nor love his peace of mind destroys,
   Nor wicked avarice of wealth.
But, if a chaste and pleasing wife,
To ease the business of his life,
Divides with him his household care,
Such as the Sabine matrons were,
Such as the swift Apulian's bride,
   Sunburnt and swarthy though she be,
Will fire for winter nights provide,
   And—without noise—will oversee
His children and his family:
And order all things till he come,
Sweaty and overlabour'd, home;
If she in pens his flocks will fold,
   And then produce her dairy store
With wine to drive away the cold,
   And unbought dainties of the poor;
Not oysters of the Lucrine lake
   My sober appetite would wish,
   Nor turbot, or the foreign fish
That rolling tempests overtake,
   And hither waft the costly dish.
Not heathpoult, or the rarer bird
   Which Phasis or Ionia yields,
More pleasing morsels would afford
   Than the fat olives of my fields;

Than shards or mallows for the pot,
  That keep the loosened body sound,
Or than the lamb, that falls by lot
  To the just guardian of my ground.
Amidst these feasts of happy swains,
  The jolly shepherd smiles to see
His flock returning from the plains.
  The farmer is as pleas'd as he,
To view his oxen sweating smoke,
Hear on their necks the loosen'd yoke;
  To look upon his menial crew,
That sit around his cheerful hearth,
  And bodies spent in toil renew
With wholesome food and country mirth.

  This Alphius said within himself;
    Resolv'd to leave the wicked town,
    And live retir'd upon his own,
    He call'd his money in:
    But the prevailing love of pelf
    Soon split him on the former shelf,—
    He put it out again.

                John Dryden

The Immortality of Verse
(ODES, IV, 9)

LEST you should think that verse shall die,
  Which sounds the silver Thames along,
Taught on the wings of truth to fly
  Above the reach of vulgar song;

Though daring Milton sits sublime,
  In Spenser native Muses play;
Nor yet shall Waller yield to time,
  Nor pensive Cowley's mortal lay.

Sages and chiefs long since had birth
  Ere Cæsar was, or Newton named;
These raised new empires o'er the earth,
  And those, new heavens and systems framed.

Vain was the chief's, the sage's pride !
  They had no poet, and they died.
In vain they schemed, in vain they bled !
  They had no poet, and are dead.

Alexander Pope

To Fuscus Aristus

(Epistles, I, 10)

HEALTH from the lover of the country, me,
Health to the lover of the city, thee.
A difference in our souls this only proves;
In all things else, we pair like married doves.
But the warm nest and crowded dove-house thou
Dost like: I loosely fly from bough to bough,
And rivers drink, and all the shining day
Upon fair trees or mossy rocks I play;
In fine, I live and reign, when I retire
From all that you equal with heaven admire;
Like one at last from the priest's service fled,
Loathing the honeyed cakes, I long for bread.
Would I a house for happiness erect,
Nature alone should be the architect;
She'd build it more convenient than great,
And doubtless in the country choose her seat:
Is there a place doth better helps supply
Against the wounds of winter's cruelty ?
Is there an aid that gentlier does assuage
The mad celestial dog's, or lion's rage ?
Is it not there that sleep (and only there)
Nor noise without, nor cares within does fear ?

Does art through pipes a purer water bring
Than that which Nature strains into a spring?
Can all your tap'stries, or your pictures, show
More beauties than in herbs and flowers do grow?
Fountains and trees our wearied pride do please,
Ev'n in the midst of gilded palaces;
And in your towns that prospect gives delight
Which opens round the country to our sight.
Men to the good from which they rashly fly,
Return at last; and their wild luxury
Does but in vain with those true joys contend,
Which Nature did to mankind recommend.
The man who changes gold for burnish'd brass,
Or small right gems for larger ones of glass,
Is not at length more certain to be made
Ridiculous, and wretched by the trade,
Than he who sells a solid good to buy
The painted goods of pride and vanity.
If thou be wise, no glorious fortune choose,
Which 'tis but pain to keep, yet grief to lose;
For, when we place ev'n trifles in the heart,
With trifles, too, unwillingly we part.
An humble roof, plain bed, and homely board
More clear untainted pleasures do afford
Than all the tumult of vain greatness brings
To kings, or to the favourites of kings.
The hornèd deer by Nature arm'd so well,
Did with the horse in common pasture dwell;
And when they fought, the field it always won;
Till the ambitious horse begg'd help of man,
And took the bridle, and thenceforth did reign
Bravely alone, as lord of all the plain.
But never after could he the rider get
From off his back, or from his mouth the bit.
So they, who poverty too much do fear,
T'avoid that weight, a greater burden bear;

That they might power above their equals have,
To cruel masters they themselves enslave.
For gold, their liberty exchang'd we see,
That fairest flower which crowns humanity.
And all this mischief does upon them light,
Only, because they know not how, aright,
That great, but secret, happiness to prize,
That's laid up in a little, for the wise:
That is the best and easiest estate
Which to a man sits close, but not too straight;
'Tis like a shoe, it pinches and it burns,
Too narrow; and too large, it overturns.
My dearest friend ! stop thy desires at last,
And cheerfully enjoy the wealth thou hast:
And, if me seeking still for more you see,
Chide and reproach, despise and laugh at me.
Money was made, not to command our will,
But all our lawful pleasures to fulfil :
Shame ! woe to us, if we our wealth obey:
The horse doth with the horseman run away.

Abraham Cowley

The Profane
(Odes, III, 1)

HENCE, ye profane ! I hate you all;
Both the great vulgar, and the small.
To virgin minds, which yet their native whiteness
    hold,
Nor yet discoloured with the love of gold,
        That jaundice of the soul,
    (Which makes it look so gilded and so foul,)
To you, ye very few, these truths I tell;
The Muse inspires my song ; hark, and observe it
    well.
    We look on men, and wonder at such odds

'Twixt things that were the same by birth;
We look on kings, as giants of the earth,
   These giants are but pigmies to the gods.
The humblest bush and proudest oak
Are but of equal proof against the thunder-stroke.
Beauty and strength, and wit, and wealth, and power,
   Have their short flourishing hour;
   And love to see themselves, and smile,
And joy in their preëminence awhile:
      Ev'n so in the same land,
Poor weeds, rich corn, gay flowers, together stand;
Alas ! death mows down all with an impartial hand:
And all ye men, whom greatness does so please,
   Ye feast, I fear, like Damocles:
   If ye your eyes could upwards move,
(But ye, I fear, think nothing is above,)
Ye would perceive by what a little thread
   The sword still hangs over your head:
   No tide of wine would drown your cares;
No mirth or music over-noise your fears:
The fear of death would you so watchful keep,
As not t'admit the image of it, Sleep.
Sleep is a god too proud to wait in palaces,
And yet so humble too, as not to scorn
   The meanest country cottages:
   His poppy grows among the corn.
The halcyon Sleep will never build his nest
      In any stormy breast.
    'Tis not enough that he does find
   Clouds and darkness in their mind;
   Darkness but half his work will do:
   'Tis not enough; he must find quiet too.
The man, who in all wishes he does make
   Does only Nature's counsel take,
That wise and happy man will never fear
    The evil aspect of the year;

Nor tremble, though two comets should appear;
He does not look in almanacs, to see
    Whether he fortunate shall be:
Let Mars and Saturn in the heavens conjoin,
And what they please against the world design,
    So Jupiter within him shine.
If of your pleasures and desires no end be found,
God to your cares and fears will set no bound.
    What would content you? who can tell?
Ye fear so much to lose what ye have got,
    As if ye liked it well:
Ye strive for more, as if ye liked it not.
    Go, level hills, and fill up seas,
Spare naught that may your wanton fancy please:
But, trust me, when you have done all this,
Much will be missing still, and much will be amiss.

Abraham Cowley

To Licinius

(ODES, II, 10)

RECEIVE, dear friend, the truths I teach;
    So shalt thou live beyond the reach
      Of adverse Fortune's power;
Not always tempt the distant deep,
Nor always timorously creep
      Along the treacherous shore.

He that holds fast the golden mean,
And lives contentedly between
      The little and the great,
Feels not the wants that pinch the poor,
Nor plagues that haunt the rich man's door,
      Embittering all his state.

The tallest pines feel most the power
Of wintry blasts; the loftiest tower
    Comes heaviest to the ground;
The bolts that spare the mountain's side,
His cloud-capt eminence divide,
    And spread the ruin round.

The well-inform'd philosopher
Rejoices with a wholesome fear,
    And hopes, in spite of pain;
If winter bellow from the north,
Soon the sweet spring comes dancing forth,
    And Nature laughs again.

What if thine heaven be overcast?
The dark appearance will not last;
    Expect a brighter sky.
The god, that strings the silver bow,
Awakes sometimes the Muses too,
    And lays his arrows by.

If hindrances obstruct thy way,
Thy magnanimity display,
    And let thy strength be seen;
But oh! if Fortune fill thy sail
With more than a propitious gale,
    Take half thy canvas in.

                        William Cowper

Persian Fopperies

(ODES, I, 38)

BOY, I hate their empty shows,
    Persian garlands I detest,
Bring not me the late-blown rose
    Lingering after all the rest:

Plainer myrtle pleases me
  Thus outstretched beneath my vine,
Myrtle more becoming thee,
  Waiting with thy master's wine.

William Cowper

To Venus

(ODES, IV, 1)

VENUS, again thou mov'st a war
  Long intermitted, pray thee, pray thee spare !
I am not such, as in the reign
  Of the good Cynara I was; refrain,
Sour mother of sweet Loves, forbear
  To bend a man, now at his fiftieth year,
Too stubborn for commands so slack:
  Go where youth's soft entreaties call thee back.
More timely hie thee to the house
  (With thy bright swans) of Paulus Maximus:
There jest and feast, make him thine host
  If a fit liver thou dost seek to toast.
For he's both noble, lovely, young,
  And for the troubled client fills his tongue:
Child of a hundred arts, and far
  Will he display the ensigns of thy war.
And when he, smiling, finds his grace
  With thee 'bove all his rivals' gifts take place,
He'll thee a marble statue make,
  Beneath a sweet-wood roof, near Alba lake;
There shall thy dainty nostril take
  In many a gum, and for thy soft ear's sake
Shall verse be set to harp and lute,
  And Phrygian hau'boy, not without the flute.
There twice a day in sacred lays,
  The youths and tender maids shall sing thy
    praise !

And in the Salian manner meet
   Thrice 'bout thy altar, with their ivory feet.
Me now, nor girl, nor wanton boy
   Delights, nor credulous hope of mutual joy;
Nor care I now healths to propound
   Or with fresh flowers to girt my temples round.
But why, oh why, my Ligurine,
   Flow my thin tears down these pale cheeks of mine ?
Or why my well-graced words among,
   With an uncomely silence, fails my tongue ?
Hard-hearted, I dream every night
   I hold thee fast ! but fled hence with the light,
Whether in Mars his field thou be,
   Or Tiber's winding streams, I follow thee.

                       Ben Jonson

To Pyrrha
(ODES, I, 5)

WHAT slender youth, bedew'd with liquid odours,
  Courts thee on roses in some pleasant cave,
     Pyrrha ?   For whom bind'st thou
     In wreaths thy golden hair,
Plain in thy neatness ?   O how oft shall he
Of faith and changed gods complain, and seas
     Rough with black winds, and storms
     Unwonted shall admire !
Who now enjoys thee credulous, all gold,
Who, always vacant, always amiable
     Hopes thee, of flattering gales
     Unmindful.   Hapless they
To whom thou untried seem'st fair.   Me, in my vow'd
Picture, the sacred wall declares to have hung
     My dank and dropping weeds
     To the stern god of sea.

                       John Milton

To Sally

(Odes, I, 22)

THE man in righteousness arrayed,
　　A pure and blameless liver,
Needs not the keen Toledo blade,
　　Nor venom-freighted quiver.
What though he wind his toilsome way
　　O'er regions wild and weary—
Through Zara's burning desert stray,
　　Or Asia's jungles dreary:

What though he plough the billowy deep
　　By lunar light, or solar,
Meet the resistless Simoom's sweep,
　　Or iceberg circumpolar !
In bog or quagmire deep and dank
　　His foot shall never settle;
He mounts the summit of Mont Blanc,
　　Or Popocatepetl.

On Chimborazo's breathless height
　　He treads o'er burning lava;
Or snuffs the Bohan Upas blight,
　　The deathful plant of Java.
Through every peril he shall pass,
　　By Virtue's shield protected;
And still by Truth's unerring glass
　　His path shall be directed.

Else wherefore was it, Thursday last,
　　While strolling down the valley,
Defenceless, musing as I passed
　　A canzonet to Sally,
A wolf, with mouth-protruding snout,
　　Forth from the thicket bounded ?
I clapped my hands and raised a shout—
　　He heard—and fled—confounded.

Tangier nor Tunis never bred
   An animal more crabbèd;
Nor Fez, dry/nurse of lions, fed
   A monster half so rabid;
Nor Ararat so fierce a beast
   Has seen since days of Noah;
Nor stronger, eager for a feast,
   The fell constrictor boa.

John Quincy Adams

To an Ambitious Friend

(Odes, II, 11)

OMIT, omit, my simple friend,
Still to inquire how parties tend,
Or what we fix with foreign powers.
If France and we are really friends,
And what the Russian Czar intends,
   Is no concern of ours.

Us not the daily quickening race
Of the invading populace
Shall draw to swell that shouldering herd.
Mourn will we not your closing hour,
Ye imbeciles in present power,
   Doomed, pompous, and absurd !

And let us bear, that they debate
Of all the engine/work of state,
Of commerce, laws, and policy,
The secrets of the world's machine,
And what the rights of man may mean,
   With readier tongue than we.

Only, that with no finer art
They cloak the troubles of the heart
With pleasant smile, let us take care;
Nor with a lighter hand dispose
Fresh garlands of this dewy rose,
    To crown Eugenia's hair.

Of little threads our life is spun,
And he spins ill, who misses one.
But is thy fair Eugenia cold?
Yet Helen had an equal grace,
And Juliet's was as fair a face,
    And now their years are told.

The day approaches, when we must
Be crumbling bones and windy dust;
And scorn us as our mistress may,
Her beauty will no better be
Than the poor face she slights in thee,
    When dawns that day, that day.

Matthew Arnold

The Ship of State

(ODES, I, 14)

O SHIP! new billows sweep thee out
Seaward. What wilt thou? Hold the port, be
    stout.
      See'st not thy mast
How rent by stiff south-western blast?

Thy side, of rowers how forlorn?
Thine hull, with groaning yards, with rigging torn,
      Can ill sustain
The fierce, and ever fiercer main;

Thy gods, no more than sails entire,
From whom yet once thy need might aid require,
　　O Pontic Pine,
The first of woodland stocks is thine,

Yet race and name are but as dust.
Not painted sterns give storm-tost seamen trust;
　　Unless thou dare
To be the sport of storms, beware.

O fold at best a weary weight,
A yearning care and constant strain of late,
　　O shun the seas
That gird those glittering Cyclades.

William Ewart Gladstone

Extremum Tanain

(ODES, III, 10)

BEFORE thy door too long of late,
O Lyce, I bewail my fate;
　　Not Don's barbarian maids, I trow,
　　Would treat their luckless lovers so;
Thou,—thou alone art obstinate.

Hast thou nor eyes nor ears, Ingrate !
Hark ! how the NORTH WIND shakes thy gate !
　　Look ! how the laurels bend with snow
　　Before thy doors !

Lay by thy pride,—nor hesitate,
Lest Love and I grow desperate;
　　If prayers, if gifts for naught must go,
　　If naught my frozen pallor show,—
Beware ! . . . I shall not always wait
　　Before thy doors !

Austin Dobson

Albi, ne doleas

(ODES, I, 33)

LOVE mocks us all. Then cast aside
These tuneful plaints, my Albius tried,
　For heartless Glycera, from thee
　Fled to a younger lover. See,
Low-browed Lycoris burns denied

For Cyrus; he—though goats shall bide
With wolves ere she in him confide—
　Turns, with base suit, to Pholoë:—
　Love mocks us all !

So Venus wills, and joys to guide
'Neath brazen yoke pairs ill-allied
　In form and mind. So linked she me
　(Whom worthier wooed) to Myrtale,
Fair, but less kind than Hadria's tide:—
　Love mocks us all !

Austin Dobson

To Chloë

(ODES, I, 23)

YOU shun me, Chloë, wild and shy
　As some stray fawn that seeks its mother
Through trackless woods. If spring winds sigh
　It vainly strives its fears to smother ;—

Its trembling knees assail each other
　When lizards stir the bramble dry;—
You shun me, Chloë, wild and shy
　As some stray fawn that seeks its mother.

And yet no Libyan lion I—
　　No ravening thing to rend another;
Lay by your tears, your tremors by—
　　A husband's better than a brother ;
Nor shun me, Chloë, wild and shy
　　As some stray fawn that seeks its mother.

Austin Dobson

To the Fountain of Bandusia

(ODES, III, 13)

O FOUNTAIN of Bandusia !
　　Whence crystal waters flow,
　　With garlands gay and wine I'll pay
　　　The sacrifice I owe;
A sportive kid with budding horns
　　I have, whose crimson blood
Anon shall dye and sanctify
　　Thy cool and babbling flood.

O fountain of Bandusia !
　　The Dog-star's hateful spell
No evil brings into the springs
　　That from thy bosom well;
Here oxen, wearied by the plough,
　　The roving cattle here
Hasten in quest of certain rest,
　　And quaff thy gracious cheer.

O fountain of Bandusia !
　　Ennobled shalt thou be,
For I shall sing the joys that spring
　　Beneath yon ilex-tree.
Yes, fountain of Bandusia,
　　Posterity shall know
The cooling brooks that from thy nooks
　　Singing and dancing go.

Eugene Field

Ad Leuconoen
(ODES, I, 11)

IT is not right for you to know, so do not ask, Leuconoë,
How long a life the gods may give or ever we are gone
  away;
Try not to read the Final Page, the ending colophonian,
Trust not the gypsy's tea/leaves, nor the prophets
  Babylonian,
Better to have what is to come enshrouded in obscurity
Than to be certain of the sort and length of our futurity.
Why, even as I monologue on wisdom and longevity
How Time has flown ! Spear some of it !
  The longest life is brevity.

F. P. Adams

Ad Xanthiam Phoceum
(ODES, II, 4)

NAY, Xanthias, feel unashamed
  That she you love is but a servant.
Remember, lovers far more famed
  Were just as fervent.

Achilles loved the pretty slave
  Brisëis for her fair complexion;
And to Tecmessa Ajax gave
  His young affection.

Why, Agamemnon at the height
  Of feasting, triumph, and anointment,
Left everything to keep, one night,
  A small appointment.

And are you sure the girl you love—
  This maid on whom you have your heart set
Is lowly—that she is not of
  The Roman smart set ?

A maiden modest as is she,
    So full of sweetness and forbearance,
Must be all right; her folks must be
    Delightful parents.

Her arms and face I can commend,
    And, as the writer of a poem,
I fain would compliment, old friend,
    The limbs below 'em.

Nay, be not jealous.   Stop your fears.
    My tendencies are far from sporty.
Besides, the number of my years
        Is over forty.

F. P. Adams

Invocation

(ODES, I, 21)

MAIDENS young and virgins tender,
Sing Diana in her splendour;
Boys at play within the hollow,
Sing the flowing-haired Apollo.

(Ye that, moved by love and duty,
Praise Diana's holy beauty,
Shall be granted joys unceasing
And, perhaps, a mate that's pleasing.)

(And if winning words we hit on,
Phœbus may present the Briton,
Persian, Parthian, and the rest, with
All the wars and plagues *we're* blessed with.)

Louis Untermeyer

ALBIUS TIBULLUS

54–18 B.C.

A Pastoral Elegy

LET others pile their yellow ingots high,
　　And see their cultured acres round them spread;
While hostile borderers draw their anxious eye,
　　And at the trumpet's blast their sleep is fled !

Me let my poverty to ease resign;
　　While my bright hearth reflects its blazing cheer;
In season let me plant the pliant vine,
　　And, with light hand, my swelling apples rear !

Hope, fail not thou ! let earth her fruitage yield;
　　Let the brimmed vat flow red with virgin wine;
For, still, some lone bare stump that marks the field,
　　Or antique cross-way stone, with flowers I twine,

In pious rite; and, when the year anew
　　Matures the blossom on the budding spray,
I bear the peasant's God his grateful due;
　　And firstling fruits upon his altar lay.

Still let thy temple's porch, O Ceres ! wear
　　The spiky garland from my harvest field;
And, midst my orchard, against the birds of air,
　　His threatening hook let red Priapus wield !

Ye too, once guardians of a rich domain,
　　Now of poor fields, domestic Gods; be kind !
Then, for unnumbered herds, a calf was slain;
　　Now to your altars is a lamb consigned !

The mighty victim of a scanty soil,
　　A lamb alone shall bleed before your shrine;
While round it shout the youthful sons of toil,
　　"Hail ! grant the harvest ! grant the generous
　　　　wine ! "

Content with little, I no more would tread
  The lengthening road, but shun the summer day,
Where some o'erbranching tree might shade my head;
  And watch the murmuring rivulet glide away.

Nor could I blush to wield the rustic prong,
  The lingering oxen goad; or some stray lamb,
Embosomed in my garment, bear along,
  Or kid forgotten by its heedless dam.

Spare my small flocks ! ye thieves, and wolves, assail
  The wealthier cotes, that ampler booty hold;
Ne'er for my shepherd due lustrations fail;
  I soothe with milk the Goddess of the fold.

Be present, Deities ! nor gifts disdain
  From homely board ; nor cups with scorn survey,
Earthen, yet pure; for such the ancient swain
  Formed for himself and shaped of ductile clay.

I envy not my sires their golden heap;
  Their garners' floors with sheafy corn bespread;
Few sheaves suffice: enough, in easy sleep
  To lay my limbs upon the accustomed bed.

How sweet ! to hear, without, the howling blast,
  And strain a yielding mistress to my breast !
Or, when the gusty torrent's rush has past,
  Sink, lulled by beating rains, to sheltered rest !

Be this my lot; be his the unenvied store,
  Who the drear storm endures and raging seas;
Ah ! perish emeralds and the golden ore,
  If the fond anxious nymph must weep for me.

Messala ! range the earth and main, that Rome
  May shine with trophies of the foes that fell;
But me a beauteous nymph enchains at home,
  At her hard door a sleepless sentinel.

I heed not praise, my Delia ! while with thee;
   Sloth brand my name, so I thy sight behold;
Let me the oxen yoke; oh, come with me !
   On desert mountains I will feed my fold.

And, while I pressed thee in my tender arms,
   Sweet were my slumber on the ragged ground;
What boots the purple couch, if cruel charms
   In wakeful tears the midnight hours have drowned ?

Not the soft plume can yield the limbs repose,
   Nor yet the broidered covering soothe to sleep;
Not the calm streamlet that in murmurs flows,
   With sound oblivious o'er the eyelids creep.

Iron is he who might thy form possess,
   Yet flies to arms and thirsts for plunder's gains;
What though his spear Cicilian squadrons press,
   What though his tent be pitched on conquered plains;

In gold and silver mail conspicuous he
   May stride the steed that, pawing, spurns the sand;
May I my last looks fondly bend on thee,
   And grasp thee with my dying, faltering hand !

And thou wilt weep when, cold, I press the bier,
   That soon shall on the flaming pyre be thrown;
And print the kiss and mingle many a tear;
   Not thine a breast of steel, a heart of stone.

Yes, thou wilt weep !   No youths shall thence return
   With tearless eye; no virgin homeward wend;
But thou forbear to violate my urn,
   Spare thy soft cheeks, nor those loose tresses rend.

Now Fate permits; now blend the sweet embrace;
   Death, cowled in darkness, creeps with stealing tread;
Ill suits with sluggish age love's sprightly grace,
   And murmured fondness with a hoary head !

The light amour be mine; the shivered door;
   The midnight fray; ye trumps and standards, hence !
Here is my camp; bleed they who thirst for ore:
   Wealth I despise in easy competence.

                             Sir Charles Abraham Elton

SEXTUS AURELIUS PROPERTIUS
51–? B.C.

When thou must home

WHEN thou must home to shades of underground,
   And there arrived, a new admirèd guest,
The beauteous spirits do ingirt thee round,
   White Iope, blithe Helen, and the rest,
To hear the stories of thy finished love
From that smooth tongue whose music hell can
     move ;

Then wilt thou speak of banqueting delights,
   Of masks and revels which sweet youth did make,
Of tourneys and great challenges of knights,
   And all these triumphs for thy beauties' sake:
When thou hast told these honours done to thee,
Then tell, O tell, how thou didst murder me.

                             Thomas Campion

Ah woe is me
(ELEGIES, I, 1)

AH woe is me, of passion naught I knew
   Till Cynthia's glances pierced my poor heart
     through.
Love ruthless pressed his heel upon my head,
My eyes cast down, my pride all vanquishèd.
He taught me soon to hate each virgin's face
And reckless live in folly's fond embrace.

And now my madness burns for all a year,
While still the anger of the gods I bear.

Milanion, friend, by labours undismayed
Conquered the scorn of the Iasian maid.
See now he wanders in Parthenian caves,
And now with shaggy monsters blindly raves,
Now the Arcadian rocks repeat his groans
As wounded by Hylæus' club he moans.
But so at last he tamed the flying fair;
Such power in love have loving deeds and prayer.

With me Love lingers still, nor tries his art
To fly his wonted way, and leave my heart.
Come then, ye seers, well skilled the moon to take
And on your altars expiation make;
Come now, my lady's heart to me incline
And make her cheeks turn still more pale than mine.
Then I shall know to you the power belongs
To draw the stars and streams with magic songs.

And you, dear friends, too late my fall to turn,
Seek me some help; with madness now I burn.
I will endure the steel, the cruel fire,
If only I may vent my bitter ire.
Take me to distant lands beyond the sea,
While so no woman knows where I shall be.
Do you remain to whom God has been kind
And grant a mutual bliss with tranquil mind.

Love haunts my days; he never gives me cease;
And Venus turns my nights to bitterness.
I warn you—shun this hell: constant remain,
Nor let your heart range loosely o'er love's plain.
For if too late you give my words belief,
To you remembrance naught will bring but grief.

F. A. Wright

Hylas

(ELEGIES, I, 20)

" THIS warning, Gallus, for thy love I send,
   Nor let it from thy heart unheeded fall.
Thou hast a Hylas too, thy fairest friend,
Whom many a wanton nymph would fain enthral
By Anio's stream, or in the forests tall,
Or at the Giant's Causeway cast her spell,
Or on some wandering river. Shun them all,
Remembering what the Minyæ befell,
And listen to the tale which now to thee I tell.

From Pagasæ—so runs the story old—
The Argo sailed to Phasis' distant land,
And passing by the waves that Hellë hold
With gliding keel drew near the Mysian strand,
Where on the quiet shore the hero band,
The voyage done, their limbs did gently lay,
Making them beds of leaves upon the sand.
There Hylas left his knight—ah woe the day !—
And sought the secret streams of fountains far away.

Scarce had he started when the wingèd twain,
Whom Orithyia by the North Wind bred,
Pursued in haste, his kisses to obtain.
Zetes and Caläis above his head
With downstretched hands in flight alternate sped
To snatch their booty from his cheeks of rose,
While he beneath their wings for refuge fled
And waved a branch to scare his treacherous foes,
And so at last escapes and to the wood-nymphs goes.

Beneath Arganthus' crest there lies a spring,
Wherein to bathe the Thynian nymphs delight.
Above uncared-for dewy apples swing,
And water meadows all around are bright .
With scarlet poppies and with lilies white.

Childlike he cared not why he had been sent;
But now would pluck such flowers as pleased his
    sight
And now in wonder o'er the fountain bent
Enraptured by his beauty's imaged blandishment.

At last, the task remembered, on his arm
He leaned, and in his hands the water took.
At once his beauty did the Naiads charm
Who 'neath the wave their wonted dance forsook,
And, as the lad bent forward, rose to look,
And drew him through the water.   Loud he cried
For help.   Alcides at his voice awoke,
And from afar with " Hylas " loud replied;
But only Echo answered from the fountain side.

Long did the hero seek him on the shore,
Vexing his weary feet against the stone
Of cruel mountains: long the pain he bore,
While every lake he searched and hillside lone,
And to untamed Ascanius made his moan.
Ah that his fate may make thee, Gallus, wise !
Guard well thy Hylas now he is thine own;
Nor trust our nymphs with so desired a prize.
For Fortune often mocks the careless lover's eyes."

F. A. Wright

Revenge to Come
(ELEGIES, III, 25)

I WAS a joke at dinners; aye, any would-be wit
  Might use me for a target, and I must stomach it.
  Five years I could be loyal; but now, you'll often
    mourn,
  Biting your nails for anguish, the faith at last outworn.

Nay, weeping will not touch me—I know that trick of
    old;
You always weep from ambush, I cannot be cajoled.
I shall depart in tears, but my wrongs will check their
    flow;
Ours was a team well sorted—you could not leave it so.
So now, my mistress' threshold, where oft my tear-drops
    fell,
And thou, the door I haunted, I bid ye both farewell.
May age afflict you, Cynthia, with ill-dissembled years,
And may you see the wrinkles your fading beauty fears.
And when your glass flings at you the ruin pictured
    there,
Go curse them, every wrinkle, and every whitening hair.
Be you in turn excluded, and suffer proud disdain,
And all you did to others be done to you again.
So fate shall soon avenge me—my page bids you give
    ear—
Your beauty waits this ending. Woman, believe—and
    fear !

Kirby Flower Smith

PUBLIUS OVIDIUS NASO

43 B.C.—A.D. 18

A Captive of Love

(ELEGIES, I, 2)

WHAT makes my bed seem hard, seeing it is soft ?
    Or why slips down the coverlet so oft ?
    Although the nights be long, I sleep not though
    My sides are sore with tumbling to and fro.
    Were Love the cause, it's like I should descry him;
    Or lies he close, and shoots where none can spy him ?
    'Twas so he struck me with a slender dart;
    'Tis cruel Love turmoils my captive heart.

Yielding or struggling, do we give him might?
Let's yield: a burden easily borne is light!
I saw a brandisht fire increase in strength;
Which being not shaked, I saw it die at length.
Young oxen newly yoked are beaten more
Than oxen which have drawn the plough before:
And rough jades' mouths with stubborn bits are torn;
But managed horses' heads are lightly borne.
Unwilling lovers Love doth more torment
Than such as in their bondage feel content.
Lo, I confess, I am thy captive, I!
And hold my conquered hands for thee to tie.
What needst thou war? I sue to thee for grace:
With arms to conquer armless men is base!
Yoke Venus' doves, put myrtles on thy hair:
Vulcan will give thee chariots rich and fair.
The people thee applauding, thou shalt stand,
Guiding the harmless pigeons with thy hand:
Young men and women shalt thou lead as thrall;
So will thy triumph seem magnifical:
I, lately caught, will have a new-made wound,
And captive-like be manacled and bound:
Good meaning, shame and such as seek Love's wrack,
Shall follow thee, their hands tied at their back:
Thee all shall fear and worship as a king;
Io-triumphing shall thy people sing;
Smooth speeches, Fear, and Rage shall by thee ride,
Which troops have always been on Cupid's side:
Thou with these soldiers conquer'st Gods and men;
Take these away, where is thine honour then?
Thy mother shall from Heaven applaud this show,
And on their faces heaps of roses strow:
With beauty of thy wings thy fair hair gilded,
Ride, golden Love, in chariot richly builded.
Unless I err, full many shalt thou burn,
And give wounds infinite at every turn:

In spite of thee, forth will thine arrows fly;
A scorching flame burns all the standers-by.
So having conquered Ind, was Bacchus' hue:
Thee pompous birds, and him two tigers drew.
Then, seeing I grace thy show in following thee,
Forbear to hurt thyself in spoiling me.
Behold thy kinsman Cæsar's prosperous bands,
Who guards the conqueror with his conquering hands.

Christopher Marlowe

Lente, Lente

(ELEGIES, I, 14)

THE old man's fair-haired consort, whose dewy axle-
    tree
Brings morning to us mortals, now rises from the Sea.
I pray you, stay, Aurora; and to your Memnon's
    shade
A sacrifice—I vow it—shall every year be made.
'Tis now my love is by me, her lips are mine to kiss,
Her arms are twined about me—is any hour like this?
'Tis cool, and one is sleepy, and from their slender
    throats
The little feathered songsters pour forth their liquid
    notes.
Now prithee, Rosy Fingers, why take such parlous
    pains
To hurry? No one wants you! Then stay those
    dewy reins.
Ere you arrive, the sailor can watch his stars and keep
His course, nor wander blindly amid the vasty deep;
With you, the weary traveller must rise and hie away,
Must rise the cruel soldier and arm him for the fray;
The hind resumes his mattock and grubs the
    stubborn soil,

The slow and patient oxen begin their day of toil;
Schoolboys you cheat of slumber, to go at your com,
 mands
Where pedagogues are waiting to smack their tender
 hands;
You summon to the courthouse the bailsmen, where
 they taste
The pain of paying dearly for one word said in haste.
The lawyers find you hateful, i' faith, and always will;
You wake them every morning to new contention still.
That girls cease toiling sometimes, 'twere surely fair
 to ask;
But no, you rouse the spinners each to her daily task.
All else I might put up with; but who was ever known
To make the girls rise early, who had one of his own?
How oft I've prayed that Darkness refuse to give you
 place,
How oft, that Stars might brave you, nor flee before
 your face;
How oft, I've prayed some whirlwind an axle,tree might
 twist,
Or that a courser stumble and stick in some thick mist!
Why hurry, spiteful goddess? I see it now, alack,
Why Memnon was so swarthy—his mother's heart was
 black!
I wish poor old Tithonus had power to testify
To what he knows—'twould make you the scandal of
 the sky!
Your spouse is old and feeble; that's why you leave
 your bower
And mount your hateful chariot at such an early hour!
If Cephalus replaced him, you know you'd clasp him
 tight,
And cry out, "Pray, go slowly, ye coursers of the
 Night!"
Why pester me, a lover? Your spouse is all but dead;

But did I urge him on you, or ever bid you wed?
How oft, the while he slumbers, our sovereign Lady
    Moon—
And she more fair than you are—comes to Endymion.
Jove joined two nights in one; I dare swear the tale is
    true,
For Jove was then a lover—and tired of seeing you!
You'd know Aurora heard me—she turned so rosy red;
The day though came no later, in spite of all I said.

Kirby Flower Smith

Winter at Tomi

(TRISTIA)

THE snow lies deep: nor sun nor melting shower
   Serves to abate the winter's icy power.
    One fall has scarcely come another's there,
    And stays in drifts unmelted all the year.
    Fierce and tempestuous is the North-wind's sway;
It levels towers of stone and carries roofs away.

    With skins and trousers men keep out the cold;
    Naught but their faces can your eyes behold.
    Into one mass their hair is frozen tight,
    Their beards with hoary rime hang glistening white.
    Nor need they jars their liquor to confine,
They do not quaff a cup, they break a bit of wine.

    Water is brittle here; you use a spade;
    And running streams by frost are solid made.
    Even the Danube flows with waves concealed,
    The dark blue surface into ice congealed.
    On foot we go across the unmoving tide
And horses' hoofs ring loud where once their oarsmen
    plied.

F. A. Wright

From the Metamorphoses

MAGIC

YE elves of hills, brooks, standing lakes, and groves,
And ye that on the sands with printless foot
Do chase the ebbing Neptune, and do fly him
When he comes back ; you demi-puppets that
By moonshine do the green sour ringlets make,
Whereof the ewe not bites; and you whose pastime
Is to make midnight mushrooms, that rejoice
To hear the solemn curfew; by whose aid,
Weak masters though ye be, I have bedimm'd
The noontide sun, call'd forth the mutinous winds,
And 'twixt the green sea and the azur'd vault
Set roaring war; to the dread rattling thunder
Have I given fire, and rifted Jove's stout oak
With his own bolt; the strong-bas'd promontory
Have I made shake, and by the spurs pluck'd up
The pine and cedar; graves at my command
Have wak'd their sleepers, op'd, and let 'em forth
By my so potent art.

William Shakespeare

BAUCIS AND PHILEMON

THEN Lelex rose, an old experienced man,
And thus, with sober gravity, began:
" Heaven's power is infinite: earth, air, and sea,
The manufactur'd mass, the making power obey:
By proof to clear your doubt; in Phrygian ground
Two neighbouring trees, with walls encompass'd
  round,
Stand on a moderate rise, with wonder shown;
One a hard oak, a softer linden one:
I saw the place, and them, by Pittheus sent
To Phrygian realms, my grandsire's government.
Not far from thence is seen a lake, the haunt

Of coots, and of the fishing cormorant:
Here Jove with Hermes came; but in disguise
Of mortal men conceal'd their deities;
One laid aside his thunder, one his rod,
And many toilsome steps together trod:
For harbour at a thousand doors they knock'd;
Not one of all the thousand but was lock'd.
At last a hospitable house they found,
A homely shed; the roof, not far from ground,
Was thatch'd with reeds and straw together bound.
There Baucis and Philemon lived, and there
Had lived long married, and a happy pair:
Now old in love, though little was their store,
Inured to want, their poverty they bore,
Nor aim'd at wealth, professing to be poor.
For master or for servant here to call
Were all alike, where only two were all.
Command was none, where equal love was paid,
Or rather both commanded, both obey'd.
    " From lofty roofs the gods repulsed before,
Now stooping, enter'd through the little door:
The man (their hearty welcome first express'd)
A common settle drew for either guest,
Inviting each his weary limbs to rest.
But ere they sat, officious Baucis lays
Two cushions stuff'd with straw, the seat to raise;
Coarse, but the best she had; then rakes the load
Of ashes from the hearth, and spreads abroad
The living coals, and, lest they should expire,
With leaves and bark she feeds her infant fire.
It smokes; and then with trembling breath she blows,
Till in a cheerful blaze the flames arose.
With brushwood and with chips she strengthens these
And adds at last the boughs of rotten trees.
The fire thus form'd, she sets the kettle on
(Like burnish'd gold the little seether shone);

Next took the coleworts which her husband got
From his own ground (a small, well-water'd spot);
She stripp'd the stalks of all their leaves; the best
She cull'd, and them with handy care she dress'd.
High o'er the hearth a chine of bacon hung;
Good old Philemon seized it with a prong,
And from the sooty rafter drew it down,
Then cut a slice, but scarce enough for one;
Yet a large portion of a little store,
Which for their sakes alone he wish'd were more.
This in the pot he plunged without delay,
To tame the flesh, and drain the salt away.
The time between, before the fire they sat,
And shorten'd the delay by pleasing chat.
  " A beam there was, on which a beechen pail
Hung by the handle, on a driven nail:
This fill'd with water, gently warmed, they set
Before their guests; in this they bathed their feet,
And after with clean towels dried their sweat.
This done, the host produced the genial bed,
Sallow the foot, the borders, and the stead,
Which with no costly coverlet they spread,
But coarse old garments; yet such robes as these
They laid alone at feasts on holidays.
The good old housewife, tucking up her gown,
The table sets; the invited gods lie down.
The trivet-table of a foot was lame,
A blot which prudent Baucis overcame,
Who thrust beneath the limping leg a sherd;
So was the mended board exactly rear'd:
Then rubb'd it o'er with newly-gather'd mint,
A wholesome herb, that breathed a grateful scent.
Pallas began the feast, where first was seen
The parti-colour'd olive, black and green:
Autumnal cornels next in order serv'd,
In lees of wine well pickled and preserved.

A garden salad was the third supply,
Of endive, radishes, and succory:
Then curds and cream, the flower of country fare,
And new-laid eggs, which Baucis' busy care
Turn'd by a gentle fire, and roasted rare.
All these in earthenware were served to board,
And, next in place, an earthen pitcher stored
With liquor of the best the cottage could afford.
This was the table's ornament and pride,
With figures wrought: like pages at his side
Stood beechen bowls; and these were shining clean,
Varnish'd with wax without, and lined within.
By this the boiling kettle had prepared,
And to the table sent the smoking lard;
On which with eager appetite they dine,
A sav'ry bit, that serv'd to relish wine;
The wine itself was suiting to the rest,
Still working in the must, and lately press'd.
The second course succeeds like that before,
Plums, apples, nuts; and of their wintry store
Dry figs, and grapes, and wrinkled dates were set
In canisters, to enlarge the little treat:
All these a milkwhite honey-comb surround,
Which in the midst a country banquet crown'd:
But the kind hosts their entertainment grace
With hearty welcome, and an open face:
In all they did, you might discern with ease
A willing mind, and a desire to please.
    "Meanwhile the beechen bowls went round, and still,
Though often emptied, were observed to fill:
Fill'd without hands, and, of their own accord,
Ran without feet, and danced about the board.
Devotion seiz'd the pair, to see the feast
With wine, and of no common grape, increased;
And up they held their hands, and fell to pray'r,
Excusing, as they could, their country fare.

" One goose they had ('twas all they could allow),
A wakeful sentry, and on duty now,
Whom to the gods for sacrifice they vow:
Her with malicious zeal the couple view'd;
She ran for life, and limping they pursued:
Full well the fowl perceived their bad intent,
And would not make her master's compliment;
But persecuted, to the powers she flies,
And close between the legs of Jove she lies:
He with a gracious ear the suppliant heard,
And saved her life; then what he was declared,
And own'd the god. ' The neighbourhood,' said he,
' Shall justly perish for impiety:
You stand alone exempted: but obey
With speed, and follow where we lead the way:
Leave these accursed, and to the mountain's height
Ascend, nor once look backward in your flight.'
 " They haste, and what their tardy feet denied,
The trusty staff (their better leg) supplied.
An arrow's flight they wanted to the top,
And there secure, but spent with travel, stop;
They turn their now no more forbidden eyes;
Lost in a lake the floated level lies:
A watery desert covers all the plains,
Their cot alone, as in an isle, remains.
Wondering, with weeping eyes, while they deplore
Their neighbours' fate, and country now no more;
Their little shed, scarce large enough for two,
Seems, from the ground increased, in height and bulk to
    grow.
A stately temple shoots within the skies,
The crotches of their cot in columns rise;
The pavement polish'd marble they behold,
The gates with sculpture graced, the spires and tiles of gold.
 " Then thus the sire of gods, with looks serene:
' Speak thy desire, thou only just of men;

And thou, O woman, only worthy found
To be with such a man in marriage bound.'
  " Awhile they whisper; then, to Jove address'd,
Philemon thus prefers their joint request:
' We crave to serve before your sacred shrine,
And offer at your altar rites divine:
And since not any action of our life
Has been polluted with domestic strife,
We beg one hour of death, that neither she
With widow's tears may live to bury me,
Nor weeping I, with wither'd arms, may bear
My breathless Baucis to the sepulchre.'
The godheads sign their suit. They run their race,
In the same tenor, all the appointed space:
Then, when their hour was come, while they relate
These past adventures at the temple gate,
Old Baucis is by old Philemon seen
Sprouting with sudden leaves of sprightly green:
Old Baucis look'd where old Philemon stood,
And saw his lengthen'd arms a sprouting wood:
New roots their fasten'd feet begin to bind,
Their bodies stiffen in a rising rind:
Then, ere the bark above their shoulders grew,
They give and take at once their last adieu.
' At once farewell, O faithful spouse,' they said;
At once the encroaching rinds their closing lips invade.
E'en yet, an ancient Tyanæan shows
A spreading oak, that near a linden grows;
The neighbourhood confirm the prodigy,
Grave men, not vain of tongue, or like to lie.
I saw myself the garlands on their boughs,
And tablets hung for gifts of granted vows;
And offering fresher up, with pious prayer,
' The good,' said I, ' are God's peculiar care,
And such as honour Heaven, shall heavenly honour
    share.' "

John Dryden

PHÆDRUS

1st century

The Purpose of Fable-writing

WHAT from the founder Æsop fell,
In neat familiar verse I tell:
Twofold's the genius of the page,
To make you smile and make you sage.
But if the critics we displease,
By wrangling brutes and talking trees,
Let them remember, ere they blame,
We're working neither sin nor shame;
'Tis but a play to form the youth
By fiction, in the cause of truth.

Christopher Smart

Æsop at Play

AS Æsop was with boys at play,
And had his nuts as well as they,
A grave Athenian, passing by,
Cast on the sage a scornful eye,
As on a dotard quite bereaved:
Which, when the moralist perceived,
(Rather himself a wit professed
Than the poor subject of a jest)
Into the public way he flung
A bow that he had just unstrung:
" There solve, thou conjurer," he cries,
" The problem, that before thee lies."
The people throng; he racks his brain,
Nor can the thing enjoined explain.
At last he gives it up—the seer
Thus then in triumph made it clear:
" As the tough bow exerts its spring,
A constant tension breaks the string;

But if 'tis let at seasons loose,
You may depend upon its use."
    Thus recreative sports and play
Are good upon a holiday,
And with more spirit they'll pursue
The studies which they shall renew.

Christopher Smart

The Dog in the River

THE churl that wants another's fare
Deserves at least to lose his share.
    As through the stream a Dog conveyed
A piece of meat, he spied his shade
In the clear mirror of the flood,
And thinking it was flesh and blood,
Snapped to deprive him of the treat:—
But mark the glutton's self-defeat,
Missed both another's and his own,
Both shade and substance, beef and bone.

Christopher Smart

The Man and the Weasel

A WEASEL, by a person caught,
And willing to get off, besought
The man to spare. "Be not severe
On him that keeps your pantry clear
Of those intolerable mice."
"This were," says he, "a work of price,
If done entirely for my sake,
And good had been the plea you make:
But since, with all these pains and care,
You seize yourself the dainty fare
On which those vermin used to fall,
And then devour the mice and all,

Urge not a benefit in vain."
This said, the miscreant was slain.
   The satire here those chaps will own,
Who, useful to themselves alone,
And bustling for a private end,
Would boast the merit of a friend.

Christopher Smart

PETRONIUS ARBITER

1st century

Encouragement to Exile

LEAVE thine own home, O youth, seek distant shores !
For thee a larger order somewhere shines—
Fear not thy fate !   For thee through unknown pines
Under the cold north-wind the Danube pours;
For thee in Egypt the untroubled lands
Wait, and strange men behold the setting sun
Fall down and rise.   Greatly be thou as one
Who disembarks, fearless, on alien sands.

Howard Mumford Jones

The Malady of Love is Nerves

NIGHT'S first sweet silence fell, and on my bed
Scarcely I closed defeated eyes in sleep
When fierce Love seized me by the hair, and said,
(Night's bitter vigil he had bade me keep,)
" Thou slave," he said, " a thousand amorous girls
Hast thou not loved ?   And canst thou lie alone ?
O hard of heart ! "   I leaped, and he was gone,
And with my garment in disordered swirls,
And with bare feet I sought his path where none
There was by which to go.   And now I run,
Being weary, and to move brings me no peace;

And turning back is bitter, and to stay
Most shames me in the midmost of my way—
And all men's voices slowly sink and cease;
The singing birds, my dogs that, faithful, keep
My house, the roaring streets, to me are still.
Alone of men, I dread my couch, my sleep—
I follow after Love, lord of my will.

Howard Mumford Jones

We are Such Stuff as Dreams . . .

DREAMS that delude with flying shade men's minds
No airy phantoms are, nor sent by gods
From any shrine of theirs, but each man only
Weaves for himself his dream.   And when in sleep,
Conquered, his limbs repose, and quiet comes,
Then the imponderable mind pursues
In darkness the slow circuit of the day.—
If towns have shook before him and sad cities
Under the weight of flames have been down-razed,
Javelins and fleeing armies he beholds,
The funerals of kings and plains wide-watered
With rivers of shed blood.   If he's an orator,
Statutes and courts appear before his eyes;
He looks with terror on tribunals thronged
With multitudes.   The miser hides his riches
And digs up buried treasure, and the huntsman
Drives through the shaken woods his yelling dogs.
The sailor dreams of shipwreck; from the waves,
Gasping, he takes his vessel, or in death
Seizes on it and sinks.   And the adultress
Dreams, and so yields herself.   The woman writes
In dreams unto her lover: why, the dog,
Sleeping, believes he follows on the hare !—
So all night long endured, the wounds of day
Doubly are sorrow to the miserable.

Howard Mumford Jones

AULUS PERSIUS FLACCUS

34–62

Prologue to the First Satire

I NEVER did on cleft Parnassus dream,
Nor taste the sacred Heliconian stream;
Nor can remember when my brain, inspir'd,
Was by the Muses into madness fir'd.
My share in pale Pyrene I resign,
And claim no part in all the mighty Nine.
Statues, with winding ivy crown'd, belong
To nobler poets, for a nobler song:
Heedless of verse, and hopeless of the crown,
Scarce half a wit, and more than half a clown,
Before the shrine I lay my rugged numbers down.
Who taught the parrot human notes to try,
Or with a voice endued the chatt'ring pie?
'Twas witty want, fierce hunger to appease;
Want taught their masters, and their masters these.
Let gain, that gilded bait, be hung on high;
The hungry witlings have it in their eye:
Pies, crows, and daws, poetic presents bring;
You say they squeak, but they will swear they sing.

John Dryden

LUCIUS VALERIUS MARTIALIS

40–104

N OT *altogether a pleasant period, those evil days of Domitian. But after dwelling in the gloom of Tacitus, after being dazzled by the lightning of Juvenal's rhetoric, it is well for us that we can see that age in the broad sunlight of Martial's genius, that we can use the keen and penetrating yet just and kindly eyes of one who saw it as it really was. As he himself said, " his page has the true relish of human life."*—
KIRBY FLOWER SMITH.

Non amo te

I DO not love thee, Doctor Fell,
The reason why I cannot tell;
But this alone I know full well,
I do not love thee, Dr. Fell.

Tom Brown

Near Neighbours

MY neighbour Hunks's house and mine
Are built so near they almost join;
The windows, too, project so much,
That through the casements we may touch.
Nay, I'm so happy, most men think,
To live so near a man of chink,
That they are apt to envy me,
For keeping such good company:
But he's as far from me, I vow,
As London is from good Lord Howe;
For when old Hunks I chance to meet,
Or one or both must quit the street;
Thus he who would not see old Roger,
Must be his neighbour or his lodger.

Jonathan Swift

Procrastination

TO-MORROW you will live, you always cry;
In what far country does this morrow lie,
That 'tis so mighty long ere it arrive?
Beyond the Indies does this morrow live?
'Tis so far fetched, this morrow, that I fear
'Twill be both very old and very dear.
To-morrow I will live, the fool does say;
To-day itself's too late: the wise lived yesterday.

Abraham Cowley

Verses on Blenheim

SEE, here's the grand approach,
That way is for his grace's coach;
There lies the bridge, and there the clock,
Observe the lion and the cock;
The spacious court, the colonnade,
And mind how wide the hall is made;
The chimneys are so well designed,
They never smoke in any wind:
The galleries contrived for walking,
The windows to retire and talk in;
The council-chamber to debate,
And all the rest are rooms of state.
Thanks, sir, cried I, 'tis very fine,
But where d'ye sleep, or where d'ye dine?
I find by all you have been telling
That 'tis a house, but not a dwelling.

Jonathan Swift

Inviting a Friend to Supper

TO-NIGHT, grave sir, both my poor house and I
Do equally desire your company.
Not that we think us worthy such a guest,
But that your worth will dignify our feast,
With those that come; whose grace may make that
seem
Something, which else could hope for no esteem.
It is the fair acceptance, sir, creates
The entertainment perfect, not the cates.
Yet shall you have, to rectify your palate,
An olive, capers, or some better salad
Ushering the mutton, with a short-legged hen
If we can get her, full of eggs, and then
Lemons, and wine for sauce; to these, a coney
Is not to be despaired of for our money;

And though fowl now be scarce, yet there are clerks,
The sky not falling, think we may have larks.
I'll tell you of more, and lie, so you will come:
Of partridge, pheasant, woodcock, of which some
May yet be there; and godwit if we can,
Knat, rail, and ruff too. Howsoe'er, my man
Shall read a piece of Virgil, Tacitus,
Livy, or of some better book to us,
Of which we'll speak our minds, amidst our meat;
And I'll profess no verses to repeat:
To this if aught appear, which I not know of,
That will the pastry, not my paper, show of.
Digestive cheese and fruit there sure will be,
But that which most doth take my Muse and me,
Is a pure cup of rich Canary wine,
Which is the Mermaid's now, but shall be mine:
Of which had Horace or Anacreon tasted,
Their lives, as do their lines, till now had lasted.
Tobacco, nectar, or the Thespian spring,
Are all but Luther's beer, to this I sing.
Of this we will sup free, but moderately,
And we will have no Pooly or Parrot by;
Nor shall our cups make any guilty men,
But, at our parting, we will be as when
We innocently met. No simple word
That shall be uttered at our mirthful board,
Shall make us sad next morning; or affright
The liberty that we'll enjoy to-night.

Ben Jonson

To his Book

TO read my book, the virgin shy
   May blush, while Brutus standeth by:
   But when he's gone, read through what's writ,
   And never stain a cheek for it.

Robert Herrick

Post-obits and the Poets

HE unto whom thou art so partial,
Oh, reader ! is the well-known Martial,
The Epigrammatist: while living,
Give him the fame thou wouldst be giving:
So shall he hear, and feel, and know it—
Post-obits rarely reach a poet.

Lord Byron

Bought Locks

THE golden hair that Gulla wears
Is hers: who would have thought it ?
She swears 'tis hers, and true she swears,
For I know where she bought it.

Sir John Harington

Critics

THE readers and the hearers like my books,
And yet some writers cannot them digest;
But what care I ? for when I make a feast,
I would my guests should praise it, not the cooks.

Sir John Harington

Quits

TO John I owed great obligation;
But John unhappily thought fit
To publish it to all the nation;
Sure John and I are more than quit.

Matthew Prior

Temperament

IN all thy humours, whether grave or mellow,
Thou'rt such a touchy, testy, pleasant fellow,
Hast so much wit and mirth and spleen about thee,
There is no living with thee nor without thee.

Joseph Addison

A Hinted Wish

YOU told me, Maro, whilst you live
You'd not a single penny give,
But that, whene'er you chanced to die,
You'd leave a handsome legacy:
You must be mad beyond redress,
If my next wish you cannot guess !

Samuel Johnson

To Chloe

I COULD resign that eye of blue
  Howe'er its splendour used to thrill me;
And even that cheek of roseate hue,—
  To lose it, Chloe, scarce would kill me.

That snowy neck I ne'er should miss,
  However much I've raved about it;
And sweetly as that lip can kiss,
  I *think* I could exist without it.

In short, so well I've learned to fast,
  That, sooth my love, I know not whether
I might not bring myself at last,
  To—do without you altogether.

Thomas Moore

What makes a Happy Life

WHAT makes a happy life, dear friend,
If thou wouldst briefly learn, attend—
An income left, not earned by toil;
Some acres of a kindly soil;
The pot unfailing on the fire;
No lawsuits, seldom town attire;
Health; strength with grace; a peaceful mind;
Shrewdness with honesty combined;
Plain living; equal friends and free ;
Evenings of temperate gayety;
A wife discreet yet blithe and bright;
Sound slumber that lends wings to night.
With all thy heart embrace thy lot,
Wish not for death, and fear it not.

Goldwin Smith

On the Death of a Young and Favourite Slave

DEAR youth, too early lost, who now art laid
Beneath the turf in green Labicum's glade,
O'er thee no storied urn, no laboured bust
I rear to crumble with the crumbling dust ;
But tapering box and shadowy vine shall wave,
And grass, with tears bedewed, shall clothe thy grave.
These gifts my sorrowing love to thee shall bring,
Gifts ever fresh and deathless as the Spring.
O when to me the fatal hour shall come,
Mine be as lowly and as green a tomb !

Goldwin Smith

Erotion

DEAR father and dear mother: Let me crave
Your loving kindness there beyond the grave
For my Erotion, the pretty maid
Who bears these lines.   Don't let her be afraid !
She's such a little lassie—only six—
To toddle down that pathway to the Styx
All by herself !   Black shadows haunt those steeps
And Cerebus the Dread who never sleeps.
May she be comforted, and may she play
About you merry as the livelong day,
And in her childish prattle often tell
Of that old master whom she loved so well.
Oh earth, bear lightly on her !   'Tis her due;
The little girl so lightly bore on you.

Kirby Flower Smith

Sextus the Usurer

WHENEVER he observes me purchasing
A slave, a cloak, or any such-like thing,
Sextus the usurer—a man, you know,
Who's been my friend for twenty years or so—
In fear that I may ask him for a loan
Thus whispers, to himself. but in a tone
Such as he knows I cannot choose but hear:
" I owe Secundus twenty thousand clear,
I owe Phileus thirty thousand more,
And then there's Phœbus—that's another four—
Besides, there's interest due on each amount,
And not one farthing in my bank account ! "
O stratagem profound of my old friend !
'Tis hard refusing when you're asked to lend;
But to refuse before you're asked displays
Inventive genius worthy of the bays !

Kirby Flower Smith

DECIMUS JUNIUS JUVENALIS

60–140

Celestial Wisdom

(FROM THE TENTH SATIRE)

MUST hapless man, in ignorance sedate,
Roll darkling down the torrent of his fate?
Must no dislike alarm, no wishes rise,
No cries invoke the mercies of the skies?
Inquirer, cease: petitions yet remain,
Which Heaven may hear: nor deem religion vain.
Still raise for good the supplicating voice,
But leave to Heaven the measure and the choice.
Safe in his power, whose eyes discern afar
The secret ambush of a specious prayer,
Implore his aid, in his decisions rest,
Secure, whate'er he gives, he gives the best.
Yet when the sense of sacred presence fires,
And strong devotion to the skies aspires,
Pour forth thy fervours for a healthful mind,
Obedient passions, and a will resigned;
For love, which scarce collective man can fill;
For patience, sovereign o'er transmuted ill;
For faith, that, panting for a happier seat,
Counts death kind Nature's signal of retreat.
These goods for man the laws of Heaven ordain,
These goods he grants, who grants the power to gain;
With these celestial Wisdom calms the mind,
And makes the happiness she does not find.

Samuel Johnson

PUBLIUS PAPINIUS STATIUS

61–96

Sleep

WHAT sin was mine, sweet, silent boy-god, Sleep,
Or what, poor sufferer, have I left undone,
That I should lack thy guerdon, I alone ?
Quiet are the brawling streams: the shuddering deep
Sinks, and the rounded mountains feign to sleep.
The high seas slumber pillowed on Earth's breast;
All flocks and birds and beasts are stilled in rest,
But my sad eyes their nightly vigil keep. . . .
    O ! if beneath the night some happier swain,
Entwined in loving arms, refuse thy boon
In wanton happiness,—come hither soon,
Come hither, Sleep.   Let happier mortals gain
The full embrace of thy soft angel wing:
But touch me with thy wand, or hovering
Above mine eyelids sweep me with thy train.

W. H. Fyfe

THE EMPEROR HADRIAN

76–138

The Dying Christian to his Soul

VITAL spark of heavenly flame !
Quit, oh quit this mortal frame:
    Trembling, hoping, lingering, flying,
    Oh the pain, the bliss of dying !
Cease, fond Nature, cease thy strife,
And let me languish into life.

Hark ! they whisper; Angels say,
Sister Spirit, come away.
    What is this absorbs me quite ?
    Steals my senses, shuts my sight,

Drowns my spirits, draws my breath ?
Tell me, my Soul, can this be Death ?

The world recedes; it disappears !
Heaven opens on my eyes ! my ears
  With sounds seraphic ring:
  Lend, lend your wings ! I mount ! I fly !
  O Grave ! where is thy Victory ?
  O Death ! where is thy Sting ?

                                Alexander Pope

ANONYMOUS

3rd century (?)

The Vigil of Venus

THE *ringing phrases turn and return, and expand and interlace and
  fold in, as though set in motion by a strain of music; the first line
perpetually repeating itself through the poem like a thread of gold in the
pattern or a phrase in the music. Flower-garlanded and myrtle-shrouded,
the Spring worshippers go dancing through the fields that break before
them into a sheet of flowers; among them the boy Love goes with his
torch and his arrows; the whole land sings with the voices of innumerable
birds.*—J. W. MACKAIL.

  *Love he to-morrow, who loved never;
  To-morrow, who hath loved, persever.*

THE spring appears, in which the earth
  Receives a new harmonious birth;
  When all things mutual love unites;
  When birds perform their nuptial rites;
  And fruitful by her watery lover
  Each grove its tresses doth recover.
  Love's Queen to-morrow, in the shade,
  Which by these verdant trees is made,
  Their sprouting tops in wreaths shall bind,
  And myrtles into arbours wind;
  To-morrow, raised on a high throne,
  Dione shall her laws make known.

> *Love he tomorrow, who loved never;*
> *Tomorrow, who hath loved, persever.*

Then the round ocean's foaming flood
Immingled with celestial blood,
'Mongst the blue purple of the main,
And horses whom two feet sustain,
Rising Dione did beget
With fruitful waters dropping wet.

> *Love he tomorrow, who loved never;*
> *Tomorrow, who hath loved, persever.*

With flowery jewels everywhere
She paints the purple-colour'd year;
She, when the rising bud receives
Favonius' breath, thrusts forth the leaves,
The naked roof with these t' adorn;
She the transparent dew o' th' morn,
Which the thick air of night still uses
To leave behind, in rain diffuses;
These tears with orient brightness shine,
Whilst they with trembling weight decline,
Whose every drop, into a small
Clear orb distill'd, sustains its fall.
Pregnant with these the bashful rose
Her purple blushes doth disclose.
The drops of falling dew that are
Shed in calm nights by every star,
She in her humid mantle holds,
And then her virgin leaves unfolds.
I' th' morn, by her command, each maid
With dewy roses is array'd;
Which from Cythera's crimson blood,
From the soft kisses Love bestow'd,
From jewels, from the radiant flame,
And the sun's purple lustre, came.
She to her spouse shall married be
Tomorrow; not ashamed that he

Should with a single knot untie
Her fiery garment's purple dye.

> *Love he to-morrow, who loved never;*
> *To-morrow, who hath loved, persever.*

The goddess bade the nymphs remove
Unto the shady myrtle grove;
The boy goes with the maids, yet none
Will trust, or think Love tame is grown,
If they perceive that anywhere
He arrows doth about him bear.
Go fearless, nymphs, for Love hath laid
Aside his arms, and tame is made.
His weapons by command resign'd,
Naked to go he is enjoin'd,
Lest he hurt any by his craft,
Either with flame, or bow, or shaft.
But yet take heed, young nymphs, beware
You trust him not, for Cupid's fair,
Lest by his beauty you be harm'd;
Love naked is completely arm'd.

> *Love he to-morrow, who loved never;*
> *To-morrow, who hath loved, persever.*

Fair Venus virgins sends to thee,
Indued with equal modesty:
One only thing we thee desire,
Chaste Delia, for a while retire;
That the wide forest, that the wood,
May be unstain'd with savage blood.
She would with prayers herself attend thee,
But that she knew she could not bend thee;
She would thyself to come have pray'd,
Did these delights beseem a maid.
Now might'st thou see with solemn rites
The Chorus celebrate three nights;

'Mongst troops whom equal pleasure crowns,
To play and sport upon thy downs;
'Mongst garlands made of various flowers,
'Mongst ever-verdant myrtle bowers.
Ceres nor Bacchus absent be,
Nor yet the poet's deity.
All night we wholly must employ
In vigils, and in songs of joy;
None but Dione must bear sway
Amongst the woods; Delia, give way.

> *Love he to-morrow, who loved never;*
> *To-morrow, who hath loved, persever.*

She the tribunal did command
Deck'd with Hyblæan flowers should stand;
She will in judgment sit; the Graces
On either side shall have their places;
Hybla, the flowers pour forth, whate'er
Was brought thee by the welcome year;
Hybla, thy flowery garment spread,
Wide as is Enna's fruitful mead;
Maids of the country here will be;
Maids of the mountain come to see;
Hither resort all such as dwell
Either in grove, or wood, or well.
The wing'd boy's mother every one
Commands in order to sit down;
Charging the virgins that they must
In nothing Love, though naked, trust.

> *Love he to-morrow, who loved never;*
> *To-morrow, who hath loved, persever.*

Let the fresh covert of a shade
Be by these early flowers display'd,
To-morrow (which with sports and play
We keep) was Æther's wedding day;

When first the father of the spring
Did out of clouds the young year bring.
The husband Shower then courts his spouse,
And in her sacred bosom flows,
That all which that vast body bred
By this defluxion may be fed:
Produced within, she all there sways
By a hid spirit, which by ways
Unknown diffused through soul and veins,
All things both governs and sustains.
Piercing through the unsounded sea,
And earth, and highest heaven, she
All places with her power doth fill,
Which through each part she doth distil;
And to the world the mystic ways
Of all production open lays.

> *Love he to-morrow, who loved never;*
> *To-morrow, who hath loved, persever.*

She to the Latins did transfer
The Trojan nephews; and by her
Was the Laurentian virgin won,
And join'd in marriage to her son.
By her assistance did Mars gain
A votaress from Vesta's fane.
To marriage Romulus betray'd
The Sabine women, by her aid,
(Of Romans the wide-spreading stem,)
And in the long descent of them
In whom that offspring was dilated,
Cæsar her nephew she created.

> *Love he to-morrow, who loved never;*
> *To-morrow, who hath loved, persever.*

The fields are fruitful made by pleasure;
The fields are rich in Venus' treasure;

And Love, Dione's son, fame yields
For truth, his birth had in the fields;
As soon as born the field reliev'd him,
Into its bosom first receiv'd him;
She bred him from his infant hours
With the sweet kisses of the flowers.

Love he to-morrow, who loved never;
To-morrow, who hath loved, persever.

See how the bulls their sides distend,
And broom-stalks with the burthen bend;
Now every one doth safely lie
Confined within his marriage tie;
See, with their husbands here are laid
The bleating flocks beneath the shade.
The warbling birds on every tree
The goddess wills not silent be.
The vocal swans on every lake,
With their hoarse voice a harsh sound make;
And Tereus' hapless maid beneath
The poplar's shade her song doth breathe;
Such as might well persuade thee, love
Doth in those trembling accents move;
Not that the sister in those strains
Of the inhuman spouse complains.
We silent are whilst she doth sing,
How long in coming is my spring?
When will the time arrive, that I
May swallow-like my voice untie?
My muse for being silent flies me,
And Phœbus will no longer prize me:
So did Amiclæ once, whilst all
Silence observed, through silence fall.

Love he to-morrow, who loved never;
To-morrow, who hath loved, persever.

                              Thomas Stanley

DECIMUS MAGNUS AUSONIUS

310–395

Idyll of the Rose

'TWAS spring, and dawn returning breathed new-born
  From saffron skies the bracing chill of morn.
Before day's orient chargers went a breeze,
That whispered: Rise, the sweets of morning seize !
In watered gardens where the cross-paths ran,
Freshness and health I sought ere noon began:
I watched from bending grasses how the rime
In clusters hung, or gemmed the beds of thyme;
How the round beads, on herb and leaf outspread,
Rolled with the weight of dews from heaven's bright
    shed ;
Saw the rose-gardens in their Pæstan bloom
Hoar 'neath the dawn-star rising through the gloom.
On every bush those separate splendours gleam,
Doomed to be quenched by day's first arrowy beam.
Here might one doubt: doth morn from roses steal
Their redness, or the rose with dawn anneal ?
One hue, one dew, one morn makes both serene;
Of star and flower one Venus reigns the queen.
Perchance one scent have they: the star's o'erhead
Far, far exhales, the flower's at hand is shed.
Goddess of star, goddess of rose no less,
The Paphian flings o'er both her crimson dress.
Now had the moment passed wherein the brood
Of clustering buds seemed one twin sisterhood.
This flower, enlaced with leaves, shows naught but
    green;
That shoots a roseate streak from forth the screen:
One opes her pyramid and purple spire,
Emerging into plenitude of fire:
Another thrusts her verdant veil aside,

Counting her petals one by one with pride:
Expands her radiant cup of gorgeous hue,
And brings dense hidden veins of gold to view:
She who had burned erewhile, a flower of flame,
Now pales and droops her fainting head with shame:—
So that I mused how swift time steals all worth,
How roses age and wither with their birth;
Yea, while I speak, the flower with crimson crowned
Hath fallen and shed her glories on the ground.
So many births, forms, fates with changes fraught,
One day begins and one day brings to naught !
Grieve we that flowers should have so short a grace,
That Nature shows and steals her gifts apace ?
Long as the day, so long the red rose lasts;
Eld following close on youth her beauty blasts:
That flower which Phosphor newly born had known,
Hesper returning finds a wrinkled crone:
Yet well if, though some brief days past she die,
Her life be lengthened through posterity !
Pluck roses, girl, when flower, when youth is new,
Mindful the while that thus time flies for you.

John Addington Symonds

To his Wife

BE life what it has been, and let us hold,
Dear wife, the names we each gave each of old;
And let not time work change upon us two,
I still your boy, and still my sweetheart you.
What though I outlive Nestor ? and what though
You in your turn a Sibyl's years should know ?
Ne'er let us know old age or late or soon,
Count not the years, but take of each its boon.

Terrot Reaveley Glover

CLAUDIUS CLAUDIANUS

c. 400

The Old Man of Verona

HAPPY the man, who his whole time doth bound
Within th' inclosure of his little ground.
Happy the man whom the same humble place,
The hereditary cottage of his race,
From his first rising infancy has known,
And by degrees sees gently bending down,
With natural propension, to that earth
Which both preserved his life, and gave him birth.
Him no false distant lights, by fortune set,
Could ever into foolish wanderings get.
He never dangers either saw or feared:
The dreadful storms at sea he never heard.
He never heard the shrill alarms of war,
Or the worse noises of the lawyers' bar.
No change of consuls marks to him the year;
The change of seasons is his calendar.
The cold and heat, winter and summer shows;
Autumn by fruits, and spring by flowers, he knows.
He measures time by landmarks, and has found
For the whole day the dial of his ground.
A neighbouring wood, born with himself, he sees,
And loves his old contemporary trees.
He has only heard of near Verona's name,
And knows it, like the Indies, but by fame.
Does with a like concernment notice take
Of the Red Sea, and of Benacus' lake.
Thus health and strength he to a third age enjoys
And sees a long posterity of boys.
About the spacious world let others roam,
The voyage, life, is longest made at home.

Abraham Cowley

Epitaph

FATE to beauty still must give
Shortened life and fugitive;
All that's noble, all that's fair
Suddenly to death repair.
Here a lovely woman lies,
Venus in her hair and eyes;
Since with these she must divide
Heaven's envy, here she died.

Howard Mumford Jones

SIDONIUS APOLLINARIS

5th century

Invitation to the Dance

SPREAD the board with linen snow,
Bid ivy and the laurel grow
Over it, and with them twine
The green branches of the vine.
Bring great baskets that shall hold
Cytisus and the marigold,
Cassia and starwort bring
And crocuses, till everything,
Couch and sideboard, all shall be
A garland of perfumery.
Then with balsam-perfumed hand
Smooth dishevelled locks; and stand
Frankincense about, to rise—
An Arabian sacrifice—
Smoking to the lofty roof.

Next, let darkness be a proof
That our lamps with day may vie,
Glittering from the chamber's sky.
Only in their bowls be spilled

Oil nor grease, but have them filled
With such odorous balm as came
From the east to give them flame.
Then bid loaded servants bring
Viands that shall please a king,
Bowing underneath the weight
Of chased silver rich and great.
Last, in bowl and patera
And in cauldron mingle a
Portion of Falernian wine
With due nard, while roses shine
Wreathed about the cup and round
The cup's tripod.   We'll confound—
Where the garlands sway in grace
From vase to alabaster vase—
All the measures of the dance;
And our languid limbs shall glance
In a mazy, Mænad play.—
Step and voice shall Bacchus sway,
And in garment let each man
Be a Dionysian !

Howard Mumford Jones

MEDIÆVAL LATIN STUDENTS' SONGS
12th–13th centuries

A Song of the Open Road

WE in our wandering,
    Blithesome and squandering,
        Tara, tantara, teino !

Eat to satiety,
Drink with propriety;
    Tara, tantara, teino !

Laugh till our sides we split,
Rags on our hides we fit;
　　Tara, tantara, teino !

Jesting eternally,
Quaffing infernally:
　　Tara, tantara, teino !

Craft's in the bone of us,
Fear 'tis unknown of us:
　　Tara, tantara, teino !

When we're in neediness,
Thieve we with greediness,
　　Tara, tantara, teino !

Brother catholical,
Man apostolical,
　　Tara, tantara, teino !

Say what you will have done,
What you ask 'twill be done !
　　Tara, tantara, teino !

Folk, fear the toss of the
Horns of philosophy !
　　Tara, tantara, teino !

Here comes a quadruple
Spoiler and prodigal !
　　Tara, tantara, teino !

Licence and vanity
Pamper insanity:
　　Tara, tantara, teino !

As the Pope bade us do,
Brother to brother's true:
　　Tara, tantara, teino !

Brother, best friend, adieu !
Now, I must part from you !
   Tara, tantara, teino !

When will our meeting be ?
Glad shall our greeting be !
   Tara, tantara, teino !

Vows valedictory
Now have the victory;
   Tara, tantara, teino !

Clasped on each other's breast,
Brother to brother pressed,
   Tara, tantara, teino !
           John Addington Symonds

A Pastoral

THERE went out in the dawning light
   A little rustic maiden;
Her flock so white, her crook so slight,
   With fleecy new wool laden.

Small is the flock, and there you'll see
   The she-ass and the wether;
This goat's a he, and that's a she,
   The bull-calf and the heifer.

She looked upon the greensward, where
   A student lay at leisure:
" What do you there, young sir, so fair ? "
   " Come, play with me, my treasure ! "
           John Addington Symonds

There's no Lust Like to Poetry

SWEET in goodly fellowship
  Tastes red wine and rare O !
But to kiss a girl's ripe lip
  Is a gift more fair O !
Yet a gift more sweet, more fine,
  Is the lyre of Maro !
While these three good gifts were mine,
  I'd not change with Pharaoh.

Bacchus wakes within my breast
  Love and love's desire,
Venus comes and stirs the blessed
  Rage of Phœbus' fire;
Deathless honour is our due
  From the laurelled sire:
Woe should I turn traitor to
  Wine and love and lyre !

Should a tyrant rise and say,
  " Give up wine ! " I'd do it;
" Love no girls ! " I would obey,
  Though my heart should rue it.
" Dash thy lyre ! " suppose he saith,
  Naught should bring me to it;
" Yield thy lyre or die ! " my breath,
  Dying, should thrill through it !

John Addington Symonds

LATIN HYMNS
Veni Creator Spiritus

CREATOR SPIRIT, by whose aid
  The world's foundations first were laid,
Come, visit ev'ry pious mind;
Come, pour thy joys on humankind;

From sin and sorrow set us free,
And make thy temples worthy thee.

   O source of uncreated light,
The Father's promis'd Paraclite !
Thrice holy fount, thrice holy fire,
Our hearts with heav'nly love inspire;
Come, and thy sacred unction bring
To sanctify us, while we sing !

   Plenteous of grace, descend from high,
Rich in thy sev'nfold energy,
Thou strength of his almighty hand,
Whose pow'r does heav'n and earth command !
Proceeding Spirit, our defence,
Who dost the gifts of tongues dispense,
And crown'st thy gift with eloquence !

   Refine and purge our earthy parts;
But, O, inflame and fire our hearts !
Our frailties help, our vice control,
Submit the senses to the soul;
And when rebellious they are grown,
Then lay thy hand, and hold 'em down.

   Chase from our minds th' infernal foe,
And peace, the fruit of love, bestow;
And lest our feet should step astray,
Protect and guide us in the way.

   Make us eternal truths receive,
And practise all that we believe:
Give us thyself, that we may see
The Father and the Son, by thee.

   Immortal honour, endless fame,
Attend th' Almighty Father's name:
The Saviour Son be glorified,
Who for lost man's redemption died;
And equal adoration be,
Eternal Paraclete, to thee.

John Dryden

The Te Deum

THEE, Sovereign God, our grateful accents praise;
We own thee Lord, and bless thy wondrous ways;
To thee, Eternal Father, earth's whole frame,
With loudest trumpets, sounds immortal fame.
Lord God of Hosts ! for thee the heavenly powers
With sounding anthems fill the vaulted towers.
Thy Cherubims thrice, Holy, Holy, Holy, cry;
Thrice, Holy, all the Seraphims reply,
And thrice returning echoes endless songs supply.
Both heaven and earth thy majesty display;
They owe their beauty to thy glorious ray.
Thy praises fill the loud apostles' choir;
The train of prophets in the song conspire.
Legions of martyrs in the chorus shine,
And vocal blood with vocal music join.
By these thy church, inspir'd by heavenly art,
Around the world maintains a second part;
And tunes her sweetest notes, O God, to thee,
The Father of unbounded majesty;
The Son, ador'd co-partner of thy seat,
And equal everlasting Paraclete.
Thou King of Glory, Christ, of the most high,
Thou co-eternal filial Deity;
Thou who, to save the world's impending doom,
Vouchsaf'dst to dwell within a Virgin's womb;
Old tyrant Death disarm'd, before thee flew
The bolts of heaven, and back the foldings drew,
To give access, and make thy faithful way;
From God's right hand thy filial beams display.
Thou art to judge the living and the dead;
Then spare those souls for whom thy veins have
   bled.
O take us up amongst thy blest above,
To share with them thy everlasting love.

Preserve, O Lord, thy people, and enhance
Thy blessing on thine own inheritance.
For ever raise their hearts, and rule their ways;
Each day we bless thee, and proclaim thy praise:
No age shall fail to celebrate thy name,
No hour neglect thy everlasting fame.
Preserve our souls, O Lord, this day from ill;
Have mercy on us, Lord, have mercy still:
As we have hop'd, do thou reward our pain;
We've hop'd in thee—let not our hope be vain.

John Dryden (?)

Hymn for St. John's Eve

O SYLVAN prophet, whose eternal fame
Echoes from Judah's hills, and Jordan's stream,
The music of our numbers raise,
And tune our voices to thy praise.

A messenger from high Olympus came
To bear the tidings of thy life and name;
And told thy sire each prodigy
That Heaven design'd to work in thee.

Hearing the news, and doubting in surprise,
His falt'ring speech in fetter'd accent dies;
But Providence, with happy choice,
In thee restor'd thy father's voice.

In the recess of nature's dark abode,
Tho' still inclos'd, yet knewest thou thy God!
Whilst each glad parent told and bless'd
The secrets of each other's breast.

John Dryden (?)

Dies Irae

HEAR'ST thou, my soul, what serious things
Both the Psalm and Sibyl sings
Of a sure Judge, from whose sharp ray
The world in flames shall fly away!

O that Fire! before whose face
Heaven and earth shall find no place:
O those Eyes! whose angry light
Must be the day of that dread night.

O that Trump! whose blast shall run
An even round with th' circling Sun,
And urge the murmuring graves to bring
Pale mankind forth to meet his King.

Horror of Nature, Hell, and Death!
When a deep groan from beneath
Shall cry, "We come, we come!" and all
The caves of night answer one call.

O that book! whose leaves so bright
Will set the world in severe light.
O that Judge! whose hand, whose eye
None can endure, yet none can fly.

Ah then, poor soul! what wilt thou say?
And to what patron choose to pray,
When stars themselves shall stagger, and
The most firm foot no more shall stand?

But Thou giv'st leave, dread Lord, that we
Take shelter from Thyself in Thee;
And with the wings of Thine own dove
Fly to Thy sceptre of soft love!

Dear [Lord], remember in that day
Who was the cause Thou cam'st this way;
Thy sheep was strayed, and Thou wouldst be
Even lost Thyself in seeking me !

Shall all that labour, all that cost
Of love, and even that loss, be lost ?
And this loved soul judged worth no less
Than all that way and weariness ?

Just mercy, then, Thy reck'ning be
With my price, and not with me;
'Twas paid at first with too much pain
To be paid twice, or once in vain.

Mercy, my Judge, mercy I cry,
With blushing cheek and bleeding eye;
The conscious colours of my sin
Are red without, and pale within.

O let Thine own soft bowels pay
Thyself, and so discharge that day !
If Sin can sigh, Love can forgive;
O, say the word, my soul shall live !

Those mercies which Thy Mary found,
Or who Thy cross confess'd and crowned,
Hope tells my heart the same loves be
Still alive, and still for me.

Though both my prayers and tears combine,
Both worthless are, for they are mine;
But Thou Thy bounteous self still be,
And show Thou art by saving me.

O when Thy last frown shall proclaim
The flocks of goats to folds of flame,
And all Thy lost sheep found shall be,
Let " Come ye blessed " then call me !

When the dread " *ITE* " shall divide
Those limbs of death from Thy left side,
Let those life-speaking lips command
That I inherit Thy right hand !

O, hear a suppliant heart all crush'd,
And crumpled into contrite dust !
My hope, my fear—my Judge, my Friend !
Take charge of me, and of my end !

Richard Crashaw

ITALIAN

CIULLO D' ALCAMO

c. 1175

Dialogue: Lover and Lady

He: THOU sweetly-smelling fresh red rose
  That near thy summer art,
Of whom each damsel and each dame
  Would fain be counterpart;
O ! from this fire to draw me forth
  Be it in thy good heart:
For night or day there is no rest with me,
Thinking of none, my lady, but of thee.
She: If thou hast set thy thoughts on me,
  Thou hast done a foolish thing.
Yea, all the pine-wood of this world
  Together might'st thou bring,
And make thee ships, and plough the sea
  Therewith for corn-sowing,
Ere any way to win me could be found:
For I am going to shear my locks all round.
He: Lady, before thou shear thy locks
  I hope I may be dead:
For I should lose such joy thereby
  And gain such grief instead.
Merely to pass and look at thee,
  Rose of the garden-bed,
Has comforted me much, once and again.
Oh ! if thou wouldst but love, what were it then !
She: Nay, though my heart were prone to love,
  I would not grant it leave.
Hark ! should my father or his kin
  But find thee here this eve,
Thy loving body and lost breath
  Our moat may well receive.

Whatever path to come here thou dost know,
By the same path I counsel thee to go.
He: And if thy kinsfolk find me here,
    Shall I be drowned then ? Marry,
I'll set, for price against my head,
    Two thousand agostari.
I think thy father would not do't
    For all his lands in Bari.
Long life to the Emperor ! Be God's the praise !
Thou hear'st, my beauty, what thy servant says.
She: And am I then to have no peace
    Morning or evening ?
I have strong coffers of my own
    And much good gold therein;
So that if thou couldst offer me
    The wealth of Saladin,
And add to that the Soldan's money-hoard,
Thy suit would not be anything toward.
He: I have known many women, love,
    Whose thoughts were high and proud,
And yet have been made gentle by
    Man's speech not over-loud.
If we but press ye long enough,
    At length ye will be bow'd;
For still a woman's weaker than a man.
When the end comes, recall how this began.
She: God grant that I may die before
    Any such end do come,—
Before the sight of a chaste maid
    Seem to me troublesome !
I marked thee here all yestereve
    Lurking about my home,
And now I say, Leave climbing, lest thou fall,
For these thy words delight me not at all.
He: How many are the cunning chains
    Thou hast wound round my heart !

Only to think upon thy voice
   Sometimes I groan apart.
For I did never love a maid
   Of this world, as thou art,
So much as I love thee, thou crimson rose.
Thou wilt be mine at last: this my soul knows.
She: If I could think it would be so,
   Small pride it were of mine
That all my beauty should be meant
   But to make thee to shine.
Sooner than stoop to that, I'd shear
   These golden tresses fine,
And make one of some holy sisterhood;
Escaping so thy love, which is not good.
He: If thou unto the cloister fly,
   Thou cruel lady and cold,
Unto the cloister I will come
   And by the cloister hold;
For such a conquest liketh me
   Much better than much gold;
At matins and at vespers I shall be
Still where thou art. Have I not conquered thee ?
She: Out and alack ! wherefore am I
   Tormented in such wise ?
Lord Jesus Christ the Saviour,
   In whom my best hope lies,
O give me strength that I may hush
   This vain man's blasphemies !
Let him seek through the earth; 'tis long and broad:
He will find fairer damsels, O my God !
He: I have sought through Calabria,
   Lombardy, and Tuscany,
Rome, Pisa, Lucca, Genoa,
   All between sea and sea:
Yea, even to Babylon I went
   And distant Barbary:

But not a woman found I anywhere
    Equal to thee, who art indeed most fair.
She: If thou have all this love for me,
      Thou canst no better do
    Than ask me of my father dear
      And my dear mother too:
    They willing, to the abbey-church
      We will together go,
    And, before Advent, thou and I will wed;
    After the which, I'll do as thou hast said.
He: These thy conditions, lady mine,
      Are altogether naught:
    Despite of them, I'll make a net
      Wherein thou shalt be caught.
    What, wilt thou put on wings to fly?
      Nay, but of wax they're wrought,—
    They'll let thee fall to earth, not rise with thee:
    So, if thou canst, then keep thyself from me.
She: Think not to fright me with thy nets
      And such-like childish gear;
    I am safe pent within the walls
      Of this strong castle here;
    A boy before he is a man
      Could give me as much fear.
    If suddenly thou get not hence again,
    It is my prayer thou mayst be found and slain.
He: Wouldst thou in very truth that I
      Were slain, and for thy sake?
    Then let them hew me to such mince
      As a man's limbs may make!
    But meanwhile I shall not stir hence
      Till of that fruit I take
    Which thou hast in thy garden, ripe enough:
    All day and night I thirst to think thereof.
She: None have partaken of that fruit,
      Not Counts nor Cavaliers:

Though many have reached up for it,
    Barons and great Seigneurs,
They all went hence in wrath because
    They could not make it theirs.
Then how canst *thou* think to succeed alone
Who hast not a thousand ounces of thine own ?
He: How many nosegays I have sent
    Unto thy house, sweet soul !
At least till I am put to proof,
    This scorn of thine control.
For if the wind, so fair for thee,
    Turn ever and wax foul,
Be sure that thou shalt say when all is done,
" Now is my heart heavy for him that's gone."
She: If by my grief thou couldst be grieved,
    God send me a grief soon !
I tell thee that though all my friends
    Prayed me as for a boon,
Saying, " Even for the love of us,
    Love thou this worthless loon,"
Thou shouldst not have the thing that thou dost hope.
No, verily: not for the realm o' the Pope.
He: Now could I wish that I in truth
    Were dead here in thy house:
My soul would get its vengeance then;
    Once known, the thing would rouse
A rabble, and they'd point and say,—
    " Lo ! she that breaks her vows,
And, in her dainty chamber, stabs ! "   Love, see:
One strikes just thus: it is soon done, pardie !
She: If now thou do not hasten hence,
    (My curse companioning,)
That my stout friends will find thee here
    Is a most certain thing:
After the which, my gallant sir,
    Thy points of reasoning

May chance, I think, to stand thee in small stead.
Thou hast no friend, sweet friend, to bring thee aid.
He: Thou sayest truly, saying that
    I have not any friend:
    A landless stranger, lady mine,
      None but his sword defend.
One year ago, my love began,
    And now, is this the end ?
Oh ! the rich dress thou worest on that day
Since when thou art walking at my side alway !
She: So 'twas my dress enamoured thee !
    What marvel ? I did wear
    A cloth of samite silver flowered,
      And gems within my hair.
But one more word; if on Christ's Book
    To wed me thou didst swear,
There's nothing now could win me to be thine:
I had rather make my bed in the sea brine.
He: And if thou make thy bed therein,
    Most courteous lady and bland,
    I'll follow all among the waves,
      Paddling with foot and hand;
Then, when the sea hath done with thee,
    I'll seek thee on the sand.
For I will not be conquered in this strife:
I'll wait, but win; or losing, lose my life.
She: For Father, Son, and Holy Ghost,
    Three times I cross myself.
    Thou art no godless heretic,
      Nor Jew, whose God's his pelf:
Even as I know it then, meseems,
    Thou needs must know thyself
That woman, when the breath in her doth cease,
Loseth all savour and all loveliness.
He: Woe's me ! Perforce it must be said
    No craft could then avail:

So that if thou be thus resolved,
I know my suit must fail.
Then have some pity, of thy grace !
Thou mayst, love, very well;
For though thou love not me, my love is such
That 'tis enough for both—yea, overmuch.
She: Is it even so ?   Learn then that I
Do love thee from my heart.
To-morrow, early in the day,
Come here, but now depart.
By thine obedience in this thing
I shall know what thou art,
And if thy love be real or nothing worth;
Do but go now, and I am thine henceforth.
He: Nay, for such promise, my own life,
I will not stir a foot.
I've said, if thou wouldst tear away
My love even from its root,
I have a dagger at my side
Which thou mayst take to do't;
But as for going hence, it will not be.
O hate me not ! my heart is burning me.
She: Think'st thou I know not that thy heart
Is hot and burns to death ?
Of all that thou or I can say,
But one word succoureth.
Till thou upon the Holy Book
Give me thy bounden faith,
God is my witness that I will not yield:
For with thy sword 'twere better to be kill'd.
He: Then on Christ's Book, borne with me still
To read from and to pray,
(I took it, fairest, in a church,
The priest being gone away,)
I swear that my whole self shall be
Thine always from this day.

And now at once give joy for all my grief,
Lest my soul fly, that's thinner than a leaf.
She: Now that this oath is sworn, sweet lord,
    There is no need to speak:
My heart, that was so strong before,
    Now feels itself grow weak.
    If any of my words were harsh,
    Thy pardon: I am meek
Now, and will give thee entrance presently.
It is best so, sith so it was to be.

D. G. Rossetti

FOLCACHIERO DE' FOLCACHIERI
KNIGHT OF SIENA

CANZONE

c. 1175

He speaks of his Condition through Love

ALL the whole world is living without war,
    And yet I cannot find out any peace.
      O God! that this should be!
  O God! what does the earth sustain me for?
  My life seems made for other lives' ill-ease:
    All men look strange to me;
    Nor are the wood-flowers now
    As once, when up above
    The happy birds in love
Made such sweet verses, going from bough to bough.

And if I come where other gentlemen
  Bear arms, or say of love some joyful thing—
    Then is my grief most sore,
And all my soul turns round upon me then:
  Folk also gaze upon me, whispering,
    Because I am not what I was before.

I know not what I am.
  I know how wearisome
  My life is now become,
And that the days I pass seem all the same.

I think that I shall die; yea, death begins;
  Though 'tis no set down sickness that I have,
    Nor are my pains set down.
But to wear raiment seems a burden since
  This came, nor ever any food I crave;
    Not any cure is known
    To me, nor unto whom
    I might commend my case:
    This evil therefore stays
Just where it is, and hope can find no room.

I know that it must certainly be Love:
  No other Lord, being thus set over me,
    Had judged me to this curse;
With such high hand he rules, sitting above,
  That of myself he takes two parts in fee,
    Only the third being hers.
    Yet if through service I
    Be justified with God,
    He shall remove this load,
Because my heart with inmost love doth sigh.

Gentle my lady, after I am gone,
  There will not come another, it may be,
    To show thee love like mine:
For nothing can I do, neither have done,
  Except what proves that I belong to thee
    And am a thing of thine.
    Be it not said that I
    Despaired and perished, then;
    But pour thy grace, like rain,
On him who is burned up, yea, visibly.

D. G. Rossetti

SAINT FRANCIS OF ASSISI

1182–1226

CANTICA

Our Lord Christ: of Order

SET Love in order, thou that lovest Me.
　　Never was virtue out of order found;
And though I fill thy heart desirously,
　　By thine own virtue I must keep My ground:
When to My love thou dost bring charity,
　　Even she must come with order girt and gown'd.
　　　　Look how the trees are bound
　　　　To order, bearing fruit;
　　　　And by one thing compute,
In all things earthly, order's grace or gain.

All earthly things I had the making of
　　Were numbered and were measured then by Me;
And each was ordered to its end by Love,
　　Each kept, through order, clean for ministry.
Charity most of all, when known enough,
　　Is of her very nature orderly.
　　　　Lo, now! what heat in thee,
　　　　Soul, can have bred this rout?
　　　　Thou putt'st all order out.
Even this love's heat must be its curb and rein.

D. G. Rossetti

GUIDO GUINICELLI

13th century

SONNET

He will praise his Lady

YEA, let me praise my lady whom I love:
　　Likening her unto the lily and rose:
　　Brighter than morning star her visage glows;
She is beneath even as her Saint above;

She is as the air in summer which God wove
Of purple and of vermilion glorious;
As gold and jewels richer than man knows.
Love's self, being love for her, must holier prove.
Ever as she walks she hath a sober grace,
Making bold men abashed and good men glad;
If she delight thee not, thy heart must err.
No man dare look on her, his thoughts being base:
Nay, let me say even more than I have said;—
No man could think base thoughts who looked
on her.

D. G. Rossetti

SONNET
Of Moderation and Tolerance

HE that has grown to wisdom hurries not,
But thinks and weighs what Reason bids him do;
And after thinking he retains his thought
Until as he conceived the fact ensue.
Let no man to o'erweening pride be wrought,
But count his state as Fortune's gift and due.
He is a fool who deems that none has sought
The truth, save he alone, or knows it true.
Many strange birds are on the air abroad,
Nor all are of one flight or of one force,
But each after his kind dissimilar:
To each was portioned of the breath of God,
Who gave them divers instincts from one source.
Then judge not thou thy fellows what they are.

D. G. Rossetti

CANZONE
He perceives his Rashness in Love, but has no Choice

I HOLD him, verily, of mean emprise,
Whose rashness tempts a strength too great to bear;
As I have done, alas! who turned mine eyes
Upon those perilous eyes of the most fair.

Unto her eyes I bow'd;
No need her other beauties in that hour
   Should aid them, cold and proud:
As when the vassals of a mighty lord,
   What time he needs his power,
Are all girt round him to make strong his sword.

With such exceeding force the stroke was dealt
  That by mine eyes its path might not be stay'd;
But deep into the heart it pierced, which felt
  The pang of the sharp wound, and waxed afraid ;
   Then rested in strange wise,
As when some creature utterly outworn
   Sinks into bed and lies.
And she the while doth in no manner care,
   But goes her way in scorn,
Beholding herself alway proud and fair.

And she may be as proud as she shall please,
  For she is still the fairest woman found:
A sun she seems among the rest; and these
  Have all their beauties in her splendour drown'd.
   In her is every grace,—
Simplicity of wisdom, noble speech,
   Accomplished loveliness;
All earthly beauty is her diadem,
   This truth my song would teach,—
My lady is of ladies chosen gem.

Love to my lady's service yieldeth me,—
  Will I, or will I not, the thing is so,—
Nor other reason can I say or see,
  Except that where it lists the wind doth blow.
   He rules and gives no sign;
Nor once from her did show of love upbuoy
   This passion which is mine.

It is because her virtue's strength and stir
    So fill her full of joy
That I am glad to die for love of her.

                              D. G. Rossetti

CANZONE

Of the Gentle Heart

WITHIN the gentle heart Love shelters him
    As birds within the green shade of the grove.
Before the gentle heart, in nature's scheme,
    Love was not, nor the gentle heart ere Love.
        For with the sun, at once,
So sprang the light immediately; nor was
        Its birth before the sun's.
And Love hath his effect in gentleness
        Of very self; even as
Within the middle fire the heat's excess.

The fire of Love comes to the gentle heart
    Like as its virtue to a precious stone;
To which no star its influence can impart
    Till it is made a pure thing by the sun:
        For when the sun hath smit
From out its essence that which there was vile
        The star endoweth it.
And so the heart created by God's breath
        Pure, true, and clean from guile,
A woman, like a star, enamoureth.

In gentle heart Love for like reason is
    For which the lamp's high flame is fanned and
        bow'd:
Clear, piercing bright, it shines for its own bliss;
    Nor would it burn there else, it is so proud.

For evil natures meet
With Love as it were water met with fire,
      As cold abhorring heat.
Through gentle heart Love doth a track divine,—
      Like knowing like; the same
As diamond runs through iron in the mine.

The sun strikes full upon the mud all day:
      It remains vile, nor the sun's worth is less.
" By race I am gentle," the proud man doth say:
      He is the mud, the sun is gentleness.
            Let no man predicate
That aught the name of gentleness should have,
            Even in a king's estate,
Except the heart there be a gentle man's.
      The star-beam lights the wave,—
Heaven holds the star and the star's radiance.

God, in the understanding of high Heaven,
      Burns more than in our sight the living sun:
There to behold His Face unveiled is given;
      And Heaven, whose will is homage paid to One,
            Fulfils the things which live
In God, from the beginning excellent.
            So should my lady give
That truth which in her eyes is glorified,
      On which her heart is bent,
To me whose service waiteth at her side.

My lady, God shall ask, " What daredst thou ? "
      (When my soul stands with all her acts review'd;)
" Thou passedst Heaven, into My sight, as now,
      To make Me of vain love similitude.
            To Me doth praise belong,
And to the Queen of all the realm of grace
            Who slayeth fraud and wrong."

Then may I plead: " As though from Thee he came,
Love wore an angel's face:
Lord, if I loved her, count it not my shame."

D. G. Rossetti

GUERZO DI MONTECANTI

13th century

SONNET

He is out of Heart with his Time

IF any man would know the very cause
Which makes me to forget my speech in rhyme,
All the sweet songs I sang in other time,—
I'll tell it in a sonnet's simple clause.
I hourly have beheld how good withdraws
To nothing, and how evil mounts the while:
Until my heart is gnawed as with a file,
Nor aught of this world's worth is what it was.
At last there is no other remedy
But to behold the universal end;
And so upon this hope my thoughts are urged:
To whom, since truth is sunk and dead at sea,
There has no other part or prayer remain'd,
Except of seeing the world's self submerged.

D. G. Rossetti

JACOPO DA LENTINO

13th century

SONNET

Of his Lady in Heaven

I HAVE it in my heart to serve God so
That into Paradise I shall repair,—
The holy place through the which everywhere
I have heard say that joy and solace flow.
Without my lady I were loth to go,—

She who has the bright face and the bright hair;
Because if she were absent, I being there,
My pleasure would be less than naught, I know.
Look you, I say not this to such intent
  As that I there would deal in any sin:
  I only would behold her gracious mien,
  And beautiful soft eyes, and lovely face,
That so it should be my complete content
  To see my lady joyful in her place.

D. G. Rossetti

SONNET

Of his Lady's Face

HER face has made my life most proud and glad;
  Her face has made my life quite wearisome;
  It comforts me when other troubles come,
And amid other joys it strikes me sad.
Truly I think her face can drive me mad;
  For now I am too loud, and anon dumb.
There is no second face in Christendom
Has a like power, nor shall have, nor has had.
What man in living face has seen such eyes,
  Or such a lovely bending of the head,
    Or mouth that opens to so sweet a smile ?
In speech, my heart before her faints and dies,
  And into Heaven seems to be spirited;
    So that I count me blest a certain while.

D. G. Rossetti

CANZONETTA

Of his Lady, and of his making her Likeness

MY Lady mine, I send
  These sighs in joy to thee,
Though, loving till the end,
  There were no hope for me

That I should speak my love;
 And I have loved indeed,
 Though, having fearful heed,
It was not spoken of.

Thou art so high and great
 That whom I love I fear;
Which thing to circumstate
 I have no messenger:
Wherefore to Love I pray,
 On whom each lover cries,
 That these my tears and sighs
Find unto thee a way.

Well have I wished, when I
 At heart with sighs have ach'd,
That there were in each sigh
 Spirit and intellect,
The which, where thou dost sit,
 Should kneel and sue for aid,
 Since I am thus afraid
And have no strength for it.

Thou, lady, killest me,
 Yet keepest me in pain,
For thou must surely see
 How, fearing, I am fain.
Ah ! why not send me still
 Some solace, small and slight,
 So that I should not quite
Despair of thy good will ?

Thy grace, all else above,
 Even now while I implore,
Enamoureth my love
 To love thee still the more.

Yet scarce should I know well
　　A greater love to gain,
　　Even if a greater pain,
Lady, were possible.

Joy did that day relax
　　My grief's continual stress,
When I essayed in wax
　　Thy beauty's life-likeness.
Ah! much more beautiful
　　Than golden-haired Yseult,—
　　Who mak'st all men exult,
Who bring'st all women dule.

And certes without blame
　　Thy love might fall to me,
Though it should chance my name
　　Were never heard of thee.
Yea, for thy love, in fine,
　　Lentino gave me birth,
　　Who am not nothing worth
If worthy to be thine.

　　　　　　　　　　D. G. Rossetti

CANZONETTA
He will neither boast nor lament to his Lady

LOVE will not have me cry
　　For grace, as others do;
Nor as they vaunt, that I
　　Should vaunt my love to you.
For service, such as all
Can pay, is counted small;
Nor is it much to praise
　　The thing which all must know;—
　　Such pittance to bestow
On you my love gainsays.

Love lets me not turn shape
  As chance or use may strike;
As one may see an ape
  Counterfeit all alike.
Then, lady, unto you
Be it not mine to sue,
For grace or pitying.
  Many the lovers be
  That of such suit are free,—
It is a common thing.

A gem, the more 'tis rare,
  The more its cost will mount:
And, be it not so fair,
  It is of more account.
So, coming from the East,
The sapphire is increased
In worth, though scarce so bright;
  I therefore seek thy face
  Not to solicit grace,
Being cheapened and made slight.

So is the colosmine
  Now cheapened, which in fame
Was once so brave and fine,
  But now is a mean gem.
So be such prayers for grace
Not heard in any place;
Would they indeed hold fast
  Their worth, be they not said,
  Nor by true lovers made
Before nine years be past.

Lady, sans sigh or groan,
  My longing thou canst see;
Much better am I known
  Than to myself, to thee.

And is there nothing else
That in my heart avails
For love but groan and sigh ?
    And wilt thou have it thus,
    This love betwixen us ?—
Much rather let me die.

                    D. G. Rossetti

GIACOMINO PUGLIESI

CANZONETTA

13th century

Of his Lady in Absence

THE sweetly-favoured face
    She has, and her good cheer,
Have filled me full of grace
    When I have walked with her.
They did upon that day:
    And everything that pass'd
    Comes back from first to last
Now that I am away.

There went from her meek mouth
    A poor low sigh which made
My heart sink down for drouth.
    She stooped, and sobbed, and said,
" Sir, I entreat of you
    Make little tarrying:
    It is not a good thing
To leave one's love and go."

But when I turned about
    Saying, " God keep you well ! "
As she looked up, I thought
    Her lips that were quite pale

Strove much to speak, but she
 Had not half strength enough:
 My own dear graceful love
Would not let go of me.

I am not so far, sweet maid,
 That now the old love's unfelt:
I believe Tristram had
 No such love for Yseult:
And when I see your eyes
 And feel your breath again,
 I shall forget this pain
And my whole heart will rise.

D. G. Rossetti

CANZONE

Of his Dead Lady

DEATH, why hast thou made life so hard to bear,
 Taking my lady hence? Hast thou no whit
Of shame? The youngest flower and the most fair
 Thou hast plucked away, and the world wanteth it.
O leaden Death, hast thou no pitying?
Our warm love's very spring
 Thou stopp'st, and endest what was holy and meet;
And of my gladdening
Mak'st a most woeful thing,
And in my heart dost bid the bird not sing
 That sang so sweet.

Once the great joy and solace that I had
 Was more than is with other gentlemen:—
Now is my love gone hence, who made me glad.
 With her that hope I lived in she hath ta'en
And left me nothing but these sighs and tears,—
Nothing of the old years
 That come not back again,
Wherein I was so happy, being hers.

Now to mine eyes her face no more appears,
Nor doth her voice make music in mine ears,
  As it did then.

O God, why hast thou made my grief so deep ?
  Why set me in the dark to grope and pine ?
Why parted me from her companionship,
  And crushed the hope which was a gift of thine ?
To think, dear, that I never any more
Can see thee as before !
  Who is it shuts thee in ?
Who hides that smile for which my heart is sore,
And drowns those words that I am longing for,
  Lady of mine ?

Where is my lady, and the lovely face
  She had, and the sweet motion when she walk'd ?—
Her chaste, mild favour—her so delicate grace—
  Her eyes, her mouth, and the dear way she talk'd ?—
Her courteous bending—her most noble air—
The soft fall of her hair ? . . .
My lady—she who to my soul so rare
  A gladness brought !
Now do I never see her anywhere,
And may not, looking in her eyes, gain there
  The blessing which I sought.

So if I had the realm of Hungary,
  With Greece, and all the Almayn even to France,
Or Saint Sophia's treasure-hoard, you see
  All could not give me back her countenance.
For since the day when my dear lady died
From us, (with God being born and glorified,)
  No more pleasaunce
Her image bringeth, seated at my side,
But only tears.   Ay me ! the strength and pride
  Which it brought once.

Had I my will, beloved, I would say
  To God, unto whose bidding all things bow,
That we were still together night and day:
  Yet be it done as His behests allow.
I do remember that while she remain'd
With me, she often called me her sweet friend ;
  But does not now,
Because God drew her towards Him, in the end.
Lady, that peace which none but He can send
  Be thine. Even so.

D. G. Rossetti

BARTOLOMEO DI SANT' ANGELO

13th century

SONNET

He jests concerning his Poverty

I AM so passing rich in poverty
  That I could furnish forth Paris and Rome,
  Pisa and Padua and Byzantium,
Venice and Lucca, Florence and Forlì;
For I possess in actual specie,
  Of nihil and of nothing a great sum;
  And unto this my hoard whole shiploads come,
What between naught and zero, annually.
In gold and precious jewels I have got
A hundred ciphers' worth, all roundly writ;
  And therewithal am free to feast my friend.
  Because I need not be afraid to spend,
  Nor doubt the safety of my wealth a whit:—
No thief will ever steal thereof, God wot.

D. G. Rossetti

FOLGORE DA SAN GEMINIANO

13th century

Of the Months

TWELVE SONNETS

Addressed to a Fellowship of Sienese Nobles

DEDICATION

UNTO the blithe and lordly Fellowship,
    (I know not where, but wheresoe'er, I know,
    Lordly and blithe,) be greeting; and thereto,
Dogs, hawks, and a full purse wherein to dip;
Quails struck i' the flight; nags mettled to the whip;
    Hart-hounds, hare-hounds, and blood-hounds
    even so;
    And o'er that realm, a crown for Niccolò,
Whose praise in Sièna springs from lip to lip.
Tingoccio, Atuin di Togno, and Ancaiàn,
    Bartolo and Mugaro and Faënot,
Who well might pass for children of King Ban,
    Courteous and valiant more than Làncelot,—
To each, God speed ! how worthy every man
    To hold high tournament in Camelot.

JANUARY

FOR January I give you vests of skins,
    And mighty fires in hall, and torches lit;
    Chambers and happy beds with all things fit;
Smooth silken sheets, rough furry counterpanes;
And sweetmeats baked; and one that deftly spins
    Warm arras; and Douay cloth, and store of it;
    And on this merry manner still to twit
The wind, when most his mastery the wind wins.
Or issuing forth at seasons in the day,
    Ye'll fling soft handfuls of the fair white snow
Among the damsels standing round, in play:
    And when you all are tired and all aglow,

Indoors again the court shall hold its sway,
And the free Fellowship continue so.

February

IN February I give you gallant sport
  Of harts and hinds and great wild boars; and all
  Your company good foresters and tall,
With buskins strong, with jerkins close and short;
And in your leashes, hounds of brave report;
  And from your purses, plenteous money-fall,
  In very spleen of misers' starveling gall,
Who at your generous customs snarl and snort.
At dusk wend homeward, ye and all your folk,
  All laden from the wilds, to your carouse,
    With merriment and songs accompanied:
And so draw wine and let the kitchen smoke;
  And so be till the first watch glorious;
    Then sound sleep to you till the day be wide.

March

IN March I give you plenteous fisheries
  Of lamprey and of salmon, eel and trout,
  Dental and dolphin, sturgeon, all the rout
Of fish in all the streams that fill the seas,
With fishermen and fishing-boats at ease,
  Sail-barques and arrow-barques, and galleons stout,
  To bear you, while the season lasts, far out,
And back, through spring, to any port you please.
But with fair mansions see that it be fill'd,
  With everything exactly to your mind,
    And every sort of comfortable folk.
No convent suffer there, nor priestly guild:
  Leave the mad monks to preach after their kind
    Their scanty truth, their lies beyond a joke.

April

I GIVE you meadow-lands in April, fair
With over-growth of beautiful green grass;
　There among fountains the glad hours shall pass,
And pleasant ladies bring you solace there.
With steeds of Spain and ambling palfreys rare;
　Provençal songs and dances that surpass;
　　And quaint French mummings; and through
　　　hollow brass
A sound of German music on the air.
And gardens ye shall have, that every one
　May lie at ease about the fragrant place;
　　And each with fitting reverence shall bow down
　　Unto that youth to whom I gave a crown
Of precious jewels like to those that grace
The Babylonian Kaiser, Prester John.

May

I GIVE you horses for your games in May,
　And all of them well trained unto the course,—
　Each docile, swift, erect, a goodly horse;
With armour on their chests, and bells at play
Between their brows, and pennons fair and gay;
　Fine nets, and housings meet for warriors,
　Emblazoned with the shields ye claim for yours;
Gules, argent, or, all dizzy at noonday.
And spears shall split, and fruit go flying up
In merry counterchange for wreaths that drop
　From balconies and casements far above;
And tender damsels with young men and youths
Shall kiss together on the cheeks and mouths;
　And every day be glad with joyful love.

JUNE

IN June I give you a close-wooded fell,
 With crowns of thicket coiled about its head,
 With thirty villas twelve times turreted,
All girdling round a little citadel;
And in the midst a springhead and fair well
 With thousand conduits branched and shining speed,
 Wounding the garden and the tender mead,
Yet to the freshened grass acceptable.
And lemons, citrons, dates, and oranges,
 And all the fruits whose savour is most rare,
Shall shine within the shadow of your trees:
 And every one shall be a lover there;
Until your life, so filled with courtesies,
 Throughout the world be counted debonair.

JULY

FOR July, in Siena, by the willow-tree,
 I give you barrels of white Tuscan wine
 In ice far down your cellars stored supine;
And morn and eve to eat in company
Of those vast jellies dear to you and me;
 Of partridges and youngling pheasants sweet,
 Boiled capons, sovereign kids: and let their treat
Be veal and garlic, with whom these agree.
Let time slip by, till by and by, all day;
 And never swelter through the heat at all,
But move at ease at home, sound, cool, and gay;
 And wear sweet-coloured robes that lightly fall;
And keep your tables set in fresh array,
 Not coaxing spleen to be your seneschal.

AUGUST

FOR August, be your dwelling thirty towers
　　Within an Alpine valley mountainous,
　　Where never the sea-wind may vex your house,
But clear life separate, like a star, be yours.
There horses shall wait saddled at all hours,
　　That ye may mount at morning or at eve:
　　On each hand either ridge ye shall perceive,
A mile apart, which soon a good beast scours.
So alway, drawing homewards, ye shall tread
　　Your valley parted by a rivulet
　　　　Which day and night shall flow sedate and
　　　　　　smooth.
There all through noon ye may possess the shade,
　　And there your open purses shall entreat
　　　　The best of Tuscan cheer to feed your youth.

SEPTEMBER

AND in September, O what keen delight !
　　Falcons and astors, merlins, sparrowhawks;
　　Decoy-birds that shall lure your game in flocks;
And hounds with bells: and gauntlets stout and tight;
　　Wide pouches; crossbows shooting out of sight;
　　Arblasts and javelins; balls and ball-cases;
　　All birds the best to fly at: moulting these,
Those reared by hand; with finches mean and slight;
And for their chase, all birds the best to fly;
　　And each to each of you be lavish still
　　　　In gifts; and robbery find no gainsaying;
And if you meet with travellers going by,
　　Their purses from your purse's flow shall fill;
　　　　And avarice be the only outcast thing.

October

NEXT, for October, to some sheltered coign
    Flouting the winds, I'll hope to find you slunk;
    Though in bird-shooting (lest all sport be sunk),
Your foot still press the turf, the horse your groin.
At night with sweethearts in the dance you'll join,
    And drink the blessed must, and get quite drunk,
    There's no such life for any human trunk;
And that's a truth that rings like golden coin !
Then, out of bed again when morning's come,
    Let your hands drench your face refreshingly,
        And take your physic roast, with flask and knife.
Sounder and snugger you shall feel at home
    Than lake-fish, river-fish, or fish at sea,
        Inheriting the cream of Christian life.

November

LET baths and wine-butts be November's due,
    With thirty mule-loads of broad gold-pieces;
    And canopy with silk the streets that freeze;
And keep your drink-horns steadily in view.
Let every trader have his gain of you:
    Clareta shall your lamps and torches send,—
    Caëta, citron-candies without end;
And each shall drink, and help his neighbour to.
And let the cold be great, and the fire grand:
    And still for fowls, and pastries sweetly wrought,
        For hares and kids, for roast and boiled, be sure
You always have your appetites at hand;
    And then let night howl and heaven fall, so naught
        Be missed that makes a man's bed-furniture.

December

LAST, for December, houses on the plain,
    Ground-floors to live in, logs heaped mountain-
      high,
    And carpets stretched, and newest games to try,
And torches lit, and gifts from man to man:
(Your host, a drunkard and a Catalan;)
    And whole dead pigs, and cunning cooks to ply
    Each throat with tit-bits that shall satisfy;
And wine-butts of Saint Galganus' brave span.
And be your coats well-lined and tightly bound,
    And wrap yourselves in cloaks of strength and
      weight,
      With gallant hoods to put your faces through.
And make your game of abject vagabond
    Abandoned miserable reprobate
      Misers; don't let them have a chance with you.

Conclusion

AND now take thought, my sonnet, who is he
    That most is full of every gentleness;
    And say to him (for thou shalt quickly guess
His name) that all his 'hests are law to me.
For if I held fair Paris town in fee,
    And were not called his friend, 'twere surely less.
    Ah ! had be but the emperor's wealth, my place
Were fitted in his love more steadily
Than is Saint Francis at Assisi. Alway
    Commend him unto me and his,—not least
      To Caian, held so dear in the blithe band.
" Folgore da San Geminiano " (say)
    " Has sent me, charging me to travel fast,
      Because his heart went with you in your hand."
                      D. G. Rossetti

SONNET

Of Virtue

THE flower of Virtue is the heart's content;
    And fame is Virtue's fruit that she doth bear;
    And Virtue's vase is fair without and fair
Within; and Virtue's mirror brooks no taint;
And Virtue by her names is sage and saint;
    And Virtue hath a steadfast front and clear;
    And Love is Virtue's constant minister;
And Virtue's gift of gifts is pure descent.
And Virtue dwells with knowledge, and therein
    Her cherished home of rest is real love;
    And Virtue's strength is in a suffering will;
And Virtue's work is life exempt from sin,
    With arms that aid; and in the sum hereof,
    All Virtue is to render good for ill.

D. G. Rossetti

On Knighthood

I

THIS morn a young squire shall be made a knight;
    Whereof he fain would be right worthy found,
    And therefore pledgeth lands and castles round
To furnish all that fits a man of might.
Meat, bread, and wine he gives to many a wight;
    Capons and pheasants on his board abound,
    Where serving men and pages march around;
Choice chambers, torches, and wax candle light.
Barbed steeds, a multitude, are in his thought,
    Mailed men at arms and noble company,
Spears, pennants, housing cloths, bells richly
        wrought;
    Musicians following with great barony
And jesters through the land his state have brought,
    With dames and damsels whereso rideth he.

II

COMES Blithesomeness with mirth and merriment,
    All decked in flowers she seemeth a rose-tree;
Of linen, silk, cloth, fur, now beareth she
To the new knight a rich habiliment;
Head-gear and cap and garland flower-besprent,
    So brave they were May-bloom he seemed to be:
    With such a rout, so many and such glee,
That the floor shook. Then to her work she went;
And stood him on his feet in hose and shoon;
    And purse and gilded girdle 'neath the fur
That drapes his goodly limbs, she buckles on;
    Then bids the singers and sweet music stir,
And showeth him to ladies for a boon
    And all who in that following went with her.

John Addington Symonds

GUIDO DELLE COLONNE
13th century
CANZONE
To Love and to his Lady

O LOVE, who all this while hast urged me on,
    Shaking the reins, with never any rest,—
    Slacken for pity somewhat of thy haste;
I am oppress'd with languor and foredone,—
Having outrun the power of sufferance,—
    Having much more endured than who, through
        faith
    That his heart holds, makes no account of death.
Love is assuredly a fair mischance,
And well may it be called a happy ill:
    Yet thou, my lady, on this constant sting,
So sharp a thing, have thou some pity still,—
Howbeit a sweet thing too, unless it kill.

O comely-favoured, whose soft eyes prevail,
　　More fair than is another on this ground,—
　　Lift now my mournful heart out of its stound,
Which thus is bound for thee in great travail:
For a high gale a little rain may end.
　　Also, my lady, be not angered thou
　　That Love should thee enforce, to whom all bow.
There is but little shame to apprehend
If to a higher strength the conquest be;
　　And all the more to Love who conquers all.
Why then appal my heart with doubts of thee?
Courage and patience triumph certainly.

I do not say that with such loveliness
　　Such pride may not beseem; it suits thee well,
　　For in a lovely lady pride may dwell,
Lest homage fail and high esteem grow less:
Yet pride's excess is not a thing to praise.
　　Therefore, my lady, let thy harshness gain
　　Some touch of pity which may still restrain
Thy hand, ere Death cut short these hours and days.
The sun is very high and full of light,
　　And the more bright the higher he doth ride:
So let thy pride, my lady, and thy height,
Stand me in stead and turn to my delight.

Still inmostly I love thee, labouring still
　　That others may not know my secret smart.
　　Oh! what a pain it is for the grieved heart
To hold apart and not to show its ill!
Yet by no will the face can hide the soul;
　　And ever with the eyes the heart has need
　　To be in all things willingly agreed.
It were a mighty strength that should control
The heart's fierce beat, and never speak a word:
　　It were a mighty strength, I say again,
To hide such pain, and to be sovran lord
Of any heart that had such love to hoard.

For Love can make the wisest turn astray:
  Love, at its most, of measure still has least;
  He is the maddest man who loves the best;
It is Love's jest, to make men's hearts alway
So hot that they by coldness cannot cool.
  The eyes unto the heart bear messages
  Of the beginnings of all pain and ease:
And thou, my lady, in thy hand dost rule
Mine eyes and heart which thou hast made thine own.
  Love rocks my life with tempests on the deep,
Even as a ship round which the winds are blown:
Thou art my pennon that will not go down.

                    D. G. Rossetti

PIER MORONELLI DI FIORENZA

                        13th century

CANZONETTA

A Bitter Song to his Lady

O LADY amorous,
  Merciless lady,
  Full blithely play'd ye
  These your beguilings.
So with an urchin
  A man makes merry,—
  In mirth grows clamorous,
  Laughs and rejoices,—
But when his choice is
  To fall aweary,
  Cheats him with silence.
  This is Love's portion:—
In much wayfaring
  With many burdens
  He loads his servants,

But at the sharing,
The underservice
And overservice
Are alike barren.

As my disaster
Your jest I cherish,
And well may perish.
Even so a falcon
Is sometimes taken
And scantly cautell'd;
Till when his master
At length to loose him,
To train and use him,
Is after all gone,—
The creature's throttled
And will not waken.
Wherefore, my lady,
If you will own me,
O look upon me !
If I'm not thought on,
At least perceive me !
O do not leave me
So much forgotten !

If, lady, truly
You wish my profit,
What follows of it
Though still you say so ?—
For all your well-wishes
I still am waiting.
I grow unruly,
And deem at last I'm
Only your pastime.
A child will play so,
Who greatly relishes
Sporting and petting

With a little wild bird:
Unaware he kills it,—
Then turns it, feels it,
Calls it with a mild word,
Is angry after,—
Then again in laughter
Loud is the child heard.

O my delightful
My own, my lady,
Upon the Mayday
Which brought me to you
Was all my haste then
But a fool's venture?
To have my sight full
Of you propitious
Truly my wish was,
And to pursue you
And let love chasten
My heart to the centre.
But warming, lady,
May end in burning.
Of all this yearning
What comes, I beg you?
In all your glances
What is't a man sees?—
Fever and ague.

D. G. Rossetti

PRINZIVALLE DORIA

13th century

CANZONE

Of his Love, with the Figure of a Sudden Storm

EVEN as the day when it is yet at dawning
   Seems mild and kind, being fair to look upon,
While the birds carol underneath their awning

Of leaves, as if they never would have done;
　Which on a sudden changes, just at noon,
And the broad light is broken into rain
　That stops and comes again;
Even as the traveller, who had held his way
　Hopeful and glad because of the bright weather,
　Forgetteth then his gladness altogether;
Even so am I, through Love, alas the day !

It plainly is through Love that I am so.
　At first, he let me still grow happier
Each day, and made her kindness seem to grow;
　But now he has quite changed her heart in her.
　And I, whose hopes throbbed and were all astir
For times when I should call her mine aloud,
　And in her pride be proud
Who is more fair than gems are, ye may say,
　Having that fairness which holds hearts in rule;—
　I have learnt now to count him but a fool
Who before evening says, A goodly day.

It had been better not to have begun,
　Since, having known my error, 'tis too late.
This thing from which I suffer, thou hast done,
　Lady: canst thou restore me my first state ?
　The wound thou gavest canst thou medicate ?
Not thou, forsooth: thou hast not any art
　To keep death from my heart.
O lady ! where is now my life's full meed
　Of peace,—mine once, and which thou took'st away ?
　Surely it cannot now be far from day:
Night is already very long indeed.

The sea is much more beautiful at rest
　Than when the storm is trampling over it.
Wherefore, to see the smile which has so bless'd
　This heart of mine, deem'st thou these eyes unfit ?
　There is no maid so lovely, it is writ,

That by such stern unwomanly regard
Her face may not be marr'd.
I therefore pray of thee, my own soul's wife,
That thou remember me who am forgot.
How shall I stand without thee? Art thou not
The pillar of the building of my life?

D. G. Rossetti

RUSTICO DI FILIPPO

1200 ?–1270

SONNET

Of the Making of Master Messerin

WHEN God had finished Master Messerin,
He really thought it something to have done:
Bird, man, and beast had got a chance in one.
And each felt flattered, it was hoped, therein.
For he is like a goose i' the windpipe thin,
And like a camelopard high i' the loins;
To which, for manhood, you'll be told, he joins
Some kinds of flesh-hues and a callow chin.
As to his singing, he affects the crow;
As to his learning, beasts in general;
And sets all square by dressing like a man.
God made him, having nothing else to do;
And proved there is not anything at all
He cannot make, if that's a thing He can.

D. G. Rossetti

NICCOLÒ DEGLI ALBIZZI

13th century

PROLONGED SONNET

When the Troops were returning from Milan

IF you could see, fair brother, how dead beat
The fellows look who came through Rome to-day,—
Black yellow smoke-dried visages,—you'd say
They thought their haste at going all too fleet.

Their empty victual-wagons up the street
  Over the bridge dreadfully sound and sway;
  Their eyes, as hanged men's, turning the wrong way;
And nothing on their backs, or heads, or feet.
One sees the ribs and all the skeletons
  Of their gaunt horses; and a sorry sight
Are the torn saddles, crammed with straw and stones.
  They are ashamed, and march throughout the night;
Stumbling, for hunger, on their marrow-bones;
  Like barrels rolling, jolting, in this plight.
Their arms all gone, not even their swords are saved;
And each as silent as a man being shaved.

D. G. Rossetti

GUIDO CAVALCANTI

1250–1301

SONNET

To Dante Alighieri

*He interprets Dante's Dream, related in the First Sonnet
of the Vita Nuova*

UNTO my thinking, thou beheld'st all worth,
  All joy, as much of good as man may know,
  If thou wert in his power who here below
Is honour's righteous lord throughout this earth.
Where evil dies, even there he has his birth,
  Whose justice out of pity's self doth grow.
  Softly to sleeping persons he will go,
And, with no pain to them, their hearts draw forth.
Thy heart he took, as knowing well, alas!
  That Death had claimed thy lady for a prey:
  In fear whereof, he fed her with thy heart.
  But when he seemed in sorrow to depart,
  Sweet was thy dream; for by that sign, I say,
Surely the opposite shall come to pass.

D. G. Rossetti

SONNET

To his Lady Joan, of Florence

FLOWERS hast thou in thyself, and foliage,
  And what is good, and what is glad to see;
The sun is not so bright as thy visàge;
  All is stark naught when one hath looked on thee;
There is not such a beautiful personage
  Anywhere on the green earth verily;
If one fear love, thy bearing sweet and sage
  Comforteth him, and no more fear hath he.
Thy lady friends and maidens ministering
  Are all, for love of thee, much to my taste:
And much I pray them that in everything
  They honour thee even as thou meritest,
  And have thee in their gentle harbouring:
  Because among them all thou art the best.

D. G. Rossetti

SONNET

*He compares all Things with his Lady, and finds them
wanting*

BEAUTY in woman; the high will's decree;
  Fair knighthood armed for manly exercise;
  The pleasant song of birds; love's soft replies;
The strength of rapid ships upon the sea ;
The serene air when light begins to be;
  The white snow, without wind that falls and lies;
  Fields of all flower; the place where waters rise;
Silver and gold; azure in jewellery:—
Weighed against these, the sweet and quiet worth
  Which my dear lady cherishes at heart
    Might seem a little matter to be shown;
  Being truly, over these, as much apart
As the whole heaven is greater than this earth.
  All good to kindred natures cleaveth soon.

D. G. Rossetti

SONNET

A Rapture concerning his Lady

WHO is she coming, whom all gaze upon,
  Who makes the air all tremulous with light,
And at whose side is Love himself? that none
  Dare speak, but each man's sighs are infinite.
  Ah me! how she looks round from left to right,
Let Love discourse: I may not speak thereon.
Lady she seems of such high benison
  As makes all others graceless in men's sight.
The honour which is hers cannot be said;
  To whom are subject all things virtuous,
    While all things beauteous own her deity.
Ne'er was the mind of man so nobly led,
  Nor yet was such redemption granted us
    That we should ever know her perfectly.

D. G. Rossetti

BALLATA

Of his Lady among other Ladies

WITH other women I beheld my love;—
  Not that the rest were women to mine eyes,
Who only as her shadows seemed to move.

I do not praise her more than with the truth,
  Nor blame I these if it be rightly read.

But while I speak, a thought I may not soothe
Says to my senses: " Soon shall ye be dead,
If for my sake your tears ye will not shed."

And then the eyes yield passage, at that thought,
To the heart's weeping, which forgets her not.

D. G. Rossetti

SONNET

Of the Eyes of a certain Mandetta, of Thoulouse, which resemble those of his Lady Joan, of Florence

A CERTAIN youthful lady in Thoulouse,
    Gentle and fair, of cheerful modesty,
    Is in her eyes, with such exact degree,
Of likeness unto mine own lady, whose
I am, that through the heart she doth abuse
    The soul to sweet desire. It goes from me
    To her; yet, fearing, saith not who is she
That of a truth its essence thus subdues.
This lady looks on it with the sweet eyes
    Whose glance did erst the wounds of Love anoint
      Through its true lady's eyes which are as they.
Then to the heart returns it, full of sighs,
    Wounded to death by a sharp arrow's point
      Wherewith this lady speeds it on its way.

D. G. Rossetti

PORTION OF A BALLATA

B EING in thought of love, I chanced to see
    Two youthful damozels.
  One sang: " Our life inhales
  All love continually."

Their aspect was so utterly serene,
    So courteous, of such quiet nobleness,
That I said to them: " Yours, I may well ween,
    'Tis of all virtue to unlock the place.
Ah ! damozels, do not account him base
    Whom thus his wound subdues:
    Since I was at Thoulouse,
    My heart is dead in me."

D. G. Rossetti

SONNET

To Dante Alighieri

*He reports, in a feigned Vision, the successful Issue of
Lapo Gianni's Love*

DANTE, a sigh that rose from the heart's core
    Assailed me, while I slumbered, suddenly:
So that I woke o' the instant, fearing sore
    Lest it came thither in Love's company:
Till, turning, I beheld the servitor
    Of Lady Lagia: "Help me," so said he,
"O help me, Pity." Though he said no more,
    So much of Pity's essence entered me,
That I was 'ware of Love, those shafts he wields
    A-whetting, and preferred the mourner's quest
        To him, who straightway answered on this wise:
"Go tell my servant that the lady yields,
    And that I hold her now at his behest:
        If he believe not, let him note her eyes."

D. G. Rossetti

SONNET

To Dante Alighieri

He mistrusts the Love of Lapo Gianni

I PRAY thee, Dante, shouldst thou meet with Love
    In any place where Lapo then may be,
    That there thou fail not to mark heedfully
If Love with lover's name that man approve;
If to our Master's will his lady move
    Aright, and if himself show fealty:
    For ofttimes, by ill custom, ye may see
This sort profess the semblance of true love.
Thou know'st that in the court where Love holds sway
    A law subsists, that no man who is vile

Can service yield to a lost woman there.
If suffering aught avail the sufferer,
Thou straightway shalt discern our lofty style,
Which needs the badge of honour must display.

D. G. Rossetti

SONNET

On the Detection of a False Friend

LOVE and the Lady Lagia, Guido and I,
　　Unto a certain lord are bounden all,
　　Who has released us—know ye from whose thrall?
Yet I'll not speak, but let the matter die:
Since now these three no more are held thereby,
　　Who in such homage at his feet did fall
　　That I myself was not more whimsical,
In him conceiving godship from on high.
Let Love be thanked the first, who first discern'd
　　The truth; and that wise lady afterward,
　　　Who in fit time took back her heart again;
And Guido next, from worship wholly turn'd;
　　And I, as he.　But if ye have not heard,
　　　I shall not tell how much I loved him then.

D. G. Rossetti

SONNET

He speaks of a Third Love of his

O THOU that often hast within thine eyes
　　A Love who holds three shafts,—know thou from
　　me
　　That this my sonnet would commend to thee
(Come from afar) a soul in heavy sighs,
Which even by Love's sharp arrow wounded lies.
　　Twice did the Syrian archer shoot, and he
　　Now bends his bow the third time, cunningly,
That, thou being here, he wound me in no wise.

Because the soul would quicken at the core
Thereby, which now is near to utter death,
From those two shafts, a triple wound that yield.
The first gives pleasure, yet disquieteth;
And with the second is the longing for
The mighty gladness by the third fulfill'd.

D. G. Rossetti

BALLATA
Of a Continual Death in Love

THOUGH thou, indeed, hast quite forgotten ruth,
Its steadfast truth my heart abandons not;
But still its thought yields service in good part
To that hard heart in thee.

Alas! who hears believes not I am so.
Yet who can know? of very surety, none.
From Love is won a spirit, in some wise,
Which dies perpetually:

And, when at length in that strange ecstasy
The heavy sigh will start,
There rains upon my heart
A love so pure and fine,
That I say: " Lady, I am wholly thine."

D. G. Rossetti

SONNET
To a Friend who does not pity his Love

IF I entreat this lady that all grace
Seem not unto her heart an enemy,
Foolish and evil thou declarest me,
And desperate in idle stubbornness.
Whence is such cruel judgment thine, whose face,
To him that looks thereon, professeth thee
Faithful, and wise, and of all courtesy,

And made after the way of gentleness ?
Alas ! my soul within my heart doth find
  Sighs, and its grief by weeping doth enhance,
    That, drowned in bitter tears, those sighs depart :
And then there seems a presence in the mind,
  As of a lady's thoughtful countenance
    Come to behold the death of the poor heart.

                    D. G. Rossetti

SONNET

Of his Pain from a New Love

WHY from the danger did mine eyes not start,—
  Why not become even blind,—ere through my
    sight
  Within my soul thou ever couldst alight
To say : " Dost thou not hear me in thy heart ? "
New torment then, the old torment's counterpart,
  Filled me at once with such a sore affright,
    That, Lady, lady, (I said,) destroy not quite
Mine eyes and me ! O help us where thou art !
Thou hast so left mine eyes, that Love is fain—
  Even Love himself—with pity uncontroll'd
    To bend above them, weeping for their loss :
Saying : " If any man feel heavy pain,
  This man's more painful heart let him behold :
    Death has it in her hand, cut like a cross."

                    D. G. Rossetti

To Dante

RETURNING from its daily quest, my Spirit
  Changed thoughts and vile in thee doth weep to
    find :
  It grieves me that thy mild and gentle mind
Those ample virtues which it did inherit,

Has lost.   Once thou didst loathe the multitude
 Of blind and maddening men: I then loved thee—
I loved thy lofty songs, and that sweet mood
 When thou wert faithful to thyself and men.
I dare not now, through thy degraded state,
 Own the delight thy strains inspire—in vain
I seek what once thou wert—we cannot meet
 As we were wont.   Again and yet again
Ponder my words: so the false Spirit shall fly,
 And leave to thee thy true integrity.

Percy Bysshe Shelley

BALLATA
Concerning a Shepherd-maid

WITHIN a copse I met a shepherd-maid,
 More fair, I said, than any star to see.

She came with waving tresses pale and bright,
 With rosy cheek, and loving eyes of flame,
Guiding the lambs beneath her wand aright.
 Her naked feet still had the dews on them,
 As, singing like a lover, so she came;
Joyful, and fashioned for all ecstasy.

I greeted her at once, and question made
 What escort had she through the woods in
  spring ?
But with soft accents she replied and said
 That she was all alone there, wandering;
 Moreover: " Do you know, when the birds sing,
My heart's desire is for a mate," said she.

While she was telling me this wish of hers,
 The birds were all in song throughout the wood.
" Even now then," said my thought, " the time
  recurs,
 With mine own longing to assuage her mood."

And so, in her sweet favour's name, I sued
That she would kiss there and embrace with me.

She took my hand to her with amorous will,
    And answered that she gave me all her heart,
And drew me where the leaf is fresh and still,
    Where spring the wood-flowers in the shade apart.
    And on that day, by Joy's enchanted art,
There Love in very presence seemed to be.

D. G. Rossetti

SONNET

Of an Ill-favoured Lady

JUST look, Manetto, at that wry-mouth'd minx;
    Merely take notice what a wretch it is;
    How well contrived in her deformities,
How beastly favoured when she scowls and blinks.
Why, with a hood on (if one only thinks)
    Or muffle of prim veils and scapularies,—
    And set together, on a day like this,
Some pretty lady with the odious sphinx;—
Why, then thy sins could hardly have such weight,
    Nor thou be so subdued from Love's attack,
    Nor so possessed in Melancholy's sway,
But that perforce thy peril must be great
    Of laughing till the very heart-strings crack:
    Either thou'dst die, or thou must run away.

D. G. Rossetti

BALLATA

In Exile at Sarzana

BECAUSE I think not ever to return,
    Ballad, to Tuscany,—
    Go therefore thou for me
      Straight to my lady's face,
      Who, of her noble grace,
      Shall show thee courtesy.

Thou seekest her in charge of many sighs,
 Full of much grief and of exceeding fear.
But have good heed thou come not to the eyes
 Of such as are sworn foes to gentle cheer:
 For, certes, if this thing should chance,—from her
   Thou then couldst only look
   For scorn, and such rebuke
   As needs must bring me pain;—
   Yea, after death again
   Tears and fresh agony.

Surely thou knowest, Ballad, how that Death
 Assails me, till my life is almost sped:
Thou knowest how my heart still travaileth
 Through the sore pangs which in my soul are bred :—
 My body being now so nearly dead,
   It cannot suffer more.
   Then, going, I implore
   That this my soul thou take
   (Nay, do so for my sake,)
   When my heart sets it free.

Ah ! Ballad, unto thy dear offices
 I do commend my soul, thus trembling;
That thou mayst lead it, for pure piteousness,
 Even to that lady's presence whom I sing.
 Ah ! Ballad, say thou to her, sorrowing,
   Whereso thou meet her then:—
   " This thy poor handmaiden
   Is come, nor will be gone,
   Being parted now from one
   Who served Love painfully."

Thou also, thou bewildered voice and weak,
 That goest forth in tears from my grieved heart,

Shalt, with my soul and with this ballad, speak
 Of my dead mind, when thou dost hence depart,
 Unto that lady (piteous as thou art !)
        Who is so calm and bright,
        It shall be deep delight
        To feel her presence there.
        And thou, Soul, worship her
        Still in her purity.

D. G. Rossetti

FRANCESCO DA BARBERINO

1264–1348

A Virgin declares her Beauties

DO not conceive that I shall here recount
   All my own beauty: yet I promise you
That you, by what I tell, shall understand
All that befits and that is well to know.

My bosom, which is very softly made,
Of a white even colour without stain,
Bears two fair apples, fragrant, sweetly-savoured,
Gathered together from the Tree of Life
The which is in the midst of Paradise.
And these no person ever yet has touched;
For out of nurse's and of mother's hands
I was, when God in secret gave them me.
These ere I yield I must know well to whom;
And for that I would not be robbed of them,
I speak not all the virtue that they have;
Yet thus far speaking:—blessed were the man
Who once should touch them, were it but a little;—
See them I say not, for that might not be.
My girdle, clipping pleasure round about,
Over my clear dress even unto my knees
Hangs down with sweet precision tenderly;
And under it Virginity abides.

Faithful and simple and of plain belief
She is, with her fair garland bright like gold;
And very fearful if she overhears
Speech of herself; the wherefore ye perceive
That I speak soft lest she be made ashamed.

Lo ! this is she who hath for company
The Son of God and Mother of the Son;
Lo ! this is she who sits with many in heaven;
Lo ! this is she with whom are few on earth.

D. G. Rossetti

Of Caution

SAY, wouldst thou guard thy son,
 That sorrow he may shun ?
 Begin at the beginning
 And let him keep from sinning.
 Wouldst guard thy house ?   One door
 Make to it, and no more.
 Wouldst guard thine orchard wall ?
 Be free of fruit to all.

D. G. Rossetti

DANTE ALIGHIERI

1265–1321

From La Vita Nuova

THE narrative of the New Life is quaint, embroidered with conceits,
deficient in artistic completeness, but it has the simplicity of youth,
the charm of sincerity, the freedom of personal confidence; and so long
as there are lovers in the world, and so long as lovers are poets, this first
and tenderest love story of modern literature will be read with appreciation
and responsive sympathy.—CHARLES ELIOT NORTON.

I

TO every heart which the sweet pain doth move,
 And unto which these words may now be brought
 For true interpretation and kind thought,
 Be greeting in our Lord's name, which is Love.

Of those long hours wherein the stars, above,
  Wake and keep watch, the third was almost naught,
  When Love was shown me with such terrors fraught
As may not carelessly be spoken of.
He seemed like one who is full of joy, and had
  My heart within his hand, and on his arm
  My lady, with a mantle round her, slept;
Whom (having wakened her) anon he made
  To eat that heart; she ate, as fearing harm.
  Then he went out; and as he went, he wept.

2

A LL ye that pass along Love's trodden way,
    Pause ye awhile and say
  If there be any grief like unto mine:
I pray you that you hearken a short space
Patiently, if my case
  Be not a piteous marvel and a sign.

Love (never, certes, for my worthless part,
But of his own great heart)
  Vouchsafed to me a life so calm and sweet
That oft I heard folk question as I went
What such great gladness meant:—
  They spoke of it behind me in the street.

But now that fearless bearing is all gone
  Which with Love's hoarded wealth was given me;
  Till I am grown to be
So poor that I have dread to think thereon.

And thus it is that I, being like as one
Who is ashamed and hides his poverty,
  Without seem full of glee,
And let my heart within travail and moan.

3

WEEP, Lovers, sith Love's very self doth weep,
  And sith the cause for weeping is so great;
  When now so many dames, of such estate
In worth, show with their eyes a grief so deep ;
For Death the churl has laid his leaden sleep
  Upon a damsel who was fair of late,
  Defacing all our earth should celebrate,—
Yea all save virtue, which the soul doth keep.
Now hearken how much Love did honour her.
  I myself saw him in his proper form
    Bending above the motionless sweet dead,
And often gazing into Heaven; for there
  The soul now sits which when her life was warm
    Dwelt with the joyful beauty that is fled.

Death, always cruel, Pity's foe in chief,
Mother who brought forth grief,
  Merciless judgment and without appeal !
  Since thou alone hast made my heart to feel
  This sadness and unweal,
My tongue upbraideth thee without relief.

And now (for I must rid thy name of ruth)
Behoves me speak the truth
  Touching thy cruelty and wickedness:
  Not that they be not known ; but ne'ertheless
  I would give hate more stress
With them that feed on love in very sooth.

Out of this world thou hast driven courtesy,
  And virtue, dearly prized in womanhood;
  And out of youth's gay mood
The lovely lightness is quite gone through thee.

Whom now I mourn, no man shall learn from me
Save by the measure of these praises given.
Whoso deserves not Heaven ⬛
May never hope to have her company.

4

A DAY agone, as I rode sullenly
    Upon a certain path that liked me not,
    I met Love midway while the air was hot,
Clothed lightly as a wayfarer might be.
And for the cheer he showed, he seemed to me
    As one who hath lost lordship he had got;
    Advancing tow'rds me full of sorrowful thought,
Bowing his forehead so that none should see.
Then as I went, he called me by my name,
    Saying: "I journey since the morn was dim
    Thence where I made thy heart to be, which now
I needs must bear unto another dame."
    Wherewith so much passed into me of him
    That he was gone, and I discerned not how.

5

S ONG, 'tis my will that thou do seek out Love,
    And go with him where my dear lady is;
    That so my cause, the which thy harmonies
Do plead, his better speech may clearly prove.

Thou goest, my Song, in such a courteous kind,
    That even companionless
    Thou mayst rely on thyself anywhere.
And yet, an thou wouldst get thee a safe mind,
    First unto Love address
    Thy steps; whose aid, mayhap, 'twere ill to spare,
    Seeing that she to whom thou mak'st thy prayer

Is, as I think, ill-minded unto me,
And that if Love do not companion thee,
    Thou'lt have perchance small cheer to tell me of.

With a sweet accent, when thou com'st to her,
    Begin thou in these words,
        First having craved a gracious audience:
" He who hath sent me as his messenger,
    Lady, thus much records,
        An thou but suffer him, in his defence.
        Love, who comes with me, by thine influence
Can make this man do as it liketh him:
Wherefore, if this fault *is* or doth but *seem*
    Do thou conceive: for his heart cannot move."

Say to her also: " Lady, his poor heart
    Is so confirmed in faith
        That all its thoughts are but of serving thee:
'Twas early thine, and could not swerve apart."
    Then, if she wavereth,
        Bid her ask Love, who knows if these things be.
        And in the end, beg of her modestly
To pardon so much boldness: saying too:—
" If thou declare his death to be thy due,
    The thing shall come to pass, as doth behove."

Then pray thou of the Master of all ruth,
    Before thou leave her there,
        That he befriend my cause and plead it well.
" In guerdon of my sweet rhymes and my truth "
    (Entreat him) " stay with her;
        Let not the hope of thy poor servant fail;
        And if with her thy pleading should prevail,
Let her look on him and give peace to him."
Gentle my Song, if good to thee it seem,
    Do this: so worship shall be thine and love.

6

ALL my thoughts always speak to me of Love,
   Yet have between themselves such difference
   That while one bids me bow with mind and sense,
A second saith, " Go to: look thou above";
The third one, hoping, yields me joy enough;
   And with the last come tears, I scarce know whence:
   All of them craving pity in sore suspense,
Trembling with fears that the heart knoweth of.
And thus, being all unsure which path to take,
   Wishing to speak I know not what to say,
   And lose myself in amorous wanderings:
Until, (my peace with all of them to make,)
   Unto mine enemy I needs must pray,
   My Lady Pity, for the help she brings.

7

EVEN as the others mock, thou mockest me;
   Not dreaming, noble lady, whence it is
   That I am taken with strange semblances,
Seeing thy face which is so fair to see:
For else, compassion would not suffer thee
   To grieve my heart with such harsh scoffs as these.
Lo ! Love, when thou art present, sits at ease,
And bears his mastership so mightily
That all my troubled senses he thrusts out,
   Sorely tormenting some, and slaying some,
      Till none but he is left and has free range
      To gaze on thee.   This makes my face to change
Into another's; while I stand all dumb,
And hear my senses clamour in their rout.

8

THE thoughts are broken in my memory,
   Thou lovely Joy, whene'er I see thy face;
   When thou art near me, Love fills up the space,
Often repeating, " If death irk thee, fly."

My face shows my heart's colour, verily,
  Which, fainting, seeks for any leaning-place;
  Till, in the drunken terror of disgrace,
The very stones seems to be shrieking, " Die ! "
It were a grievous sin, if one should not
  Strive then to comfort my bewildered mind
  (Though merely with a simple pitying)
For the great anguish which thy scorn has wrought
  In the dead sight o' the eyes grown nearly blind,
  Which look for death as for a blessed thing.

9

AT whiles (yea oftentimes) I muse over
  The quality of anguish that is mine
  Through Love: then pity makes my voice to pine,
Saying, " Is any else thus, anywhere ? "
Love smiteth me, whose strength is ill to bear;
  So that of all my life is left no sign
  Except one thought; and that, because 'tis thine,
Leaves not the body but abideth there.
And then if I, whom other aid forsook,
  Would aid myself, and innocent of art
  Would fain have sight of thee as a last hope,
No sooner do I lift mine eyes to look
  Than the blood seems as shaken from my heart,
  And all my pulses beat at once and stop.

10

LADIES that have intelligence in love,
  Of mine own lady I would speak with you;
  Not that I hope to count her praises through,
  But telling what I may, to ease my mind.
And I declare that when I speak thereof,
  Love sheds such perfect sweetness over me
  That if my courage failed not, certainly

To him my listeners must be all resign'd.
Wherefore I will not speak in such large kind
That mine own speech should foil me, which were base;
But only will discourse of her high grace
    In these poor words, the best that I can find,
With you alone, dear dames and damozels:
'Twere ill to speak thereof with any else.

An angel, of his blessed knowledge, saith
    To God: " Lord, in the world that Thou hast made,
    A miracle in action is display'd,
      By reason of a soul whose splendours fare
Even hither: and since Heaven requireth
    Naught saving her, for her it prayeth Thee,
    Thy Saints crying aloud continually."
    Yet Pity still defends our earthly share
    In that sweet soul; God answering thus the prayer:
" My well-belovèd, suffer that in peace
Your hope remain, while so My pleasure is,
    There where one dwells who dreads the loss of her:
And who in Hell unto the doomed shall say,
' I have looked on that for which God's chosen pray.' "

My lady is desired in the high Heaven:
    Wherefore, it now behoveth me to tell,
    Saying: Let any maid that would be well
      Esteemed keep with her: for as she goes by,
Into foul hearts a deathly chill is driven
By Love, that makes ill thought to perish there:
While any who endures to gaze on her
    Must either be ennobled, or else die.
    When one deserving to be raised so high
Is found, 'tis then her power attains its proof,
Making his heart strong for his soul's behoof
    With the full strength of meek humility.
Also this virtue owns she, by God's will:
Who speaks with her can never come to ill.

Love saith concerning her: " How chanceth it
  That flesh, which is of dust, should be thus pure ? "
  Then, gazing always, he makes oath: " For sure,
    This is a creature of God till now unknown."
She hath that paleness of the pearl that's fit
In a fair woman, so much and not more;
She is as high as Nature's skill can soar;
    Beauty is tried by her comparison.
    Whatever her sweet eyes are turned upon,
Spirits of love do issue thence in flame,
Which through their eyes who then may look on them
    Pierce to the heart's deep chamber every one.
And in her smile Love's image you may see;
Whence none can gaze upon her steadfastly.

Dear Song, I know thou wilt hold gentle speech
  With many ladies, when I send thee forth:
  Wherefore (being mindful that thou hadst thy birth
    From Love, and art a modest, simple child,)
Whomso thou meetest, say thou this to each:
" Give me good speed !   To her I wend along
In whose much strength my weakness is made strong."
    And if, i' the end, thou wouldst not be beguiled
    Of all thy labour, seek not the defiled
And common sort; but rather choose to be
Where man and woman dwell in courtesy.
    So to the road thou shalt be reconciled,
And find the Lady, and with the lady, Love.
Commend thou me to each, as doth behove.

II

LOVE and the gentle heart are one same thing,
  Even as the wise man in his ditty saith:
  Each, of itself, would be such life in death
  As rational soul bereft of reasoning.

'Tis Nature makes them when she loves: a king
  Love is, whose palace where he sojourneth
  Is called the Heart; there draws he quiet breath
At first, with brief or longer slumbering.
Then beauty seen in virtuous womankind
  Will make the eyes desire, and through the heart
  Send the desiring of the eyes again;
Where often it abides so long enshrin'd
  That Love at length out of his sleep will start.
  And women feel the same for worthy men.

12

MY lady carries love within her eyes;
  All that she looks on is made pleasanter;
  Upon her path men turn to gaze at her;
He whom she greeteth feels his heart to rise,
And droops his troubled visage, full of sighs,
  And of his evil heart is then aware:
  Hate loves, and pride becomes a worshipper.
O women, help to praise her in somewise.
Humbleness, and the hope that hopeth well,
  By speech of hers into the mind are brought,
  And who beholds is blessèd oftenwhiles.
  The look she hath when she a little smiles
Cannot be said, nor holden in the thought;
  'Tis such a new and gracious miracle.

13

YOU that thus wear a modest countenance
  With lids weigh'd down by the heart's heaviness,
  Whence come you, that among you every face
Appears the same, for its pale troubled glance?
Have you beheld my lady's face, perchance,
  Bow'd with the grief that Love makes full of grace?
  Say now, " This thing is thus "; as my heart says,

Marking your grave and sorrowful advance.
And if indeed you come from where she sighs
   And mourns, may it please you (for his heart's
      relief)
   To tell how it fares with her unto him
Who knows that you have wept, seeing your eyes,
   And is so grieved with looking on your grief
      That his heart trembles and his sight grows dim.

Canst thou indeed be he that still would sing
   Of our dear lady unto none but us?
For though thy voice confirms that it is thus,
Thy visage might another witness bring.
And wherefore is thy grief so sore a thing
   That grieving thou mak'st others dolorous?
   Hast thou too seen her weep, that thou from us
Canst not conceal thine inward sorrowing?
Nay, leave our woe to us: let us alone:
   'Twere sin if one should strive to soothe our woe,
      For in her weeping we have heard her speak:
Also her look's so full of her heart's moan
   That they who should behold her, looking so,
      Must fall aswoon, feeling all life grow weak.

14

A VERY pitiful lady, very young,
   Exceeding rich in human sympathies,
      Stood by, what time I clamour'd upon Death;
And at the wild words wandering on my tongue
   And at the piteous look within mine eyes
      She was affrighted, that sobs choked her breath.
      So by her weeping where I lay beneath,
Some other gentle ladies came to know
   My state, and made her go:

Afterward, bending themselves over me,
One said, " Awaken thee ! "
  And one, " What thing thy sleep disquieteth ? "
With that, my soul woke up from its eclipse,
The while my lady's name rose to my lips:

But utter'd in a voice so sob/broken,
 So feeble with the agony of tears,
  That I alone might hear it in my heart;
And though that look was on my visage then
 Which he who is ashamed so plainly wears,
  Love made that I through shame held not apart,
  But gazed upon them. And my hue was such
That they look'd at each other and thought of death;
Saying under their breath
Most tenderly, " O let us comfort him":
Then unto me: " What dream
  Was thine, that it hath shaken thee so much ? "
And when I was a little comforted,
" This, ladies, was the dream I dreamt," I said.

" I was a/thinking how life fails with us
 Suddenly after such a little while;
  When Love sobb'd in my heart, which is his home.
Whereby my spirit wax'd so dolorous
 That in myself I said, with sick recoil:
  ' Yea, to my lady too this Death must come.'
  And therewithal such a bewilderment
Possess'd me, that I shut mine eyes for peace;
And in my brain did cease
Order of thought, and every healthful thing.
Afterwards, wandering
 Amid a swarm of doubts that came and went,
Some certain women's faces hurried by,
And shrieked to me, ' Thou too shalt die, shalt die ! '

" Then saw I many broken hinted sights
  In the uncertain state I stepp'd into.
    Meseem'd to be I know not in what place,
Where ladies through the streets, like mournful lights,
    Ran with loose hair, and eyes that frighten'd you,
      By their own terror, and a pale amaze:
      The while, little by little, as I thought,
The sun ceased, and the stars began to gather,
And each wept at the other;
And birds dropp'd in mid‑flight out of the sky;
And earth shook suddenly;
    And I was 'ware of one, hoarse and tired out,
Who ask'd of me: ' Hast thou not heard it said ? . . .
Thy lady, she that was so fair, is dead.'

" Then lifting up mine eyes, as the tears came,
  I saw the Angels, like a rain of manna,
    In a long flight flying back Heavenward;
Having a little cloud in front of them,
    After the which they went and said, ' Hosanna ';
      And if they had said more, you should have heard.
      Then Love said, ' Now shall all things be made
        clear:
Come and behold our lady where she lies.'
These 'wildering phantasies
Then carried me to see my lady dead.
Even as I there was led,
    Her ladies with a veil were covering her;
And with her was such very humbleness
That she appeared to say, ' I am at peace.' "

15

I FELT a spirit of love begin to stir
    Within my heart, long time unfelt till then;
    And saw Love coming towards me fair and fain,
  (That I scarce knew him for his joyful cheer,)

Saying, " Be now indeed my worshipper ! "
　And in his speech he laugh'd and laugh'd again.
　Then, while it was his pleasure to remain,
I chanced to look the way he had drawn near,
And saw the Ladies Joan and Beatrice
　Approach me, this the other following,
　One and a second marvel instantly.
And even as now my memory speaketh this,
　Love spake it then: " The first is christen'd Spring;
　The second Love, she is so like to me."

16

MY lady looks so gentle and so pure
　When yielding salutation by the way,
　That the tongue trembles and has naught to say,
And the eyes, which fain would see, may not endure.
And still, amid the praise she hears secure,
　She walks with humbleness for her array;
　Seeming a creature sent from Heaven to stay
On earth, and show a miracle made sure.
She is so pleasant in the eyes of men
　That through the sight the inmost heart doth gain
　A sweetness which needs proof to know it by:
And from between her lips there seems to move
A soothing essence that is full of love,
　Saying for ever to the spirit, " Sigh ! "

17

FOR certain he hath seen all perfectness
　Who among other ladies hath seen mine:
　They that go with her humbly should combine
To thank their God for such peculiar grace.
So perfect is the beauty of her face
　That it begets in no wise any sign
　Of envy, but draws round her a clear line
Of love, and blessed faith, and gentleness.

Merely the sight of her makes all things bow:
  Not she herself alone is holier
    Than all; but hers, through her, are raised above.
From all her acts such lovely graces flow
  That truly one may never think of her
    Without a passion of exceeding love.

18

L OVE hath so long possessed me for his own
  And made his lordship so familiar
That he, who at first irked me, is now grown
  Unto my heart as its best secrets are.
    And thus, when he in such sore wise doth mar
My life that all its strength seems gone from it,
  Mine inmost being then feels throughly quit
    Of anguish, and all evil keeps afar.
Love also gathers to such power in me
  That my sighs speak, each one a grievous thing,
    Always soliciting
My lady's salutation piteously.
Whenever she beholds me, it is so,
Who is more sweet than any words can show.

19

T HE eyes that weep for pity of the heart
  Have wept so long that their grief languisheth,
    And they have no more tears to weep withal:
And now, if I would ease me of a part
  Of what, little by little, leads to death,
    It must be done by speech, or not at all.
    And because often, thinking, I recall
How it was pleasant, ere she went afar,
  To talk of her with you, kind damozels,
    I talk with no one else,

But only with such hearts as women's are.
  And I will say,—still sobbing as speech fails,—
That she hath gone to Heaven suddenly,
And hath left Love below, to mourn with me.

Beatrice is gone up into high Heaven,
  The kingdom where the angels are at peace;
    And lives with them: and to her friends is dead.
Not by the frost of winter was she driven
  Away, like others; nor by summer-heats;
    But through a perfect gentleness, instead.
    For from the lamp of her meek lowlihead
Such an exceeding glory went up hence
  That it woke wonder in the Eternal Sire,
    Until a sweet desire
Entered Him for that lovely excellence,
  So that He bade her to Himself aspire;
Counting this weary and most evil place
Unworthy of a thing so full of grace.

Wonderfully out of the beautiful form
  Soared her clear spirit, waxing glad the while;
    And is in its first home, there where it is.
Who speaks thereof, and feels not the tears warm
  Upon his face, must have become so vile
    As to be dead to all sweet sympathies.
    Out upon him ! an abject wretch like this
May not imagine anything of her,—
  He needs no bitter tears for his relief.
  But sighing comes, and grief,
And the desire to find no comforter,
  (Save only Death, who makes all sorrow brief,)
To him who for a while turns in his thought
How she hath been among us, and is not.

With sighs my bosom always laboureth
  In thinking, as I do continually,

Of her for whom my heart now breaks apace;
And very often when I think of death,
  Such a great inward longing comes to me
    That it will change the colour of my face;
    And, if the idea settles in its place,
All my limbs shake as with an ague-fit:
  Till, starting up in wild bewilderment,
    I do become so shent
That I go forth, lest folk misdoubt of it.
  Afterward, calling with a sore lament
On Beatrice, I ask, " Canst thou be dead ? "
And calling on her, I am comforted.

Grief with its tears, and anguish with its sighs,
  Come to me now whene'er I am alone;
    So that I think the sight of me gives pain.
And what my life hath been, that living dies,
  Since for my lady the New Birth's begun,
    I have not any language to explain.
    And so, dear ladies, though my heart were fain,
I scarce could tell indeed how I am thus.
  All joy is with my bitter life at war;
    Yea, I am fallen so far
That all men seem to say, " Go out from us,"
  Eyeing my cold white lips, how dead they are.
But she, though I be bowed unto the dust,
Watches me; and will guerdon me, I trust.

Weep, pitiful Song of mine, upon thy way,
  To the dames going and the damozels
    For whom and for none else
Thy sisters have made music many a day.
Thou, that art very sad and not as they,
  Go dwell thou with them as a mourner dwells.

20

STAY now with me, and listen to my sighs,
  Ye piteous hearts, as pity bids ye do.
  Mark how they force their way out and press
    through:
If they be once pent up, the whole life dies.
Seeing that now indeed my weary eyes
  Oftener refuse than I can tell to you
  (Even though my endless grief is ever new,)
To weep and let the smothered anguish rise.
Also in sighing ye shall hear me call
  On her whose blessed presence doth enrich
    The only home that well befitteth her:
And ye shall hear a bitter scorn of all
  Sent from the inmost of my spirit in speech
    That mourns its joy and its joy's minister.

21

WHATEVER while the thought comes over me
    That I may not again
      Behold that lady whom I mourn for now,
  About my heart my mind brings constantly
    So much of extreme pain
      That I say, Soul of mine, why stayest thou?
      Truly the anguish, soul, that we must bow
  Beneath, until we win out of this life,
    Gives me full oft a fear that trembleth:
    So that I call on Death
  Even as on Sleep one calleth after strife,
  Saying, Come unto me. Life showeth grim
  And bare; and if one dies, I envy him.

  For ever, among all my sighs which burn,
    There is a piteous speech
      That clamours upon death continually:

Yea, unto him doth my whole spirit turn
   Since first his hand did reach
      My lady's life with most foul cruelty.
        But from the height of woman's fairness, she,
Going up from us with the joy we had,
   Grew perfectly and spiritually fair;
   That so she spreads even there
A light of Love which makes the Angels glad,
And even unto their subtle minds can bring
A certain awe of profound marvelling.

22

THAT lady of all gentle memories
   Had lighted on my soul;—whose new abode
   Lies now, as it was well ordained of God,
Among the poor in heart, where Mary is.
Love, knowing that dear image to be his,
   Woke up within the sick heart sorrow-bow'd,
   Unto the sighs which are its weary load
Saying, " Go forth."   And they went forth, I wis;
Forth went they from my breast that throbbed and
      ached;
   With such a pang as oftentimes will bathe
    Mine eyes with tears when I am left alone.
   And still those sighs which drew the heaviest breath
Came whispering thus : " O noble intellect !
   It is a year to-day that thou art gone."

23

MINE eyes beheld the blessed pity spring
   Into thy countenance immediately
   A while agone, when thou beheldst in me
The sickness only hidden grief can bring;
And then I knew thou wast considering
   How abject and forlorn my life must be;
   And I became afraid that thou shouldst see

My weeping, and account it a base thing.
Therefore I went out from thee; feeling how
  The tears were straightway loosened at my heart
  Beneath thine eyes' compassionate control.
  And afterwards I said within my soul:
  " Lo ! with this lady dwells the counterpart
Of the same Love who holds me weeping now."

24

LOVE'S pallor and the semblance of deep ruth
  Were never yet shown forth so perfectly
  In any lady's face, chancing to see
Grief's miserable countenance uncouth,
As in thine, lady, they have sprung to soothe,
  When in mine anguish thou hast looked on me;
  Until sometimes it seems as if, through thee,
My heart might almost wander from its truth.
Yet so it is, I cannot hold mine eyes
  From gazing very often upon thine
    In the sore hope to shed those tears they keep;
And at such time, thou mak'st the pent tears rise
  Even to the brim, till the eyes waste and pine;
    Yet cannot they, while thou art present, weep.

25

THE very bitter weeping that ye made
  So long a time together, eyes of mine,
  Was wont to make the tears of pity shine
In other eyes full oft, as I have said.
But now this thing were scarce rememberèd
  If I, on my part, foully would combine
  With you, and not recall each ancient sign
Of grief, and her for whom your tears were shed.
It is your fickleness that doth betray

My mind to fears, and makes me tremble thus
    What while a lady greets me with her eyes.
Except by death, we must not any way
    Forget our lady who is gone from us.
        So far doth my heart utter, and then sighs.

26

A GENTLE thought there is will often start,
    Within my secret self, to speech of thee:
    Also of Love it speaks so tenderly
That much in me consents and takes its part.
" And what is this," the soul saith to the heart,
    " That cometh thus to comfort thee and me,
    And thence where it would dwell, thus potently
Can drive all other thoughts by its strange art ? "
And the heart answers: " Be no more at strife
    'Twixt doubt and doubt: this is Love's messenger
        And speaketh but his words,from him received;
And all the strength it owns and all the life
    It draweth from the gentle eyes of her
        Who, looking on our grief,hath often grieved."

27

WOE'S me ! by dint of all these sighs that come
    Forth of my heart, its endless grief to prove,
    Mine eyes are conquered, so that even to move
Their lids for greeting is grown troublesome.
They wept so long that now they are grief's home
    And count their tears all laughter far above;
    They wept till they are circled now by Love
With a red circle in sign of martyrdom.
These musings, and the sighs they bring from me,
    Are grown at last so constant and so sore
        That love swoons in my spirit with faint breath;
Hearing in those sad sounds continually

The most sweet name that my dead lady bore,
  With many grievous words touching her death.

28

YE pilgrim-folk, advancing pensively
    As if in thought of distant things, I pray,
  Is your own land indeed so far away—
  As by your aspect it would seem to be—
  That this our heavy sorrow leaves you free
    Though passing through the mournful town mid-
      way;
    Like unto men that understand to-day
  Nothing at all of her great misery?
  Yet if he will but stay, whom I accost,
    And listen to my words a little space,
      At going ye shall mourn with a loud voice.
  It is her Beatrice that she hath lost;
    Of whom the least word spoken holds such grace
      That men weep hearing it, and have no choice.

29

BEYOND the sphere which spreads to widest space
    Now soars the sigh that my heart sends above;
  A new perception born of grieving Love
  Guideth it upward the untrodden ways.
  When it hath reached unto the end, and stays,
    It sees a lady round whom splendours move
    In homage; till, by the great light thereof
  Abashed, the pilgrim spirit stands at gaze.
  It sees her such, that when it tells me this
    Which it hath seen, I understand it not,
      It hath a speech so subtile and so fine.
  And yet I know its voice within my thought
  Often remembereth me of Beatrice:
    So that I understand it, ladies mine.

D. G. Rossetti

SONNET

To Guido Cavalcanti

GUIDO, I would that Lapo, thou, and I,
    Led by some strong enchantment, might ascend
    A magic ship, whose charmèd sails should fly
    With winds at will, where'er our thoughts might
        wend.
And that no change, nor any evil chance,
    Should mar our joyous voyage; but it might be
    That even satiety should still enhance
    Between our hearts their strict community,
And that the bounteous wizard then would place
    Vanna and Bice and my gentle love,
    Companions of our wandering, and would grace
With passionate talk, wherever we might rove,
    Our time, and each were as content and free
    As I believe that thou and I should be.

                      Percy Bysshe Shelley

SONNET

To Brunetto Latini
Sent with the Vita Nuova

MASTER BRUNETTO, this my little maid
    Is come to spend her Easter-tide with you:
    Not that she reckons feasting as her due,—
Whose need is hardly to be fed, but read.
Not in a hurry can her sense be weigh'd,
    Nor mid the jests of any noisy crew:
    Ah! and she wants a little coaxing too
Before she'll get into another's head.
But if you do not find her meaning clear,
    You've many Brother Alberts hard at hand,
    Whose wisdom will respond to any call.

Consult with them and do not laugh at her;
    And if she still is hard to understand,
      Apply to Master Janus last of all.

D. G. Rossetti

SONNET

Of Beatrice de' Portinari, on All Saints' Day

LAST All Saints' holy-day, even now gone by,
    I met a gathering of damozels:
      She that came first, as one doth who excels,
Had Love with her, bearing her company:
A flame burned forward through her steadfast eye,
    As when in living fire a spirit dwells:
      So, gazing with the boldness which prevails
O'er doubt, I knew an angel visibly.
As she passed on, she bowed her mild approof
    And salutation to all men of worth,
Lifting the soul to solemn thoughts aloof.
    In Heaven itself that lady had her birth,
I think, and is with us for our behoof:
    Blessed are they who meet her on the earth.

D. G. Rossetti

SONNET

To certain Ladies; when Beatrice was lamenting her Father's Death

WHENCE come you, all of you so sorrowful?
    An it may please you, speak for courtesy.
      I fear for my dear lady's sake, lest she
Have made you to return thus filled with dule.
O gentle ladies, be not hard to school
    In gentleness, but to some pause agree,
      And something of my lady say to me,
For with a little my desire is full.

Howbeit it be a heavy thing to hear:
　For Love now utterly has thrust me forth,
With hand for ever lifted, striking fear.
　See if I be not worn unto the earth;
Yea, and my spirit must fail from me here,
　If, when you speak, your words are of no worth.

D. G. Rossetti

SONNET

To the same Ladies; with their Answer

YE ladies, walking past me piteous-eyed,
　Who is the lady that lies prostrate here?
　Can this be even she my heart holds dear?
Nay, if it be so, speak, and nothing hide.
Her very aspect seems itself beside,
　And all her features of such altered cheer
　That to my thinking they do not appear
Hers who makes others seem beatified.

" If thou forget to know our lady thus,
　Whom grief o'ercomes, we wonder in no wise,
For also the same thing befalleth us.
　Yet if thou watch the movement of her eyes,
Of her thou shalt be straightway conscious.
　O weep no more; thou art all wan with sighs."

D. G. Rossetti

BALLATA

He will gaze upon Beatrice

BECAUSE mine eyes can never have their fill
　Of looking at my lady's lovely face,
　　I will so fix my gaze
That I may become blessed beholding her.
Even as an angel, up at his great height
Standing amid the light,

Becometh blessed by only seeing God:—
So, though I be a simple earthly wight,
Yet none the less I might,
  Beholding her who is my heart's dear load,
  Be blessed, and in the spirit soar abroad.
Such power abideth in that gracious one;
Albeit felt of none
  Save of him who, desiring, honours her.

                                        D. G. Rossetti

CANZONE

He beseeches Death for the Life of Beatrice

DEATH, since I find not one with whom to grieve,
    Nor whom this grief of mine may move to tears,
      Whereso I be or whitherso I turn:
Since it is thou who in my soul wilt leave
    No single joy, but chill'st it with just fears
      And makest it in fruitless hopes to burn:
      Since thou, Death, and thou only, canst decern
Wealth to my life, or want, at thy free choice:
It is to thee that I lift up my voice,
    Bowing my face that's like a face just dead.
I come to thee, as to one pitying,
In grief for that sweet rest which naught can bring
    Again, if thou but once be enterèd
Into her life whom my heart cherishes
Even as the only portal of its peace.

Death, how most sweet the peace is that thy grace
    Can grant to me, and that I pray thee for,
      Thou easily mayst know by a sure sign,
If in mine eyes thou look a little space
    And read in them the hidden dread they store,—
      If upon all thou look which proves me thine.
      Since the fear only maketh me to pine
After this sort,—what will mine anguish be

When her eyes close, of dreadful verity,
    In whose light is the light of mine own eyes?
But now I know that thou wouldst have my life
As hers, and joy'st thee in my fruitless strife.
    Yet I do think this which I feel implies
That soon, when I would die to flee from pain,
I shall find none by whom I may be slain.

Death, if indeed thou smite this gentle one
    Whose outward worth but tells the intellect
        How wondrous is the miracle within,—
Thou biddest Virtue rise up and begone,
    Thou dost away with Mercy's best effect,
        Thou spoil'st the mansion of God's sojourning.
        Yea, unto naught her beauty thou dost bring
Which is above all other beauties, even
In so much as befitteth one whom Heaven
    Sent upon earth in token of its own.
Thou dost break through the perfect trust which hath
Been alway her companion in Love's path:
    The light once darkened which was hers alone,
Love needs must say to them he ruleth o'er,
"I have lost the noble banner that I bore."

Death, have some pity then for all the ill
    Which cannot choose but happen if she die,
        And which will be the sorest ever known.
Slacken the string, if so it be thy will,
    That the sharp arrow leave it not,—thereby
        Sparing her life, which if it flies is flown.
        O Death, for God's sake, be some pity shown!
Restrain within thyself, even at its height,
The cruel wrath which moveth thee to smite
    Her in whom God hath set so much of grace.
Show now some ruth if 'tis a thing thou hast!
I seem to see Heaven's gate, that is shut fast,

Open, and angels filling all the space
About me,—come to fetch her soul whose laud
Is sung by saints and angels before God.

Song, thou must surely see how fine a thread
 This is that my last hope is holden by,
  And what I should be brought to without her.
Therefore for thy plain speech and lowlihead
 Make thou no pause: but go immediately,
  Knowing thyself for my heart's minister,
  And with that very meek and piteous air
Thou hast, stand up before the face of Death,
To wrench away the bar that prisoneth
 And win unto the place of the good fruit.
And if indeed thou shake by thy soft voice
Death's mortal purpose,—haste thee and rejoice
 Our lady with the issue of thy suit.
So yet awhile our earthly nights and days
Shall keep the blessed spirit that I praise.

D. G. Rossetti

SONNET

On the 9th of June, 1290

UPON a day, came Sorrow in to me,
 Saying, "I've come to stay with thee a while";
 And I perceived that she had ushered Bile
And Pain into my house for company.
Wherefore I said, "Go forth—away with thee!"
 But like a Greek she answered, full of guile,
 And went on arguing in an easy style.
Then looking, I saw Love come silently,
Habited in black raiment, smooth and new,
 Having a black hat set upon his hair;
And certainly the tears he shed were true.
 So that I asked, "What ails thee, trifler?"

Answering he said: "A grief to be gone through;
For our own lady's dying, brother dear."

D. G. Rossetti

SONNET

Of Beauty and Duty

TWO ladies to the summit of my mind
    Have clomb, to hold an argument of love.
    The one has wisdom with her from above,
For every noblest virtue well designed:
The other, beauty's tempting power refined
    And the high charm of perfect grace approve:
    And I, as my sweet Master's will doth move,
At feet of both their favours am reclined.
Beauty and Duty in my soul keep strife,
    At question if the heart such course can take
      And 'twixt the two ladies hold its love complete.
      The fount of gentle speech yields answer meet,
    That Beauty may be loved for gladness' sake,
And Duty in the lofty ends of life.

D. G. Rossetti

SESTINA

Of the Lady Pietra degli Scrovigni

TO the dim light and the large circle of shade
I have clomb, and to the whitening of the hills,
There where we see no colour in the grass.
Natheless my longing loses not its green,
It has so taken root in the hard stone
Which talks and hears as though it were a lady.

Utterly frozen is this youthful lady,
Even as the snow that lies within the shade;
For she is no more moved than is the stone
By the sweet season which makes warm the hills

And alters them afresh from white to green,
Covering their sides again with flowers and grass.

When on her hair she sets a crown of grass
The thought has no more room for other lady,
Because she weaves the yellow with the green
So well that Love sits down there in the shade,—
Love who has shut me in among low hills
Faster than between walls of granite‹stone.

She is more bright than is a precious stone;
The wound she gives may not be healed with grass:
I therefore have fled far o'er plains and hills
For refuge from so dangerous a lady;
But from her sunshine nothing can give shade,—
Not any hill, nor wall, nor summer‹green.

A while ago, I saw her dressed in green,—
So fair, she might have wakened in a stone
This love which I do feel even for her shade;
And therefore, as one woos a graceful lady,
I wooed her in a field that was all grass
Girdled about with very lofty hills.

Yet shall the streams turn back and climb the hills
Before Love's flame in this damp wood and green
Burn, as it burns within a youthful lady,
For my sake, who would sleep away in stone
My life, or feed like beasts upon the grass,
Only to see her garments cast a shade.

How dark soe'er the hills throw out their shade,
Under her summer‹green the beautiful lady
Covers it, like a stone cover'd in grass.

D. G. Rossetti

SONNET

To the Lady Pietra degli Scrovigni

MY curse be on the day when first I saw
    The brightness in those treacherous eyes of
      thine,—
The hour when from my heart thou cam'st to draw
My soul away, that both might fail and pine:
My curse be on the skill that smooth'd each line
Of my vain songs,—the music and just law
Of art, by which it was my dear design
That the whole world should yield thee love
    and awe.
Yea, let me curse mine own obduracy,
    Which firmly holds what doth itself con-
      found—
    To wit, thy fair perverted face of scorn:
    For whose sake Love is oftentimes forsworn
So that men mock at him: but most at me
    Who would hold fortune's wheel and turn it
      round.

                D. G. Rossetti

CINO DA PISTOIA

1270–1336

SONNET

To Dante Alighieri

*He interprets Dante's Dream, related in the First Sonnet
of the* Vita Nuova

EACH lover's longing leads him naturally
    Unto his lady's heart his heart to show;
    And this it is that Love would have thee know
By the strange vision which he sent to thee.
With thy heart therefore, flaming outwardly,

In humble guise he fed thy lady so,
Who long had lain in slumber, from all woe
Folded within a mantle silently.
Also, in coming, Love might not repress
His joy, to yield thee thy desire achieved,
    Whence heart should unto heart true service
    bring.
But understanding the great lovesickness
Which in thy lady's bosom was conceived,
He pitied her, and wept in vanishing.

D. G. Rossetti

SONNET

To Dante Alighieri

He conceives of some Compensation in Death

DANTE, whenever this thing happeneth,—
    That Love's desire is quite bereft of Hope,
    (Seeking in vain at ladies' eyes some scope
Of joy, through what the heart for ever saith,)—
I ask thee, can amends be made by Death ?
    Is such sad pass the last extremity ?—
    Or may the Soul that never feared to die
Then in another body draw new breath ?
Lo ! thus it is through her who governs all
    Below,—that I, who entered at her door,
        Now at her dreadful window must fare forth.
Yea, and I think through her it doth befall
    That even ere yet the road is travelled o'er
        My bones are weary and life is nothing worth.

D. G. Rossetti

MADRIGAL

To his Lady Selvaggia Vergiolesi; likening his Love to a Search for Gold

I AM all bent to glean the golden ore
    Little by little from the river-bed;
        Hoping the day to see
When Crœsus shall be conquered in my store.
    Therefore, still sifting where the sands are spread,
        I labour patiently:
Till, thus intent on this thing and no more,—
    If to a vein of silver I were led,
        It scarce could gladden me.
And, seeing that no joy's so warm i' the core
    As this whereby the heart is comforted
        And the desire set free,—
Therefore thy bitter love is still my scope,
    Lady, from whom it is my life's sore theme
More painfully to sift the grains of hope
    Than gold out of that stream.

D. G. Rossetti

SONNET

To Love, in great Bitterness

O LOVE, O thou that, for my fealty,
    Only in torment dost thy power employ,
    Give me, for God's sake, something of thy joy,
That I may learn what good there is in thee.
Yea, for, if thou art glad with grieving me,
    Surely my very life thou shalt destroy
    When thou renew'st my pain, because the joy
Must then be wept for with the misery.
He that had never sense of good, nor sight,
    Esteems his ill estate but natural,
        Which so is lightlier borne: his case is mine.

But, if thou wouldst uplift me for a sign,
Bidding me drain the curse and know it all,
I must a little taste its opposite.

D. G. Rossetti

SONNET

Death is not without but within him

THIS fairest lady, who, as well I wot,
    Found entrance by her beauty to my soul,
    Pierced through mine eyes my heart, which erst
        was whole,
Sorely, yet makes as though she knew it not;
Nay, turns upon me now, to anger wrought;
    Dealing me harshness for my pain's best dole,
    And is so changed by her own wrath's control,
That I go thence, in my distracted thought
Content to die; and, mourning, cry abroad
    On Death, as upon one afar from me;
        But Death makes answer from within my
        heart.
    Then, hearing her so hard at hand to be,
I do commend my spirit unto God;
    Saying to her too, " Ease and peace thou art."

D. G. Rossetti

SONNET

A Trance of Love

VANQUISHED and weary was my soul in me,
    And my heart gasped after its much lament,
    When sleep at length the painful languor sent.
And, as I slept (and wept incessantly),—
Through the keen fixedness of memory
    Which I had cherished ere my tears were spent,
    I passed to a new trance of wonderment;
Wherein a visible spirit I could see,

Which caught me up, and bore me to a place
Where my most gentle lady was alone;
And still before us a fire seemed to move,
Out of the which methought there came a moan,
Uttering, " Grace, a little season, grace !
I am of one that hath the wings of Love."

D. G. Rossetti

SONNET

Of the Grave of Selvaggia, on the Monte della Sambuca

I WAS upon the high and blessed mound,
   And kissed, long worshipping, the stones and grass,
   There on the hard stones prostrate, where, alas !
That pure one laid her forehead in the ground.
Then were the springs of gladness sealed and bound,
   The day that unto Death's most bitter pass
   My sick heart's lady turned her feet, who was
Already in her gracious life renown'd.
So in that place I spake to Love, and cried:
   " O sweet my god, I am one whom Death may claim
   Hence to be his; for lo ! my heart lies here."
   Anon, because my Master lent no ear,
   Departing, still I called Selvaggia's name.
So with my moan I left the mountain-side.

D. G. Rossetti

CANZONE

His Lament for Selvaggia

A Y me, alas ! the beautiful bright hair
   That shed reflected gold
      O'er the green growths on either side of the way:
Ay me ! the lovely look, open and fair,
   Which my heart's core doth hold

With all else of that best remembered day;
　　Ay me ! the face made gay
With joy that Love confers;
　　Ay me ! that smile of hers
　　Where whiteness as of snow was visible
Among the roses at all seasons red !
　　Ay me ! and was this well,
O Death, to let me live when she is dead ?

D. G. Rossetti

DANTE DA MAIANO

c. 1300

SONNET

To Dante Alighieri

*He interprets Dante Alighieri's Dream, related in the
First Sonnet of the* Vita Nuova

OF that wherein thou art a questioner
　　Considering, I make answer briefly thus,
　　Good friend, in wit but little prosperous:
And from my words the truth thou shalt infer,—
So hearken to thy dream's interpreter.
　　If, sound of frame, thou soundly canst discuss
　　In reason,—then, to expel this overplus
Of vapours which hath made thy speech to err,
See that thou lave and purge thy stomach soon.
　　But if thou art afflicted with disease,
　　　　Know that I count it mere delirium.
　　　　Thus of my thought I write thee back the sum:
　　Nor my conclusions can be changed from these
Till to the leech thy water I have shown.

D. G. Rossetti

SONNET

He craves interpreting of a Dream of his

THOU that art wise, let wisdom minister
  Unto my dream, that it be understood.
To wit: A lady, of her body fair,
  And whom my heart approves in womanhood,
  Bestowed on me a wreath of flowers, fair-hued
And green in leaf, with gentle loving air;
  After the which, meseemed I was stark nude
Save for a smock of hers that I did wear.
Whereat, good friend, my courage gat such growth
  That to mine arms I took her tenderly:
With no rebuke the beauty laughed unloath,
  And as she laughed I kissed continually.
I say no more, for that I pledged mine oath,
  And that my mother, who is dead, was by.

D. G. Rossetti

CECCO ANGIOLIERI, DA SIENA

c. 1300

SONNET

To Dante Alighieri

On the Last Sonnet of the Vita Nuova

DANTE ALIGHIERI, Cecco, your good friend
  And servant, gives you greeting as his lord,
  And prays you for the sake of Love's accord,
(Love being the Master before whom you bend,)
That you will pardon him if he offend,
  Even as your gentle heart can well afford.
  All that he wants to say is just one word
Which partly chides your sonnet at the end.
For where the measure changes, first you say
  You do not understand the gentle speech
  A spirit made touching your Beatrice:

And next you tell your ladies how, straightway,
    You understand it.   Wherefore (look you) each
    Of these your words the other's sense denies.

                     D. G. Rossetti

SONNET

He will not be too deeply in Love

I AM enamoured, and yet not so much
    But that I'd do without it easily;
    And my own mind thinks all the more of me
That Love has not quite penned me in his hutch.
Enough if for his sake I dance and touch
    The lute, and serve his servants cheerfully:
    An overdose is worse than none would be:
Love is no lord of mine, I'm proud to vouch.
So let no woman who is born conceive
    That I'll be her liege slave, as I see some,
    Be she as fair and dainty as she will.
Too much of love makes idiots, I·believe:
    I like not any fashion that turns glum
    The heart, and makes the visage sick and ill.

                     D. G. Rossetti

SONNET

Of Love in Men and Devils

THE man who feels not, more or less, somewhat
    Of love in all the years his life goes round
    Should be denied a grave in holy ground
Except with usurers who will bate no groat;
Nor he himself should count himself a jot
    Less wretched than the meanest beggar found.
    Also the man who in Love's robe is gown'd
May say that Fortune smiles upon his lot.

Seeing how love has such nobility
    That if it entered in the lord of Hell
        'Twould rule him more than his fire's ancient
            sting;
He should be glorified to eternity,
    And all his life be always glad and well
        As is a wanton woman in the spring.

D. G. Rossetti

SONNET

Of Love, in honour of his Mistress Becchina

WHATEVER good is naturally done
    Is born of Love as fruit is born of flower:
    By Love all good is brought to its full power:
Yea, Love does more than this; for he finds none
So coarse but from his touch some grace is won,
    And the poor wretch is altered in an hour.
    So let it be decreed that Death devour
The beast who says that Love's a thing to shun.
A man's just worth the good that he can hold,
    And where no love is found, no good is there;
        On that there's nothing that I would not stake.
So now, my Sonnet, go as you are told
    To lovers and their sweethearts everywhere,
        And say I made you for Becchina's sake.

D. G. Rossetti

SONNET

Of Becchina, the Shoemaker's Daughter

WHY, if Becchina's heart were diamond,
    And all the other parts of her were steel,
    As cold to love as snows when they congeal
In lands to which the sun may not get round;
And if her father were a giant crown'd

And not a donkey born to stitching shoes,
  Or I were but an ass myself;—to use
Such harshness, scarce could to her praise redound.
Yet if she'd only for a minute hear,
  And I could speak if only pretty well,
  I'd let her know that I'm her happiness;
That I'm her life should also be made clear,
  With other things that I've no need to tell;
  And then I feel quite sure she'd answer Yes.

D. G. Rossetti

SONNET
Of the 20th June, 1291

I'M full of everything I do not want,
  And have not that wherein I should find ease;
  For alway till Becchina brings me peace
The heavy heart I bear must toil and pant;
That so all written paper would prove scant
  (Though in its space the Bible you might squeeze)
  To say how like the flames of furnaces
I burn, remembering what she used to grant.
Because the stars are fewer in heaven's span
  Than all those kisses wherewith I kept tune
  All in an instant (I who now have none !)
Upon her mouth (I and no other man !)
  So sweetly on the twentieth day of June
  In the new year twelve hundred ninety-one.

D. G. Rossetti

SONNET
Of Becchina in a Rage

WHEN I behold Becchina in a rage,
  Just like a little lad I trembling stand
  Whose master tells him to hold out his hand.

Had I a lion's heart, the sight would wage
Such war against it, that in that sad stage
  I'd wish my birth might never have been plann'd,
  And curse the day and hour that I was bann'd
With such a plague for my life's heritage.
Yet even if I should sell me to the Fiend,
  I must so manage matters in some way
    That for her rage I may not care a fig;
Or else from death I cannot long be screen'd.
So I'll not blink the fact, but plainly say
  It's time I got my valour to grow big.

D. G. Rossetti

SONNET
In Absence from Becchina

MY heart's so heavy with a hundred things
  That I feel dead a hundred times a day;
Yet death would be the least of sufferings,
  For life's all suffering save what's slept away;
Though even in sleep there is no dream but brings
  From dream-land such dull torture as it may.
And yet one moment would pluck out these stings,
  If for one moment she were mine to-day
Who gives my heart the anguish that it has.
  Each thought that seeks my heart for its abode
    Becomes a wan and sorrow-stricken guest:
Sorrow has brought me to so sad a pass
  That men look sad to meet me on the road;
    Nor any road is mine that leads to rest.

D. G. Rossetti

SONNET
He rails against Dante, who had censured his Homage to Becchina

DANTE ALIGHIERI in Becchina's praise
  Won't have me sing and bears him like my lord.
  He's but a pinchbeck florin, on my word;

Sugar he seems, but salt's in all his ways;
He looks like wheaten bread, who's bread of maize;
   He's but a sty, though like a tower in height;
   A falcon, till you find that he's a kite;
Call him a cock !—a hen's more like his case.
Go now to Florence, Sonnet of my own,
   And there with dames and maids hold pretty parles,
   And say that all he is doth only seem.
And I meanwhile will make him better known
   Unto the Court of Provence, good King Charles;
   And in this way we'll singe his skin for him.

D. G. Rossetti

SONNET
Of all he would do

IF I were fire, I'd burn the world away;
   If I were wind, I'd turn my storms thereon;
   If I were water, I'd soon let it drown;
If I were God, I'd sink it from the day;
If I were Pope, I'd never feel quite gay
   Until there was no peace beneath the sun;
      If I were Emperor, what would I have done ?—
I'd lop men's heads all round in my own way.
If I were Death, I'd look my father up;
   If I were Life, I'd run away from him;
      And treat my mother to like calls and runs.
If I were Cecco (and that's all my hope),
   I'd pick the nicest girls to suit my whim,
      And other folk should get the ugly ones.

D. G. Rossetti

SONNET
He is past all Help

FOR a thing done, repentance is no good,
   Nor to say after, Thus would I have done:
In life, what's left behind is vainly rued;
   So let a man get used his hurt to shun;

For on his legs he hardly may be stood
  Again, if once his fall be well begun.
But to show wisdom's what I never could;
  So where I itch I scratch now, and all's one.
I'm down, and cannot rise in any way;
  For not a creature of my nearest kin
    Would hold me out a hand that I could reach.
I pray you do not mock at what I say;
  For so my love's good grace may I not win
    If ever sonnet held so true a speech !

D. G. Rossetti

SONNET
Of why he is unhanged

WHOEVER without money is in love
  Had better build a gallows and go hang;
  He dies not once, but oftener feels the pang
Than he who was cast down from Heaven above.
And certes, for my sins, it's plain enough,
  If Love's alive on earth, that he's myself,
    Who would not be so cursed with want of pelf
If others paid my proper dues thereof.
Then why am I not hanged by my own hands ?
  I answer: for this empty narrow chink
    Of hope;—that I've a father old and rich,
And that if once he dies I'll get his lands;
  And die he must, when the sea's dry, I think.
    Meanwhile God keeps him whole and me i'
    the ditch.

D. G. Rossetti

SONNET
Of why he would be a Scullion

I AM so out of love through poverty
  That if I see my mistress in the street
  I hardly can be certain whom I meet,
And of her name do scarce remember me.

Also my courage it has made to be
   So cold, that if I suffered some foul cheat,
   Even from the meanest wretch that one could beat,
Save for the sin I think he should go free.
Aye, and it plays me a still nastier trick:
   For, meeting some who erewhile with me took
   Delight, I seem to them a roaring fire.
So here's a truth whereat I need not stick;—
   That if one could turn scullion to a cook,
   It were a thing to which one might aspire.

D. G. Rossetti

SONNET

He argues his Case with Death

GRAMERCY, Death, as you've my love to win,
   Just be impartial in your next assault;
   And that you may not find yourself in fault,
Whate'er you do, be quick now and begin.
As oft may I be pounded flat and thin
   As in Grosseto there are grains of salt,
   If now to kill us both you be not call'd,—
Both me and him who sticks so in his skin.
Or better still, look here; for if I'm slain
   Alone,—his wealth, it's true, I'll never have,
Yet death is life to one who lives in pain:
   But if you only kill Saldagno's knave,
I'm left in Siena (don't you see your gain?)
   Like a rich man who's made a galley-slave.

D. G. Rossetti

SONNET

To Dante Alighieri

He writes to Dante, then in exile at Verona, defying him as no better than himself

DANTE ALIGHIERI, if I jest and lie,
  You in such lists might run a tilt with me:
  I get my dinner, you your supper, free;
And if I bite the fat, you suck the fry;
I shear the cloth and you the teazel ply;
  If I've a strut, who's prouder than you are?
  If I'm foul-mouthed, you're not particular.
And you've turned Lombard, even if Roman I.
So that, 'fore Heaven! if either of us flings
  Much dirt at the other, he must be a fool:
For lack of luck and wit we do these things.
  Yet if you want some lessons at my school,
Just say so, and you'll find the next touch stings—
  For, Dante, I'm the goad and you're the bull.

D. G. Rossetti

SIMONE DALL' ANTELLA

c. 1300

PROLONGED SONNET

In the Last Days of the Emperor Henry VII

ALONG the road all shapes must travel by,
  How swiftly, to my thinking, now doth fare
  The wanderer who built his watchtower there
Where wind is torn with wind continually!
Lo! from the world and its dull pain to fly,
  Unto such pinnacle did he repair,
  And of her presence was not made aware,
Whose face, that looks like Peace, is Death's own lie.

Alas, Ambition, thou his enemy,
   Who lurest the poor wanderer on his way,
But never bring'st him where his rest may be,—
   O leave him now, for he is gone astray
Himself out of his very self through thee,
   Till now the broken stems his feet betray,
And, caught with boughs before and boughs behind,
Deep in thy tangled wood he sinks entwin'd.

D. G. Rossetti

GIOVANNI QUIRINO

c. 1300

SONNET

To Dante Alighieri

*He commends the Work of Dante s Life, then drawing
to its close; and deplores his own Deficiencies*

GLORY to God and to God's Mother chaste,
   Dear friend, is all the labour of thy days:
   Thou art as he who evermore uplays
That heavenly wealth which the worm cannot waste:
So shalt thou render back with interest
   The precious talent given thee by God's grace:
   While I, for my part, follow in their ways
Who by the cares of this world are possess'd.
For, as the shadow of the earth doth make
   The moon's globe dark, when so she is debarr'd
     From the bright rays which lit her in the sky,—
So now, since thou my sun didst me forsake,
   (Being distant from me,) I grow dull and hard,
     Even as a beast of Epicurus' sty.

D. G. Rossetti

FRANCESCO PETRARCA

1304–74

*W*HAT *he had achieved for the modern world was not merely to
bequeath to his Italian imitators masterpieces of lyrical art unrivalled
for perfection of workmanship, but also, and far more, to open out for
Europe a new sphere of mental activity. Standing within the threshold
of the Middle Ages, he surveyed the kingdom of the modern spirit, and,
by his own inexhaustible industry in the field of scholarship, he determined
what we call the revival of learning.*—J. A. SYMONDS.

Visions

I

BEING one day at my window all alone
  So manie strange things happened me to see,
As much it grieveth me to thinke thereon.
   At my right hand a hynde appear'd to mee,
So faire as mote the greatest god delite;
   Two eager dogs did her pursue in chace,
Of which the one was blacke, the other white:
  With deadly force so in their cruell race
They pincht the haunches of that gentle beast,
   That at the last, and in short time, I spide,
Under a rocke, where she alas, opprest,
   Fell to the ground, and there untimely dide.
Cruell death vanquishing so noble beautie
Oft makes me wayle so hard a destenie.

II

After, at sea a tall ship did appeare,
  Made all of heben and white yvorie;
The sailes of golde, of silke the tackle were:
  Milde was the winde, calme seem'd the sea to bee,
The skie eachwhere did show full bright and faire:
  With rich treasures this gay ship fraighted was:
But sudden storme did so turmoyle the aire,
  And tumbled up the sea, that she (alas)

Strake on a rock, that under water lay,
　And perished past all recoverie.
O ! how great ruth, and sorrowful assay,
　Doth vex my spirite with perplexitie,
Thus in a moment to see lost, and drown'd,
So great riches, as like cannot be found.

III

The heavenly branches did I see arise
　Out of the fresh and lustie lawrell tree,
Amidst the young greene wood of paradise;
　Some noble plant I thought my selfe to see:
Such store of birds therein yshrowded were
　Chaunting in shade their sundrie melodie,
That with their sweetnes I was ravisht nere.

　While on this lawrell fixed was mine eie,
The skie gan everie where to overcast,
　And darkened was the welkin all about,
When sudden flash of heavens fire out brast,
　And rent this royall tree quite by the roote;
Which makes me much and ever to complaine;
For no such shadow shal be had againe.

IV

Within this wood, out of a rocke did rise
　A spring of water, mildly rumbling downe,
Whereto approched not in anie wise
　The homely shepheard, nor the ruder clown;
But manie muses, and the nymphes withall,
　That sweetly in accord did tune their voyce
To the soft sounding of the waters fall;
　That my glad heart thereat did much rejoyce.
But, while herein I tooke my chiefe delight,
　I saw (alas) the gaping earth devoure

The spring, the place, and all cleane out of sight;
　　Which yet aggreeves my hart even to this houre,
And wounds my soule with rufull memorie,
To see such pleasures go so suddenly.

V

I saw a phœnix in the wood alone,
　　With purple wings, and crest of golden hewe;
Strange bird he was, whereby I thought anone,
　　That of some heavenly wight I have the vewe;
Untill he came unto the broken tree,
　　And to the spring, that late devoured was.
What say I more? each thing at last we see
　　Doth passe away: the phœnix there alas,
Spying the tree destroid, the water dride,
　　Himselfe smote with his beake, as in disdain,
And so foorthwith in great despight he dide;
　　That yet my heart burnes, in exceeding paine,
For ruth and pitie of so hapless plight:
O! let mine eyes no more see such a sight.

VI

At last so faire a ladie did I spie,
　　That thinking yet on her I burne and quake;
On hearbs and flowres she walked pensively,
　　Milde, but yet love she proudly did forsake:
White seem'd her robes, yet woven so they were,
　　As snow and golde together had been wrought:
Above the wast a darke clowde shrouded her,
　　A stinging serpent by the heele her caught;
Wherewith she languisht as the gathered floure;
　　And, well assur'd, she mounted up to ioy.
Alas, on earth so nothing doth endure,
　　But bitter griefe and sorrowfull annoy:
Which makes their life wretched and miserable,
Tossed with stormes of fortune variable.

VII

When I beheld this fickle trustles state
  Of vaine worlds glorie, flitting too and fro,
And mortall men tossed by troublous fate
  In restles seas of wretchedness and woe;
I wish I might this wearie life forgoe,
  And shortly turne unto my happie rest,
Where my free spirite might not anie moe
  Be vext with sights, that doo her peace molest.
And ye, faire ladie, in whose bounteous brest
  All heavenly grace and vertue shrined is,
When ye these rythmes doo read, and vew the rest,
  Loath this base world, and thinke of heavens blis:
And though ye be the fairest of Gods creatures,
Yet thinke, that Death shall spoyle your godly features.

Edmund Spenser

The Song of Troylus

IF no love is, O God, what fele I so?
  And if love is, what thinge and whiche is he?
  If love be gode, from whennes comth my wo?
  If it be wykke, a wonder thynketh me,
  Whenne every torment and adversite,
  That cometh of him, may to me savory thynke;
  For ay thirst I the more that Iche it drynke.

  And if that in myn owne lust I brenne,
  From whennes cometh my wailynge and my pleynte?
  If harme agree me, whereto pleyne I thenne?
  I noot, ne why, unwery, that I feynte.
  O quyke deth! O swete harm so queynte!
  How may I se in me swiche quantite,
  But if that I consente that it so be?

  And if that I consente, I wrongfully
  Compleyne ywis; thus possed to and fro,
  Al sterelees withinne a boot am I

Amyd the see, betwexen windes two,
That in contrarie standen ever mo.
Allas ! what is this wonder maladye ?
For hete of cold, for cold of hete I dye.

Geoffrey Chaucer

Summer is come

THE soote season, that bud and bloom forth brings
With green hath clad the hill, and eke the vale.
The nightingale with feathers new she sings;
The turtle to her mate hath told her tale.
Summer is come, for every spray now springs;
The hart has hung his old head on the pale;
The buck in brake his winter coat he flings;
The fishes flete with new repairèd scale;
The adder all her slough away she slings;
The swift swallow pursueth the flies smale;
The busy bee her honey now she mings.
Winter is worn that was the flowers' bale,
And thus I see among these pleasant things
Each care decays, and yet my sorrow springs !

The Earl of Surrey

A Complaint by Night of the Lover not beloved

ALAS, so all things now do hold their peace !
Heaven and earth disturbèd in no thing;
The beasts, the air, the birds their song do cease,
The nightès car the stars about doth bring;
Calm is the sea; the waves work less and less:
So am not I, whom love, alas ! doth wring,
Bringing before my face the great increase
Of my desires, whereat I weep and sing,
In joy and woe, as in a doubtful case.
For my sweet thoughts sometime do pleasure bring;

But by and by, the cause of my disease
  Gives me a pang that inwardly doth sting,
When that I think what grief it is again
To live and lack the thing should rid my pain.

The Earl of Surrey

Complaint of a Lover rebuked

LOVE, that liveth and reigneth in my thought,
  That built his seat within my captive breast,
Clad in the arms wherein with me he fought,
  Oft in my face he doth his banner rest.
She, that me taught to love, and suffer pain:
  My doubtful hope and eke my hot desire
With shamefaced cloak to shadow and restrain;
  Her smiling grace converteth straight to ire,
And coward Love then to the heart apace
  Taketh his flight, whereas he lurks, and plains
His purpose lost, and dare not show his face.
  For my lord's guilt thus faultless bide I pains;
Yet from my lord shall not my foot remove:
Sweet is his death, that takes his end by love.

The Earl of Surrey

Love's Fidelity

SET me whereas the sun doth parch the green,
  Or where his beams do not dissolve the ice:
In temperate heat, where he is felt and seen;
  In presence prest of people mad or wise;
Set me in high, or yet in low degree;
  In longest night, or in the shortest day;
In clearest sky, or where clouds thickest be;
  In lusty youth, or when my hairs are grey:
Set me in heaven, in earth, or else in hell,
  In hill or dale, or in the foaming flood;

Thrall, or at large, alive whereso I dwell,
  Sick or in health, in evil fame or good,
Hers will I be; and only with this thought
Content myself although my chance be naught.

The Earl of Surrey

Love's Inconsistency

I FIND no peace, and all my war is done;
  I fear and hope, I burn and freeze likewise;
  I fly above the wind, yet cannot rise;
And naught I have, yet all the world I seize on;
That looseth, nor locketh, holdeth me in prison,
  And holds me not, yet can I 'scape no wise;
  Nor lets me live, nor die, at my devise,
And yet of death it giveth none occasion.
Without eyes I see, and without tongue I plain;
  I wish to perish, yet I ask for health;
  I love another, and yet I hate myself;
I feed in sorrow, and laugh in all my pain;
  Lo, thus displeaseth me both death and life,
  And my delight is causer of my grief.

Sir Thomas Wyatt

The Heart on the Hill

THOU green and blooming, cool and shaded hill,
  Where sits, now songful, now in thought, thy guest,
  By whom the world's of glory dispossessed,
And heavenly spirits are made credible—
My heart, which quitted me for her (what skill
  He showed; and if he come not back, shows best!)
  Goes on relating, how that foot hath pressed,
And how those eyes the sward are softening still.
He says, and with a shrug at every pace,
  " Oh were that caitiff here a little now,

Who is so tired of tears and of his lot ! "
She smiles, and how unequal is the case,
   I being heartless stone, and Eden thou,
   Oh hallowed, fortunate, delightsome spot !

C. B. Cayley

Signs of Love

IF amorous faith, a heart of guileless ways,
   Soft languors, courteously controlled desire,
   And virtuous will, kindled with noble fire,
And lengthened wanderings in a lightless maze;
If thoughts, which evermore the brow displays,
   Or words that faint and brokenly suspire,
   Still checked with fear and shame; if hues no higher
Than the pale violet hath, or love displays;
If holding some one than one's self more dear,
   If sorrowing and sighing evermore,
   If chewing grief, and rage, and many a cross,
If burning far away, and freezing near,
   Are signs that Love consumes me to the core,
   Yours, lady, is the fault and mine the loss.

C. B. Cayley

If it be destined

IF it be destined that my Life, from thine
   Divided, yet with thine shall linger on
Till, in the later twilight of Decline,
   I may behold those Eyes, their lustre gone;
When the gold tresses that enrich thy brow
   Shall all be faded into silver-grey,
From which the wreaths that well bedeck them now
   For many a Summer shall have fall'n away;
Then should I dare to whisper in your ears
   The pent-up Passion of so long ago,

That Love which hath survived the wreck of years
　　Hath little else to pray for, or bestow,
Thou wilt not to the broken heart deny
　　The boon of one too⸗late relenting Sigh.

Edward FitzGerald

GIOVANNI BOCCACCIO

SONNETS

1313–75

I

To one who had censured his Public Exposition of Dante

IF Dante mourns, there wheresoe'er he be,
　　That such high fancies of a soul so proud
　　Should be laid open to the vulgar crowd,
(As, touching my Discourse, I'm told by thee,)
This were my grievous pain; and certainly
　　My proper blame should not be disavow'd;
　　Though hereof somewhat, I declare aloud,
Were due to others, not alone to me.
False hopes, true poverty, and therewithal
　　The blinded judgment of a host of friends,
　　　　And their entreaties, made that I did thus.
But of all this there is no gain at all
　　Unto the thankless souls with whose base ends
　　　　Nothing agrees that's great or generous.

II

Inscription for a Portrait of Dante

DANTE ALIGHIERI, a dark oracle,
　　Of wisdom and of art, I am; whose mind
　　Has to my country such great gifts assign'd
That men account my powers a miracle.
My lofty fancy passed as low as Hell,
　　As high as Heaven, secure and unconfin'd;
　　And in my noble book doth every kind

Of earthly lore and heavenly doctrine dwell.
Renownèd Florence was my mother,—nay,
  Stepmother unto me her piteous son,
    Through sin of cursed slander's tongue and
      tooth.
Ravenna sheltered me so cast away;
  My body is with her,—my soul with One
    For whom no envy can make dim the truth.

III

To Dante in Paradise, after Fiammetta's Death

DANTE, if thou within the sphere of Love,
  As I believe, remain'st contemplating
  Beautiful Beatrice, whom thou didst sing
Erewhile, and so wast drawn to her above;—
Unless from false life true life thee remove
  So far that Love's forgotten, let me bring
  One prayer before thee: for an easy thing
This were, to thee whom I do ask it of.
I know that when all joy doth most abound
  In the Third Heaven, my own Fiammetta sees
    The grief which I have borne since she is dead.
O pray her (if mine image be not drown'd
  In Lethe) that her prayers may never cease
    Until I reach her and am comforted.

IV

Of Fiammetta singing

LOVE steered my course, while yet the sun rode high,
  On Scylla's waters to a myrtle-grove:
  The heaven was still and the sea did not move;
Yet now and then a little breeze went by
Stirring the tops of trees against the sky:

And then I heard a song as glad as love,
So sweet that never yet the like thereof
Was heard in any mortal company.
" A nymph, a goddess, or an angel sings
Unto herself, within this chosen place,
Of ancient loves "; so said I at that sound.
And there my lady, 'mid the shadowings
Of myrtle-trees, 'mid flowers and grassy space,
Singing I saw, with others who sat round.

V

Of his Last Sight of Fiammetta

ROUND her red garland and her golden hair
I saw a fire about Fiammetta's head;
Thence to a little cloud I watched it fade,
Than silver or than gold more brightly fair;
And like a pearl that a gold ring doth bear,
Even so an angel sat therein, who sped
Alone and glorious throughout heaven, array'd
In sapphires and in gold that lit the air.
Then I rejoiced as hoping happy things,
Who rather should have then discerned how God
Had haste to make my lady all His own,
Even as it came to pass. And with these stings
Of sorrow, and with life's most weary load
I dwell, who fain would be where she is gone.

VI

Of Three Girls and of their Talk

BY a clear well, within a little field
Full of green grass and flowers of every hue,
Sat three young girls, relating (as I knew)
Their loves. And each had twined a bough to shield
Her lovely face; and the green leaves did yield

The golden hair their shadow; while the two
Sweet colours mingled, both blown lightly through
With a soft wind for ever stirred and still'd.
After a little while one of them said,
   (I heard her,) " Think ! If, ere the next hour
     struck,
     Each of our lovers should come here to*day,
Think you that we should fly or feel afraid ? "
   To whom the others answered, " From such luck
   A girl would be a fool to run away."

                  D. G. Rossetti

FAZIO DEGLI UBERTI

1326–60

CANZONE

His Portrait of his Lady, Angiola of Verona

I LOOK at the crisp golden*threaded hair
   Whereof, to thrall my heart, Love twists a net,
   Using at times a string of pearls for bait,
     And sometimes with a single rose therein.
I look into her eyes which unaware
   Through mine own eyes to my heart penetrate;
   Their splendour, that is excellently great,
     To the sun's radiance seeming near akin,
     Yet from herself a sweeter light to win.
So that I, gazing on that lovely one,
   Discourse in this wise with my secret thought:—
   " Woe's me ! why am I not,
Even as my wish, alone with her alone,—
   That hair of hers, so heavily uplaid,
   To shed down braid by braid,
And make myself two mirrors of her eyes
Within whose light all other glory dies ? "

I look at the amorous beautiful mouth,
  The spacious forehead which her locks enclose,
  The small white teeth, the straight and shapely
    nose,
    And the clear brows of a sweet pencilling.
And then the thought within me gains full growth,
  Saying, " Be careful that thy glance now goes
  Between her lips, red as an open rose,
    Quite full of every dear and precious thing;
    And listen to her gracious answering,
Born of the gentle mind that in her dwells,
  Which from all things can glean the nobler half.
  Look thou when she doth laugh
How much her laugh is sweeter than aught else."
  Thus evermore my spirit makes avow
  Touching her mouth; till now
I would give anything that I possess,
Only to hear her mouth say frankly, " Yes."

I look at her white easy neck, so well
  From shoulders and from bosom lifted out;
  And at her round cleft chin, which beyond doubt
    No fancy in the world could have design'd.
And then, with longing grown more voluble,
  " Were it not pleasant now," pursues my thought,
  " To have that neck within thy two arms caught
    And kiss it till the mark were left behind ? "
    Then, urgently: " The eyelids of thy mind
Open thou: if such loveliness be given
  To sight here,—what of that which she doth hide ?
  Only the wondrous ride
Of sun and planets through the visible heaven
  Tells us that there beyond is Paradise.
  Thus, if thou fix thine eyes,
Of a truth certainly thou must infer
That every earthly joy abides in her."

I look at the large arms, so lithe and round,—
  At the hands, which are white and rosy too,—
  At the long fingers, clasped and woven through,
    Bright with the ring which one of them doth
      wear.
Then my thought whispers: " Were thy body wound
  Within those arms, as loving women's do,
  In all thy veins were born a life made new
    Which thou couldst find no language to declare.
    Behold if any picture can compare
With her just limbs, each fit in shape and size,
  Or match her angel's colour like a pearl.
  She is a gentle girl
To see; yet when it needs, her scorn can rise.
  Meek, bashful, and in all things temperate,
  Her virtue holds its state;
In whose least act there is that gift express'd
Which of all reverence makes her worthiest."

Soft as a peacock steps she, or as a stork
  Straight on herself, taller and statelier:
    'Tis a good sight how every limb doth stir
    For ever in a womanly sweet way.
" Open thy soul to see God's perfect work,"
  (My thought begins afresh,) " and look at her
  When with some lady-friend exceeding fair
    She bends and mingles arms and locks in play.
    Even as all lesser lights vanish away,
When the sun moves, before his dazzling face,
  So is this lady brighter than all these.
  How should she fail to please,—
Love's self being no more than her loveliness?
  In all her ways some beauty springs to view;
  All that she loves to do
Tends alway to her honour's single scope;
And only from good deeds she draws her hope."

Song, thou canst surely say, without pretence,
    That since the first fair woman ever made,
    Not one can have display'd
        More power upon all hearts than this one doth;
        Because in her are both
Loveliness and the soul's true excellence:—
And yet (woe's me !) is pity absent thence ?

                    D. G. Rossetti

Of England, and of its Marvels

NOW to Great Britain we must make our way,
    Unto which kingdom Brutus gave its name
    What time he won it from the giants' rule.
    'Tis thought at first its name was Albion,
    And Anglia, from a damsel, afterwards.
    The island is so great and rich and fair,
    It conquers others that in Europe be,
    Even as the sun surpasses other stars.
    Many and great sheep-pastures bountifully
    Nature has set there, and herein more bless'd,
    That they can hold themselves secure from wolves.
    Black amber also doth the land enrich,
    (Whose properties my guide Solinus here
    Told me, and how its colour comes to it;)
    And pearls are found in great abundance too.
    The people are as white and comely-faced
    As they of Ethiop land are black and foul.
    Many hot springs and limpid fountain-heads
    We found about this land, and spacious plains,
    And divers beasts that dwell within thick woods.
    Plentiful orchards too and fertile fields
    It has, and castle-forts, and cities fair
    With palaces and girth of lofty walls.
    And proud wide rivers without any fords
    We saw, and flesh, and fish, and crops enough.
    Justice is strong throughout those provinces.

Now this I saw not; but so strange a thing
It was to hear, and by all men confirm'd,
That it is fit to note it as I heard;—
To wit, there is a certain islet here
Among the rest, where folk are born with tails,
Short, as are found in stags and such-like beasts.

For this I vouch,—that when a child is freed
From swaddling bands, the mother without stay
Passes elsewhere, and 'scapes the care of it.

I put no faith herein; but it is said
Among them, how such marvellous trees are there
That they grow birds, and this is their sole fruit.

Forty times eighty is the circuit ta'en,
With ten times fifteen, if I do not err,
By our miles reckoning its circumference.
Here every metal may be dug; and here
I found the people to be given to God,
Steadfast, and strong, and restive to constraint.
Nor is this strange, when one considereth;
For courage, beauty, and large-heartedness,
Were there, as it is said, in ancient days.

North Wales, and Orkney, and the banks of Thames,
Land's End and Stonehenge and Northumberland,
I chose with my companion to behold.
We went to London, and I saw the Tower
Where Guenevere her honour did defend,
With the Thames river which runs close to it;
I saw the castle which by force was ta'en
With the three shields by gallant Lancelot,
The second year that he did deeds of arms.
I beheld Camelot despoiled and waste;
And was where one and the other had her birth,
The maids of Corbonek and Astolat.

Also I saw the castle where Geraint
Lay with his Enid; likewise Merlin's stone
Which for another's love I joyed to see.
I found the tract where is the pine-tree well,
And where of old the knight of the black shield
With weeping and with laughter kept the pass,
What time the pitiless and bitter dwarf
Before Sir Gawaine's eyes discourteously
With many heavy stripes led him away.
I saw the valley which Sir Tristram won
When having slain the giant hand to hand
He set the stranger knights from prison free.
And last I viewed the field, at Salisbury,
Of that great martyrdom which left the world
Empty of honour, valour, and delight.

So, compassing that Island round and round,
I saw and hearkened many things and more
Which might be fair to tell but which I hide.

D. G. Rossetti

FRANCO SACCHETTI

1335–1400 ?

BALLATA

His Talk with Certain Peasant-girls

" YE graceful peasant-girls and mountain-maids,
   Whence come ye homeward through these evening
     shades ? "

" We come from where the forest skirts the hill;
   A very little cottage is our home,
Where with our father and our mother still
   We live, and love our life, nor wish to roam.
   Back every evening from the field we come
And bring with us our sheep from pasturing there."

" Where, tell me, is the hamlet of your birth,
  Whose fruitage is the sweetest by so much ?
Ye seem to me as creatures worship-worth,
  The shining of your countenance is such.
  No gold about your clothes, coarse to the touch,
Nor silver; yet with such an angel's air !

" I think your beauties might make great complaint
  Of being thus shown over mount and dell;
Because no city is so excellent
  But that your stay therein were honourable.
  In very truth, now, does it like ye well
To live so poorly on the hill-side here ? "

" Better it liketh one of us, pardie,
  Behind her flock to seek the pasture-stance,
Far better than it liketh one of ye
  To ride unto your curtained rooms and dance.
  We seek no riches, neither golden chance
Save wealth of flowers to weave into our hair."

Ballad, if I were now as once I was,
  I'd make myself a shepherd on some hill,
And, without telling any one, would pass
  Where these girls went, and follow at their will;
  And " Mary " and " Martin " we would murmur still,
And I would be for ever where they were.

D. G. Rossetti

CATCH

On a Wet Day

AS I walked thinking through a little grove,
  Some girls that gathered flowers came passing me,
  Saying, " Look here ! look there ! " delightedly.
  " Oh, here it is ! " " What's that ? " " A lily, love."
  " And there are violets ! "

" Further for roses !   Oh, the lovely pets—
The darling beauties !   Oh, the nasty thorn !
Look here, my hand's all torn ! "
" What's that that jumps ! "   " Oh, don't ! it's a grass-
　　hopper ! "
" Come run, come run,
Here's bluebells ! "   " Oh, what fun ! "
" Not that way !   Stop her ! "
" Yes, this way ! "   " Pluck them, then ! "
" Oh, I've found mushrooms !   Oh, look here ! "
　　" Oh, I'm
Quite sure that further on we'll get wild thyme."

" Oh, we shall stay too long, it's going to rain !
There's lightning, oh there's thunder ! "
" Oh, shan't we hear the vesper bell, I wonder ? "
" Why, it's not nones, you silly little thing;
And don't you hear the nightingales that sing
Fly away O die away ? "
" Oh, I hear something !   Hush ! "
" Why, where ? what is it, then ? "   " Ah ! in that
　　bush ! "
So every girl here knocks it, shakes and shocks it,
Till with the stir they make
Out skurries a great snake.
" O Lord !   O me !   Alack !   Ah me ! alack ! "
They scream, and then all run and scream again,
And then in heavy drops down comes the rain.

Each running at the other in a fright,
Each trying to get before the other, and crying,
And flying, stumbling, tumbling, wrong or right;
One sets her knee
There where her foot should be;
One has her hands and dress
All smothered up with mud in a fine mess;
And one gets trampled on by two or three.

What's gathered is let fall
About the wood and not picked up at all.
The wreaths of flowers are scattered on the ground;
And still as screaming, hustling, without rest
They run this way and that and round and round,
She thinks herself in luck who runs the best.

I stood quite still to have a perfect view,
And never noticed till I got wet through.

D. G. Rossetti

ANONYMOUS

14th century

SONNET

A Lady laments for her Lost Lover, by Similitude of a Falcon

ALAS for me, who loved a falcon well !
   So well I loved him, I was nearly dead:
   Ever at my low call he bent his head,
And ate of mine, not much, but all that fell.
Now he has fled, how high I cannot tell,
   Much higher now than ever he has fled,
   And is in a fair garden housed and fed;
Another lady, alas ! shall love him well.
Oh, my own falcon whom I taught and rear'd !
   Sweet bells of shining gold I gave to thee
That in the chase thou shouldst not be afeard.
   Now thou hast risen like the risen sea,
Broken thy jesses loose, and disappear'd,
   As soon as thou wast skilled in falconry.

D. G. Rossetti

BALLATA

One speaks of the Beginning of his Love

THIS fairest one of all the stars, whose flame,
   For ever lit, my inner spirit fills,
   Came to me first one day between the hills.

I wondered very much; but God the Lord
Said, " From Our Virtue, lo ! this light is pour'd."
So in a dream it seemed that I was led
By a great Master to a garden spread
With lilies underfoot and overhead.

D. G. Rossetti

BALLATA

Of True and False Singing

A LITTLE wild bird sometimes at my ear
   Sings his own verses very clear:
Others sing louder that I do not hear.

For singing loudly is not singing well;
   But ever by the song that's soft and low
The master-singer's voice is plain to tell.
   Few have it and yet all are masters now,
And each of them can trill out what he calls
His ballads, canzonets, and madrigals.
The world with masters is so covered o'er,
There is no room for pupils any more.

D. G. Rossetti

ANGELO POLIZIANO

1454-94

THREE BALLATE

I

I FOUND myself one day all, all alone,
For pastime in a field with blossoms strewn.

I do not think the world a field could show
   With herbs of perfume so surpassing rare;
But when I passed beyond the green hedge-row,
   A thousand flowers around me flourished fair,
   White, pied and crimson, in the summer air;
Among the which I heard a sweet bird's tone.

I found myself one day all, all alone,
For pastime in a field with blossoms strewn.

Her song it was so tender and so clear
  That all the world listened with love; then I
With stealthy feet a-tiptoe drawing near,
  Her golden head and golden wings could spy,
  Her plumes that flashed like rubies 'neath the sky,
Her crystal beak and throat and bosom's zone.

I found myself one day all, all alone,
For pastime in a field with blossoms strewn.

Fain would I snare her, smit with mighty love;
  But arrow-like she soared, and through the air
Fled to her nest upon the boughs above;
  Wherefore to follow her is all my care,
  For haply I might lure her by some snare
Forth from the woodland wild where she is flown.

I found myself one day all, all alone,
For pastime in a field with blossoms strewn.

Yea, I might spread some net or woven wile;
  But since of singing she doth take such pleasure,
Without or other art or other guile
  I seek to win her with a tuneful measure;
  Therefore in singing spend I all my leisure,
To make by singing this sweet bird my own.

I found myself one day all, all alone,
For pastime in a field with blossoms strewn.

II

HE who knows not what thing is Paradise,
Let him look fixedly on Myrrha's eyes.

From Myrrha's eyes there flieth, girt with fire,
  An angel of our lord, a laughing boy,

Who lights in frozen hearts a flaming pyre,
 And with such sweetness doth the soul destroy,
 That while it dies, it murmurs forth its joy:
Oh blessed am I to dwell·in Paradise !

He who knows not what thing is Paradise,
Let him look fixedly on Myrrha's eyes.

From Myrrha's eyes a virtue still doth move,
 So swift and with so fierce and strong a flight,
That it is like the lightning of high Jove,
 Riving of iron and adamant the might;
 Nathless the wound doth carry such delight
That he who suffers dwells in Paradise.

He who knows not what thing is Paradise,
Let him look fixedly on Myrrha's eyes.

From Myrrha's eyes a lovely messenger
 Of joy so grave, so virtuous, doth flee,
That all proud souls are bound to bend to her;
 So sweet her countenance, it turns the key
 Of hard hearts locked in cold security:
Forth flies the prisoned soul to Paradise.

He who knows not what thing is Paradise,
Let him look fixedly on Myrrha's eyes.

In Myrrha's eyes beauty doth but make her throne,
 And sweetly smile and sweetly speak her mind:
Such grace in her fair eyes a man hath known
 As in the whole wide world he scarce may find:
 Yet if she slay him with a glance too kind,
He lives again beneath her gazing eyes.

He who knows not what thing is Paradise,
Let him look fixedly on Myrrha's eyes.

III

I WENT a roaming, maidens, one bright day,
In a green garden in mid month of May.

Violets and lilies grew on every side
 Mid the green grass, and the young flowers
  wonderful,
Golden and white and red and azure-eyed;
 Toward which I stretched my hands, eager to pull
 Plenty to make my fair curls beautiful,
To crown my rippling curls with garlands gay.

I went a roaming, maidens, one bright day,
In a green garden in mid month of May.

But when my lap was full of flowers I spied
 Roses at last, roses of every hue;
Therefore I ran to pluck their ruddy pride,
 Because their perfume was so sweet and true
 That all my soul went forth with pleasure new,
With yearning and desire too soft to say.

I went a roaming, maidens, one bright day,
In a green garden in mid month of May.

I gazed and gazed. Hard task it were to tell
 How lovely were the roses in that hour:
One was but peeping from her verdant shell,
 And some were faded, some were scarce in flower:
 Then Love said: Go, pluck from the blooming bower
Those that thou seest ripe upon the spray.

I went a roaming, maidens, one bright day,
In a green garden in mid month of May.

For when the full rose quits her tender sheath,
 When she is sweetest and most fair to see,

Then is the time to place her in thy wreath,
  Before her beauty and her freshness flee.
  Gather ye therefore roses with great glee,
Sweet girls, or e'er their perfume pass away.

I went a roaming, maidens, one bright day,
In a green garden in mid month of May.

John Addington Symonds .

LORENZO DE' MEDICI

1448–92

TWO LYRICS

I

INTO a little close of mine I went
  One morning, when the sun with his fresh light
  Was rising all refulgent and unshent.
Rose-trees are planted there in order bright,
  Whereto I turned charmed eyes, and long did stay,
  Taking my fill of that new-found delight.
Red and white roses bloomed upon the spray;
  One opened, leaf by leaf, to greet the morn,
  Shyly at first, then in sweet disarray;
Another, yet a youngling, newly born,
  Scarce struggled from the bud, and there were some
  Whose petals closed them from the air forlorn;
Another fell, and showered the grass with bloom;
  Thus I behold the roses dawn and die,
  And one short hour their loveliness consume.
But while I watched those languid petals lie
  Colourless on cold earth, I could but think
  How vain a thing is youthful bravery.
Trees have their time to bloom on winter's brink;
  Then the rathe blossoms wither in an hour,
  When the brief days of spring towards summer sink
The fruit, as yet unformed, is tart and sour;
  Little by little it grows large, and weighs

The strong boughs down with slow persistent power;
Nor without peril can the branches raise
    Their burden; now they stagger 'neath the weight
    Still growing, and are bent above the ways;
Soon autumn comes, and the ripe, ruddy freight
    Is gathered: the glad season will not stay;
    Flowers, fruit, and leaves are now all desolate.
Pluck the rose, therefore, maiden, while 'tis May.

II

HOW can I sing light-souled and fancy-free,
When my loved lord no longer smiles on me?

    Dances and songs and merry wakes I leave
      To lovers fair, more fortunate and gay;
    Since to my heart so many sorrows cleave
      That only doleful tears are mine for ay:
      Who hath heart's ease, may carol, dance, and play;
    While I am fain to weep continually.

How can I sing light-souled and fancy-free,
When my loved lord no longer smiles on me?

    I too had heart's ease once, for so Love willed,
      When my lord loved me with love strong and great:
    But envious fortune my life's music stilled,
      And turned to sadness all my gleeful state.
      Ah me! Death surely were less desolate
    Than thus to live and love-neglected be!

How can I sing light-souled and fancy-free,
When my loved lord no longer smiles on me?

    One only comfort soothes my heart's despair,
      And mid this sorrow lends my soul some cheer;
    Unto my lord I ever yielded fair
      Service of faith untainted pure and clear;
      If then I die thus guiltless, on my bier
    It may be she will shed one tear for me.

How can I sing light-souled and fancy-free,
When my loved lord no longer smiles on me ?

John Addington Symonds

MICHELANGELO BUONARROTI

1475–1564

The Doom of Beauty

CHOICE soul, in whom, as in a glass, we see,
    Mirrored in thy pure form and delicate,
    What beauties heaven and nature can create,
    The paragon of all their works to be !
Fair soul, in whom love, pity, piety,
    Have found a home, as from thy outward state
    We clearly read, and are so rare and great
    That they adorn none other like to thee !
Love takes me captive; beauty binds my soul;
    Pity and mercy with their gentle eyes
    Wake in my heart a hope that cannot cheat.
What law, what destiny, what fell control,
    What cruelty, or late or soon, denies
    That death should spare perfection so complete ?

John Addington Symonds

Celestial Love

NO mortal thing enthralled these longing eyes
    When perfect peace in thy fair face I found;
    But far within, where all is holy ground,
    My soul felt Love, her comrade of the skies:
For she was born with God in Paradise;
    Nor all the shows of beauty shed around
    This fair false world her wings to earth have
      bound:
    Unto the Love of Loves aloft she flies.

Nay, things that suffer death, quench not the fire
   Of deathless spirits; nor eternity
   Serves sordid Time, that withers all things rare.
Not love but lawless impulse is desire:
   That slays the soul; our love makes still more fair
   Our friends on earth, fairer in death on high.

                    John Addington Symonds

Love, the Light-giver

WITH your fair eyes a charming light I see,
   For which my own blind eyes would peer in vain;
   Stayed by your feet the burden I sustain
   Which my lame feet find all too strong for me;
Wingless upon your pinions forth I fly;
   Heavenward your spirit stirreth me to strain;
   E'en as you will, I blush and blanch again,
   Freeze in the sun, burn 'neath a frosty sky.
Your will includes and is the lord of mine;
   Life to my thoughts within your heart is given;
   My words begin to breathe upon your breath:
Like to the moon am I, that cannot shine
   Alone; for lo ! our eyes see naught in heaven
   Save what the living sun illumineth.

                    John Addington Symonds

Love's Entreaty

THOU knowest, love, I know that thou dost know
   That I am here more near to thee to be,
   And knowest that I know thou knowest me:
   What means it then that we are sundered so ?
If they are true, these hopes that from thee flow,
   If it is real, this sweet expectancy,
   Break down the wall that stands 'twixt me and thee;
   For pain in prison pent hath double woe.

Because in thee I love, O my loved lord,
    What thou best lovest, be not therefore stern:
    Souls burn for souls, spirits to spirits cry!
I seek the splendour in thy fair face stored;
    Yet living man that beauty scarce can learn,
    And he who fain would find it, first must die.
                    John Addington Symonds

On the Brink of Death

NOW hath my life across a stormy sea
    Like a frail bark reached that wide port where all
    Are bidden, ere the final reckoning fall
Of good and evil for eternity.
Now know I well how that fond phantasy
    Which made my soul the worshipper and thrall
    Of earthly art, is vain; how criminal
Is that which all men seek unwillingly.
Those amorous thoughts which were so lightly
    dressed,
    What are they when the double death is nigh?
    The one I know for sure, the other dread.
Painting nor sculpture now can lull to rest
    My soul that turns to His great love on high,
    Whose arms to clasp us on the cross were spread.
                    John Addington Symonds

A Prayer for Purification

PERCHANCE that I might learn what pity is,
    That I might laugh at erring men no more,
    Secure in my own strength as heretofore,
    My soul hath fallen from her state of bliss:
Nor know I under any flag but this
    How fighting I may 'scape those perils sore,
    Or how survive the rout and horrid roar
    Of adverse hosts, if I thy succour miss.

O flesh ! O blood ! O cross ! O pain extreme !
By you may those foul sins be purified,
Wherein my fathers were, and I was born !
Lo, Thou alone art good: let Thy supreme
Pity my state of evil cleanse and hide—
So near to death, so far from God, forlorn.

John Addington Symonds

The Transfiguration of Beauty
(A Dialogue with Love)

NAY, prithee tell me, Love, when I behold
My lady, do mine eyes her beauty see
In truth, or dwells that loveliness in me
Which multiplies her grace a thousandfold ?
Thou needs must know; for thou with her of old
Comest to stir my soul's tranquillity;
Yet would I not seek one sigh less, or be
By loss of that loved flame, more simply cold.—
The beauty thou discernest, all is hers;
But grows in radiance as it soars on high,
Through mortal eyes unto the soul above:
'Tis there transfigured; for the soul confers
On what she holds, her own divinity:
And this transfigured beauty wins thy love.

John Addington Symonds

The Garland and the Girdle

WHAT joy hath yon glad wreath of flowers that is
Around her golden hair so deftly twined,
Each blossom pressing forward from behind,
As though to be the first her brows to kiss !
The livelong day her dress hath perfect bliss,
That now reveals her breast, now seems to bind:
And that fair woven net of gold refined
Rests on her cheek and throat in happiness !

Yet still more blissful seems to me the band
Gilt at the tips, so sweetly doth it ring
And clasp the bosom that it serves to lace:
Yea, and the belt, to such as understand,
    Bound round her waist, saith: Here I'd ever
    cling.—
What would my arms do in that girdle's place?

John Addington Symonds

Joy may kill

TOO much good luck no less than misery
May kill a man condemned to mortal pain,
If, lost to hope and chilled in every vein,
A sudden pardon comes to set him free.
Thus thy unwonted kindness shown to me
Amid the gloom where only sad thoughts reign,
With too much rapture bringing light again,
Threatens my life more than that agony.
Good news and bad may bear the self-same knife;
And death may follow both upon their flight;
For hearts that shrink or swell, alike will break.
Let then thy beauty, to preserve my life,
Temper the source of this supreme delight,
Lest joy so poignant slay a soul so weak.

John Addington Symonds

Love's Justification

YES! hope may with my strong desire keep pace,
And I be undeluded, unbetrayed;
For if of our affections none find grace
In sight of Heaven, then wherefore hath God made
The world which we inhabit? Better plea
Love cannot have, than that in loving thee
Glory to that eternal peace is paid,

Who such divinity to thee imparts
As hallows and makes pure all gentle hearts.
His hope is treacherous only whose love dies
With beauty, which is varying every hour:
But, in chaste hearts uninfluenced by the power
Of outward change, there blooms a deathless flower,
That breathes on earth the air of paradise.

William Wordsworth

To the Supreme Being

THE prayers I make will then be sweet indeed,
If Thou the spirit give by which I pray:
My unassisted heart is barren clay,
Which of its native self can nothing feed:
Of good and pious works Thou art the seed,
Which quickens only where Thou say'st it may;
Unless Thou show to us Thine own true way,
No man can find it. Father ! Thou must lead.
Do Thou, then, breathe those thoughts into my mind
By which such virtue may in me be bred
That in Thy holy footsteps I may tread;
The fetters of my tongue do Thou unbind,
That I may have the power to sing of Thee,
And sound Thy praises everlastingly.

William Wordsworth

To Vittoria Colonna

WHEN the prime mover of my many sighs
      Heaven took through death from out her earthly
          place,
      Nature, that never made so fair a face,
      Remained ashamed, and tears were in all eyes.
  O fate, unheeding my impassioned cries !
  O hopes fallacious ! O thou spirit of grace,

Where art thou now ?   Earth holds in its embrace
Thy lovely limbs, thy holy thoughts the skies.
Vainly did cruel death attempt to stay
    The rumour of thy virtuous renown,
    That Lethe's waters could not wash away !
A thousand leaves, since he hath stricken thee down,
    Speak of thee, nor to thee could Heaven convey,
    Except through death, a refuge and a crown.

                                    H. W. Longfellow

Dante

WHAT should be said of him cannot be said;
    By too great splendour is his name attended;
    To blame is easier those who him offended,
    Than reach the faintest glory round him shed.
This man descended to the doomed and dead
    For our instruction; then to God ascended;
    Heaven opened wide to him its portals splendid,
    Who from his country's, closed against him, fled.
Ungrateful land !   To its own prejudice
    Nurse of his fortunes; and this showeth well
    That the most perfect most of grief shall see.
Among a thousand proofs let one suffice,
    That as his exile hath no parallel,
    Ne'er walked the earth a greater man than he.

                                    H. W. Longfellow

GIOVANNI DELLA CASA

1503-56

To Sleep

O SLEEP, O tranquil son of noiseless Night,
    Of humid, shadowy Night; O dear repose
    For wearied men, forgetfulness of woes
    Grievous enough the bloom of life to blight !

Succour this heart that hath outworn delight,
  And knows no rest; these tired limbs compose;
  Fly to me, Sleep; thy dusky vans disclose
Over my languid eyes, then cease thy flight.
Where, where is Silence, that avoids the day?
  Where the light dreams, that with a wavering tread
  And unsubstantial footing follow thee?
Alas! in vain I call thee; and these grey,
  These frigid shades flatter in vain. O bed,
  How rough with thorns! O nights, how harsh
    to me!

John Addington Symonds

GIOVANNI BATTISTA GUARINI
1537–1612

From Il Pastor Fido

HOW I forsook
Elias and Pisa after, and betook
Myself to Argos and Mycenæ, where
An earthly god I worshipped, with what there
I suffered in that hard captivity,
Would be too long for thee to hear, for me
Too sad to utter.   Only thus much know;—
I lost my labour, and in sand did sow:
I writ, wept, sung; hot and cold fits I had;
I rid, I stood, I bore, now sad, now glad,
Now high, now low, now in esteem, now scorned;
And as the Delphic iron, which is turned
Now to heroic, now mechanic use,
I feared no danger,—did no pains refuse;
Was all things,—and was nothing; changed my hair,
Condition, custom, thoughts, and life,—but ne'er
Could change my fortune.   Then I knew at last,
And panted after, my sweet freedom past.

So, flying smoky Argos, and the great
Storms that attend on greatness, my retreat
I made to Pisa,—my thought's quiet port.

Who would have dreamed 'midst plenty to grow poor;
Or to be less, by toiling to be more ?
I thought, by how much more in princes' courts
Men did excel in titles and supports,
So much the more obliging they would be,
The best enamel of nobility.
But now the contrary by proofs I've seen:
Courtiers in name, and courteous in their mien,
They are; but in their actions I could spy
Not the least transient spark of courtesy.
People, in show, smooth as the calmed waves,
Yet cruel as the ocean when it raves:
Men in appearance only did I find,—
Love in the face, but malice in the mind;
With a straight look and tortuous heart, and least
Fidelity where greatest was professed.
That which elsewhere is virtue is vice there:
Plain truth, fair dealing, love unfeigned, sincere
Compassion, faith inviolable, and
An innocence both of the heart and hand,
They count the folly of a soul that's vile
And poor,—a vanity worthy their smile.
To cheat, to lie, deceit and theft to use,
And under show of pity to abuse,
To rise upon the ruins of their brothers,
And seek their own by robbing praise from others,
The virtues are of that perfidious race.
No worth, no valour, no respect of place,
Of age, or law,—bridle of modesty,—
No tie of love or blood, nor memory
Of good received; nothing's so venerable,
Sacred, or just, that is inviolable

By that vast thirst of riches, and desire
Unquenchable of still ascending higher.
Now I, not fearing, since I meant not ill,
And in court-craft not having any skill,
Wearing my thoughts charactered on my brow,
And a glass window in my heart,—judge thou
How open and how fair a mark my heart
Lay to their envy's unsuspected dart.

Sir Richard Fanshawe

Claim to Love

ALAS! alas! thou turn'st in vain
   Thy beauteous face away,
Which, like young sorcerer, rais'd a pain
   Above its power to lay.

Love moves not as thou turn'st thy look,
   But here doth firmly rest:
He long ago thine eyes forsook
   To revel in my breast.

Thy power on him why hop'st thou more
   Than his on me should be?
The claim thou lay'st to him is poor
   To that he owns from me.

His substance in my heart excels,
   His shadow, in thy sight;
Fire where it burns more truly dwells
   Than where it scatters light.

Thomas Stanley

Spring

O SPRING, thou youthful beauty of the year,
Mother of flowers, bringer of warbling choirs,
Of all sweet new green things and new desires,
Thou, Spring, returnest; but, alas! with thee

No more return to me
The calm and happy days these eyes were used to see.
Thou, thou returnest, thou,
But with these returns now
Naught else but dread remembrance of the pleasure
I took in my lost treasure.
Thou still, thou still, art the same blithe, sweet thing
Thou ever wast, O Spring;
But I, in whose weak orbs these tears arise,
Am what I was no more, dear to another's eyes.

Leigh Hunt

TORQUATO TASSO

1544–95

From Aminta

THE GOLDEN AGE

O LOVELY age of gold !
Not that the rivers rolled
With milk, or that the woods wept honeydew;
Not that the ready ground
Produced without a wound,
Or the mild serpent had no tooth that slew;
Not that a cloudless blue
For ever was in sight,
Or that the heaven, which burns
And now is cold by turns,
Looked out in glad and everlasting light;
No, nor that even the insolent ships from far
Brought war to no new lands nor riches worse
    than war:

But solely that that vain
And breath-invented pain,
That idol of mistake, that worshipped cheat,
That Honour,—since so called
By vulgar minds appalled,—

Played not the tyrant with our nature yet.
It had not come to fret
The sweet and happy fold
Of gentle human kind;
Nor did its hard law bind
Souls nursed in freedom; but that law of gold,
That glad and golden law, all free, all fitted,
Which Nature's own hand wrote,—What pleases is
    permitted.

Then among streams and flowers
The little winged powers
Went singing carols without torch or bow;
The nymphs and shepherds sat
Mingling with innocent chat
Sports and low whispers; and with whispers low,
Kisses that would not go.
The maiden, budding o'er,
Kept not her bloom uneyed,
Which now a veil must hide,
Nor the crisp apples which her bosom bore;
And oftentimes, in river or in lake,
The lover and his love their merry bath would take.

'Twas thou, thou, Honour, first
That didst deny our thirst
Its drink, and on the fount thy covering set;
Thou bad'st kind eyes withdraw
Into constrained awe,
And keep the secret for their tears to wet;
Thou gather'dst in a net
The tresses from the air,
And mad'st the sports and plays
Turn all to sullen ways,
And putt'st on speech a rein, in steps a care.
Thy work it is,—thou shade, that wilt not move,—
That what was once the gift is now the theft of Love.

Our sorrows and our pains,
These are thy noble gains.
But, O, thou Love's and Nature's masterer,
Thou conqueror of the crowned,
What dost thou on this ground,
Too small a circle for thy mighty sphere?
Go, and make slumber dear
To the renowned and high;
We here, a lowly race,
Can live without thy grace,
After the use of mild antiquity.
Go, let us love; since years
No truce allow, and life soon disappears;
Go, let us love; the daylight dies, is born;
But unto us the light
Dies once for all; and sleep brings on eternal night.

Leigh Hunt

To his Mistress in Absence

FAR from thy dearest self, the scope
　　Of all my aims,
　　I waste in secret flames;
And only live because I hope.

O when will Fate restore
　　The joys, in whose bright fire
　　My expectation shall expire,
That I may live because I hope no more!

Thomas Stanley

Love

LOVE, the great master of true eloquence,
　　Disdains the tribute of a vulgar tongue:
　　Cold are the words, and vain the affected song
Of him whose boasted passion is pretence;

The favoured few that to his court belong
With noblest gifts the mighty god presents;
Their vigorous accents chain the admiring sense,
And their warm words in torrents stream along.
Oft too—O wondrous excellence of Love !—
Unuttered vows and sighs and accents broken
With far more force the gentle bosom move
Than smoothest phrase with courtly action spoken.
E'en Silence oft has found the power to prove
Both word and prayer, when it is true love's token.

John Herman Merivale

GIORDANO BRUNO

1548–1600

The Philosophic Flight

NOW that these wings to speed my wish ascend,
The more I feel vast air beneath my feet,
The more toward boundless air on pinions fleet,
Spurning the earth, soaring to heaven, I tend:
Nor makes them stoop their flight the direful end
Of Dædal's son; but upward still they beat.
What life the while with this death could compete,
If dead to earth at last I must descend ?
My own heart's voice in the void air I hear.
Where wilt thou bear me, O rash man ! Recall
Thy daring will ! This boldness waits on fear !
Dread not, I answer, that tremendous fall:
Strike through the clouds, and smile when death
is near,
If death so glorious be our doom at all !

John Addington Symonds

GABRIELLO CHIABRERA

1562-1637

Epitaphs

1

WEEP not, belovèd friends ! nor let the air
For me with sighs be troubled.   Not from life
Have I been taken; this is genuine life,
And this alone,—the life which now I live
In peace eternal; where desire and joy
Together move in fellowship without end.—
Francesco Ceni after death enjoined
That thus his tomb should speak for him.   And
    surely
Small cause there is for that fond wish of ours
Long to continue in this world,—a world
That keeps not faith, nor yet can point a hope
To good, whereof itself is destitute.

2

PERHAPS some needful service of the state
Drew Titus from the depth of studious bowers,
And doomed him to contend in faithless courts,
Where gold determines between right and wrong.
Yet did at length his loyalty of heart,
And his pure native genius, lead him back
To wait upon the bright and gracious Muses,
Whom he had early loved.   And not in vain
Such course he held.   Bologna's learnèd schools
Were gladdened by the sage's voice, and hung
With fondness on those sweet Nestorian strains.
There pleasure crowned his days; and all his thoughts
A roseate fragrance breathed.   O human life,
That never art secure from dolorous change !
Behold, a high injunction suddenly

To Arno's side hath brought him, and he charmed
A Tuscan audience: but full soon was called
To the perpetual silence of the grave.
Mourn, Italy, the loss of him who stood
A champion steadfast and invincible,
To quell the rage of literary war !

3

O THOU who movest onward with a mind
Intent upon thy way, pause, though in haste !
'Twill be no fruitless moment. I was born
Within Savona's walls, of gentle blood.
On Tiber's banks my youth was dedicate
To sacred studies; and the Roman Shepherd
Gave to my charge Urbino's numerous flock.
Well did I watch, much laboured, nor had power
To escape from many and strange indignities;
Was smitten by the great ones of the world,
But did not fall; for Virtue braves all shocks,
Upon herself resting immovably.
Me did a kindlier fortune then invite
To serve the glorious Henry, king of France,
And in his hands I saw a high reward
Stretched out for my acceptance: but Death came.
Now, reader, learn from this my fate, how false,
How treacherous to her promise, is the world,
And trust in God,—to whose eternal doom
Must bend the sceptred potentates of earth.

4

THERE never breathed a man who, when his life
Was closing, might not of that life relate
Toils long and hard. The warrior will report
Of wounds, and bright swords flashing in the field,
And blast of trumpets. He who hath been doomed
To bow his forehead in the courts of kings

Will tell of fraud and never-ceasing hate,
Envy and heart-inquietude, derived
From intricate cabals of treacherous friends.
I, who on shipboard lived from earliest youth,
Could represent the countenance horrible
Of the vexed waters, and the indignant rage
Of Auster and Boötes.   Fifty years
Over the well-steered galleys did I rule.
From huge Pelorus to the Atlantic Pillars,
Rises no mountain to mine eyes unknown;
And the broad gulfs I traversed oft—and—oft.
Of every cloud which in the heavens might stir
I knew the force; and hence the rough sea's pride
Availed not to my vessel's overthrow.
What noble pomp, and frequent, have not I
On regal decks beheld ! yet in the end
I learned that one poor moment can suffice
To equalize the lofty and the low.
We sail the sea of life,—a calm one finds,
And one a tempest,—and, the voyage o'er,
Death is the quiet haven of us all.
If more of my condition ye would know,
Savona was my birth-place, and I sprang
Of noble parents: seventy years and three
Lived I,—then yielded to a slow disease.

5

TRUE is it that Ambrosio Salinero,
With an untoward fate, was long involved
In odious litigation; and full long,
Fate harder still ! had he to endure assaults
Of racking malady.   And true it is
That not the less a frank, courageous heart
And buoyant spirit triumphed over pain;
And he was strong to follow in the steps
Of the fair Muses.   Not a covert path

Leads to the dear Parnassian forest's shade,
That might from him be hidden; not a track
Mounts to pellucid Hippocrene, but he
Had traced its windings.   This Savona knows,
Yet no sepulchral honours to her son
She paid; for in our age the heart is ruled
Only by gold.   And now a simple stone,
Inscribed with this memorial, here is raised
By his bereft, his lonely, Chiabrera.
Think not, O passenger who read'st the lines,
That an exceeding love hath dazzled me:
No,—he was one whose memory ought to spread
Where'er Permessus bears an honoured name,
And live as long as its pure stream shall flow.

6

DESTINED to war from very infancy
Was I, Roberto Dati, and I took
In Malta the white symbol of the Cross.
Nor in life's vigorous season did I shun
Hazard or toil; among the sands was seen
Of Libya, and not seldom, on the banks
Of wide Hungarian Danube, 'twas my lot
To hear the sanguinary trumpet sounded.
So lived I, and repined not at such fate:
This only grieves me, for it seems a wrong,
That stripped of arms I to my end am brought
On the soft down of my paternal home.
Yet haply Arno shall be spared all cause
To blush for me.   Thou, loiter not nor halt
In thy appointed way, and bear in mind
How fleeting and how frail is human life !

7

O FLOWER of all that springs from gentle blood,
And all that generous nurture breeds, to make
Youth amiable ! O friend so true of soul
To fair Aglaia ! by what envy moved,
Lelius, has Death cut short thy brilliant day
In its sweet opening ? and what dire mishap
Has from Savona torn her best delight ?
For thee she mourns, nor e'er will cease to mourn;
And, should the outpourings of her eyes suffice not
For her heart's grief, she will entreat Sebeto
Not to withhold his bounteous aid,—Sebeto,
Who saw thee on his margin yield to death,
In the chaste arms of thy beloved love !
What profit riches ? what does youth avail ?
Dust are our hopes !—I, weeping bitterly,
Penned these sad lines, nor can forbear to pray
That every gentle spirit hither led
May read them not without some bitter tears.

8

NOT without heavy grief of heart did he
On whom the duty fell (for at that time
The father sojourned in a distant land)
Deposit in the hollow of this tomb
A brother's child, most tenderly beloved !
Francesco was the name the youth had borne,—
Possobònnelli his illustrious house;
And when beneath this stone the corse was laid,
The eyes of all Savona streamed with tears.
Alas ! the twentieth April of his life
Had scarcely flowered: and at this early time,
By genuine virtue he inspired a hope
That greatly cheered his country; to his kin
He promised comfort; and the flattering thoughts

His friends had in their fondness entertained
He suffered not to languish or decay.
Now is there not good reason to break forth
Into a passionate lament?   O soul!
Short while a pilgrim in our nether world,
Do thou enjoy the calm empyreal air;
And round this earthly tomb let roses rise,—
An everlasting spring!—in memory
Of that delightful fragrance which was once
From thy mild manners quietly exhaled.

9

PAUSE, courteous spirit!—Balbi supplicates,
That thou, with no reluctant voice, for him
Here laid in mortal darkness, wouldst prefer
A prayer to the Redeemer of the world.
This to the dead by sacred right belongs;
All else is nothing.   Did occasion suit
To tell his worth, the marble of this tomb
Would ill suffice: for Plato's lore sublime,
And all the wisdom of the Stagyrite,
Enriched and beautified his studious mind;
With Archimedes, also, he conversed,
As with a chosen friend; nor did he leave
Those laureate wreaths ungathered which the Nymphs
Twine near their beloved Permessus.   Finally,
Himself above each lower thought uplifting,
His ears he closed to listen to the songs
Which Sion's kings did consecrate of old;
And his Permessus found on Lebanon.
A blessed man! who of protracted days
Made not, as thousands do, a vulgar sleep;
But truly did he live his life.   Urbino,
Take pride in him!—O passenger, farewell!

William Wordsworth

TOMASSO CAMPANELLA
1568–1639

The People

THE people is a beast of muddy brain
That knows not its own force, and therefore stands
Loaded with wood and stone; the powerless hands
Of a mere child guide it with bit and rein:
One kick would be enough to break the chain;
But the beast fears, and what the child demands,
It does; nor its own terror understands,
Confused and stupefied by bugbears vain.
Most wonderful ! with its own hand it ties
And gags itself—gives itself death and war
For pence doled out by kings from its own store.
Its own are all things between earth and heaven;
But this it knows not; and if one arise
To tell this truth, it kills him unforgiven.

John Addington Symonds

GIAMBATTISTA MARINI
1569–1625

Fading Beauty

BEAUTY—a beam, nay, flame,
Of the great lamp of light—
Shines for a while with fame,
But presently makes night:
Like Winter's short-lived bright,
Or Summer's sudden gleams;
As much more dear, so much less lasting beams.

Winged Love away doth fly,
And with him Time doth bear;
And both take suddenly
The sweet, the fair, the dear:
To shining day and clear

Succeeds the obscure night;
And sorrow is the heir of sweet delight.

With what, then, dost thou swell,
  O youth of new-born day?
Wherein doth thy pride dwell,
  O Beauty, made of clay?
  Not with so swift a way
The headlong current flies,
As do the lively rays of two fair eyes.

That which on Flora's breast,
  All fresh and flourishing,
Aurora newly dressed
  Saw in her dawning spring;
  Quite dry and languishing,
Deprived of honour quite,
Day-closing Hesperus beholds at night.

Fair is the lily; fair
  The rose, of flowers the eye!
Both wither in the air,
  Their beauteous colours die:
  And so at length shall lie,
Deprived of former grace,
The lilies of thy breasts, the roses of thy face.

Do not thyself betray
  With shadows; with thy years,
O Beauty (traitors gay!)
  This melting life, too, wears,—
  Appearing, disappears;
And with thy flying days,
Ends all thy good of price, thy fair of praise.

Trust not, vain creditor,
    Thy oft-deceived view
In thy false counsellor,
    That never tells thee true:
    Thy form and flattered hue,
Which shall so soon transpass,
Are far more frail than is thy looking-glass.

Enjoy thy April now,
    Whilst it doth freely shine:
This lightning flash and show,
    With that clear spirit of thine,
    Will suddenly decline;
And those fair murdering eyes
Shall be Love's tomb, where now his cradle lies.

Old trembling age will come,
    With wrinkled cheeks and stains,
With motion troublesome,
    With void and bloodless veins;
    That lively visage wanes,
And, made deformed and old,
Hates sight of glass it loved so to behold.

Thy gold and scarlet shall
    Pale silver-colour be;
Thy row of pearls shall fall
    Like withered leaves from tree;
    And thou shalt shortly see
Thy face and hair to grow
All ploughed with furrows, over-swollen with snow.

What, then, will it avail,
    O youth advised ill,
In lap of beauty frail
    To nurse a wayward will,
    Like snake in sun-warm hill ?

Pluck, pluck betime thy flower,
That springs and parches in the self-same hour.

Samuel Daniel

FRANCESCO REDI

1626-98

From Bacchus in Tuscany

BACCHUS'S OPINION OF WINE, AND OTHER BEVERAGES

GIVE me, give me Buriano,
Trebbiano, Colombano,—
Give me bumpers, rich and clear !
'Tis the true old Aurum Potabile,
Gilding life when it wears shabbily:
Helen's old Nepenthe 'tis,
That in the drinking
Swallowed thinking,
And was the receipt for bliss.
Thence it is, that ever and ay,
When he doth philosophize,
Good old glorious Rucellai
Hath it for light unto his eyes;
He lifteth it, and by the shine
Well discerneth things divine:
Atoms with their airy justles,
And all manner of corpuscles;
And, as through a crystal skylight,
How morning differeth from evening twilight;
And further telleth us the reason why go
Some stars with such a lazy light, and some with
 a vertigo.

O, how widely wandereth he,
Who in search of verity
Keeps aloof from glorious wine !
Lo, the knowledge it bringeth to me !

For Barbarossa, this wine so bright,
With its rich red look and its strawberry light,
So inviteth me,
So delighteth me,
I should infallibly quench my inside with it,
Had not Hippocrates
And old Andromachus
Strictly forbidden it
And loudly chidden it,
So many stomachs have sickened and died with it.
Yet, discordant as it is,
Two good biggins will not come amiss;
Because I know, while I'm drinking them down,
What is the finish and what is the crown.
A cup of good Corsican
Does it at once;
Or a glass of old Spanish
Is neat for the nonce:
Quackish resources are things for a dunce.

Talk of Chocolate !
Talk of Tea !
Medicines made—ye gods !—as they are,
Are no medicines made for me.
I would sooner take to poison
Than a single cup set eyes on
Of that bitter and guilty stuff ye
Talk of by the name of Coffee.
Let the Arabs and the Turks
Count it 'mongst their cruel works:
Foe of mankind, black and turbid,
Let the throats of slaves absorb it.
Down in Tartarus,
Down in Erebus,
'Twas the detestable Fifty invented it;
The Furies then took it
To grind and to cook it,

And to Proserpina all three presented it.
If the Mussulman in Asia
Doats on a beverage so unseemly,
I differ with the man extremely.

There's a squalid thing, called Beer:
The man whose lips that thing comes near
Swiftly dies; or falling foolish,
Grows, at forty, old and owlish.
She that in the ground would hide her,
Let her take to English Cider:
He who'd have his death come quicker,
Any other Northern liquor.
Those Norwegians and those Laps
Have extraordinary taps:
Those Laps especially have strange fancies;
To see them drink,
I verily think,
Would make me lose my senses.
But a truce to such vile subjects,
With their impious, shocking objects.
Let me purify my mouth
In a holy cup o' th' South;
In a golden pitcher let me
Head and ears for comfort get me,
And drink of the wine of the vine benign
That sparkles warm in Sansovine.

Leigh Hunt

VINCENZO FILICAJA
1642–1707

Italy

ITALIA ! O Italia ! thou who hast
The fatal gift of beauty, which became
A funeral dower of present woes and past,
On thy sweet brow is sorrow plough'd by shame,

And annals graved in characters of flame.
O God ! that thou wert in thy nakedness
Less lovely or more powerful, and couldst claim
Thy right, and awe the robbers back, who press
To shed thy blood, and drink the tears of thy distress;

Then might'st thou more appal, or, less desired,
Be homely and be peaceful, undeplored
For thy destructive charms; then, still untired,
Would not be seen the armèd torrents pour'd
Down the steep Alps; nor would the hostile horde
Of many-nation'd spoilers from the Po
Quaff blood and water; nor the stranger's sword
Be thy sad weapon of defence, and so,
Victor or vanquished, thou the slave of friend or foe.

Lord Byron

VITTORIO ALFIERI

1749–1803

To Dante

" GREAT father Alighier, if from the skies
This thy disciple prostrate thou dost see
Before thy gravestone, shaken with deep sighs,
O turn thou not in wrathfulness from me !
O of thy kindness, favouring pure desires,
Illuminate me with a ray of thine;
Must who to pristine, deathless fame aspires
Take arms 'gainst envy and each fell design ? "
     " I did so, son, to my great sorrow, for
Thereby the names of men too vile to tread
Under my feet are heard for evermore.
If thou dost trust in me, why droop thy head ?
Go thunder, triumph, and if thou shouldst chance
To meet with such, pass by nor deign a glance."

Lorna De' Lucchi

JACOPO VITTORELLI

1749–1835

On a Nun

OF two fair virgins, modest, though admired,
    Heaven made us happy; and now, wretched sires,
    Heaven for a nobler doom their worth desires,
    And gazing upon *either*, *both* required.
Mine, while the torch of Hymen newly fired
    Becomes extinguish'd, soon—too soon—expires:
    But thine, within the closing grate retired,
    Eternal captive, to her God aspires.
But *thou*, at least, from out the jealous door,
    Which shuts between your never-meeting eyes,
    May'st hear her sweet and pious voice once more:
I to the marble, where *my* daughter lies,
    Rush,—the swoln flood of bitterness I pour,
    And knock, and knock, and knock—but none
        replies.

Lord Byron

GIACOMO LEOPARDI

1798–1837

To Italy

O ITALY, I see the lonely towers,
The arches and the columns and the walls
Of bygone days. The glory and the steel
That girt our fathers I behold not. Now
Unarmed, thou show'st a naked breast, a brow
Undiademed. Ah me, what wounds, what blood !
How art thou fallen, O most beautiful !
I cry to heaven, unto earth I cry:
Say, say, who brought her to so dire a pass ?
Her arms are bound in chains; with scattered locks
And face unveiled, she sits disconsolate,

Forgotten, and her head between her knees
Hiding, she weeps. Ah, weep, my Italy,
Thou hast good cause, thou who wert born to rule,
Now fallen on so dark a destiny.

Were thy dim eyes two gushing founts of tears
They ne'er could quench thy sorrow and thy shame,
Who wert a queen, and art become a slave.
Who now doth speak of thee, remembering
Thy vaunted past, but saith: She once was great,
She is no more ?   Why ?   Why ?   Where is thy might,
Thine ancient valour, arms, and constancy ?
Who hath unclasped thy sword ?   Who thee betrayed ?
What subtle craft, what labour, or what power
Despoiled thee of thy mantle and thy crown ?
How, when didst fall from majesty so low ?
Will none defend thee, will none fight for thee
Among thy children ?   Arms, to arms !   Alone
I'll fight for thee, I'll fall for thee alone,
And be my blood a brand to fire cold hearts.

Where are thy children ?   Noise of arms I hear,
Of chariots and of shouting and of drums:
In foreign lands thy sons are combating.
Attend, O Italy.   I see afar
A swaying throng of horses and of men,
Whirling of smoke and dust, and in the midst,
As lightning streaks the cloud, a flash of blades.
Art thou not comforted ?   Thy tear-dimmed eyes
Upon th' uncertain battle canst not bend ?
What moves thy youth to fight upon those fields ?
Ye gods, for alien lands Italian steel
Is bared.   Unhappy he who fighting falls,
Not for his native shores and children dear,
But for the stranger, slain by others' foe,

And dying cannot say: O sacred soil,
I give thee back the life thou gavest me.

Oh fortunate and blest those days of old
When for their country peoples thronged to die.
Be ye for ever honoured and most praised,
O Thessalonian passes, where dark fate
To Persian arms allied proved powerless
Against a handful of intrepid souls.
Methinks your waves and plants, your very stones
And watching mountains with incessant voice
Proclaim how all that coast was covered thick
With those undaunted hosts that fell for Greece.
Then, wild with fear, Xerxes o'er Hellespont
Fled, for all time a spectacle and scorn.
Simonides with failing steps did climb
Anthela's mount, where that heroic band
Dying were freed from death, and all about
Gazing with streaming eyes at hills and sea,
Took up his lyre and sang: O blessed ye
Who bared your breasts unto the foe's sharp steel
For love of her who gave you to the light,
Whom Greece hath tested, and the world reveres.
What mighty love your youthful spirits moved
To face 'mid clash of arms such bitter doom?
O children, with what shining countenance
Was Death to you revealed, that smiling thus
Ye ran to him 'mid pain and wounds so sore?
It seemed ye went to dance and feasting gay,
Yet night awaited you, and Tartarus;
Nor child nor spouse stood by when on that shore,
Without a kiss, without a tear, ye died.

But for the Persian 'twas dread chastisement,
Undying anguish. For as 'mid a drove
Of bulls a lion plunging, now on one
Now on another leaps, with claws and teeth

Tearing their flesh, so 'mid the Persian hordes
Raged the heroic fury of the Greeks.
See horses prone and men; see broken tents
And chariots trip the vanquished in their flight.
And see among the foremost, wild-eyed, pale,
The tyrant.   See how with barbaric blood
Encrimsoned, the pursuing heroes fall,
One after one, by wounds o'ercome at last.
Live, live, most blessed ones, while yet the world
Hath tongue and hand to blaze your glorious deed!

The stars, uprooted, shall be hurled from heaven
Into the deep, and their majestic fires
'Mid hissing ruin quenched, ere memory
Your image shall unclasp, or spurn your love.
Your tomb an altar is, whereto shall come
Mothers, unto their children showing there
The shining traces of your blood.   Behold,
O glorious ones, bowed on this hallowed ground,
I kiss these stones, this sod; may they be blest
And praised eternally from pole to pole.
Ah would that I were buried here with you,
And that this soil were sodden with my blood.
But since fate wills not that my dying eyes
Should close in battle for a land oppressed,
May the gods grant your poet's humble fame
Mingled with yours shall through the ages last.

Romilda Rendel

To Himself

NOW rest for evermore, my weary heart!
Perished the last illusion I believed
Eternal, perished!   Truly I can tell
How of our cherished dreams
The hope is quenched and the desire as well.
Now rest for evermore!

Enough of strife !
There's nothing worth one throb of thine; this earth
Deserveth not a sigh !   Bitter is life
And wearisome, naught else;
The world's defiled !
Despair for the last time and then be still !
Fate made us at our birth no gift save death;
Scorn nature now, and brutal destiny
Who ruleth hidden for the common ill,
And of all things the infinite vanity !

Lorna De' Lucchi

The Infinite

I ALWAYS loved this solitary hill,
This ledge as well, which takes so large a share
Of the far-flung horizon from my view;
But seated here, in contemplation lost,
My thought discovers vaster space beyond
Supernal silence and unfathomed peace;
Almost I am afraid; then, since I hear
The murmur of the wind among the leaves,
I match that infinite calm unto this sound
And with my mind embrace eternity,
The vivid, speaking present and dead past;
In such immensity my spirit drowns,
And sweet to me is shipwreck in this sea.

Lorna De' Lucchi

GIOSUÈ CARDUCCI

1836–1907

Snowfall

SILENTLY, slowly falls the snow from an ashen sky ;
Cries and sounds of life from the city rise no more ;

No more the hawker's shout and the sound of running
wheels,
No more the joyous song of love and youth arise.

Raucously from the sombre spire through the leaden
air
The hours moan, like sighs of a world removed from
time.

Wandering birds insistent knock on the glowing panes.
My ghostly friends return, and gaze, and call to me.

Soon, my dear ones, soon—be still, O dauntless heart—
Down to the silence I come, in the shadow I will rest.

Romilda Rendel

Petrarch

MASTER FRANCESCO, I have come to thee
  And to thy friend, that gentle, fair-haired dame,
To calm my angry spirit and set free
  My grim soul by sweet Sorga's crystal stream.
Look ! shade and rest I find beneath this tree !
  I sit, and to the lonely shore I call;
Thou comest, and a choir encircles thee
  Who greet me with a friendly welcome all.
And that sweet choir—they are those songs of thine,
  Down whose fair sides their golden tresses fall—
Escaping from the rose-wreaths that entwine
  Their gathered folds, in ringlets prodigal;
And one doth shake her locks, and the rebel cry
Breaks from her tuneful lips, " Rome ! Italy ! "

William Dudley Foulke

Primo Vere

BEHOLD, from sluggish winter's arm
  Spring lifts herself again:
Naked before the steel-cold air
  She shivers as in pain;

Look, Lalage, is that a tear
In the sun's eye which yet shines clear ?

From beds of snow the flowers awake,
  Lifting in deep amaze
To heaven their eager eyes: but yet
  More in that wistful gaze
Than wonder lies: sure trembles there,
O Lalage, some memory fair,

Some dream which 'neath the coverlet white
  Of winter snow they dreamed,
Some sleeping sight of dewy dawns
  And summer suns that gleamed,
And thy bright eyes, O Lalage;
Was not the dream a prophecy ?

To-day my spirit sleeps and dreams;
  Where do my far thoughts fly ?
Close to thy beauty's face we stand
  And smile, the spring and I;—
Yet, Lalage, whence come these tears ?
Has spring, too, felt the doom of years ?

John Bailey

POPULAR SONGS OF TUSCANY

I

SLEEPING or waking, thou sweet face,
Lift up thy fair and tender brow:
  List to thy love in this still place;
  He calls thee to thy window now:
  But bids thee not the house to quit,
  Since in the night this were not meet.
  Come to thy window, stay within;
  I stand without, and sing and sing:
  Come to thy window, stay at home;
  I stand without, and make my moan.

2

I see the dawn e'en now begin to peer:
Therefore I take my leave, and cease to sing.
See how the windows open far and near,
And hear the bells of morning, how they ring!
Through heaven and earth the sounds of ringing swell;
Therefore, bright jasmine flower, sweet maid, farewell!
Through heaven and Rome the sound of ringing goes;
Farewell, bright jasmine flower, sweet maiden rose!

3

It was the morning of the first of May,
Into the close I went to pluck a flower;
And there I found a bird of woodland gay,
Who whiled with sings of love the silent hour.
O bird, who fliest from fair Florence, how
Dear love begins, I prithee teach me now!—
Love it begins with music and with song,
And ends with sorrow and with sighs ere long.

4

Passing across the billowy sea,
I let, alas, my poor heart fall;
I bade the sailors bring it me;
They said they had not seen it fall.
I asked the sailors, one and two;
They said that I had given it you.
I asked the sailors, two and three;
They said that I had given it thee.

5

That time I see you passing by,
I sit and count the steps you take:
You take the steps; I sit and sigh:
Step after step, my sighs awake.

Tell me, dear love, which more abound,
My sighs or your steps on the ground ?
Tell me, dear love, which are the most,
Your light steps or the sighs they cost ?

6

I would I were a bird so free,
That I had wings to fly away:
Unto that window I would flee,
Where stands my love and grinds all day.
Grind, miller, grind; the water's deep !
I cannot grind; love makes me weep.
Grind, miller, grind; the waters flow !
I cannot grind; love wastes me so.

7

On Sunday morning well I knew
Where gayly dressed you turned your feet;
And there were many saw it too,
And came to tell me through the street:
And when they spoke, I smiled, ah me !
But in my room wept privately;
And when they spoke, I sang for pride,
But in my room alone I sighed.

Strew me with blossoms when I die,
Nor lay me 'neath the earth below;
Beyond those walls, there let me lie,
Where oftentimes we used to go.
There lay me to the wind and rain;
Dying for you, I feel no pain:
There lay me to the sun above;
Dying for you, I die of love.

John Addington Symonds

SPANISH

JUAN RUIZ DE HITA

c. 1343

Praise of Little Women

I WISH to make my sermon brief,—to shorten my
    oration,—
For a never‑ending sermon is my utter detestation:
I like short women,—suits at law without procrastina‑
    tion,—
And am always most delighted with things of short
    duration.

A babbler is a laughing‑stock; he's a fool who's always
    grinning;
But little women love so much, one falls in love with
    sinning.
There are women who are very tall, and yet not
    worth the winning,
And in the change of short for long repentance finds
    beginning.

To praise the little women Love besought me in my
    musing;
To tell their noble qualities is quite beyond refusing:
So I'll praise the little women, and you'll find the
    thing amusing;
They are, I know, as cold as snow, whilst flames
    around diffusing.

They're cold without, whilst warm within the flame
    of Love is raging;
They're gay and pleasant in the street,—soft, cheerful,
    and engaging;

They're thrifty and discreet at home,—the cares of life
    assuaging:
All this and more;—try, and you'll find how true is
    my presaging.

In a little precious stone what splendour meets the eyes !
In a little lump of sugar how much of sweetness lies !
So in a little woman love grows and multiplies:
You recollect the proverb says,—*A word unto the wise.*

A pepper-corn is very small, but seasons every dinner
More than all other condiments, although 'tis sprinkled
    thinner:
Just so a little woman is, if Love will let you win her,—
There's not a joy in all the world you will not find
    within her.

And as within the little rose you find the richest dyes,
And in a little grain of gold much price and value lies,
As from a little balsam much odour doth arise,
So in a little woman there's a taste of paradise.

Even as the little ruby its secret worth betrays,
Colour, and price, and virtue, in the clearness of its
    rays,—
Just so a little woman much excellence displays,
Beauty, and grace, and love, and fidelity always.

The skylark and the nightingale, though small and light
    of wing,
Yet warble sweeter in the grove than all the birds that
    sing:
And so a little woman, though a very little thing,
Is sweeter far than sugar, and flowers that bloom in
    spring.

The magpie and the golden thrush have many a thrilling
    note,
Each as a gay musician doth strain his little throat,—

A merry little songster in his green and yellow coat:
And such a little woman is, when Love doth make her
dote.

There's naught can be compared to her, throughout the
wide creation;
She is a paradise on earth,—our greatest consolation,—
So cheerful, gay, and happy, so free from all vexation:
In fine, she's better in the proof than in anticipation.

If as her size increases are woman's charms decreased,
Then surely it is good to be from all the great released.
Now of two evils choose the less,—said a wise man of
the East.
By consequence, of woman-kind be sure to choose the
least.

H. W. Longfellow

JUAN II OF CASTILE

1405-54

Canción

O LOVE, I never, never thought
Thy power had been so great,
That thou couldst change my fate
By changes in another wrought,
Till now, alas! I know it.

I thought I knew thee well,
For I had known thee long;
But though I felt thee strong,
I felt not all thy spell.

Nor ever, ever had I thought
Thy power had been so great,
That thou couldst change my fate
By changes in another wrought,
Till now, alas! I know it.

George Ticknor

DIEGO DE SALDAÑA

15th century

Eyes So Tristful

EYES so tristful, eyes so tristful,
Heart so full of care and cumber,
I was lapped in rest and slumber,
Ye have made me wakeful, wistful !
In this life of labour endless
Who shall comfort my distresses ?
Querulous my soul and friendless
In its sorrow shuns caresses.
Ye have made me, ye have made me
Querulous of you, that care not,
Eyes so tristful, yet I dare not
Say to what ye have betrayed me.

H. W. Longfellow

ANONYMOUS

15th century

Villancico

THREE dark maids,—I loved them when
In Jaën,—
Axa, Fatima, Marien.

Three dark maids who went together
Picking olives in clear weather,
My, but they were in fine feather
In Jaën,—
Axa, Fatima, Marien !—

There the harvests they collected,
Turning home with hearts dejected,
Haggard where the sun reflected
In Jaën,—
Axa, Fatima, Marien—

Three dark Moors so lovely they—
Three dark Moors so lovely, they
Plucked the apples on that day
Near Jaën,—
Axa, Fatima, Marien.

Thomas Walsh [1]

CRISTOBAL DE CASTILLEJO   1490–1550
Some Day, Some Day

SOME day, some day,
O troubled breast,
Shalt thou find rest.
If Love in thee
To grief give birth,
Six feet of earth
Can more than he;
There calm and free
And unoppressed
Shalt thou find rest.
The unattained
In life at last,
When life is passed
Shall all be gained;
And no more pained,
No more distressed,
Shalt thou find rest.

H. W. Longfellow

ANONYMOUS   16th century?
The Siesta

AIRS! that wander and murmur round,
Bearing delight where'er ye blow,—
Make in the elms a lulling sound,
While my lady sleeps in the shade below.

[1] Courtesy of the Hispanic Society of America.

Lighten and lengthen her noonday rest,
    Till the heat of the noonday sun is o'er:
Sweet be her slumbers,—though in my breast
    The pain she has waked may slumber no more !
Breathing soft from the blue profound,
    Bearing delight where'er ye blow,
Make in the elms a lulling sound,
    While my lady sleeps in the shade below.

Airs ! that over the bending boughs,
    And under the shadows of the leaves,
Murmur soft, like my timid vows,
    Or the secret sighs my bosom heaves,—
Gently sweeping the grassy ground,
    Bearing delight where'er ye blow,
Make in the elms a lulling sound,
    While my lady sleeps in the shade below.

William Cullen Bryant

OLD SPANISH BALLADS

16th century ?

Gentle River, Gentle River

GENTLE river, gentle river,
    Lo, thy streams are stained with gore.
Many a brave and noble captain
Floats along thy willowed shore.

All beside thy limpid waters,
All beside thy sands so bright,
Moorish chiefs and Christian warriors
Joined in fierce and mortal fight.

Lords and dukes and noble princes
On thy fatal banks were slain;
Fatal banks that gave to slaughter
All the pride and flower of Spain.

There the hero, brave Alonso,
Full of wounds and glory died;
There the fearless Urdiales
Fell a victim by his side.

Lo ! where yonder, Don Saavedra
Through their squadrons slow retires;
Proud Seville, his native city,
Proud Seville his worth admires.

Close behind a renegado
Loudly shouts with taunting cry:
" Yield thee, yield thee, Don Saavedra.
Dost thou from the battle fly ?

" Well I know thy aged parents,
Well thy blooming bride I know;
Seven years I was thy captive,
Seven years of pain and woe.

" May our Prophet grant my wishes,
Haughty chief, thou shalt be mine;
Thou shalt drink that cup of sorrow
Which I drank when I was thine."

Like a lion turns the warrior,
Back he sends an angry glare;
Whizzing came the Moorish javelin,
Vainly whizzing through the air.

Back the hero full of fury
Sent a deep and mortal wound;
Instant sank the renegado
Mute and lifeless on the ground.

With a thousand Moors surrounded,
Brave Saavedra stands at bay;
Wearied out but never daunted,
Cold at length the warrior lay.

Near him, fighting, great Alonso
Stout resists the Paynim bands;
From his slaughtered steed dismounted
Firm entrenched behind him stands.

Furious press the hostile squadrons,
Furious he repels their rage;
Loss of blood at length enfeebles;
Who can war with thousands wage?

Where yon rock the plain o'ershadows
Close behind its foot retired,
Fainting sank the bleeding hero,
And without a groan expired.

Thomas Percy

Abenamar, Abenamar

O THOU Moor of Morería,
There were mighty signs and aspects
On the day when thou wert born,
Calm and lovely was the ocean,
Bright and full the moon above.
Moor, the child of such an aspect
Never ought to answer falsely.
Then replied the Moorish captive,
(You shall hear the Moor's reply):

Nor will I untruly answer,
Though I died for saying truth.
I am son of Moorish sire.
My mother was a Christian slave.
In my childhood, in my boyhood,
Often would my mother bid me
Never know the liar's shame.
Ask thou, therefore, King, thy question.
Truly will I answer thee.

Thank thee, thank thee, Abenamar,
For thy gentle answer, thanks.
What are yonder lofty castles,
Those that shine so bright on high ?

That, O King, is the Alhambra,
Yonder is the Mosque of God.
There you see the Alixares,
Works of skill and wonder they;
Ten times ten doubloons the builder
Daily for his hire received;
If an idle day he wasted
Ten times ten doubloons he paid.
Farther is the Generalife,
Peerless are its garden groves.
Those are the Vermilion Towers,
Far and wide their fame is known.

Then spake up the King Don Juan
(You shall hear the Monarch's speech):
Wouldst thou marry me Granada,
Gladly would I for thy dowry
Cordoba and Seville give.

I am married, King Don Juan.
King, I am not yet a widow.
Well I love my noble husband.
Well my wedded Lord loves me.

Robert Southey

The Song of the Galley

YE mariners of Spain,
    Bend strongly on your oars,
And bring my love again,—
    For he lies among the Moors !

Ye galleys fairly built,
    Like castles on the sea,
O, great will be your guilt,
    If ye bring him not to me !

The wind is blowing strong,—
    The breeze will aid your oars;
O, swiftly fly along,—
    For he lies among the Moors !

The sweet breeze of the sea
    Cools every cheek but mine;
Hot is its breath to me,
    As I gaze upon the brine.

Lift up, lift up your sail,
    And bend upon your oars;
O, lose not the fair gale,—
    For he lies among the Moors !

It is a narrow strait,—
    I see the blue hills over;
Your coming I'll await,
    And thank you for my lover.

To Mary I will pray,
    While ye bend upon your oars;
'Twill be a blessed day,
    If ye fetch him from the Moors !
                    John Gibson Lockhart

The Lamentation for Celin

AT the gate of old Granada, when all its bolts are
    barred,
    At twilight, at the Vega-gate, there is a trampling
        heard;
    There is a trampling heard, as of horses treading
        slow,

And a weeping voice of women, and a heavy sound
of woe !—
" What tower is fallen ? what star is set ? what chief
come these bewailing ? "
" A tower is fallen ! a star is set !—Alas ! alas for
Celin ! "

Three times they knock, three times they cry,—and
wide the doors they throw;
Dejectedly they enter, and mournfully they go;
In gloomy lines they mustering stand beneath the hollow
porch,
Each horseman grasping in his hand a black and flaming
torch;
Wet is each eye as they go by, and all around is wail
ing,—
For all have heard the misery,—" Alas ! alas for Celin ! "

Him yesterday a Moor did slay, of Bencerrage's blood,—
'Twas at the solemn jousting,—around the nobles stood;
The nobles of the land were by, and ladies bright and
fair
Looked from their latticed windows, the haughty sight
to share:
But now the nobles all lament,—the ladies are bewail
ing,—
For he was Granada's darling knight,—" Alas ! alas for
Celin ! "

Before him ride his vassals, in order two by two,
With ashes on their turbans spread, most pitiful to view;
Behind him his four sisters, each wrapped in sable veil,
Between the tambour's dismal strokes take up their
doleful tale;
When stops the muffled drum, ye hear their brotherless
bewailing,
And all the people, far and near, cry,—" Alas ! alas for
Celin ! "

O, lovely lies he on the bier, above the purple pall,
The flower of all Granada's youth, the loveliest of them
    all !
His dark, dark eyes are closed, his rosy lip is pale,
The crust of blood lies black and dim upon his bur=
    nished mail;
And evermore the hoarse tambour breaks in upon their
    wailing,—
Its sound is like no earthly sound,—" Alas ! alas for
    Celin ! "

The Moorish maid at the lattice stands,—the Moor
    stands at his door;
One maid is wringing of her hands, and one is weeping
    sore;
Down to the dust men bow their heads, and ashes black
    they strew
Upon their broidered garments, of crimson, green, and
    blue;
Before each gate the bier stands still,—then bursts the
    loud bewailing,
From door and lattice, high and low,—" Alas ! alas for
    Celin ! "

An old, old woman cometh forth, when she hears the
    people cry,—
Her hair is white as silver, like horn her glazèd eye;
'Twas she that nursed him at her breast,—that nursed
    him long ago:
She knows not whom they all lament, but soon she well
    shall know !
With one deep shriek, she through doth break, when
    her ears receive their wailing,—
" Let me kiss my Celin, ere I die !—Alas ! alas for
    Celin ! "

John Gibson Lockhart

The Death of Don Pedro

HENRY and King Pedro, clasping,
  Hold in straining arms each other;
Tugging hard, and closely grasping,
  Brother proves his strength with brother.

Harmless pastime, sport fraternal,
  Blends not thus their limbs in strife:
Either aims, with rage infernal,
  Naked dagger, sharpened knife.

Close Don Henry grapples Pedro,
  Pedro holds Don Henry strait,—
Breathing, this, triumphant fury,
  That, despair and mortal hate.

Sole spectator of the struggle,
  Stands Don Henry's page afar,
In the chase who bore his bugle,
  And who bore his sword in war.

Down they go in deadly wrestle,
  Down upon the earth they go;
Fierce King Pedro has the vantage,
  Stout Don Henry falls below.

Marking then the fatal crisis,
  Up the page of Henry ran,
By the waist he caught Don Pedro,
  Aiding thus the fallen man.

" King to place, or to depose him,
  Dwelleth not in my desire;
But the duty which he owes him
  To his master pays the squire."

Now Don Henry has the upmost,
  Now King Pedro lies beneath;
In his heart his brother's poniard
  Instant finds its bloody sheath.

Thus with mortal gasp and quiver,
  While the blood in bubbles welled,
Fled the fiercest soul that ever
  In a Christian bosom dwelled.

John Gibson Lockhart

GIL VICENTE

16th century

Song

IF thou art sleeping, maiden,
  Awake and open thy door.
'Tis the break of day, and we must away
  O'er meadow, and mount, and moor.

Wait not to find thy slippers,
  But come with thy naked feet;
We shall have to pass through the dewy grass
  And waters wide and fleet.

H. W. Longfellow

SISTER MARCELA DE CARPIO DE SAN FELIX

16th century

Amor Mysticus

LET them say to my lover
  That here I lie !
The thing of His pleasure,—
  His slave am I.

Say that I seek Him
Only for love,
And welcome are tortures
My passion to prove.

Love giving gifts
Is suspicious and cold;
I have all, my Belovèd,
When Thee I hold.

Hope and devotion
The good may gain;
I am but worthy
Of passion and pain.

So noble a Lord
None serves in vain,
For the pay of my love
Is my love's sweet pain.

I love Thee, to love Thee,—
No more I desire;
By faith is nourished
My love's strong fire.

I kiss Thy hands
When I feel their blows;
In the place of caresses
Thou givest me woes.

But in Thy chastising
Is joy and peace.
O Master and Love,
Let Thy blows not cease.

Thy beauty, Belovèd,
With scorn is rife,
But I know that Thou lovest me
Better than life.

And because Thou lovest me,
Lover of mine,
Death can but make me
Utterly Thine.

I die with longing
Thy face to see;
Oh ! sweet is the anguish
Of death to me !

John Hay

SAINT TERESA

1515–82

Lines written in her Breviary

LET nothing disturb thee,
Nothing affright thee;
All things are passing;
God never changeth;
Patient endurance
Attaineth to all things;
Who God possesseth
In nothing is wanting;
Alone God sufficeth.

H. W. Longfellow

If, Lord, Thy Love for me is Strong

IF, Lord, Thy love for me is strong
As this which binds me unto Thee,
What holds me from Thee, Lord, so long,
What holds Thee, Lord, so long from me ?

O soul, what then desirest thou ?
—Lord, I would see Thee, who thus choose Thee.
What fears can yet assail thee now ?
—All that I fear is but to lose Thee.

Love's whole possession I entreat,
Lord, make my soul Thine own abode,
And I will build a nest so sweet
It may not be too poor for God.

O soul in God hidden from sin,
What more desires for thee remain,
Save but to love, and love again,
And, all on flame with love within,
Love on, and turn to love again?

Arthur Symons

Let mine Eyes see Thee

LET mine eyes see Thee,
Sweet Jesus of Nazareth,
Let mine eyes see Thee,
And then see death.

Let them see that care
Roses and jessamine;
Seeing Thy face most fair
All blossoms are therein,
Flower of seraphim.
Sweet Jesus of Nazareth,
Let mine eyes see Thee,
And then see death.

Nothing I require
Where my Jesus is;
Anguish all desire,
Saving only this;
All my help is His,
He only succoureth.
Let mine eyes see Thee,
Sweet Jesus of Nazareth,
Let mine eyes see Thee,
And then see death.

Arthur Symons

To∗day a Shepherd

TO∗DAY a shepherd and our kin,
O Gil, to ransom us is sent,
And He is God Omnipotent.
For us hath He cast down the pride
And prison wall of Satanas;
But He is of the kin of Bras,
Of Menga, also of Llorent.
O is not God Omnipotent?

If He is God, how then is He
Come hither and here crucified?
—With His dying sin also died,
Enduring death the innocent.
Gil, how is God Omnipotent!

Why, I have seen Him born, pardie,
And of a most sweet shepherdess.
—If He is God how can He be
With such poor folk as these content?
—Seest not He is Omnipotent?

Give over idle parleyings
And let us serve Him, you and I,
And since He came on earth to die,
Let us die with Him too, Llorent;
For He is God Omnipotent.

Arthur Symons

Shepherd, Shepherd, Hark

SHEPHERD, shepherd, hark that calling!
Angels they are, and the day is dawning.
What is this ding∗dong,
Or loud singing is it?

Come, Bras, now the day is here,
The shepherdess we'll visit.
Shepherd, shepherd, hark that calling !
Angels they are, and the day is dawning.

Oh, is this the Alcalde's daughter,
Or some lady come from far ?
She is the daughter of God the Father,
And she shines like a star.
Shepherd, shepherd, hark that calling !
Angels they are, and the day is dawning.

Arthur Symons

LUIS VAZ DE CAMOËNS
1524–80

On the Death of Catarina de Attayda

THOSE charming eyes within whose starry sphere
Love whilom sat, and smiled the hours away,—
Those braids of light, that shamed the beams of
day,—
That hand benignant, and that heart sincere,—
Those virgin cheeks, which did so late appear
Like snow-banks scattered with the blooms of May,
Turned to a little cold and worthless clay,
Are gone, for ever gone, and perished here,—

But not unbathed by Memory's warmest tear !
Death, thou hast torn, in one unpitying hour,
That fragrant plant, to which, while scarce a flower,
The mellower fruitage of its prime was given;
Love saw the deed,—and as he lingered near
Sighed o'er the ruin, and returned to heaven !

R. F. Burton

On revisiting Cintra after the Death of Catarina

APPAREL of green woods and meadows gay;
  Clear and fresh waters innocent of stain,
  Wherein the field and grove are found again,
As from high rocks ye take your downward way;
And shaggy peaks, and ordered disarray
  Of crags abrupt, know that ye strive in vain,
  Till grief consent, to soothe the eye of pain,
Shown the same scene that Pleasure did survey.
Nor as erst seen am I beheld by you,
  Rejoiced no more by fields of pleasant green,
    Or lively runnels laughing as they dart;
Sown be these fields with seeds of ruth and rue,
  And wet with brine of welling tears, till seen
    Sere with the herb that suits the broken heart.

Richard Garnett

Babylon and Sion (Goa and Lisbon)

HERE, where fecundity of Babel frames
  Stuff for all ills wherewith the world doth teem,
  Where loyal Love is slurred with disesteem,
For Venus all controls, and all defames;
Where vice's vaunts are counted virtue's shames;
  Where Tyranny o'er Honour lords supreme;
  Where blind and erring sovereignty doth deem
That God for deeds will be content with names;

Here in this world where whatso is, is wrong,
  Where Birth and Worth and Wisdom begging go
    To doors of Avarice and Villainy,—

Trammelled in the foul chaos, I prolong
My days, because I must. Woe to me ! Woe !
Sion, had I not memory of thee !

Richard Garnett

Sonnet

LEAVE me, all sweet refrains my lip hath made;
Leave me, all instruments attuned for song;
Leave me, all fountains pleasant meads among;
Leave me, all charms of garden and of glade;
Leave me, all melodies the pipe hath played;
Leave me, all rural feast and sportive throng;
Leave me, all flocks the reed beguiles along;
Leave me, all shepherds happy in the shade.

Sun, moon and stars, for me no longer glow;
Night would I have, to wail for vanished peace;
Let me from pole to pole no pleasure know;
Let all that I have loved and cherished cease;
But see that thou forsake me not, my Woe,
Who wilt, by killing, finally release.

Richard Garnett

Sonnet

TIME and the mortal will stand never fast;
Estrangèd fates man's confidence estrange;
Ay with new quality imbued, the vast
World seems but victual of voracious change.

New endless growth surrounds on every side,
Such as we deemed not earth could ever bear,
Only doth sorrow for past woe abide,
And sorrow for past good, if good it were.

Now Time with green hath made the meadows gay,
Late carpeted with snow by winter frore,

And to lament hath turned my gentle lay;
Yet of all change this chiefly I deplore,
  The human lot, transformed to ill alway,
Not chequered with rare blessing as of yore.

Richard Garnett

FRA LUIS DE LEON

1528-91

The Life of the Blessed

REGION of life and light !
Land of the good whose earthly toils are o'er !
  Nor frost nor heat may blight
  Thy vernal beauty, fertile shore,
Yielding thy blessed fruits for evermore !

  There, without crook or sling,
Walks the Good Shepherd; blossoms white and red
  Round his meek temples cling;
  And, to sweet pastures led,
His own loved flock beneath his eye is fed.

  He guides, and near him they
Follow delighted; for he makes them go
  Where dwells eternal May,
  And heavenly roses blow,
Deathless, and gathered but again to grow.

  He leads them to the height
Named of the infinite and long-sought Good,
  And fountains of delight;
  And where his feet have stood,
Springs up, along the way, their tender food.

  And when, in the mid skies,
The climbing sun has reached his highest bound,
  Reposing as he lies,
  · With all his flock around,
He witches the still air with numerous sound.

From his sweet lute flow forth
Immortal harmonies, of power to still
    All passions born of earth,
    And draw the ardent will
Its destiny of goodness to fulfil.

    Might but a little part,
A wandering breath, of that high melody
    Descend into my heart,
    And change it till it be
Transformed and swallowed up, O love ! in thee:

    Ah ! then my soul should know,
Beloved ! where thou liest at noon of day;
    And from this place of woe
    Released, should take its way
To mingle with thy flock, and never stray.

William Cullen Bryant

MIGUEL DE CERVANTES

1547–1616

Sonnet

WHEN I was marked for suffering, Love forswore
    All knowledge of my doom; or else at ease
    Love grows a cruel tyrant, hard to please;
Or else a chastisement exceeding sore
A little sin hath brought me.   Hush !   No more
    Love is a god !   All things he knows and sees !
    And gods are bland and mild !   Who then
      decrees
The dreadful woe I bear and yet adore ?

If I should say, O Chloe, that 'twas thou,
    I should speak falsely since, being wholly good
      Like Heaven itself, from thee no ill can come.

There is no hope; I must die shortly now,
  Not knowing why, since, sure, no witch hath
    brewed
  The drug that might avert my martyrdom.
                              Sir Edmund Gosse

SAINT JOHN OF THE CROSS
1549–91

The Obscure Night of the Soul

UPON an obscure night
Fevered with love in love's anxiety
(O hapless-happy plight !)
I went, none seeing me,
Forth from my house where all things be.

By night, secure from sight,
And by the secret stair, disguisedly
(O hapless-happy plight !)
By night, and privily,
Forth from my house where all things quiet be.

Blest night of wandering,
In secret, where by none might I be spied,
Nor I see anything;
Without a light or guide,
Save that which in my heart burnt in my side.

That light did lead me on,
More surely than the shining of noontide,
Where well I knew that one
Did for my coming bide;
Where He abode, might none but He abide.

O night that didst lead thus,
O night more lovely than the dawn of light,
O night that broughtest us,
Lover to lover's sight,
Lover with loved in marriage of delight !

Upon my flowery breast
Wholly for Him, and save Himself for none,
There did I give sweet rest
To my belovèd one;
The fanning of the cedars breathed thereon.

When the first moving air
Blew from the tower and waved His locks aside,
His hand, with gentle care,
Did wound me in the side,
And in my body all my senses died.

All things I then forgot,
My cheek on Him who for my coming came;
All ceased, and I was not,
Leaving my cares and shame
Among the lilies, and forgetting them.

Arthur Symons

O Flame of Living Love

O FLAME of living love,
That dost eternally
Pierce through my soul with so consuming heat,
Since there's no help above,
Make thou an end of me,
And break the bond of this encounter sweet.

O burn that burns to heal!
O more than pleasant wound!
And O soft hand, O touch most delicate,
That dost new life reveal,
That lost in grace abound,
And, slaying, dost from death to life translate!

O lamps of fire that shined
With so intense a light
That those deep caverns where the senses live,
Which were obscure and blind,
Now with strange glories bright,
Both heat and light to His belovèd give !

With how benign intent
Rememberest thou my breast,
Where thou alone abidest secretly;
And in thy sweet ascent,
With glory and good possessed,
How delicately thou teachest love to me !

Arthur Symons

LUIS DE GÓNGORA

1561–1627

The Rosemary Spray

THE flowers upon the rosemary spray,
Young Maid, may school thy sorrow;
The blue-eyed flower, that blooms to-day,
To honey turns to-morrow.

A tumult stirs thy tender breast,
With jealous pain true-hearted,
That he, whom thy first love hath bless'd,
From thee hath coldly parted.

Ungracious boy, who slights thy love,
And overbold disdaining
To ask forgiveness, and remove
The cause of thy complaining.

Hope, come and drive those tears away !
For lovers' jealous sorrow,
Like dewy blue-eyed flower on spray
To honey turns to-morrow.

By thine own joy thou wast undone:
A bliss thou couldst not measure,
Like star at dawn too near the sun,
Eclipsed thee by its pleasure.

Walk forth with eyes serene and fair;
The pearls, that deck the morning,
Are wasted in the day's fierce glare;
With calmness tame his scorning.

Disperse those clouds that but dismay;
Distrust that jealous sorrow:
The blue-eyed flower, that blooms to-day,
To honey turns to-morrow.

E. Churton

The Rose of Life

BLOWN in the morning, thou shalt fade ere noon:
  What boots a life which in such haste forsakes thee ?
Th'art wondrous frolick being to die so soon:
  And passing proud a little colour makes thee.
If thee thy brittle beauty so deceives,
  Know then the thing that swells thee is thy bane;
For the same beauty doth in bloody leaves
  The sentence of thy early death contain.
Some clown's coarse lungs will poison thy sweet flower
  If by the careless plough thou shalt be torn:
And many Herods lie in wait each hour
  To murther thee as soon as thou art born,
Nay, force thy bud to blow; their tyrant breath,
Anticipating life, to hasten death.

Sir Richard Fanshawe

Let me go Warm

LET me go warm and merry still;
  And let the world laugh, an' it will.

Let others muse on earthly things,—
The fall of thrones, the fate of kings,
  And those whose fame the world doth fill;
Whilst muffins sit enthroned in trays,
And orange-punch in winter sways
The merry sceptre of my days;—
  And let the world laugh, an' it will.

He that the royal purple wears
From golden plate a thousand cares
  Doth swallow as a gilded pill:
On feasts like these I turn my back,
Whilst puddings in my roasting-jack
Beside the chimney hiss and crack;—
  And let the world laugh, an' it will.

And when the wintry tempest blows,
And January's sleets and snows
  Are spread o'er every vale and hill,
With one to tell a merry tale
O'er roasted nuts and humming ale,
I sit, and care not for the gale;—
  And let the world laugh, an' it will.

Let merchants traverse seas and lands,
For silver mines and golden sands;
  Whilst I beside some shadowy rill,
Just where its bubbling fountain swells,
Do sit and gather stones and shells,
And hear the tale the blackbird tells;—
  And let the world laugh, an' it will.

For Hero's sake the Grecian lover
The stormy Hellespont swam over:
  I cross, without the fear of ill,
The wooden bridge that slow bestrides
The Madrigal's enchanting sides,
Or barefoot wade through Yepes' tides;—
  And let the world laugh, an' it will.

But since the Fates so cruel prove,
That Pyramus should die of love,
  And love should gentle Thisbe kill;
My Thisbe be an apple tart,
The sword I plunge into her heart
The tooth that bites the crust apart;—
  And let the world laugh, an' it will.

H. W. Longfellow

LOPE DE VEGA

1562–1635

To morrow

LORD, what am I, that, with unceasing care,
  Thou didst seek after me,—that thou didst wait,
  Wet with unhealthy dews, before my gate,
And pass the gloomy nights of winter there?
O, strange delusion, that I did not greet
  Thy blest approach! and, O, to heaven how lost,
  If my ingratitude's unkindly frost
Has chilled the bleeding wounds upon thy feet!
How oft my guardian angel gently cried,
  "Soul, from thy casement look and thou shalt see
How he persists to knock and wait for thee!"
And, O, how often to that voice of sorrow,
  "To morrow we will open," I replied!
And when the morrow came, I answered still,
  "To morrow."

H. W. Longfellow

FRANCISCO DE QUEVEDO Y VILLEGAS

1580–1645

Sonnet: Death Warnings

I SAW the ramparts of my native land,
  One time so strong, now dropping in decay,
  Their strength destroyed by this new age's way
That has worn out and rotted what was grand.

I went into the fields; there I could see
The sun drink up the waters newly thawed,
And on the hills the moaning cattle pawed;
Their miseries robbed the day of light for me.

I went into my house; I saw how spotted,
Decaying things made that old home their prize;
My withered walking-staff had come to bend.
I felt the age had won; my sword was rotted,
And there was nothing on which to set my eyes
That was not a reminder of the end.

John Masefield

PEDRO CALDERÓN DE LA BARCA

1600–81

HE exceeds all modern dramatists, with the exception of Shakespeare, whom he resembles, however, in the depth of thought and subtlety of imagination of his writings, and in the rare power of interweaving delicate and powerful comic traits with the most tragical situations.— PERCY BYSSHE SHELLEY.

The Dream called Life

A DREAM it was in which I found myself.
And you that hail me now, then hailed me king,
In a brave palace that was all my own,
Within, and all without it, mine; until,
Drunk with excess of majesty and pride,
Methought I towered so big and swelled so wide
That of myself I burst the glittering bubble
Which my ambition had about me blown
And all again was darkness.   Such a dream
As this, in which I may be walking now,
Dispensing solemn justice to you shadows,
Who make believe to listen; but anon
Kings, princes, captains, warriors, plume and steel,
Aye, even with all your airy theatre,

May flit into the air you seem to rend
With acclamations, leaving me to wake
In the dark tower; or dreaming that I wake
From this that waking is; or this and that,
Both waking and both dreaming; such a doubt
Confounds and clouds our mortal life about.
But whether wake or dreaming, this I know,
How dreamwise human glories come and go;
Whose momentary tenure not to break,
Walking as one who knows he soon may wake,
So fairly carry the full cup, so well
Disordered insolence and passion quell,
That there be nothing after to upbraid
Dreamer or doer in the part he played;
Whether to-morrow's dawn shall break the spell,
Or the last trumpet of the Eternal Day,
When dreaming, with the night, shall pass away.

Edward FitzGerald

From "Life is a Dream"

WE live, while we see the sun,
  Where life and dreams are as one;
And living has taught me this,
Man dreams the life that is his,
  Until his living is done.
The king dreams he is king, and he lives
  In the deceit of a king,
  Commanding and governing;
And all the praise he receives
  Is written in wind, and leaves
  A little dust on the way
When death ends all with a breath.
Where then is the gain of a throne,
That shall perish and not be known
In the other dream that is death?

Dreams the rich man of riches and fears,
The fears that his riches breed;
The poor man dreams of his need,
And all his sorrows and tears;
Dreams he that prospers with years,
Dreams he that feigns and foregoes,
Dreams he that rails on his foes;
And in all the world, I see,
Man dreams whatever he be,
And his own dream no man knows.
And I too dream and behold,
I dream and I am bound with chains,
And I dreamed that these present pains
Were fortunate ways of old.
What is life ? a tale that is told;
What is life ? a frenzy extreme,
A shadow of things that seem;
And the greatest good is but small,
That all life is a dream to all,
And that dreams themselves are a dream.

Arthur Symons

GUSTAVO ADOLFO BECQUÉR
1836–70

They closed her Eyes

THEY closed her eyes,
They were still open;
They hid her face
With a white linen,
And, some sobbing,
Others in silence,
From the sad bedroom
All came away.

The nightlight in a dish
Burned on the floor;

It threw on the wall
The bed's shadow,
And in that shadow
One saw sometimes
Drawn in sharp line
The body's shape.

The dawn appeared.
At its first whiteness,
With its thousand noises,
The town awoke.
Before that contrast
Of light and darkness,
Of life and strangeness,
I thought a moment,—
   My God, how lonely
   The dead are !

On the shoulders of men
To church they bore her,
And in a chapel
They left her bier.
There they surrounded
Her pale body
With yellow candles
And black stuffs.

At the last stroke
Of the ringing for the souls
An old crone finished
Her last prayers.
She crossed the narrow nave,
The doors moaned,
And the holy place
Remained deserted.

From a clock one heard
The measured ticking,

And from a candle
The guttering.
All things there
Were so dark and mournful,
So cold and rigid,
That I thought a moment,—
    My God, how lonely
    The dead are !

From the high belfry
The tongue of iron
Clanged, giving out
A last farewell.
Crape on their clothes,
Her friends and kindred
Passed by in line
In homage to her.

In the last vault,
Dark and narrow,
The pickaxe opened
A niche at one end;
They laid her away there.
Soon they bricked the place up,
And with a gesture
Bade grief farewell.

Pickaxe on shoulder,
The gravedigger,
Singing between his teeth,
Passed out of sight.
The night came down,
It was all silent.
Alone in darkness,
I thought a moment,—
    My God, how lonely
    The dead are !

In the dark nights
Of bitter winter,
When the wind makes
The rafters creak,
When the violent rain
Lashes the windows,
Lonely I remember
That poor girl.

There falls the rain
With its noise eternal,
There the north-wind
Fights with the rain.
Stretched in the hollow
Of the damp bricks,
Perhaps her bones
Freeze with the cold.

Does the dust return to dust?
Does the soul fly to heaven?
Or is all vile matter,
Rottenness, filthiness?
I know not, but
There is something—something—
Something which gives me
Loathing, terror,
To leave the dead
So alone, so wretched.

John Masefield

ANTONIO MACHADO

1879–

Poems

I

A FRAIL sound of a tunic trailing
across the infertile earth,
and the sonorous weeping
of the old bells.

The dying embers
of the horizon smoke.
White ancestral ghosts
go lighting the stars.

—Open the balcony window.   The hour
of illusion draws near. . . .
The afternoon has gone to sleep
and the bells dream.

2

FIGURES in the fields against the sky !
Two slow oxen plough
on a hill side early in autumn,
and between the black heads bent down
under the weight of the yoke,
hangs and sways a basket of reeds,
a child's cradle;
And behind the yoke stride
a man who leans towards the earth
and a woman who, into the open furrows,
throws the seed.
Under a cloud of carmine and flame,
in the liquid green gold of the setting,
their shadows grow monstrous.

3

NAKED is the earth
and the soul howls to the wan horizon
like a hungry she wolf.
                              What do you seek,
poet, in the sunset ?
Bitter going, for the path
weighs one down, the frozen wind,
and the coming night and the bitterness

of distance. . . . On the white path
the trunks of frustrate trees show black,
on the distant mountains
there is gold and blood. The sun dies. . . .
               What do you seek,
poet, in the sunset ?

4

WE think to create festivals
of love out of our love,
to burn new incense
on untrodden mountains;
and to keep the secret
of our pale faces,
and why in the bacchanals of life
we carry empty glasses,
while with tinkling echoes and laughing
foams the gold must of the grape. . . .
A hidden bird among the branches
of the solitary park
whistles mockery. . . . We feel
the shadow of a dream in our wine-glass,
and something that is earth in our flesh
feels the dampness of the garden like a caress.

                              John Dos Passos

SPANISH FOLK SONGS

I

LET the rich man fill his belly;
   Let him fast that has no bread;
And he may sleep in the moonlight
   That cannot find a bed.
            *   *   *

If the sea were one great ink-pot
    And the sky of paper made,
The evil that's in women
    Could not all be said.
        *   *   *

If the sea were one great ink-pot
    And of paper all the sky,
It were not enough for telling
    How deeply men can lie.
        *   *   *

To love with no return
    Is a sad thing to befall;
But a sadder, to come to die
    Before having loved at all.

2

MY father was a sailor,
    My brother, a sailor was he,
And the man who would be my lover
    A sailor he must be.
        *   *   *

Oh, a pearl is a thing of much value,
    And a diamond yet more than this;
But I know what to me is most precious,
    And that is a student's kiss.
        *   *   *

Do not look at my face;
    I am brown, I am not fair;
When you look, look below my waist,
    I am sweet altogether there.
        *   *   *

My lover is but a small man,
    So would I have him be;
Fewer leaves and more fruit ever
    We find on the little tree.
                    Havelock Ellis

FRENCH

FROM THE PROVENÇAL

*D*ANCE, *and Provençal song, and sun-burnt mirth !*—JOHN KEATS

GUILLAUME DE POITIERS

11th century

Behold the Meads

BEHOLD, the meads are green again,
The orchard-bloom is seen again,
Of sky and stream the mien again
    Is mild, is bright !
Now should each heart that loves obtain
    Its own delight.

But I will say no ill of Love,
However slight my guerdon prove:
Repining doth not me behove:
    And yet—to know
How lightly she I fain would move
    Might bliss bestow !

There are who hold my folly great,
Because with little hope I wait;
But one old saw doth animate
    And me assure:
Their hearts are high, their might is great,
    Who will endure.

Harriet Waters Preston

MARCABRUN

12th century

At the Fountain

A FOUNT there is, doth overfling
Green turf and garden walks; in spring
A glory of white blossoming
Shines underneath its guardian tree;
And new-come birds old music sing;
And there, alone and sorrowing,
I found a maid I could not cheer,—

Of beauty meet to be adored,
The daughter of the castle's lord;
Methought the melody outpour'd
By all the birds unceasingly,
The season sweet, the verdant sward,
Might gladden her, and eke my word
Her grief dismiss, would she but hear.—

Her tears into the fountain fell;
With sorry sighs her heart did swell;
"O Jesus, King Invisible!"
She cried,—" of Thee is my distress!
Through Thy deep wrong bereft I dwell:
Earth's best have bidden us farewell,
On Thee at Thine own shrine to wait.

"And my true Love is also gone,
The free, fair, gentle, valiant One;
So what can I but make my moan,
And how the sad desire suppress
That Louis' name were here unknown,
The prayers, the mandates, all undone
Whereby I am made desolate?"

Soon as I heard this plaintive cry,
Moving the limpid wave anigh,
" Weep not, fair maid ! so piteously,
Nor waste thy roses ! " thus I cried,—
" Neither despair, for He is by
Who brought this leafy greenery,
And He will give thee joy one day."

" Seigneur ! I well believe," she said,—
" Of God I shall be comforted
In yonder world when I am dead;
And many a sinful soul beside;—
But now hath He prohibited
My chief delight.   I bow my head,—
But heaven is very far away."

Harriet Waters Preston

BERNARD DE VENTADOUR

12th century

No Marvel is It

NO marvel is it if I sing
Better than other minstrels all:
For more than they I am Love's thrall,
And all myself therein I fling,—
Knowledge and sense, body and soul,
And whatso power I have beside;
The rein that doth my being guide
Impels me to this only goal.

His heart is dead whence did not spring
Love's odour, sweet and magical;
His life doth ever on him pall
Who knoweth not that blessed thing;

Yea ! God, who doth my life control,
Were cruel did He bid me bide
A month, or even a day, denied
The love whose rapture I extol.

How keen, how exquisite the sting
Of that sweet odour !   At its call
An hundred times a day I fall
And faint, an hundred rise and sing.
So fair the semblance of my dole,
'Tis lovelier than another's pride:
If such the ill doth me betide,
Good hap were more than I could thole.

Yet haste, kind heaven ! the sundering
True swains from false, great hearts from small !
The traitor in the dust bid crawl !
The faithless to confession bring !
Ah ! if I were the master sole
Of all earth's treasures multiplied,
To see my Lady satisfied
Of my pure faith, I'd give the whole.

Harriet Waters Preston

ARNAUT DANIEL
Mot eran Dous miei Cossir

SWEET my musings used to be,
Without shadow of distress,
Till the queen of loveliness,
Lowly, mild, yet frank as day,
Bade me put her love away;
    Love so deeply wrought in me.
And because I answered not,
Nay, nor e'en her mercy sought,
All the joy of life is gone,
For it lived in her alone.

O my lady, hearken thee !
For thy wondrous tenderness,
Nor my faltering cry repress;
Bid thy faithful servant stay;
Deign to keep my love, I pray;
    Let me not my rival see !
That which never cost thee aught
Were to me with rapture fraught.
Who would grudge the sick man's moan
When his pain is all his own ?

Thou art wise as thou art fair,
And thy voice is ever kind;
Thou for all dost welcome find,
With a courtesy so bright,
Praise of all it doth invite.
    Hope and comforting of care
In thy smile are born and live
Wheresoe'er thou dost arrive.
Not my love doth canonize,
But the truth and thine own price.

Unto one thus everywhere
In the praise of men enshrined,
What's my tribute unrefined ?
And yet, lady of delight,
True it is, however trite.
    He shall sway the balance fair
Who a single grain doth give,
Be the poise right sensitive.
So might one poor word suffice
To enhance thy dignities.

Harriet Waters Preston

Bel m'es quan lo Vens m'alena

SOFTLY sighs the April air,
  Ere the coming of the May;
Of the tranquil night aware,
  Murmur nightingale and jay;
Then, when dewy dawn doth rise,
  Every bird in his own tongue
Wakes his mate with happy cries;
  All their joy abroad is flung.

Gladness, lo ! is everywhere
  When the first leaf sees the day;
And shall I alone despair,
  Turning from sweet love away ?
Something to my heart replies,
  Thou too wast for rapture strung;
Wherefore else the dreams that rise
  Round thee when the year is young ?

One, than Helen yet more fair,
  Loveliest blossom of the May,
Rose-tints hath and sunny hair,
  And a gracious mien and gay;
Heart that scorneth all disguise,
  Lips where pearls of truth are hung,—
God, who gives all sovereignties,
  Knows her like was never sung.

Though she lead through long despair,
  I would never say her nay,
If one kiss—reward how rare !—
  Each new trial might repay.
Swift returns I'd then devise,
  Many labours, but not long.
Following so fair a prize
  I could nevermore go wrong.

                              Harriet Waters Preston

MARIE DE FRANCE

13th century

Song from Chartivel

HATH any loved you well, down there,
 Summer or winter through?
Down there, have you found any fair
 Laid in the grave with you?
Is death's long kiss a richer kiss
 Than mine was wont to be—
Or have you gone to some far bliss
 And quite forgotten me?

What soft enamouring of sleep
 Hath you in some soft way?
What charmed death holdeth you with deep
 Strange lure by night and day?
A little space below the grass,
 Out of the sun and shade;
But worlds away from me, alas,
 Down there where you are laid.

My brightest waved and wasted gold,
 What is it now to thee—
Whether the rose-red life I hold
 Or white death holdeth me?
Down there you love the grave's own green,
 And evermore you rave
Of some sweet seraph you have seen
 Or dreamt of in the grave.

There you shall lie as you have lain,
 Though in the world above,
Another live your life again,
 Loving again your love:
Is it not sweet beneath the palm?
 Is it not warm day rife

With some long mystic golden calm
    Better than love and life ?

The broad quaint odorous leaves like hands
    Weaving the fair day through,
Weave sleep no burnished bird withstands,
    While death weaves sleep for you;
And many a strange rich breathing sound
    Ravishes morn and noon:
And in that place you must have found
    Death a delicious swoon—

Hold me no longer for a word
    I used to say or sing:
Ah, long ago you must have heard
    So many a sweeter thing:
For rich earth must have reached your heart
    And turned the faith to flowers;
And warm wind stolen, part by part,
    Your soul through faithless hours.

And many a soft seed must have won
    Soil of some yielding thought,
To bring a bloom up to the sun
    That else had ne'er been brought;
And, doubtless, many a passionate hue
    Hath made that place more fair,
Making some passionate part of you
    Faithless to me down there.

                  Arthur O'Shaughnessy

Would I might go Far Over Sea

WOULD I might go far over sea,
    My Love, or high above the air,
    And come to land or heaven with thee,
    Where no law is, and none shall be,
    Against beholding the most rare
    Strange beauty that thou hast for me.

Alas, for, in this bitter land,
Full many a written curse doth stand
Against the kiss thy lips should bear;
Against the sweet gift of thy hands;
Against the knowing that thou art fair,
And too fond loving of thy hair.

Arthur O'Shaughnessy

THE VIDAME DE CHARTRES

13th century

April

WHEN the fields catch flower
    And the underwood is green,
And from bower unto bower
    The songs of the birds begin,
    I sing with sighing between.
When I laugh and sing,
    I am heavy at heart for my sin;
I am sad in the spring
    For my love that I shall not win,
For a foolish thing.

This profit I have of my woe,
    That I know, as I sing,
I know he will needs have it so
    Who is master and king,
    Who is lord of the spirit of spring.
I will serve her and will not spare
    Till her pity awake
Who is good, who is pure, who is fair,
    Even her for whose sake
Love hath ta'en me and slain unaware.

O my lord, O Love,
    I have laid my life at thy feet;

Have thy will thereof,
　　Do as it please thee with it,
　　For what shall please thee is sweet.
I am come unto thee
　　To do thee service, O Love;
Yet cannot I see
　　Thou wilt take any pity thereof,
Any mercy on me.

But the grace I have long time sought
　　Comes never in sight,
If in her it abideth not,
　　Through thy mercy and might,
　　Whose heart is the world's delight.
Thou hast sworn without fail I shall die,
　　For my heart is set
On what hurts me, I wot not why,
　　But cannot forget
What I love, what I sing for and sigh.

She is worthy of praise,
　　For this grief of her giving is worth
All the joy of my days
　　That lie between death's day and birth,
　　All the lordship of things upon earth.
Nay, what have I said?
　　I would not be glad if I could;
My dream and my dread
　　Are of her, and for her sake I would
That my life were fled.

Lo, sweet, if I durst not pray to you,
　　Then were I dead;
If I sang not a little to say to you,
　　(Could it be said)
　　O my love, how my heart would be fed;

Ah, sweet, who hast hold of my heart,
  For thy love's sake I live,
Do but tell me, ere either depart,
  What a lover may give
For a woman so fair as thou art.

The lovers that disbelieve,
  False rumours shall grieve
And evil-speaking shall part.

Algernon Charles Swinburne

JEAN FROISSART

1337–1404

Rondel

LOVE, love, what wilt thou with this heart of mine?
  Naught see I fixed or sure in thee!
I do not know thee,—nor what deeds are thine:
Love, love, what wilt thou with this heart of mine?
  Naught see I fixed or sure in thee!

Shall I be mute, or vows with prayers combine?
  Ye who are blessed in loving, tell it me:
Love, love, what wilt thou with this heart of mine?
  Naught see I permanent or sure in thee!

H. W. Longfellow

CHARLES D'ORLÉANS

1391–1465

Rondel

*(To his mistress, to succour his heart that is beleaguered
by jealousy)*

STRENGTHEN, my Love, this castle of my heart,
  And with some store of pleasure give me aid,
For Jealousy, with all them of his part,
  Strong siege about the weary tower has laid.

Nay, if to break his bands thou art afraid,
Too weak to make his cruel force depart,
Strengthen at least this castle of my heart,
    And with some store of pleasure give me aid.
Nay, let not Jealousy, for all his art
    Be master, and the tower in ruin laid,
      That still, ah, Love, thy gracious rule obeyed.
Advance, and give me succour of thy part;
Strengthen, my Love, this castle of my heart.

Andrew Lang

Spring

THE year has changed his mantle cold
    Of wind, of rain, of bitter air;
And he goes clad in cloth of gold,
    Of laughing suns and season fair;
No bird or beast of wood or wold
    But doth with cry or song declare
The year lays down his mantle cold.
All founts, all rivers, seaward rolled,
    The pleasant summer livery wear,
    With silver studs on broidered vair;
The world puts off its raiment old,
The year lays down his mantle cold.

Andrew Lang

Alons au Bois le May Cueillir

WE'LL to the woods and gather may
    Fresh from the footprints of the rain;
    We'll to the woods, at every vein
To drink the spirit of the day.

The winds of spring are out at play,
    The needs of spring in heart and brain.
We'll to the woods and gather may
    Fresh from the footprints of the rain.

The world's too near her end, you say ?—
    Hark to the blackbird's mad refrain.
    It waits for her, the vast Inane ?—
Then, girls, to help her on the way
We'll to the woods and gather may.

                W. E. Henley

ANONYMOUS
John of Tours

JOHN of Tours is back with peace,
But he comes home ill at ease.

" Good-morrow, mother." " Good-morrow, son ;
Your wife has borne you a little one."

" Go now, mother, go before,
Make me a bed upon the floor.

" Very low your foot must fall,
That my wife hear not at all."

As it neared the midnight toll,
John of Tours gave up his soul.

" Tell me now, my mother my dear,
What's the crying that I hear ? "

" Daughter, it's the children wake,
Crying with their teeth that ache."

" Tell me though, my mother my dear,
What's the knocking that I hear ? "

" Daughter, it's the carpenter
Mending planks upon the stair."

" Tell me too, my mother my dear,
What's the singing that I hear ? "

" Daughter, it's the priests in rows
Going round about our house."

" Tell me then, my mother my dear,
What's the dress that I should wear ? "

" Daughter, any reds or blues,
But the black is most in use."

" Nay, but say, my mother my dear,
Why do you fall weeping here ? "

" Oh, the truth must be said,—
It's that John of Tours is dead."

" Mother, let the sexton know
That the grave must be for two;

" Aye, and still have room to spare,
For you must shut the baby there."

D. G. Rossetti

My Father's Close

INSIDE my father's close,
  (Fly away, O my heart, away !)
Sweet apple-blossom blows
  So sweet.

Three kings' daughters fair,
  (Fly away, O my heart, away !)
They lie below it there
  So sweet.

"Ah," says the eldest one,
  (Fly away, O my heart, away!)
"I think the day's begun
  So sweet."

"Ah," says the second one,
  (Fly away, O my heart, away!)
"Far off I hear the drum
  So sweet."

"Ah," says the youngest one,
  (Fly away, O my heart, away!)
"It's my true love, my own,
  So sweet."

"Oh, if he fight and win,
  (Fly away, O my heart, away!)
"I keep my love for him,
  So sweet:
  Oh, let him lose or win,
  He hath it still complete."

D. G. Rossetti

MEDIÆVAL NORMAN SONGS

I

FAIR is her body, bright her eye,
With smiles her mouth is kind to me;
Then, think no evil, this is she
Whom God hath made my only joy.

Between the earth and heaven high
There is no maid so fair as she;
The beauty of her sweet body
Doth ever fill my heart with joy.

He is a knave, nor do I lie,
Who loveth her not heartily;
The grace that shines from her body
Giveth to lovers all great joy.

2

Sad, lost in thought, and mute I go:
  The cause, ah me ! you know full well:
  But see that naught thereof you tell,
For men will only laugh at woe—
For men will only laugh at woe.

3

Kiss me then, my merry May,
By the soul of love I pray !
  Prithee, nay !   Tell, tell me why ?
If with you I sport and play,
My mother will be vexed to day.
  Tell me why, oh tell me why.

4

Before my lady's window gay,
The little birds they sing all day,
  The lark, the mavis, and the dove;
But the sweet nightingale of May,
She whiles the silent hours away,
  Chanting of sorrow, joy, and love.

5

I found at daybreak yester morn,
Close by the nest where she was born,
  A tender turtle dove:
  Oha ! ohé ! ohesa, hesa, hé !

She fluttered, but she could not fly:
I heard, but would not heed her cry:
She had not learned to love:
    Oha ! ohé ! ohesa, hesa, hé !

Now she is quiet on my breast,
And from her new and living nest
She doth not seek to rove:
    Oha ! ohé ! ohesa, hesa, hé !

6

This month of May, one pleasant eventide,
    I heard a young girl singing on the green;
I came upon her where the ways divide,
    And said: " God keep you, maiden, from all teen.

" Maiden, the God of love you keep and save,
    And give you all your heart desires," I cried.
Then she: " Pray tell me, gentle sir and brave,
    Whither you wend this pleasant eventide ? "

" To you I come, a lover leal and true,
    To tell you all my hope and all my care;
Your love alone is what I seek; than you
    No woman ever seemed to me more fair."

7

In this merry morn of May,
    When as the year grows young and green,
Into the wood I went my way,
    To say farewell unto my queen.

And when we could no longer stay,
    Weeping upon my neck she fell:
Oh, send me news from far away,
    Farewell, sweet heart of mine, farewell.

8

O Love, my love, and perfect bliss !
God in His goodness grant me this—
   I see thee soon again.
Naught else I need to take away
The grief that for thy sake alway
   Doth keep me in great pain.

Alas, I know not what to do,
Nor how to get good news and true:
   Dear God, I pray to Thee;
If else Thou canst not comfort me,
Of Thy great mercy make that he
   Send speedy news to me.

Within my father's garden walls
There is a tree—when April falls
   It blossometh alway.
There wend I oft in winter drear,
Yes, and in spring, the winds to hear,
   The sweet winds at their play.

9

Alas, poor heart, I pity thee
   For all the grief thou hast and care.
   My love I see not anywhere;
He is so far away from me.
Until once more his face I see
   I shall be sad by night and day;

And if his face I may not see
Then I shall die most certainly:
For other pleasures have I none,
And all my hope is this alone.
   No ease I take by night and day:
   O Love, my love, to thee I pray
   Have pity upon me !

Dear nightingale of woodland gay,
   Who singest on the leafy tree,
Go, take a message, I thee pray,
   A message to my love from me;
Tell, tell him that I waste away
And weaker grow from day to day.

Ah, God! what pain and grief have we
   Who are poor lovers, leal and true:
   For every week that we pass through,
Five hundred thousand griefs have we:
   One cannot think, or count, or tell
   The griefs and pains that we know well!

10

Now who is he on earth that lives,
   Who knows or with his tongue can say
What grief to poor lovers it gives
   To love with loyal heart alway?

So bitter is their portion, yea,
   So hard their part!
   But this doth more confound my heart;
Unloved to love, and still to pray!
Thinking thereon I swoon away.

11

Sweet flower, that art so fair and gay,
   Come tell me if thou lovest me.
   Think well, and tell me presently:
For sore it irks me, by my fay.

For sore it irketh me alway,
   That I know not the mind of thee:
I pray thee, gentle lady gay,
   If so thou wilt, tell truth to me.

For I do love thee so, sweet May,
  That if my heart thou wert to see,
  In sooth I know, of courtesy,
Thou wouldst have pity on me this day.

12

  My love for him shall be
    Fair love and true:
      For he loves me, I know,
  And I love him, pardie !

  And for I know that he
    Doth love me so,
      I should be all untrue
  To love but him, pardie !

13

Beneath the branch of the green may
  My merry heart sleeps happily,
  Waiting for him who promised me
To meet me here again this day.

And what is that I would not do
  To please my love so dear to me ?
He loves me with leal heart and true,
  And I love him no less, pardie.

Perchance I see him but a day;
  Yet maketh he my heart so free—
  His beauty so rejoiceth me—
That month thereafter I am gay.

14

They have said evil of my dear;
Therefore my heart is vexed and drear:
  But what is it to them
If he be fair or foul to see,
Since he is perfect joy to me ?

He loves me well: the like do I:
I do not look with half an eye,
  But seek to pleasure him.

From all the rest I choose him here;
I want no other for my dear:
  How then should he displease
Those who may leave him if they please?
  God keep him from all fear.

15

They lied, those lying traitors all,
Disloyal, hypocritical,
  Who feigned that I spake ill of thee.
  Heed not their words of charity;
For they are flatterers tongued with gall,
    And liars all.

They make the tales that they let fall,
Coining falsehoods, where withal
  They swear that I spake ill of thee:
  Heed not their lies of charity;
For they are flatterers tongued with gall,
    And liars all.

Believe them not, although they call
Themselves thy servants; one and all,
  They lie, or God's curse light on me,—
  Whatever oaths they swear to thee,
Or were they thrice as stout and tall,
    They're liars all.

16

O nightingale of woodland gay,
  Go to my love and to her tell
  That I do love her passing well;
And bid her also think of me,
For I to her will bring the may.

The may that I shall bring will be
  Nor rose nor any opening flower;
  But with my heart I will her dower;
And kisses on her lips I'll lay,
And pray God keep her heartily.

17

Maid Marjory sits at the castle gate:
  With groans and sighs
  She weeps and cries:
Her grief it is great.
Her father asks, "Daughter, what is your woe?
Seek you a husband or lord I trow?"
  "Let husbands be.
  Give my love to me,
Who pines in the dungeon dark below."

"I' faith, my daughter, thou'll long want him;
For he hangs to-morrow when dawn is dim."

"Then bury my corpse at the gallows' feet;
And men will say they were true lovers sweet."

18

Drink, gossips mine! we drink no wine.
They were three wives that had one heart for wine;
One to the other said—We drink no wine!
  Drink, gossips mine! we drink no wine.

Drink, gossips mine! we drink no wine.
The varlet stood in jerkin tight and fine
To serve the dames with service of good wine.
  Drink, gossips mine! we drink no wine.

Drink, gossips mine ! we drink no wine.
These wives they cried—Here's service of good wine!
Make we good cheer, nor stint our souls of wine !
Drink, gossips mine ! we drink no wine.

Drink, gossips mine ! we drink no wine.
The gallant fills, nor seeketh further sign,
But crowns the cups with service of good wine.
Drink, gossips mine ! we drink no wine.

Drink, gossips mine ! we drink no wine.
Sinning beginneth, and sweet notes combine
With joyance to proclaim the praise of wine !
Drink, gossips mine ! we drink no wine.

Drink, gossips mine ! we drink no wine.
For fear of husbands will we never pine;
They are not here to mar the taste of wine.
Drink, gossips mine ! we drink no wine.

John Addington Symonds

BALLADS
The Three Captains
(*Collected by Gérard de Nerval*)

ALL beneath the white-rose tree
    Walks a lady fair to see ;
  She is as white as the snows,
  She is as fair as the day:
    From her father's garden close
  Three knights have ta'en her away.

He has ta'en her by the hand,
    The youngest of the three—
  "Mount and ride, my bonnie bride,
  On my white horse with me."

And ever they rode, and better rode,
    Till they came to Senlis town.
The hostess she looked hard at them
    As they were lighting down.

" And are ye here by force," she said,
    " Or are ye here for play ? "
" From out my father's garden close
    Three knights me stole away.

" And fain would I win back," she said,
    " The weary way I come:
And fain would see my father dear,
    And fain go maiden home."

" Oh, weep not, lady fair," said she;
    " You shall win back," she said,
" For you shall take this draught from me
    Will make you lie for dead."

" Come in and sup, fair lady," they said,
    " Come busk ye and be bright;
It is with three bold captains
    That ye must be this night."

When they had eaten well and drunk,
    She fell down like one slain;
" Now, out and alas, for my bonnie may
    Shall live no more again."

" Within her father's garden stead
    There are three white lilies;
With her body to the lily bed,
    With her soul to Paradise."

They bore her to her father's house,
    They bore her all the three;
They laid her in her father's close,
    Beneath the white rose tree.

She had not lain a day, a day,
   A day but barely three,
When the may awakes, " Oh, open, father,
   Oh, open the door for me.

" 'Tis I have lain for dead, father,
   Have lain the long days three,
That I might maiden come again
   To my mother and to thee."

Andrew Lang

The Bridge of Death

" THE dance is on the Bridge of Death,
   And who will dance with me ? "
  " There's never a man of living men
   Will dare to dance with thee."

Now Margaret's gone within her bower
   Put ashes in her hair,
And sackcloth on her bonny breast,
   And on her shoulders bare.

There came a knock to her bower door,
   And blithe she let him in;
It was her brother from the wars,
   The dearest of her kin.

" Set gold within your hair, Margaret,
   Set gold within your hair,
And gold upon your girdle band,
   And on your breast so fair.

" For we are bidden to dance to night,
   We may not bide away;
This one good night, this one fair night,
   Before the red new day."

"Nay, no gold for my head, brother,
  Nay, no gold for my hair;
It is the ashes and dust of earth
  That you and I must wear.

"No gold work for my girdle band,
  No gold work on my feet;
But ashes of the fire, my love,
  But dust that the serpents eat."

They danced across the Bridge of Death,
  Above the black water,
And the marriage-bell was tolled in hell
  For the souls of him and her.

Andrew Lang

Le Père Sévère

KING LOUIS on his bridge is he,
He holds his daughter on his knee.

She asks a husband at his hand
That is not worth a rood of land.

"Give up your lover speedily,
Or you within the tower must lie."

"Although I must the prison dree,
I will not change my love for thee.

"I will not change my lover fair,
Not for the mother that me bare.

"I will not change my true lover
For friends or for my father dear."

"Now where are all my pages keen,
And where are all my serving men?

" My daughter must lie in the tower alway,
Where she shall never see the day."

Seven long years are past and gone
And there has seen her never one.

At ending of the seventh year
Her father goes to visit her.

" My child, my child, how may you be ? "
" O father, it fares ill with me.

" My feet are wasted in the mould,
The worms they gnaw my side so cold."

" My child, change your love speedily
Or you must still in prison lie."

" 'Tis better far the cold to dree
Than give my true love up for thee."

Andrew Lang

The Milk-white Doe

IT was a mother and a maid
 That walked the woods among,
And still the maid went slow and sad,
 And still the mother sung.

" What ails you, daughter Margaret ?
 Why go you pale and wan ?
Is it for a cast of bitter love,
 Or for a false leman ? "

" It is not for a false lover
 That I go sad to see;
But it is for a weary life
 Beneath the greenwood tree.

" For ever in the good daylight
 A maiden may I go,
But always on the ninth midnight
 I change to a milk-white doe.

" They hunt me through the green forest
 With hounds and hunting men;
And ever it is my fair brother
 That is so fierce and keen."

" Good-morrow, mother." " Good-morrow, son;
 Where are your hounds so good ? "
" Oh, they are hunting a white doe
 Within the glad greenwood.

" And three times have they hunted her
 And thrice she's won away;
The fourth time that they follow her
 That white doe they shall slay."

Then out and spoke the forester,
 As he came from the wood,
" Now never saw I maid's gold hair
 Among the wild deer's blood.

" And I have hunted the wild deer
 In east lands and in west;
And never saw I white doe yet
 That had a maiden's breast."

Then up and spake her fair brother,
 Between the wine and bread,
" Behold, I had but one sister,
 And I have seen her dead.

" But ye must bury my sweet sister
 With a stone at her foot and her head,
And ye must cover her fair body
 With the white roses and red.

"And I must out to the greenwood;
The roof shall never shelter me;
And I shall lie for seven long years
On the grass below the hawthorn tree."

Andrew Lang

A Lady of High Degree

I be pareld most of prise,
I ride after the wild fee.

WILL ye that I should sing
Of the love of a goodly thing,
     Was no vilein's may?
'Tis sung of a knight so free,
Under the olive tree,
     Singing this lay.

Her weed was of samite fine,
Her mantle of white ermine,
     Green silk her hose;
Her shoon with silver gay,
Her sandals flowers of May,
     Laced small and close.

Her belt was of fresh spring buds,
Set with gold clasps and studs,
     Fine linen her shift;
Her purse it was of love,
Her chain was the flower thereof,
     And Love's gift.

Upon a mule she rode,
The selle was of brent gold,
     The bits of silver made;
Three red rose trees there were
That overshadowed her,
     For a sun shade.

She riding on a day,
Knights met her by the way,
  They did her grace;
"Fair lady, whence be ye?"
"France it is my country,
  I come of a high race.

"My sire is the nightingale,
That sings, making his wail,
  In the wild wood, clear;
The mermaid is mother to me,
That sings in the salt sea,
  In the ocean mere."

"Ye come of a right good race,
And are born of a high place,
  And of high degree;
Would to God that ye were
Given unto me, being fair,
  My lady and love to be."

Andrew Lang

Lost for a Rose's Sake

I LAVED my hands
  By the water side;
With the willow leaves
  My hands I dried.

The nightingale sang
  On the bough of the tree;
Sing, sweet nightingale,
  It is well with thee.

Thou hast heart's delight,
  I have sad heart's sorrow
For a false, false maid
  That will wed to-morrow.

'Tis all for a rose,
That I gave her not,
And I would that it grew
In the garden plot.

And I would the rose-tree
Were still to set,
That my love Marie
Might love me yet.

Andrew Lang

FRANÇOIS VILLON

1431–89

N O one has ever more skilfully communicated his own disenchant-
ments; no one ever blown a more ear-piercing note of sadness. It is
in death that he finds his truest inspiration; in the swift and sorrowful
change that overtakes beauty; in the strange revolution by which great
fortunes and renowns are diminished to a handful of churchyard dust;
and in the utter passing away of what was once lovable and mighty.—
ROBERT LOUIS STEVENSON.

Ballade of the Gibbet

*An Epitaph in the form of a ballade that François Villon
wrote of himself and his company, they expecting shortly
to be hanged.*

B ROTHERS and men that shall after us be,
Let not your hearts be hard to us:
For pitying this our misery
Ye shall find God the more piteous.
Look on us six that are hanging thus,
And for the flesh that so much we cherished
How it is eaten of birds and perished,
And ashes and dust fill our bones' place.
Mock not at us that so feeble be,
But pray God pardon us out of His grace.

Listen, we pray you, and look not in scorn,
  Though justly, in sooth, we are cast to die;
Ye wot no man so wise is born
  That keeps his wisdom constantly.
  Be ye then merciful, and cry
To Mary's Son that is piteous,
That His mercy take no stain from us,
  Saving us out of the fiery place.
We are but dead, let no soul deny
  To pray God succour us of His grace.

The rain out of heaven has washed us clean,
  The sun has scorched us black and bare,
Ravens and rooks have pecked at our eyne,
  And feathered their nests with our beards and
    hair.
  Round are we tossed, and here and there,
This way and that, at the wild wind's will,
Never a moment my body is still;
  Birds they are busy about my face.
Live not as we, nor fare as we fare;
  Pray God pardon us out of His grace.

L'envoy

Prince Jesus, Master of all, to Thee
We pray Hell gain no mastery,
  That we come never anear that place;
And, ye men, make no mockery,
  Pray God, pardon us out of His grace.

Andrew Lang

Rondel

GOOD‚BYE, the tears are in my eyes;
  Farewell, farewell, my prettiest;
  Farewell, of women born the best;
Good‚bye, the saddest of good‚byes.

Farewell, with many vows and sighs
  My sad heart leaves you to your rest;
Farewell, the tears are in my eyes;
Farewell, from you my miseries
  Are more than now may be confessed,
  And most by thee have I been blessed,
Yea, and for thee have wasted sighs;
Good-bye, the last of my good-byes.

Andrew Lang

Arbor Amoris

I HAVE a tree, a graft of love,
  That in my heart has taken root;
Sad are the buds and blooms thereof,
  And bitter sorrow is its fruit;
  Yet, since it was a tender shoot,
So greatly hath its shadow spread,
That underneath all joy is dead,
  And all my pleasant days are flown,
  Nor can I slay it, nor instead
  Plant any tree, save this alone.

Ah, yet, for long and long enough
  My tears were rain about its root,
And though the fruit be harsh thereof,
  I scarcely looked for better fruit
  Than this, that carefully I put
In garner, for the bitter bread
Whereon my weary life is fed:
  Ah, better were the soil unsown
That bears such growths; but Love instead
  Will plant no tree, but this alone.

Ah, would that this new spring, whereof
  The leaves and flowers flush into shoot,
I might have succour and aid of Love,
  To prune these branches at the root,

That long have borne such bitter fruit,
And graft a new bough, comforted
With happy blossoms white and red;
  So pleasure should for pain atone,
Nor Love slay this tree, nor instead
  Plant any tree, but this alone.

L'envoy

Princess, by whom my hope is fed,
My heart thee prays in lowlihead
  To prune the ill boughs overgrown,
Nor slay Love's tree, nor plant instead
  Another tree, save this alone.

Andrew Lang

No, I am not as Others are

NO, I am not, as others are,
  Child of the angels, with a wreath
Of planets or of any star.
My father's dead, and lies beneath
The churchyard stone: God rest his breath!
I know that my poor old mother
(And she too knows) must come to death,
And that her son must follow her.

I know that rich and poor and all,
Foolish and wise, and priest and lay,
Mean folk and noble, great and small,
High and low, fair and foul, and they
That wore rich clothing on the way,
Being of whatever stock or stem,
And are coiffed newly every day,
Death shall take every one of them.

Paris and Helen are both dead.
Whoever dies, dies with much pain;

For when his wind and breath are sped
His gall breaks on his heart, and then
He sweats, God knows that sweat of men !
Then shall he pray against his doom
Child, brother, sister, all in vain:
None will be surety in his room.

Death makes him tremble and turn pale,
His veins stretch and his nose fall in,
His flesh grow moist and his neck swell,
Joints and nerves lengthen and wax thin;
Body of woman, that hath been
Soft, tender, precious, smooth and even,
Must thou be spoiled in bone and skin ?
Yes, or else go alive to heaven.

Arthur Symons

Villon's Straight Tip to All Cross Coves

SUPPOSE you screeve ? or go cheap-jack ?
   Or fake the broads ? or fig a nag ?
Or thimble-rig ? or knap a yack ?
   Or pitch a snide ? or smash a rag ?
   Suppose you duff ? or nose and lag ?
Or get the straight, and land your pot ?
   How do you melt the multy swag ?
Booze and the blowens cop the lot.

Fiddle, or fence, or mace, or mack;
   Or moskeneer, or flash the drag;
Dead-lurk a crib, or do a crack;
   Pad with a slang, or chuck a fag;
   Bonnet, or tout, or mump and gag;
Rattle the tats, or mark the spot;
   You cannot bank a single stag;
Booze and the blowens cop the lot.

Suppose you try a different tack,
    And on the square you flash your flag ?
At penny/a/lining make your whack,
    Or with the mummers mug and gag ?
    For nix, for nix the dibbs you bag !
At any graft, no matter what,
    Your merry goblins soon stravag:
Booze and the blowens cop the lot.

The Moral

It's up the spout and Charley Wag
With wipes and tickers and what not.
Until the squeezer nips your scrag,
Booze and the blowens cop the lot.

                W. E. Henley

The Ballade of Dead Ladies

TELL me now in what hidden way is
    Lady Flora the lovely Roman ?
Where's Hipparchia, and where is Thais,
    Neither of them the fairer woman ?
    Where is Echo, beheld of no man,
Only heard on river and mere,—
    She whose beauty was more than human ? . . .
But where are the snows of yester/year ?

Where's Héloise, the learned nun,
    For whose sake Abeillard, I ween,
Lost manhood and put priesthood on ?
    (From Love he won such dule and teen !)
    And where, I pray you, is the Queen
Who willed that Buridan should steer
    Sewed in a sack's mouth down the Seine ? . . .
But where are the snows of yester/year ?

White Queen Blanche, like a queen of lilies,
  With a voice like any mermaiden,—
Bertha Broadfoot, Beatrice, Alice,
  And Ermengarde the lady of Maine,—
  And that good Joan whom Englishmen
At Rouen doomed and burned her there,—
  Mother of God, where are they then ? . . .
But where are the snows of yester-year ?

Nay, never ask this week, fair lord,
  Where they are gone, nor yet this year,
Save with thus much for an overword,—
  But where are the snows of yester-year ?

D. G. Rossetti

To Death, of his Lady

DEATH, of thee do I make my moan,
  Who hadst my lady away from me,
  Nor wilt assuage thine enmity
Till with her life thou hast mine own;
For since that hour my strength has flown.
  Lo ! what wrong was her life to thee,
            Death ?

Two we were, and the heart was one;
  Which now being dead, dead I must be,
  Or seem alive as lifelessly
As in the choir the painted stone,
            Death !

D. G. Rossett

His Mother's Service to Our Lady

LADY of Heaven and Earth, and therewithal
　Crowned Empress of the nether clefts of Hell,—
I, thy poor Christian, on thy name do call,
　Commending me to thee, with thee to dwell,
　Albeit in naught I be commendable.
But all mine undeserving may not mar
Such mercies as thy sovereign mercies are;
　Without the which (as true words testify)
No soul can reach thy Heaven so fair and far.
　Even in this faith I choose to live and die.

Unto thy Son say thou that I am His,
　And to me graceless make Him gracious.
Sad Mary of Egypt lacked not of that bliss,
　Nor yet the sorrowful clerk Theophilus,
　Whose bitter sins were set aside even thus
Though to the Fiend his bounden service was.
Oh help me, lest in vain for me should pass
　(Sweet Virgin that shalt have no loss thereby !)
The blessed Host and sacring of the Mass.
　Even in this faith I choose to live and die.

A pitiful poor woman, shrunk and old,
　I am, and nothing learn'd in letter-lore.
Within my parish-cloister I behold
　A painted Heaven where harps and lutes adore,
　And eke an Hell whose damned folk seethe full
　　sore:
One bringeth fear, the other joy to me.
That joy, great Goddess, make thou mine to be,—
　Thou of whom all must ask it even as I;
And that which faith desires, that let it see.
　For in this faith I choose to live and die.

O excellent Virgin Princess ! thou didst bear
   King Jesus, the most excellent comforter,
Who even of this our weakness craved a share
   And for our sake stooped to us from on high,
Offering to death His young life sweet and fair.
Such as He is, Our Lord, I Him declare,
   And in this faith I choose to live and die.

D. G. Rossetti

The Complaint of the Fair Armouress

MESEEMETH I heard cry and groan
   That sweet who was the armourer's maid;
For her young years she made sore moan,
   And right upon this wise she said:
   " Ah fierce old age with foul bald head,
To spoil fair things thou art over fain;
   Who holdeth me? who? would God I were dead !
Would God I were well dead and slain !

" Lo, thou hast broken the sweet yoke
   That my high beauty held above
All priests and clerks and merchant-folk;
   There was not one but for my love
   Would give me gold and gold enough,
Though sorrow his very heart had riven,
   To win from me such wage thereof
As now no thief would take if given.

" I was right chary of the same,
   God wot it was my great folly,
For love of one sly knave of them,
   Good store of that same sweet had he;
   For all my subtle wiles, perdie,
God wot I loved him well enow;
   Right evilly he handled me,
But he loved well my gold, I trow.

" Though I gat bruises green and black,
   I loved him never the less a jot;
Though he bound burdens on my back,
   If he said, ' Kiss me, and heed it not,'
   Right little pain I felt, God wot,
When that foul thief's mouth, found so sweet,
   Kissed me—Much good thereof I got !
I keep the sin and the shame of it.

" And he died thirty year agone.
   I am old now, no sweet thing to see;
By God, though, when I think thereon,
   And of that good glad time, woe's me,
   And stare upon my changed body
Stark naked, that has been so sweet,
   Lean, wizen, like a small dry tree,
I am nigh mad with the pain of it.

" Where is my faultless forehead's white,
   The lifted eyebrows, soft gold hair,
Eyes wide apart and keen of sight,
   With subtle skill in the amorous air;
   The straight nose, great nor small, but fair,
The small carved ears of shapeliest growth,
   Chin dimpling, colour good to wear,
And sweet red splendid kissing mouth ?

" The shapely slender shoulders small,
   Long arms, hands wrought in glorious wise,
Round little breasts, the hips withal
   High, full of flesh, not scant of size,
   Fit for all amorous masteries;
      .   .   .
      .   .   .

" A writhled forehead, hair gone grey,
   Fallen eyebrows, eyes gone blind and red,

Their laughs and looks all fled away,
  Yea, all that smote men's hearts are fled;
The bowed nose, fallen from goodlihead;
Foul flapping ears like water-flags;
  Peaked chin, and cheeks all waste and dead,
And lips that are two skinny rags:

" Thus endeth all the beauty of us.
  The arms made short, the hands made lean,
The shoulders bowed and ruinous,
  The breasts, alack ! all fallen in;
The flanks too, like the breasts, grown thin;

  For the lank thighs, no thighs but skin,
They are speckled with spots like sausage-meat.

" So we make moan for the old sweet days,
  Poor old light women, two or three
Squatting above the straw-fire's blaze,
  The bosom crushed against the knee,
  Like fagots on a heap we be,
Round fires soon lit, soon quenched and done;
  And we were once so sweet, even we !
Thus fareth many and many an one."

Algernon Charles Swinburne

A Double Ballade of Good Counsel

NOW take your fill of love and glee,
  And after balls and banquets hie;
In the end ye'll get no good for fee,
  But just heads broken by and by;
  Light loves make beasts of men that sigh;
They changed the faith of Solomon,
  And left not Samson lights to spy;
Good luck has he that deals with none !

Sweet Orpheus, lord of minstrelsy,
   For this with flute and pipe came nigh
The danger of the dog's heads three
   That ravening at hell's door doth lie;
   Fain was Narcissus, fair and shy,
For love's love lightly lost and won,
   In a deep well to drown and die;
Good luck has he that deals with none !

Sardana, flower of chivalry,
   Who conquered Crete with horn and cry,
For this was fain a maid to be
   And learn with girls the thread to ply;
   King David, wise in prophecy,
Forgot the fear of God for one
   Seen washing either shapely thigh;
Good luck has he that deals with none !

For this did Amnon, craftily
   Feigning to eat of cakes of rye,
Deflower his sister fair to see,
   Which was foul incest; and hereby
   Was Herod moved, it is no lie,
To lop the head of Baptist John
   For dance and jig and psaltery;
Good luck has he that deals with none !

Next to myself I tell, poor me,
   How thrashed like clothes at wash was I
Stark naked, I must needs agree;
   Who made me eat so sour a pie
   But Katherine of Vaucelles ? thereby
Noé took third part of that fun;
   Such wedding-gloves are ill to buy;
Good luck has he that deals with none !

But for that young man fair and free
   To pass those young maids lightly by,

Nay, would you burn him quick, not he;
　Like broom-horsed witches though he fry,
They are sweet as civet in his eye;
But trust them, and you're fooled anon;
　For white or brown, and low or high,
Good luck has he that deals with none !

Algernon Charles Swinburne

Fragment on Death

AND Paris be it or Helen dying,
　Who dies soever, dies with pain.
He that lacks breath and wind for sighing,
　His gall bursts on his heart; and then
　He sweats, God knows what sweat !—again,
No man may ease him of his grief;
　Child, brother, sister, none were fain
To bail him thence for his relief.

Death makes him shudder, swoon, wax pale,
　Nose bend, veins stretch, and breath surrender,
Neck swell, flesh soften, joints that fail
　Crack their strained nerves and arteries slender.
　O woman's body found so tender,
Smooth, sweet, so precious in men's eyes,
　Must thou too bear such count to render ?
Yes; or pass quick into the skies.

Algernon Charles Swinburne

Ballade of the Lords of Old Time

(*After the former argument*)

WHAT more ?　Where is the third Calixt,
　Last of that name now dead and gone,
Who held four years the Papalist ?
　Alphonso king of Aragon,
　The gracious lord, duke of Bourbon,

650

And Arthur, duke of old Britaine ?
  And Charles the Seventh, that worthy one ?
Even with the good knight Charlemain.

The Scot too, king of mount and mist,
  With half his face vermilion,
Men tell us, like an amethyst
  From brow to chin that blazed and shone;
  The Cypriote king of old renown,
Alas ! and that good king of Spain,
  Whose name I cannot think upon ?
Even with the good knight Charlemain.

No more to say of them I list;
  'Tis all but vain, all dead and done:
For death may no man born resist,
  Nor make appeal when death comes on.
  I make yet one more question;
Where's Lancelot, king of far Bohain ?
  Where's he whose grandson called him son ?
Even with the good knight Charlemain.

Where is Guesclin, the good Breton ?
  The lord of the eastern mountain-chain,
And the good late duke of Alençon ?
  Even with the good knight Charlemain.
                    Algernon Charles Swinburne

Ballade of the Women of Paris

ALBEIT the Venice girls get praise
  For their sweet speech and tender air,
And though the old women have wise ways
  Of chaffering for amorous ware,
  Yet at my peril dare I swear,
Search Rome, where God's grace mainly tarries
  Florence and Savoy, everywhere,
There's no good girl's lip out of Paris.

The Naples women, as folk prattle,
　　Are sweetly spoken and subtle enough;
German girls are good at tattle,
　　And Prussians make their boast thereof;
　　Take Egypt for the next remove,
Or that waste land the Tartar harries,
　　Spain or Greece, for the matter of love,
There's no good girl's lip out of Paris.

Breton and Swiss know naught of the matter,
　　Gascony girls or girls of Toulouse;
Two fishwomen with a half-hour's chatter
　　Would shut them up by threes and twos;
　　Calais, Lorraine, and all their crews,
(Names enow the mad song marries,)
　　England and Picardy, search them and choose,
There's no good girl's lip out of Paris.

Prince, give praise to our French ladies
　　For the sweet sound their speaking carries;
'Twixt Rome and Cadiz many a maid is,
　　But no good girl's lip out of Paris.

Algernon Charles Swinburne

Ballade Written for a Bride-groom

*Which Villon gave to a gentleman newly married to send to
his wife whom he had won with the sword*

AT daybreak, when the falcon claps his wings,
　　No whit for grief, but noble heart and high,
With loud glad noise he stirs himself and springs,
　　And takes his meat and toward his lure draws nigh;
　　Such good I wish you! Yea, and heartily
I am fired with hope of true love's meed to get;
　　Know that Love writes it in his book; for why,
This is the end for which we twain are met.

Mine own heart's lady with no gainsayings
　　You shall be always wholly till I die;
And in my right against all bitter things
　　Sweet laurel with fresh rose its force shall try;
　　Seeing reason wills not that I cast love by
(Nor here with reason shall I chide or fret)
　　Nor cease to serve, but serve more constantly;
This is the end for which we twain are met.

And, which is more, when grief about me clings
　　Through Fortune's fit or fume of jealousy,
Your sweet kind eye beats down her threatenings
　　As wind doth smoke; such power sits in your eye.
　　Thus in your field my seed of harvestry
Thrives, for the fruit is like me that I set;
　　God bids me tend it with good husbandry;
This is the end for which we twain are met.

Princess, give ear to this my summary;
　　That heart of mine your heart's love should forget,
Shall never be: like trust in you put I:
　　This is the end for which we twain are met.

Algernon Charles Swinburne

Ballade Against the Enemies of France

MAY he fall in with beasts that scatter fire,
　　Like Jason, when he sought the fleece of gold,
Or change from man to beast three years entire,
　　As King Nebuchadnezzar did of old;
　　Or else have times as shameful and as bad
As Trojan folk for ravished Helen had;
　　Or gulfed with Proserpine and Tantalus
Let hell's deep fen devour him dolorous,
　　With worse to bear than Job's worst sufferance
Bound in his prison-maze with Dædalus,
　　Who could wish evil to the state of France!

May he four months, like bitterns in the mire,
    Howl with head downmost in the lake/springs
      cold,
Or to bear harness like strong bulls for hire
    To the Great Turk for money down be sold;
Or thirty years like Magdalen live sad,
With neither wool nor web of linen clad;
Drown like Narciss', or swing down pendulous
Like Absalom with locks luxurious,
    Or liker Judas fallen to reprobance;
Or find such death as Simon sorcerous,
    Who could wish evil to the state of France !

May the old times come of fierce Octavian's ire,
    And in his belly molten coin be told;
May he like Victor in the mill expire,
    Crushed between moving millstones on him rolled,
Or in deep sea drenched breathless, more adrad
Than in the whale's bulk Jonas, when God bade:
From Phœbus' light, from Juno's treasure/house
Driven, and from joys of Venus amorous,
    And cursed of God most high to the utterance,
As was the Syrian king Antiochus,
    Who could wish evil to the state of France !

Envoy

Prince, may the bright/winged brood of Æolus
To sea/king Glaucus' wild wood cavernous
    Bear him bereft of peace and hope's least glance,
For worthless is he to get good of us,
    Who could wish evil to the state of France !
                Algernon Charles Swinburne

The Dispute of the Heart and Body of François Villon

WHO is this I hear ?—Lo, this is I, thine heart,
　That holds on merely now by a slender string.
Strength fails me, shape and sense are rent apart,
　The blood in me is turned to a bitter thing,
　Seeing thee skulk here like a dog shivering.—
Yea, and for what ?—For that thy sense found
　　sweet.—
What irks it thee ?—I feel the sting of it.—
　Leave me at peace.—Why ?—Nay now, leave me
　　at peace;
I will repent when I grow ripe in wit.—
　I say no more.—I care not though thou cease.—

What art thou, trow ?—A man worth praise,
　　perfay.—
　This is thy thirtieth year of wayfaring.—
'Tis a mule's age.—Art thou a boy still ?—Nay.—
　Is it hot lust that spurs thee with its sting,
　Grasping thy throat ?　Know'st thou not any⸗
　　thing ?—
Yea, black and white, when milk is specked with
　　flies,
I can make out.—No more ?—Nay, in no wise.
　Shall I begin again the count of these ?—
Thou art undone.—I will make shift to rise.—
　I say no more.—I care not though thou cease.—

I have the sorrow of it, and thou the smart.
　Wert thou a poor mad fool or weak of wit,
Then might'st thou plead this pretext with thine
　　heart;
　But if thou know not good from evil a whit,
　Either thy head is hard as stone to hit,
Or shame, not honour, gives thee most content.

655

What canst thou answer to this argument ?—
    When I am dead I shall be well at ease.—
God ! what good luck !—Thou art over eloquent.—
    I say no more.—I care not though thou cease.—

Whence is this ill ?—From sorrow and not from sin.
    When Saturn packed my wallet up for me
I well believe he put these ills therein.—
    Fool, wilt thou make thy servant lord of thee ?
    Hear now the wise king's counsel; thus saith he:
All power upon the stars a wise man hath;
There is no planet that shall do him scathe.—
    Nay, as they made me I grow and I decrease.—
What say'st thou ?—Truly this is all my faith.—
    I say no more.—I care not though thou cease.—

Wouldst thou live still ?—God help me that I may !—
Then thou must—What ? turn penitent and pray ?—
Read always—What ?—Grave words and good to say;
    Leave off the ways of fools, lest they displease.—
Good; I will do it.—Wilt thou remember ?—Yea.—
Abide not till there come an evil day.
    I say no more.—I care not though thou cease.

Algernon Charles Swinburne

Epistle in Form of a Ballade to his Friends

HAVE pity, pity, friends, have pity on me,
    Thus much at least, may it please you, of your
        grace !
    I lie not under hazel or hawthorn-tree
        Down in this dungeon ditch, mine exile's place
        By leave of God and fortune's foul disgrace.
    Girls, lovers, glad young folk and newly wed,

'Jumpers and jugglers, tumbling heel o'er head,
  Swift as a dart, and sharp as needle-ware,
Throats clear as bells that ring the kine to shed,
  Your poor old friend, what, will you leave him there ?

Singers that sing at pleasure, lawlessly,
  Light, laughing, gay of word and deed, that race
And run like folk light-witted as ye be
  And have in hand nor current coin nor base,
  Ye wait too long, for now he's dying apace.
Rhymers of lays and roundels sung and read,
  Ye'll brew him broth too late when he lies dead.
Nor wind nor lightning, sunbeam nor fresh air,
May pierce the thick wall's bound where lies his bed;
  Your poor old friend, what, will you leave him there ?

O noble folk, from tithes and taxes free,
  Come and behold him in this piteous case,
Ye that nor king nor emperor holds in fee,
  But only God in heaven; behold his face
  Who needs must fast, Sundays and holidays,
Which makes his teeth like rakes; and when he hath fed
With never a cake for banquet but dry bread,
  Must drench his bowels with much cold watery fare,
With board nor stool, but low on earth instead;
  Your poor old friend, what, will you leave him there ?

Princes afore-named, old and young foresaid,
Get me the king's seal and my pardon sped,
  And hoist me in some basket up with care:
So swine will help each other ill bested,
For where one squeaks they run in heaps ahead,
  Your poor old friend, what, will you leave him there ?
                   Algernon Charles Swinburne

MELLIN DE SAINT-GELAIS
1491–1558

The Sonnet of the Mountain

WHEN from afar these mountain tops I view,
I do but mete mine own distress thereby;
High is their head, and my desire is high;
Firm is their foot, my faith is certain, too.

E'en as the winds about their summits blue,
From me, too, breaks betimes the wistful sigh;
And as from them the brooks and streamlets hie,
So from mine eyes the tears run down anew.

A thousand flocks upon them feed and stray;
As many loves within me see the day,
And all my heart for pasture ground divide.

No fruit have they, my lot as fruitless is;
And 'twixt us now naught diverse is but this—
In them the snows, in me the fires abide.

Austin Dobson

CLÉMENT MAROT
1495–1544

A Love-Lesson

A SWEET " No ! no ! " with a sweet smile beneath
Becomes an honest girl,—I'd have you learn it;
As for plain " Yes ! " it may be said, i' faith,
Too plainly and too soft,—pray, well discern it !

Not that I'd have my pleasure incomplete,
Or lose the kiss for which my lips beset you;
But that in suffering me to take it, sweet !
I'd have you say—" No ! no ! I will not let you ! "

Leigh Hunt

Madame D'Albert's Laugh

YES ! that fair neck, too beautiful by half,
Those eyes, that voice, that bloom, all do her honour;
Yet, after all, that little giddy laugh
Is what, in my mind, sits the best upon her.

Good God ! 'twould make the very streets and ways,
Through which she passes, burst into a pleasure !
Did melancholy come to mar my days
And kill me in the lap of too much leisure,
No spell were wanting, from the dead to raise me,
But only that sweet laugh wherewith she slays me.

Leigh Hunt

Friar Lubin

TO gallop off to town post-haste,
    So oft, the times I cannot tell;
To do vile deed, nor feel disgraced,—
    Friar Lubin will do it well.
But a sober life to lead,
    To honour virtue, and pursue it,
That's a pious, Christian deed,—
    Friar Lubin cannot do it.

To mingle, with a knowing smile,
    The goods of others with his own,
And leave you without cross or pile,
    Friar Lubin stands alone.
To say 'tis yours is all in vain,
    If once he lays his finger to it;
For as to giving back again,
    Friar Lubin cannot do it.

With flattering words and gentle tone,
    To woo and win some guileless maid,
Cunning pander need you none,—
    Friar Lubin knows the trade.
Loud preacheth he sobriety,
    But as for water, doth eschew it;
Your dog may drink it,—but not he;
    Friar Lubin cannot do it.

Envoy

When an evil deed's to do,
Friar Lubin is stout and true;
Glimmers a ray of goodness through it,
Friar Lubin cannot do it.

H. W. Longfellow

JACQUES TAHUREAU

1527-55

Shadows of his Lady

WITHIN the sand of what far river lies
    The gold that gleams in tresses of my Love?
    What highest circle of the Heavens above
Is jewelled with such stars as are her eyes?
And where is the rich sea whose coral vies
    With her red lips, that cannot kiss enough?
    What dawn-lit garden knew the rose, whereof
The fled soul lives in her cheeks' rosy guise?

What Parian marble that is loveliest
Can match the whiteness of her brow and breast?
    When drew she breath from the Sabæan glade?
Oh, happy rock and river, sky and sea,
Gardens and glades Sabæan, all that be
    The far-off splendid semblance of my maid.

Andrew Lang

Moonlight

THE high Midnight was garlanding her head
  With many a shining star in shining skies,
And, of her grace, a slumber on mine eyes,
  And, after sorrow, quietness was shed.
Far in dim fields cicalas jargonèd
  A thin shrill clamour of complaints and cries;
  And all the woods were pallid, in strange wise,
With pallor of the sad moon overspread.

Then came my lady to that lonely place,
And, from her palfrey stooping, did embrace
  And hang upon my neck, and kissed me over;
Wherefore the day is far less dear than night,
And sweeter is the shadow than the light,
  Since night has made me such a happy lover.

Andrew Lang

JEAN PASSERAT

1534–1602

Love in May

OFF with sleep, love, up from bed,
    This fair morn;
  See, for our eyes the rosy red
    New dawn is born;
  Now that skies are glad and gay
  In this gracious month of May,
    Love me, sweet;
  Fill my joy in brimming measure;
  In this world he hath no pleasure
    That will none of it.

Come, love, through the woods of spring,
    Come walk with me;
  Listen, the sweet birds jargoning
    From tree to tree.

List and listen, over all
Nightingale most musical
   That ceases never;
Grief begone, and let us be
For a space as glad as he;
   Time's flitting ever.

Old Time, that loves not lovers, wears
   Wings swift in flight;
All our happy life he bears
   Far in the night.
Old and wrinkled on a day,
Sad and weary shall you say,
   " Ah, fool was I,
That took no pleasure in the grace
Of the flower that from my face
   Time has seen die."

Leave then sorrow, teen, and tears
   Till we be old;
Young we are, and of our years,
   Till youth be cold,
Pluck the flower; while Spring is gay
In this happy month of May
   Love me, love;
Fill our joy in brimming measure;
In this world he hath no pleasure
   That will none thereof.

Andrew Lang

PIERRE DE RONSARD

1524–85

Fragment of a Sonnet

NATURE withheld Cassandra in the skies,
For more adornment, a full thousand years;
She took their cream of Beauty, fairest dies,
And shaped and tinted her above all Peers:

Meanwhile Love kept her dearly with his wings,
And underneath their shadow filled her eyes
With such a richness that the cloudy Kings
Of high Olympus uttered slavish sighs.
When from the Heavens I saw her first descend,
My heart took fire, and only burning pains,
They were my pleasures—they my Life's sad end;
Love poured her beauty into my warm veins.

John Keats

Roses

I SEND you here a wreath of blossoms blown,
    And woven flowers at sunset gathered;
    Another dawn had seen them ruined, and shed
Loose leaves upon the grass at random strown.
By this, their sure example, be it known,
    That all your beauties, now in perfect flower,
    Shall fade as these, and wither in an hour,
Flowerlike, and brief of days, as the flower sown.

Ah, time is flying, lady,—time is flying;
    Nay, 'tis not time that flies but we that go,
Who in short space shall be in churchyard lying,
    And of our loving parley none shall know,
Nor any man consider what we were;
Be therefore kind, my love, whiles thou art fair.

Andrew Lang

The Rose

SEE, Mignonne, hath not the Rose,
    That this morning did unclose
        Her purple mantle to the light,
    Lost before the day be dead
    The glory of her raiment red,
        Her colour, bright as yours is bright?

Ah, Mignonne, in how few hours
The petals of her purple flowers
    All have faded, fallen, died;
Sad Nature, mother ruinous,
That seest thy fair child perish thus
    'Twixt matin song and eventide.

Hear me, my darling, speaking sooth,
Gather the fleet flower of your youth,
    Take ye your pleasure at the best;
Be merry ere your beauty flit,
For length of days will tarnish it
    Like roses that were loveliest.

Andrew Lang

To the Moon

HIDE this one night thy crescent, kindly Moon;
    So shall Endymion faithful prove, and rest
Loving and unawakened on thy breast;
So shall no foul enchanter importune
Thy quiet course; for now the night is boon,
    And through the friendly night unseen I fare,
    Who dread the face of foemen unaware,
And watch of hostile spies in the bright noon.
    Thou knowest, Moon, the bitter power of Love;
    'Tis told how shepherd Pan found ways to move,
For little price, thy heart; and of your grace,
    Sweet stars, be kind to this not alien fire,
    Because on earth ye did not scorn desire,
Bethink ye, now ye hold your heavenly place.

Andrew Lang

To his Young Mistress

FAIR flower of fifteen springs, that still
    Art scarcely blossomed from the bud,
Yet hast such store of evil will,
    A heart so full of hardihood,

Seeking to hide in friendly wise
The mischief of your mocking eyes.

If you have pity, child, give o'er;
Give back the heart you stole from me,
Pirate, setting so little store
On this your captive from Love's sea,
Holding his misery for gain,
And making pleasure of his pain.

Another, not so fair of face,
But far more pitiful than you,
Would take my heart, if of his grace,
My heart would give her of Love's due;
And she shall have it, since I find
That you are cruel and unkind.

Nay, I would rather that I died,
Within your white hands prisoning,
Would rather that it still abide
In your ungentle comforting,
Than change its faith, and seek to her
That is more kind, but not so fair.

Andrew Lang

Deadly Kisses

AH, take these lips away; no more,
No more such kisses give to me.
My spirit faints for joy; I see
Through mists of death the dreamy shore,
And meadows by the water-side,
Where all about the Hollow Land
Fare the sweet singers that have died,
With their lost ladies, hand in hand;
Ah, Love, how fireless are their eyes,
How pale their lips that kiss and smile!
So mine must be in little while
If thou wilt kiss me in such wise.

Andrew Lang

Of his Lady's Old Age

WHEN you are very old, at evening
    You'll sit and spin beside the fire, and say,
    Humming my songs, "Ah well, ah well a day!
When I was young, of me did Ronsard sing."
None of your maidens that doth hear the thing,
    Albeit with her weary task foredone,
    But wakens at my name, and calls you one
Blest, to be held in long remembering.

I shall be low beneath the earth, and laid
On sleep, a phantom in the myrtle shade,
    While you beside the fire, a grandame grey,
My love, your pride, remember and regret;
Ah, love me, love! we may be happy yet,
    And gather roses, while 'tis called to day.

                    Andrew Lang

On his Lady's Waking

MY lady woke upon a morning fair,
    What time Apollo's chariot takes the skies,
    And, fain to fill with arrows from her eyes
His empty quiver, Love was standing there:
I saw two apples that her breast doth bear;
    None such the close of the Hesperides
    Yields; nor hath Venus any such as these,
Nor she that had of nursling Mars the care.

Even such a bosom, and so fair it was,
Pure as the perfect work of Phidias,
    That sad Andromeda's discomfiture
Left are, when Perseus passed her on a day,
And pale as death for fear of death she lay,
    With breast as marble cold, as marble pure.

                    Andrew Lang

His Lady's Death

TWAIN that were foes, while Mary lived, are fled;
One laurel-crowned abides in heaven, and one
Beneath the earth has fared, a fallen sun,
A light of love among the loveless dead.
The first is Chastity, that vanquished
The archer Love, that held joint empery
With the sweet beauty that made war on me,
When laughter of lips with laughing eyes was wed.

Their strife the Fates have closed, with stern control,
The earth holds her fair body, and her soul
An angel with glad angels triumpheth;
Love has no more than he can do; desire
Is buried, and my heart a faded fire,
And for Death's sake, I am in love with Death.

Andrew Lang

His Lady's Tomb

AS in the gardens, all through May, the rose,
Lovely, and young, and fair apparelled,
Makes sunrise jealous of her rosy red,
When dawn upon the dew of dawning glows;
Graces and Loves within her breast repose,
The woods are faint with the sweet odour shed,
Till rains and heavy suns have smitten dead
The languid flower, and the loose leaves unclose,—

So this, the perfect beauty of our days,
When earth and heaven were vocal of her praise,
The fates have slain, and her sweet soul reposes;
And tears I bring, and sighs, and on her tomb
Pour milk, and scatter buds of many a bloom,
That dead, as living, she may be with roses.

Andrew Lang

The Paradox of Time

(A variation on Ronsard)

Le temps s'en va, le temps s'en va, madame !
Las ! le temps non: mais " NOUS nous en allons ! "

TIME goes, you say ?　Ah, no !
Alas, Time stays, *we* go;
　Or else, were this not so,
What need to chain the hours,
For Youth were always ours ?
　Time goes, you say ?—ah, no !

Ours is the eyes' deceit
Of men whose flying feet
　Lead through some landscape low;
We pass, and think we see
The earth's fixed surface flee:—
　Alas, Time stays,—we go !

Once in the days of old,
Your locks were curling gold,
　And mine had shamed the crow.
Now, in the self-same stage,
We've reached the silver age;
　Time goes, you say ?—ah, no !

Once, when my voice was strong,
I filled the woods with song
　To praise your " rose " and " snow ";
My bird, that sang, is dead;
Where are your roses fled ?
　Alas, Time stays,—we go !

See, in what traversed ways,
What backward Fate delays
　The hopes we used to know;
Where are your old desires ?—

Ah, where those vanished fires ?
    Times goes, you say ?—ah, no !

How far, how far, O Sweet,
The past behind our feet
    Lies in the even‑glow !
Now on the forward way,
Let us fold hands, and pray;
    Alas, Time stays,—*we* go.

Austin Dobson

The Revenge

FAIR rebel to thyself and Time,
    Who laugh'st at all my tears,
When thou hast lost thy youthful prime,
    And age his trophy rears,

Weighing thy inconsiderate pride,
    Thou shalt in vain accuse it:
" Why beauty am I now denied,
    Or knew not then to use it ? "

Then shall I wish, ungentle Fair,
    Thou in like flames may'st burn !
Venus, if just, will hear my prayer,
    And I shall laugh my turn.

Thomas Stanley

JOACHIM DU BELLAY

1525–60.

From the Visions

I

IT was the time, when rest, soft sliding downe
    From heavens hight into mens heavy eyes,
In the forgetfulness of sleepe doth drowne
    The carefull thoughts of mortall miseries;

Then did a ghost before mine eyes appeare,
  On that great rivers banck, that runnes by Rome;
Which, calling me by name, bad me to reare
  My lookes to heaven, whence all good gifts do come
And crying lowd, " Lo ! now beholde," quoth hee,
  " What under this great temple placed is:
Lo, all is nought but flying vanitee ! "
  So I, that know this world's inconstancies,
Sith onely God surmounts all times decay,
In God alone my confidence do stay.

2

On high hills top I saw a stately frame,
  An hundred cubits high by iust assize,
With hundreth pillours fronting faire the same,
  All wrought with diamond after Dorick wize;
Nor brick not marble was the wall in view,
  But shining christall, which from top to base
Out of her womb a thousand rayons threw,
  One hundred steps of Afrike golds enchase:
Golde was the parget; and the seeling bright
  Did shine all scaly with great plates of golde;
The floore of iasp and emeraude was dight.
  O, worlds vainesse ! Whiles thus I did behold,
An earthquake shooke the hill from lowest seat,
And overthrew this frame with ruine great.

3

Then did a sharped spyre of diamond bright,
  Ten feete each way in square, appeare to mee,
Justly proportion'd up unto his hight,
  So far as archer might his level see:
The top thereof a pot did seeme to beare,
  Made of the metall which we most do honour;
And in this golden vessel couched weare
  The ashes of a mightie emperor:

Upon foure corners of the base were pight,
　　To beare the frame, foure great lyons of gold;
A worthy tombe for such a worthy wight.
　　Alas ! this world doth nought but grievance hold !
I saw a tempest from the heaven descend,
Which this brave monument with flash did rend.

4

I saw raysde up on yvorie pillowes tall,
　　Whose bases were of richest mettals warke,
The chapters alabaster, the fryses christall,
　　The double front of a triumphall arke:
On each side purtraid was a Victorie,
　　Clad like a nimph, that winges of silver weares,
And in triumphant chayre was set on hie
　　The auncient glory of the Romaine peares.
No worke it seem'd of earthly craftsmans wit,
　　But rather wrought by his owne industry,
That thunder-dartes for Iove his syre doth fit.
　　Let me no more see faire thing under sky,
Sith that mine eyes have seene so faire a sight
With sodain fall to dust consumed quight.

5

Then was the faire Dodonian tree far seene
　　Upon seaven hills to spread his gladsom gleame,
And conquerours bedecked with his greene,
　　Along the bancks of the Ausonian streame:
There many an auncient trophee was addrest,
　　And many a spoyle, and many a goodly show,
Which that brave races greatnes did attest,
　　That whilome from the Troyan blood did flow.
Ravisht I was so rare a thing to vew;
　　When, lo ! a barbarous troupe of clownish fone

The honour of these noble boughs down threw:
    Under the wedge I heard the tronck to grone;
And, since, I saw the roote in great disdaine
    A twinne of forked trees send forth againe.

6

I saw a wolfe under a rockie cave
    Noursing two whelps; I saw her little ones
In wanton dalliance the teate to crave,
    While she her neck wreath'd from them for the nones:
I saw her raunge abroad to seeke her food,
    And, roming through the field with greedie rage,
T' embrew her teeth and clawes with lukewarm blood
Of the small heards, her thirst for to asswage:
I saw a thousand huntsmen, which descended
    Downe from the mountaines bordring Lombardie,
That with an hundred speares her flank wide rended:
    I saw her on the plaine outstretched lie,
Throwing out thousand throbs in her owne soyle;
Soone on a tree uphang'd I saw her spoyle.

Edmund Spenser

Hymn to the Winds

(The winds are invoked by the winnowers of corn)

TO you, troop so fleet,
    That with winged wandering feet,
        Through the wide world pass,
    And with soft murmuring
    Toss the green shades of spring
        In woods and grass,
    Lily and violet
    I give, and blossoms wet,
        Roses and dew;
    This branch of blushing roses,

Whose fresh bud uncloses,
    Wind-flowers too.
Ah, winnow with sweet breath,
Winnow the holt and heath,
    Round this retreat;
Where all the golden morn
We fan the gold o' the corn,
    In the sun's heat.

Andrew Lang

A Vow to Heavenly Venus

WE that with like hearts love, we lovers twain,
New wedded in the village by thy fane,
Lady of all chaste love, to thee it is
We bring these amaranths, these white lilies,
A sign, and sacrifice; may Love, we pray,
Like amaranthine flowers, feel no decay;
Like these cool lilies may our loves remain,
Perfect and pure, and know not any stain;
And be our hearts, from this thy holy hour,
Bound each to each, like flower to wedded flower.

Andrew Lang

To his Friend in Elysium

SO long you wandered on the dusky plain,
    Where flit the shadows with their endless cry,
    You reach the shore where all the world goes by,
You leave the strife, the slavery, the pain;
But we, but we, the mortals that remain
    In vain stretch hands; for Charon sullenly
    Drives us afar, we may not come anigh
Till that last mystic obolus we gain.
But you are happy in the quiet place,

And with the learned lovers of old days,
    And with your love, you wander evermore
In the dim woods, and drink forgetfulness
Of us your friends, a weary crowd that press
    About the gate, or labour at the oar.

Andrew Lang

A Sonnet to Heavenly Beauty

IF this our little life is but a day
    In the Eternal,—if the years in vain
    Toil after hours that never come again,—
If everything that hath been must decay,
Why dreamest thou of joys that pass away,
    My soul, that my sad body doth restrain ?
    Why of the moment's pleasure art thou fain ?
Nay, thou hast wings,—nay, seek another stay.
There is the joy whereto each soul aspires,
And there the rest that all the world desires,
    And there is love, and peace, and gracious mirth;
And there in the most highest heavens shalt thou
Behold the Very Beauty, whereof now
    Thou worshippest the shadow upon earth.

Andrew Lang

Heureux Qui, comme Ulysse, a Fait un Beau Voyage

HAPPY who like Ulysses, or that lord
    That raped the fleece; returning full and sage,
With usage and the world's wide reason stored,
    With his own kin can wait the end of age.
When shall I see, when shall I see, God knows !
    My little village smoke; or pass the door,
The old dear door of that unhappy house,
    That is to me a kingdom and much more ?

Mightier to me the house my fathers made,
   Than your audacious heads, O Halls of Rome;
More than immortal marbles undecayed,
   The thin sad slates that cover up my home;
More than your Tiber is my Loire to me,
   Than Palatine my little Lyré there;
And more than all the winds of all the sea
   The quiet kindness of the Angevin air.

                          Gilbert K. Chesterton

REMY BELLEAU

                          1528–77

April

APRIL, pride of woodland ways,
   Of glad days,
April, bringing hope and prime,
To the young flowers that beneath
   Their bud sheath
Are guarded in their tender time;

April, pride of fields that be
   Green and free,
That in fashion glad and gay,
Stud with flowers red and blue,
   Every hue,
Their jewelled spring array;

April, pride of murmuring
   Winds of spring,
That beneath the winnowed air,
Trap with subtle nets and sweet
   Flora's feet,
Flora's feet, the fleet and fair;

April, by thy hand caressed,
   From her breast
Nature scatters everywhere

Handfuls of all sweet perfumes,
   Buds and blooms,
Making faint the earth and air.

April, joy of the green hours,
   Clothes with flowers
Over all her locks of gold
My sweet lady; and her breast
   With the blest
Buds of summer manifold.

April, with thy gracious wiles,
   Like the smiles,
Smiles of Venus; and thy breath
Like her breath, the gods' delight,
   (From their height
They take the happy air beneath ;)

It is thou that, of thy grace,
   From their place
In the far-off isles dost bring
Swallows over earth and sea,
   Glad to be
Messengers of thee, and Spring.

Daffodil and eglantine,
   And woodbine,
Lily, violet, and rose
Plentiful in April fair,
   To the air,
Their pretty petals do unclose.

Nightingales ye now may hear,
   Piercing clear,
Singing in the deepest shade;
Many and many a babbled note
   Chime and float,
Woodland music through the glade.

April, all to welcome thee,
　　Spring sets free
Ancient flames, and with low breath
Wakes the ashes grey and old
　　That the cold
Chilled within our hearts to death.

Thou beholdest in the warm
　　Hours, the swarm
Of the thievish bees, that flies
Evermore from bloom to bloom
　　For perfume,
Hid away in tiny thighs.

Her cool shadows May can boast,
　　Fruits almost
Ripe, and gifts of fertile dew,
Manna-sweet and honey-sweet,
　　That complete
Her flower garland fresh and new.

Nay, but I will give my praise
　　To these days,
Named with the glad name of Her
That from out the foam o' the sea
　　Came to be
Sudden light on earth and air.

Andrew Lang

PHILIPPE DESPORTES

1545-1606

Conquest

THOSE eyes that set my fancy on a fire,
　Those crispèd hairs that hold my heart in chains,
Those dainty hands which conquered my desire,
　That wit which of my thoughts doth hold the reins:

Those eyes for clearness do the stars surpass,
  Those hairs obscure the brightness of the sun,
Those hands more white than ever ivory was,
  That wit even to the skies hath glory won.
O eyes that pierce our hearts without remorse !
  O hairs of right that wear a royal crown !
O hands that conquer more than Cæsar's force !
  O wit that turns huge kingdoms upside down !
Then, Love, be judge, what heart may therewith
    stand
Such eyes, such hair, such wit, and such a hand ?
(Anonymous: From William Barley's New Book
of Tabliture, 1596)

JEAN DE LA FONTAINE

1621–95

*L*A FONTAINE *is the one French poet who speaks to all the*
world. No one is more truly and variously human than he. We
love him, and laugh with him, even at him sometimes, and should like
some day to come across him in the Elysian fields.—JOHN BAILEY.

The Cock and the Fox

UPON a tree there mounted guard
    A veteran cock, adroit and cunning;
    When to the roots a fox up running
Spoke thus, in tones of kind regard:—
" Our quarrel, brother, 's at an end;
Henceforth I hope to live your friend;
    For peace now reigns
    Throughout the animal domains.
I bear the news.   Come down, I pray,
And give me the embrace fraternal;
    And please, my brother, don't delay:
So much the tidings do concern all,
    That I must spread them far to-day.

Now you and yours can take your walks
Without a fear or thought of hawks;
And should you clash with them or others,
In us you'll find the best of brothers;—
    For which you may, this joyful night,
    Your merry bonfires light.
      But, first, let's seal the bliss
      With one fraternal kiss."
" Good friend," the cock replied, " upon my word,
A better thing I never heard;
    And doubly I rejoice
    To hear it from your voice:
And, really, there must be something in it,
  For yonder come two greyhounds, which, I flatter
  Myself, are couriers on this very matter;
They come so fast, they'll be here in a minute.
    I'll down, and all of us will seal the blessing
    With general kissing and caressing."
    " Adieu," said Fox, " my errand's pressing;
      I'll hurry on my way,
      And we'll rejoice some other day."
So off the fellow scampered, quick and light,
To gain the fox-holes of a neighbouring height,—
Less happy in his stratagem than flight.
    The cock laughed sweetly in his sleeve;—
    'Tis doubly sweet deceiver to deceive.

                    Elizur Wright

Love and Folly

LOVE'S worshippers alone can know
    The thousand mysteries that are his;
His blazing torch, his twanging bow,
    His blooming age are mysteries.
A charming science—but the day
    Were all too short to con it o'er;

So take of me this little lay,
  A sample of its boundless lore.

As once, beneath the fragrant shade
  Of myrtles fresh in heaven's pure air,
The children, Love and Folly, played,
  A quarrel rose betwixt the pair.
Love said the gods should do him right—
  But Folly vowed to do it then,
And struck him, o'er the orbs of sight,
  So hard he never saw again.

His lovely mother's grief was deep,
  She called for vengeance on the deed;
A beauty does not vainly weep,
  Nor coldly does a mother plead.
A shade came o'er the eternal bliss
  That fills the dwellers of the skies;
Even stony-hearted Nemesis
  And Rhadamanthus wiped their eyes.

"Behold," she said, "this lovely boy,"
  While streamed afresh her graceful tears—
"Immortal, yet shut out from joy
  And sunshine, all his future years.
The child can never take, you see,
  A single step without a staff—
The hardest punishment would be
  Too lenient for the crime by half."

All said that Love had suffered wrong,
  And well that wrong should be repaid;
Then weighed the public interest long,
  And long the party's interest weighed.
And thus decreed the court above:
  "Since Love is blind from Folly's blow,
Let Folly be the guide of Love,
  Where'er the boy may choose to go."

                    William Cullen Bryant

The Hag and the Slavies

THERE was a Hag who kept two Chambermaids ;
So well they spun that the Three Sister Spinners,
Compared with them, were bunglers and beginners,
And her sole study was to give them work.
The moment Phœbus left his watery bed,
Up wheel, up distaffs, spin, spin, spin,
Morning out and evening in,
She kept 'em at it like a Turk.
The moment Eos raised her golden head,
A shabby cock would crow his punctual note:
The Hag, still shabbier, from her pallet leaping,
Would huddle on a greasy petticoat,
Light a cracked lamp, and scurry to the bed
Where the poor slaves with all their might
Were fiercely, ravenously sleeping.
One stretched an arm, one opened half an eye,
And both with concentrated spite
Swore through their teeth that the damned cock
    should die.

  No sooner said than done—that scrannel crow
Was hushed; but did the assassins profit ?   No—
The Hag became her own alarum,
And lest the hour should slip her unbeknown,
Began to hustle harum-scarum
Almost before the pair had lain them down.

Thus oft a struggle to escape
But lands us in a still worse scrape:
To exchange the cock for old Sibylla
Was *From Charybdis into Scylla.*

Edward Marsh

JEAN-BAPTISTE POQUELIN MOLIÈRE

1622–73

To Monsieur De La Mothe Le Vayer

(*Upon the death of his son*)

LET thy tears, Le Vayer, let them flow;
None of scant cause thy sorrowing can accuse,
Since, losing that which thou for aye dost lose,
E'en the most wise might find a ground for woe.

Vainly we strive with precepts to forego
The drops of pity that are Pity's dues;
And Nature's self, indignant, doth refuse
To count for fortitude that heartless show.

No grief, alas! can now bring back again
The son too dear, by Death untimely ta'en;
Yet, not the less, his loss is hard to bear,
Graced as he was by all the world reveres,
Large heart, keen wit, a lofty soul and rare,
—Surely these claim eternity of tears!

Austin Dobson

ANDRÉ CHÉNIER

1760–94

Elegies

I

EVERY man has his sorrows; yet each still
Hides under a calm forehead his own will.
Each pities but himself. Each in his grief
Envies his neighbour: he too seeks relief;
For one man's pain is of no other known:
They hide their sorrows as he hides his own;

And each, with tears and aching heart, can sigh:
All other men are happy, but not I.
They are unhappy all.   They, desolate,
Cry against heaven and bid heaven change their fate.
Their fate is changed; they soon, with fresh tears, know
They have but changed one for another woe.

2

A white nymph wandering in the woods by night
Spies a swift satyr, and pretends a flight;
She runs, and, running, feigns to call him back !
The goat-foot, following on her flying track,
Falls down and flounders in the stagnant pool:
Whereat they, while he whimpers, mock the fool.

3

Well, I would have it so.   I should have known
How many times I made her will my own.
For once, at least, I should have let her be,
And waited, till I made her come to me.
No.   I forget what fretful cries last night
Drove me to bitter silence and to flight;
This morning, O weak heart, I long
To have her back, yet do her pride no wrong.

I fly to her, take all her wrongs, but she
Whom I would pardon will not pardon me.
I it is who am false, unjust, and seek
To show my horrid strength where she is weak.
And floods and tempest come, and tears that flow
Obediently, as she would have them go.
And I, to have some peace, must own defeat,
Kneel down, and take her pardon at her feet.

Arthur Symons

PIERRE JEAN DE BÉRANGER

1780–1857

The King of Yvetot

THERE flourished once a potentate,
  Whom history doesn't name;
He rose at ten, retired at eight,
  And snored unknown to fame!
A night-cap for his crown he wore,
  A common cotton thing,
Which Jeannette to his bedside bore,
  This jolly little king!
Ho, ho, ho, ho! Ha, ha, ha, ha!
  This jolly little king!

With four diurnal banquets he
  His appetite allayed,
And on a jackass leisurely
  His royal progress made.
No cumbrous state his steps would clog,
  Fear to the winds he'd fling;
His single escort was a dog,
  This jolly little king!
Ho, ho, ho, ho! Ha, ha, ha, ha!
  This jolly little king!

He owned to only one excess,—
  He doted on his glass,—
But when a king gives happiness,
  Why that, you see, will pass!
On every bottle, small or great,
  For which he used to ring,
He laid a tax inordinate,
  This jolly little king!
Ho, ho, ho, ho! Ha, ha, ha, ha!
  This jolly little king!

Such crowds of pretty girls he found
  Occasion to admire,
It gave his subjects double ground
  For greeting him as Sire !
To shoot for coconuts he manned
  His army every spring,
But all conscription sternly banned
  This jolly little king !
Ho, ho, ho, ho ! Ha, ha, ha, ha !
  This jolly little king !

He eyed no neighbouring domain
  With envy or with greed,
And, like a pattern sovereign,
  Took Pleasure for his creed !
Yet, it was not, if aright I ween,
  Until his life took wing,
His subjects saw that he had been
  A jolly little king.
Ho, ho, ho, ho ! Ha, ha, ha, ha !
  This jolly little king !

This worthy monarch, readers mine,
  You even now may see,
Embellishing a tavern⁄sign
  Well known to you and me !
There, when the fête⁄day bottle flows,
  Their bumpers they will bring,
And toast beneath his very nose
  This jolly little king.
Ho, ho, ho, ho ! Ha, ha, ha, ha !
  This jolly little king !

William Toynbee

ALPHONSE MARIE LOUIS DE LAMARTINE
1790–1869

The Cedars of Lebanon

EAGLES, that wheel above our crests,
Say to the storms that round us blow,
They cannot harm our gnarled breasts,
Firm-rooted as we are below.
Their utmost efforts we defy.
They lift the sea-waves to the sky;
But when they wrestle with our arms
Nervous and gaunt, or lift our hair,
Balanced within its cradle fair
The tiniest bird has no alarms.

Sons of the rock, no mortal hand
Here planted us: God-sown we grew.
We are the diadem green and grand
On Eden's summit that He threw.
When waters in a deluge rose,
Our hollow flanks could well enclose
Awhile the whole of Adam's race;
And children of the Patriarch
Within our forest built the Ark
Of Covenant, foreshadowing grace.

We saw the Tribes as captives led,
We saw them back return anon;
As rafters have our branches dead
Cover'd the porch of Solomon;
And later, when the Word, made man,
Came down in God's salvation-plan
To pay for sin the ransom-price,
The beams that form'd the Cross we gave:
These, red in blood of power to save,
Were altars of that Sacrifice.

In memory of such great events,
Men come to worship our remains;
Kneel down in prayer within our tents,
And kiss our old trunks' weather-stains.
The saint, the poet, and the sage,
Hear and shall hear from age to age
Sounds in our foliage like the voice
Of many waters; in these shades
Their burning words are forged like blades,
While their uplifted souls rejoice.

Toru Dutt

ALFRED DE VIGNY

1797–1863

The Sound of the Horn

I LOVE the sound of the horn in the deep, dim wood-
      land,
   Whether it wail with the doe that is nigh to death,
Or cry the hunter's farewell on the echoes waning,
   From leaf to leaf borne on by the north wind's
      breath.

How often alone, in the shadow at midnight straying,
   I have smiled to hear it, how often have wept still
      more !
For I seemed to hear the rumour of things foreboding
   The death of the Paladin knights that lived of yore.

O azure Mountain ! O land that my heart is fain of !
   Franzona fells, and summits of Marboré,
Fountains that fall with the drifted snows for a burden,
   Torrents and brooks of the Pyrenees' chill spray,

Mountains frozen or fertile, throning the seasons,
   Who have ice for crown and the meadows about
      your feet,

'Tis there would I dwell, 'tis there would I wait to
    hearken
    The far-borne sound of the horn blow sad and sweet.

A traveller strayed mayhap when the air is stilly,
    Lifts up this brazen voice that the night repeats;
With the sound of his cadenced songs for a while is
    blending
    The tiny bell of the tethered lamb that bleats.

A doe that heareth the sound flies not but rather
    Stands still as a stone on the hill-top, while waters
    chime
In vast uproar with the music for ever calling
    From the old romance of the immemorial time.

Souls of the Paladins, say, do your ghosts still haunt us ?
    Is it you who speak to us still in the blare of the horn ?
Roncevaux ! Roncevaux ! deep in thy sombre valley
    The shade of the noble Roland is still forlorn !

Wilfrid Thorley

Nature

I AM the stage, impassive, mute and cold,
    That thrills not where the actor's foot hath trod.
My alabaster halls, my emerald
    Stairs, and my tones were sculptured by a god:
Your voice of crying I know not, no, nor see
The passing of the human comedy
    That looks to heaven to find its period.

I roll, and to my deep disdain I thrust
    The seed of ants and human populations;
Their tenements I know not from their dust,
    Their names I know not—I that bear the nations;
Mother in name, in deed a very room
For death; my winter takes its hecatomb,
    My spring is careless of your adorations.

Before you, always essenced, always fair,
   I shook my locks abroad the winds of heaven,
And trod my customary path in air,
   While the divine hands held the balance even:
And onward, to that void where all things roll
I shall be carried silently and sole,
   And by my breast and brows the airs be riven.

                 Margaret Jourdain

VICTOR HUGO

1802–85

A Sunset

(From Les Feuilles d'Automne)

I LOVE the evenings, passionless and fair, I love the
   evens,
   Whether old manor-fronts their ray with golden
      fulgence leavens,
      In numerous leafage bosomed close;
Whether the mist in reefs of fire extend its reaches
   sheer,
Or a hundred sunbeams splinter in an azure atmosphere
      On cloudy archipelagos.

Oh, gaze ye on the firmament! a hundred clouds in
   motion,
Up-piled in the immense sublime beneath the winds'
   commotion,
      Their unimagined shapes accord:
Under their waves at intervals flames a pale levin
   through,
As if some giant of the air amid the vapours drew
      A sudden elemental sword.

The sun at bay with splendid thrusts still keeps the
    sullen fold;
And momently at distance sets, as a cupola of gold,
    The thatched roof of a cot a-glance;
Or on the blurred horizon joins his battle with the haze;
Or pools the glooming fields about with inter-isolate
    blaze,
    Great moveless meres of radiance.

Then mark you how there hangs athwart the firma-
    ment's swept track,
Yonder, a mighty crocodile with vast irradiant back,
    A triple row of pointed teeth ?
Under its burnished belly slips a ray of eventide,
The flickerings of a hundred glowing clouds its tene-
    brous side
    With scales of golden mail ensheathe.

Then mounts a palace, then the air vibrates—the vision
    flees.
Confounded to its base, the fearful cloudy edifice
    Ruins immense in mounded wrack;
Afar the fragments strew the sky, and each envermeiled
    cone
Hangeth, peak downward, overhead, like mountains
    overthrown
    When the earthquake heaves its hugy back.

These vapours, with their leaden, golden, iron, bronzèd
    glows,
Where the hurricane, the waterspout, thunder, and hell
    repose,
    Muttering hoarse dreams of destined harms,—
'Tis God who hangs their multitude amid the skiey deep,
As a warrior that suspendeth from the roof-tree of his
    keep
    His dreadful and resounding arms !

All vanishes ! The sun, from topmost heaven precipi⸗
tated,
Like to a globe of iron which is tossed back fiery red
Into the furnace stirred to fume,
Shocking the cloudy surges, plashed from its impetuous
ire,
Even to the zenith spattereth in a flecking scud of fire
The vaporous and inflamèd spume.

O contemplate the heavens ! Whenas the vein⸗drawn
day dies pale,
In every season, every place, gaze through their every⸗
veil,
With love that has not speech for need !
Beneath their solemn beauty is a mystery infinite:
If winter hue them like a pall, or if the summer night
Fantasy them with starry brede.

Francis Thompson

Heard on the Mountain

(From Les Feuilles d'Automne)

HAVE you sometimes, calm, silent, let your tread
aspirant rise
Up to the mountain's summit, in the presence of
the skies ?
Was't on the borders of the South ? or on the
Bretagne coast ?
And at the basis of the mount had you the Ocean
tossed ?
And there, leaned o'er the wave and o'er the
immeasurableness,
Calm, silent, have you hearkened what it says ? Lo,
what it says !
One day at least, whereon my thought, enlicensèd
to muse,

Had drooped its wing above the beachèd margent of
    the ooze,
And, plunging from the mountain height into the
    immensity,
Beheld upon one side the land, on the other side the sea,
I hearkened, comprehended,—never, as from those
    abysses,
No, never issued from a mouth, nor moved an ear such
    voice as this is !

A sound it was, at outset, immeasurable, confused,
Vaguer than is the wind among the tufted trees effused,
Full of magnificent accords, suave murmurs, sweet as is
The evensong, and mighty as the shock of panoplies
When the hoarse mêlée in its arms the closing squadrons
    grips,
And pants, in furious breathings, from the clarions'
    brazen lips.
Unutterable the harmony, unsearchable its deep,
Whose fluid undulations round the world a girdle
    keep,
And through the vasty heavens, which by its surges are
    washed young,
Its infinite volutions roll, enlarging as they throng,
Even to the profound arcane, whose ultimate chasms
    sombre
Its shattered flood englut with time, with space and
    form and number.
Like to another atmosphere, with thin o'erflowing robe,
The hymn eternal covers all the inundated globe:
And the world, swathed about with this investuring
    symphony,
Even as it trepidates in the air, so trepidates in the
    harmony.

And pensive, I attended the ethereal lutany,
Lost within this containing voice as if within the sea.

Soon I distinguished, yet as tone which veils confuse and
    smother,
Amid this voice two voices, one commingled with the
    other,
Which did from off the land and seas even to the
    heavens aspire;
Chanting the universal chant in simultaneous choir.
And I distinguished them amid that deep and rumorous
    sound,
As who beholds two currents thwart amid the fluctuous
    profound.

The one was of the waters; a be-radiant hymnal speech !
That was the voice o' the surges, as they parleyed each
    with each.
The other, which arose from our abode terranean,
Was sorrowful; and that, alack ! the murmur was of
    man;
And in this mighty choir, whose chantings day and
    night resound,
Every wave had its utterance, and every man his sound.

Now, the magnificent Ocean, as I said, unbannering,
A voice of joy, a voice of peace, did never stint to sing,
Most like in Sion's temples to a psaltery psaltering,
And to creation's beauty reared the great lauds of his
    song.
Upon the gale, upon the squall, his clamour borne along
Unpausingly arose to God in more triumphal swell;
And every one among his waves, that God alone can
    quell,
When the other of its song made end, into the singing
    pressed.
Like that majestic lion whereof Daniel was the guest,
At intervals the Ocean his tremendous murmur awed;
And, toward where the sunset fires fell shaggily and
    broad,

Under his golden mane, methought that I saw pass the
hand of God.

Meanwhile, and side by side with that august fanfaron-
nade
The other voice, like the sudden scream of a destrier
affrayed,
Like an infernal door that grates ajar its rusty throat,
Like to a bow of iron that gnarls upon an iron rote,
Grinded; and tears, and shriekings, the anathema, the
lewd taunt,
Refusal of viaticum, refusal of the font,
And clamour, and malediction, and dread blasphemy,
among
That hurtling crowd of rumour from the diverse human
tongue,
Went by as who beholdeth, when the valleys thick
t'ward night,
The long drifts of the birds of dusk pass, blackening
flight on flight.
What was this sound whose thousand echoes vibrated
unsleeping?
Alas! the sound was earth's and man's, for earth and
man were weeping.

Brothers! of these two voices strange, most unimagin-
ably,
Unceasingly regenerated, dying unceasingly,
Hearkenèd of the Eternal throughout His Eternity,
The one voice uttereth NATURE, and the other voice
HUMANITY.

Then I alit in reverie; for my ministering sprite,
Alack! had never yet deployed a pinion of an ampler
flight,
Nor ever had my shadow endured so large a day to
burn:

And long I rested dreaming, contemplating turn by turn
Now that abyss obscure which lurked beneath the
water's roll,
And now that other untemptable abyss which opened
in my soul.
And I made question of me, to what issues are we here,
Whither should tend the thwarting threads of all this
ravelled gear;
What doth the soul; to be or live if better worth it is;
And why the Lord, Who, only, reads within that book
of His,
In fatal hymeneals hath eternally entwined
The vintage chant of nature with the dirging cry of
humankind ?

Francis Thompson

The Grave and the Rose

THE Grave said to the Rose,
" What of the dews of dawn,
Love's flower, what end is theirs ? "
" And what of spirits flown,
The souls whereon doth close
The tomb's mouth unawares ? "
The Rose said to the Grave.

The Rose said, " In the shade
From the dawn's tears is made
A perfume faint and strange,
Amber and honey sweet."
" And all the spirits fleet
Do suffer a sky change,
More strangely than the dew,
To God's own angels new,"
The Grave said to the Rose.

Andrew Lang

The Genesis of Butterflies

THE dawn is smiling on the dew that covers
The tearful roses; lo, the little lovers
That kiss the buds, and all the flutterings
In jasmine bloom, and privet, of white wings,
That go and come, and fly, and peep and hide,
With muffled music, murmured far and wide !
Ah, the Spring time, when we think of all the lays
That dreamy lovers send to dreamy mays,
Of the fond hearts within a billet bound,
Of all the soft silk paper that pens wound,
The messages of love that mortals write
Filled with intoxication of delight,
Written in April and before the May time
Shredded and flown, playthings for the wind's play
    time,
We dream that all white butterflies above,
Who seek through clouds or waters souls to love,
And leave their lady mistress in despair,
To flit to flowers, as kinder and more fair,
Are but torn love letters, that through the skies
Flutter, and float, and change to butterflies.

Andrew Lang

More Strong than Time

SINCE I have set my lips to your full cup, my sweet,
Since I my pallid face between your hands have laid,
Since I have known your soul, and all the bloom of it,
And all the perfume rare, now buried in the shade;

Since it was given to me to hear one happy while,
The words wherein your heart spoke all its mysteries,
Since I have seen you weep, and since I have seen
    you smile,
Your lips upon my lips, and your eyes upon my eyes;

Since I have known above my forehead glance and
    gleam,
A ray, a single ray, of your star, veiled always,
Since I have felt the fall, upon my lifetime's stream,
Of one rose petal plucked from the roses of your days;

I now am bold to say to the swift changing hours,
Pass, pass upon your way, for I grow never old,
Fleet to the dark abysm with all your fading flowers,
One rose that none may pluck, within my heart I hold.

Your flying wings may smite, but they can never spill
The cup fulfilled of love, from which my lips are wet;
My heart has far more fire than you can frost to chill,
My soul more love than you can make my soul forget.

Andrew Lang

The Poor Children

TAKE heed of this small child of earth;
    He is great; he hath in him God most high.
Children before their fleshly birth
    Are lights alive in the blue sky.

In our light bitter world of wrong
    They come; God gives us them awhile.
His speech is in their stammering tongue,
    And His forgiveness in their smile.

Their sweet light rests upon our eyes.
    Alas! their right to joy is plain.
If they are hungry, Paradise
    Weeps, and, if cold, Heaven thrills with pain.

The want that saps their sinless flower
    Speaks judgment on sin's ministers.
Man holds an angel in his power.
    Ah! deep in Heaven what thunder stirs,

When God seeks out these tender things
  Whom in the shadow where we sleep
He sends us clothed about with wings,
  And finds them ragged babes that weep !
Algernon Charles Swinburne

GÉRARD DE NERVAL
1808–55

An Old Tune

THERE is an air for which I would disown
  Mozart's, Rossini's, Weber's melodies,—
A sweet sad air that languishes and sighs,
  And keeps its secret charm for me alone.

Whene'er I hear that music vague and old,
  Two hundred years are mist that rolls away;
The thirteenth Louis reigns, and I behold
  A green land golden in the dying day.

An old red castle, strong with stony towers,
  The windows gay with many-coloured glass;
Wide plains, and rivers flowing among flowers,
  That bathe the castle basement as they pass.

In antique weed, with dark eyes and gold hair,
  A lady looks forth from her window high;
It may be that I knew and found her fair,
  In some forgotten life, long time gone by.
Andrew Lang

ALFRED DE MUSSET
1810–57

Juana

AGAIN I see you, ah my queen,
  Of all my old loves that have been
  The first love, and the tenderest;

Do you remember or forget—
Ah me, for I remember yet—
　How the last summer days were blest?

Ah lady, when we think of this,
The foolish hours of youth and bliss,
　How fleet, how sweet, how hard to hold!
How old we are, ere spring be green!
You touch the limit of eighteen
　And I am twenty winters old.

My rose, that 'mid the red roses
Was brightest, ah, how pale she is!
　Yet keeps the beauty of her prime;
Child, never Spanish lady's face
Was lovely with so wild a grace;
　Remember the dead summer-time.

Think of our loves, our feuds of old,
And how you gave your chain of gold
　To me for a peace offering;
And how all night I lay awake
To touch and kiss it for your sake,—
　To touch and kiss the lifeless thing.

Lady, beware, for all we say,
This love shall live another day,
　Awakened from his deathly sleep;
The heart that once has been your shrine
For other loves is too divine;
　A home, my dear, too wide and deep.

What did I say,—why do I dream?
Why should I struggle with the stream
　Whose waves return not any day?
Close heart, and eyes, and arms from me;
Farewell, farewell, so must it be,
　So runs, so runs, the world away.

The season bears upon its wing
The swallows and the songs of spring,
    And days that were, and days that flit;
The loved lost hours are far away;
And hope and fame are scattered spray
For me, that gave you love a day,
    For you that not remember it.

Andrew Lang

THÉOPHILE GAUTIER

1811–72

Posthumous Coquetry

LET there be laid, when I am dead,
Ere 'neath the coffin-lid I lie,
Upon my cheek a little red,
A little black about the eye.

For I in my close bier would fain,
As on the night his vows were made,
Rose-red eternally remain,
With khol beneath my blue eye laid.

Wind me no shroud of linen down
My body to my feet, but fold
The white folds of my muslin gown
With thirteen flounces as of old.

This shall go with me where I go:
I wore it when I won his heart;
His first look hallowed it, and so,
For him, I laid the gown apart.

No immortelles, no broidered grace
Of tears upon my cushions be;
Lay me on my pillow's lace,
My hair across it like a sea.

That pillow, those mad nights of old,
Has seen our slumbering brows unite,
And neath the gondola's black fold
Has counted kisses infinite.

Between my hands of ivory,
Together set for prayer and rest,
Place then the opal rosary
The holy Pope at Rome has blest.

I will lie down then on that bed
And sleep the sleep that shall not cease;
His mouth upon my mouth has said
Pater and *Ave* for my peace.

Arthur Symons

Clarimonde

WITH elbow buried in the downy pillow
    I've lain and read,
All through the night, a volume strangely written
    In tongues long dead.

For at my bedside lie no dainty slippers;
    And, save my own,
Under the paling lamp I hear no breathing:—
    I am alone !

But there are yellow bruises on my body
    And violet stains;
Though no white vampire came with lips blood,
      crimsoned
    To suck my veins !

Now I bethink me of a sweet weird story,
    That in the dark
Our dead loves thus with seal of chilly kisses
    Our bodies mark.

Gliding beneath the coverings of our couches
  They share our rest,
And with their dead lips sign their loving visit
  On arm and breast.

Darksome and cold the bed where now she slumbers,
  I loved in vain,
With sweet eyelids closed, to be reopened
  Never again.

Dead sweetheart, can it be that thou hast lifted
  With thy frail hand
Thy coffin-lid, to come to me again
  From shadowland?

Thou who, one joyous night, didst, pale and speechless,
  Pass from us all,
Dropping thy silken mask and gift of flowers
  Amidst the ball?

Oh, fondest of my loves, from that far heaven
  Where thou must be,
Hast thou returned to pay the debt of kisses
  Thou owest to me?

       Lafcadio Hearn

Love at Sea

WE are in love's land to-day;
  Where shall we go?
Love, shall we start or stay,
  Or sail or row?
There's many a wind and way,
And never a May but May;
We are in love's land to-day;
  Where shall we go?

Our landwind is the breath
Of sorrows kissed to death
   And joys that were;
Our ballast is a rose;
Our way lies where God knows
   And love knows where.
      We are in love's land to-day—

Our seamen are fledged loves,
Our masts are bills of doves,
   Our decks fine gold;
Our ropes are dead maids' hair,
Our stores are love-shafts fair
   And manifold.
      We are in love's land to-day—

Where shall we land you, sweet?
On fields of strange men's feet,
   Or fields near home?
Or where the fire-flowers blow,
Or where the flowers of snow
   Or flowers of foam?
      We are in love's land to-day—

Land me, she says, where love
Shows but one shaft, one dove,
   One heart, one hand.
—A shore like that, my dear,
Lies where no man will steer,
   No maiden land.

Algernon Charles Swinburne

CHARLES BAUDELAIRE

1821–67

IN the poetry of Baudelaire there is a deliberate science of sensual and sexual-perversity which has something curious in its accentuation of vice with horror, in its passionate devotion to passions. Baudelaire lived and died solitary, secret, a confessor of sins who had never told the whole truth, an ascetic of passion, a hermit of the brothel.—ARTHUR SYMONS.

Don Juan in Hell

THE night Don Juan came to pay his fees
  To Charon, by the caverned water's shore,
A beggar, proud-eyed as Antisthenes,
  Stretched out his knotted fingers on the oar.

Mournful, with drooping breasts and robes unsewn,
  The shapes of women swayed in ebon skies,
Trailing behind him with a restless moan
  Like cattle herded for a sacrifice.

Here, grinning for his wage, stood Sganarelle,
  And here Don Luis pointed, bent and dim,
To show the dead who lined the holes of hell,
  This was that impious son who mocked at him.

The hollow-eyed, the chaste Elvira came,
  Trembling and veiled, to view her traitor spouse.
Was it one last bright smile she thought to claim,
  Such as made sweet the morning of his vows?

A great stone man rose like a tower on board,
  Stood at the helm and cleft the flood profound:
But the calm hero, leaning on his sword,
  Gazed back, and would not offer one look round.

James Elroy Flecker

Epilogue

WITH heart at rest I climbed the citadel's
Steep height, and saw the city as from a tower,
Hospital, brothel, prison, and such hells,

Where evil comes up softly like a flower.
Thou knowest, O Satan, patron of my pain,
Not for vain tears I went up at that hour;

But, like an old sad faithful lecher, fain
To drink delight of that enormous trull
Whose hellish beauty makes me young again.

Whether thou sleep, with heavy vapours full,
Sodden with day, or, new apparelled, stand
In gold-laced veils of evening beautiful,

I love thee, infamous city! Harlots and
Hunted have pleasures of their own to give,
The vulgar herd can never understand.

Arthur Symons

Les Hiboux

UNDER the yew-tree's heavy weight
The owls stand in their sullen fashions,
Like Pagan gods of Pagan passions
They dart their eyes and meditate.
Unmoving they stare with living flame
Until the end of the melancholy
Hour sees the oblique sun set in folly,
And darkness falls in shades of shame.
Their aspect to the wise man teaches
All that he needs, all he beseeches,
Tumult and change and discontent;
The man drunk of a shadow that passes

Keeps always the imperishable scent
That makes the wind change and the grasses.

Arthur Symons

Parfum Exotique

WHEN with eyes closed as in an opium dream
I breathe the odour of thy passionate breast,
I see in vision hell's infernal stream
And the sunset fires that have no instant's rest

An idle island where the unnatural scheme
Of Nature is by savourous fruits oppressed,
And where men's bodies are their women's guest
And women's bodies are not what they seem.

Guided by thine odour towards the heat of veils,
I see a harbour filled with masts and sails,
Wearied by the sea wind that wearies me,

And in the perfume of the tamarind there clings
I know not what of marvellous luxury
Mixed in my soul with the song the mariner sings.

Arthur Symons

Elevation

ABOVE the pools, above the valley of fears,
Above the woods, the clouds, the hills, the trees,
Beyond the sun's and the moon's mad mysteries,
Beyond the confines of the starry spheres,

My spirit, you move with a pure ardency,
And, as one who swoons in the senses of sound,
You furrow furiously the immensity profound
With an indicible and male sensuality.

Fly from those morbid miasmas and their mire;
Purify your own self in the mid air malign,
And there drink, as a delicious and rare wine,
The enormity and the intensity of fire.

Beyond the universe and the vast chagrins
Which load the smoky air with their existence,
Joyous is he who can with a bird's persistence
Rush toward the heavens not fashioned by our sins !

He whose thoughts, like the lark that sings and wings
Its way at dawn toward the sky in a higher flight,
Wandering over the immensity of the night,
Knows the flowers' speech and the speech of silent
    things !

Arthur Symons

Correspondences

ALL Nature is a temple where the alive
Pillars breathe often a tremor of mixed words;
Man wanders in a forest of accords
That peer familiarly from each ogive.

Like thinning echoes tumbling to sleep, beyond,
In a unity umbrageous and infinite,
Vast as the night tremendously moonlit,
Perfumes and colours and sounds correspond.

Perfumes blown sweet as infants' naked flesh,
Soft as oboes, green as a studded plain,
—Others, corrupt, rich and triumphant, thresh

Expansions to the infinite of pain:
Amber and myrrh, benzoin and musk condense
To transports in the spirit and the sense !

Allen Tate

A Carrion

REMEMBER now, my Love, what piteous thing
  We saw on a summer's gracious day:
By the roadway a hideous carrion, quivering
  On a clean bed of pebbly clay,

With legs flexed in the air like a courtesan,
  Burning and sweating venomously,
Calmly disclosed its belly, ironic and wan,
  Clamorous with foul ecstasy.

The sun bore down upon this rottenness
  As if to roast it with gold fire,
And render back to Nature her own largess
  A hundredfold of her desire.

Heaven observed the vaunting carcass there
  Blooming with the richness of a flower;
And that almighty stink which corpses wear
  Choked you with sleepy power !

The flies swarmed on that putrid vulva; then
  A black tumbling rout would seethe
Of maggots, thick like a torrent in a glen,
  Over those rags that lived and seemed to breathe.

They darted down and ascended like a wave
  Or buzzed impetuously as before;
One would have thought the corpse was held a slave
  To living by the life it bore !

This world made music, had its own swift emotion
  Like water and the wind running,
Or corn that a winnower, in rhythmic motion,
  Fans with fiery cunning.

All forms receded—as in a dream, were still,
  Where white visions vaguely start
From the sketch of a painter's long-neglected idyl
  Into a perfect art !

Behind the rocks a restless bitch looked on,
  Regarding us with jealous eyes,
Waiting to tear from the livid skeleton
  Her loosed morsel quick with flies.

—And even you will come to this foul shame,
  This horrible infection,
Star of my eyes, my being's inner flame,
  My angel and my passion !

Yes: such you shall be, O queen of heavenly grace,
  Beyond the last sacrament,
When through your bones the sucking flowers and grass
  Weave their rank cerement.

Speak, then, my Beauty, to this dire putrescence,
  To the worm that shall kiss your proud estate,
That I have kept the divine Form and the Essence
  Of my festered loves inviolate !

                                        Allen Tate

Le Balcon

MOTHER of Memories ! O mistress-queen !
  Oh ! all my joy and all my duty thou !
    The beauty of caresses that have been,
    The evenings and the hearth remember now,
    Mother of Memories ! O mistress-queen !

    The evenings burning with the glowing fire,
    And on the balcony, the rose-stained nights !
    How sweet, how kind you were, my soul's desire.
    We said things wonderful as chrysolites,
    When evening burned beside the glowing fire.

How fair the sun is in the evening !
How strong the soul, how high the heaven's high tower !
O first and last of every worshipped thing,
Your odorous heart's-blood filled me like a flower.
How fair the sun is in the evening !

The night grew deep between us like a pall,
And in the dark I guessed your shining eyes,
And drank your breath, O sweet, O honey-gall !
Your little feet slept on me sister-wise.
The night grew deep between us like a pall.

I can call back the days desirable,
And live all bliss again between your knees,
For where else can I find that magic spell
Save in your heart and in your Mysteries ?
I can call back the days desirable.

These vows, these scents, these kisses infinite,
Will they like young suns climbing up the skies
Rise up from some unfathomable pit,
Washed in the sea from all impurities ?
O vows, O scents, O kisses infinite !

Lord Alfred Douglas

Harmonie du Soir

NOW is the hour when, swinging in the breeze,
Each flower, like a censer, sheds its sweet.
The air is full of scents and melodies,
O languorous waltz ! O swoon of dancing feet !

Each flower, like a censer, sheds its sweet,
The violins are like sad souls that cry,
O languorous waltz ! O swoon of dancing feet !
A shrine of Death and Beauty is the sky.

The violins are like sad souls that cry,
Poor souls that hate the vast black night of Death;
A shrine of Death and Beauty is the sky.
Drowned in red blood, the Sun gives up his breath.

This soul that hates the vast black night of Death
Takes all the luminous past back tenderly.
Drowned in red blood, the Sun gives up his breath.
Thine image like a monstrance shines in me.

Lord Alfred Douglas

HENRI MURGER

1822–61

Spring in the Students' Quarter

WINTER is passing, and the bells
    For ever with their silver lay
Murmur a melody that tells
    Of April and of Easter Day.
High in sweet air the light vane sets,
    The weathercocks all southward twirl;
A sou will buy her violets
    And make Nini a happy girl.

The winter to the poor was sore,
    Counting the weary winter days,
Watching his little firewood store,
    The bitter snowflakes fell always;
And now his last log dimly gleamed,
    Lighting the room with feeble glare,
Half cinder and half smoke it seemed
    That the wind wafted into air.

Pilgrims from ocean and far isles
    See where the east is reddening,
The flocks that fly a thousand miles
    From sunsetting to sunsetting;

Look up, look out, behold the swallows,
  The throats that twitter, the wings that beat;
And on their song the summer follows,
  And in the summer life is sweet.

With the green tender buds that know
  The shoot and sap of lusty spring
My neighbour of a year ago
  Her casement, see, is opening;
Through all the bitter months that were,
  Forth from her nest she dared not flee,
She was a study for Boucher,
  She now may sit to Gavarni.

Andrew Lang

Old Loves

LOUISE, have you forgotten yet
  The corner of the flowery land,
The ancient garden where we met,
  My hand that trembled in your hand?
Our lips found words scarce sweet enough,
  As low beneath the willow trees
We sat: have you forgotten, love?
  Do you remember, love Louise?

Marie, have you forgotten yet
  The loving barter that we made?
The rings we changed, the suns that set,
  The woods fulfilled with sun and shade?
The fountains that were musical
  By many an ancient trysting tree—
Marie, have you forgotten all?
  Do you remember, love Marie?

Christine, do you remember yet
  Your room with scents and roses gay?

My garret—near the sky 'twas set—
　The April hours, the nights of May?
The clear calm nights—the stars above
　That whispered they were fairest seen
Through no cloud-veil?　Remember, love!
　Do you remember, love Christine?

Louise is dead, and, well-a-day!
　Marie a sadder path has ta'en;
And pale Christine has passed away
　In southern suns to bloom again.
Alas, for one and all of us—
　Marie, Louise, Christine forget;
Our bower of love is ruinous,
　And I alone remember yet.

Andrew Lang

FRÉDÉRIC MISTRAL

1830–1914

The Cocooning

(From the Mirèio)

WHEN the crop is fair in the olive-yard,
　And the earthen jars are ready
For the golden oil from the barrels poured,
　And the big cart rocks unsteady
With its tower of gathered sheaves, and strains
And groans on its way through fields and lanes:

When brawny and bare as an old athlete
　Comes Bacchus the dance a-leading,
And the labourers all, with juice-dyed feet,
　The vintage of Crau are treading,
And the good wine pours from the brimful presses,
And the ruby foam in the vats increases;

When under the leaves of the Spanish broom
　The clear silk-worms are holden,

An artist each, in a tiny loom,
Weaving a web of golden,
Fine, frail cells out of sunlight spun,
Where they creep and sleep by the million,—

Glad is Provence on a day like that,
'Tis the time of jest and laughter:
The Ferigoulet and the Baume Muscat
They quaff, and they sing thereafter.
And lads and lasses, their toils between,
Dance to the tinkling tambourine.

Harriet Waters Preston

The Leaf-picking

SING, magnarello, merrily,
As the green leaves you gather !
In their third sleep the silk-worms lie,
And lovely is the weather.
Like brown bees that in open glades
From rosemary gather honey,
The mulberry-trees swarm full of maids,
Glad as the air is sunny !

Sing, magnarello, merrily,
The green leaves are piling !
Two comely children sit on high,
Amid the foliage, smiling.
Sing, magnarello, loud and oft:
Your merry labour hasten.
The guileless pair who laugh aloft
Are learning love's first lesson.

Sing, magnarello, merrily,
As the green leaves you gather !
The sun of May is riding higher,
And ardent is the weather.

Sing, magnarello, heap your leaves,
 While sunny is the weather !
He comes to aid her when she grieves:
 The two are now together.

    Harriet Waters Preston

SULLY PRUDHOMME

1839–1907

The Struggle

NIGHTLY tormented by returning doubt,
I dare the sphinx with faith and unbelief;
And through lone hours when no sleep brings relief
The monster rises all my hopes to flout.

In a still agony, the light blown out,
I wrestle with the unknown; nor long nor brief
The night appears, my narrow couch of grief
Grown like the grave with Death walled round about.

Sometimes my mother, coming with her lamp,
Seeing my brow as with a death-sweat damp,
Asks, "Ah, what ails thee, child? Hast thou no
 rest?"

And then I answer, touched by her look of yearning,
Holding my beating heart and forehead burning,
"Mother, I strove with God, and was hard prest."

    Arthur O' Shaughnessy

CATULLE MENDÈS

1841–1909

I go by Road

I GO by road, I go by street—
 Lira, la, la !
O white high roads, ye know my feet !
A loaf I carry and, all told,

Three broad bits of lucky gold—
  Lira, la, la !
And oh, within my flowering heart,
(Sing, dear nightingale !) is my Sweet.

A poor man met me and begged for bread—
  Lira, la, la !
" Brother, take all the loaf," I said,
I shall but go with lighter cheer—
  Lira, la, la !
And oh, within my flowering heart
(Sing, sweet nightingale !) is my Dear.

A thief I met on the lonely way—
  Lira, la, la !
He took my gold; I cried to him, " Stay !
And take my pocket and make an end."
  Lira, la, la !
And oh, within my flowering heart
(Sing, soft nightingale !) is my Friend.

Now on the plain I have met with death—
  Lira, la, la !
My bread is gone, my gold, my breath.
But oh, this heart is not afraid—
  Lira, la la !
For oh, within this lonely heart
(Sing, sad nightingale !) is my Maid.

Alice Meynell

STÉPHANE MALLARMÉ

1842–98

L'Après≀Midi d'un Faune

I WOULD immortalize these nymphs: so bright
Their sunlit colouring, so airy light,
It floats like drowsy down.   Loved I a dream ?
My doubts, born of oblivious darkness, seem

A subtle tracery of branches grown
The tree's true self—proving that I have known,
Thinking it love, the blushing of a rose.
But think.   These nymphs, their loveliness . . .
    suppose
They bodied forth your senses' fabulous thirst?
Illusion! which the blue eyes of the first,
As cold and chaste as is the weeping spring,
Beget: the other, sighing, passioning,
Is she the wind, warm in your fleece at noon?
No; through this quiet, when a weary swoon
Crushes and chokes the latest faint essay
Of morning, cool against the encroaching day,
There is no murmuring water, save the gush
Of my clear fluted notes; and in the hush
Blows never a wind, save that which through my reed
Puffs out before the rain of notes can speed
Upon the air, with that calm breath of art
That mounts the unwrinkled zenith visibly,
Where inspiration seeks its native sky.
You fringes of a calm Sicilian lake,
The sun's own mirror which I love to take,
Silent beneath your starry flowers, tell
How here I cut the hollow rushes, well
Tamed by my skill, when on the glaucous gold
Of distant lawns about their fountain cold
A living whiteness stirs like a lazy wave;
And at the first slow notes my panpipes gave
These flocking swans, these naiads, rather, fly
Or dive.   Noon burns inert and tawny dry,
Nor marks how clean that Hymen slipped away
From me who seek in song the real A.
Wake, then, to the first ardour and the sight,
O lonely faun, of the old fierce white light,
With, lilies, one of you for innocence.
Other than their lips' delicate pretence,

The light caress that quiets treacherous lovers,
My breast, I know not how to tell, discovers
The bitten print of some immortal's kiss.

But hush ! a mystery so great as this
I dare not tell, save to my double reed,
Which, sharer of my every joy and need,
Dreams down its cadenced monologues that we
Falsely confuse the beauties that we see
With the bright palpable shapes our song creates:
My flute, as loud as passion modulates,
Purges the common dream of flank and breast,
Seen through closed eyes and inwardly caressed,
Of every empty and monotonous line.

Bloom then, O Syrinx, in thy flight malign,
A reed once more beside our trysting-lake.
Proud of my music, let me often make
A song of goddesses and see their rape
Profanely done on many a painted shape.
So when the grape's transparent juice I drain,
I quell regret for pleasures past and feign
A new real grape.   For holding towards the sky
The empty skin, I blow it tight and lie
Dream-drunk till evening, eyeing it.
                                    Tell o'er
Remembered joys and plump the grape once more.
Between the reeds I saw their bodies gleam
Who cool no mortal fever in the stream,
Crying to the woods the rage of their desire;
And their bright hair went down in jewelled fire
Where crystal broke and dazzled shudderingly.
I check my swift pursuit: for see where lie,
Bruised, being twins in love, by languor sweet,
Two sleeping girls, clasped at my very feet.
I seize and run with them, nor part the pair,
Breaking this covert of frail petals, where

Roses drink scent of the sun and our light play
'Mid tumbled flowers shall match the death of day.
I love that virginal fury—ah, the wild
Thrill when a maiden body shrinks, defiled,
Shuddering like arctic light, from lips that sear
Its nakedness . . . the flesh in secret fear !
Contagiously through my linked pair it flies
Where innocence in either, struggling, dies,
Wet with fond tears or some less piteous dew.
Gay in the conquest of these fears, I grew
So rash that I must needs the sheaf divide
Of ruffled kisses heaven itself had tied.
For as I leaned to stifle in the hair
Of one my passionate laughter (taking care
With a stretched finger, that her innocence
Might stain with her companion's kindling sense
To touch the younger little one, who lay
Child-like unblushing) my ungrateful prey
Slips from me, freed by passion's sudden death
Nor heeds the frenzy of my sobbing breath.

Let it pass ! others of their hair shall twist
A rope to drag me to those joys I missed.
See how the ripe pomegranates bursting red
To quench the thirst of the mumbling bees have bled;
So too our blood, kindled by some chance fire,
Flows for the swarming legions of desire.
At evening, when the woodland green turns gold
And ashen grey, 'mid the quenched leaves, behold !
Red Etna glows, by Venus visited,
Walking the lava with her snowy tread
Whene'er the flames in thunderous slumber die.
I hold the goddess !

                              Ah, sure penalty !

But the unthinking soul and body swoon
At last beneath the heavy hush of noon.

Forgetful let me lie where summer's drouth
Sifts fine the sand and then with gaping mouth
Dream planet‹struck by the grape's round wine‹red star.

Nymphs, I shall see the shade that now you are.

Aldous Huxley

Sigh

MY soul, calm sister, towards thy brow, whereon
    scarce grieves
    An autumn strewn already with its russet leaves,
    And towards the wandering sky of thine angelic
      eyes,
    Mounts, as in melancholy gardens may arise
    Some faithful fountain sighing whitely towards the
      blue !
    Towards the blue, pale and pure, that sad October
      knew,
    When, in those depths, it mirrored languors infi‹
      nite,
    And agonizing leaves upon the waters white,
    Windily drifting, traced a furrow cold and dun,
    Where, in one long last ray, lingered the yellow sun.

Arthur Symons

Sea‹wind

THE flesh is sad, alas ! and all the books are read.
Flight, only flight ! I feel that birds are wild to tread
The floor of unknown foam, and to attain the skies !
Naught, neither ancient gardens mirrored in the eyes,
Shall hold this heart that bathes in waters its delight,
O nights ! nor yet my waking lamp, whose lonely
    light
Shadows the vacant paper, whiteness profits best,
Nor the young wife who rocks her baby on her breast.

I will depart !   O steamer, swaying rope and spar,
Lift anchor for exotic lands that lie afar !
A weariness, outworn by cruel hopes, still clings
To the last farewell handkerchief's last beckonings !
And are not these, the masts inviting storms, not
    these
That an awakening wind bends over wrecking seas,
Lost, not a sail, a sail, a flowering isle, ere long ?
But, O my heart, hear thou, hear thou, the sailors'
    song !

Arthur Symons

Anguish

TO-NIGHT I do not come to conquer thee,
   O Beast that dost the sins of the whole world bear,
Nor with my kisses' weary misery
Wake a sad tempest in thy wanton hair;
It is that heavy and that dreamless sleep
I ask of the close curtains of thy bed,
Which, after all thy treacheries, folds thee deep,
Who knowest oblivion better than the dead.
For Vice, that gnaws with keener tooth than time,
Brands me as thee, of barren conquest proud;
But while thou guardest in thy breast of stone
A heart that fears no fang of any crime,
I wander palely, haunted by my shroud,
Fearing to die if I but sleep alone.

Arthur Symons

JOSÉ-MARIA DE HEREDIA
1842–1905

The Flute: A Pastoral

EVENING !   A flight of pigeons in clear sky !
   What wants there to allay love's fever now,
   Goatherd ! but that thy pipe should overflow,
While through the reeds the river murmurs by ?

Here in the plane-tree's shadow where we lie
    Deep grows the grass and cool.   Sit and allow
    The wandering goat to scale yon rocky brow
And graze at will, deaf to the weanling's cry.

My flute—a simple thing, seven oaten reeds
Glued with a little wax—sings, plains, or pleads
    In accents deep or shrill as I require;
Come ! thou shalt learn Silenus' sacred art,
    And through this channel breath'd will fierce desire
Rise, wing'd with music, from the o'er-laboured heart.

H. J. C. Grierson

The Labourer

HERE is the yoke, with arrow and share near by,
    The goad, the scythe that in a day hath mown
    Swathes that would make the wide barn-flooring
        groan,
And here the fork the brown haymakers ply.
Too heavy tools !   He hath vowed them utterly
    Unto immortal Rhea, who alone
    Brings seed to blossom from hard tilth.   His own
Labour is done and he not loth to die.

Fourscore long years, sun-blistered, poor, he drave
    The coulter, without mirth, through stubborn soil,
Who now goes grimly onward to the grave.
    Yet he bewails the labour too long borne,
    And dreads to find more fallow for his toil
    In sunless fields of Erebus forlorn.

Wilfrid Thorley

PAUL VERLAINE

1844–96

HE was the purest lyrical singer that France has ever known. He strikes a discreet and troubling note that leaves its vibrations in the heart and in the nerves for ever.—LUDWIG LEWISOHN.

"Il Pleut Doucement sur la Ville"

TEARS fall within mine heart,
As rain upon the town:
Whence does this languor start,
Possessing all mine heart?

O sweet fall of the rain
Upon the earth and roof,
Unto a heart in pain,
O music of the rain.

Tears that have no reason
Fall in my sorry heart:
What, there was no treason?
This grief hath no reason.

Nay, the more desolate
Because I know not why
(Neither for love nor hate)
Mine heart is desolate.

Ernest Dowson

Spleen

AROUND were all the roses red,
The ivy all around was black.

Dear, so thou only move thine head,
Shall all mine old despairs awake.

Too blue, too tender was the sky,
The air too soft, too green the sea.

Always I fear, I know not why,
Some lamentable flight from thee.

I am so tired of holly-sprays
And weary of the bright box-tree,

Of all the endless country ways;
Of everything, alas, save thee.

Ernest Dowson

The Sky is up above the Roof

THE sky is up above the roof
   So blue, so soft.
A tree there, up above the roof,
   Swayeth aloft.

A bell within that sky we see,
   Chimes low and faint;
A bird upon that tree we see,
   Maketh complaint.

Dear God, is not the life up there
   Simple and sweet?
How peacefully are borne up there
   Sounds of the street.

What hast thou done, who comest here,
   To weep alway?
Where hast thou laid, who comest here,
   Thy youth away?

Ernest Dowson

A Clymène

MYSTICAL strains unheard,
   A song without a word,
   Dearest, because thine eyes,
   Pale as the skies,

Because thy voice, remote
As the far clouds that float
Veiling for me the whole
Heaven of the soul,

Because the stately scent
Of thy swan's whiteness, blent
With the white lily's bloom
Of thy perfume,

Ah, because thy dear love,
The music breathed above
By angels halo-crowned,
Odour and sound,

Hath, in my subtle heart,
With some mysterious art
Transposed thy harmony,
So let it be.

Arthur Symons

Fantoches

SCARAMOUCHE waves a threatening hand
To Pulcinella, and they stand,
  Two shadows, black against the moon.

The old doctor of Bologna pries
For simples with impassive eyes,
  And mutters o'er a magic rune.

The while his daughter, scarce half-dressed,
Glides slyly 'neath the trees, in quest
  Of her bold pirate lover's sail;

Her pirate from the Spanish main,
Whose passion thrills her in the pain
  Of the loud languorous nightingale.

Arthur Symons

Pantomime

PIERROT, no sentimental swain;
Washes a pâté down again
   With furtive flagons, white and red.

Cassandre, to chasten his content,
Greets with a tear of sentiment
   His nephew disinherited.

That blackguard of a Harlequin
Pirouettes, and plots to win
   His Colombine that flits and flies.

Colombine dreams, and starts to find
A sad heart sighing in the wind,
   And in her heart a voice that sighs.

                              Arthur Symons

Cythère
(Fêtes Galantes)

BY favourable breezes fanned,
A trellised arbour is at hand
   To shield us from the summer airs;

The scent of roses, fainting sweet,
Afloat upon the summer heat,
   Blends with the perfume that she wears.

True to the promise her eyes gave,
   She ventures all, and her mouth rains
   A dainty fever through my veins;

And Love, fulfilling all things, save
   Hunger, we 'scape, with sweets and ices,
   The folly of Love's sacrifices.

                              Arthur Symons

Dans l'Allée
(Fêtes Galantes)

AS in the age of shepherd king and queen,
Painted and frail amid her nodding bows,
Under the sombre branches, and between
The green and mossy garden-ways she goes,
With little mincing airs one keeps to pet
A darling and provoking perroquet.
Her long-trained robe is blue, the fan she holds
With fluent fingers girt with heavy rings,
So vaguely hints of vague erotic things
That her eye smiles, musing among its folds.
—Blonde too, a tiny nose, a rosy mouth,
Artful as that sly patch that makes more sly,
In her divine unconscious pride of youth,
The slightly simpering sparkle of the eye.

Arthur Symons

Mandoline
(Fêtes Galantes)

THE singers of serenades
  Whisper their faded vows
Unto fair listening maids
  Under the singing boughs.

Tircis, Aminte, are there,
  Clitandre has waited long,
And Damis for many a fair
  Tyrant makes many a song.

Their short vests, silken and bright,
  Their long pale silken trains,
Their elegance of delight,
  Twine soft blue silken chains.

And the mandolines and they,
Faintlier breathing, swoon
Into the rose and grey
Ecstasy of the moon.

Arthur Symons

Clair de Lune
(*Fêtes Galantes*)

YOUR soul is a sealed garden, and there go
With masque and bergamasque fair companies
Playing on lutes and dancing and as though
Sad under their fantastic fripperies.

Though they in minor keys go carolling
Of love the conqueror and of live boon
They seem to doubt the happiness they sing
And the song melts into the light of the moon,

The sad light of the moon, so lovely fair
That all the birds dream in the leafy shade
And the slim fountains sob into the air
Among the marble statues in the glade.

Arthur Symons

A la Promenade
(*Fêtes Galantes*)

THE sky so pale, and the trees, such frail things,
Seem as if smiling on our bright array
That flits so light and grey upon the way
With indolent airs and fluttering as of wings.

The fountain wrinkles under a faint wind,
And all the sifted sunlight falling through
The lime-trees of the shadowy avenue
Comes to us blue and shadowy-pale and thinned.

Faultlessly fickle, and yet fond enough,
With fond hearts not too tender to be free,
We wander whispering deliciously,
And every lover leads a lady-love,

Whose imperceptible and roguish hand
Darts now and then a dainty tap, the lip
Revenges on an extreme finger-tip,
The tip of the left little finger, and,

The deed being so excessive and uncouth,
A duly freezing look deals punishment,
That in the instant of the act is blent
With a shy pity pouting in the mouth.

Arthur Symons

Cortège

(Fêtes Galantes)

A SILVER-VESTED monkey trips
And pirouettes before the face
Of one who twists a kerchief's lace
Between her well-gloved finger-tips.

A little negro, a red elf,
Carries her drooping train, and holds
At arm's-length all the heavy folds,
Watching each fold displace itself.

The monkey never lets his eyes
Wander from the fair woman's breast,
White wonder that to be possessed
Would call a god out of the skies.

Sometimes the little negro seems
To lift his sumptuous burden up
Higher than need be, in the hope
Of seeing what all night he dreams.

She goes by corridor and stair,
Still to the insolent appeals
Of her familiar animals
Indifferent or unaware.

Arthur Symons

En Bateau

(Fêtes Galantes)

THE shepherd's star with trembling glint
Drops in black water; at the hint
The pilot fumbles for his flint.

Now is the time, or never, sirs.
No hand that wanders wisely errs:
I touch a hand, and is it hers?

The Knightly Atys strikes the strings,
And to the faithless Chloris flings
A look that speaks of many things.

The Abbé has absolved again
Eglé, the viscount all in vain
Has given his hasty heart the rein.

Meanwhile the moon is up and streams
Upon the skiff that flies and seems
To float upon a tide of dreams.

Arthur Symons

Chanson d'Automne

(From Poèmes Saturniens)

WHEN a sighing begins
In the violins
Of the autumn-song,

My heart is drowned
In the slow sound
Languorous and long.

Pale as with pain,
Breath fails me when
The hour tolls deep.
My thoughts recover
The days that are over,
And I weep.

And I go
Where the winds know,
Broken and brief,
To and fro,
As the winds blow
A dead leaf.

Arthur Symons

Femme et Chatte

(From Poèmes Saturniens)

THEY were at play, she and her cat,
And it was marvellous to mark
The white paw and the white hand pat
Each other in the deepening dark.

The stealthy little lady hid
Under her mittens' silken sheath
Her deadly agate nails that thrid
The silk-like dagger-points of death.

The cat purred primly and drew in
Her claws that were of steel filed thin:
The devil was in it all the same.

And in the boudoir, while a shout
Of laughter in the air rang out,
Four sparks of phosphor shone like flame.

Arthur Symons

Art Poétique

(From Jadis et Naguère)

MUSIC first and foremost of all !
Choose your measure of odd not even,
Let it melt in the air of heaven,
Pose not, poise not, but rise and fall.

Choose your words, but think not whether
Each to other of old belong:
What so dear as the dim grey song
Where clear and vague are joined together ?

'Tis veils of beauty for beautiful eyes,
'Tis the trembling light of the naked noon,
'Tis a medley of blue and gold, the moon
And stars in the cool of autumn skies.

Let every shape of its shade be born;
Colour, away ! come to me, shade !
Only of shade can the marriage be made
Of dream with dream and of flute with horn.

Shun the Point, lest death with it come,
Unholy laughter and cruel wit
(For the eyes of the angels weep at it)
And all the garbage of scullery-scum.

Take Eloquence, and wring the neck of him !
You had better, by force, from time to time,
Put a little sense in the head of Rhyme:
If you watch him not, you will be at the beck of
  him.

O, who shall tell us the wrongs of Rhyme ?
What witless savage or what deaf boy
Has made for us this two'penny toy
Whose bells ring hollow and out of time ?

Music always and music still !
Let your verse be the wandering thing
That flutters in the light from a soul on the wing
Towards other skies at a new whim's will.

Let your verse be the luck of the lure
Afloat on the winds that at morning hint
Of the odours of thyme and the savour of mint . . .
And all the rest is literature.

Arthur Symons

From Sagesse

I

SLUMBER dark and deep
Falls across my life;
I will put to sleep
Hope, desire and strife.

All things pass away,
Good and evil seem
To my soul to'day
Nothing but a dream;

I a cradle laid
In a hollow cave,
By a great hand swayed:
Silence, like the grave.

2

FAIRER is the sea
Than the minster high,
Faithful nurse is she,
And last lullaby,
And the Virgin prays
Over the sea's ways.

Gifts or grief and guerdons
From her bounty come,
And I hear her pardons
Chide her angers home;
Nothing in her is
Unforgivingness.

She is piteous,
She the perilous !
Friendly things to us
The wave sings to us:
You whose hope is past,
Here is peace at last.

And beneath the skies,
Brighter-hued than they,
She has azure dyes,
Rose and green and grey.
Better is the sea
Than all fair things or we.

Arthur Symons

TRISTAN CORBIÈRE

1845-75

Epitaph

For Himself

OF many things adulterate:
No penny, yet the friend of fate;
Power enough but naught of will,
Thus free and yet a prisoner still.
Full-hearted, yet without full spirit,
A breast for friends—no comrade near it;
Imagination—no ideas.
Love, without the lip that cheers.
Idleness, but no repose.
In him virtue wore vice's clothes.

Blasé although insatiate,
Dead, though not cured of living yet.
Spoiler of life, inopportune;
Parched body, head a tipsy moon.
Hoping, the future he'd deny;
Deceased while waiting life to try
He lived while waiting but to die.

Joseph T. Shipley

ARTHUR RIMBAUD

1854–91

Sensation

ON summer evenings blue, pricked by the wheat
   On rustic paths the thin grass I shall tread,
And feel its freshness underneath my feet,
   And, dreaming, let the wind bathe my bare head.

I shall not speak, nor think, but, walking slow
   Through Nature, I shall rove with Love my guide,
As gypsies wander, where, they do not know,
   Happy as one walks by a woman's side.

Jethro Bithell

The Sleeper of the Valley

THERE'S a green hollow where a river sings,
Silvering the torn grass in its glittering flight,
And where the sun from the proud mountain flings
Fire—and the little valley brims with light.

A soldier young, with open mouth, bare head,
Sleeps with his neck in dewy watercress,
Under the sky and on the grass his bed,
Pale in the deep green and the light's excess.

He sleeps amid the iris and his smile
Is like a sick child's slumbering for a while.
Nature, in thy warm lap his chilled limbs hide !

The perfume does not thrill him from his rest.
He sleeps in sunshine, hand upon his breast,
Tranquil—with two red holes in his right side.

Ludwig Lewisohn

Hunger

IF I have any taste, it is hardly
For more than earth and stones.
I always breakfast on air,
Rock, cinders, and iron.

Round, my hungers.   Crop, hungers,
The field of sounds.
Suck the sweet venom
Of convolvulus.

Eat the stones someone breaks,
The old stones of churches;
The shingle of ancient floods,
Bread sown in grey valleys.

.   .   .   .

The wolf cries under the leaves,
Spitting out the gay feathers
Of his meal of poultry:
Like him I consume myself.

Green stuffs and fruits
Await but the gathering,
But the hedge spider
Eats only violets.

May I sleep !   May I boil
On the altars of Solomon.
The broth flows over the rust
And mingles with Kedron.

Edgell Rickword

Song of the Highest Tower

MAY they come, may they come,
The days which enchant us.

I have been so long resigned
That I forget it all.
Fears and sufferings
To the skies are gone,
And the unclean thirst
Darkens my veins.

May they come, may they come,
The days which enchant us.

Like the meadows
Left to ruin,
Spreading and overgrown
With flowers and weeds,
In the angry humming
Of filthy flies.

May they come, may they come,
The days which enchant us.

Edgell Rickword

EMILE VERHAEREN

1855–1916

The Poor

WITH hearts of poor men it is so:
That they are full of tears that flow,
That they are pale as head-stones white
In the moonlight.

And so with poor men's backs it is—
More bent with heavy miseries
Than sagging roofs of brown huts be
Beside the sea.

And it is so with poor men's hands,
Like leaves along autumnal lands,
Leaves that lie sere and dead and late
Beside the gate.

And it is so with poor men's eyes,
Humble and in all sorrow wise,
And like the cattle's, sad and dumb,
When the storms come.

Oh, it is so with the poor folk
That under misery's iron yoke
Have gestures weary and resigned
On earth's far plains of sun and wind.

Ludwig Lewisohn

ALBERT SAMAIN

1858–1900

Pannyra of the Golden Heel

THE revel pauses and the room is still:
The silver flute invites her with a thrill,
And, buried in her great veils fold and fold,
Rises to dance Pannyra, Heel of Gold.
Her light steps cross; her subtle arm impels
The clinging drapery; it shrinks and swells,
Hollows and floats, and bursts into a whirl:
She is a flower, a moth, a flaming girl.
All lips are silent; eyes are all trance:
She slowly wakes the madness of the dance,
Windy and wild the golden torches burn;
She turns, and swifter yet she tries to turn,
Then stops: a sudden marble stiff she stands.
The veil that round her coiled its spiral bands,
Checked in its course, brings all its folds to rest,
And clinging to bright limb and pointed breast

Shows, as beneath silk waters woven fine,
Pannyra naked in a flash divine !

James Elroy Flecker

From Summer Hours

FLOWER petals fall.
    Dull flares the torch's mane;
    Mine eyes to weep were fain,
Mine eyes possess thee all.

Yielded beyond recall,
    Heart, naught shall heal thee again,
    O clay moulded unto pain . . .
Flower petals fall.

The roses all are dying . . .
I am saying nothing, thou hearest
Under thy motionless hair.

Love is heavy. My soul is sighing . . .
What wing brushes both of us, dearest,
In the sick and soundless air ?

Jethro Bithell

REMY DE GOURMONT

1858–1915

Hair

THERE is great mystery, Simone,
    In the forest of your hair.

It smells of hay, and of the stone
Cattle have been lying on;
Of timber, and of new-baked bread
Brought to be one's breakfast fare;
And of the flowers that have grown
Along a wall abandonèd;
Of leather and of winnowed grain;

Of briars and ivy washed by rain;
You smell of rushes and of ferns
Reaped when day to evening turns;
You smell of withering grasses red
Whose seed is under hedges shed;
You smell of nettles and of broom;
Of milk, and fields in clover‑bloom;
You smell of nuts, and fruits that one
Gathers in the ripe season;
And of the willow and the lime
Covered in their flowering time;
You smell of honey, of desire;
You smell of air the noon makes shiver;
You smell of earth and of the river;
You smell of love, you smell of fire.

There is great mystery, Simone,
In the forest of your hair.

Jethro Bithell

JULES LAFORGUE

1860–87

For the Book of Love

I MAY be dead to‑morrow, uncaressed.
My lips have never touched a woman's, none
Has given me in a look her soul, not one
Has ever held me swooning at her breast.

I have but suffered for all nature, trees
Whipped by the winds, wan flowers, the ashen sky,
Suffered with all my nerves, minutely, I
Have suffered for my soul's impurities.

And I have spat on love, and, mad with pride,
Slaughtered my flesh, and life's revenge I brave,
And, while the whole world else was Instinct's slave,
With bitter laughter Instinct I defied.

In drawing‚rooms, the theatre, the church,
  Before cold men, the greatest, most refined,
  And women with eyes jealous, proud, or kind,
Whose tender souls no lust would seem to smirch,

I thought: This is the end for which they work.
  Beasts coupling with the groaning beasts they
  capture.
  And all this dirt for just three minutes' rapture !
Men, be correct ! And women, purr and smirk !

Jethro Bithell

MAURICE MAETERLINCK

1862–

Song

THREE little maidens they have slain,
  To find out what their hearts contain.

The first of them was brimmed with bliss,
  And everywhere her blood was shed,
For full three years three serpents hiss.

The second full of kindness sweet,
  And everywhere her blood was shed,
Three lambs three years have grass to eat.

The third was full of pain and rue,
  And everywhere her blood was shed,
Three seraphim watch three years through.

Jethro Bithell

The Last Words

AND if he ever should come back,
  What am I to say ?
    —Tell him that I watch'd for him
    All my life away.

And if he should ask me more,
  Nor know my face again?
—Speak gently as a sister speaks,
  He may be in pain.

If he ask me where you are,
  How shall I reply?
—Then give him my golden ring,
  Very silently.

And if he should want to know
  Why the hall stands bare?
—Then show him the burnt-out lamp
  And the door ajar.

And if he should ask me then
  How you fell asleep?
—Tell him that I smiled and died.
  Do not let him weep.
                    Frederick York Powell

HENRI DE REGNIER

1864-

Night

AN odorous shade lingers the fair day's ghost,
  And the frail moon now by no wind is tost,
And shadow-laden scents of tree and grass
  Build up again a world our eyes have lost.

Now all the wood is but a murmured light
  Where leaf on leaf falls softly from the height;
The hidden freshness of the river seems
  A breath that mingles with the breath of night.

And time and shade and silence seem to say,
  Close now your eyes nor fear to die with day;
For if the daylight win to earth again,
  Will not its beauty also find a way?

742

And flower and stream and forest, will they not
  Bring back to-morrow, as to-day they brought,
This shadow-hidden scent—this odorous shade ?
  Yea, and with more abiding memories fraught.

Seumas O'Sullivan

ANDRÉ SPIRE

1868-

Lonely

THEY pity me.
  " Look at him, see.
  Taking his walking stick, and going out.   So lonely.
  He flees us.   Look at his strange eyes.
  Not even a book does he take with him.   Only
  His stick.   What does he mean to do ?
  Is he intent on evil ?   In revolt ?   Or fever-sick ? "

Alone, O beautiful white road,
Between your ditches full of grass and flowers,
Over your pebbles telling tales of old !
Alone, O forest, with the blue bark of your pines;
And with your wind that parleys with your trees;
And with your ants processioning that drag
Bodies of little beetles on their backs !
Alone, with you, you sun-drenched fields,
All full of cries, and noises, and heads raised alert !
Alone with you, flies, merlins, buzzards, kites,
Rocks, brambles, sources, crevices,
Fogs, clouds, mists, cones, peaks, precipices,
Heat, odour, order, chaos, and disorder,
Among the dialogues your rival mouths
Exchange for ever !
Alone with my stick, alone with my fatigue,
My dust, my throbbing temples, and my dizziness,
And the proud sweat glued to my skin.

Jethro Bithell

Spring

NOW hand in hand, you little maidens, walk.
Pass in the shadow of the crumbling wall.
Arch your proud bellies under rosy aprons.
And let your eyes so deeply lucid tell
Your joy at feeling flowing into your heart
Another loving heart that blends with yours;
You children faint with being hand in hand.

Walk hand in hand, you languorous maidens, walk.
The boys are turning round, and drinking in
Your sensual petticoats that beat your heels.
And, while you swing your interlacing hands,
Tell, with your warm mouths yearning each to each,
The first books you have read, and your first kisses.
Walk hand in hand, you maidens, friend with friend.

Walk hand in hand, you lovers loving silence.
Walk to the sun that veils itself with willows.
Trail your uneasy limbs by languorous banks,
The stream is full of dusk, your souls are heavy.
You silent lovers, wander hand in hand.

Jethro Bithell

Nudities

The hair is a nudity.—The Talmud.

YOU said to me: But I will be your comrade;
And visit you, but never chafe your blood;
And we will pass long evenings in your room,
Thinking of our brethren they are murdering;
And through the cruel universe we two
Will seek some country which shall give them rest.
But I shall never see your eye-balls burning,
Nor on your temples purple veins distend,—
I am your equal, I am not your prey.

For see ! my clothes are chaste, and almost poor,
You see not even the bottom of my neck.

But I gave answer: Woman, thou art naked.
Fresh as a cup the hair is on thy neck;
Thy chignon, falling down, shakes like a breast;
Thy headbands are as lustful as a herd of goats. . . .
Shear thy hair.

Woman, thou art naked.
Thy naked hands rest on our open book;
Thy hands, the subtle ending of thy body,
Thy hands without a ring will touch mine by and
    by. . . .
Mutilate thy hands.

Woman, thou art naked.
Thy singing voice mounts from thy breast;
Thy voice, thy breath, the very warmth of thy flesh,
Spreads itself on my body and penetrates my flesh. . . .
Woman, tear out thy voice.

Jethro Bithell

FRANCIS JAMMES

1868–

Amsterdam

THE pointed houses lean so you would swear
That they were falling.   Tangled vessel masts
Like leafless branches lean against the sky
Amid a mass of green, and red, and rust,
Red herrings, sheepskins, coal along the quays.

Robinson Crusoe passed through Amsterdam,
(At least I think he did,) when he returned
From the green isle shaded with cocoa-trees.

What were the feelings of his heart before
These heavy knockers and these mighty doors ! . . .

Did he look through the window-panes and watch
The clerks who write in ledgers all day long ?
Did tears come in his eyes when he remembered
His parrot, and the heavy parasol
Which shaded him in the sad and clement isle ?

" Glory to thee, good Lord," he would exclaim,
Looking at chests with tulip-painted lids.
But, saddened by the joy of the return,
He must have mourned his kid left in the vines
Alone, and haply on the island dead.

I have imagined this before the shops
Which make you think of Jews who handle scales,
With bony fingers knotted with green rings.
See ! Amsterdam under a shroud of snow
Sleeps in a scent of fog and bitter coal.

Last night the white globes of the lighted inns,
Whence issue heavy women's whistled calls,
Were hanging down like fruits resembling gourds.
Posters blue, red, and green shone on their walls.
The bitter pricking of their sugared beer
Rasped on my tongue and gave my nose the itch.

And in the Jewry where detritus lies,
You smell the raw, cold reek of fresh-caught fish.
The slippery flags are strown with orange-peel.
Some swollen face would open staring eyes,
A wrangling arm moved onions to and fro.

Rebecca, from your little tables you
Were selling sticky sweets, a scanty show. . . .
The sky seemed pouring, like a filthy sea,
A tide of vapour into the canals.

Smoke that one does not see, commercial calm
Rose from the husked roofs and rich table-cloths,
And from the houses' comfort India breathed.

Fain had I been one of those merchant princes,
Who sailed in olden days from Amsterdam
To China, handing over their estate
And home affairs to trusty mandatories.
Like Robinson before a notary
I would have signed my pompous procuration.

Then honesty had piled from day to day
My riches more, and flowered them like a moon-beam
Upon my laden ships' imposing prows.
And in my house the nabobs of Bombay
Would have been tempted by my florid spouse.

The Mogul would have sent a gold-ringed negro
To traffic, with a smiling row of teeth,
Under his spreading parasol. And he
Would have enchanted with his savage tales
My eldest girl, to whom he would have given
A robe of rubies cut by cunning slaves.

I should have had my family portrayed
By some poor wretch whose paintings lived and breathed:
My plump and sumptuous wife with rosy face,
My sons, whose beauty would have charmed the town,
My daughters, with their pure and different grace.

And so to-day, instead of being myself,
I should have been another, visiting
A pompous mansion of old Amsterdam,
Launching my soul before the plain devise,
Under a gable: Here lived Francis Jammes.

Jethro Bithell

Prayer to go to Paradise with the Asses

O GOD, when You send for me, let it be
Upon some festal day of dusty roads.
I wish, as I did ever here below
By any road that pleases me, to go
To Paradise, where stars shine all day long.
Taking my stick out on the great highway,
To my dear friends the asses I shall say:
I am Francis Jammes going to Paradise,
For there is no hell where the Lord God dwells.
Come with me, my sweet friends of azure skies,
You poor, dear beasts who whisk off with your ears
Mosquitoes, peevish blows, and buzzing bees. . . .

Let me appear before You with these beasts,
Whom I so love because they bow their head
Sweetly, and halting join their little feet
So gently that it makes you pity them.
Let me come followed by their million ears,
By those that carried panniers on their flanks,
And those that dragged the cars of acrobats,
Those that had battered cans upon their backs,
She-asses limping, full as leather-bottles,
And those too that they breech because of blue
And oozing wounds round which the stubborn flies
Gather in swarms.   God, let me come to You
With all these asses into Paradise.
Let angels lead us where your rivers soothe
Their tufted banks, and cherries tremble, smooth
As is the laughing flesh of tender maids.
And let me, where Your perfect peace pervades,
Be like Your asses, bending down above
The heavenly waters through eternity,

To mirror their sweet, humble poverty
In the clear waters of eternal love.

Jethro Bithell

Love

LASS, when they talk of love, laugh in their face.
They find not love who seek it far and wide.
Man is a cold, hard brute. Your timid grace
Will leave his coarse desires unsatisfied.

He only lies. And he will leave you lone
Upon your hearth with children to look after,
And you will feel so old when he reels home,
To fill the morning hours with obscene laughter.

Do not believe there is any love for the winning.
But go to the garden where the blue skies pour,
And watch, at the greenest rose-tree's dusky core,
The silver spider living alone, and spinning.

Jethro Bithell

The Child Reads an Almanac

THE child reads on; her basket of eggs stands by.
She sees the weather signs, the Saints with awe,
And watches the fair houses of the sky:
The *Goat*, the *Bull*, the *Ram*, et cetera.

And so the little peasant maiden knows
That in the constellations we behold,
Are markets like the one to which she goes
Where goats and bulls and rams are bought and sold.

She reads about the market in the sky.
She turns a page and sees the *Scales* and then
Says that in Heaven, as at the grocery,
They weigh salt, coffee, and the souls of men.

Ludwig Lewisohn

PAUL FORT

1872–

Pan and the Cherries

I RECOGNIZED him by his skips and hops,
And by his hair I knew that he was Pan.
Through sunny avenues he ran,
And leapt for cherries to the red tree-tops.
Upon his fleece were pearling water drops
Like little silver stars.   How pure he was !

And this was when my spring was arched with blue.

Now, seeing a cherry of a smoother gloss,
He seized it, and bit the kernel from the pulp.
I watched him with great joy. . . . I came anigh. . . .

He spat the kernel straight into my eye.
I ran to kill Pan with my knife !
He stretched his arm out, swirled—
And the whole earth whirled !

Let us adore Pan, god of the world !

Jethro Bithell

Ballade

THE pretty maid she died, she died, in love-bed as
she lay;
They took her to the churchyard, all at the break of
day;
They laid her all alone there, all in her white array;
They laid her all alone there, a-coffined in the clay;
And they came back so merrily, all at the dawn of
day;
A-singing, all so merrily, " *The dog must have his
day !* "

The pretty maid is dead, is dead, in love-bed as she
  lay;
And they went off a-field to work, as they do every
  day.

Frederick York Powell

PAUL VALÉRY

1872–

Narcissus

PERHAPS you expected a face that was free from tears,
You calms, you always decked with leaves and flowers,
And haunted depths of the incorruptible,
O nymphs ! . . . . But yielding to the enchanted slopes
That were my irretrievable roadway to you,
Permit this fair reflection of man's disorder.
Happy your blended forms, you deep and level
  waters !
I am alone . . . if the gods, the waves, and the echoes
And so many sighs allow ! I am alone !
But still I am he who comes unto himself
When he comes near the banks this growth adorns.

On the peaks the light has halted its pure plunder,
The voice of the fountains turns to talk of dusk,
Calm concord hearkens, wherein I hear hope.
I hear the night grass grow in the holy shadows,
And the perfidious moon now elevates her mirror
Even to the secrets of the dying pool.

And I ! My body cast upon these reeds,
I languish, Sapphire, in my mournful beauty !
I must henceforth adore the magic waters
Where I have forgotten the olden smile and the rose.
Let me bewail your pure and fatal glory,
Fountain so softly closed around by me,

Where my eyes draw forth from the lethal azure
Those same dark eyes of their astounded soul !
What loss within oneself so calm a place affords !
The soul, even unto destruction, seeks a god
Demanding of the wave, the lonely wave
That gleams inviting soft advent of swan. . . .
Never have thirsty flocks bemired these waters !
Others who have wandered here have found repose,
And in the dark earth a clear, opening tomb;
But it is not calm, alas ! that I shall find,
When the opaque delight where the splendour sleeps
Yields to my body the horror of widening leafage
And, driving back the shade and the frightening thick-
ness,
I see ! I fall ! and come from this tyrant body
Peacefully to share the eternal charms !

There, nude between the arms that spring from the
forest,
A tender gleam of daylight doubtfully plays;
And there the glimmer of day becomes a bridegroom,
Pure in the pale place where the sad water lures me,
Delightful spirit, desirable and cold !
I behold in the water my flesh of moon and the dawn-
dew,
Obedient form opposed to my desires !
There are the pure stirrings of my silver arms !
My lingering hands in the adorable gold grow weary
Of seeking the captive whom the leaves entwine,
And I cry to echo the names of the hidden gods !

But how fair his mouth in that mute blasphemy !
O likeness ! . . . . Yet more perfect than myself,
Immortal ephemeron, clear before my eyes,
Pale limbs of pearl and softly silken hair,
Must the shadow darken us who scarce have loved,

Must the night already part us, O Narcissus,
And press between us the blade that halves a fruit !

What is it ?
My plaint is baneful ? . . .
The mere stir
Of the breath I set upon your lips, my double,
Has coursed a tremor on your limpid wave ! . . .
You tremble ! But these words I, kneeling, breathe
Are still no more than a hesitant soul between us,
Between that clear brow and my spent memory. . . .
I am so near you I can drink you in,
O countenance ! . . . My thirst is a naked slave. . . .
Till this rapt hour I did not know myself,
Nor how to cherish, how attain my soul ! . . .
But watching you, dear slave, obey the least
Of the shadows sadly retreating in my heart,
And on my brow a secret fire and storm,
Watching, O marvel ! watching my murmurous mouth
Betray . . . snare on the water a flower of fancy,
And mad events that sparkle in the eye !
I have found a treasure of impotence and pride !
May no sweet virgin whom the satyr stalks,
None ! swift in flight, deft in unfeeling fall,
No nymph, no maiden, ever lure me on
As you within the waters, my illimitable soul !

Joseph T. Shipley

Helen, the Sad Queen

AZURE, I come ! from the caves of death withdrawn
To hear the waves break rhythmic on the shores,
To see swift galleys clear, across the dawn,
Lifting from darkness on the blades of golden oars.

My lonely hands now summon forth the kings
Whose salt-grey beards amuse my chaste fingers. . . .

I wept. . . . And each his gloomy triumph sings
And behind the stern of his bark the furrow lingers.

I hear sonorous conches and clarion calls
Marking the lift of the oars and their even falls.
The clear chant of the undulant oarsmen charms
The tumult; and the gods ! heroic at the prow,
With their olden smile and the spray hurled at their
    brow,
Stretch toward me their indulgent, graven arms.
                                   Joseph T. Shipley

CHARLES GUÉRIN
                                           1873–1907
Partings

O TRAGIC hours when lovers leave each other !
Then every mistress feels herself a mother,
And, making of her lap a chair of ease,
Cradles us in the hollow of her knees,
And turns aside her brimful, dreaming eyes,
And with brief voice to our vain vows replies,
And hums a tune, and whispers, and at whiles
Smooths with slow, gliding hand our hair, and smiles
As laughs a babe to angels over him.
In her strange eyes her heart's dark sorrows swim;
Convulsively her arms strain us to her;
She moans and trembles, and, with sudden stir,
Presses her lips upon our eyes, and bids
Silence, and drinks our soul through closed eye-lids.
                                   Jethro Bithell

CHARLES VILDRAC

1882–

After Midnight

IT is at morning twilight they expire;
Death takes in hand, when midnight sounds,
Millions of bodies in their beds,
And scarcely anybody thinks of it. . . .

O men and women, you
About to die at break of day,
I see your hands' uneasy multitude,
Which now the blood deserts for ever !

White people in the throes of death,
Wrestling in all the world to night,
And whom the weeping dawn will silence,
Fearful I hear your gasping breath !

How many of you there are dying !
How can so many other folks be lying
Asleep upon the shore of your death rattles !

. . . Here is noise in the house;
I am not the only one who hears you:
Someone has stepped about a room,
Someone has risen to watch over you.

But no !   It is a little song I hear.
If someone stepped about a room,
It was to go and rock a little child
Who has been born this evening in the house.

                                        Jethro Bithell

JULES ROMAINS

1885–

Another Spirit Advances

WHAT is it so transforms the boulevard?
The lure of the passers-by is not of the flesh;
There are no movements; there are flowing rhythms
And I have no need of eyes to see them there.
The air I breathe is fresh with spirit-savour.
Men are ideas that a mind sends forth.
From them to me all flows, yet is internal;
Cheek to cheek we lie across the distance,
Space in communion binds us in one thought.

Joseph T. Shipley

GERMAN

FROM THE MINNESINGERS

*IT is a bright, animated, eventful age which we find reflected in the
literature of the Minnesingers; not trivial, for the stern premonition
of coming struggle is felt; frank, artless, and natural; original, because
reaped on fresh fields, by fresh hands; and with a direct impress of Nature,
which we find for the first time in any literature.*—BAYARD TAYLOR.

DIETMAR VON AIST

12th century

Parting at Morning

(Slâfest, dû mîn friedel)

"DEAR love, dost thou sleep fairly?
Alas, there wakes us early
A pretty bird that flew but now
And perched aloft upon the linden-bough."
  "Full softly I was sleeping,
Child, till I heard thee weeping.
Sweet must have its sorrow still;
But all thou bid'st me, sweetheart, I'll fulfil."
  The lady fell a-moaning:
"Thou'lt ride and leave me lonely.
And when wilt thou come back to me?
Alas, thou takest all my joy with thee!"

Frank C. Nicholson

A Bird was singing

A BIRD was singing on the linden tree,
Filling the fields with music by the wood;
My heart was lifted, and did long to be
In the old hollow where the rose-bush stood:
Its wilding blossoms I again could see,
Many and fragrant clustered on the briar,

As are my thoughts of her I most admire.
"It seems indeed a thousand years ago,
Since in the arms of my dear love I lay;
And not for any fault of mine I know
He has been strange to me this many a day;
But since I heed not if birds sing or no,
And since the flowers for me have had no sheen,
Short has my pleasure, long my sorrow been."

Jethro Bithell

A Lady Stood

A LADY stood on the turret-stone
Looking away o'er the moorlands lone,
If that her love were riding there.
She saw a falcon in the air:
"O happy falcon flying free,
Flying where thy heart would be!
In all the wood one single tree
Thou choosest to be dear to thee.
And so chose I.
My eyes have singled out a knight;
Now other ladies in their spite
Are envious, and spy.
Why will they plot against my happiness?
I grudge them not the men their arms caress."

Jethro Bithell

HEINRICH VON RUGGE

12th century

He that loves a Rosy Cheek

ASK not overmuch for fair
Form and face: let women be
Good: beauty is but a snare:
Gladly woo, if good is she.

After the strewn leaves of roses
Richer the rich mind uncloses.
Boorish is he, and unwise,
Who judges women by the eyes.

Jethro Bithell

REINMAR VON HAGENAU

12th century

As on the Heather

I HAVE marked, as on the heather now I strayed,
Fresh-springing sweetly-fashioned violets,
And bolder flowers in flaunting red arrayed;
And this is why the nightingale forgets
The stubborn woe that all the winter long
Weighed on her heart the cheerless trees among.
I have heard her song.

My heart's heaviness, soon as the burgeons burst,
Like to a carried burden I laid by:
For the lady for whose love I was athirst
Filled such a chalice for my lips that I,
Revived, the lightsome mood of nature share;
And all that she shall do to me I swear
Is good and fair.

She sundered sorrow from my soul that smiles
Like these pure skies whence all the clouds are flown;
Yet not a thousand women with their wiles
Could have achieved it: my true love alone
Routed the cares that surged by day and night:
So I have chosen her my life's delight
In the world's despite.

My portion shall be rapture without end:
I wot I have no need to nurse alarms;
And, if it come to pass as I intend,
She yet shall lie in secret in my arms.

I shall, when my embraces hold her fast,
Believe that I to Paradise have passed.
If dreams would last !

There are among our friends who love me not
That in my happy face my joy I show:
Their venomed glances are as arrows shot
Beyond the mark: I heed not friend nor foe.
What profit all the pitfalls they devise ?
That love is ripening while they surmise
Escapes their eyes !

Jethro Bithell

A Childish Game

LONG as I can call to mind,
Never was so much of ill.
In the world you shall not find
One who does attain his will.
So it was, and is, alas !
Grief did ever hearts harass.
Joy and sorrow both shall pass.

He whose passion is misprized
Vainly suffers agony.
Where's the gain, to be despised ?—
Only sorrow's usury.
That is all that I have got.
She I loved so well hath not
Deigned assuage my cruel lot.

"Constancy is lovers' aid."—
This is but a juggler's tale.
Since on her my eyes first strayed,
Never did my service fail.
From that service I depart.—
No, I cannot rend my heart.—
Love, a childish game thou art !

Jethro Bithell

HARTMANN VON AUE

12th century

None is Happy

NONE is happy, free from care
In this world, an't be not he
Who in love has ne'er a share,
And who shuns in love to be.
Troubled not with sighs his breath—
Sighs of yearning that to death
Bring full many who have earned,
But receive not, love's caress.
He by passion is not burned,
Such as that which I confess
Is my furnace of distress.

Jethro Bithell

WALTHER VON DER VOGELWEIDE

13th century

There is a Lady

THERE is a lady conquering with glances:
Happy the hour she was to me revealed !
A hard-embattled legion of my fancies
Against her sent, were forced and fain to yield.
And sure I know that ransom there is none.
Her excellence and beauty have done this,
And her red, laughing mouth that were so sweet to kiss.

And so my soul and senses serve and crave her,
Who is so sweet, and pure, and excellent;
And, lest I die of longing for her favour,
I dare to hope that she may yet relent,
And grant the greatest guerdon e'er I won.
Her excellence and beauty have done this,
And her red, laughing mouth that were so sweet to kiss.

Jethro Bithell

Awake!

AWAKE! The day is coming now
That brings the sweat of anguish to the brow
Of Christians, Jews, and Pagans all!
Many a token in the sky
And on the earth shows it is nigh:
Foretold in Holy Writ withal.
The sun no longer shows
His face; and treason sows
His secret seeds that no man can detect;
Fathers by their children are undone;
The brother would the brother cheat;
And the cowled monk is a deceit,
Who should the way to Heaven direct;
Might is right, and justice there is none.
Arise! we slept, nor of the peril recked.

Jethro Bithell

With a Rod no Man Alive

WITH a rod no man alive
Goodness in a child can drive:
Whom you may to honour bring
As a blow a word will sting.
As a blow a word will sting
Whom you may to honour bring:
Goodness in a child can drive
With a rod no man alive.

Have a good care of your tongue,
Guarded speech beseems the young;
Shoot the bolt the door behind,
Lock within the words unkind.
Lock within the words unkind,
Shoot the bolt the door behind;

Guarded speech beseems the young,
Have a good care of your tongue.
 Have a good care of your eyes,
They were never meant for spies:
Noble manners let them mind,
Be they to ignoble blind.
Be they to ignoble blind,
Noble manners let them mind:
They were never meant for spies,
Have a good care of your eyes.
 Have a good care of your ears,
Foolish is who all things hears:
Evil speech if they admit,
You will be defiled by it.
You will be defiled by it,
Evil speech if they admit;
Foolish is who all things hears,
Have a good care of your ears.
 Have good care of all the three,
They are often all too free:
Tongue and eyes and ears are bent
On delight and devilment.
On delight and devilment
Tongue and eyes and ears are bent:
They are often all too free,
Have good care of all the three.

Jethro Bithell

WOLFRAM VON ESCHENBACH

13th century

His Own True Wife

HIDDEN lovers' woes
 Thou wast wont to sing ere dawn arose:
 Bitter parting after raptured meetings.
 Whosoever love and lady's greeting
 So received that he was torn

From her breast my fear of men,
Thou wouldst sing him counsel, when
Shone the star of morn.
Warder, sing it now no more, lay by thy bugle-horn !
    He to whom is given
Not to be from love by morning riven—
Whom the watchers think not to beleaguer,
Hath no need to be alert and eager
To avert the peril rife
In the day: his rest is pure,
Nor a warder makes secure
His unhappy life.
Love so sweet bestows in all men's sight his own true
    wife !

Jethro Bithell

NEIDHART VON REUENTAL
13th century

On the Mountain

ON the mountain, in the valley,
Singing birds again do rally;
Now is seen
Clover green;
Winter, take away thy teen !
    Trees that erst were grey to view
Now their verdant robes renew;
In their shade
Nests are made;
Thence the toll of May is paid.
    Fought an aged wife for breath
Day and night, and baffled death;
Now she rushes
Like a ram about, and pushes
All the young ones into the bushes.

Jethro Bithell

ULRICH VON LIECHTENSTEIN

13th century

Love, Whose Month was Ever May

WHEN with May the air is sweet,
When the forest fair is clad,
All that have a love to meet
Pair in pleasure, lass and lad.
Merrily arm in arm they go,
For the time will have it so.
    Love and love, when linked together,
Love goes with to keep them gay:
All the three, this sunshine weather,
They are making holiday.
Sorrow cannot come between
Hearts where Love and May are seen.
    Where to love sweet love is plighted,
Constant and with all the soul,
And the pair are so united
That their love is sound and whole:
God shall make them man and wife
For the bliss of all their life.
    He that finds a constant heart,
Constant love, and constant mind,
All his sorrows shall depart.
Love, when constant, is so kind
That it makes a constant breast
Evermore content and blest.
    Could I find affection true,
So sincere should be mine own:
We should conquer, being two,
Care I cannot kill alone.
Constant love is all my care:
Love inconstant I forbear.

Jethro Bithell

REINMAR VON ZWETER

13th century

I Came A-riding

I CAME a-riding in a far countrie
On a blue goose, and strange things I did see.
There was a crow and hawk that in a brook
Fished many a swine; a falcon by a bear
Was hunted in the upper realms of air;
Midges were playing chess; and I did look
Upon a stag that span the fine silk thread;
A wolf was shepherd of the lambs that fed
In the willow tops; a cock caught in a trap
Three giants; and a coney trained a hound;
A crab raced with a dove and won a pound.
If this is true, an ass can sew a cap.

Jethro Bithell

ANONYMOUS

13th century

Truelove

TRUELOVE, come O come to me,
I am waiting here for thee:
I am waiting here for thee,
Truelove, come O come to me !
Sweetest mouth red as the rose,
Come and heal me of my woes:
Come and heal me of my woes,
Sweetest mouth red as the rose.

Jethro Bithell

ANONYMOUS

14th century ?

Serenade

COME now, and let us wake them: time
It is that they arise !
But gently to the window climb,
Where love with love together sleeping lies.

I heard a gently flowing river:
Methought it was the Rhine.
And at her window, with his quiver,
Stood Cupid shooting at a love of mine.

I brake three lilies from their stem,
And in at the window threw:
Sleeping or waking, cherish them;
And rise, sweet love, and let me in to you.

" How would it be, were I asleep,
And could not let you in ?
For I am lying now so deep
My truelove's arms within."

If you do in your love's arms lie,
Deep in the arms of love,
And if your love should not be I:
On me have mercy God in Heaven above !

And he who made this little song,
And set it to the tune,
He thought it over well and long,
And sang it for " Good-night " beneath the moon.

Jethro Bithell

ANONYMOUS

16th century

Westphalian Song

WHEN thou to my true love com'st
Greet her from me kindly;
When she asks thee how I fare?
Say, folks in Heaven fare finely.

When she asks, " What ! Is he sick ? "
Say, dead !—and when for sorrow
She begins to sob and cry,
Say, I come to morrow.

Samuel Taylor Coleridge

ANONYMOUS

16th century

A Lovely Rose is Sprung

A LOVELY rose is sprung
Out of a tender root,
As men of old have sung,
From Jesse's stem a shoot.
And so a flower bright
Has bloomed in coldest winter
E'en in the deepest night.

The little rose I mean
Whereof Isaiah told,
Pure Mary, maid serene,
Brought forth alone—behold:
Through God's eternal might
A little child she bore us
E'en in the deepest night.

Margarete Münsterberg

MARTIN LUTHER

1483–1546

A Mighty Fortress is our God

A MIGHTY fortress is our God,
A bulwark never failing,
Our helper He, amid the flood
Of mortal ill prevailing;
For still our ancient foe
Doth seek to work us woe,
His craft and power are great,
And armed with cruel hate,
On earth is not his equal.

Did we in our strength confide,
Our striving would be losing,
Were not the right man on our side,
The man of God's own choosing.
Dost ask who that may be?
Christ Jesus, it is he,
Lord Sabaoth his name,
From age to age the same,
And he must win the battle.

And though this world, with devils filled,
Should threaten to undo us,
We will not fear, for God hath willed
His truth to triumph through us.
The Prince of Darkness grim,
We tremble not at him,
His rage we can endure,
For lo! his doom is sure,
One little word shall fell him.

That word above all earthly powers—
No thanks for them—abideth;
The spirit and the gift is ours,
Through him who with us sideth.

Let goods and kindred go,
This mortal life also;
The body they may kill,
God's truth abideth still,
· His kingdom is for ever.

F. H. Hedge

JOHANN GOTTFRIED VON HERDER
1744–1803

Sir Olaf

SIR OLAF he rideth west and east
To bid the folk to his bridal feast.

On the wold are dancing an elvish band,
And Erl-king's daughter proffers her hand.

" Now welcome, Sir Olaf: what haste's with thee ?
Step into our circle and dance with me."

" To dance I neither will nor may,
To-morrow's dawn is my bridal-day."

" Nay, stay, Sir Olaf, and dance with me,
And golden spurs will I give to thee."

" To dance I neither will nor may,
To-morrow's dawn is my bridal-day."

" Nay, stay, Sir Olaf, and dance with me,
A heap of gold will I give to thee."

" For all thy gold I will not stay,
And dance I neither will nor may."

" If thou wilt not dance, Sir Olaf, with me,
Then Pest and Sickness shall follow thee."

She touched Sir Olaf upon the heart—
Ne'er in his life had he felt such smart.

She lifted him up on his steed that tide,
" Ride home ! ride fast to thy troth-plight bride ! "

And when he came to his castle-door,
His mother stood there, and trembled sore.

" Now say, sweet son, right speedilie
Why art thou wan, and white of blee ? "

"Well may my face be wan and white.
I was in Erl-king's realm last night."

" Now tell me, my son so true and tried,
What thing shall I say to thy plighted bride ? "

" Say that I hunt in the good greenwood,
With hound and horse as a good knight should."

When scarce the dawn in heaven shone red,
Came the train with the bride Sir Olaf should wed.

They sat at meat, they sat at wine;
" Now where is Sir Olaf, bridegroom of mine ? "

" Sir Olaf rode out to the greenwood free,
With horse and hound to the hunt rode he."

The bride she lifted a cloth of red:
Beneath, Sir Olaf was lying dead.

Elizabeth Craigmyle

Esthonian Bridal Song

DECK thyself, maiden,
  With the hood of thy mother;
Put on the ribands
Which thy mother once wore:
On thy head the band of duty,
On thy forehead the band of care.
Sit in the seat of thy mother,
And walk in thy mother's footsteps.

And weep not, weep not, maiden:
If thou weepest in thy bridal attire,
Thou wilt weep all thy life.

W. Taylor

LUDWIG HEINRICH CHRISTOPH HÖLTY

1748–76

Harvest Song

Sickles sound;
On the ground
Fast the ripe ears fall;
Every maiden's bonnet
Has blue blossoms on it;
Joy is over all.

Sickles ring,
Maidens sing
To the sickle's sound;
Till the moon is beaming,
And the stubble gleaming,
Harvest songs go round.

All are springing,
All are singing,
Every lisping thing.
Man and master meet;
From one dish they eat;
Each is now a king.

Hans and Michael
Whet the sickle,
Piping merrily.
Now they mow; each maiden
Soon with sheaves is laden,
Busy as a bee.

Now the blisses,
And the kisses !
Now the wit doth flow
Till the beer is out;
Then, with song and shout,
Home they go, yo ho !

Charles T. Brooks

JOHANN WOLFGANG VON GOETHE

1749–1832

PERENNIAL, *as a possession for ever, Goethe's History and Writings abide there ; a thousand-voiced " Melody of Wisdom" which he that has ears may hear.*—THOMAS CARLYLE.

The Erl-King

O WHO rides by night thro' the woodland so wild ?
It is the fond father embracing his child;
And close the boy nestles within his loved arm,
To hold himself fast, and to keep himself warm.

" O father, see yonder ! see yonder ! " he says;
" My boy, upon what dost thou fearfully gaze ? "
" O, 'tis the Erl-King with his crown and his
     shroud."
" No, my son, it is but a dark wreath of the cloud."

THE ERL-KING SPEAKS

" O come and go with me, thou loveliest child;
By many a gay sport shall thy time be beguiled;
My mother keeps for thee full many a fair toy,
And many a fine flower shall she pluck for my boy."

" O father, my father, and did you not hear
The Erl-King whisper so low in my ear ? "
" Be still, my heart's darling—my child, be at ease;
It was but the wild blast as it sung thro' the trees."

ERL-KING

" O wilt thou go with me, thou loveliest boy ?
My daughter shall tend thee with care and with joy;
She shall bear thee so lightly thro' wet and thro' wild,
And press thee, and kiss thee, and sing to my child."

" O father, my father, and saw you not plain
The Erl-King's pale daughter glide past thro' the rain ? "
" O yes, my loved treasure, I knew it full soon;
It was the grey willow that danced to the moon."

ERL-KING

" O come and go with me, no longer delay,
Or else, silly child, I will drag thee away."
" O father ! O father ! now, now, keep your hold,
The Erl-King has seized me—his grasp is so cold ! "

Sore trembled the father; he spurr'd thro' the wild,
Clasping close to his bosom his shuddering child;
He reaches his dwelling in doubt and in dread,
But, clasp'd to his bosom, the infant was dead.

Sir Walter Scott

Wanderer's Night-songs

I

THOU that from the heavens art,
Every pain and sorrow stillest,
And the doubly wretched heart
Doubly with refreshment fillest,
I am weary with contending !
Why this rapture and unrest ?
Peace descending
Come, ah, come into my breast !

2

O'er all the hill-tops
Is quiet now,
In all the tree-tops
Hearest thou
Hardly a breath;
The birds are asleep in the trees:
Wait ; soon like these
Thou too shalt rest.

H. W. Longfellow

The Lay of the Captive Count

THE COUNT

I KNOW a Flower of beauty rare,
    And long with sweetest anguish
To go and cull this Flower so fair;
    But here in thrall I languish.
All day I murmur, " Woe is me ! "
For, while as yet my steps were free,
This lovely flower was in my power.

From these blank walls I gaze in vain
    To find my cherished Flower;
The dell is lost, and dim the plain,
    So lofty is this tower !
But, be he knave, or be he knight,
Who brings me here my heart's delight,
I'll call him nearest friend and dearest.

THE ROSE

Behold ! a Flower divinely bright
    Below thy trellis bloweth;
Thou surely meanest me, Sir Knight,
    The Rose that richly gloweth:

A princely mind is thine, I ween,
The flower of flowers, the garden-queen,
Methinks must blossom on thy bosom.

THE COUNT

O Rose ! we prize thy damask dyes
    Through leafy darkness peering:
As precious thou in maiden's eyes
    As pearl, or gold, or ear-ring.
Thou deckest well her braided hair;
Yet art not thou the wonder fair
Whereon I ponder, ever fonder.

THE LILY

The flaunting Rose is proud of port,
    And proud are they who seek her,
But modest minds will fainer court
    A coyer flower and meeker.
The soft in soul, the pure in heart,
Methinks will choose the better part,
And love with stilly love the Lily.

THE COUNT

I hold myself unstained and chaste,
    And free from darker failings;
Yet here, a captive wretch, I waste
    My heart in bitter wailings !
Meet emblem of the Undefiled
Art thou, a spotless flower and mild,
But mine is rarer, dearer, fairer.

THE PINK

That rarer, fairer flower am I,
    I bud and bloom so gayly
Here in mine arbour, tended by
    The heedful warden daily;

With clustering petals breathing out
Voluptuous perfume round‿about,
And thousand glowing colours showing.

THE COUNT

The brilliant Pink let no man slight,—
   The gardener's minion‿floweret,
Now must it bask in garish light,
   Now shadow must embower it;
But such will never heal my woe;
Mine is a meek‿eyed flower, and, though
Serene and tender, hath no splendour.

THE VIOLET

Uneyed and hidden here I bloom,
   Wrapped in communings lonely;
Yet will I now, Sir Knight, presume
   To speak, though this time only.
If I, the Violet, be thy flower,
It grieves me that I want the power
To lightly clamber tow'rds thy chamber.

THE COUNT

I love the vestal Violet,
   Her odour and her colour,
But even for her can ne'er forget
   My lonely doom of dolour.
Hear, friends, my mournful riddle right:
In vain all round this rocky height
I cast mine eye for what I sigh for.

But far beneath, by streams and groves,
   Her bosom overladen
With sorrow for my thraldom, roves
   Earth's truest‿hearted maiden.

And when she weeps my dreary lot,
And plucks the blue Forget-Me-Not,
It wakes Affection's recollections.

For love like hers hath mystic might,
   Which breathes through sundering distance;
And feeds, even in my dungeon's night,
   My lamp of pale existence.
And, when my heart would break, this thought
Steals over it, Forget-Me-Not !
And I inherit Strength and Spirit.

James Clarence Mangan

The Minstrel

" WHAT voice, what harp. are those we hear
   Beyond the gate in chorus ?
Go, page !—the lay delights our ear,
   We'll have it sung before us ! "
So speaks the king: the stripling flies—
He soon returns; his master cries—
   " Bring in the hoary minstrel ! "

" Hail, princes mine !   Hail, noble knights !
   All hail, enchanting dames !
What starry heaven !   What blinding lights !
   Whose tongue may tell their names ?
In this bright hall, amid this blaze,
Close, close, mine eyes !   Ye may not gaze
   On such stupendous glories ! "

The Minnesinger closed his eyes;
   He struck his mighty lyre:
Then beauteous bosoms heaved with sighs,
   And warriors felt on fire;
The king, enraptured by the strain,
Commanded that a golden chain
   Be given the bard in guerdon.

" Not so !   Reserve thy chain, thy gold,
    For those brave knights whose glances,
Fierce flashing through the battle bold,
    Might shiver sharpest lances !
Bestow it on thy Treasurer there—
The golden burden let him bear
    With other glittering burdens.

" I sing as in the greenwood bush
    The cageless wild,bird carols—
The tones that from the full heart gush
    Themselves are gold and laurels !
Yet, might I ask, then thus I ask,
Let one bright cup of wine in flask
    Of glowing gold be brought me ! "

They set it down: he quaffs it all—
    " O ! draught of richest flavour !
O ! thrice divinely happy hall,
    Where that is scarce a favour !
If Heaven shall bless ye, think on me,
And thank your GOD as I thank ye
    For this delicious wine,cup ! "

James Clarence Mangan

The Rose

ONCE a boy beheld a bright
    Rose in dingle growing;
Far, far off it pleased his sight;
Near he viewed it with delight:
    Soft it seemed and glowing.
Lo ! the rose, the rose so bright,
    Rose so brightly blowing !

Spake the boy, " I'll pluck thee, grand
    Rose all wildly blowing."
Spake the rose, " I'll wound thy hand,

Thus the scheme thy wit hath planned
  Deftly overthrowing."
O ! the rose, the rose so grand,
  Rose so grandly glowing.

But the stripling plucked the red
  Rose in glory growing,
And the thorn his flesh hath bled,
And the rose's pride is fled,
  And her beauty's going.
Woe ! the rose, the rose once red,
  Rose once redly glowing.

James Clarence Mangan

The King of Thulé

OH ! true was his heart while he breathèd,
  That King over Thulé of old,
So she that adored him bequeathèd
  Him, dying, a beaker of gold.

At banquet and supper for years has
  He brimmingly filled it up,
His eyes overflowing with tears as
  He drank from that beaker-cup.

When Death came to wither his pleasures
  He parcelled his cities wide,
His castle, his lands, and his treasures,
  But the beaker he laid aside.

They drank the red wine from the chalice,
  His barons and marshals brave;
The monarch sat in his rock-palace
  Above the white foam of the wave.

And now, growing weaker and weaker,
  He quaffed his last Welcome to Death,
And hurled the golden beaker
  Down into the flood beneath.

He saw it winking and sinking,
 And drinking the foam so hoar;
The light from his eyes was shrinking,
 Nor drop did he ever drink more.

James Clarence Mangan

A Voice from the Invisible World

HIGH o'er his mouldering castle walls
 The warrior's phantom glides,
And loudly to the skiff it calls
 That on the billow rides—

"Behold! these arms once vaunted might,
 This heart beat wild and bold—
Behold! these ducal veins ran bright
 With wine-red blood of old.

"The noon in storm, the eve in rest,
 So sped my life's brief day.
What then? *Young bark on Ocean's breast,
 Cleave thou thy destined way!*"

James Clarence Mangan

An Irish Lamentation

O! RAISE the woeful *Pillalu*,
 And let your tears in streams be shed;
Och, orro, orro, ollalu!
 The Master's eldest hope is dead!

Ere broke the morning dim and pale
 The owlet flapped his heavy wing:
We heard the winds at evening wail,
 And now our dirge of death we sing,
 Och, orro, orro, ollalu!

Why wouldst thou go ? How couldst thou die ?
  Why hast thou left thy parents dear ?
Thy friends, thy kindred far and nigh,
  Whose cries, *mo vrone !* thou dost not hear ?
    Och, orro, orro, ollalu !

Thy mother, too !—how could she part
  From thee, her darling fair and sweet,
The heart that throbbed within her heart,
  The pulse, the blood that bade it beat ?
    Och, orro, orro, ollalu !

Oh ! lost to her and all thy race,
  Thou sleepest in the House of Death;
She sees no more thy cherub face,
  She drinks no more thy violet breath;
    Och, orro, orro, ollalu !

By strand and road, by field and fen,
  The sorrowing clans come thronging all;
From camp and dun, from hill and glen,
  They crowd around the castle wall.
    Och, orro, orro, ollalu !

From East and West, from South and North,
  To join the funeral train they hie;
And now the mourners issue forth,
  And far they spread the keening cry,
    Och, orro, orro, ollalu !

Then raise the woeful *Pillalu,*
  And let your tears in streams be shed,
Och, orro, orro, ollalu !
  The Chieftain's pride, his heir, is dead.
                    James Clarence Mangan

Prometheus

BLACKEN thy heavens, Jove,
With thunder-clouds,
And exercise thee, like a boy
Who thistles crops,
With smiting oaks and mountain-tops !
Yet must leave me standing
My own firm Earth;
Must leave my cottage, which thou didst not build,
And my warm hearth,
Whose cheerful glow
Thou enviest me.

I know naught more pitiful
Under the sun than you, Gods !
Ye nourish scantily,
With altar-taxes
And with cold lip-service,
This your majesty;—
Would perish, were not
Children and beggars
Credulous fools.

When I was a child,
And knew not whence or whither,
I would turn my wildered eye
To the sun, as if up yonder were
An ear to hear to my complaining,—
A heart, like mine,
On the oppressed to feel compassion.

Who helped me,
When I braved the Titans' insolence ?
Who rescued me from death,
From slavery ?
Hast thou not all thyself accomplished,

Holy-glowing heart ?
And, glowing young and good,
Most ignorantly thanked
The slumberer above there ?

I honour thee ?   For what ?
Hast thou the miseries lightened
Of the down-trodden ?
Hast thou the tears ever banished
From the afflicted ?
Have I not to manhood been moulded
By omnipotent Time,
And by Fate everlasting,—
My lords and thine ?

Dreamedst thou ever
I should grow weary of living,
And fly to the desert,
Since not all our
Pretty dream-buds ripen ?
Here sit I, fashion men
In mine own image,—
A race to be like me,
To weep and to suffer,
To be happy and to enjoy themselves,—
All careless of *thee* too,
As I !

John S. Dwight

To the Parted One

AND thou art now no longer near !
   From me, O fairest, thou hast flown !
Nor rings in my accustomed ear
   A single word—a single tone.

As when, at morn, the wanderer's eye
  Pierces the air in vain to see
Where, hidden in the deep-blue sky,
  High up the lark goes singing free,—

So wanders anxiously my gaze
  Piercing the field, the bush, the grove;
On thee still call my frequent lays:
  O, come to me again, dear love.

Christopher Pearse Cranch

To a Golden Heart, worn Round his Neck

REMEMBRANCER of joys long passed away,
  Relic, from which as yet I cannot part,
  O, hast thou power to lengthen love's short day?
    Stronger thy chain than that which bound the
      heart?
Lili, I fly!—yet still thy fetters press me
  In distant valley, or far lonely wood.
Still with a struggling sigh of pain confess thee
  The mistress of my soul in every mood.

The bird may burst the silken chain that bound him,
  Flying to the green home, which fits him best;
But, ah! he bears the prisoner's badge around him,
  Still by the piece about his neck distressed.
He ne'er can breathe his free wild notes again;
They're stifled by the pressure of his chain.

Margaret Fuller Ossoli

The Shepherd's Lament

UP yonder on the mountain
  A thousand times I stand,
Leant on my crook, and gazing
  Down on the valley-land.

I follow the flock to the pasture;
  My little dog watches them still.
I have come below, but I know not
  How I descended the hill.

The beautiful meadow is covered
  With blossoms of every hue;
I pluck them, alas! without knowing
  Whom I shall give them to.

I seek, in the rain and the tempest,
  A refuge under the tree:
Yonder the doors are fastened,
  And all is a dream to me.

Right over the roof of the dwelling
  I see a rainbow stand;
But she has departed for ever,
  And gone far out in the land.

Far out in the land, and farther,—
  Perhaps to an alien shore:
Go forward, ye sheep! go forward,—
  The heart of the shepherd is sore.

Bayard Taylor

From Faust

Prologue in Heaven

Raphael

THE sun makes music as of old
  Amid the rival spheres of Heaven,
On its predestined circle rolled
  With thunder speed: the Angels even
Draw strength from gazing on its glance,
  Though none its meaning fathom may;
The world's unwithered countenance
  Is bright as at creation's day.

GABRIEL

And swift and swift, with rapid lightness,
    The adorned Earth spins silently,
Alternating Elysian brightness
    With deep and dreadful night, the sea
Foams in broad billows from the deep
    Up to the rocks, and rocks and ocean,
Onward, with spheres which never sleep,
    Are hurried in eternal motion.

MICHAEL

And tempests in contention roar
    From land to sea, from sea to land;
And, raging, weave a chain of power,
    Which girds the earth, as with a band.
A flashing desolation there
    Flames before the thunder's way;
But Thy servants, Lord, revere
    The gentle changes of Thy day.

CHORUS OF THE THREE

The Angels draw strength from Thy glance,
    Though no one comprehend Thee may;
Thy world's unwithered countenance
    Is bright as on creation's day.

                    Percy Bysshe Shelley

SOLDIER'S SONG

CASTLES with lofty
        Ramparts and towers,—
    Maidens disdainful
        In Beauty's array,—
        All shall be ours !
    Bold is the venture,
        Splendid the pay !

Lads, let the trumpets
 For us be suing,
Calling to pleasure,
 Calling to ruin !
Stormy our life is;
 Such is its boon:
Maidens and castles
 Capitulate soon.
Bold is the venture,
 Splendid the pay !
And the soldiers go marching,
 Marching away.

Bayard Taylor

The Thought Eternal

WHETHER day my spirit's yearning
Unto far, blue hills has led,
Or the night lit all the burning
Constellations at my head—
Hours of light or hours nocturnal
Do I praise our mortal fate:
If man think the thought eternal
He is ever fair and great.

Ludwig Lewisohn

FRIEDRICH VON SCHILLER

1759–1805

Thekla's Song
From The Piccolomini

THE cloud doth gather, the green wood roar,
The damsel paces along the shore;
 The billows they tumble with might, with might;
 And she flings out her voice to the darksome night;
 Her bosom is swelling with sorrow;

The world it is empty, the heart will die,
There's nothing to wish for beneath the sky:
Thou Holy One, call Thy child away !
I've lived and loved, and that was to-day—
  Make ready my grave-clothes to-morrow.

Samuel Taylor Coleridge

The Maid of Orleans

AT thee *the Mocker* sneers in cold derision,
  Through thee he seeks to desecrate and dim
Glory for which he hath no soul or vision,
  For " God " and " Angel " are but sounds with
    him.
He makes the jewels of the heart his booty,
And scoffs at Man's Belief and Woman's Beauty.

Yet thou—a lowly shepherdess !—descended
  Not from a kingly but a godly race,
Art crowned by Poësy ! Amid the splendid
  Of Heaven's high stars she builds thy dwelling-
    place,
Garlands thy temples with a wreath of glory,
And swathes thy memory in eternal Story.

The Base of this weak world exult at seeing
  The Fair defaced, the Lofty in the dust;
Yet grieve not ! There are godlike hearts in being
  Which worship still the Beautiful and Just.
Let Momus and his mummers please the crowd,
Of nobleness alone a noble mind is proud.

James Clarence Mangan

The Unrealities

AND dost thou faithlessly abandon me ?
  Must thy chameleon phantasies depart ?
Thy griefs, thy gladnesses, take wing and flee
  The bower they builded in this lonely heart ?

O, Summer of Existence, golden, glowing !
　　Can naught avail to curb thine onward motion ?
In vain !　The river of my years is flowing,
　　And soon shall mingle with the eternal ocean.

Extinguished in dead darkness lies the sun
　　That lighted up my shrivelled world of wonder;
Those fairy bands Imagination spun
　　Around my heart have long been rent asunder.
Gone, gone for ever is the fine belief,
　　The all-too-generous trust in the Ideal:
All my Divinities have died of grief,
　　And left me welded to the Rude and Real.

As clasped the enthusiastic Prince of old
　　The lovely statue, stricken by its charms,
Until the marble, late so dead and cold,
　　Glowed into throbbing life beneath his arms,
So fondly round enchanting Nature's form,
　　I too entwined my passionate arms, till, pressed
In my embraces, she began to warm
　　And breathe and revel in my bounding breast.

And, sympathizing with my virgin bliss,
　　The speechless things of Earth received a tongue;
They gave me back Affection's burning kiss,
　　And loved the Melody my bosom sung:
Then sparkled hues of Life on tree and flower,
　　Sweet music from the silver fountain flowed;
All soulless images in that brief hour
　　The Echo of my Life divinely glowed !

How struggled all my feelings to extend
　　Themselves afar beyond their prisoning bounds !
O, how I longed to enter Life and blend
　　Me with its words and deeds, its shapes and sounds.

This human theatre, how fair it beamed
  While yet the curtain hung before the scene !
Uprolled, how little then the arena seemed !
  That little how contemptible and mean !

How roamed, imparadised in blest illusion,
  With soul to which the upsoaring Hope lent pinions,
And heart as yet unchilled by Care's intrusion,
  How roamed the stripling-lord through his dominions !
Then Fancy bore him to the palest star
  Pinnacled in the lofty æther dim:
Was naught so elevated, naught so far,
  But thither the Enchantress guided him !

With what rich reveries his brain was rife !
  What adversary might withstand him long ?
How glanced and danced before the Car of Life
  The visions of his thought, a dazzling throng !
For there was FORTUNE with her golden crown,
  There flitted LOVE with heart-bewitching boon,
There glittered starry-diademed RENOWN,
  And TRUTH, with radiance like the sun of noon !

But ah ! ere half the journey yet was over,
  That gorgeous escort wended separate ways ;
All faithlessly forsook the pilgrim-rover,
  And one by one evanished from his gaze.
Away inconstant-handed FORTUNE flew;
  And, while the thirst of Knowledge burned alway,
The dreary mists of Doubt arose and threw
  Their shadow over TRUTH's resplendent ray.

I saw the sacred garland-crown of FAME
  Around the common brow its glory shed:
The rapid Summer died, the Autumn came,
  And LOVE, with all his necromancies, fled,

And ever lonelier and silenter
  Grew the dark images of Life's poor dream,
Till scarcely o'er the dusky scenery there
  The lamp of HOPE itself could cast a gleam.

And now, of all, Who, in my day of dolour,
  Alone survives to clasp my willing hand?
Who stands beside me still, my best consoler,
  And lights my pathway to the Phantom-strand?
Thou, FRIENDSHIP! stancher of our wounds and sorrows,
  From whom this lifelong pilgrimage of pain
A balsam for its worst afflictions borrows;
  Thou whom I early sought, nor sought in vain!

And thou whose labours by her light are wrought,
  Soother and soberer of the spirit's fever,
Who, shaping all things, ne'er destroyest aught,
  Calm OCCUPATION! thou that weariest never!
Whose efforts rear at last the mighty Mount
  Of Life, though merely grain on grain they lay,
And, slowly toiling, from the vast Account
  Of Time strike minutes, days, and years away.

James Clarence Mangan

To My Friends

BELOVÈD friends! More glorious times than ours
Of old existed: men of loftier powers
    Than we can boast have flourished:—who shall
      doubt it?
A million stones dug from the depths of Earth
Will bear this witness for the ancient worth,
    If History's chronicles be mute about it.
        But, all are gone—those richly-gifted souls—
          That constellation of illustrious names:
        For Us, for Us, the current moment rolls,
          And We, We live, and have our claims.

My friends ! The wanderer tells us—and we own—
That Earth shows many a more luxuriant zone
  Than that whereunder we sedately live;
But, if denied a paradise, our hearts
Are still the home of science and the arts,
  And glow and gladden in the light they give;
    And if beneath our skies the laurel pines,
      And winter desolates our myrtle boughs,
    The curling tendrils of our joyous vines
      Shed freshest greenness round our brows.

May burn more feverish life, more maddening pleasures,
Where four assembled worlds exchange their treasures,
  At London, in the world's Commercial Hall;
A thousand stately vessels come and go,
And costly sights are there, and pomp and show,
  And Gold is lord and idolgod of all !
    But will the sun be mirrored in the stream
      Sullied and darkened by the flooding rains ?
    No ! On the still smooth lake alone his beam
      Is brightly imaged, and remains.

The beggar at St. Angelo's might gaze
With scorn upon our North, for he surveys
  The one, lone, only, everliving Rome—
All shapes of beauty fascinate his eye;
He sees a brilliant heaven below the sky
  Shine in Saint Peter's wonderwaking dome.
    But, even while beaming with celestial glory,
      Rome is the grave of long-departed years;
    It is the green young plant and not the hoary
      And time-worn trunk that blooms and cheers.

Prouder achievements may perchance appear
Elsewhere than signalize our humble sphere,
  But newer nowhere underneath the sun.
We see in pettier outlines on our stage,

Which miniatures the world of every age,
   The storied feats of bypassed eras done.
      All things are but redone, reshown, retold,
         Fancy alone is ever young and new;
      Man and the universe shall both grow old,
         But not the forms her pencil drew !

James Clarence Mangan

JOHANN GAUDENZ VON SALIS
1762–1834

Song of the Silent Land

INTO the Silent Land !
   Ah ! who shall lead us thither ?
Clouds in the evening sky more darkly gather,
   And shattered wrecks lie thicker on the strand.
      Who leads us with a gentle hand
         Thither, O, thither,
         Into the Silent Land ?

      Into the Silent Land !
      To you, ye boundless regions
Of all perfection !   Tender morning-visions
   Of beauteous souls !   The Future's pledge and band !
      Who in Life's battle firm doth stand
         Shall bear Hope's tender blossoms
         Into the Silent Land !

         O Land !   O Land !
      For all the broken-hearted
The mildest herald by our fate allotted
   Beckons, and with inverted torch doth stand
      To lead us with a gentle hand
      Into the land of the great departed,
         Into the Silent Land !

H. W. Longfellow

SIEGFRIED AUGUST MAHLMANN

1771–1826

Allah

ALLAH gives light in darkness,
Allah gives rest in pain,
Cheeks that are white with weeping
Allah paints red again.

The flowers and the blossoms wither,
Years vanish with flying feet;
But my heart will live on for ever,
That here in sadness beat.

Gladly to Allah's dwelling
Yonder would I take flight;
There will the darkness vanish,
There will my eyes have sight.

H. W. Longfellow

JOHANN LUDWIG TIECK

1773–1853

Autumn Song

A LITTLE bird flew through the dell,
And where the failing sunbeams fell
He warbled thus his wondrous lay,
" Adieu ! adieu ! I go away:
Far, far,
Must I voyage ere the twilight star ! "

It pierced me through, the song he sang,
With many a sweet and bitter pang:
For wounding joy, delicious pain,
My bosom swelled and sank again.
Heart ! heart !
Is it drunk with bliss or woe thou art ?

Then, when I saw the drifted leaves,
I said, "Already Autumn grieves!
To sunnier skies the swallow hies:
So Love departs and Longing flies,
Far, far,
Where the Radiant and the Beauteous are."

But soon the Sun shone out anew,
And back the little flutterer flew:
He saw my grief, he saw my tears,
And sang, "Love knows no Winter years!
No! no!
While it lives its breath is Summer's glow!"

James Clarence Mangan

JUSTINUS KERNER

1786–1862

Home-sickness

THERE calleth me ever a marvellous Horn,
  "Come away! Come away!"
Is it earthly music faring astray,
  Or is it air-born?
Oh, whether it be a spirit-wile
  Or a forest voice,
It biddeth mine ailing heart rejoice,
  Yet sorrow the while!

In the greenwood glades—o'er the garlanded bowl—
  Night, Noontide, and Morn,
The summoning call of that marvellous Horn
  Tones home to my soul!
In vain have I sought for it east and west,
  But I darkly feel
That so soon as its music shall cease to peal
  I go to my rest!

James Clarence Mangan

LUDWIG UHLAND

1787–1862

Spirits Everywhere

A MANY a summer is dead and buried
Since over this flood I last was ferried;
And then, as now, the Noon lay bright
On strand, and water, and castled height.

Beside me then in this bark sat nearest
Two companions the best and dearest;
One was a gentle and thoughtful sire,
The other a youth with a soul of fire.

One, outworn by Care and Illness,
Sought the grave of the Just in stillness;
The other's shroud was the bloody rain
And thunder‹smoke of the battle plain.

Yet still, when Memory's necromancy
Robes the Past in the hues of Fancy,
Medreameth I hear and see the Twain
With talk and smiles at my side again !

Even the grave is a bond of union;
Spirit and spirit best hold communion !
Seen through Faith, by the Inward Eye,
It is *after* Life they are truly nigh !

Then, ferryman, take this coin, I pray thee,
Thrice thy fare I cheerfully pay thee;
For, though thou seest them not, there stand
Anear me Two from the Phantomland !

                    James Clarence Mangan

Ichabod! the Glory has Departed

I RIDE through a dark, dark Land by night,
Where moon is none and no stars lend light,
   And rueful winds are blowing,
Yet oft have I trodden this way ere now,
With summer zephyrs a׳fanning my brow,
   And the gold of the sunshine glowing.

I roam by a gloomy Garden׳wall;
The deathstricken leaves around me fall;
   And the night׳blast wails its dolours;
How oft with my love I have hitherward strayed
When the roses flowered, and all I surveyed
   Was radiant with Hope's own colours!

But the gold of the sunshine is shed and gone,
And the once bright roses are dead and wan,
   And my love in her low grave moulders,
And I ride through a dark, dark Land by night
With never a star to bless me with light,
   And the Mantle of Age on my shoulders.

James Clarence Mangan

Durand of Blonden

TOW'RDS the lofty walls of Balbi, lo! Durand of
   Blonden hies;
   Thousand songs are in his bosom; Love and Pleasure
     light his eyes.
   There, he dreams, his own true maiden, beauteous
     as the evening׳star,
   Leaning o'er her turret׳lattice, waits to hear her
     knight's guitar.

In the linden-shaded courtyard soon Durand begins his
lay.
But his eyes glance vainly upwards; there they meet no
answering ray.
Flowers are blooming in the lattice, rich of odour, fair to
see.
But the fairest flower of any, Lady Blanca, where is she?

Ah! while yet he chants the ditty, draws a mourner near
and speaks—
" She is dead, is dead for ever, whom Durand of Blonden
seeks!"
And the knight replies not, breathes not: darkness
gathers round his brain:
He is dead, is dead for ever, and the mourners weep the
twain.

In the darkened castle-chapel burn a many tapers bright:
There the lifeless maiden lies, with whitest wreaths and
ribands dight.
There . . . But lo! a mighty marvel! She hath oped her
eyes of blue!
All are lost in joy and wonder! Lady Blanca lives anew!

Dreams and visions flit before her, as she asks of those
anear,
" Heard I not my lover singing?—Is Durand of Blonden
here?"
Yes, O Lady, thou hast heard him; he has died for thy
dear sake!
He could wake his trancèd mistress: him shall none for
ever wake!

He is in a realm of glory, but as yet he weets not where;
He but seeks the Lady Blanca: dwells she not already
there?

Till he finds her must he wander to and fro, as one
    bereaven,
Ever calling, "Blanca! Blanca!" through the desert
    halls of Heaven.

James Clarence Mangan

The Luck of Edenhall

OF Edenhall the youthful lord
    Bids sound the festal trumpet's call;
He rises at the banquet board,
    And cries, 'mid the drunken revellers all,
    " Now bring me the Luck of Edenhall ! "

The butler hears the words with pain,—
    The house's oldest seneschal,—
Takes slow from its silken cloth again
    The drinking-glass of crystal tall;
    They call it *The Luck of Edenhall.*

Then said the lord, " This glass to praise,
    Fill with red wine from Portugal ! "
The greybeard with trembling hand obeys;
    A purple light shines over all;
    It beams from the Luck of Edenhall.

Then speaks the lord, and waves it light,—
    " This glass of flashing crystal tall
Gave to my sires the Fountain-Sprite;
    She wrote in it, *If this glass doth fall,*
    Farewell then, O Luck of Edenhall !

" 'Twas right a goblet the fate should be
    Of the joyous race of Edenhall !
We drink deep draughts right willingly;
    And willingly ring, with merry call,
    Kling ! klang ! to the Luck of Edenhall ! "

First rings it deep, and full, and mild,
  Like to the song of a nightingale;
Then like the roar of a torrent wild;
  Then mutters, at last, like the thunder's fall,
  The glorious Luck of Edenhall.

" For its keeper, takes a race of might
  The fragile goblet of crystal tall;
It has lasted longer than is right;
  Kling ! klang !—with a harder blow than all
  Will I try the Luck of Edenhall ! "

As the goblet, ringing, flies apart,
  Suddenly cracks the vaulted hall;
And through the rift the flames upstart;
  The guests in dust are scattered all
  With the breaking Luck of Edenhall !

In storms the foe, with fire and sword !
  He in the night had scaled the wall;
Slain by the sword lies the youthful lord,
  But holds in his hand the crystal tall,
  The shattered Luck of Edenhall.

On the morrow the butler gropes alone,
  The greybeard, in the desert hall;
He seeks his lord's burnt skeleton;
  He seeks in the dismal ruin's fall
  The shards of the Luck of Edenhall.

" The stone wall," saith he, " doth fall aside;
  Down must the stately columns fall;
Glass is this earth's Luck and Pride;
  In atoms shall fall this earthly ball,
  One day, like the Luck of Edenhall ! "

                              H. W. Longfellow

The Castle by the Sea

"HAST thou seen that lordly castle,
  That castle by the sea?
Golden and red above it
  The clouds float gorgeously.

"And fain it would stoop downward
  To the mirrored wave below;
And fain it would soar upward
  In the evening's crimson glow."

"Well have I seen that castle,
  That castle by the sea,
And the moon above it standing,
  And the mist rise solemnly."

"The winds and the waves of ocean,
  Had they a merry chime?
Didst thou hear, from those lofty chambers,
  The harp and the minstrel's rhyme?"

"The winds and the waves of ocean,
  They rested quietly;
But I heard on the gale a sound of wail,
  And tears came to mine eye."

"And sawest thou on the turrets
  The king and his royal bride,
And the wave of their crimson mantles,
  And the golden crown of pride?

"Led they not forth, in rapture,
  A beauteous maiden there,
Resplendent as the morning sun,
  Beaming with golden hair?"

"Well saw I the ancient parents,
   Without the crown of pride;
They were moving slow, in weeds of woe;
   No maiden was by their side!"

H. W. Longfellow

In a Lovely Garden Walking

IN a lovely garden walking
   Two lovers went hand in hand;
Two wan, worn figures, talking
   They sat in the flowery land.

On the cheek they kissed one another,
   On the mouth with sweet refrain;
Fast held they each the other,
   And were young and well again.

Two little bells rang shrilly—
   The dream went with the hour:
She lay in the cloister stilly,
   He far in the dungeon-tower!

George MacDonald

A Leaf

A LEAF falls softly at my feet,
   Sated with rain and summer heat;
What time this leaf was green and new,
I still had parents dear and true.

A leaf—how soon it fades away!
Child of the spring, the autumn's prey,
Yet has this leaf outlived, I see,
So much that was most dear to me.

John S. Dwight

The Hostess's Daughter

THREE fellows were marching over the Rhine,
They stopped where they saw the hostess's sign.

" Dear Hostess, have you good beer and wine ?
Where have you your daughter so fair and fine ? "

" My beer is good, my wine is clear,
My daughter is lying upon the bier."

Now into the chamber she led the way,
There in a black coffin the maiden lay.

The first man drew the veil aside,
And full of sorrow the maid espied.

" Ah, beautiful maiden, if thou couldst live !
To thee alone my love I would give ! "

The second laid back the veil again,
And turned away and wept in pain.

" Oh, why must thou lie upon the bier !
Alas, I have loved thee for many a year."

The third man lifted again the veil,
And kissed her upon the lips so pale:

" I loved thee always, I love thee to day,
And I will love thee for ever, and ay."

Margarete Münsterberg

FRIEDRICH RUECKERT

1789–1866

The Ride Round the Parapet

SHE said, " I was not born to mope at home in loneli‚
ness,"—
>> The Lady Eleanora von Alleyne.
She said, " I was not born to mope at home in loneli‚
ness ;
When the heart is throbbing sorest there is balsam in
the forest,
>> There is balsam in the forest for its pain,"
>>> Said the Lady Eleanora,
>>> Said the Lady Eleanora von Alleyne.

She doffed her silks and pearls, and donned instead
her hunting‚gear,
>> The Lady Eleanora von Alleyne.
She doffed her silks and pearls, and donned instead
her hunting‚gear,
And, till summer‚time was over, as a huntress and a
rover
>> Did she couch upon the mountain and the
plain,
>>> She, the Lady Eleanora.
>> Noble Lady Eleanora von Alleyne.

Returning home again, she viewed with scorn the
tournaments—
>> The Lady Eleanora von Alleyne.
Returning home again, she viewed with scorn the
tournaments;
She saw the morions cloven and the crowning chaplets
woven,
>> And the sight awakened only the disdain
>>> Of the Lady Eleanora,
>> Of the Lady Eleanora von Alleyne.

" My feeling towards Man is one of utter scornfulness,"
  Said Lady Eleanora von Alleyne.
" My feeling towards Man is one of utter scornfulness,
And he that would o'ercome it, let him ride around the
    summit
      Of my battlemented Castle by the Maine,"
        Said the Lady Eleanora,
      Said the Lady Eleanora von Alleyne.

So came a knight anon to ride around the parapet,
  For Lady Eleanora von Alleyne.
So came a knight anon to ride around the parapet,
Man and horse were hurled together o'er the crags that
    beetled nether.
        Said the Lady, " There, I fancy, they'll re-
        main ! "
        Said the Lady Eleanora,
      Queenly Lady Eleanora von Alleyne !

Then came another knight to ride around the parapet,
  For Lady Eleanora von Alleyne.
Then came another knight to ride around the parapet,
Man and horse fell down, asunder, o'er the crags that
    beetled under.
        Said the Lady, " They'll not leap the leap
        again ! "
        Said the Lady Eleanora,
      Lovely Lady Eleanora von Alleyne !

Came other knights anon to ride around the parapet,
  For Lady Eleanora von Alleyne.
Came other knights anon to ride around the parapet,
Till six and thirty corses of both mangled men and
    horses
        Had been sacrificed as victims at the fane
          Of the Lady Eleanora,
        Stately Lady Eleanora von Alleyne !

That woeful year was by, and Ritter none came after⸗
    wards
      To Lady Eleanora von Alleyne.
That woeful year was by, and Ritter none came after⸗
    wards;
The Castle's lonely basscourt looked a wild o'ergrown⸗
    with⸗grass court.
      'Twas abandoned by the Ritters and their train
        To the Lady Eleanora,
      Haughty Lady Eleanora von Alleyne !

She clomb the silent wall, she gazed around her sovran⸗
    like,
      The Lady Eleanora von Alleyne !
She clomb the silent wall, she gazed around her sovran⸗
    like;
" And wherefore have departed all the Brave, the lion⸗
    hearted,
      Who have left me here to play the Castellain ? "
      Said the Lady Eleanora,
      Said the Lady Eleanora von Alleyne.

" And is it fled for ay, the palmy time of Chivalry ? "
      Cried Lady Eleanora von Alleyne.
" And is it fled for ay, the palmy time of Chivalry ?
Shame light upon the cravens ! May their corpses gorge
    the ravens,
      Since they tremble thus to wear a woman's
      chain ! "
      Said the Lady Eleanora,
      Said the Lady Eleanora von Alleyne.

The story reached at Gratz the gallant Margrave Gondi⸗
    bert
      Of Lady Eleanora von Alleyne.
The story reached at Gratz the gallant Margrave Gondi⸗
    bert.

Quoth he, " I trow the woman must be more or less than
 human;
   She is worth a little peaceable campaign,
    Is the Lady Eleanora,
    Is the Lady Eleanora von Alleyne ! "

He trained a horse to pace round narrow stones laid
 merlonwise,
   For Lady Eleanora von Alleyne.
He trained a horse to pace round narrow stones laid
 merlonwise,
" Good Grey ! do thou thy duty, and this rocky-bosomed
 beauty
   Shall be taught that all the vauntings are in
   vain
    Of the Lady Eleanora,
    Of the Lady Eleanora von Alleyne ! "

He left his castle-halls, he came to Lady Eleanor's,
   The Lady Eleanora von Alleyne.
He left his castle-halls, he came to Lady Eleanor's.
" O, lady, best and fairest, here am I,—and, if thou
 carest,
   I will gallop round the parapet amain,
    Noble Lady Eleanora,
    Noble Lady Eleanora von Alleyne ! "

She saw him spring to horse, that gallant Margrave Gon-
 dibert,
   The Lady Eleanora von Alleyne.
She saw him spring to horse, that gallant Margrave Gon-
 dibert.
" O bitter, bitter sorrow ! I shall weep for this to-morrow !
 It were better that in battle he were slain,"
   Said the Lady Eleanora,
   Said the Lady Eleanora von Alleyne.

Then rode he round and round the battlemented parapet,
    For Lady Eleanora von Alleyne.
Then rode he round and round the battlemented parapet:
The Lady wept and trembled, and her paly face resembled,
      As she looked away, a lily wet with rain;
        Hapless Lady Eleanora !
    Hapless Lady Eleanora von Alleyne !

So rode he round and round the battlemented parapet,
    For Lady Eleanora von Alleyne !
So rode he round and round the battlemented parapet:
" Accurst be my ambition !   He but rideth to perdition,
    He but rideth to perdition without rein ! "
        Wept the Lady Eleanora,
      Wept the Lady Eleanora von Alleyne.

Yet rode he round and round the battlemented parapet,
    For Lady Eleanora von Alleyne.
Yet rode he round and round the battlemented parapet.
Meanwhile her terror shook her—yea, her breath well
    nigh forsook her.
      Fire was burning in the bosom and the brain
        Of the Lady Eleanora,
      Of the Lady Eleanora von Alleyne !

Then rode he round and off the battlemented parapet
    To Lady Eleanora von Alleyne.
Then rode he round and off the battlemented parapet.
" Now blest be GOD for ever !   This is marvellous !   I
    never
      Cherished hope of laying eyes on thee again,"
        Cried the Lady Eleanora,
      Joyous Lady Eleanora von Alleyne !

" The Man of Men thou art, for thou hast fairly conquered me,
      The Lady Eleanora von Alleyne !

The Man of Men thou art, for thou hast fairly con‑
    quered me.
I greet thee as my lover, and, ere many days be over,
      Thou shalt wed me and be Lord of my do‑
      main,"
        Said the Lady Eleanora,
        Said the Lady Eleanora von Alleyne.

Then bowed the graceful knight, the gallant Margrave
    Gondibert,
      To Lady Eleanora von Alleyne.
Then bowed the graceful knight, the gallant Margrave
    Gondibert,
And thus he answered coldly, " There be many who as
    boldly
      Will adventure an achievement they disdain,
      For the Lady Eleanora,
      For the Lady Eleanora von Alleyne.

" Mayest bide until they come, O stately Lady Eleanor !
      O, Lady Eleanora von Alleyne !
Mayest bide until they come, O stately Lady Eleanor !
And thou and they may marry, but, for me, I must not
    tarry,
      I have won a wife already out of Spain,
      Virgin Lady Eleanora,
      Virgin Lady Eleanora von Alleyne ! "

Thereon he rode away, the gallant Margrave Gondibert,
    From Lady Eleanora von Alleyne.
Thereon he rode away, the gallant Margrave Gondibert.
And long in shame and anguish did that haughty Lady
    languish,
      Did she languish without pity for her pain,
      She the Lady Eleanora,
      She the Lady Eleanora von Alleyne.

And year went after year, and still in barren maiden‑
hood
Lived Lady Eleanora von Alleyne.
And wrinkled Eld crept on, and still her lot was maiden‑
hood.
And, woe ! her end was tragic; she was changed, at
length, by magic,
To an ugly wooden image, they maintain;
She, the Lady Eleanora,
She, the Lady Eleanora von Alleyne !

And now, before the gate, in sight of all, transmogrified,
Stands Lady Eleanora von Alleyne.
Before her castle‑gate, in sight of all, transmogrified ;
And he that won't salute her must be fined in foaming
pewter,
If a boor—but, if a burgher, in champagne,
For the Lady Eleanora,
Wooden Lady Eleanora von Alleyne !

James Clarence Mangan

Barbarossa

THE ancient Barbarossa, the Kaiser Frederick old,
In subterranean castle ensorcelled state doth hold.

Dead was the Kaiser never. he lives in mystic sleep.
Long has he slumbered lonely in that enchanted
keep.

The glory of the Empire with him has passed away;
But Emperor and Empire shall have one wakening‑
day.

The throne is all of ivory where sits the Kaiser dread,
Of porphyry the table whereon he leans his head.

Like fire not flax the beard is, that thick and long has
    grown
Right through the propping table that is of marble
    stone.

He nods as if a-dreaming, half-closed his eye of fire.
After long space of silence he beckons to a squire.

To him in sleep he mutters, "Around the castle-hill
See if the ravens flutter, and soar in circles still.

"And if the ancient ravens still circle far and near,
So must I sleep enchanted another hundred year."

Elizabeth Craigmyle

WILHELM MÜLLER

1794–1827

Whither?

I HEARD a brooklet gushing
    From its rocky fountain near,
Down into the valley rushing,
    So fresh and wondrous clear.

I know not what came o'er me,
    Nor who the counsel gave:
But I must hasten downward,
    All with my pilgrim-stave;

Downward, and ever farther,
    And ever the brook beside;
And ever fresher murmured,
    And ever clearer, the tide.

Is this the way I was going?
    Whither, O brooklet, say!
Thou hast, with thy soft murmur,
    Murmured my senses away.

What do I say of a murmur ?
 That can no murmur be ;
'Tis the water-nymphs, that are singing
 Their roundelays under me.

Let them sing, my friend, let them murmur,
 And wander merrily near ;
The wheels of a mill are going
 In every brooklet clear.

H. W. Longfellow

HEINRICH HEINE

1799–1856

*THE comfort of coming to a man of genius, who finds in verse his freest and most perfect expression, whose voyage over the deep of poetry destiny makes smooth ! The magic of Heine's poetical form is incomparable; he employs this form with the most exquisite lightness and ease, and yet it has at the same time the inborn fullness, pathos, and old-world charm of all true forms of popular poetry. Thus in Heine's poetry, too, one perpetually blends the impression of French modernism and clearness with that of German sentiment and fullness.—*MATTHEW ARNOLD.

Proem

OUT of my own great woe
 I make my little songs,
Which rustle their feathers in throngs
 And beat on her heart even so.

They found the way, for their part,
 Yet come again, and complain :
Complain, and are not fain
 To say what they saw in her heart.

Elizabeth Barrett Browning

Ad Finem

THE years they come and go,
  The races drop in the grave,
Yet never the love doth so
  Which here in my heart I have.

Could I see thee but once, one day,
  And sink down so on my knee,
And die in thy sight while I say,
  " Lady, I love but thee ! "

Elizabeth Barrett Browning

Mein Kind, wir waren Kinder

MY child, we were two children,
  Small, merry by childhood's law;
  We used to creep to the henhouse,
  And hide ourselves in the straw.

We crowed like cocks, and whenever
  The passers near us drew—
  " Cock·a·doodle ! " they thought
  'Twas a real cock that crew.

The boxes about our courtyard
  We carpeted to our mind,
  And lived there both together—
  Kept house in a noble kind.

The neighbour's old cat often
  Came to pay us a visit;
  (We have made the very same speeches
  Each with a compliment in it.)

After her health we asked,
  Our care and regard to evince—
  (We have made the very same speeches
  To many an old cat since).

We also sat and wisely
Discoursed, as old folks do,
Complaining how all went better
In those good old times we knew;—

How love, and truth, and believing
Had left the world to itself,
And how so dear was the coffee,
And how so rare was the pelf.

The children's games are over,
The rest is over with youth—
The world, the good games, the good times,
The belief, and the love, and the truth.

Elizabeth Barrett Browning

Ich weiss nicht was soll es bedeuten

I CANNA tell what has come ower me
  That I am sae eerie and wae;
An auld-warld tale comes before me,
  It haunts me by nicht and by day.

From the cool lift the gloamin' draps dimmer,
  And the Rhine slips saftly by;
The taps of the mountains shimmer
  I' the lowe o' the sunset sky.

Up there, in a glamour entrancin',
  Sits a maiden wondrous fair;
Her gowden adornments are glancing,
  She is kaimin' her gowden hair.

As she kaims it the gowd kaim glistens,
  The while she is singin' a song
That hauds the rapt soul that listens,
  With its melody sweet and strong.

The boy, floating by in vague wonder,
  Is seized with a wild weird love;
He sees na the black rocks under,—
  He sees but the vision above.

The waters their waves are flingin'
  Ower boatie and boatman anon;
And this, with her airtful singin',
  The Waterwitch Lurley hath done.

Alexander Macmillan

The Sea hath its Pearls

THE sea hath its pearls,
  The heaven hath its stars;
But my heart, my heart,
  My heart hath its love.

Great are the sea, and the heaven;
  Yet greater is my heart,
And fairer than pearls or stars
  Flashes and beams my love.

Thou little, youthful maiden,
  Come unto my great heart;
My heart, and the sea, and the heaven
  Are melting away with love!

H. W. Longfellow

Sag' mir wer einst die Uhren erfund

WHO was it, tell me, that first of men reckon'd
Time by the hour and the minute and second?
A soulless man, without heart or light,
He sat and he mused in the long winter's night,
And counted the pittering steps of the mouse,
And the pick of the woodworm that gnawed at the
  house.

Kisses, now tell me, who first did discover ?
It was the warm happy mouth of a lover:
He kiss'd without ceasing, he kiss'd without care,
He kiss'd his first kiss in the May-season fair;
The flowers from their emerald cradle upsprang,
The sun brightly beam'd, the birds sweetly sang.

Richard Garnett

Warum sind denn die Rosen so blass

O DEAREST, canst thou tell me why
 The rose should be so pale ?
And why the azure violet
 Should wither in the vale ?

And why the lark should in the cloud
 So sorrowfully sing ?
And why from loveliest balsam-buds
 A scent of death should spring ?

And why the sun upon the mead
 So chillingly should frown ?
And why the earth should, like a grave,
 Be mouldering and brown ?

And why it is that I myself
 So languishing should be ?
And why it is, my heart of hearts,
 That thou forsakest me ?

Richard Garnett

Es fällt ein Stern herunter

SEE yonder, where a gem of night
Falls helpless from its heavenly height !
It is the brilliant star of Love
That thus forsakes the realms above.

And one by one the wind bereaves
The apple-tree of silvery leaves;
The breezes, in their reckless play,
Spurn them with dancing feet away.

And round and round swims on the pool
The tuneful swan so beautiful,
And ever singing sweet and slow
He sinks into his grave below.

It is so dreary and so dread !
The leaf is wholly witherèd,
The fallen star has flamed away,
The swan has sung his dying lay.

Richard Garnett

Mir träumte von einem Königskind

IT was a mighty monarch's child,
Her cheek was pale, her eye was wild;
Beneath a linden's shade I press'd
The maiden to my panting breast.

" I will not have thy father's throne,
I will not have his golden crown,
I will not have his realm so wide,
I will have thee, and naught beside."

" That cannot be," the maiden said,
" Because I am already dead;
And but by night the sods above
I burst for thee, and thy dear love."

Richard Garnett

Die Rose, die Lilie, die Taube, die Sonne

THE rose and the lily, the moon and the dove,
  Once loved I them all with a perfect love.
I love them no longer, I love alone
  The Lovely, the Graceful, the Pure, the One
Who twines in one wreath all their beauty and love,
And rose is, and lily, and moon and dove.

Richard Garnett

Auf meiner Herzliebsten Äugelein

UPON my darling's beaming eyes
  I plied my rhyming trade;
Upon my darling's cherry lips
  An epigram I made;
My darling has a blooming cheek,
  I penn'd a song upon it;
And if she had but had a heart,
  Her heart had had a sonnet.

Richard Garnett

Mein Liebchen, wir sassen zusammen

MY darling, we sat together,
  We two, in our frail boat:
The night was calm o'er the wide sea
  Whereon we were afloat.

The Spectre-Island, the lovely,
  Lay dim in the moon's mild glance;
There sounded sweetest music,
  There waved the shadowy dance.

It sounded sweeter and sweeter,
  It waved there to and fro;
But we slid past forlornly
  Upon the great sea-flow.

James Thomson

Es stehen unbeweglich

FOR many thousand ages
  The steadfast stars above
Have gazed upon each other
  With ever mournful love.

They speak a certain language,
  So beautiful, so grand,
Which none of the philologians
  Could ever understand.

But I have learned it, learned it,
  For ever, by the grace
Of studying one grammar,
  My heart's own darling's face.

James Thomson

Die Lotosblume ängstigt

THE Lotus-flower doth languish
  Beneath the sun's fierce light;
With drooping head she waiteth
  All dreamily for night.

The Moon is her true lover,
  He wakes her with his glance:
To him she unveils gladly
  Her gentle countenance.

She blooms and glows and brightens,
    Intent on him above;
Exhaling, weeping, trembling
    With ever-yearning love.

James Thomson

Die Welt ist dumm, die Welt ist blind

THE world is dull, the world is blind,
    And daily grows more silly !
It says of you, my lovely child,
    You are not quite a lily.

The world is dull, the world is blind,
    And judges in stupid fashion;
It knows not how sweet your kisses are,
    And how they burn with passion.

James Thomson

Die blauen Veilchen der Äugelein

THE violets blue of the eyes divine,
And the rose of the cheeks as red as wine,
And the lilies white of the hands so fine,
They flourish and flourish from year to year,
And only the heart is withered and sere.

James Thomson

Ein Fichtenbaum steht einsam

A PINE-TREE standeth lonely
    In the North on an upland bare;
It standeth whitely shrouded
    With snow, and sleepeth there.

It dreameth of a Palm Tree
Which far in the East alone,
In mournful silence standeth
On its ridge of burning stone.

James Thomson

Mir träumte wieder der alte Traum

THE old dream comes again to me:
With May-night stars above,
We two sat under the linden-tree
And swore eternal love.

Again and again we plighted troth,
We chattered, and laughed, and kissed;
To make me well remember my oath
You gave me a bite in the wrist.

O darling with the eyes serene,
And with the teeth so white !
The vows were proper to the scene,
Superfluous was the bite.

James Thomson

Mein Herz, mein Herz ist traurig

MY heart, my heart is mournful,
Yet joyously shines the May;
I stand by the linden leaning,
High on the bastion grey.

The blue town-moat thereunder
Glides peacefully along;
A boy in a boat is angling,
And whistling a careless song.

Beyond, like a well-known picture,
    All small and fair, are strewed
Houses and gardens and people,
    Oxen and meadows and wood.'

The maidens bleach the linen,
    And dance in the grass for glee;
The mill-wheel scatters diamonds,
    Its far hum reaches me.

Upon the hoary tower
    A sentry-box stands low;
A youth in his coat of scarlet
    There passes to and fro.

He trifles with his musket,
    Which gleams in the sunshine red ;
He shoulders and presents it,—
    I would he shot me dead !

James Thomson

Der Mond ist aufgegangen

THE moon is fully risen,
    And shineth o'er the sea;
And I embrace my darling,
    Our hearts are swelling free.

In the arms of the lovely maiden
    I lie alone on the strand;—
" What sounds in the breezes sighing ?
    Why trembles your white hand ? "

" That is no breeze's sighing,
    That is the mermaiden's song,
The singing of my sisters
    Whom the sea hath drowned so long."

James Thomson

Sag', wo ist dein schönes Liebchen?

"SAY, where is the maiden sweet,
    Whom you once so sweetly sung,
When the flames of mighty heat
    Filled your heart and fired your tongue?"

Ah, those flames no longer burn,
    Cold and drear the heart that fed;
And this book is but the urn
    Of the ashes of love dead.

James Thomson

Wie langsam kriechet sie dahin

OLD Time is lame and halt,
    The snail can barely crawl:
But how should I find fault,
    Who cannot move at all?

No gleam of cheerful sun!
    No hope my life to save!
I have two rooms, the one
    I die in and the grave.

Maybe, I've long been dead;
    Maybe, a giddy train
Of phantoms fills my head,
    And haunts what was my brain.

These dear old gods or devils,
    Who see me stiff and dull,
May like to dance their revels
    In a dead Poet's skull.

Their rage of weird delight
Is luscious pain to me:
And my bony fingers write
What daylight must not see.

Lord Houghton

Enfant Perdu

IN Freedom's War, of " Thirty Years " and more,
A lonely outpost have I held—in vain !
With no triumphant hope or prize in store,
Without a thought to see my home again.

I watched both day and night: I could not sleep
Like my well-tented comrades far behind,
Though near enough to let their snoring keep
A friend awake, if e'er to doze inclined.

And thus, when solitude my spirits shook,
Or fear—for all but fools know fear sometimes,—
To rouse myself and them, I piped and took
A gay revenge in all my wanton rhymes.

Yes ! there I stood, my musket always ready,
And when some sneaking rascal showed his head,
My eye was vigilant, my aim was steady,
And gave his brains an extra dose of lead.

But war and justice have far different laws,
And worthless acts are often done right well;
The rascals' shots were better than their cause,
And I was hit—and hit again, and fell !

That outpost was abandoned: while the one
Lies in the dust, the rest in troops depart;
Unconquered—I have done what could be done,
With sword unbroken, and with broken heart.

Lord Houghton

Zu fragmentarisch ist Welt und Leben

THIS world and this life are so scattered, they try me,
　And so to a German professor I'll hie me.
He can well put all the fragments together
　Into a system convenient and terse;
While with his night-cap and dressing-robe tatters
　He'll stop up the chink of the wide Universe.

Charles G. Leland

Du bist wie eine Blume

E'EN as a lovely flower,
　So fair, so pure thou àrt;
　I gaze on thee, and sadness
　　Comes stealing o'er my heart.

My hands I fain had folded
　Upon thy soft brown hair,
Praying that God may keep thee
　So lovely, pure, and fair.

Kate Freiligrath Kroeker

The Message

UP, boy! arise, and saddle quick,
　And mount your swiftest steed,
　And to King Duncan's castle ride
　O'er bush and brake with speed.

There slip into the stable soft,
　Till one shall see you hide,
Then ask him: Which of Duncan's girls
　Is she that is a bride?

And if he say, The dark-haired one,
Then give your mare the spur;
But if he say, The fair-haired one,
You need not hurry here.

You only need, if that's the case,
Buy me a hempen cord,
Ride slowly back and give it me,
But never speak a word.

Kate Freiligrath Kroeker

To my Mother

I 'VE kept a haughty heart thro' grief and mirth,
And borne my head perchance a thought too high;
If even a king should look me in the eye
I would not bend it humbly to the earth:
Yet, dearest mother, such the gentle worth
Of thy benignant presence, angel-mild,
It ever hath my proudest moods beguiled,
And given to softer, humbler feelings birth.
Was it thy mind's calm penetrative power,
Thy purer mind, that secretly came o'er me,
And unto Heaven's clearer light upbore me;
Or did remembrance sting me in that hour,
With thought of words and deeds which pierced
    unkindly
That gentle heart, loving me still so blindly.

Matilda Dickson

Im Traum sah ich ein Männchen klein und putzig

I SAW in dream a dapper mannikin
That walked on stilts, each stride an ell or more;
White linen and a dainty dress he wore,
But it was coarse and smirched and stained within.

All inwardly was mean and poor and thin,
   Yet with a stately seeming lacquered o'er;
   His words were full of bluster, and he bore
Himself like one well used to fight and win.
"And know'st thou who he is ? Come, look and guess!"
So spake the God of Dreams, and showed me then
Within a glass a billowy multitude.
The mannikin before an altar stood,
My love beside him: both of them said, Yes !
And countless fiends laughed loud and cried
                           " Amen ! "
                    Sir Theodore Martin

Mädchen mit dem rothen Mündchen

LASSIE, with the lips sae rosy,
   With the eyne sae saft and bricht,
Dear wee lassie, I keep thinkin',
   Thinkin' on thee day and nicht.

Winter nichts are lang and eerie;
   Oh, gin I were with thee, dear,
Arms about thee, cracking couthly,
   With nae mortal by to hear !

With my kisses I would smother
   Thy white hand sae jimp and sma',
And my tears for very rapture
   On that wee white hand should fa'.
                    Sir Theodore Martin

Anno 1829

I CRAVE an ampler, worthier sphere;
   I'd liefer bleed at every vein
Than stifle 'mid these hucksters here,
   These lying slaves of paltry gain.

They eat, they drink; they're every whit
 As happy as their type, the mole;
Large are their bounties—as the slit
 Through which they drop the poor man's dole.

With pipe in mouth they go their way,
 With hands in pockets; they are blest
With grand digestions: only *they*
 Are such hard morsels to digest !

The hand that's red with some dark deed,
 Some giant crime, were white as wool
Compared with these sleek saints, whose creed
 Is paying all their debts in full.

Ye clouds that sail to far-off lands,
 O waft me to what clime ye will !
To Lapland's snows, to Lybia's sands,
 To the world's end—but onward still !

Take me, O clouds ! They ne'er look down;
 But (proof of a discerning mind)
One moment hung o'er Hamburg town,
 The next they leave it leagues behind.

      Charles Stuart Calverley

The Azra

DAILY walked the fair and lovely
 Sultan's daughter in the twilight,—
In the twilight by the fountain,
 Where the sparkling waters plash.

Daily stood the young slave silent
 In the twilight by the fountain,
Where the plashing waters sparkle,
 Paler and paler every day.

Once by twilight came the princess
Up to him with rapid question:
" I would know thy name, thy nation,
Whence thou comest, who thou art."

And the young slave said, " My name is
Mahomet, I come from Yemen.
I am of the sons of Azra,
Men who perish if they love."

John Hay

Dear Maiden

DEAR maiden, as each morning
   Thy house I saunter by,
    It glads me when at the window
    Thy winsome face I spy.

My face with a silent question
   Thy brown eyes gravely scan :
" Who art thou, and what ails thee,
   Thou strange sick-looking man ? "

I am a German Poet,
   In German land well known;
When the best names are spoken,
   They also speak my own.

And what ails me, dear maiden,
   Makes many a German groan;
When the worst woes are spoken,
   They also speak my own.

John Todhunter

I met by Chance

I MET by chance, as I travelled,
   My Darling's whole family,
Small sister, and father, and mother,
   And gladly they greeted me.

They asked how I was most kindly,
    And said, ere I told my tale:
I was not the least bit altered,
    Except that my face was pale.

I asked after aunts and cousins,
    And many a bore of mark,
And after the little puppy
    With his wheezy little bark.

Then after my married Sweetheart
    I asked with polite *sangfroid;*
They beamed on me with the answer
    That she was then in the straw.

With cordial congratulations
    I begged them, stammeringly,
To greet her with heartiest good wishes
    A thousand times from me.

Then out burst the little sister:
    " That small fat puppy of mine
Grew big, went mad, got so horrid,
    We drowned him in the Rhine."

The young one is like her sister,
    In laughing especially:
She has the self-same eyes too
    That wrought me such misery.

John Todhunter

I Wept as I Lay Dreaming

I WEPT as I lay dreaming,
    I dreamed thou wert laid in thy grave.
I woke, and my cheeks o'erstreaming,
    My tears flowed wave on wave.

I wept as I lay sleeping,
　I dreamed thou wert false to me.
I woke, and I was weeping,
　And long wept bitterly.

I wept as I lay dreaming,
　I dreamed thou wert mine again.
I woke, and my tears were streaming,
　And ever they stream in vain.

John Todhunter

I'm Black and Blue

I'M black and blue from their worrying,
　They've tortured me early and late,
Some with their love—God help me !
　The others with their hate.

They've poisoned the wine on my table,
　They've poisoned the bread on my plate,
Some with their love—God help me !
　The others with their hate.

But she who most has worried,
　And tortured and troubled—she
Has never either loved me,
　Or even hated me.

John Todhunter

We Cared for Each Other

WE cared for each other as boy and maid,
　Yet gave Mrs. Grundy no cause for huffing.
At " Man and Wife " we have often played,
　Yet never quarrelled or came to cuffing.
We have joked together, and shouted for glee,
And kissed and fondled most tenderly.

At last, through the woods in our childish sport
Playing hide-and-seek, like sister and brother,
We hid ourselves in such clever sort
That never again we could find each other.

John Todhunter

Farewell

THE linden blossomed, the nightingale sang,
  The sun laughed out with a kindly zest,
You kissed me, and round me your arms you flung,
  And clasped me close to your heaving breast.

Hoarse croaked the raven, the green leaves fell,
  The sun frowned greeting with sullen smile;
Then each of us frostily said: " Farewell ! "
  You dropped me a curtsy in courtliest style.

John Todhunter

Fresco-sonnets to Christian Sethe

I

I LAUGH at each dull bore, taste's parasite
  Who stares upon me with his goatish eyes;
  And those raw freshmen, lean as hungry flies,
  Who gape and sniff at me in petty spite.
I laugh, too, at those apes, whose learning trite
  Puffs them with pride to pose as critics wise;
  And at those dastard rogues, my enemies,
  'Gainst poisoned weapons daring me to fight.
Yet when Joy's nosegay of delightful things
  Is shattered for us by the hand of Fate,
  And at our feet flung withered, without scent,
And when the heart within the breast is rent,
  Rent, and stabbed through, sore-wounded, desper-
    ate—
  What's left us but the laugh that shrilly rings ?

2

Give me a mask, I'll join the masquerade,
   Playing the knave that charlatans I see,
   Flaunting in gaudy robes of dignity,
   May count me not a craftsman of their trade.
Come vulgar words and manners to my aid,
   In popular art I'll take my base degree,
   All those rare sparks of genius banned shall be,
   Wherewith stale rogues of late fine tricks have played.
And thus will I dance at the grand masked ball,
   'Mid German knights, monks, kings in motley crew,
   Capped to by Harlequin, known to but few,
With their blunt swords of lath cudgelled by all.
   That is their sport.   Should I unmask, beware !
   I should dumbfounder every jail-bird there.

John Todhunter

The Voyage

I STOOD and leant upon the mast
   And counted every wave.
Farewell, my beautiful Fatherland !
   Fast sails my bark so brave !

My fair Love's house, I passed it by,
   The window-panes were glaring;
I gazed my eyes out of my head,
   But none made sign of caring.

O tears, come not into mine eyes,
   Lest ye should dim their seeing !
My sick heart, break not in my breast
   With woe too vast for being !

John Todhunter

The Window=glance

PALE Heinrich he came sauntering by,
  Fair Hedwig leaned from her garret.
"God keep me safe!" she said with a sigh,
  "Yon lad looks pale as a spirit!"

The lad his languishing eyes from below
  Uplifted to Hedwig's garret.
They filled fair Hedwig's with lovers' woe,
  She too grew pale as a spirit.

Fair Hedwig, hurt with love's secret harms,
  Looked daily down from her garret.
But soon she lay nightly in Heinrich's arms,
  When wanders each churchyard spirit.

John Todhunter

When Two are Parted

WHEN two who love are parted,
  They talk, as friend to friend,
Clasp hands and weep a little,
  And sigh without an end.

We did not weep, my darling,
  Not sigh "Why must this be . . ."
The tears, the sighs, the anguish
  Came later—and to me.

Louis Untermeyer

I Love but Thee

WHENE'ER I look into your eyes
Then all my grief and sorrow flies;
And when I kiss your mouth, oh then
I am made well and strong again.

And when I lean upon your breast
My soul is soothed with godlike rest;
But when you swear, " I love but thee ! "
Then I must weep—and bitterly.

Louis Untermeyer

When Young Hearts Break

WHEN young hearts break with passion
    The stars break into laughter,
They laugh and, in their fashion,
    Gossip a long time after:

" Poor souls, those mortals languish
    With Love; 'tis all they cherish.
It pays them back with anguish
    And pain until they perish.

" We never can discover
    This Love, so brief and breathless,
So fatal to each lover—
    And hence we stars are deathless."

Louis Untermeyer

From the North Sea

A NIGHT BY THE SEA

STARLESS and chill is the night;
    The sea yawns wide,
And stretched on the sea, flat on his paunch,
Lies the shapeless form of the North Wind,
Who snivels and groans in stealthy mumblings,
A peevish old grumbler in garrulous humour,
Babbling down to the waves.
And he tells them wild, lawless stories,
Giant tales of gloom and murder,
Ancient sagas from Norway,

And again, with wide-clanging laughter he bellows
The witching spells of the Edda
And crafty rime-runes,
So darkly strong and so potent with magic
That the snowy sea-children
Leap up the waves with shouting,
Hissing in wild joy.

But meanwhile across the flat sea-beach
Over the clinging, spray-soaked sand
Strideth a stranger, whose heart within him
Is far more wild than winds and waters.
Where'er he steps
Sparks are scattered and sea-conches crackle;
And he wraps him close in his gloomy mantle
And presses on through the wind-driven night,
Safely led by the tiny candle,
Enticing and sweet, that glimmers
From a lonely fisher cottage.
Father and brother are out at sea,
And lone as a mother's soul she lives
In the cottage, the fisher-maiden,
The wondrous lovely fisher-maiden,
And by the fireside
Sits hearkening to the kettle
Purr in sweet and secret surmise,
And heaps the crackling boughs on the fire,
And blows on it
Till the flapping flames of crimson
Mirrored are in wizard beauty
On her face, set a-glowing,
On her white and tender shoulders
That peer so piteously
From her coarse and faded costume,
And on the heedful little hand
Which more closely binds the under-garment
Round her slender hips.

Then suddenly the door springs wide,
And he enters there, the nocturnal stranger;
Sure of love, his eyes he resteth
On the pale and slender maiden
Who shrinks before his gaze
Like a frail, terrified lily;
And he throws to the ground his mantle
And laughs and speaks:

" Behold, my child, I keep our troth.
I am come, and with me come
The ancient years when the gods from the heavens
To the daughters of mortals descended
And the daughters of mortals embraced them
And with them engendered
Kingly races, the sceptre-carriers,
And heroes, wonders o' the world . . .
Don't puzzle, my child, any further
About my divinity,
But I beg of you, mix me some tea with rum;
For outside 'twas cold,—
Before such a night-wind
Even we gods might freeze, though eternal,
And easily catch the godliest sneezings,
A cough like the gods without ending."

Howard Mumford Jones

Evening Twilight

ON the wan sea-strand
Lonely I lay, and in sorrowful brooding.
The sun sank lower and lower, and flung
His red rays, glowing, on the water,
And I watched the far white billows,
In the grip of the flood,
Foaming and roaring, nigher and nigher—
Strange medley of sounds ! a whispering and wailing,

A laughing and murmuring, sobbing and sighing,
Low voices, the while, a strange lullaby singing.
Methought I heard long-forgotten legends,
World-old adorable folk-tales,
That long since in boyhood
From neighbours' children I learnt;
When, of a summer evening,
On the steps of stone by the house-door,
We squatted for quiet story-telling,
With small hearts eagerly listening
And young eyes keen for wonders;
While the fair grown-up maidens
Sat, 'mid balm-breathing pots of flowers,
At a window over the way there,
With rosy faces,
Smiling and lit by the moon.

John Todhunter

EPILOGUE

LIKE the ears of wheat in a wheat-field growing,
So a thousand thoughts spring and tremble
In the minds of men.
But the tender fancies of love
Are like the happy colours that leap among them;
Red and blue flowers.

Red and blue flowers!
The sullen reaper destroys you as worthless;
Block-headed fools will scornfully thresh you;
Even the penniless wayfarer
Who is charmed and cheered by your faces,
Shakes his poor head,
And calls you pretty weeds!
But the young girl from the village,
Twining her garland,
Honours and gathers you.

And with you she brightens her lovely tresses.
And thus adorned, she hurries to the dancing,
Where fiddles and flutes are sweetly sounding;
Or runs to the sheltering beech-tree,
Where the voice of her lover sounds even sweeter
Than fiddles and flutes.

Louis Untermeyer

EDUARD MÖRICKE

1804–75

Beauty Rohtraut

WHAT is the name of King Ringang's daughter?
    Rohtraut, Beauty Rohtraut!
And what does she do the livelong day,
Since she dare not knit and spin alway?
O hunting and fishing is ever her play!
And, heigh! that her huntsman I might be!
I'd hunt and fish right merrily!
    Be silent, heart!

And it chanced that, after this some time,
    Rohtraut, Beauty Rohtraut!
The boy in the Castle has gained access,
And a horse he has got and a huntsman's dress,
To hunt and to fish with the merry Princess;
And, O! that a king's son I might be!
Beauty Rohtraut I love so tenderly.
    Hush! hush! my heart.

Under a grey old oak they sat,
    Beauty, Beauty Rohtraut!
She laughs: "Why look you so slyly at me?
If you have heart enough, come, kiss me."
Cried the breathless boy, "Kiss thee?"
But he thinks kind fortune has favoured my youth;
And thrice he has kissed Beauty Rohtraut's mouth.
    Down! down! mad heart.

Then slowly and silently they rode home,—
Rohtraut, Beauty Rohtraut !
The boy was lost in his delight:
" And, wert thou Empress this very night,
I would not heed or feel the blight;
Ye thousand leaves of the wild wood wist
How Beauty Rohtraut's mouth I kiss'd.
  Hush ! hush ! wild heart."

George Meredith

ARTHUR FITGER

1840–1909

Evening Prayer

" DAUGHTER, how the door is creaking,
 In the dead of night it shakes ! "—
Mother o' mine, the wind is shrieking,
 Never mind the noise it makes.
On the window beats the rain.
 Lie you still,
 And I will
Read the evening prayers again.

Ye daughters of Jerusalem, give heed !
Hark to my friend's feet coming o'er the mead.
I hear his feet o'er the dark meadow tripping,
With nightly dew his locks are dripping.

" Daughter, some one's in the house !
 To the stairs I hear him creeping."—
Mother, it's the little mouse
 Nibbling, or the cricket cheeping.
On the window beats the rain.
 Lie you still,
 And I will
Read the evening prayers again.

Ye daughters of Jerusalem, my friend
Comes from the orchard where the blue grapes bend,
From where the brown fig is to purple grown,
He comes, seeks, longs to be with me alone.

" Daughter, are there ghosts that haunt thee ?
  Soft feet in thy room I hear."—
Mother, ghosts will never daunt me:
  There will be an angel near.
On the window beats the rain.
  Lie you still,
  And I will
Read the evening prayers again.

O friend, belovèd, loveliest and best,
My heart beats loud and louder in my breast;
All eyes now sleep, there shines no candle-ray:
Watchmen of Zion, ye will not betray.

Jethro Bithell

FRIEDRICH WILHELM NIETZSCHE
1844–1900

Star Morals

UNTO a heavenly course decreed,
  Star of the darkness, take no heed.

Roll onward through this time and range !
Its woe to thee be far and strange !

To utmost worlds thy light secure:
No pity shall thy soul endure !

But one command is thine: be pure !

Ludwig Lewisohn

The Solitary

HARSH cry the crows
And townward take their whirring flight;
Soon come the snows—
Happy who has a home this night.

With glances dead
Thou gazest backward as of old !
Why hadst thou fled
Unto the world from winter's cold ?

The world—a gate
To freezing deserts dumb and bare !
Who lost what late
Thou lost is homeless everywhere.

Pale one, to bleak
And wintry pilgrimages driven,
Smoke-like to seek
The ever colder heights of heaven.

Soar, bird, fling wide
That song of birds in deserts born !
O madman, hide
Thy bleeding heart in ice and scorn.

Harsh cry the crows
And townward take their whirring flight;
Soon come the snows—
Woe unto him who has no home this night.

Ludwig Lewisohn

DETLEV VON LILIENCRON 1844–1909

Who Knows Where

Battle of Kolin, June 18, 1757

ON blood, smoke, rain and the dead,
On trampled grass unharvested
The sun poured light.
Dark fell.   The battle's rage was o'er,
And many a one came home no more
From Kolin's fight.

A lad, half boy, had shared the fray,
Had first heard bullets whiz that day.
He had to go . . .
And though he swung his flag on high,
Fate touched him, it was his to die,
He had to go. . . .

Near him there lay a pious book,
Which still the youngster bore and took
With sword and cup.
A grenadier from Bevern found
The small, stained volume on the ground
And picked it up.

And swiftly to the father brought
This last farewell with silence fraught
And with despair.
Then wrote therein the trembling hand:
" Kolin.   My son hid in the sand,
Who knows where ! "

And he who here has sung this song,
And he who reads it, both are strong
Of life and fair.
But once art thou and once am I
Hid in the sand eternally,
Who knows where !

Ludwig Lewisohn

After the Hunt

TIRED and thirsty, weary of the way,
I seek the forest-inn that is my own;
Rifle and cap upon a bench I lay,
Beside the water pail my dog lies prone.
The inn's young mistress in the dying day
Stands still as one from whom all joy has flown;
Then she smiles shyly and half turns away—
The guests' departure leaves us soon alone.

Ludwig Lewisohn

Autumn

A FLOCK of crows high from the Northland flies,
On their dark wings the evening sunshine plays.
Below the Ursulines' calm convent lies
And an old man dreams in its garden ways.
From the cool chapel float the harmonies
Upward in rapture deep of peace and grace
And fall and fade. . . . All sound of living dies
While the old man unto Our Lady prays.

Ludwig Lewisohn

GUSTAV FALKE

1853–1916

Strand-thistle

THE lady walked by the ocean strand
O'er the white sand at the fall of day,
Till a shy red flower stood in her way.
She plucked it, and cast it out of her hand.

She bent down to the grey, forlorn,
Tall thistle that beside it stood.
But this was clad in hardihood,
And through her frail hand drove its thorn.

But she brake it, and walked, and sang a lay,
 With tired mouth a tired lay she sang,
 Over the darkening bay it rang,
And on the salt wind died away.

Jethro Bithell

God's Harp

THE wind, stirring in the dark foliage, brings
Songs to me of the wakeful nightingale;
At intervals a stranger music rings.
Whence are these voices that now light,
Now deeply echo from the night
And now of their own beauty fail?

The apple bough of white
That at my open window rocks and sways,
Against the pane its dewy blossom lays,
Shines magically in the blanchèd light,
A sabbath radiance covers all the ways;
My vision waxes vast and wide:

Oh, there arises now a solemn tide
For those who live in dreams, the delicate
Souls that to every subtle tone vibrate
Which from God's harp rings forth and prophesies
That He for ever
His busy hand in ancient music plies,
And will not end the song of His delight.

Thus ends it never—
Hark, what a tone of love passed through the night!

Ludwig Lewisohn

PETER HILLE

1854–1904

The Maiden

AWKWARD was she yesterday,
Pitiful, and poor, and grey,
Nothing to be seen in her.
Must be on her guard to-day,
As when blossoms snow in May,
Lest they all should blow away.

As there were a Queen in her,
As though God had, unawares,
Planted her in a garden of cares,
Blossoms delicate she bears.
There is courage keen in her,
Though upon the ground she stares

Because she is in blossoms rich,
Because the wind breaks blossoms which
Do not blush for dreams that sinned,
Are not full of innocence,
Caution, shyness, and pretence—
　　O foolish wind !

Jethro Bithell

Beauty

Sappho to Chloe

FRIEND !
Poor, foolish blossom !
How thou shinest for him who
Dishevels thee, and withers thee.

Lo, such a man.
The thrall he is !
His doings loud and running.

Could we be so?
Only a woman walks.
She is, and beàuty tarries thence,
Red little ears of curls are opened.

Scents my blood to thee as thine to me?
No, Chloe.
It scenteth not.
Beauty thou knowest not, nor beauty's longing,
The seeking wind of the May of flowers,
Thou knowest it not.

Without a soul through me thou roamest.
Thou glowest hence to other haunts than I.
O fie for shame!
Thou my degenerated one!
How else could I feel thee, thou truant from me!

List: fortunate like to the gods seemeth the man
    to me,
Who face to face with thee may sit quite near,
And listen into him thy chatter of twittering lips,
That sets the soul on fire.

Jethro Bithell

RICHARD DEHMEL

1863–1920

My Drinking Song

YET one more hour, then comes the night;
Drink till the very soul o'erflows.
Glasses, ring!
Look how the sun in wild delight
Drowns in its crimson blood and glows.
Drink and sing:
Sing me the song of living and of dying.
Lo, upon earth the withered vines are lying.
But grapes they gave us ere the fall went flying.
Ho!

Yet one more hour, then comes the night;
In the pale river glints and spins
Sombre glow.
'Tis the red moon's awakened light
That peers across the hill and grins;
Sun, oho !
Sing me the song of life, the song of death !
Open your lips ! Sinful resounds our mood ;
Cling, clang, sinful as mortal breath—
To drink and laugh one must have flesh and blood.

Yet one more hour, then comes the night;
A bridge grows over the river wide.
Hail !   O hail !
It creaks beneath a horseman's might !
Saw ye yon sable horseman ride ?
Hail !   Thrice hail !
The song of death and life we still are singing !
Crash !   A new glass !   For upward we go winging
Above this life to which our lives are clinging !
Hail !

Ludwig Lewisohn

Before the Storm

THE sky grew darker with each minute
Outside my room, I felt within it
The clouds, disconsolate and grey.
The ash-tree yonder moved its crown
With heavy creaking up and down,
The dead leaves whirled across the way.

Then ticked, through the close room, unhurried,
As in still vaults where men are buried
The woodworm gnaws, and ticks my watch.
And through the open door close by,
Wailed the piano, thin and shy,
Beneath her touch.

Slate-like upon us weighed the heaven,
Her playing grew more sorrow-riven,
· I saw her form.
Sharp gusts upon the ash-tree beat ;
The air, aflame with dust and heat,
Sighed for the storm.

Pale through the walls the sounds came sobbing,
Her blind, tear-wasted hands passed throbbing
Across the keys.
Crouching she sang that song of May
That once had sung my heart away,
She panted lest the song should cease.

In the dull clouds no shadow shivered,
The aching music moaned and quivered
Like dull knives in me, stroke on stroke—
And in that song of love was blent
Two children's voices' loud lament—
Then first the lightning broke.

Ludwig Lewisohn

Vigil

THE crimson roses burn and glow,
Softly the dark leaves stir and shake,
And I am in the grass awake,
Oh, wert thou here . . . .
For soon the mid of night will break !

Into the lake the moonbeams flow,
The garden-gate hides her from view,
The moveless willows stand arow,
My burning forehead seeks the dew;
Oh, I have never loved thee so !

Oh, I have never so deeply known
As often as our close embrace
Made each the other, why thy face
Grew pallid and thy heart made moan
When all my being sought thy grace.

And now—oh, hadst thou seen how there
Two little fire-flies crept alow,
I never more from thee will fare,
Oh, wert thou here,
Or still the crimson roses glow.

Ludwig Lewisohn

Harvest Song

A FIELD of golden wheat there grows,
Even to the world's end it goes.
Grind, O mill, keep grinding !

The wind falters in all the land,
The mills on the horizon stand.
Grind, O mill, keep grinding !

The evening sky turns sombre red;
Many poor people cry for bread.
Grind, O mill, keep grinding !

The night's womb holds a storm within;
To-morrow shall the task begin.
Grind, O mill, keep grinding !

The storm shall sweep the fields of earth
Until no man cries out for dearth !
Grind, O mill, keep grinding !

Ludwig Lewisohn

The Silent Town

A TOWN lies in the valley,
A pale day fades and dies;
And it will not be long before
Neither moon nor starlight,
Night only fills the skies.

From all the mountain ridges
Creeps mist, and swathes the town;
No farm, no house, no wet red roof
Can pierce the thickly woven woof,
And scarce even spires and bridges.

But as the wanderer shudders,
Deep down a streak of light rejoices
His heart; and, through the smoke and haze,
Children's voices
Begin a gentle hymn of praise.

Jethro Bithell

To ——?

I HAVE baptized thee Withy, because of thy slender
limbs,
And since thou art the rod for God to chastise me
withal,
Yea, and because a yearning in thy posture overbrims
Even as in April days sways in the willows tall.

I know thee not—but in the tempest shock,
Some day, I shall hear thee at my door,
And I shall straightway open to thy knock,
Upon thy tameless breasts my tameless breast to lock
To beat with equal beat for evermore.

For I know thee—thy eyes like buds are glowing,
And thou wouldst flower, flower, flower !
And thy young ideas scatter like the shower
From shrubs with cataracts bespattered;
And thou wert fain as I do to defy God's tempests
   blowing
Or—be shattered !

Jethro Bithell

A Trysting

SO was it even then.   So soundlessly
  Over the land the clouded air hung hot,
And underneath the weeping beech's roof
  Were tangled, where is hedged the garden-plot,
The blossom-vapours of the elder-tree;
  My sultry hand she fondled, speaking not,
Voiceless with joy.

There was an odour of graves. . . . No guilt is mine !
  Thou pale light up above there in the sky,
Why stand'st thou like a ghost pent in his shroud !
  Why wilt thou pore upon me like God's eye ?
Monitor image of the spirit bowed,
  Be quenched !   I broke her not !   She willed to die.
Why should an alien anguish torture me ? . . .

The land grows grey.   And every willow-trunk
  Like smoke stands in the fog's deep starless sea.
Upon the corn the heavy sky seems sunk.
  Motionless cling the wet leaves to the tree,
As though they all had poison drunk.
  So silent now lies she.
I wish that I were dead.

Jethro Bithell

The Labourer

WE have a bed, and a baby too,
  My wife !
  We have work besides, we have work for two,
  And we have the sun, and the wind, and the rain,
  And we only need one little thing more
  To be as free as the birds that soar:
  Only time.

When we go through the fields on the Sunday morn,
  My child,
  And far and away o'er the bending corn,
  We see the swarming swallows flash,
  Then we only need a bit of a dress
  To have the birds' bright loveliness:
  Only time.

The storm is gathering black as jet,
  Feel the poor.
  Only a little eternity yet;
  We need nothing else, my wife, my child,
  Except all things through us that thrive,
  To be bold as the birds through the air that drive:
  Only time !

Jethro Bithell

Voice in Darkness

THERE'S moaning somewhere in the dark.
  I want to know what it may be.
  The wind is angry with the night—
  Yet the wind's moan sounds not so near.
  The wind will always moan at night.
  'Tis in my ear my blood that moans—
  My blood, forsooth.

Yet not so strangely moans my blood.
My blood is tranquil like the night.
I think a heart must moan somewhere.

Margarete Münsterberg

CÄSAR FLAISCHLEN

1864–1920

Most Quietly at Times

MOST quietly at times and like a dream
In thee re-echoes a far distant song. . . .
Thou knowest not whence suddenly it came,
Thou knowest not what it would have of thee. . . .
And like a dream most peacefully and still
It dies in distant music, even as it came. . . .

As suddenly as in the crowded street,
And in the very winter's frozen heart,
An odour of roses will around thee breathe,
Or as a picture unawares will rise
From far-forgotten happy childhood's days,
And gaze at thee with eyes inquisitive. . . .

Most quietly, and lightly as a dream. . . .
Thou knowest not whence suddenly it came,
Thou knowest not what it would have of thee,
And like a dream most peacefully and still
It pales and passes, fading whence it came.

Jethro Bithell

OTTO JULIUS BIERBAUM

1865–1910

Kindly Vision

NOT in sleep I saw it, but in daylight,
Clear and beautiful by day before me:
Saw a meadow overgrown with daisies,
Round a cottage white in green embowered;

Statues of the gods gleam in the arbour.
And the lady that I walk with loves me,
With a quiet spirit in the coolness
And the peacefulness of this white dwelling,
Full of beauty waiting till we enter.

Jethro Bithell

Blacksmith Pain

PAIN is a blacksmith,
Hard is his hammer;
With flying flames
His hearth is hot;
A straining storm
Of forces ferocious
Blows his bellows.
He hammers hearts
And tinkers them,
With blows tremendous,
Till hard they hold.—
Well, well forges Pain.—
No storm destroys,
No frost consumes,
No rust corrodes,
What Pain has forged.

Jethro Bithell

Jeannette

I

WHAT'S my sweetheart ?—A laundress is she.
Where does she live ?—Down by the river.
Where the Isar roars, and the bridge stands high,
And the fluttering shirts hang out to dry:
There lives my pleasure-giver.

In the little cot with the garden plot,
  And the shutters green a-showing,
There at the ironing-board she stands,
With the smoothing-iron in her clever hands:
  And how her cheeks are glowing !

There she stands in a lily-white blouse
  Figured with many a blossom;
No corset fastens the soft wavy billows
That bob underneath it, the easiest of pillows,
  The swelling rounds of her bosom.

2

A bed, a cupboard, a table, a bench,
And in the midst a strapping wench,
  My dolly, my jolly Jeannette.
Her eyes are brown, and so is her hair,
With its curls here, there, and everywhere,
And of cherry-ripe lips she's a swelling pair,
  Jeannette ! Jeannette !

There's ivy growing right up to the eaves,
And love at the lattice peeps through the leaves,
  My dolly, my jolly Jeannette.
Bang goes the door, on my neck she springs,
We are alone, and the old wind sings
The song of a couple of happy things.
  Jeannette ! Jeannette !

                                        Jethro Bithell

Oft in the Silent Night

OFT in the silent night
    When faint our breathing grows
    And sickle-bright the moon
    In the dark heaven glows,

When all is quieted
And no desires command,
Then my soul leadeth me
Into my childhood's land.

Then I see how infirm
My little feet did go,
And see my childish eye
And my small hands also,

And hear how then my mouth
Spoke ever pure and plain
And sink my head and of
My life take thought again:

Didst thou, didst thou always
Tread paths as white and sweet
As thou didst walk upon
With little childish feet?

Hast thou, hast thou always
Spoken as clear and true
As long ago thy voice
Faltering was wont to do?

And hast thou ever looked
So straight into the face
Of the great sun as once
With childhood's fearless grace?

My glance, O Moon, I lift
Unto thy splendour white;
Deep, deep am I made sad
Oft in the silent night.

Ludwig Lewisohn

STEFAN GEORGE

1868–

Stanzas Concerning Love

A NOVICE when I came beneath thy gaze,
There was no wonder in mine eyes before
And no desire till I beheld thy grace.
Be thou benign to young hands folded where
I pray to be thy servant evermore,
And with long‚suffering compassion spare
The feet still faltering on alien ways.

Now that my lips are very still and burn
Do I behold whither have gone my feet:
Into a splendid realm for others meet.
Ah, yet perchance it was the hour to turn,
When thro’ the lofty gateway seemed to shine
The eyes whose light my bended knees entreat
Seeking my own and giving me a sign.

Dead for ever is my world of old.
Sense and spirit for thy presence reaches,
Interchange of unimagined speeches,
Grace, withdrawal, service manifold.
Only thee would I in dreams behold,
And I mourn the visions fugitive
With the golden dark wherein they live,
When the cloudless morning rises cold.

Ludwig Lewisohn

Invocation and Prelude

I

G RANT me the great and solemn breath withdrawn,
The glow that with eternal youth is gifted,
Wherewith the wings of childhood once uplifted
Soared in the sacrificial smoke of dawn.

I would not live but in thy breath divine.
Enclose me wholly in thy sanctuary !
One crumb from thy rich table let me carry !
Thus from dark caves rises this prayer of mine.

The Angel spoke: These stormy cries I hear
Speak strange desires among themselves divided.
The granting of such precious gifts unguided
Is not my office, and my grace austere

By zeal or force cannot commanded be !
But I in prayer my arms beside him bending,
Heard all my wakeful yearning's voice ascending:
I loose thee not except thou blessest me.

2

In my life, too, were angry days and evil
And music that rang dissonant and shrill.
Now a kind spirit holds the balance level
And all my deeds are at an Angel's will.

Though often still my faltering soul be broken
Even unto sobbing in a joyless world,
Swift at the anchorage the words are spoken:
To fairer shorelands be thy sails unfurled.

And when storm-driven upon farthest ocean
'Twixt death and madness I am all unmanned,
He grasps the rudder and the wild commotion
Of powers tumultuous hearkens his command.

The embattled waves yield them unto his chiding.
From the pure azure clouds and shadows cease.
On foamless waters soon thy feet are gliding
To blessed islands and a port of peace.

Ludwig Lewisohn

Rapture

1

I FEEL a breath from other planets blowing
And pallid through the darkness wax the faces
That even now so kind and near were glowing.

Grey and more grey are tree and path and meadow
So that I scarcely know familiar places,
And thou, dear summoner of my pain, bright shadow,

Too far in deeper glow dissolved hast floated
To deem me, after this wild tumult's mazes,
To any earthly love or awe devoted.

Melted I am in music, circling, driven,
In boundless gratitude and nameless praises
Will and desireless to the eternal given.

2

A tempest wafts me and I am elated
In passionate madness of the women grieving
Who deep in dust their prayers have consecrated.

Then I behold the milky mists dislimning,
A noble clearness filled with sunshine leaving
Wherein the farthest mountain peaks are swimming.

The ground beneath me, white and soft, is shaken . . .
By monstrous chasms I mount high and higher
Above the last cloud's silver edge to waken,

In seas of crystal radiance to dip under—
I am a spark of the eternal fire,
And of the eternal voice I am the thunder !

Ludwig Lewisohn

The Lord of the Isle

FISHERMEN will relate that in the South
Upon an island rich in spice and oil
And precious stones that glitter in the sand,
There dwelt a bird who, standing upon earth,
Could tear the crowns of lofty trees asunder
With his strong beak; who, lifting up his wings
Dyed as with ichor of the Tyrian snail,
Unto his low and heavy flight, had been
A shadow in seeming, like a sombre cloud.
By day he vanished in the olive groves,
But evening ever brought him to the shore
Where in the coolness of the salt sea-breeze
He raised up his sweet voice and dolphins came,
Who are the friends of song, across the sea
With golden feathers filled and golden sparks.
Thus lived he since the making of the world
And only ship-wrecked sailors saw his form.
But when for the first time the snowy sails
Of man, guided by fortunate winds, had turned
Unto his island—to its topmost hill
He rose surveying that beloved place,
And spreading out his mighty pinions
Departed with a muffled cry of pain.

Ludwig Lewisohn

PETER BAUM

1869–

Horror

THIS is a fearful thing to bear,
That oft to me it seems
I have thine eyes and hair.
Then, helpless, my hands supplicate,

Even as thine own,
And my lips curse me in hate,
And moan.

Thou comest over me so every evening late.

Twin carrion birds
Then o'er the churchyard fly.

Jethro Bithell

Psalms of Love

1

THY nights moan into my days,
Through my dreams courses the blood of thy feet.
O I will drink thy tears away,
I will bear thee up under the crown of my leaves.

The crown of my leaves is cool and full of peace,
Bathed high in waters deep.
Down upon us shall drip the depths of the sky,
From seas eternal through the holy crown of leaves.

Slumber deep in my arms !
My eyes are steel-hard angels watching
Over thy peace.

2

Thine eyes with gloom are gleaming,
And a spinning weeping
Of thy raven hair
Over the linen.

O thy pale face,
And how thy slender fingers
Over the pillows are creeping :—

Touching stammering
Of a sprouting song,
That fain would flower.

My soul with thee is seeking.

3

When the roses wonder open at morn
Fain would I come to thee !
Bring cool dew to thy brow,
And laughter to thy lips.

In my nights thy loneliness affrights me;
Nestle deep in the pinions of my soul !
Darkly they rustle over the seas,
To find a way to thee.

4

When the night goes hence,
Let us from goblets dark
Reach to each other our blood.

And be one eye, one soul,
Shivering over the valleys,
Burning chalices clear.

Seest thou the morning wind ?   It bears
Hovering life from bush to bush,
Blade of grass to blade.
Be thou mine !

Jethro Bithell

ALFRED MOMBERT

1872–

Sleeping They bear Me

SLEEPING they bear me
Into my homeland.
From far away I come,

Hither over peaks and chasms
Over a dark ocean
Into my homeland.

Now that I have quelled the strongest
　　of the giants,
Out of the darkest land
Won my way home,
Led by a white fairy hand—

Echo heavy the bells.
And I stagger through the streets
Sleep-bound.

Jethro Bithell

Idyl

AND my young sweetheart sat at board with me.
I ate and drank and cried most bitterly.
Delicate linen on the board she laid.
And of her own small shift that cloth was made.
She gave to me a little silvern cup.
And it was her own blood that filled it up.
She took a loaf and gave me bread thereof.
And that was her young body warm with love.

Then, as of some strange mystery aware,
She smiled, and put a rose into her hair.

Ludwig Lewisohn

CARL BUSSE

1872–

In the Night of the Full Moon

ALL the full-moon night in the coomb
　　Roars a fallow deer in rut,
Wading through the silvered broom,
　　With a timid mouse-soft foot.

I am strangely seized, oppressed
  By his stifled rage of yearning,
And I feel in my own breast
  Tears withholden wildly burning.

Jethro Bithell

The Quiet Kingdom

THERE is a quiet kingdom's strand,
Like to no other earthly land,
The clouds and winds divide us—
Ah me, and who shall guide us ?

It will be found, I say to thee,
By one who yearneth deep as we.

Ludwig Lewisohn

RICHARD SCHAUKAL

1874–

Images

1

OVER the lids of thine eyes
With soft and light
Gliding of plumage flies
The magical bird of night.

His great, green, lustrous wings
Are heavy with dreamy freight.
Hearken, he sings
Of palm-forests and very strange, sweet things.
Who comes afar and late. . . .

2

And there came mighty birds floating thro' night
With crooked and contemptuous strong beaks,
Who looked upon all life with bitterness

And evil wisdom of their cold, grey eyes,
And onward to the dark horizon flew
On their far-shadowing and soundless wings.

Ludwig Lewisohn

HUGO VON HOFMANNSTHAL

1874-

The Two

HER hand a goblet bore for him—
Her chin and mouth curved like its rim—
So gentle yet so sure her tread,
No drop was from the goblet shed.

So gentle and so firm his hand:
A tameless steed allured his daring
And with a gesture swift, uncaring
He forced its trembling form to stand.

But when at last from her pale hand
He was to take the cup of gold,
Too heavy for them both it was:
For they so trembled like the grass,
That neither hand the other found
And on the ground the dark wine rolled.

Ludwig Lewisohn

A Venetian Night

ALL thro' the breathing night there seemed to flow,
Thro' the blue night, strange voices to and fro.
There was no sleep in Nature anywhere.
With dewy lips and deep intake of breath
She lay and listened in the vastness darkling
Of all the web of secret things aware.
And streaming, raining, fell the star-light sparkling
Upon the vigil of the garden there.

And ichor of all heavy fruits was swelling
Under the yellow moon and upward welling
Bubbled the glimmering fountains under trees.
And there awakened heavy harmonies.
And where in haste the clouds' dark shadows glided,
A sound of soft and naked steps abided. . . .
Softly I rose—by all the magic drawn—
Then floated through the night a sweet intoning
As of the poignant flute's impassioned moaning
Which in his marble hand in thoughtful wise
By the dark laurel holds the dreamy faun,
Yonder where the deep bed of violets lies.
I saw him in his still, marmoreal gleaming,
With rays of blue and silver o'er him streaming;
And where pomegranates open to the night
I heard the murmur of the bees in flight,
And saw them suck, upon the scarlet sunken,
With ripeness and nocturnal passion drunken.
And when the darkness with low breathing now
Brought all the garden fragrance to my brow,
Over the grass I seemed to hear the trailing
Of long and billowy garments thro' the land,
And feel the warm touch of a gentle hand.
In silken whiteness of moonlight were sailing
Impassioned midges in a maddened dance,
And on the lake lay softest radiance
Swaying in silver of its watery path.
I know not whether swans were plashing there
Or the white limbs of Naiads in their bath,
But lovely odour as of woman's hair
Blended with budding aloes everywhere. . . .
And all that splendour met in me and I
Was by excess of beauty overcome
That makes words empty and the senses dumb.

Ludwig Lewisohn

868

Ballad of the Outer Life

AND deep-eyed children cannot long be children,
Knowing of nothing they grow up and die,
And all men go their ways upon the earth.

And bitter fruits are sweetened by and by,
And fall at night like dead birds to the floor,
And in a few days rot even where they lie.

And ever blows the wind, and evermore
A multitude of words we speak and hear,
And now are happy, and now tired and sore.

And roads run through the grass, and towns uprear
Their torch-filled toils, some menacingly live,
And some cadaverously dry and drear.

Why are these built aloft ?   And ever strive,
So countless many, not to be the same ?
And tears drive laughter out till death arrive ?

What profits man this ever-changing game ?
Full-grown are we, yet still like chartless ships,
And wandering never follow any aim.

What profit hath he who the furthest roams ?
And yet he sayeth much who " evening " saith,
A word from which deep melancholy drips

Like heavy honey out of hollow combs.

Jethro Bithell

Many Indeed must Perish in the Keel

MANY indeed must perish in the keel,
Chained where the heavy oars of vessels smite ;
Others direct the rudder on the bridge,
And know the flight of birds and charted stars.

Others with weary limbs lie evermore
By the inextricable roots of life ;
For others chairs are with the sibyls set,
The Queens, in whose abode they dwell at home,
With brain untaxed and soft unhampered hands.

But from those lives a shadow falls athwart
On these the lighter, and as to earth and air
The light is with the hard life bound in one.

I cannot free my eyelids from fatigues
Of nations long-forgotten, no, nor guard
My soul in terror from the soundless fall
Of stars remote in deeps of cosmic dark.

Existence plies her shuttle through the woof
Of many fates indissolubly one,
And my own portion of this common life
Is more than taper flame or slender lyre.

Jethro Bithell

Stanzas on Mutability

I

STILL on my cheeks I feel their fondling breath:
   How can it be that days so very nigh
Are gone, for ever gone, and merged in death !

This is a thing that no man fathoms quite,
   And far too cruel for complaint or cry,
That all things slip and drip out of men's sight.

And that my own untrammelled I hath found
   Out of a little child its gradual stair,
To me unearthly, dumb, strange as a hound.

Then: that I was a hundred summers ere
   My birth, and that my forebears underground
Are closely kin to me as my own hair.

As much at one with me as my own hair.

2

The hours ! when we are gazing at the peerless
 Blue of the sea, and read Death's riddle stark
So easily and solemnly and fearless.

As little pale-faced maidens stand and hark,
 Cold always, with their great eyes opened wide,
Hearken in silence looking into the dark,

Out of their sleep-drunk limbs they feel life glide
 Noiselessly into grass, and trees of the wood,
And smiling tiredly know some little pride,

Even as a holy martyr sheds her blood.

Jethro Bithell

ARNO HOLZ

1863–

A Leave-taking

HIS friend the watchman was still awake,
 The Town-hall roof one silver flake,
 And the moon hung over it.

He scarcely knew what grief he bore,
 At every step his heart beat sore,
 And his knapsack weighed him down.

The street it was so long, so long,
 And he heard a voice singing a song:
 When the breeze of the May is blowing !

Now elder boughs o'er the hedgerow nod,
 And he sees the marble Mother of God
 Standing white at the Minster door.

Here he stood for a moment still,
 And heard what the jackdaw whistled shrill
 Up above on the steeple cross.

Then the landlord of the Lion Hotel
Put out his lights, and slowly the bell
Of the Minster clock pealed ten.

Everything was as it used to be,
The nightingale sang on the linden-tree,
And the fountain dreamily ran.

Out of his coat the rose he dashed,
The flower with his stick on the flags he thrashed,
Till the sparks flew, then he went.

The lamp o'er the gateway flickered red,
And the wood into which his pathway led
Stood black in the moonlight there. . . .

And where the path the Saints' Stone reaches,
Just where it bends around the beeches,
It all came back to him.

The leaves rustled, he stood and stood:
He stared down where, beneath the wood,
The roofs were glistening.

He saw the house in the garden gleaming,
And this was the end, was the end of the dreaming,
And—the roofs were glistening !

His heart beat wild with piteous pain !
When I come, when I come, when I come back again !

But he never came back any more.

Jethro Bithell

Roses Red

ROSES red
Wind themselves around my lance severe.

Through white woods of lilies
Snorts my stallion.

Out of emerald lakes,
Reeds in hair,
Slender, veilless virgins rise.

I ride as I were bronze.

Ever,
Hard before me,
Flies the Phœnix bird,
Singing.

Jethro Bithell

Buddha

BY night around my temple grove
watch seventy brazen cows.
A thousand mottled stone lampions flicker.

Upon a red throne of lac
I sit in the Holy of Holies.

Over me
thro' the beams of sandalwood,
in the ceiling's open square,
stand the stars.

I blink.

Were I now to rise up
my ivory shoulders would splinter the roof;
and the oval diamond upon my brow
would stave in the moon.

The chubby priests may snore away.
I rise not up.
I sit with legs crossed under
and observe my navel.

It is a blood-red ruby
in a naked belly of gold.

William Ellery Leonard

Phantasus

ITS roof among the stars projected,
The courtyard throbbed with factory roar,
The common human hive erected,
With hurdy-gurdies at the door.
The dark rat scurried in the basement,
A shop served brandy, grog, and beer,
And to the top-floor's broken casement
Man's wretchedness was native here.

There by his lamp he sat in fever—
Wild scorn of men, speak not at all !
And wrote his songs to last for ever,
A dreamer and a prodigal.
Into his garret could be taken
Table and bed—just room for breath;
He was as poor and as forsaken
As once that God from Nazareth.

And tho' the world, a venal harlot,
Her old taunt: " Crazed and useless ! " hissed,
A radiant spirit girth with scarlet
His forehead and his eyes had kissed.
And when in lonely awe he wondered
The verse beneath his hand to see,
For ever more from him were sundered
The world in its banality.

His only coat was ripped and tattered,
Dry bread a neighbour's hand would share,
He sighed: O Muse ! and nothing mattered,
Of want and misery unaware.
Thus by his lamp he sat in fever,
When day had fled and night would fall,
And wrote his songs to last for ever,
A dreamer and a prodigal.

                                    Ludwig Lewisohn

KARL BULCKE

1875–

There is an Old City

AN old town lies afar
From where the great towns be;
The storm roars over the town;
Beside it thunders the sea.

There is an ancient house ;
Long locked the gate has been.
On its grey walls the trembling
Blades of the grass are green.

There is a lonely heart,
Strange, full of fears,
That town and that house and that heart
Shut in my boyhood's years. . . .

Ludwig Lewisohn

RAINER MARIA RILKE

1875–1926

Prayer of the Maidens to Mary

I

O SEE how narrow are our days,
How full of fear our bed;
We reach out awkward arms always
To gather the roses red.

Thou must be mild to us, Mary,
Out of Thy blood we blow;
And what a pain is yearning
Thou alone canst know;

For Thou hast known this maiden's woe
   In Thine own soul's desire;
It feels as cold as Christmas snow,
   And yet is all on fire. . . .

2

AFTER THE PRAYER

But I feel how my heart is glowing
   Warmer and warmer in my breast,
And every evening poorer growing,
   Nor any night can bring me rest.

I tear at the white silken tissue,
And my shy dreams cry out to Thee:
   Let me be sorrow of Thy sorrow,
   O let us both
By the same wonder wounded be.

Jethro Bithell

Abishag

SHE lay, and serving-men her lithe arms took,
  And bound them round the withering old man,
And on him through the long sweet hours she lay,
A little fearful of his many years.

And many times she turned amidst his beard
Her face, as often as the night-owl screeched,
And all that was the night around them reached
Its feelers manifold of longing fears.

As they had been the sisters of the child
The stars trembled, and fragrance searched the room,
The curtain stirring sounded with a sign
Which drew her gentle glances after it.

But she clung close upon the dim old man,
And, by the night of nights not over-taken,
Upon the cooling of the King she lay
Maidenly, and lightly as a soul.

2

The King sate thinking out the empty day
Of deeds accomplished and untasted joys,
And of his favourite bitch that he had bred—
But with the evening Abishag was arched
Above him. His dishevelled life lay bare,
Abandoned as diffamèd coasts, beneath
The quiet constellation of her breasts.

But many times, as one in women skilled,
He through his eyebrows recognized the mouth
Unmoved, unkissed; and saw: the comet green
Of her desires reached not to where he lay.
He shivered. And he listened like a hound,
And sought himself in his remaining blood.

Jethro Bithell

For, Lord, the Crowded Cities be . . .

FOR, Lord, the crowded cities be
Desolate and divided places,
Flight as from flames upon their ways is,
And comfortless of any graces
Their little time fades utterly.
And men who dwell there heavy and humbly move
About dark rooms with dread in all their bearing,
Less than the spring-time flocks in fire and daring;
And somewhere breathes and watches earth for faring,
But they are here and do not know thereof.

And children grow up where the shadows falling
From wall and window have the light exiled,
And know not that without the flowers are calling
Unto a day of distance, wind and wild—
And every child must be a saddened child.
There blossom virgins to the unknown turning
And for their childhood's faded rest are fain
And do not find for what their soul is burning,
And trembling, close their timid buds again,
And bear in chambers shadowed and unsleeping
The days of disappointed motherhood,
And the long night's involuntary weeping,
And the cold years devoid of glow or good.
In utter darkness stand their deathbeds lowly,
For which thro' gradual years the grey heart pants;
And die as tho' in chains, and dying slowly
Go forth from life in guise of mendicants.

Ludwig Lewisohn

The Youth Dreams

OH, I should love to be like one of those
Who thro' the night on tameless horses ride,
With torches like dishevelled tresses wide
Which the great wind of gallop streaming blows.
And I would stand as on a shallop's prow,
Slender and tall and like a banner rolled,
Dark but for helmeting of ruddy gold
That glints and gleams.   Behind me in a row
Ten men whom from the equal darkness glow
With helmets of the changeful gold designed,
Now clear as glass, now dark and old and blind.
And one by me blows me a vision of space
Upon a trumpet glittering that cries,
Or makes a solitary blackness rise
Thro' which as in a rapid dream we race:

The houses slant behind us to their knees,
The crooked streets to meet us bend and strain,
The squares flee from us; but we grapple these,
And still our horses rustle like the rain.

Ludwig Lewisohn

The Song of Love

HOW shall I guard my soul so that it be
Touched not by thine? And how shall it be
brought,
Lifted above thee, unto other things?
Ah, gladly would I hide it utterly
Lost in the dark where are no murmurings,
In strange and silent places that do not
Vibrate when thy deep soul quivers and sings.
But all that touches us two makes us twin,
Even as the bow crossing the violin
Draws but one voice from the two strings that meet.
Upon what instrument are we two spanned?
And what great player has us in his hand?
O song most sweet.

Ludwig Lewisohn

Silent Hour

WHOEVER weeps somewhere out in the world
Weeps without cause in the world
Weeps over me.

Whoever laughs somewhere out in the night
Laughs without cause in the night
Laughs at me.

Whoever wanders somewhere in the world
Wanders in vain in the world
Wanders to me.

Whoever dies somewhere in the world
Dies without cause in the world
Looks at me.

Jessie Lemont

Presaging

I AM like a flag unfurled in space,
I scent the oncoming winds and must bend with them,
While the things beneath are not yet stirring,
While the doors close gently and there is silence in the
chimneys
And the windows do not yet tremble and the dust is
still heavy—
Then I feel the storm and am vibrant like the sea
And expand and withdraw into myself
And thrust myself forth and am alone in the great
storm.

Jessie Lemont

ERNST HARDT

1876–

The Spectre

THE ashen feelers of the frigid morrow
Were groping at my forehead pale with sorrow,
And colder than these walls that round me stand.

Sleep fled from me, and ciphers half and whole
In phalanx upon phalanx chased my soul;
I raised my head and, horribly unmanned,

I glared upon a curling, crooked thing,
A griffin shape down by thee cowering,
That held thy loved heart in a cruel hand,

And gnawed at it with teeth most steep and hard,
Until the cock's crow sounded from the yard,
Then fled it—and the young day scaled the land.

I pressed my fevered head and wept, undone,
I knew that also this made us as one,
The torture that is low and like a brand,

Which eats up nights and days and all our life.

Jethro Bithell

HERMANN HESSE

1877–

Spring Song

THE storm cries every night,
Its great, moist wing falters and sweeps,
In dreamy flight the plover falls;
Now nothing sleeps
And through the land stirs new delight,
For the Spring calls.

Oh in these nights I cannot sleep
Youth stirs my heart !
From the blue wells of memory start
The ardent glories of that dawn
And look at me with eyes so deep,
And tremble, and are gone.

Be still, my heart, give o'er !
Though in the heavy blood holds sway
The passionate sweet pain
And lead thee the old paths again—
Unto youth's land no more
For ever goes thy way.

Ludwig Lewisohn

Night

OFTEN this thought wakens me unawares,
That through the chill of night a vessel fares
Seeking an ocean, touching on a shore
For which my soul must yearn for evermore;

That in still places which no sailor knows
A crimson, undiscovered Northlight glows,
That an unknown and lovely lady's arm
Pulses amid the pillows white and warm;
That one long destined to become my friend
Finds in an alien sea a sombre end,
And that my mother, strange and far apart,
Speaks at this hour my name within her heart.

Ludwig Lewisohn

KARL GUSTAVE VOLLMOELLER

1878–

Nocturne in G Minor

THE nightwind sings and rustles through the reeds.
The pallid lilacs by the lake are sweet.
" I wait for thee ! Ah, when will come thy feet
Down the chill steps ? . . . Hush . . . 'tis the gate
. . . none heeds. . . ."

The nightwind sings and rustles through the reeds.
The nightwind sweeps and whispers by the boat.
The lake is calm. " Ah, hide me in thine arm,
Against that bosom, young and white and warm. . . .
How scarlet are thy lips, how wild thy throat ! "

The nightwind sweeps and whispers by the boat.

The frosty nightwind trembles through the reeds.
" Hark ! Birds of dawn ! " " If ever this rapture
die !"
" Thou weepest ? " " Sweet and bitter is my cry."
The gate is closed. The harsh moon upward speeds.

The nightwind storms and shivers through the reeds.

Ludwig Lewisohn

SCANDINAVIAN

OLD NORSE

FROM THE ELDER EDDA

c. 1000

THE Poetic Edda is the original storehouse of Germanic mythology. It is, indeed, in many ways the greatest literary monument preserved to us out of the antiquity of the kindred races which we call Germanic. The mythological poems include, in the Voluspo, one of the vastest conceptions of the creation and ultimate destruction of the world ever crystallized in literary form.—HENRY ADAMS BELLOWS.

Voluspo

The Wise-woman's Prophecy

HEARING I ask from the holy races,
From Heimdall's sons, both high and low;
Thou wilt, Valfather, that well I relate
Old tales I remember of men long ago.

I remember yet the giants of yore,
Who gave me bread in the days gone by;
Nine worlds I knew, the nine in the tree
With mighty roots beneath the mould.

Of old was the age when Ymir lived;
Sea nor cool waves nor sand there were;
Earth had not been, nor heaven above,
But a yawning gap, and grass nowhere.

Then Bur's sons lifted the level land,
Mithgarth the mighty there they made;
The sun from the south warmed the stones of earth,
And green was the ground with growing leeks.

The sun, the sister of the moon, from the south
Her right hand cast over heaven's rim;
No knowledge she had where her home should be,
The moon knew not what might was his,
The stars knew not where their stations were.

Then sought the gods their assembly-seats,
The holy ones, and council held;
Names then gave they to noon and twilight,
Morning they named, and the waning moon,
Night and evening, the years to number.

At Ithavoll met the mighty gods,
Shrines and temples they timbered high;
Forges they set, and they smithied ore,
Tongs they wrought, and tools they fashioned.

In their dwellings at peace they played at tables,
Of gold no lack did the gods then know,—
Till thither came up giant-maids three,
Huge of might, out of Jotunheim.

Then sought the gods their assembly-seats,
The holy ones, and council held,
To find who should raise the race of dwarfs
Out of Brimir's blood and the legs of Blain.

There was Motsognir the mightiest made
Of all the dwarfs, and Durin next;
Many a likeness of men they made,
The dwarfs in the earth, as Durin said.

Nyi and Nithi, Northri and Suthri,
Austri and Vestri, Althjof, Dvalin,
Nar and Nain, Niping, Dain,
Bifur, Bofur, Bombur, Nori,
An and Onar, Ai, Mjothvitnir.

Vigg and Gandalf, Vindalf, Thrain,
Thekk and Thorin, Thror, Vit and Lit,
Nyr and Myrath,—now have I told—
Regin and Rathsvith—the list aright.

Fili, Kili, Fundin, Nali,
Heptifili, Hannar, Sviur,
Frar, Hornbori, Fraeg and Loni,
Aurvang, Jari, Eikinskjaldi.

The race of the dwarfs in Dvalin's throng
Down to Lofar the list must I tell;
The rocks they left, and through wet lands
They sought a home in the fields of sand.

There were Draupnir and Dolgthrasir,
Hor, Haugspori, Hlevang, Gloin,
Dori, Ori, Duf, Andvari,
Skirfir, Virfir, Skafith, Ai,

Alf and Yngvi, Eikinskjaldi,
Fjalar and Frosti, Fith and Ginnar;
So for all time shall the tale be known,
The list of all the forbears of Lofar.

Then from the throng did three come forth
From the home of the gods, the mighty and gracious;
Two without fate on the land they found,
Ask and Embla, empty of might.

Soul they had not, sense they had not,
Heat nor motion, nor goodly hue;
Soul gave Othin, sense gave Hönir,
Heat gave Lothur and goodly hue. .

An ash I know, Yggdrasil its name,
With water white is the great tree wet;
Thence come the dews that fall in the dales,
Green by Urth's well does it ever grow.

Thence come the maidens mighty in wisdom,
Three from the dwelling down 'neath the tree;
Urth is one named, Verthandi the next,—
On the wood they scored,—and Skuld the third.
Laws they made there, and life allotted
To the sons of men, and set their fates.

The war I remember, the first in the world,
When the gods with spears had smitten Gollveig,
And in the hall of Hor had burned her,—
Three times burned, and three times born,
Oft and again, yet ever she lives.

Heith they named her who sought their home,
The wide-seeing witch, in magic wise;
Minds she bewitched that were moved by her magic,
To evil women a joy she was.

On the host his spear did Othin hurl,
Then in the world did war first come;
The wall that girdled the gods was broken,
And the field by the warlike Wanes was trodden.

Then sought the gods their assembly-seats,
The holy ones, and council held,
Whether the gods should tribute give,
Or to all alike should worship belong.

Then sought the gods their assembly-seats,
The holy ones, and council held,
To find who with venom the air had filled,
Or had given Oth's bride to the giants' brood.

In swelling rage then rose up Thor,—
Seldom he sits when he such things hears,—
And the oaths were broken, the words and bonds,
The mighty pledges between them made.

I know of the horn of Heimdall, hidden
Under the high-reaching holy tree;
On it there pours from Valfather's pledge
A mighty stream: would you know yet more?

Alone I sat when the Old One sought me,
The terror of gods, and gazed in mine eyes:
" What hast thou to ask? why comest thou hither?
Othin, I know where thine eye is hidden."

I know where Othin's eye is hidden,
Deep in the wide-famed well of Mimir;
Mead from the pledge of Othin each morn
Does Mimir drink: would you know yet more?

Necklaces had I and rings from Heerfather,
Wise was my speech and my magic wisdom;
.   .   .   .
Widely I saw over all the worlds.

On all sides saw I Valkyries assemble,
Ready to ride to the ranks of the gods;
Skuld bore the shield, and Skogul rode next,
Guth, Hild, Gondul, and Geirskogul.
Of Herjan's maidens the list have ye heard,
Valkyries ready to ride o'er the earth.

I saw for Baldr, the bleeding god,
The son of Othin, his destiny set:
Famous and fair in the lofty fields,
Full grown in strength the mistletoe stood.

From the branch which seemed so slender and fair
Came a harmful shaft that Hoth should hurl;
But the brother of Baldr was born ere long,
And one night old fought Othin's son.

His hands he washed not, his hair he combed not,
Till he bore to the bale-blaze Baldr's foe,
But in Fensalir did Frigg weep sore
For Valhall's need: would you know yet more?

One did I see in the wet woods bound,
A lover of ill, and to Loki like;
By his side does Sigyn sit, nor is glad
To see her mate: would you know yet more?

From the east there pours through poisoned vales
With swords and daggers the river Slith.

.   .   .   .

Northward a hall in Nithavellir
Of gold there rose for Sindri's race;
And in Okolnir another stood,
Where the giant Brimir his beer-hall had.

A hall I saw, far from the sun,
On Nastrond it stands, and the doors face north;
Venom drops through the smoke-vent down,
For around the walls do serpents wind.

I saw there wading through rivers wild
Treacherous men and murderers too,
And workers of ill with wives of men;
There Nithogg sucked the blood of the slain,
And the wolf tore men; would you know yet more?

The giantess old in Ironwood sat,
In the east, and bore the brood of Fenrir;
Among these one in monster's guise
Was soon to steal the sun from the sky.

There feeds he full on the flesh of the dead,
And the home of the gods he reddens with gore;
Dark grows the sun, and in summer soon
Come mighty storms: would you know yet more?

On a hill there sat, and smote on his harp,
Eggther the joyous, the giants' warder;
Above him the cock in the bird-wood crowed,
Fair and red did Fjalar stand.

Then to the gods crowed Gollinkambi,
He wakes the heroes in Other's hall;
And beneath the earth does another crow,
The rust-red bird at the bars of Hel.

Now Garm howls loud before Gnipahellir,
The fetters will burst, and the wolf run free;
Much do I know, and more can see
Of the fate of the gods, the mighty in fight.

Brothers shall fight and fell each other,
And sisters' sons shall kinship stain;
Hard is it on earth, with mighty whoredom;
Axe-time, sword-time, shields are sundered,
Wind-time, wolf-time, ere the world falls;
Nor ever shall men each other spare.

Fast move the sons of Mim, and fate
Is hard in the note of the Ghallarhorn;
Loud blows Heimdall, the horn is aloft,
In fear quake all who on Hel-roads are.

Yggdrasil shakes, and shiver on high
The ancient limbs, and the giant is loose;
To the head of Mim does Othin give heed,
But the kinsman of Surt shall slay him soon.

How fare the gods? how fare the elves?
All Jotunheim groans, the gods are at council;
Loud roar the dwarfs by the doors of stone,
The masters of the rocks: would you know yet more?

Now Garm howls loud before Gnipahellir,
The fetters will burst, and the wolf run free;
Much do I know, and more can see
Of the fate of the gods, the mighty in fight.

From the east comes Hrym with shield held high;
In giant-wrath does the serpent writhe;
O'er the waves he twists, and the tawny eagle
Gnaws corpses screaming; Naglfar is loose.

O'er the sea from the north there sails a ship
With the people of Hel, at the helm stands Loki;
After the wolf do wild men follow,
And with them the brother of Byleist goes.

Surt fares from the south with the scourge of branches;
The sun of the battle-gods shone from his sword;
The crags are sundered, the giant-women sink,
The dead throng Hel-way, and heaven is cloven.

Now comes to Hlin yet another hurt,
When Othin fares to fight with the wolf,
And Beli's fair slayer seeks out Surt,
For there must fall the joy of Frigg.

Then comes Sigfather's mighty son,
Vithar, to fight with the foaming wolf;
In the giant's son does he thrust his sword
Full to the heart: his father is avenged.

Hither there comes the son of Hlothyn,
The bright snake gapes to heaven above;
        .   .   .   .
Against the serpent goes Othin's son.

In anger smites the warder of earth,—
Forth from their homes must all men flee;—
Nine paces fares the son of Fjorgyn,
And, slain by the serpent, fearless he sinks.

The sun turns black, earth sinks in the sea,
The hot stars down from heaven are whirled;
Fierce grows the steam and the life-feeding flame,
Till fire leaps high about heaven itself.

Now Garm howls loud before Gnipahellir,
The fetters will burst, and the wolf run free;
Much do I know, and more can see
Of the fate of the gods, the mighty in fight.

Now do I see the earth anew
Rise all green from the waves again;
The cataracts fall, and the eagle flies,
And fish he catches beneath the cliffs.

The gods in Ithavoll meet together,
Of the terrible girdler of earth they talk,
And the mighty past they call to mind,
And the ancient runes of the Ruler of Gods.

In wondrous beauty once again
Shall the golden tables stand mid the grass,
Which the gods had owned in the days of old,

.   .   .

Then fields unsowed bear ripened fruit,
All ills grow better, and Baldr comes back;
Baldr and Hoth dwell in Hropt's battle-hall,
And the mighty gods: would you know yet more ?

Then Hönir wins the prophetic wand,

.   .   .

And the sons of the brothers of Tveggi abide
In Vindheim now: would you know yet more ?

More fair than the sun, a hall I see,
Roofed with gold, on Gimle it stands;
There shall the righteous rulers dwell,
And happiness ever there shall they have.

There comes on high, all power to hold,
A mighty lord, all lands he rules.

From below the dragon dark comes forth,
Nithhogg flying from Nithalfjoll;
The bodies of men on his wings he bears,
The serpent bright: but now must I sink.

Henry Adams Bellows [1]

The First Lay of Gudrun

*F*OR *this is the Great Story of the North, which should be to all our race what the Tale of Troy was to the Greeks.*—WILLIAM MORRIS.

GUDRUN of old days
Drew near to dying
As she sat in sorrow
Over Sigurd;
Yet she sighed not
Nor smote hand on hand,
Nor wailed she aught
As other women.

Then went earls to her,
Full of all wisdom,
Fain help to deal
To her dreadful heart:
Hushed was Gudrun
Of wail or greeting,
But with heavy woe
Was her heart a-breaking.

Bright and fair
Sat the great earls' brides,
Gold arrayed
Before Gudrun;

[1] Courtesy of the American-Scandinavian Foundation.

Each told the tale
Of her great trouble,
The bitterest bale
She erst abode.

Then spake Giaflaug,
Giuki's sister:
" Lo upon earth
I live most loveless
Who of five mates
Must see the ending,
Of daughters twain
And three sisters,
Of brethren eight,
And abide behind lonely."

Naught gat Gudrun
Of wail or greeting,
So heavy was she
For her dead husband,
So dreadful-hearted
For the King laid dead there.

Then spake Herborg
Queen of Hunland—
" Crueller tale
Have I to tell of,
Of my seven sons
Down in the Southlands,
And the eighth man, my mate,
Felled in the death-mead.

" Father and mother,
And four brothers,
On the wide sea
The winds and death played with;
The billows beat
On the bulwark boards.

" Alone must I sing o'er them,
Alone must I array them,
Alone must my hands deal with
Their departing;
And all this was
In one season's wearing,
And none was left
For love or solace.

" Then was I bound
A prey of the battle,
When that same season
Wore to its ending;
As a tiring may
Must I bind the shoon
Of the duke's high dame,
Every day at dawning.

" From her jealous hate
Gat I heavy mocking,
Cruel lashes
She laid upon me,
Never met I
Better master
Or mistress worser
In all the wide world."

Naught gat Gudrun
Of wail or greeting,
So heavy was she
For her dead husband,
So dreadful-hearted
For the King laid dead there.

Then spake Gullrond,
Giuki's daughter—
" O foster-mother,
Wise as thou mayst be,
Naught canst thou better

The young wife's bale."
And she bade uncover
The dead King's corpse.

She swept the sheet
Away from Sigurd,
And turned his cheek
Towards his wife's knees—
" Look on thy loved one,
Lay lips to his lips,
E'en as thou wert clinging
To thy King alive yet ! "

Once looked Gudrun—
One look only,
And saw her lord's locks
Lying all bloody,
The great man's eyes
Glazed and deadly,
And his heart's bulwark
Broken by sword-edge.

Back then sank Gudrun,
Back on the bolster,
Loosed was her head array,
Red did her cheeks grow,
And the rain-drops ran
Down over her knees.

Then wept Gudrun,
Giuki's daughter,
So that the tears flowed
Through the pillow;
As the geese withal
That were in the homefield,
The fair fowls the may owned,
Fell a-screaming.

Then spake Gullrond,

Giuki's daughter—
" Surely knew I
No love like your love
Among all men,
On the mould abiding;
Naught wouldst thou joy in
Without or within doors,
O my sister,
Save beside Sigurd."

Then spake Gudrun,
Giuki's daughter—
" Such was my Sigurd
Among the sons of Giuki,
As is the king leek
O'er the low grass waxing,
Or a bright stone
Strung on band,
Or a pearl of price
On a prince's brow.

" Once was I counted
By the king's warriors
Higher than any
Of Herjan's mays;
Now am I as little
As the leaf may be
Amid wind-swept wood,
Now when dead he lieth.

" I miss from my seat,
I miss from my bed,
My darling of sweet speech.
Wrought the sons of Giuki,
Wrought the sons of Giuki,
This sore sorrow,
Yea, for their sister,
Most sore sorrow.

" So may your lands
Lie waste on all sides,
As ye have broken
Your bounden oaths !
Ne'er shalt thou, Gunnar,
The gold have joy of,
The dear-bought rings
Shall drag thee to death,
Whereon thou swarest
Oath unto Sigurd.

" Ah, in the days by-gone
Great mirth in the homefield
When my Sigurd
Set saddle on Grani,
And they went their ways
For the wooing of Brynhild !
An ill day, an ill woman,
And most ill hap ! "

Then spake Brynhild,
Budli's daughter—
" May the woman lack
Both love and children,
Who gained greeting
For thee, O Gudrun !
Who gave thee this morning
Many words ! "

Then spake Gullrond,
Giuki's daughter—
" Hold peace of such words,
Thou hated of all folk !
The bane of brave men
Hast thou been ever,
All waves of ill
Wash over thy mind,

To seven great kings
Hast thou been a sore sorrow,
And the death of good will
To wives and women."

Then spake Brynhild,
Budli's daughter—
" None but Atli
Brought bale upon us,
My very brother
Born of Budli.

" When we saw in the hall
Of the Hunnish people
The gold a'gleaming
On the kingly Giukings;
I have paid for that faring
Oft and full,
And for the sight
That then I saw."

By a pillar she stood
And strained its wood to her;
From the eyes of Brynhild,
Budli's daughter,
Flashed out fire,
And she snorted forth venom,
As the sore wounds she gazed on
Of the dead'slain Sigurd.

William Morris and Eirikr Magnusson

The Lay of Sigurd

SIGURD of yore
Sought the dwelling of Giuki,
As he fared, the young Volsung,
After fight won;

Troth he took
From the two brethren;
Oath swore they betwixt them,
Those bold ones of deed.

A may they gave to him
And wealth manifold,
Gudrun the young,
Giuki's daughter;
They drank and gave doom
Many days together,
Sigurd the young,
And the sons of Giuki.

Until they wended
For Brynhild's wooing,
Sigurd a*riding
Amidst their rout;
The wise young Volsung
Who knew of all ways—
Ah ! he had wed her,
Had fate so willed it.

Southlander Sigurd
A naked sword,
Bright, well grinded,
Laid betwixt them;
No kiss he won
From the fair woman,
Nor in arms of his
Did the Hun King hold her,
Since he gat the young maid
For the son of Giuki.

No lack in her life
She wotted of now,
And at her death*day
No dreadful thing

For a shame indeed
Or a shame in seeming;
But about and betwixt
Went baleful fate.

Alone, abroad,
She sat of an evening,
Of full many things
She fell a-talking:
" O for my Sigurd !
I shall have death,
Or my fair, my lovely,
Laid in mine arms.

" For the word once spoken,
I sorrow sorely—
His queen is Gudrun,
I am wed to Gunnar;
The dread Norns wrought for us
A long while of woe."

Oft with heart deep
In dreadful thoughts
O'er ice-fields and ice-hills
She fared a-night time
When he and Gudrun
Were gone to their fair bed
And Sigurd wrapped
The bed-gear round her.

" Ah ! now the Hun King
His queen in arms holdeth,
While love I go lacking,
And all things longed for
With no delight
But in dreadful thought."

These dreadful things
Thrust her toward murder:
—" Listen, Gunnar,
For thou shalt lose
My wide lands,
Yea, me myself!
Never love I my life,
With thee for my lord—

" I will fare back thither
From whence I came,
To my nighest kin
And those that know me.
There shall I sit
Sleeping my life away,
Unless thou slayest
Sigurd the Hun King,
Making thy might more
E'en than his might was !

" Yea, let the son fare
After the father,
And no young wolf
A long while nourish !
For on each man lieth
Vengeance lighter,
And peace shall be surer
If the son live not."

Adrad was Gunnar,
Heavy-hearted was he,
And in doubtful mood
Day-long he sat.
For naught he wotted,
Nor might see clearly
What was the seemliest
Of deeds to set hand to;

What of all deeds
Was best to be done:
For he minded the vows
Sworn to the Volsung,
And the sore wrong
To be wrought against Sigurd.

Wavered his mind
A weary while,
No wont it was
Of those days worn by,
That queens should flee
From the realms of their kings.

" Brynhild to me
Is better than all,
The child of Budli
Is the best of women.
Yea, and my life
Will I lay down,
Ere I am twinned
From that woman's treasure."

He bade call Hogni
To the place where he bided;
With all the trust that might be,
Trowed he in him.

" Wilt thou bewray Sigurd
For his wealth's sake ?
Good it is to rule
O'er the Rhine's metal;
And well content
Great wealth to wield,
Biding in peace
And blissful days."

One thing alone Hogni
Had for an answer:

" Such doings for us
Are naught seemly to do;
To rend with sword
Oaths once sworn,
Oaths once sworn,
And troth once plighted.

" Nor know we on mould
Men of happier days,
The while we four
Rule over the folk;
While the bold in battle,
The Hun King, bides living.

" And no nobler kin
Shall be known afield,
If our five sons
We long may foster;
Yea, a goodly stem
Shall surely wax.
—But I clearly see
In what wise it standeth,
Brynhild's sore urging
O'ermuch on thee beareth."

" Guttorm shall we
Get for the slaying,
Our younger brother
Bare of wisdom;
For he was out of
All the oaths sworn,
All the oaths sworn,
And the plighted troth."

Easy to rouse him
Who of naught recketh !
—Deep stood the sword
In the heart of Sigurd.

There, in the hall,
Gat the high-hearted vengeance;
For he cast his sword
At the reckless slayer:
Out at Guttorm
Flew Gram the mighty,
The gleaming steel
From Sigurd's hand.

Down fell the slayer
Smitten asunder;
The heavy head
And the hands fell one way,
But the feet and such-like
Aback where they stood.

Gudrun was sleeping
Soft in the bed,
Empty of sorrow
By the side of Sigurd:
When she awoke
With all pleasure gone,
Swimming in blood
Of Frey's beloved.

So sore her hands
She smote together,
That the great-hearted
Gat raised in bed;
—" O Gudrun, weep not
So woefully,
Sweet lovely bride,
For thy brethren live for thee !

" A young child have I
For heritor;
Too young to win forth

From the house of his foes.—
Black deeds and ill
Have they been a-doing,
Evil rede
Have they wrought at last.

"Late, late, rideth with them
Unto the Thing,
Such sister's son,
Though seven thou bear,—
—But well I wot
Which way all goeth;
Alone wrought Brynhild
This bale against us.

"That maiden loved me
Far before all men,
Yet wrong to Gunnar
I never wrought;
Brotherhood I heeded
And all bounden oaths,
That none should deem me
His queen's darling."

Weary sighed Gudrun,
As the king gat ending,
And so sore her hands
She smote together,
That the cups arow
Rang out therewith,
And the geese cried on high
That were in the homefield.

Then laughed Brynhild,
Budli's daughter,
Once, once only,
From out her heart;

When to her bed
Was borne the sound
Of the sore greeting
Of Giuki's daughter.

Then, quoth Gunnar,
The king, the hawk-bearer,
" Whereas thou laughest,
O hateful woman,
Glad on thy bed,
No good it betokeneth:
Why lackest thou else
Thy lovely hue ?
Feeder of foul deeds,
Fey do I deem thee,

" Well worthy art thou
Before all women,
That thine eyes should see
Atli slain of us;
That thy brother's wounds
Thou shouldst see a-bleeding,
That his bloody hurts
Thine hands should bind."

" No man blameth thee, Gunnar,
Thou hast fulfilled death's measure.
But naught Atli feareth
All thine ill will;
Life shall he lay down
Later than ye,
And still bear more might
Aloft than thy might.

" I shall tell thee, Gunnar,
Though well the tale thou knowest,
In what early days
Ye dealt abroad your wrong:

Young was I then,
Worn with no woe,
Good wealth I had
In the house of my brother !

" No mind had I
That a man should have me,
Or ever ye Giukings
Rode into our garth;
There ye sat on your steeds
Three kings of the people—
—Ah ! that that faring
Had never befallen !

" Then spake Atli
To me apart,
And said that no wealth
He would give unto me,
Neither gold nor lands
If I would not be wedded;
Nay, and no part
Of the wealth apportioned,
Which in my first days
He gave me duly;
Which in my first days
He counted down.

" Wavered the mind
Within me then,
If to fight I should fall
And the felling of folk,
Bold in byrny
Because of my brother;
A deed of fame
Had that been to all folk,
But to many a man
Sorrow of mind.

" So I let all sink
Into peace at the last:
More grew I minded
For the mighty treasure,
The red/shining rings
Of Sigmund's son;
For no man's wealth else
Would I take unto me.

" For myself had I given
To that great king
Who sat amid gold
On the back of Grani:
Naught were his eyen
Like to your eyen,
Nor in any wise
Went his visage with yours;
Though ye might deem you
Due kings of men.

" One I loved,
One, and none other,
The gold/decked may
Had no doubtful mind;
Thereof shall Atli
Wot full surely,
When he getteth to know
I am gone to the dead.

" Far be it from me,
Feeble and wavering,
Ever to love
Another's love—
—Yet shall my woe
Be well avenged."

Up rose Gunnar,
The great men's leader,

And cast his arms
About the queen's neck ;
And all went nigh
One after other,
With their whole hearts
Her heart to turn.

But then all these
From her neck she thrust,
Of her long journey
No man should let her.

Then called he Hogni
To have talk with him :
" Let all folk go
Forth into the hall,
Thine with mine—
—O need sore and mighty !—
To wot if we yet
My wife's parting may stay,
Till with time's wearing
Some hindrance wax."

One answer Hogni
Had for all :
" Nay, let hard need
Have rule thereover,
And no man let her
Of her long journey !
Never born again,
May she come back thence !

" Luckless she came
To the lap of her mother,
Born into the world
For utter woe,
To many a man
For heart whole mourning."

Unpraised he turned
From the talk and the trouble,
To where the gem-field
Dealt out goodly treasure;
As she looked and beheld
All the wealth that she had,
And the hungry bondmaids,
And maids of the hall.

With no good in her heart
She donned her gold byrny,
Ere she thrust the sword-point
Through the midst of her body:
On the bolster's far side
Sank she adown,
And, smitten with sword,
Still bethought her of redes.

" Let all come forth
Who are fain the red gold,
Or things less worthy
To win from my hands;
To each one I give
A necklace gilt over,
Wrought hangings and bed-gear
And bright woven weed."

All they kept silence,
And thought what to speak,
Then all at once
Answer gave:
" Full enow are death-doomed,
Fain are we to live yet,
Maids of the hall
All meet work winning."

From her wise heart at last
The linen-clad damsel,

The one of few years
Gave forth the word:
" I will that none driven
By hand or by word,
For our sake should lose
Well-loved life.

" Thou on the bones of you
Surely shall burn,
Less dear treasure
At your departing
Nor with Menia's Meal
Shall ye come to see me."

" Sit thee down, Gunnar,
A word must I say to thee
Of the life's ruin
Of thy lightsome bride—
—Nor shall thy ship
Swim soft and sweetly
For all that I
Lay life adown.

" Sooner than ye might deem
Shall ye make peace with Gudrun,
For the wise woman
Shall lull in the young wife
The hard memory
Of her dead husband.

" There is a may born
Reared by her mother,
Whiter and brighter
Than is the bright day;
She shall be Swanhild,
She shall be Sunbeam.

" Thou shalt give Gudrun
Unto a great one,
Noble, well-praised
Of the world's folk;
Not with her goodwill,
Or love shalt thou give her;
Yet will Atli
Come to win her,
My very brother,
Born of Budli.

—" Ah ! many a memory
Of how ye dealt with me,
How sorely, how evilly
Ye ever beguiled me,
How all pleasure left me
The while my life lasted !—

" Fain wilt thou be
Oddrun to win,
But thy good liking
Shall Atli let;
But in secret wise
Shall ye win together,
And she shall love thee
As I had loved thee,
If in such wise
Fate had willed it.

" But with all ill
Shall Atli sting thee,
Into the strait worm-close
Shall he cast thee.

" But no long space
Shall slip away
Ere Atli too
All life shall lose.

Yea, all his weal
With the life of his sons,
For a dreadful bed
Dights Gudrun for him,
From a heart sore laden,
With the sword's sharp edge.

" More seemly for Gudrun,
Your very sister,
In death to wend after
Her love first wed;
Had but good rede
To her been given,
Or if her heart
Had been like to my heart.

—" Faint my speech groweth—
But for our sake
Ne'er shall she lose
Her life beloved;
The sea shall have her,
High billows bear her
Forth unto Jonakr's
Fair land of his fathers.

" There shall she bear sons,
Stays of a heritage,
Stays of a heritage,
Jonakr's sons;
And Swanhild shall she
Send from the land,
That may born of her,
The may born of Sigurd.

" Her shall bite
The rede of Bikki,
Whereas for no good
Wins Jormunrek life;

And so is clean perished
All the kin of Sigurd,
Yea, and more greeting,
And more for Gudrun.

" And now one prayer
Yet pray I of thee—
The last word of mine
Here in the world—
So broad on the field
Be the burg of the dead
That fair space may be left
For us all to lie down,
All those that died
At Sigurd's death !

" Hang round that burg
Fair hangings and shields,
Web by Gauls woven,
And folk of the Gauls:
There burn the Hun King
Lying beside me.

" But on the other side
Burn by the Hun King
Those who served me
Strewn with treasure;
Two at the head,
And two at the feet,
Two hounds therewith,
And two hawks moreover:
Then is all dealt
With even dealing.

" Lay there amidst us
The ring-dight metal,
The sharp-edged steel,
That so lay erst;

When we both together
Into one bed went,
And were called by the name
Of man and wife.

" Never, then, belike
Shall clash behind him
Valhall's bright door
With rings bedight:
And if my fellowship
Followeth after,
In no wretched wise
Then shall we wend.

" For him shall follow
My five bondmaids,
My eight bondsmen,
No borel folk:
Yea, and my fosterer,
And my father's dower
That Budli of old days
Gave to his dear child.

" Much have I spoken,
More would I speak,
If the sword would give me
Space for speech;
But my words are waning,
My wounds are swelling—
Naught but truth have I told—
—And now make I ending."

William Morris and Eirikr Magnusson

Counsels of Sigrdrifa

NOW this is my first counsel:
That thou with thy kin
Be guiltless, guileless ever;
Nor hasty of wrath

Despite of wrong done,—
Unto the Dead good that doeth.
        —Lo ! the second counsel:
        That oath thou swearest never
But trusty oath and true;
        Grim tormenting
        Gripes troth-breakers,
Cursèd wretch is the wolf of vows.
        —This is my third rede:
        That thou at the Thing
Deal not with the fools of folk;
        For unwise man
        From mouth lets fall
Worser word than well he wotteth.
        Yet hard it is
        That holding of peace
When men shall deem thee dastard,
Or deem the lie said soothly;
But woeful is home witness
Unless right good thou gettest it:
        Ah ! on another day
        Drive the life from out him
And pay the liar back for his lying !
        —Now behold the fourth rede:
        If ill witch thee bideth,
Woe-begetting by the way,
        Good going farther
        Rather than guesting,
Though thick night be on thee !
        Far-seeing eyes
        Need all sons of men
Who wend in wrath to war;
        For baleful women
        Bide oft by the highway,
Swords and hearts to soften.
        —And now the fifth rede:

As fair as thou seèst
Brides on the bench abiding,
Let not love's silver
Rule over thy sleeping;
Draw no woman to kind kissing!
—For the sixth thing I rede:
When men sit a-drinking
Amid ale-words and ill words,
Deal thou naught
With the drunken fight-staves!
For wine stealeth wit from many.
Brawling and drink
Have brought unto men
Sorrow sore oft enow;
Yea! bane unto some,
And to some weary bale;
Many are the griefs of mankind.
—For the seventh I rede thee:
If strife thou raisest
With a man right high of heart,
Better fight a-field
Than burn in the fire
Within thine hall fair to behold.
—The eighth rede that I give thee:
Unto all ill look thou,
And hold thine heart from all beguiling!
Draw to thee no maiden!
No man's wife bewray thou!
Urge them not to unmeet pleasure!
—This is the ninth counsel:
That thou have heed of dead folk
Whereso thou findest them a-field;
Be they sick-dead,
Be they sea-dead,
Or come to ending by war-weapons.
Let bath be made

For such men foredone !
Wash thou hands and feet thereof,
   Comb their hair and dry them
   Ere the coffin has them;
Then bid them sleep full sweetly !
   —This for the tenth counsel:
   That thou give trust never
Unto oaths of foeman's kin,
Beest thou bane of his brother,
Or hast thou fell'd his father;
Wolf in young son waxes,
Though he with gold be gladden'd.
   For wrong and hatred
   Shall rest them never,
Nay ! nor sore sorrow;
   Both wit and weapons
   Must the king have
Who is fain to be the foremost.
   —The last rede and eleventh:
   Unto all ill look thou,
And watch thy friends' ways ever !

William Morris and Eirikr Magnusson

DANISH

ANONYMOUS

14th–16th centuries

Ballads

THE ELECTED KNIGHT

SIR OLUF he rideth over the plain,
   Full seven miles broad and seven miles wide;
But never, ah ! never, can meet with the man
   A tilt with him dare ride.

He saw under the hill-side
  A knight full well equipped;
His steel was black, his helm was barred;
  He was riding at full speed.

He wore upon his spurs
  Twelve little golden birds;
Anon he spurred his steed with a clang,
  And there sat all the birds and sang.

He wore upon his mail
  Twelve little golden wheels;
Anon in eddies the wild wind blew,
  And round and round the wheels they flew.

He wore before his breast
  A lance that was poised in rest,
And it was sharper than diamond-stone;
  It made Sir Oluf's heart to groan.

He wore upon his helm
  A wreath of ruddy gold;
And that gave him the Maidens Three,
  The youngest was fair to behold.

Sir Oluf questioned the knight eftsoon
  If he were come from heaven down;
" Art thou Christ of Heaven ? " quoth he
  " So will I yield me unto thee."

" I am not Christ the Great,
  Thou shalt not yield thee yet;
I am an Unknown Knight,
  Three modest Maidens have me bedight."

" Art thou a knight elected ?
  And have three maidens thee bedight ?
So shalt thou ride a tilt this day,
  For all the maidens' honour ! "

The first tilt they together rode,
    They put their steeds to the test;
The second tilt they together rode,
    They proved their manhood best.

The third tilt they together rode,
    Neither of them would yield;
The fourth tilt they together rode,
    They both fell on the field.

Now lie the lords upon the plain,
    And their blood runs unto death;
Now sit the Maidens in the high tower,
    The youngest sorrows till death.

H. W. Longfellow

THE MER-MAN, AND MARSTIG'S DAUGHTER

"NOW rede me, dear mither, a sonsy rede;
    A sonsy rede swythe rede to me,
How Marstig's daughter I may fa',
    My love and lemman gay to be."

She's made him a steed o' the clear water;
    A saddle and bridle o' sand made she;
She's shap'd him into a knight sae fair,
    Syne into Mary's kirk-yard rade he.

He's tied his steed to the kirk-stile,
    Syne wrang-gates round the kirk gaed he;
When the Mer-man entered the kirk-door,
    Awa the sma' images turned their ee'.

The priest afore the altar stood:
    " O, what for a gude knight may this be ? "
The may leugh till hersell, and said,
    " God gif that gude knight were for me ! "

The Mer-man he stept o'er ae deas,
  And he has steppit over three:
" O maiden, pledge me faith and troth !
  O Marstig's daughter, gang wi' me ! "

And she raught out her lily hand,
  And pledg'd it to the knight sae free:
" Hae; there's my faith and troth, Sir Knight,
  And willingly I'll gang wi' thee."

Out frae the kirk gaed the bridal train,
  And on they danc'd wi' fearless glee;
And down they danc'd unto the strand,
  Till twasome now alane they be:
" O Marstig's daughter, haud my steed,
  And the bonniest ship I'll bigg for thee ! "

And whan they came to the white sand,
  To shore the sma' boats turning came;
And whan they came to the deep water,
  The maiden sank in the saut sea faem.

The shriek she shriek'd amang the waves
  Was heard far up upo' the land:
" I rede gude ladies, ane and a',
  They dance wi' nae sic unco man."

Robert Jamieson

ELFER HILL

I LAID my haffet on Elfer Hill;
  Saft slooming clos'd my ee';
And there twa selcouth ladies came,
  Sae fain to speak to me.

Ane clappit me then, wi' cheek sae white,
  Ane rown'd intill mine ear:
" Rise up, fair youth, and join our dance;
  Rise up, nor doubt nor fear !

" Wake up, fair youth, and join the dance,
 And we will tread the ring,
While mair nor eardly melody
 My ladies for thee sing."

Syne ane, the fairest may on mould,
 Sae sweet a sang began;
The hurling stream was still'd therewi',
 Sae fast afore that ran.

The striving stream was still'd therewi',
 Sae fast that wont to rin;
The sma' fish, in the flood that swam,
 Amo' their faes now blin'.

The fishes a', in flood that were,
 Lay still, baith fin and tail;
The sma' fowls in the shaw began
 To whitter in the dale.

" O, hear, thou fair, thou young swain !
 And thou wi' us will dwell,
Then will we teach thee book and rune,
 To read and write sae well.

" I'll lear thee how the bear to bind,
 And fasten to the aik tree;
The dragon, that liggs on mickle goud,
 Afore thee fast shall flee."

They danced out, and they danced in,
 In the Elfer ring sae green;
All silent sat the fair young swain,
 And on his sword did lean.

" Now hear, thou fair, thou young swain,
 But and thou till us speak,
Then shall on sword and sharp knife
 Thy dearest heart-blood reek."

Had God nae made my luck sae gude,
　　That the cock did wap his wing,
I boot hae bidden on Elfer Hill,
　　In the Elf ladies' ring.

I rede the Danish young swains,
　　That to the court will ride,
That they ne'er ride to Elfer Hill,
　　Nor sleep upon its side.

Robert Jamieson

JOHANNES EVALD

1743–81

King Christian

KING CHRISTIAN stood by the lofty mast
　　In mist and smoke;
His sword was hammering so fast
Through Gothic helm and brain it passed;
Then sank each hostile hulk and mast
　　In mist and smoke.
" Fly ! " shouted they, " fly, he who can !
Who braves of Denmark's Christian
　　The stroke ? "

Nils Juel gave heed to the tempest's roar;
　　Now is the hour !
He hoisted his blood red flag once more,
And smote upon the foe full sore,
And shouted loud, through the tempest's roar,
　　" Now is the hour ! "
" Fly ! " shouted they, " for shelter fly !
Of Denmark's Juel who can defy
　　The power ? "

North Sea ! a glimpse of Wessel rent
　　Thy murky sky !
Then champions to thine arms were sent;
Terror and Death glared where he went;

From the waves was heard a wail that rent
    Thy murky sky !
From Denmark thunders Tordenskiol';
Let each to Heaven commend his soul,
    And fly !

Path of the Dane to fame and might !
    Dark-rolling wave !
Receive thy friend, who, scorning flight,
Goes to meet danger with despite,
Proudly as thou the tempest's might,
    Dark-rolling wave !
And, amid pleasures and alarms,
And war and victory, be thine arms
    My grave !

H. W. Longfellow

JENS BAGGESEN

1764–1826

Childhood

THERE was a time when I was very small,
    When my whole frame was but an ell in height;
Sweetly, as I recall it, tears do fall,
    And therefore I recall it with delight.

I sported in my tender mother's arms,
    And rode a-horseback on best father's knee;
Alike were sorrows, passions, and alarms,
    And gold, and Greek, and love, unknown to me.

Then seemed to me this world far less in size,
    Likewise it seemed to me less wicked far;
Like points in heaven, I saw the stars arise,
    And longed for wings that I might catch a star.

I saw the moon behind the island fade,
  And thought, " O , were I on that island there,
I could find out of what the moon is made,
  Find out how large it is, how round, how fair ! "

Wondering, I saw God's sun, through western skies,
  Sink in the ocean's golden lap at night,
And yet upon the morrow early rise,
  And paint the eastern heaven with crimson light;

And thought of God, the gracious Heavenly Father,
  Who made me, and that lovely sun on high,
And all those pearls of heaven thick-strung together,
  Dropped, clustering, from His hand o'er all the sky.

With childish reverence, my young lips did say
  The prayer my pious mother taught to me:
" O gentle God ! O, let me strive alway
  Still to be wise, and good, and follow Thee ! "

So prayed I for my father and my mother,
  And for my sister, and for all the town;
The king I knew not, and the beggar-brother,
  Who, bent with age, went, sighing, up and down.

They perished, the blithe days of boyhood perished,
  And all the gladness, all the peace I knew !
Now have I but their memory, fondly cherished;—
  God ! may I never, never lose that too !

H. W. Longfellow

ADAM OEHLENSCHLAGER

1779–1850

There is a Charming Land

THERE is a charming land
  Where grow the wide-armed beeches
  By the salt eastern Strand.
  Old Denmark, so we call

These rolling hills and valleys,
And this is Freia's Hall.

Here sat in days of yore
The warriors in armour,
Well rested from the war.
They scattered all their foes,
And now beneath great barrows
Their weary bones repose.

The land is lovely still,
With blue engirdling ocean
And verdant vale and hill,
Fair women, comely maids,
Strong men and lads are dwelling
In Denmark's island glades.

Robert Hillyer [1]

NORWEGIAN

HENRIK IBSEN

1828–1906

In the Orchard

IN the sunny orchard closes,
  While the warblers sing and swing,
Care not whether blustering Autumn
  Break the promises of Spring !
Rose and white, the apple blossom
  Hides you from the sultry sky—
Let it flutter, blown and scatter'd,
  On the meadows by and by !

Will you ask about the fruitage
  In the season of the flowers ?
Will you murmur, will you question,
  Count the run of weary hours ?

[1] Courtesy of the American-Scandinavian Foundation.

Will you let the scarecrow clapping
  Drown all happy sounds and words?
Brothers! there is better music
  In the singing of the birds.

From your heavy-laden garden
  Will you hunt the mellow thrush?
He will pay you for protection
  With his crown-song's liquid rush.
O but you will win the bargain,
  Though your fruit be spare and late,
For remember Time is flying
  And will shut the garden gate.

With my living, with my singing,
  I will tear the hedges down,
Sweep the grass and heap the blossom!
  Let it shrivel, pale and brown!
Swing the wicket! Sheep and cattle,
  Let them graze among the best!
I broke off the flowers; what matter
  Who may revel with the rest?

                                   Sir Edmund Gosse

BJÖRNSTERNE BJÖRNSON

                                   1832–1910

Fatherland Song
(Norwegian National Hymn)

YES, we love this land together,
  Where the wild sea foams,
Furrowed, beat by wind and weather,
  With the thousand homes.
Yes, we love her; with her blending
Father, mother, birth,
And that saga-twilight sending
Dreams upon our earth.

This the land that Harold savèd
With his warriors young;
All for this land Haakon bravèd,
Whilst that Oevin sung.
Olaf with his blood hath printed
Cross upon her loam;
From her highlands Swerre stinted
Not to talk to Rome.

Peasants ground their axes' edges
At the call to go;
Tordenskjold along the ledges
Homeward lit the foe.
Women too stood up that day,
Smote as they were men;
Others could but weep and pray,
Nor was that in vain.

Evil times could not undo us,
We outstood the same;
But when straits were sorest, to us
Blue-eyed Freedom came.
That gave strength of olden story
Hunger, war, to face;
That gave even death its glory,
Gave new ties of race.

Foe its weapon cast, and slew them—
Up our visors then !
We in wonder hastened to them,
For they were our kin.
Southward, sped by shame, we thither
Fared into their land:
Now we stand three sons together
And shall ever stand.

Norsemen, ye in hut and hall,
Thank the Lord of Hosts !

Guard He will the land and all,
Howso dark the coasts.
All for which the fathers perished,
And the mothers wept,
Hath the Lord in stillness cherished—
So we won and kept.

Yes, we love this land together,
Where the wild sea foams,
Furrowed, beat by wind and weather,
With the thousand homes.
As our fathers' battles freed us
Out of old distress,
We'll to war, if once she need us,
For her peace no less.

William Ellery Leonard

The Boy and the Flute

THROUGH the forest the boy wends all day long:
For there he has heard such a wonderful song.
He carved him a flute of the willow-tree,
And tried what the tune within it might be.
The tune came out of it sad and gay;
But while he listen'd it pass'd away.
He fell asleep, and once more it sung,
And over his forehead it lovingly hung.
He thought he would catch it, and wildly woke;
And the tune in the pale night faded and broke.
" O God ! my God ! take me up to Thee !
For the tune Thou hast made is consuming me."
And the Lord God said: " 'Tis a friend divine,
Though never one hour shalt thou hold it thine.
Yet all other music is poor and thin
By the side of this which thou never shalt win ! "

Sir Edmund Gosse

SWEDISH

GUSTAV ROSENHANE

1619–84

SONNETS

1

DEEP in a vale where rocks on every side
  Shut out the winds, and scarcely let the sun
  Between them dart his rays down one by one,
Where all was still and cool in summer-tide,
And softly, with her whispering waves that sighed,
  A little river, that had scarce begun
  Her silver course, made bold to fleet and run
Down leafy falls to woodlands dense and wide,
There stood a tiny plain, just large enow
  To give small mountain-folk right room to dance,
  With oaks and limes and maples ringed around;
Hither I came, and viewed its turf askance,
  Its solitude with beauty seemed aglow,—
  My Love had walked there and 'twas holy ground !

2

AND then I sat me down, and gave the rein
  To my wild thoughts, till many a song that rang
  From boughs around where hidden warblers sang
Recalled me from myself; then " Ah ! in vain,"
I said, " do these outpour the tender strain ?
  Can these sweet birds that with such airs harangue
  Their feathered loves, like me, feel sorrow's pang ?
Ah ! would that I, like them, had pinions twain !
Straight would I fly to her whom I love best,
  Nor vainly warbling in the woodland sing,
But chirp my prayer, and preen my plumèd crest,
  And to this spot once more her beauty bring,
  And flutter round her flight with supple wing,
And lead her to my secret leafy nest."

Sir Edmund Gosse

ERIK JOHANN STAGNELIUS

1793–1823

Memory

O CAMP of flowers, with poplars girdled round,
  Grey guardians of life's soft and purple bud !
  O silver spring, beside whose brimming flood
My pensive childhood its Elysium found !
O happy hours by love and fancy crowned,
  Whose horn of plenty flatteringly subdued
  My heart into a trance, whence, with a rude
And horrid blast, fate came my soul to hound !
Who was the goddess that empowered you all
  Thus to bewitch me ?   Out of wasting snow
  And lily-leaves her head-dress should be made !
Weep, my poor lute ! nor on Astræa call,
  She will nor smile, nor I, who mourn below,
  Till I, a shade in heaven, clasp her, a shade.

Sir Edmund Gosse

ESAIAS TEGNER

1782–1846

From Frithiof's Saga

FRITHIOF'S HOMESTEAD

THREE miles extended around the fields of the homestead; on three sides
  Valleys and mountains and hills, but on the fourth
  side was the ocean.
Birch-woods crowned the summits, but over the
  down-sloping hill-sides
Flourished the golden corn, and man-high was
  waving the rye-field.
Lakes, full many in number, their mirror held up
  for the mountains,

Held for the forest up, in whose depths the high-
  antlered reindeers
Had their kingly walk, and drank of a hundred
  brooklets.
But in the valleys, full widely around, there fed on
  the green-sward
Herds with sleek, shining sides, and udders that
  longed for the milk-pail.
'Mid these were scattered, now here and now there,
  a vast countless number
Of white-woolled sheep, as thou seest the white-looking
  stray clouds,
Flock-wise, spread o'er the heavenly vault, when it
  bloweth in spring-time.
Twice twelve swift-footed coursers, mettlesome, fast-
  fettered storm-winds,
Stamping stood in the line of stalls, all champing their
  fodder,
Knotted with red their manes, and their hoofs all
  whitened with steel shoes.
The banquet-hall, a house by itself, was timbered of
  hard fir.
Not five hundred men (at ten times twelve to the
  hundred)
Filled up the roomy hall, when assembled for drinking
  at Yule-tide.
Thorough the hall, as long as it was, went a table of
  holm-oak,
Polished and white, as of steel; the columns twain of the
  high-seat
Stood at the end thereof, two gods carved out of an elm-
  tree;
Odin with lordly look, and Frey with the sun on his
  frontlet.
Lately between the two, on a bear-skin (the skin, it was
  coal-black,

Scarlet-red was the throat, but the paws were shodden
  with silver),
Thorsten sat with his friends, Hospitality sitting with
  Gladness.
Oft, when the moon among the night clouds flew, related
  the old man
Wonders from far distant lands he had seen, and cruises
  of Vikings
Far on the Baltic and Sea of the West, and the North
  Sea.
Hushed sat the listening bench, and their glances hung
  on the greybeard's
Lips, as a bee on the rose; but the Skald was thinking
  of Bragé,
Where, with silver beard, and runes on his tongue, he is
  seated
Under the leafy beech, and tells a tradition by Mimer's
Ever-murmuring wave, himself a living tradition.
Mid-way the floor (with thatch was it strewn), burned
  for ever the fire-flame
Glad on its stone-built hearth; and through the wide-
  mouthed smoke-flue
Looked the stars, those heavenly friends, down into the
  great hall.
But round the walls, upon nails of steel, were hanging in
  order
Breastplate and helm with each other, and here and
  there in among them
Downward lightened a sword, as in winter evening a
  star shoots.
More than helmets and swords, the shields in the
  banquet-hall glistened,
White as the orb of the sun, or white as the moon's disc
  of silver.
Ever and anon went a maid round the board and filled
  up the drink-horns;

Ever she cast down her eyes and blushed; in the shield
her reflection
Blushed too, even as she;—this gladdened the hard‑
drinking champions.

H. W. Longfellow

Frithiof's Farewell

" NO more shall I see
        In its upward motion
The smoke of the Northland.   Man is a slave;
    The Fates decree.
        On the waste of the ocean,
There is my fatherland, there is my grave.

    " Go not to the strand,
        Ring, with thy bride,
After the stars spread their light through the sky.
    Perhaps in the sand,
        Washed up by the tide,
The bones of the outlawed Viking may lie.

    Then quoth the king,
        " 'Tis mournful to hear
A man like a whimpering maiden cry,
    The death‑song they sing
        Even now in mine ear.
What avails it ?   He who is born must die."

H. W. Longfellow

RUSSIAN

FOLK SONGS
The Plaint of the Wife

THE WIFE

FAIN would I be sleeping, dreaming:
Heavy lies my head upon the pillow.
Up and down the passage goes my husband's father,
Angrily about it keeps he pacing.

CHORUS

Thumping, scolding, thumping, scolding,—
Never lets his daughter sleep.

FATHER-IN-LAW

Up, up, up, thou sloven there!
Up, up, up, thou sluggard there!
Slovenly, slatternly, sluggardish slut!

THE WIFE

Fain would I be sleeping, dreaming:
Heavy lies my head upon the pillow.
Up and down the passage goes my husband's mother,
Angrily about it keeps she pacing.

CHORUS

Thumping, scolding, thumping, scolding,—
Never lets her daughter sleep.

MOTHER-IN-LAW

Up, up, up, thou sloven there!
Up, up, up, thou sluggard there!
Slovenly, slatternly, sluggardish slut!

THE WIFE

Fain would I be sleeping, dreaming:
Heavy lies my head upon the pillow.
Up and down the passage steals my well-beloved
   One,—
All so lightly, softly, keeps he whispering.

THE LOVER

Sleep, sleep, sleep, my darling One!
Sleep, sleep, sleep, my precious One!
Driven out, thrown away, married too soon!

W. R. S. Ralston

Sorrow

WHITHER shall I, the fair maiden, flee from Sorrow?
If I fly from Sorrow into the dark forest,—
After me runs Sorrow with an axe:
" I will fell, I will fell the green oaks;
I will seek, I will find the fair maiden."
If I fly from Sorrow into the open field,—
After me runs Sorrow with a scythe:
" I will mow, I will mow the open field;
I will seek, I will find the fair maiden."
Whither then shall I flee from Sorrow?
If I rush from Sorrow into the blue sea,—
After me comes Sorrow as a huge fish:
" I will drink, I will swallow the blue sea;
I will seek, I will find the fair maiden."
If I seek refuge from Sorrow in marriage,—
Sorrow follows me as my dowry;
If I take to my bed to escape from Sorrow,—
Sorrow sits beside my pillow;
And when I shall have fled from Sorrow into the
   damp earth,—
Sorrow will come after me with a spade.

Then will Sorrow stand over me, and cry triumphantly,
" I have driven, I have driven, the maiden into the
    damp earth ! "

W. R. S. Ralston

Love=song

THE little wild birds have come flying
    From beyond the sea, the blue sea;
The little birds go fluttering
About the bushes, over the open field:
All have their mates and rejoice in love.
Only the good youth, Alexàndrushka,
A homeless orphan in the wide world,
Grieves like a pining cuckoo,
And melts away in burning tears.
The poor lad has no one,
No one in the wide world to fondle him,—
No one ever brings joy to the orphan,
Uttering words of kind endearment.
Should he go out into the open field,
There to trample under foot his cares,
His misery and his bitter longing,
His longing and his misery not to be shaken off,—
Or should he go out into the dark forest,
His sorrow will not fly away.
The heart of the good youth
Is eaten up with care;
He fades, he withers in his loneliness,
Like a blade of grass in the midst of a wild plain.
To the youth not even God's light is dear.
But Dunya dear has taken pity
On the poor fellow, on the orphan;
She has caress'd the homeless One,
She has spoken to him terms of endearment,—
The beautiful maiden has fallen in love
With the lad Alexàndrushka.

She has cover'd him with her silken veil,
She has call'd him her darling, her Belovèd One:
And his sorrow and sighing have pass'd away.

W. R. S. Ralston

IVAN ANDREEVICH KRILOFF

1768–1844

The Peasant and the Sheep

A PEASANT haled a sheep to court,
  And pressed against her there a serious objection.
A fox, as judge, is ready for a fault's detection,
Hears plaintiff first and and, then, defendant in retort;
  Taking in turn each point, and cool, though others
    stammer,
  He seeks the cause of all the clamour.
The peasant says:—"My lord! when visiting my
    yard,
  I found two chickens missing; 'twas in early morn‹
    ing;
Only their bones and feathers served me as a warning;
  This sheep alone was there on guard!"
The sheep replies:—"No strange event my slumbers
    marred;
  Prithee, the evidence of neighbours don't discard;
Against me ne'er was brought a charge of thieving
    Or other crime
    At any time;
  As to my tasting flesh, 'tis notion past conceiving."
Here are the fox's judgments from their earliest weav‹
    ing:—
  "I noway can accept the pleadings of this sheep,
    Because all rogues are skilled to keep
      Their wicked purposes from others.
  'Tis clear from plaintiff's words that, on the given
    night,

Defendant held the fowl-house well in sight;
  Now, who can think she smothers
An inborn wish for viands choice?
So I decide, by conscience' sacred voice,
  She cannot have admitted
  Hens were for her unfitted!
Her guilt is clear and lets the peasant win;
  The carcase comes to me, and he will get the skin."

C. Fillingham Coxwell

ALEXANDER SERGEYEVICH PUSHKIN

1799–1837

*H*E *is placed in the company of Dante, Shakespeare, and Goethe by his compatriots. The intensity of his passionate nature was governed by a wide intelligence, a capacity for detachment, and above all by a sense of measure and harmony.*—BABETTE DEUTSCH and AVRAHM YARMO-
LINSKY.

Autumn

OCTOBER at last has come! The thicket has shaken
The last leaf lingering down from the naked branch.
Autumn is breathing cold, the road is frozen—
The brook still runs with a murmur behind the mill,
But the pond is still; my neighbour is up and away
With a hunt, away to the farthest dreaming field,
Where the winter wheat will suffer from his mad
    sport,
And the bark of dogs will startle the forest oaks.

It is my time now! I never could love the spring,
The dragging thaw, the mud, the stench—I am sick
In spring: my blood's astray, my mind is oppressed
With a yearning pain. Winter is better for me.
I love the serious snow-fields under the moon!
How the light run of the sled is swift and free,
And the hand of a love down under the sables
    warm! . . .

And oh the fun, to be shod with the sharpened steel,
And glide on the glassy face of the standing river !
The shining alarm of a winter holiday !
But still there's a limit in things !—A half-year's
    snow—
Even at last to the old cave-dweller, the bear,
It is long enough ! You cannot for ever and ever
Slide in a sled with the beautiful young Armida,
Or sulk behind double glass by a friendly stove. . . .

They commonly scold the last days of autumn: to me,
My reader and friend, they are dear; their beauty is
    quiet,
Their modesty brilliant; they draw me to them like a
    child
Whom the family does not love. I will tell you frankly:
Of all the seasons of time I can love but one;
I find in her—I am not a vainglorious lover,
Though wilful of fancy—I find in my love much good.

How shall I tell you ? She ravishes me
As a dying virgin, perhaps, might ravish you.
Condemned, and bending meekly, and murmuring not.
Not angry—a smile on the fading lips—
She does not perceive the abysmal opening mouth
Of the tomb—the purplish light on her features, plays—
To-day she is here—she lives—and to-morrow not.

Sweet mournful days, charm of the dreaming eyes,
Your beauty is dear to me that says farewell !
I love the sumptuous decline of nature's life,
The tents of the forest adorned with purple and gold,
And loud with the sound of the faster breath of the
    wind,
A billowy curtain of fog concealing the sky,
And the sun's rare beam, and the early frost,
And the threat of the grey-head winter standing off !

With every autumn that comes I bloom again;
It is good for my health, it is good, this Russian cold;
I fall afresh in love with the habit of being;
Sleep flies early, and hunger is in its place,
The blood romps joyfully through my heart,
Desire seethes up—I laugh again, I am young,
I am living life—such is my organism
(If you will excuse me, please, the prosaism).

So saddle my horse; and into the plentiful open
With fluttering mane he will carry me flying, and under
His body his glittering hoofs will ring like a tune
Through the frozen valley, will crackle and crash on the
    ice—
Till the brief day dies ! And then the chimney, for‹
    gotten,
Will waken again with fire—will pour sharp light,
Or dimly glow, while I sit reading long,
And nourishing the long thoughts in my soul. . . .

Max Eastman

Message to Siberia

DEEP in the Siberian mine,
    Keep your patience proud;
      The bitter toil shall not be lost,
      The rebel thought unbowed.

    The sister of misfortune, Hope,
    In the under‹darkness dumb
      Speaks joyful courage to your heart:
      The day desired will come.

    And love and friendship pour to you
    Across the darkened doors,
      Even as round your galley‹beds
      My free music pours.

The heavy-hanging chains will fall,
The walls will crumble at a word;
And Freedom greet you in the light,
And brothers give you back the sword.

Max Eastman

Work

HERE is the long-bided hour: the labour of years is
accomplished.

Why should this sadness unplumbed secretly weigh
on my heart?

Is it, my work being done, I stand like a labourer,
useless,

One who has taken his pay, a stranger to tasks that
are new?

Is it the work I regret, the silent companion of midnight,

Friend of the golden-haired Dawn, friend of the
gods of the hearth?

Babette Deutsch and Avrahm Yarmolinsky

The Prophet

ATHIRST in spirit, through the gloom
Of an unpeopled waste I blundered,
And saw a six-winged Seraph loom
Where the two pathways met and sundered.
He laid his fingers on my eyes:
His touch lay soft as slumber lies,—
And like an eagle's, his crag shaken,
Did my prophetic eyes awaken.
Upon my ears his fingers fell
And sound rose,—stormy swell on swell:
I heard the spheres revolving, chiming,
The angels in their soaring sweep,
The monsters moving in the deep,
The green vine in the valley climbing.

And from my mouth the Seraph wrung
Forth by its roots my sinful tongue;
The evil things and vain it babbled
His hand drew forth and so effaced,
And the wise serpent's tongue he placed
Between my lips with hand blood-dabbled;
And with a sword he clove my breast,
Plucked out the heart he made beat higher,
And in my stricken bosom pressed
Instead a coal of living fire.
Upon the wastes, a lifeless clod,
I lay, and heard the voice of God:
" Arise, oh, prophet, watch and hearken,
And with my Will thy soul engird,
Roam the grey seas, the roads that darken,
And burn men's hearts with this, my Word."

Babette Deutsch and Avrahm Yarmolinsky

FYODOR TYUTCHEV

1803–73

As Ocean's Stream

AS ocean's stream girdles the ball of earth,
From circling seas of dream man's life emerges,
And as night moves in silence up the firth
The secret tide around our mainland surges.

The voice of urgent waters softly sounds;
The magic skiff uplifts white wings of wonder.
The tide swells swiftly and the white sail rounds,
Where the blind waves in shoreless darkness thunder.

And the wide heavens, starred and luminous,
Out of the deep in mystery aspire.
The strange abyss is burning under us;
And we sail onward, and our wake is fire.

Babette Deutsch and Avrahm Yarmolinsky

NIKOLAY PLATONOVICH OGAREV

1813–79

The Road

FAINT shines the far moon
  Through misty night,
Sad lies the dead field
  In the moon's light.
White with frost along
  The road without end,
Bare-branched their long line
  Birches extend.
Bells tinkle, the team
  Swiftly whirls along,
My drowsy driver hums
  Softly his song.
Onward I travel
  In my crazy cart,
Sadly, pitying
  The land of my heart.

P. E. Matheson

MIKHAIL YURYEVICH LERMONTOV

1814–41

THIS brilliant bully and egotistic rake was, after his own fashion, a knight of the Grail and a poetic genius such as rarely graces any language.—BABETTE DEUTSCH and AVRAHM YARMOLINSKY.

A Sail

WHITE is the sail and lonely
  On the misty infinite blue;
Flying from what in the homeland?
  Seeking for what in the new?

The waves romp, and the winds whistle,
   And the mast leans and creaks;
Alas ! He flies not from fortune,
   And no good fortune he seeks.

Beneath him the stream, luminous, azure,
   Above him the sun's golden breast;
But he, a rebel, invites the storms,
   As though in the storms were rest.

Max Eastman

A Thought

I GAZE with grief upon our generation,
   Its future black or vacant—and to-day,
Bent with a load of doubt and understanding,
In sloth and cold stagnation it grows old.
When scarcely from the cradle we were rich
In follies, in our fathers' tardy wits.
Life wearied us—a road without a goal,
A feast upon a foreign holiday.
Toward good and evil shamefully impassive,
In mid-career we fade without a fight.
Before a danger pusillanimous,
Before a power that scorns us we are slaves.
Precocious fruit, untimely ripe, we hang,
Rejoicing neither sight nor touch nor tongue,
A wrinkled orphan runt among the blossoms,
Their beauty's hour the hour of its decay.

The hues of poetry, the shapes of art,
Wake in our minds no lovely ecstasy.
We hoard the dregs of feelings that are dead ;
Misers, we dig and hide a debased coin.
We hate by chance, we love by accident;
We make no sacrifice to hate or love.
Within our minds presides a secret chill
Even while the flame is burning in our blood.

A bore to us our fathers' gorgeous sporting,
Their conscientious childish vast debauch.
We hasten tomb-wards without joy or glory,
With but a glance of ridicule thrown back.
A surly-hearted crowd and soon forgotten,
We pass in silence, trackless from the world,
Tossing no fruit of dreaming to the ages,
No deed of genius even half begun.
Our dust the justice of the citizen
In future time will judge in songs of venom. . . .
Will celebrate the weak and squandering father
In bitter mockery the cheated son.

Max Eastman

The Mountain

A GOLDEN cloud slept for her pleasure
All night on the gaunt hill's breast;
Light-heart to her play-ground of azure,
How early she sped from the nest.

But the soft moist trace of her sleeping
Lay in the folds of the hill.
He pondered; his tears are creeping
Down to the desert still.

Max Eastman

The Reed

THERE sat a happy fisherman
Upon a river bank.
Before him on the wind's wings
Tall reeds swayed rank on rank.

He cut him down a dry reed,
He pierced it through and through,
Then pinched one end together,
And in the other blew.

As if to life awaking,
The reed to speak began.
Was it the wind's voice calling
Or was it voice of man ?

The reed sang slow and sadly—
" Oh let me, let me be,
Oh happy, happy fisherman,
For you are killing me.

" I was a comely maiden
With life and joy aglow.
In my step-mother's house
I flowered long ago.

" And many tears and bitter
I innocently shed,
And often in the darkness
I wished that I was dead.

" She had a son beloved
Of her and none besides,
Who frightened honest people
And ravished girlish brides.

" And once we went at evening
Upon the steep high shore
To look upon the sunset
And hear the waters roar.

" He gave me gold and silver—
I would not take his gold.
He asked me for my true love—
My heart grew sad and cold.

" Then in my soft young bosom
His heavy knife-blade sank,
And here my corpse he buried
Upon the river bank.

" Out of my stricken bosom
A great dry reed uprose,
And in it live my dolour,
My pain and all my woes.

" Oh happy, happy fisherman,
Pray let me, let me be,
Or have you never suffered
And tasted misery ? "

J. J. Robbins

From The Dæmon (Part I, xv)

ON the sightless seas of ether,
Rudderless, without a sail,
Choirs of stars uplift their voices,
Where the mist waves rise and fail.

Through the hemless fields of heaven
Wander wide and tracelessly
Clouds, unshepherded, unnumbered,
Pale, ephemeral, and free.

Hour of parting, hour of meeting,
Neither gladden them nor fret;
Theirs no yearning toward the future,
Theirs no haunting of regret.

On the grim day of disaster
These remember, worlds away:
Be beyond earth's reach as they are,
And indifferent as they.

Babette Deutsch and Avrahm Yarmolinsky

AFANASY AFANASYEVICH FOETH (SHENSHIN)

1820–92

Morning Song

I CAME to you with a greeting,
To tell you the sun has arisen,
With his hot happy light
He is trembling among the leaves;

To tell you the forest is waking,
Every twig is awaking,
And every bird is shaking his wings,
Is full of the thirst of spring;

With all of the midnight's passion
Again in the morning I come,
And my spirit is still as eager
To wait upon joy and you;

And all of the winds of the heaven
Blow happiness to me,
And I know not the theme of the singing,
But a song is lifting its wings.

Max Eastman

NIKOLAI NEKRASOV

1821–77

The Capitals are Rocked

THE capitals are rocked with thunder
Of orators in wordy feuds.
But in the depths of Russia, yonder
An age-old awful silence broods.
Only the wind in wayside willows,
Coming and going, does not cease;

And corn-stalks touch in curving billows
The earth that cherishes and pillows,
Through endless fields of changeless peace.
                    Babette Deutsch and Avrahm Yarmolinsky

IVAN SAVVICH NIKITIN

1824–61

A Night in a Village

SULTRY air, the smoke of shavings,
    Dirt spread over all,
Feet and benches dirty; cobwebs
    To adorn the wall:
Smoke-begrimed each cottage chamber;
    Bread and water stale;
Spinners coughing, children crying—
    Want and woe prevail.
Hand to mouth lifelong they labour,
    Then a pauper's grave—
Ah ! what need to learn the lesson—
    " Trust, my soul, be brave ! "

                    P. E. Matheson

FYODOR SOLOGUB

1863–

The Amphora

IN a gay jar upon his shoulder
The slave morosely carries wine.
His road is rough with bog and boulder,
And in the sky no planets shine.
Into the dark with stabbing glances
He peers, his careful steps are slow,
Lest on his breast as he advances
The staining wine should overflow.
I bear my amphora of sorrow,
Long brimming with the wine it hides;

There poison for each waiting morrow
Ferments within the painted sides.
I follow secret ways and hidden
To guard the evil vessel, lest
A careless touch should pour unbidden
Its bitterness upon my breast.

    Babette Deutsch and Avrahm Yarmolinsky

Austere the Music of my Songs

AUSTERE the music of my songs:
The echo of sad utterance fills them,
A bitter breath, far-wafted, chills them;
And is my back not bent to thongs?

The mists of day on darkness fall;
To reach my promised land I follow
A vain road that the shadows swallow;
The world rears round me like a wall.

At times from that far land the vain
Faint voice will sound like distant thunder.
Can the long waiting on a wonder
Obliterate the long bleak pain?

    Babette Deutsch and Avrahm Yarmolinsky

VYACHESLAV IVANOV

1866–

The Holy Rose

THE holy Rose her leaves will soon unfold.
The tender bud of dawn already lies
Reddening on the wide, transparent skies.
Love's star is a white sail the still seas hold.
Here in the light-soaked space above the wold,
Through the descending dew the arches rise

Of the unseen cathedral, filled with cries
From the winged weavers threading it with gold.
Here on the hill, the cypress, in accord
With me, stands praying: a cowled eremite.
And on the rose's cheeks the tears fall light.
Upon my cell the patterned rays are poured.
And in the East, the purple vines bleed bright,
And seething overflow. . . . Hosanna, Lord !

Babette Deutsch and Avrahm Yarmolinsky

IVAN BUNIN

1870–

Flax

SHE sits on tumulus Savoor, and stares,
Old woman Death, upon the crowded road.
Like a blue flame the small flax-flower flares
Thick through the meadows sowed.

And says old woman Death: " Hey, traveller !
Does anyone want linen, linen fit
For funeral wear ?   A shroud, madam or sir,
I'll take cheap coin for it ! "

And says serene Savoor: " Don't crow so loud !
Even the winding-sheet is dust, and cracks
And crumbles into earth, that from the shroud
May spring the sky-blue flax."

Babette Deutsch and Avrahm Yarmolinsky

VALERY BRYUSOV

1873–1924

Radiant Ranks of Seraphim

RADIANT ranks of seraphim
Stir the air about our bed.
With their windy wings and dim
Our hot cheeks are comforted.

Low the circling seraphs bend,
And we tremble and rejoice
At hosannas that ascend,
Winged with their unearthly voice.

Cloudy luminous faces hover,
And the wing⹀swept candles wane.
And our fiery breasts they cover
As with hidden holy rain.

Babette Deutsch and Avrahm Yarmolinsky

ALEXANDER BLOK

1880–1921

Russia

TO sin, unshamed, to lose, unthinking,
The count of careless nights and days,
And then, while the head aches with drinking,
Steal to God's house, with eyes that glaze;

Thrice to bow down to earth, and seven
Times cross oneself beside the door,
With the hot brow, in hope of heaven,
Touching the spittle⹀covered floor;

With a brass farthing's gift dismissing
The offering, the holy Name
To mutter with loose lips, in kissing
The ancient, kiss⹀worn icon⹀frame;

And coming home, then, to be tricking
Some wretch out of the same small coin,
And with an angry hiccup, kicking
A lean cur in his trembling groin;

And where the icon's flame is quaking
Drink tea, and reckon loss and gain,
From the fat chest of drawers taking
The coupons wet with spittle⹀stain;

And sunk in feather-beds to smother
In slumber, such as bears may know,—
Dearer to me than every other
Are you, my Russia, even so.

Babette Deutsch and Avrahm Yarmolinsky

From The Twelve

IT was given to this delicate and remote lyricist to produce the out-standing poem of the Proletarian Revolution. He wrote his brief, crowded epic, " The Twelve," in January, 1918, with, as he said, the tumult of a falling world assailing his ears, and it is told that the composition took him a single night. The piece is known far beyond the confines of Russia and is accessible in many languages.—BABETTE DEUTSCH and AVRAHM YARMOLINSKY.

I

BLACK night.
White snow.
The wind, the wind !
It will not let you go.
The wind, the wind !
Through God's whole world it blows.

The wind is weaving
The white snow.
Brother ice peeps from below.
Stumbling and tumbling,
Folk slip and fall.
God pity all ! . . .

The wind lashes at the cross-roads
And the frost stings to the bone.
With his nose stuck in his collar
A bourgeois stands alone.

And who's this fellow tosses his long hair
And mutters with a mournful air:
" Renegades !
Russia is dead " ?

One of those pen-pushing blades—
Gently bred.

Here's a frocked one, black and bulky,
Sidling like a beast.
Why so sulky,
Comrade priest ?
You used to strut,
Do you recall,
Your belly with its pendent cross
Shining on one and all ? . . .

It is late.
One flickering lamp
In the street.   A stooping tramp
Goes past with shuffling gait.
The shrill winds hiss.

" Come here,
Poor dear,
Give us a kiss."
" Bread ! "
" Oh, get ahead ! "

Pitchy sky; no stars, no chart.
Hate, sorrowful hate,
Bursts the heart.
Black, holy hate.
Comrade,
Watch your gait.

2

The wind is a whirl, the snow is a dance.
In the night twelve men advance.

Black, narrow rifle-straps,
Cigarettes, tilted caps.

A convict's stripes would fit their backs.
Fires mark their nightly tracks.

Freedom, ekh, freedom—
Unhallowed, unblessed !
Trah,tah,tah ! . . .

Fires blaze upon their track.
Their rifle,straps are gleaming black.

March to the revolution's pace;
We've a fierce enemy to face.

More daring, friends, take aim, the lot !
At Holy Russia let's fire a shot.

At hutted Russia,
Fat,rumped and solid,
Russia, the stolid !

Ekh, ekh, unhallowed, unblessed. . . .

9

The city's roar is far away,
Black silence broods on Neva's brink.
No more police !   We can be gay,
Comrades, without a drop to drink.

A bourgeois, a lonely mourner,
His nose tucked in his ragged fur,
Stands lost and idle on the corner,
Tagged by a cringing, mangy cur.

The bourgeois like a hungry mongrel,—
A silent question,—stands and begs;
The old world like a kinless mongrel
Stands there, its tail between its legs. . . .

11

And the twelve, unblessed, uncaring,
Still go marching on,
Ripe for death and daring,
Pitying none.

On, with rifles lifted
At the hidden enemy.
Through deaf alleys where the snow is sifted,
Where the lonely tempest tosses free.
Onward, where the snow has drifted
Clutching at the marcher's knee.

The red flag
Flaunts in their faces.

Steady beat
Their sounding paces.

Grimly followed
Are their traces.

Ruthlessly the storm-wind smites
Days and nights.

Forward, forward, the thundering beat
Of the workers' marching feet !

12

Onward as a haughty host they march.
Ho ! Who else is there ? Come out !
Only wind, wind bellying the flag,
Tossing the red flag about.

On ahead a snowdrift towers sheer.
Who is hiding in the drift ? Come out !
A starving mongrel shambles in the rear,
Limping off as though he feared a clout.

" Skip ! or I'll prick your mangy fur
With this tickling bayonet !
The old world is a mongrel cur. . . .
Beatings are the best you'll get."

Teeth keen-gleaming in a hungry grin,
Furtively he follows on behind.
The mongrel has nor kith nor kin . . .
" Hey ! Who goes there ? Answer quickly, mind !

" Who's waving the red flag ? You cannot see
In the darkness, through the blinding snow.
There is someone stirring stealthily
In the shadows, secretly and slow.

" We will get you and your comrades too !
Best surrender while you're breathing still,
Comrade . . . it will be the worse for you.
Come ! or else we'll shoot to kill."

Crrack-crack-crack ! But solitary
Echo answers, from the houses thrown,
While the storm-wind, wild and merry,
Laughs among the snows alone.

Crrack-crack-crack !
Crrack-crack-crack !

Forward as a haughty host they tread.
A hungry mongrel shambles in the rear.
Bearing forth the banner's windy red,
Where the vagrant snow-veils veer,
In dim hands no bullets sear,
On the tempest gently thrown,
Like a snow of diamonds blown
In mist-white roses garlanded—
Christ marches on. And twelve are led.

Babette Deutsch and Avrahm Yarmolinsky

The Scythians

YOU are the millions, we are multitude
And multitude and multitude.
Come, fight! Yea, we are Scythians,
Yea, Asians, a squint-eyed, greedy brood.

For you—the centuries, for us—one hour.
Like slaves, obeying and abhorred,
We were the shield between the breeds
Of Europe and the raging Mongol horde.

For centuries the hammers on your forge
Drowned out the avalanche's boom;
You heard like wild, fantastic tales
Old Lisbon's and Messina's sudden doom.

Yea, you have long since ceased to love
As our hot blood can love; the taste
You have forgotten, of a love
That burns like fire and like fire lays waste.

All things we love: cold numbers' burning chill,
The ecstasies that secret bloom.
All things we know: the Gallic light
And the parturient Germanic gloom.

And we remember all: Parisian hells,
The breath of Venice's lagoons,
Far fragrance of green lemon groves,
And dim Cologne's cathedral-splintered moons.

And flesh we love, its colour and its taste,
Its deathly odour, heavy, raw.
And is it our guilt if your bones
May crack beneath our powerful supple paw?

It is our wont to seize wild colts at play:
They rear and impotently shake
Wild manes—we crush their mighty croups.
And shrewish women slaves we tame—or break.

Come unto us, from the black ways of war,
Come to our peaceful arms and rest.
Comrades, while it is not too late,
Sheathe the old sword. May brotherhood be blest.

If not, we have not anything to lose.
We also know old perfidies.
By sick descendants you will be
Accursed for centuries and centuries.

To welcome pretty Europe, we shall spread
And scatter in the tangled space
Of our wide thickets. We shall turn
To you our alien Asiatic face.

For centuries your eyes were toward the East.
Our pearls you hoarded in your chests,
And mockingly you bode the day
When you could aim your cannon at our breasts.

The time has come. Disaster beats its wings.
With every day the insults grow.
The hour will strike, and without ruth
Your proud and powerless Pæstums be laid low.

Oh, pause, old world, while life still beats in you,
Oh, weary one, oh, worn, oh, wise !
Halt here, as once did Œdipus
Before the Sphinx's enigmatic eyes.

Yea, Russia is a Sphinx. Exulting, grieving,
And sweating blood, she cannot sate
Her eyes that gaze and gaze and gaze
At you with stone-lipped love for you, and hate.

Go, all of you, to Ural fastnesses.
We clear the ground for the appalling scenes
Of war between the savage Mongol hordes
And pitiless science with its massed machines.

But we, we shall no longer be your shield.
But, careless of the battle-cries,
Will watch the deadly duel seethe,
Aloof, with indurate and narrow eyes.

We will not move when the ferocious Hun
Despoils the corpse and leaves it bare,
Burns towns, herds cattle in the church,
And smell of white flesh roasting fills the air.

For the last time, old world, we bid you come,
Feast brotherly within our walls.
To share our peace and glowing toil
Once only the barbarian lyre calls.

Babette Deutsch and Avrahm Yarmolinsky

VLADIMIR MAYAKOVSKY

1894–

Our March

SLOG brute streets with rebel tramping !
Higher, the crags of haughty heads !
We will wash all the planets' cities
In the surge of a second flood.

Pied days, these.
Slow drags the dray of years.
Our god's Speed.
Our hearts are drums.

Who can match the glow of our golds ?
Will the waspy bullets bite ?
We strike back with songs for weapons.
Massive gold—our thundering voices.

Lacquer the lawn, green,
Carpet the days, grass;
Harness the quick years, sky,
Under a rainbow yoke.

Look at heaven, gaping with boredom:
We have shut it out from our songs.
Hey, Great Dipper, demand
That they hoist us to heaven alive.

Drink to joy ! Shout !
Spring has flooded our blood.
Heart, exult, beat !
Our breasts are as crashing brass.

Babette Deutsch and Avrahm Yarmolinsky

ENGLISH

ANONYMOUS

c. 1250

Sumer is Icumen in

SUMER is icumen in,
Lhude sing cuccu;
Groweth sed and bloweth med
And springth the wude nu.
Sing cuccu !

Awe bleteth after lomb,
Lhouth after calve cu;
Bulluc sterteth, bucke verteth,
Murie sing cuccu.

Cuccu, cuccu, wel
Singes thu, cuccu:
Na swike thu naver nu;
Sing cuccu, nu,
Sing cuccu,
Sing cuccu, sing cuccu, nu.

GEOFFREY CHAUCER

1340 ?–1400

Balade

From The Prologue to the Legend of Good Women

HYD, Absolon, they gilte tresses clere;
Ester, ley thou thy meknesse al a-doun;
Hyd, Jonathas, al thy frendly manere;
Penalopee, and Marcia Catoun,
Mak of your wyfhod no comparisoun;
Hyde ye your beautes, Isoude and Eleyne,
Alceste is here, that al that may desteyne.

Thy faire bodye, lat hit nat appere,
Lavyne; and thou, Lucresse of Rome toun,
And Polixene, that boghte love so dere,
Eek Cleopatre, with al thy passioun,
Hyde ye your trouthe in love and your renoun;
And thou, Tisbe, that hast for love swich peyne:
Alceste is here, that al that may desteyne.

Herro, Dido, Laudomia, alle in-fere,
Eek Phyllis, hanging for thy Demophoun,
And Canace, espyed by thy chere,
Ysiphile, betrayed with Jasoun,
Mak of your trouthe in love no bost ne soun;
Nor Ypermistre or Adriane, ne pleyne;
Alceste is here, that al that may desteyne.

ANONYMOUS

16th–17th centuries

Ballads

SIR PATRICK SPENS

THE king sits in Dumferling toune,
  Drinking the blude-reid wine:
" O whar will I get a guid sailor,
  To sail this schip of mine ? "

Up and spak an eldern knicht,
  Sat at the kings richt kne:
" Sir Patrick Spens is the best sailor,
  That sails upon the se."

The king has written a braid letter,
  And signd it wi his hand,
And sent it to Sir Patrick Spens,
  Was walking on the sand.

The first line that Sir Patrick red,
　A loud lauch lauchèd he;
The next line that Sir Patrick red,
　The teir blinded his ee.

" O what is this has don this deid,
　This ill deid done to me,
To send me out this time o' the yeir,
　To sail upon the se !

" Mak hast, mak hast, my mirry men all,
　Our guid schip sails the morne:"
" O say na sae, my master deir,
　For I feir a deadlie storme.

" Late late yestreen I saw the new moone,
　Wi the auld moone in hir arme,
And I feir, I feir, my deir master,
　That we will cum to harme."

O our Scots nobles were richt laith
　To weet their cork-heild schoone;
Bot lang owre a' the play wer playd,
　Thair hats they swam aboone.

O lang, lang may their ladies sit,
　Wi thair fans into their hand,
Or eir they se Sir Patrick Spens
　Cum sailing to the land.

O lang, lang may the ladies stand,
　Wi thair gold kems in their hairs,
Waiting for thair ain deir lords,
　For they'll se thame na mair.

Haf owre, haf owre to Aberdour,
　It's fiftie fadom deip,
And thair lies guid Sir Patrick Spens,
　Wi the Scots lords at his feit.

THE WIFE OF USHER'S WELL

THERE lived a wife at Usher's Well,
    And a wealthy wife was she;
She had three stout and stalwart sons,
    And sent them o'er the sea.

They hadna been a week from her,
    A week but barely ane,
Whan word came to the carlin wife
    That her three sons were gane.

They hadna been a week from her,
    A week but barely three,
Whan word came to the carlin wife
    That her sons she'd never see.

" I wish the wind may never cease,
    Nor fashes in the flood,
Till my three sons come hame to me,
    In earthly flesh and blood."

It fell about the Martinmass,
    When nights are lang and mirk,
The carlin wife's three sons came hame,
    And their hats were o' the birk.

It neither grew in syke nor ditch,
    Nor yet in ony sheugh;
But at the gates o' Paradise,
    That birk grew fair eneugh.

    *   *   *   *

" Blow up the fire, my maidens,
    Bring water from the well;
For a' my house shall feast this night,
    Since my three sons are well."

And she has made to them a bed,
    She's made it large and wide,
And she's taen her mantle her about,
    Sat down at the bed-side.

    *   *   *   *

Up then crew the red, red cock,
    And up and crew the grey;
The eldest to the youngest said,
    " 'Tis time we were away."

The cock he hadna crawd but once,
    And clappd his wings at a',
When the youngest to the eldest said,
    " Brother, we must awa.

" The cock doth craw, the day doth daw,
    The channerin worm doth chide;
Gin we be mist out o' our place,
    A sair pain we maun bide.

" Fare ye weel, my mother dear !
    Fareweel to barn and byre !
And fare ye weel, the bonny lass
    That kindles my mother's fire ! "

Bonny Barbara Allan

IT was in and about the Martinmas time,
    When the green leaves were a falling,
That Sir John Græme, in the West Country,
    Fell in love with Barbara Allan.

He sent his man down through the town,
    To the place where she was dwelling:
" O haste and come to my master dear,
    Gin ye be Barbara Allan."

O hooly, hooly rose she up,
 To the place where he was lying,
And when she drew the curtain by,
 " Young man, I think you're dying."

" O it's I'm sick, and very, very sick,
 And 'tis a' for Barbara Allan ":
" O the better for me ye's never be,
 Tho your heart's blood were a spilling.

" O dinna ye mind, young man," said she,
 " When ye was in the tavern a drinking,
That ye made the healths gae round and round,
 And slighted Barbara Allan ? "

He turnd his face unto the wall,
 And death was with him dealing:
" Adieu, adieu, my dear friends all,
 And be kind to Barbara Allan."

And slowly, slowly raise she up,
 And slowly, slowly left him,
And sighing said, she could not stay,
 Since death of life had reft him.

She had not gane a mile but twa,
 When she heard the dead-bell ringing,
And every jow that the dead-bell geid,
 It cry'd, Woe to Barbara Allan !

" O mother, mother, make my bed !
 O make it saft and narrow !
Since my love died for me to-day,
 I'll die for him to-morrow."

LORD RANDAL

" O WHERE hae ye been, Lord Randal, my son ?
 O where hae ye been, my handsome young man?"
 " I hae been to the wild wood; mother, make my
  bed soon,
 For I'm weary wi' hunting, and fain wald lie down."

" Where gat ye your dinner, Lord Randal, my son ?
Where gat ye your dinner, my handsome young man ? "
" I din'd wi my true-love; mother, make my bed soon,
For I'm weary wi' hunting, and fain wald lie down."

" What gat ye to your dinner, Lord Randal, my son ?
What gat ye to your dinner, my handsome young man?"
" I gat eels boiled in broo;-mother, make my bed soon,
For I'm weary wi' hunting, and fain wald lie down."

" What became of your bloodhounds, Lord Randal,
    my son ?
What became of your bloodhounds, my handsome young
    man ? "
" O they swelld and they died; mother, make my bed
    soon,
For I'm weary wi' hunting, and fain wald lie down."

" O I fear ye are poisond, Lord Randal, my son !
O I fear ye are poisond, my handsome young man ! "
" O yes ! I am poisond; mother, make my bed soon,
For I'm sick at the heart, and I fain wald lie down."

EDMUND SPENSER
Amoretti
1552-99

LXX

FRESH Spring, the herald of loves mighty king,
  In whose cote-armor richly are displayd
  All sorts of flowers the which on earth do spring,
  In goodly colours gloriously arrayd,
  Goe to my love, where she is carelesse layd,
  Yet in her winters bowre, not well awake;
  Tell her the joyous time wil not be staid,
  Unlesse she doe him by the forelock take:
  Bid her therefore her selfe soone ready make,
  To wayt on Love amongst his lovely crew,
  Where every one that misseth then her make

Shall be by him amearst with penance dew.
Make hast therefore, sweet love, whilest it is prime;
For none can call againe the passèd time.

LXXV

One day I wrote her name upon the strand,
But came the waves and washed it away:
Agayne I wrote it with a second hand,
But came the tyde, and made my paynes his pray.
Vayne man, sayd she, that doest in vaine assay,
A mortall thing so to immortalize,
For I my selve shall lyke to this decay,
And eek my name bee wyped out lykewize.
Not so, (quod I) let baser things devize
To dy in dust, but you shall live by fame:
My verse your vertues rare shall eternize,
And in the hevens wryte your glorious name.
Where whenas death shall al the world subdew,
Our love shall live, and later life renew.

LXXIX

Men call you fayre, and you doe credit it,
For that your selfe ye dayly such doe see:
But the trew fayre, that is the gentle wit,
And vertuous mind, is much more praysd of me.
For all the rest, how ever fayre it be,
Shall turne to nought and loose that glorious hew:
But onely that is permanent and free
From frayle corruption, that doth flesh ensew.
That is true beautie: that doth argue you
To be divine and borne of heavenly seed:
Deriv'd from that fayre Spirit, from whom al true
And perfect beauty did at first proceed.
He onely fayre, and what he fayre hath made,
All other fayre lyke flowres untymely fade.

SIR PHILIP SIDNEY

1554-86

A Ditty

MY true-love hath my heart, and I have his,
By just exchange one for another given:
I hold his dear, and mine he cannot miss,
There never was a better bargain driven:
  My true-love hath my heart, and I have his.

His heart in me keeps him and me in one,
My heart in him his thoughts and senses guides:
He loves my heart, for once it was his own,
I cherish his because in me it bides:
  My true-love hath my heart, and I have his.

Astrophel and Stella

I

LOVING in truth, and fain in verse my love to show
That she, dear she, might take some pleasure of my
  pain,—
Pleasure might cause her read, reading might make
  her know,
Knowledge might pity win, and pity grace obtain,—
I sought fit words to paint the blackest face of woe,
Studying inventions fine, her wits to entertain,
Oft turning others' leaves, to see if thence would flow
Some fresh and fruitful showers upon my sunburnt
  brain.
But words came halting forth, wanting Invention's
  stay;
Invention, Nature's child, fled step-dame Study's
  blows;
And others' feet still seemed but strangers' in my way.
Thus, great with child to speak, and helpless in my
  throes,

Biting my truant pen, beating myself for spite,
"Fool," said my Muse to me, "look in thy heart,
   and write!"

XXXI

With how sad steps, O Moon, thou climb'st the skies!
How silently, and with how wan a face!
What, may it be that even in heavenly place
That busy archer his sharp arrows tries?
Sure, if that long‑with‑love‑acquainted eyes
Can judge of love, thou feel'st a lover's case,
I read it in thy looks; thy languished grace,
To me, that feel the like, thy state descries.
Then, even of fellowship, O Moon, tell me,
Is constant love deemed there but want of wit?
Are beauties there as proud as here they be?
Do they above love to be loved, and yet
Those lovers scorn whom that love doth possess?
Do they call virtue there ungratefulness?

MICHAEL DRAYTON

1563–1631

From Idea

SINCE there's no help, come, let us kiss and part!
Nay, I have done, you get no more of me;
And I am glad, yea, glad with all my heart,
That thus so cleanly I myself can free.
Shake hands for ever, cancel all our vows;
And when we meet at any time again,
Be it not seen in either of our brows
That we one jot of former love retain.
Now at the last gasp of Love's latest breath,
When, his pulse failing, Passion speechless lies,
When Faith is kneeling by his bed of death,
And Innocence is closing up his eyes,—

Now, if thou wouldst, when all have given him over,
From death to life thou might'st him yet recover.

CHRISTOPHER MARLOWE
1564-93

The Passionate Shepherd to his Love

COME live with me and be my love,
And we will all the pleasures prove,
That valleys, groves, hills and fields,
Woods or steepy mountains yields.

And we will sit upon the rocks,
Seeing the shepherds feed their flocks
By shallow rivers, to whose falls
Melodious birds sing madrigals.

And I will make thee beds of roses,
And a thousand fragrant posies,
A cap of flowers and a kirtle
Embroidered all with leaves of myrtle;

A gown made of the finest wool,
Which from our pretty lambs we pull;
Fair-linèd slippers for the cold,
With buckles of the purest gold;

A belt of straw and ivy buds,
With coral clasps and amber studs;
And if these pleasures may thee move,
Come live with me and be my love.

The shepherd swains shall dance and sing
For thy delight each May morning;
If these delights thy mind may move,
Then live with me and be my love.

WILLIAM SHAKESPEARE

1564–1616

Sonnets

XII

WHEN I do count the clock that tells the time,
And see the brave day sunk in hideous night;
When I behold the violet past prime,
And sable curls all silvered o'er with white;
When lofty trees I see barren of leaves,
Which erst from heat did canopy the herd,
And summer's green all girded up in sheaves
Borne on the bier with white and bristly beard,
Then of thy beauty do I question make,
That thou among the wastes of time must go,
Since sweets and beauties do themselves forsake
And die as fast as they see others grow;
And nothing 'gainst Time's scythe can make defence
Save breed, to brave him when he takes thee hence.

XXIX

When, in disgrace with fortune and men's eyes,
I all alone beweep my outcast state
And trouble deaf heaven with my bootless cries
And look upon myself and curse my fate,
Wishing me like to one more rich in hope,
Featured like him, like him with friends possessed,
Desiring this man's art and that man's scope,
With what I most enjoy contented least;
Yet in these thoughts myself almost despising,
Haply I think on thee, and then my state,
Like to the lark at break of day arising
From sullen earth, sings hymns at heaven's gate;
For thy sweet love remembered such wealth brings
That then I scorn to change my state with kings.

XXX

When to the sessions of sweet silent thought
I summon up remembrance of things past,
I sigh the lack of many a thing I sought,
And with old woes new wail my dear time's waste:
Then can I drown an eye, unused to flow,
For precious friends hid in death's dateless night,
And weep afresh love's long since cancelled woe,
And moan the expense of many a vanished sight:
Then can I grieve at grievances foregone,
And heavily from woe to woe tell o'er
The sad account of fore-bemoanèd moan,
Which I new pay as if not paid before.
But if the while I think on thee, dear friend,
All losses are restored and sorrows end.

XXXIII

Full many a glorious morning have I seen
Flatter the mountain-tops with sovereign eye,
Kissing with golden face the meadows green,
Gilding pale streams with heavenly alchemy;
Anon permit the basest clouds to ride
With ugly rack on his celestial face,
And from the forlorn world his visage hide,
Stealing unseen to west with this disgrace:
Even so my sun one early morn did shine
With all-triumphant splendour on my brow;
But out, alack ! he was but one hour mine;
The region cloud hath masked him from me now.
Yet him for this my love no with disdaineth;
Suns of the world may stain when heaven's sun staineth.

LIV

O, how much more doth beauty beauteous seem
By that sweet ornament which truth doth give !

The rose looks fair, but fairer we it deem
For that sweet odour which doth in it live.
The canker-blooms have full as deep a dye
As the perfumèd tincture of the roses,
Hang on such thorns, and play as wantonly
When summer's breath their maskèd buds discloses:
But, for their virtue only is their show,
They live unwooed and unrespected fade,
Die to themselves. Sweet roses do not so;
Of their sweet deaths are sweetest odours made:
And so of you, beauteous and lovely youth,
When that shall fade, my verse distills your truth.

LV

Not marble, nor the gilded monuments
Of princes, shall outlive this powerful rhyme;
But you shall shine more bright in these contents
Than unswept stone besmeared with sluttish time.
When wasteful war shall statues overturn,
And broils root out the work of masonry,
Nor Mars his sword nor war's quick fire shall burn
The living record of your memory.
'Gainst death and all-oblivious enmity
Shall you pace forth; your praise shall still find room
Even in the eyes of all posterity
That wear this world out to the ending doom.
So, till the judgment that yourself arise,
You live in this, and dwell in lovers' eyes.

LXIV

When I have seen by Time's fell hand defaced
The rich proud cost of outworn buried age;
When sometime lofty towers I see down-razed
And brass eternal slave to mortal rage;
When I have seen the hungry ocean gain
Advantage on the kingdom of the shore,

And the firm soil win of the watery main,
Increasing store with loss and loss with store;
When I have seen such interchange of state,
Or state itself confounded to decay;
Ruin hath taught me thus to ruminate,
That Time will come and take my love away.
This thought is as a death, which cannot choose
But weep to have that which it fears to lose.

LXV

Since brass, nor stone, nor earth, nor boundless sea,
But sad mortality o'er-sways their power,
How with this rage shall beauty hold a plea,
Whose action is no stronger than a flower?
O, how shall summer's honey breath hold out
Against the wreckful siege of battering days,
When rocks impregnable are not so stout,
Nor gates of steel so strong, but Time decays?
O fearful meditation! where, alack,
Shall Time's best jewel from Time's chest lie hid?
Or what strong hand can hold his swift foot back?
Or who his spoil of beauty can forbid?
O, none, unless this miracle have might,
That in black ink my love may still shine bright.

LXVI

Tired with all these, for restful death I cry,
As, to behold desert a beggar born,
And needy nothing trimmed in jollity,
And purest faith unhappily forsworn,
And gilded honour shamefully misplaced,
And maiden virtue rudely strumpeted,
And right perfection wrongfully disgraced,
And strength by limping sway disabled,
And art made tongue-tied by authority,
And folly doctor-like controlling skill,

And simple truth miscalled simplicity,
And captive good attending captain ill:
Tired with all these, from these would I be gone,
Save that, to die, I leave my love alone.

LXXI

No longer mourn for me when I am dead
Than you shall hear the surly sullen bell
Give warning to the world that I am fled
From this vile world, with vilest worms to dwell:
Nay, if you read this line, remember not
The hand that writ it; for I love you so
That I in your sweet thoughts would be forgot
If thinking on me then should make you woe.
O, if, I say, you look upon this verse
When I perhaps compounded am with clay,
Do not so much as my poor name rehearse,
But let your love even with my life decay,
Lest the wise world should look into your moan
And mock you with me after I am gone.

LXXIII

That time of year thou mayst in me behold
When yellow leaves, or none, or few, do hang
Upon those boughs which shake against the cold,
Bare ruined choirs, where late the sweet birds sang.
In me thou see'st the twilight of such day
As after sunset fadeth in the west,
Which by and by black night doth take away,
Death's second self, that seals up all in rest.
In me thou see'st the glowing of such fire
That on the ashes of his youth doth lie,
As the death-bed whereon it must expire
Consumed with that which it was nourished by.
This thou perceivest, which makes thy love more strong,
To love that well which thou must leave ere long.

XC

Then hate me when thou wilt; if ever, now;
Now, while the world is bent my deeds to cross,
Join with the spite of fortune, make me bow,
And do not drop in for an after-loss:
Ah, do not, when my heart hath 'scaped this sorrow,
Come in the rearward of a conquered woe;
Give not a windy night a rainy morrow,
To linger out a purposed overthrow.
If thou wilt leave me, do not leave me last,
When other petty griefs have done their spite,
But in the onset come: so shall I taste
At first the very worst of fortune's might,
And other strains of woe, which now seem woe,
Compared with loss of thee will not seem so.

XCVII

How like a winter hath my absence been
From thee, the pleasure of the fleeting year !
What freezings have I felt, what dark days seen !
What old December's bareness everywhere !
And yet this time removed was summer's time,
The teeming autumn, big with rich increase,
Bearing the wanton burden of the prime,
Like widowed wombs after their lords' decease:.
Yet this abundant issue seemed to me
But hope of orphans and unfathered fruit;
For summer and his pleasures wait on thee,
And, thou away, the very birds are mute;
Or, if they sing, 'tis with so dull a cheer
That leaves look pale, dreading the winter's near.

XCVIII

From you have I been absent in the spring,
When proud-pied April dressed in all his trim

Hath put a spirit of youth in every thing,
That heavy Saturn laughed and leaped with him.
Yet nor the lays of birds nor the sweet smell
Of different flowers in odour and in hue
Could make me any summer's story tell,
Or from their proud lap pluck them where they grew;
Nor did I wonder at the lily's white,
Nor praise the deep vermilion in the rose;
They were but sweet, but figures of delight,
Drawn after you, you pattern of all those.
Yet seemed it winter still, and, you away,
As with your shadow I with these did play.

CVI

When in the chronicle of wasted time
I see descriptions of the fairest wights,
And beauty making beautiful old rhyme
In praise of ladies dead and lovely knights,
Then, in the blazon of sweet beauty's best,
Of hand, of foot, of lip, of eye, of brow,
I see their antique pen would have expressed
Even such a beauty as you master now.
So all their praises are but prophecies
Of this our time, all you prefiguring;
And, for they looked but with divining eyes,
They had not skill enough your worth to sing:
For we, which now behold these present days,
Have eyes to wonder, but lack tongues to praise.

CVII

Not mine own fears, nor the prophetic soul
Of the wide world dreaming on things to come,
Can yet the lease of my true love control,
Supposed as forfeit to a confined doom.
The mortal moon hath her eclipse endured
And the sad augurs mock their own presage;

Incertainties now crown themselves assured
And peace proclaims olives of endless age.
Now with the drops of this most balmy time
My love looks fresh, and Death to me subscribes,
Since, spite of him, I'll live in this poor rhyme,
While he insults o'er dull and speechless tribes:
And thou in this shalt find thy monument,
When tyrants' crests and tombs of brass are spent.

CXVI

Let me not to the marriage of true minds
Admit impediments.   Love is not love
Which alters when it alteration finds,
Or bends with the remover to remove:
O, no ! it is an ever-fixèd mark
That looks on tempests and is never shaken;
It is the star to every wandering bark,
Whose worth's unknown, although his height be taken.
Love's not Time's fool, though rosy lips and cheeks
Within his bending sickle's compass come;
Love alters not with his brief hours and weeks,
But bears it out even to the edge of doom.
If this be error and upon me proved,
I never writ, nor no man ever loved.

CXXIX

The expense of spirit in a waste of shame
Is lust in action; and till action, lust
Is perjured, murderous, bloody, full of blame,
Savage, extreme, rude, cruel, not to trust,
Enjoyed no sooner but despisèd straight;
Past reason hunted, and no sooner had
Past reason hated, as a swallowed bait
On purpose laid to make the taker mad;
Mad in pursuit and in possession so;
Had, having, and in quest to have, extreme;

A bliss in proof, and proved, a very woe;
Before, a joy proposed; behind, a dream.
All this the world well knows; yet none knows well
To shun the heaven that leads men to this hell.

CXXX

My mistress' eyes are nothing like the sun;
Coral is far more red than her lips' red:
If snow be white, why then her breasts are dun;
If hairs be wires, black wires grow on her head.
I have seen roses damasked, red and white,
But no such roses see I in her cheeks ;
And in some perfumes is there more delight
Than in the breath that from my mistress reeks.
I love to hear her speak, yet well I know
That music hath a far more pleasing sound;
I grant I never saw a goddess go;
My mistress, when she walks, treads on the ground:
And yet, by heaven, I think my love as rare
As any she belied with false compare.

CXLVI

Poor soul, the centre of my sinful earth,
Thrall to these rebel powers that thee array,
Why dost thou pine within and suffer dearth,
Painting thy outward walls so costly gay ?
Why so large cost, having so short a lease,
Dost thou upon thy fading mansion spend ?
Shall worms, inheritors of this excess,
Eat up thy charge ? Is this thy body's end ?
Then, soul, live thou upon thy servant's loss,
And let that pine to aggravate thy store;
Buy terms divine in selling hours of dross;
Within be fed, without be rich no more:
So shalt thou feed on Death, that feeds on men,
And Death once dead, there's no more dying then.

Songs from the Plays

From Love's Labour's Lost

WHEN icicles hang by the wall,
　　And Dick the shepherd blows his nail,
And Tom bears logs into the hall,
　　And milk comes frozen home in pail,
When blood is nipped and ways be foul,
Then nightly sings the staring owl,
　　" Tu-whit, tu-whoo ! " a merry note,
While greasy Joan doth keel the pot.

When all aloud the wind doth blow,
　　And coughing drowns the parson's saw,
And birds sit brooding in the snow,
　　And Marian's nose looks red and raw,
When roasted crabs hiss in the bowl,
Then nightly sings the staring owl,
　　" Tu-whit, tu-whoo ! " a merry note,
While greasy Joan doth keel the pot.

From Much Ado About Nothing

SIGH no more, ladies, sigh no more,
　　Men were deceivers ever,
One foot in sea and one on shore,
　　To one thing constant never:
Then sigh not so, but let them go,
　　And be you blithe and bonny,
Converting all your sounds of woe
　　Into Hey nonny, nonny.

Sing no more ditties, sing no moe,
　　Of dumps so dull and heavy !
The fraud of men was ever so,
　　Since summer first was leavy:

Then sigh not so, but let them go,
And be you blithe and bonny,
Converting all your sounds of woe
Into Hey nonny, nonny.

From AS YOU LIKE IT

UNDER the greenwood tree
Who loves to lie with me,
And turn his merry note
Unto the sweet birds' throat,
Come hither, come hither, come hither:
Here shall he see
No enemy
But winter and rough weather.

Who doth ambition shun
And loves to live i' the sun,
Seeking the food he eats
And pleased with what he gets,
Come hither, come hither, come hither:
Here shall he see
No enemy
But winter and rough weather.

———————

Blow, blow, thou winter wind,
Thou art not so unkind
As man's ingratitude;
Thy tooth is not so keen,
Because thou art not seen,
Although thy breath be rude.
Heigh ho ! sing, heigh ho ! unto the green holly:
Most friendship is feigning, most loving mere folly:
Then, heigh ho, the holly !
This life is most jolly.

Freeze, freeze, thou bitter sky,
That dost not bite so nigh
   As benefits forgot:
Though thou the waters warp,
Thy sting is not so sharp
   As friend remembered not.
Heigh ho ! sing, heigh ho ! etc.

It was a lover and his lass,
   With a hey, and a ho, and a hey nonino,
That o'er the green corn-field did pass
   In the spring time, the only pretty ring time,
When birds do sing, hey ding a ding, ding;
Sweet lovers love the spring.

Between the acres of the rye,
   With a hey, and a ho, and a hey nonino,
These pretty country folks would lie,
   In spring time, etc.

This carol they began that hour,
   With a hey, and a ho, and a hey nonino,
How that a life was but a flower
   In spring time, etc.

And therefore take the present time,
   With a hey, and a ho, and a hey nonino;
For love is crownèd with the prime
   In spring time, etc.

From TWELFTH NIGHT

O MISTRESS mine, where are you roaming ?
   O, stay and hear, your true love's coming,
     That can sing both high and low:
Trip no further, pretty sweeting,
Journeys end in lovers meeting,
   Every wise man's son doth know.

What is love ?   'Tis not hereafter;
Present mirth hath present laughter;
    What's to come is still unsure:
In delay there lies no plenty;
Then come kiss me, sweet and twenty,
    Youth's a stuff will not endure.

From MEASURE FOR MEASURE

TAKE, O, take those lips away,
    That so sweetly were forsworn;
And those eyes, the break of day,
    Lights that do mislead the morn:
But my kisses bring again,
                Bring again;
Seals of love, but sealed in vain,
                Sealed in vain.

From CYMBELINE

HARK, hark ! the lark at heaven's gate sings,
    And Phœbus 'gins arise,
His steeds to water at those springs
    On chaliced flowers that lies;
And winking Mary-buds begin
    To ope their golden eyes:
With every thing that pretty is,
    My lady sweet, arise;
    Arise, arise.

FEAR no more the heat o' the sun,
    Nor the furious winter's rages;
Thou thy worldly task hast done,
    Home art gone, and ta'en thy wages:
Golden lads and girls all must,
As chimney-sweepers, come to dust.

Fear no more the frowns o' the great;
    Thou art past the tyrant's stroke;

Care no more to clothe and eat;
　　To thee the reed is as the oak:
The sceptre, learning, physic, must
All follow this, and come to dust.

Fear no more the lightning-flash,
　　Nor the all-dreaded thunder-stone;
Fear not slander, censure rash;
　　Thou hast finished joy and moan:
All lovers young, all lovers must
Consign to thee, and come to dust.

No exorciser harm thee !
　　Nor no witchcraft charm thee !
Ghost unlaid forbear thee !
　　Nothing ill come near thee !
Quiet consummation have;
And renownèd be thy grave !

From THE TEMPEST

FULL fathom five thy father lies;
　　Of his bones are coral made;
Those are pearls that were his eyes:
　　Nothing of him that doth fade
But doth suffer a sea-change
Into something rich and strange.
Sea-nymphs hourly ring his knell:
　　　　　　　　　　Ding-dong.
Hark ! now I hear them,—ding-dong, bell.

Where the bee sucks, there suck I;
In a cowslip's bell I lie;
There I couch when owls do cry.
On the bat's back I do fly
After summer merrily.
Merrily, merrily shall I live now
Under the blossom that hangs on the bough.

BEN JONSON

1573–1637

Hymn to Diana

From CYNTHIA'S REVELS

QUEEN and huntress, chaste and fair,
  Now the sun is laid to sleep,
Seated in thy silver chair,
    State in wonted manner keep:
      Hesperus entreats thy light,
      Goddess excellently bright.

Earth, let not thy envious shade
  Dare itself to interpose;
Cynthia's shining orb was made
    Heaven to clear when day did close:
      Bless us then with wishèd sight,
      Goddess excellently bright.

Lay thy bow of pearl apart
  And thy crystal-shining quiver;
Give unto the flying hart
    Space to breathe, how short soever:
      Thou that mak'st a day of night—
      Goddess excellently bright !

Song to Celia

DRINK to me only with thine eyes,
  And I will pledge with mine;
Or leave a kiss but in the cup,
  And I'll not look for wine.
The thirst that from the soul doth rise
  Doth ask a drink divine;
But might I of Jove's nectar sup,
  I would not change for thine.

I sent thee late a rosy wreath,
   Not so much honouring thee
As giving it a hope that there
   It could not withered be.
But thou thereon didst only breathe,
   And sent'st it back to me;
Since when it grows, and smells, I swear,
   Not of itself but thee.

Simplex Munditiis

From EPICŒNE; OR, THE SILENT WOMAN

STILL to be neat, still to be dressed,
   As you were going to a feast;
Still to be powdered, still perfumed:
   Lady, it is to be presumed,
Though art's hid causes are not found,
All is not sweet, all is not sound.

Give me a look, give me a face
That makes simplicity a grace;
Robes loosely flowing, hair as free:
Such sweet neglect more taketh me
Than all the adulteries of art;
They strike mine eyes, but not my heart.

JOHN DONNE

1573–1631

Song

GO and catch a falling star,
   Get with child a mandrake root,
Tell me where all past years are,
   Or who cleft the devil's foot,

Teach me to hear mermaids' singing,
  Or to keep off envy's stinging,
    And find
    What wind
Serves to advance an honest mind.

If thou be'st born to strange sights,
  Things invisible go see,
Ride ten thousand days and nights,
  Till Age snow white hairs on thee;
Thou, when thou return'st, wilt tell me
All strange wonders that befell thee,
    And swear
    No where
Lives a woman true and fair.

If thou find'st one, let me know;
  Such a pilgrimage were sweet.
Yet do not; I would not go,
  Though at next door we might meet.
Though she were true when you met her,
And last till you write your letter,
    Yet she
    Will be
False, ere I come, to two or three.

Love's Deity

I LONG to talk with some old lover's ghost
  Who died before the god of love was born.
I cannot think that he who then loved most,
  Sunk so low as to love one which did scorn.
But since this god produced a destiny
And that vice-nature, custom, lets it be,
  I must love her that loves not me.

Sure, they which made him god, meant not so much,
  Nor he in his young godhead practised it.
But when an even flame two hearts did touch,
  His office was indulgently to fit
Actives to passives.   Correspondency
Only his subject was; it cannot be
  Love, till I love her who loves me.

But every modern god will not extend
  His vast prerogative as far as Jove.
To rage, to lust, to write to, to commend,
  All is the purlieu of the god of love.
O ! were we wakened by this tyranny
To ungod this child again, it could not be
  I should love her who loves not me.

Rebel and atheist too, why murmur I,
  As though I felt the worst that love could do ?
Love may make me leave loving, or might try
  A deeper plague, to make her love me too;
Which, since she loves before, I'm loth to see.
Falsehood is worse than hate; and that must be,
  If she whom I love, should love me.

The Funeral

WHOEVER comes to shroud me, do not harm
      Nor question much
  That subtle wreath of hair about mine arm;
  The mystery, the sign you must not touch,
      For 'tis my outward soul,
  Viceroy to that which, unto heav'n being gone,
      Will leave this to control
  And keep these limbs, her provinces, from dissolu-
      tion.

  For if the sinewy thread my brain lets fall
      Through every part

Can tie those parts, and make me one of all;
Those hairs, which upward grew, and strength and
    art
    Have from a better brain,
Can better do 't: except she meant that I
    By this should know my pain,
As prisoners then are manacled, when they're
    condemned to die.

Whate'er she meant by 't, bury it with me,
    For since I am
Love's martyr, it might breed idolatry
If into other hands these reliques came;
    As 't was humility
To afford to it all that a soul can do,
    So 't is some bravery
That, since you would have none of me, I bury
    some of you.

A Hymn to God the Father

WILT thou forgive that sin where I begun,
    Which was my sin, though it were done before?
Wilt thou forgive that sin through which I run,
    And do run still, though still I do deplore?
When thou hast done, thou hast not done;
    For I have more.

Wilt thou forgive that sin which I have won
    Others to sin, and made my sins their door?
Wilt thou forgive that sin which I did shun
    A year or two, but wallowed in a score?
When thou hast done, thou hast not done;
    For I have more.

I have a sin of fear, that when I've spun
    My last thread, I shall perish on the shore;

But swear by thyself that at my death thy Son
  Shall shine as he shines now and heretofore;
And having done that, thou hast done;
  I fear no more.

RICHARD BARNEFIELD

1574–1627

The Nightingale

AS it fell upon a day
  In the merry month of May,
  Sitting in a pleasant shade
  Which a grove of myrtles made,
  Beasts did leap and birds did sing,
  Trees did grow and plants did spring;
  Everything did banish moan
  Save the Nightingale alone:
  She, poor bird, as all forlorn,
  Leaned her breast up till a thorn,
  And there sung the dolefull'st ditty
  That to hear it was great pity.
  Fie, fie, fie, now would she cry;
  Teru, teru, by and by;
  That to hear her so complain
  Scarce I could from tears refrain;
  For her griefs so lively shown
  Made me think upon mine own.
  Ah! thought I, thou mourn'st in vain,
  None takes pity on thy pain:
  Senseless trees they cannot hear thee,
  Ruthless beasts they will not cheer thee:
  King Pandion he is dead,
  All thy friends are lapped in lead;
  All thy fellow birds do sing
  Careless of thy sorrowing:
  Even so, poor bird, like thee
  None alive will pity me.

JOHN FLETCHER

1579–1625

Aspatia's Song

From THE MAID'S TRAGEDY

LAY a garland on my hearse
　　Of the dismal yew;
Maidens, willow branches bear;
　　Say I dièd true.

My love was false, but I was firm
　　From my hour of birth;
Upon my buried body lie
　　Lightly, gentle earth!

GEORGE WITHER

1588–1667

The Lover's Resolution

SHALL I, wasting in despair,
Die, because a woman's fair?
　Or make pale my cheeks with care
　'Cause another's rosy are?
　Be she fairer than the day,
　Or the flowery meads in May,
　　If she think not well of me,
　　What care I how fair she be?

Shall my silly heart be pined,
'Cause I see a woman kind?
　Or a well disposèd nature
　Joinèd with a lovely feature?
　Be she meeker, kinder, than
　Turtle-dove or pelican,
　　If she be not so to me,
　　What care I how kind she be?

Shall a woman's virtues move
Me to perish for her love ?
Or her well deserving known
Make me quite forget my own ?
Be she with that goodness blest
Which may merit name of Best,
   If she be not such to me,
   What care I how good she be ?

'Cause her fortune seems too high,
Shall I play the fool and die ?
She that bears a noble mind,
If not outward helps she find,
Thinks what with them he would do
That without them dares her woo;
   And unless that mind I see,
   What care I how great she be ?

Great, or good, or kind, or fair,
I will ne'er the more despair;
If she love me, this believe,
I will die ere she shall grieve;
If she slight me when I woo,
I can scorn, and let her go;
   For if she be not for me,
   What care I for whom she be ?

WILLIAM BROWNE
1590 ?–1645 ?

On the Countess of Pembroke

UNDERNEATH this sable hearse
Lies the subject of all verse:
Sidney's sister, Pembroke's mother:
Death, ere thou hast slain another
Fair, and learned, and good as she,
Time shall throw a dart at thee.

Marble piles let no man raise
To her name: in after days,
Some kind woman, born as she,
Reading this, like Niobe
Shall turn marble, and become
Both her mourner and her tomb.

ROBERT   HERRICK   *1591–1674*

An Ode for Ben Jonson

AH, Ben!
Say how, or when
Shall we, thy guests,
Meet at those lyric feasts
Made at the Sun,
The Dog, the Triple Tun?
Where we such clusters had,
As made us nobly wild, not mad;
And yet each verse of thine
Out/did the meat, out/did the frolic wine.

My Ben!
Or come again,
Or send to us
Thy wit's great overplus;
But teach us yet
Wisely to husband it,
Lest we that talent spend;
And having once brought to an end
That precious stock, the store
Of such a wit the world should have no more.

To Daffodils

FAIR daffodils, we weep to see
You haste away so soon;
As yet the early rising sun
Has not attained his noon.

Stay, stay,
Until the hasting day
Has run
But to the even-song:
And, having prayed together, we
Will go with you along.

We have short time to stay as you,
We have as short a spring;
As quick a growth to meet decay,
As you, or anything.
We die,
As your hours do, and dry
Away,
Like to the summer's rain,
Or as the pearls of morning's dew,
Ne'er to be found again.

Upon Julia's Clothes

WHENAS in silks my Julia goes,
Then, then, methinks, how sweetly flows
That liquefaction of her clothes.

Next, when I cast mine eyes, and see
That brave vibration, each way free,
O, how that glittering taketh me !

Sweet Disorder

A SWEET disorder in the dress
Kindles in clothes a wantonness:
A lawn about the shoulders thrown
Into a fine distraction—
An erring lace, which here and there
Enthrals the crimson stomacher—
A cuff neglectful, and thereby
Ribbands to flow confusedly—

A winning wave, deserving note,
In the tempestuous petticoat—
A careless shoe-string, in whose tie
I see a wild civility—
Do more bewitch me than when art
Is too precise in every part.

Grace for a Child

HERE a little child I stand,
Heaving up my either hand;
Cold as paddocks though they be,
Here I lift them up to Thee,
For a benison to fall
On our meat and on us all.   Amen.

To the Virgins to make Much
of Time

GATHER ye rosebuds while ye may,
Old Time is still a-flying;
And this same flower that smiles to-day,
To-morrow will be dying.

The glorious lamp of heaven, the sun,
The higher he's a-getting,
The sooner will his race be run,
And nearer he's to setting.

That age is best which is the first,
When youth and blood are warmer;
But being spent, the worse and worst
Times still succeed the former.

Then be not coy, but use your time,
And while ye may, go marry;
For, having lost but once your prime,
You may for ever tarry.

GEORGE HERBERT

1593–1633

Virtue

SWEET day, so cool, so calm, so bright,
  The bridal of the earth and sky;
The dew shall weep thy fall to-night,
  For thou must die.

Sweet rose, whose hue, angry and brave,
  Bids the rash gazer wipe his eye,
Thy root is ever in its grave,
  And thou must die.

Sweet spring, full of sweet days and roses,
  A box where sweets compacted lie,
My music shows ye have your closes,
  And all must die.

Only a sweet and virtuous soul,
  Like seasoned timber, never gives;
But though the whole world turn to coal,
  Then chiefly lives.

Peace

SWEET Peace, where dost thou dwell? I humbly
    crave,
    Let me once know.
  I sought thee in a secret cave,
    And ask'd, if Peace were there,
A hollow wind did seem to answer, No:
    Go seek elsewhere.

I did; and going did a rainbow note:
    Surely, thought I,
  This is the lace of Peace's coat:
    I will search out the matter.

But while I lookt the clouds immediately
Did break and scatter.

Then went I to a garden and did spy
A gallant flower,
The crown Imperiall: Sure, said I,
Peace at the root must dwell.
But when I digg'd, I saw a worm devoure
What show'd so well.

At length I met a rev'rend good old man;
Whom when for Peace
I did demand, he thus began:
There was a Prince of old
At Salem dwelt, who liv'd with good increase
Of flock and fold.

He sweetly liv'd; yet sweetnesse did not save
His life from foes.
But after death out of his grave
There sprang twelve stalks of wheat;
Which many wondring at, got some of those
To plant and set.

It prosper'd strangely, and did soon disperse
Through all the earth:
For they that taste it do rehearse,
That vertue lies therein;
A secret vertue, bringing peace and mirth
By flight of sinne.

Take of this grain, which in my garden grows,
And grows for you;
Make bread of it: and that repose .
And peace, which ev'ry where
With so much earnestness you do pursue
Is onely there.

The Collar

I STRUCK the board, and cried, " No more;
     I will abroad !
What, shall I ever sigh and pine ?
My lines and life are free; free as the road,
    Loose as the wind, as large as store.
      Shall I be still in suit ?
    Have I no harvest but a thorn
    To let me blood, and not restore
What I have lost with cordial fruit ?
      Sure there was wine
    Before my sighs did dry it; there was corn
    Before my tears did drown it;
    Is the year only lost to me ?
    Have I no bays to crown it,
No flowers, no garlands gay ? all blasted,
      All wasted ?
    Not so, my heart; but there is fruit,
     And thou hast hands.
    Recover all thy sigh-blown age
On double pleasures; leave thy cold dispute
Of what is fit and not; forsake thy cage,
     Thy rope of sands
Which petty thoughts have made; and made to thee
    Good cable, to enforce and draw,
     And be thy law,
    While thou didst wink and wouldst not see.
      Away ! take heed;
      I will abroad.
Call in thy death's head there, tie up thy fears:
     He that forbears
    To suit and serve his need
    Deserves his load."
But as I raved, and grew more fierce and wild
     At every word,

Methought I heard one calling, " Child " ;
And I replied, " My Lord."

THOMAS CAREW
1594 ?–1639

Disdain Returned

HE that loves a rosy cheek,
    Or a coral lip admires,
Or from star-like eyes doth seek
    Fuel to maintain his fires;
As old Time makes these decay,
So his flames must waste away.

But a smooth and steadfast mind,
    Gentle thoughts, and calm desires,
Hearts with equal love combined,
    Kindle never-dying fires.
Where these are not, I despise
Lovely cheeks or lips or eyes.

No tears, Celia, now shall win
    My resolved heart to return;
I have searched that soul within,
    And find naught but pride and scorn:
I have learned thy arts, and now
Can disdain as much as thou.
    Some power in my revenge convey
    That love to her I cast away.

Ask me no more

ASK me no more where Jove bestows,
    When June is past, the fading rose;
For in your beauty's orient deep
These flowers, as in their causes, sleep.

Ask me no more whither do stray
The golden atoms of the day,
For, in pure love, heaven did prepare
Those powders to enrich your hair.

Ask me no more whither doth haste
The nightingale when May is past;
For in your sweet dividing throat
She winters, and keeps warm her note.

Ask me no more where those stars light
That downwards fall in dead of night,
For in your eyes they sit, and there
Fixèd become as in their sphere.

Ask me no more if east or west
The phœnix builds her spicy nest;
For unto you at last she flies,
And in your fragrant bosom dies.

JAMES SHIRLEY

1596-1666

A Dirge

From THE CONTENTION OF AJAX AND ULYSSES

THE glories of our blood and state
  Are shadows, not substantial things;
 There is no armour against fate;
 Death lays his icy hand on kings:
    Sceptre and crown
    Must tumble down,
And in the dust be equal made
With the poor crooked scythe and spade.

Some men with swords may reap the field,
  And plant fresh laurels where they kill;

But their strong nerves at last must yield;
　They tame but one another still:
　　　Early or late
　　　They stoop to fate,
And must give up their murmuring breath
When they, pale captives, creep to death.

The garlands wither on your brow;
　Then boast no more your mighty deeds;
Upon Death's purple altar now
　See where the victor victim bleeds:
　　　Your heads must come
　　　To the cold tomb;
Only the actions of the just
Smell sweet, and blossom in their dust.

WILLIAM DAVENANT

1606–68

Song

THE lark now leaves his watery nest,
　And climbing shakes his dewy wings.
He takes this window for the East,
　And to implore your light he sings—
Awake, awake! the morn will never rise
Till she can dress her beauty at your eyes.

The merchant bows unto the seaman's star,
　The ploughman from the sun his season takes;
But still the lover wonders what they are
　Who look for day before his mistress wakes.
Awake, awake! break through your veils of lawn!
Then draw your curtains, and begin the dawn!

EDMUND WALLER

1606–87

Go, Lovely Rose !

GO, lovely Rose !
Tell her that wastes her time and me
That now she knows,
When I resemble her to thee,
How sweet and fair she seems to be.

Tell her that's young,
And shuns to have her graces spied,
That hadst thou sprung
In deserts, where no men abide,
Thou must have uncommended died.

Small is the worth
Of beauty from the light retired;
Bid her come forth,
Suffer herself to be desired,
And not blush so to be admired.

Then die ! that she
The common fate of all things rare
May read in thee;
How small a part of time they share
That are so wondrous sweet and fair !

On a Girdle

THAT which her slender waist confined,
Shall now my joyful temples bind;
No monarch but would give his crown,
His arms might do what this has done.

It was my heaven's extremest sphere,
The pale which held that lovely deer,
My joy, my grief, my hope, my love,
Did all within this circle move !

A narrow compass ! and yet there
Dwelt all that's good, and all that's fair !
Give me but what this ribband bound,
Take all the rest the sun goes round !

JOHN MILTON

1608–74

Lycidas

In this Monody the Author bewails a learned Friend, unfortu‚
nately drowned in his passage from Chester on the Irish Seas, 1637;
and, by occasion, foretells the ruin of our corrupted Clergy, then in
their height.

YET once more, O ye laurels, and once more,
  Ye myrtles brown, with ivy never sere,
  I come to pluck your berries harsh and crude,
  And with forced fingers rude
  Shatter your leaves before the mellowing year.
  Bitter constraint and sad occasion dear
  Compels me to disturb your season due;
  For Lycidas is dead, dead ere his prime,
  Young Lycidas, and hath not left his peer.
  Who would not sing for Lycidas ? he knew
  Himself to sing, and build the lofty rhyme.
  He must not float upon his watery bier
  Unwept, and welter to the parching wind,
  Without the meed of some melodious tear.
    Begin then, Sisters of the sacred well
  That from beneath the seat of Jove doth spring;
  Begin, and somewhat loudly sweep the string.
  Hence with denial vain and coy excuse:
  So may some gentle Muse
  With lucky words favour my destined urn,
  And as he passes turn,
  And bid fair peace be to my sable shroud !
    For we were nursed upon the self‚same hill,
  Fed the same flock, by fountain, shade, and rill;

Together both, ere the high lawns appeared
Under the opening eyelids of the Morn,
We drove a-field, and both together heard
What time the grey-fly winds her sultry horn,
Battening our flocks with the fresh dews of night,
Oft till the star that rose at evening bright
Toward heaven's descent had sloped his westering wheel.
Meanwhile the rural ditties were not mute;
Tempered to the oaten flute
Rough Satyrs danced, and Fauns with cloven heel
From the glad sound would not be absent long;
And old Damœtas loved to hear our song.

But, oh! the heavy change, now thou art gone,
Now thou art gone and never must return!
Thee, Shepherd, thee the woods and desert caves,
With wild thyme and the gadding vine o'ergrown,
And all their echoes, mourn.
The willows, and the hazel copses green,
Shall now no more be seen
Fanning their joyous leaves to thy soft lays.
As killing as the canker to the rose,
Or taint-worm to the weanling herds that graze,
Or frost to flowers that their gay wardrobe wear,
When first the white-thorn blows;
Such, Lycidas, thy loss to shepherd's ear.

Where were ye, Nymphs, when the remorseless deep
Closed o'er the head of your loved Lycidas?
For neither were ye playing on the steep
Where your old bards, the famous Druids, lie,
Nor on the shaggy top of Mona high,
Nor yet where Deva spreads her wizard stream.
Ay me! I fondly dream,
"Had ye been there," . . . for what could that have
    done?
What could the Muse herself that Orpheus bore,
The Muse herself, for her enchanting son,

Whom universal nature did lament,
When, by the rout that made the hideous roar,
His gory visage down the stream was sent,
Down the swift Hebrus to the Lesbian shore ?
 Alas ! what boots it with uncessant care
To tend the homely, slighted, shepherd's trade,
And strictly meditate the thankless Muse ?
Were it not better done, as others use,
To sport with Amaryllis in the shade,
Or with the tangles of Neæra's hair ?
Fame is the spur that the clear spirit doth raise
(That last infirmity of noble mind)
To scorn delights and live laborious days;
But the fair guerdon when we hope to find,
And think to burst out into sudden blaze,
Comes the blind Fury with the abhorrèd shears
And slits the thin-spun life.   "But not the praise,"
Phœbus replied, and touched my trembling ears:
" Fame is no plant that grows on mortal soil,
Nor in the glistering foil
Set off to the world, nor in broad rumour lies,
But lives and spreads aloft by those pure eyes
And perfect witness of all-judging Jove;
As he pronounces lastly on each deed,
Of so much fame in heaven expect thy meed."
 O fountain Arethuse, and thou honoured flood,
Smooth-sliding Mincius, crowned with vocal reeds,
That strain I heard was of a higher mood.
But now my oat proceeds,
And listens to the Herald of the Sea
That came in Neptune's plea.
He asked the waves, and asked the felon winds,
What hard mishap hath doomed this gentle swain ?
And questioned every gust of rugged wings,
That blows from off each beakèd promontory.
They knew not of his story;

And sage Hippotades their answer brings,
That not a blast was from his dungeon strayed:
The air was calm, and on the level brine
Sleek Panopé with all her sisters played.
It was that fatal and perfidious bark,
Built in the eclipse, and rigged with curses dark,
That sunk so low that sacred head of thine.
    Next, Camus, reverend sire, went footing slow,
His mantle hairy, and his bonnet sedge,
Inwrought with figures dim, and on the edge
Like to that sanguine flower inscribed with woe.
" Ah ! who hath reft," quoth he, " my dearest pledge ? "
Last came, and last did go,
The Pilot of the Galilean Lake;
Two massy keys he bore of metals twain
(The golden opes, the iron shuts amain).
He shook his mitred locks, and stern bespake:—
" How well could I have spared for thee, young swain,
Enow of such as, for their bellies' sake,
Creep, and intrude, and climb into the fold !
Of other care they little reckoning make
Than how to scramble at the shearers' feast
And shove away the worthy bidden guest.
Blind mouths ! that scarce themselves know how to hold
A sheep-hook, or have learned aught else the least
That to the faithful herdman's art belongs !
What recks it them ? What need they ? They are sped;
And, when they list, their lean and flashy songs
Grate on their scrannel pipes of wretched straw;
The hungry sheep look up, and are not fed,
But, swoln with wind and the rank mist they draw,
Rot inwardly, and foul contagion spread;
Besides what the grim wolf with privy paw
Daily devours apace, and nothing said.
But that two-handed engine at the door
Stands ready to smite once, and smite no more."

Return, Alphëus; the dread voice is past
That shrunk thy streams; return, Sicilian Muse,
And call the vales, and bid them hither cast
Their bells and flowerets of a thousand hues.
Ye valleys low, where the mild whispers use
Of shades, and wanton winds, and gushing brooks,
On whose fresh lap the swart star sparely looks,
Throw hither all your quaint enamelled eyes
That on the green turf suck the honeyed showers,
And purple all the ground with vernal flowers.
Bring the rathe primrose that forsaken dies,
The tufted crow-toe, and pale jessamine,
The white pink, and the pansy freaked with jet,
The glowing violet,
The musk-rose, and the well-attired woodbine,
With cowslips wan that hang the pensive head,
And every flower that sad embroidery wears;
Bid amaranthus all his beauty shed,
And daffadillies fill their cups with tears,
To strew the laureate hearse where Lycid lies.
For so, to interpose a little ease,
Let our frail thoughts dally with false surmise.
Ay me ! whilst thee the shores and sounding seas
Wash far away, where'er thy bones are hurled;
Whether beyond the stormy Hebrides,
Where thou perhaps under the whelming tide,
Visit'st the bottom of the monstrous world;
Or whether thou, to our moist vows denied,
Sleep'st by the fable of Bellerus old,
Where the great Vision of the guarded mount
Looks towards Namancos and Bayona's hold.
Look homeward, Angel, now, and melt with ruth:
And, O ye dolphins, waft the hapless youth.

Weep no more, woeful shepherds, weep no more,
For Lycidas, your sorrow, is not dead,
Sunk though he be beneath the watery floor.

So sinks the day-star in the ocean bed,
And yet anon repairs his drooping head,
And tricks his beams, and with new-spangled ore
Flames in the forehead of the morning sky:
So Lycidas sunk low, but mounted high,
Through the dear might of Him that walked the waves,
Where, other groves and other streams along,
With nectar pure his oozy locks he laves,
And hears the unexpressive nuptial song,
In the blest kingdoms meek of joy and love.
There entertain him all the Saints above,
In solemn troops, and sweet societies,
That sing, and singing in their glory move,
And wipe the tears for ever from his eyes.
Now, Lycidas, the shepherds weep no more;
Henceforth thou art the Genius of the shore,
In thy large recompense, and shalt be good
To all that wander in that perilous flood.

    Thus sang the uncouth swain to the oaks and rills,
While the still morn went out with sandals grey;
He touched the tender stops of various quills,
With eager thought warbling his Doric lay:
And now the sun had stretched out all the hills,
And now was dropped into the western bay.
At last he rose, and twitched his mantle blue:
To-morrow to fresh woods, and pastures new.

On his having arrived at the Age of Twenty-three

HOW soon hath Time, the subtle thief of youth,
    Stolen on his wing my three-and-twentieth year !
My hasting days fly on with full career,
But my late spring no bud or blossom shew'th.

Perhaps my semblance might deceive the truth
  That I to manhood am arrived so near;
  And inward ripeness doth much less appear,
  That some more timely happy spirits endu'th.
Yet, be it less or more, or soon or slow,
  It shall be still in strictest measure even
  To that same lot, however mean or high,
Toward which Time leads me, and the will of
    Heaven.
  All is, if I have grace to use it so,
  As ever in my great Task Master's eye.

To Mr. H. Lawes on his Airs

HARRY, whose tuneful and well measured song
  First taught our English music how to span
  Words with just note and accent, not to scan
With Midas' ears, committing short and long,
Thy worth and skill exempts thee from the throng,
  With praise enough for Envy to look wan;
  To after age thou shalt be writ the man
That with smooth air couldst humour best our
    tongue.
Thou honour'st Verse, and Verse must lend her wing
  To honour thee, the priest of Phœbus' choir,
  That tunest their happiest lines in hymn or story.
Dante shall give Fame leave to set thee higher
  Than his Casella, whom he wooed to sing,
  Met in the milder shades of Purgatory.

To Mr. Lawrence

LAWRENCE, of virtuous father virtuous son,
  Now that the fields are dank, and ways are mire,
  Where shall we sometimes meet, and by the fire
  Help waste a sullen day, what may be won

From the hard season gaining ?   Time will run
  On smoother, till Favonius reinspire
  The frozen earth, and clothe in fresh attire
  The lily and rose, that neither sowed nor spun.
What neat repast shall feast us, light and choice,
  Of Attic taste, with wine, whence we may rise
  To hear the lute well touched or artful voice
Warble immortal notes and Tuscan air ?
  He who of those delights can judge, and spare
  To interpose them oft, is not unwise.

On his Blindness

WHEN I consider how my light is spent
  Ere half my days in this dark world and wide,
  And that one talent which is death to hide
  Lodged with me useless, though my soul more
    bent
To serve therewith my Maker, and present
  My true account, lest he returning chide,
  " Doth God exact day-labour, light denied ? "
  I fondly ask.   But Patience, to prevent
That murmur, soon replies, " God doth not need
  Either man's work or his own gifts.   Who best
  Bear his mild yoke, they serve him best.   His state
Is kingly: thousands at his bidding speed,
  And post o'er land and ocean without rest;
  They also serve who only stand and wait."

On the Late Massacre in Piedmont

AVENGE, O Lord, thy slaughtered saints, whose bones
  Lie scattered on the Alpine mountains cold;
  Even them who kept thy truth so pure of old,
  When all our fathers worshipped stocks and stones,
Forget not: in thy book record their groans
  Who were thy sheep, and in their ancient fold

Slain by the bloody Piedmontese, that rolled
Mother with infant down the rocks. Their moans
The vales redoubled to the hills, and they
To heaven. Their martyred blood and ashes sow
O'er all the Italian fields, where still doth sway
The triple Tyrant; that from these may grow
A hundredfold, who, having learnt thy way,
Early may fly the Babylonian woe.

SIR JOHN SUCKLING

1609–42

Why so Pale and Wan?

From AGLAURA

WHY so pale and wan, fond lover?
Prithee, why so pale?
Will, when looking well can't move her,
Looking ill prevail?
Prithee, why so pale?

Why so dull and mute, young sinner?
Prithee, why so mute?
Will, when speaking well can't win her,
Saying nothing do 't?
Prithee, why so mute?

Quit, quit for shame! This will not move;
This cannot take her.
If of herself she will not love,
Nothing can make her:
The devil take her!

The Constant Lover

OUT upon it, I have loved
Three whole days together!
And am like to love three more,
If it prove fair weather.

Time shall moult away his wings,
 Ere he shall discover
In the whole world wide again
 Such a constant lover.

But the spite on 't is, no praise
 Is due at all to me:
Love with me had made no stays,
 Had it any been but she.

Had it any been but she,
 And that very face,
There had been at least ere this
 A dozen dozen in her place.

RICHARD LOVELACE

1618–58

To Lucasta, on going to the Wars

TELL me not, sweet, I am unkind,
 That from the nunnery
Of thy chaste breast and quiet mind
 To war and arms I fly.

True, a new mistress now I chase,
 The first foe in the field;
And with a stronger faith embrace
 A sword, a horse, a shield.

Yet this inconstancy is such
 As thou too shalt adore;
I could not love thee, dear, so much,
 Loved I not honour more.

To Althea, from Prison

WHEN Love with unconfinèd wings
    Hovers within my gates,
And my divine Althea brings
    To whisper at the grates;
When I lie tangled in her hair
    And fettered to her eye,
The birds that wanton in the air
    Know no such liberty.

When flowing cups run swiftly round
    With no allaying Thames,
Our careless heads with roses bound,
    Our hearts with loyal flames;
When thirsty grief in wine we steep,
    When healths and draughts go free,
Fishes that tipple in the deep
    Know no such liberty.

When, like committed linnet, I
    With shriller throat shall sing
The sweetness, mercy, majesty,
    And glories of my king;
When I shall voice aloud how good
    He is, how great should be,
Enlargèd winds, that curl the flood,
    Know no such liberty.

Stone walls do not a prison make,
    Nor iron bars a cage;
Minds innocent and quiet take
    That for an hermitage;
If I have freedom in my love,
    And in my soul am free,
Angels alone, that soar above,
    Enjoy such liberty.

ANDREW MARVELL

1621–78

The Garden

HOW vainly men themselves amaze,
To win the palm, the oak, or bays,
And their incessant labours see
Crowned from some single herb or tree
Whose short and narrow-vergèd shade
Does prudently their toils upbraid,
While all the flowers and trees do close
To weave the garlands of repose !

Fair quiet, have I found thee here,
And Innocence, thy sister dear ?
Mistaken long, I sought you then
In busy companies of men.
Your sacred plants, if here below,
Only among the plants will grow;
Society is all but rude
To this delicious solitude.

No white nor red was ever seen
So amorous as this lovely green.
Fond lovers, cruel as their flame,
Cut in these trees their mistress' name.
Little, alas ! they know or heed,
How far these beauties hers exceed !
Fair trees ! wheres'e'r your bark I wound,
No name shall but your own be found.

When we have run our passion's heat,
Love hither makes his best retreat.
The gods, that mortal beauty chase,
Still in a tree did end their race;
Apollo hunted Daphne so,
Only that she might laurel grow;

And Pan did after Syrinx speed,
Not as a nymph, but for a reed.

What wondrous life is this I lead !
Ripe apples drop about my head;
The luscious clusters of the vine
Upon my mouth do crush their wine;
The nectarine, and curious peach,
Into my hands themselves do reach;
Stumbling on melons, as I pass,
Insnared with flowers, I fall on grass.

Meanwhile the mind, from pleasure less,
Withdraws into its happiness;—
The mind, that ocean where each kind
Does straight its own resemblance find;
Yet it creates, transcending these,
Far other worlds, and other seas,
Annihilating all that's made
To a green thought in a green shade.

Here at the fountain's sliding foot,
Or at some fruit/tree's mossy root,
Casting the body's vest aside,
My soul into the boughs does glide:
There, like a bird, it sits and sings,
Then whets and combs its silver wings,
And, till prepared for longer flight,
Waves in its plumes the various light.

Such was that happy garden/state,
While man there walked without a mate:
After a place so pure and sweet,
What other help could yet be meet !
But 'twas beyond a mortal's share
To wander solitary there:
Two paradises 'twere in one,
To live in paradise alone.

How well the skilful gardener drew
Of flowers, and herbs, this dial new;
Where, from above, the milder sun
Does through a fragrant zodiac run,
And, as it works, the industrious bee
Computes its time as well as we !
How could such sweet and wholesome hours
Be reckoned but with herbs and flowers ?

To his Coy Mistress

HAD we but world enough, and time,
This coyness, lady, were no crime.
We would sit down, and think which way
To walk, and pass our long love's day.
Thou by the Indian Ganges' side
Shouldst rubies find: I by the tide
Of Humber would complain.   I would
Love you ten years before the flood,
And you should, if you please, refuse
Till the conversion of the Jews;
My vegetable love should grow
Vaster than empires and more slow;
An hundred years should go to praise
Thine eyes, and on thy forehead gaze;
Two hundred to adore each breast,
But thirty thousand to the rest;
An age at least to every part,
And the last age should show your heart.
For, lady, you deserve this state,
Nor would I love at lower rate.
    But at my back I always hear
Time's wingèd chariot hurrying near,
And yonder all before us lie
Deserts of vast eternity.
Thy beauty shall no more be found,
Nor, in thy marble vault, shall sound

My echoing song; then worms shall try
That long-preserved virginity,
And your quaint honour turn to dust,
And into ashes all my lust:
The grave's a fine and private place,
But none, I think, do there embrace.
  Now, therefore, while the youthful hue
Sits on thy skin like morning dew,
And while thy willing soul transpires
At every pore with instant fires,
Now let us sport us while we may,
And now, like amorous birds of prey,
Rather at once our time devour,
Than languish in his slow-chapped power.
Let us roll all our strength and all
Our sweetness up into one ball,
And tear our pleasures with rough strife
Thorough the iron gates of life;
Thus, though we cannot make our sun
Stand still, yet we will make him run.

HENRY VAUGHAN

1622–95

The Retreat

HAPPY those early days, when I
Shined in my angel-infancy!
Before I understood this place
Appointed for my second race,
Or taught my soul to fancy aught
But a white, celestial thought;
When yet I had not walked above
A mile or two from my first love,
And looking back—at that short space—
Could see a glimpse of his bright face;
When on some gilded cloud or flower
My gazing soul would dwell an hour,

And in those weaker glories spy
Some shadows of eternity;
Before I taught my tongue to wound
My conscience with a sinful sound,
Or had the black art to dispense
A several sin to every sense,
But felt through all this fleshly dress
Bright shoots of everlastingness.
    O, how I long to travel back,
And tread again that ancient track !
That I might once more reach that plain,
Where first I left my glorious train;
From whence the enlightened spirit sees
That shady city of palm trees.
But ah ! my soul with too much stay
Is drunk, and staggers in the way !
Some men a forward motion love,
But I by backward steps would move;
And when this dust falls to the urn,
In that state I came, return.

JOHN DRYDEN

1631–1700

To the Memory of Mr. Oldham

FAREWELL, too little, and too lately known,
  Whom I began to think and call my own:
For sure our souls were near allied, and thine
Cast in the same poetic mould with mine.
One common note on either lyre did strike,
And knaves and fools we both abhorr'd alike.
To the same goal did both our studies drive;
The last set out the soonest did arrive.
Thus Nisus fell upon the slippery place,
While his young friend perform'd and won the race.
O early ripe ! to thy abundant store

What could advancing age have added more?
It might (what nature never gives the young)
Have taught the numbers of thy native tongue.
But satire needs not those, and wit will shine
Thro' the harsh cadence of a rugged line:
A noble error, and but seldom made,
When poets are by too much force betray'd.
Thy generous fruits, tho' gather'd ere their prime,
Still show'd a quickness; and maturing time
But mellows what we write to the dull sweets of
    rhyme.
Once more, hail and farewell; farewell, thou young,
But ah too short, Marcellus of our tongue;
Thy brows with ivy, and with laurels bound;
But fate and gloomy night encompass thee around.

Song

From MARRIAGE À LA MODE

WHY should a foolish marriage vow,
    Which long ago was made,
Oblige us to each other now,
    When passion is decay'd?
We lov'd, and we lov'd, as long as we could,
    Till our love was lov'd out in us both;
But our marriage is dead, when the pleasure is fled:
    'Twas pleasure first made it an oath.

If I have pleasures for a friend,
    And farther love in store,
What wrong has he whose joys did end,
    And who could give no more?
'Tis a madness that he should be jealous of me,
    Or that I should bar him of another:
For all we can gain is to give ourselves pain,
    When neither can hinder the other.

Song

From AMPHITRYON

FAIR Iris I love, and hourly I die,
But not for a lip, nor a languishing eye:
She's fickle and false, and there we agree,
For I am as false and as fickle as she.
We neither believe what either can say;
And, neither believing, we neither betray.
'Tis civil to swear, and say things of course;
We mean not the taking for better or worse.
When present, we love; when absent, agree:
I think not of Iris, nor Iris of me.
The legend of love no couple can find,
So easy to part, or so equally join'd.

Song

From SECRET LOVE

I FEED a flame within, which so torments me,
That it both pains my heart, and yet contents me:
'Tis such a pleasing smart, and I so love it,
That I had rather die than once remove it.

Yet he for whom I grieve shall never know it;
My tongue does not betray, nor my eyes show it;
Not a sigh, nor a tear, my pain discloses,
But they fall silently, like dew on roses.

Thus to prevent my love from being cruel,
My heart's the sacrifice, as 't is the fuel:
And while I suffer this, to give him quiet,
My faith rewards my love, tho' he deny it.

On his eyes will I gaze, and there delight me;
Where I conceal my love, no frown can fright me:
To be more happy, I dare not aspire;
Nor can I fall more low, mounting no higher.

A Song for St. Cecilia's Day
1687

FROM harmony, from heavenly harmony
 This universal frame began:
When Nature underneath a heap
 Of jarring atoms lay
And could not heave her head,
The tuneful voice was heard from high,
 " Arise, ye more than dead ! "
Then cold and hot and moist and dry
In order to their stations leap,
 And Music's power obey.
From harmony, from heavenly harmony
 This universal frame began:
 From harmony to harmony
Through all the compass of the notes it ran,
The diapason closing full in man.

What passion cannot Music raise and quell ?
 When Jubal struck the chorded shell,
 His listening brethren stood around,
 And, wondering, on their faces fell
 To worship that celestial sound:
Less than a god they thought there could not dwell
 Within the hollow of that shell
 That spoke so sweetly and so well.
What passion cannot Music raise and quell ?

 The trumpet's loud clangour
  Excites us to arms,
 With shrill notes of anger
  And mortal alarms.
 The double double double beat
  Of the thundering drum
  Cries " Hark ! the foes come;
Charge, charge ! 'tis too late to retreat ! "

The soft complaining flute
   In dying notes discovers
   The woes of hopeless lovers,
Whose dirge is whispered by the warbling lute.

   Sharp violins proclaim
Their jealous pangs and desperation,
Fury, frantic indignation,
Depth of pain, and height of passion
    For the fair disdainful dame.
   But oh ! what art can teach,
   What human voice can reach
    The sacred organ's praise ?
Notes inspiring holy love,
Notes that wing their heavenly ways
    To mend the choirs above.

Orpheus could lead the savage race,
And trees unrooted left their place,
   Sequacious of the lyre:
But bright Cecilia raised the wonder higher:
When to her organ vocal breath was given,
   An angel heard, and straight appeared—
   Mistaking earth for heaven.

Grand Chorus

As from the power of sacred lays
   The spheres began to move,
And sung the great Creator's praise
   To all the blest above;
So when the last and dreadful hour
This crumbling pageant shall devour,
The trumpet shall be heard on high,
The dead shall live, the living die,
And Music shall untune the sky.

Characters from the Satires

ACHITOPHEL

OF these the false Achitophel was first,
A name to all succeeding ages curst:
For close designs and crooked counsels fit,
Sagacious, bold, and turbulent of wit,
Restless, unfixed in principles and place,
In power unpleased, impatient of disgrace;
A fiery soul, which working out its way,
Fretted the pigmy body to decay
And o'er-informed the tenement of clay.
A daring pilot in extremity,
Pleased with the danger, when the waves went high,
He sought the storms; but, for a calm unfit,
Would steer too nigh the sands to boast his wit.
Great wits are sure to madness near allied
And thin partitions do their bounds divide;
Else, why should he, with wealth and honour blest,
Refuse his age the needful hours of rest?
Punish a body which he could not please,
Bankrupt of life, yet prodigal of ease?
And all to leave what with his toil he won
To that unfeathered two-legged thing, a son,
Got, while his soul did huddled notions try,
And born a shapeless lump, like anarchy.
In friendship false, implacable in hate,
Resolved to ruin or to rule the state;
To compass this the triple bond he broke,
The pillars of the public safety shook,
And fitted Israel for a foreign yoke;
Then, seized with fear, yet still affecting fame,
Usurped a patriot's all-atoning name.
So easy still it proves in factious times
With public zeal to cancel private crimes.

Zimri

SOME of their chiefs were princes of the land;
In the first rank of these did Zimri stand,
A man so various that he seemed to be
Not one, but all mankind's epitome:
Stiff in opinions, always in the wrong,
Was everything by starts and nothing long;
But in the course of one revolving moon
Was chymist, fiddler, statesman, and buffoon;
Then all for women, painting, rhyming, drinking,
Besides ten thousand freaks that died in thinking.
Blest madman, who could every hour employ
With something new to wish or to enjoy!
Railing and praising were his usual themes,
And both, to show his judgment, in extremes:
So over violent or over civil
That every man with him was God or Devil.
In squandering wealth was his peculiar art;
Nothing went unrewarded but desert.
Beggared by fools whom still he found too late,
He had his jest, and they had his estate.
He laughed himself from Court; then sought relief
By forming parties, but could ne'er be chief:
For spite of him, the weight of business fell
On Absalom and wise Achitophel;
Thus wicked but in will, of means bereft,
He left not faction, but of that was left.

Og and Doeg

AND hasten Og and Doeg to rehearse,
Two fools that crutch their feeble sense on verse,
Who by my Muse to all succeeding times
Shall live in spite of their own doggrel rhymes.
Doeg, though without knowing how or why,
Made still a blundering kind of melody;

Spurred boldly on, and dashed through thick and thin,
Through sense and nonsense, never out nor in;
Free from all meaning, whether good or bad,
And, in one word, heroically mad,
He was too warm on picking-work to dwell,
But faggoted his notions as they fell,
And, if they rhymed and rattled, all was well.
Spiteful he is not, though he wrote a satire,
For still there goes some thinking to ill-nature;
He needs no more than birds and beasts to think,
All his occasions are to eat and drink.
If he call rogue and rascal from a garret,
He means you no more mischief than a parrot;
The words for friend and foe alike were made,
To fetter them in verse is all his trade. . . .
Railing in other men may be a crime,
But ought to pass for mere instinct in him;
Instinct he follows and no farther knows,
For to write verse with him is to *transprose*;
'Twere pity treason at his door to lay
Who makes heaven's gate a lock to its own key;
Let him rail on, let his invective Muse
Have four and twenty letters to abuse,
Which if he jumbles to one line of sense,
Indict him of a capital offence.
In fire-works give him leave to vent his spite,
Those are the only serpents he can write;
The height of his ambition is, we know,
But to be master of a puppet-show;
On that one stage his works may yet appear,
And a month's harvest keeps him all the year.

Now stop your noses, readers, all and some,
For here's a tun of midnight work to come,
Og from a treason-tavern rolling home.
Round as a globe, and liquored every chink,
Goodly and great he sails behind his link.

With all this bulk there's nothing lost in Og,
For every inch that is not fool is rogue: . . .
When wine has given him courage to blaspheme,
He curses God, but God before cursed him;
And if man could have reason, none has more,
That made his paunch so rich and him so poor.
With wealth he was not trusted, for Heaven knew
What 'twas of old to pamper up a Jew;
To what would he on quail and pheasant swell
That even on tripe and carrion could rebel ?
But though Heaven made him poor, with reverence
    speaking,
He never was a poet of God's making;
The midwife laid her hand on his thick skull,
With this prophetic blessing—*Be thou dull;*
Drink, swear, and roar, forbear no lewd delight
Fit for thy bulk, do anything but write.
Thou art of lasting make, like thoughtless men,
A strong nativity—but for the pen;
Eat opium, mingle arsenic in thy drink,
Still thou mayest live, avoiding pen and ink.
I see, I see, 'tis counsel given in vain,
For treason, botched in rhyme, will be thy bane;
Rhyme is the rock on which thou art to wreck,
'Tis fatal to thy fame and to thy neck.
Why should thy metre good king David blast ?
A psalm of his will surely be thy last.
Darest thou presume in verse to meet thy foes,
Thou whom the penny pamphlet foiled in prose ?
Doeg, whom God for mankind's mirth has made,
O'ertops thy talent in thy very trade;
Doeg to thee, thy paintings are so coarse,
A poet is, though he's the poet's horse.
A double noose thou on thy neck dost pull
For writing treason and for writing dull;
To die for faction is a common evil,

But to be hanged for nonsense is the devil.
Hadst thou the glories of thy King exprest,
Thy praises had been satires at the best;
But thou in clumsy verse, unlicked, unpointed,
Hast shamefully defied the Lord's anointed:
I will not rake the dunghill of thy crimes,
For who would read thy life that reads thy rhymes?
But of king David's foes be this the doom,
May all be like the young man Absalom;
And for my foes may this their blessing be,
To talk like Doeg and to write like thee.

SIR CHARLES SEDLEY

1639 ?–1701

To Celia

NOT, Celia, that I juster am,
　Or better than the rest!
For I would change each hour like them,
　Were not my heart at rest.

But I am tied to very thee
　By every thought I have;
Thy face I only care to see,
　Thy heart I only crave.

All that in woman is adored
　In thy dear self I find;
For the whole sex can but afford
　The handsome and the kind.

Why then should I seek further store
　And still make love anew?
When change itself can give no more,
　'Tis easy to be true.

MATTHEW PRIOR

1664–1721

A Better Answer

DEAR Chloe, how blubbered is that pretty face !
　Thy cheek all on fire, and thy hair all uncurled !
Prithee quit this caprice, and (as old Falstaff says)
　Let us e'en talk a little like folks of this world.

How canst thou presume thou hast leave to destroy
　The beauties which Venus but lent to thy keeping?
Those looks were designed to inspire love and joy;
　More ordinary eyes may serve people for weeping.

To be vexed at a trifle or two that I writ,
　Your judgment at once and my passion you wrong;
You take that for fact which will scarce be found wit:
　Od's life ! must one swear to the truth of a song ?

What I speak, my fair Chloe, and what I write, shows
　The difference there is betwixt nature and art:
I court others in verse, but I love thee in prose;
　And they have my whimsies, but thou hast my
　　heart.

The god of us verse-men (you know, child), the sun,
　How after his journeys he sets up his rest;
If at morning o'er earth 'tis his fancy to run,
　At night he reclines on his Thetis's breast.

So when I am wearied with wandering all day,
　To thee, my delight, in the evening I come:
No matter what beauties I saw in my way;
　They were but my visits, but thou art my home.

Then finish, dear Chloe, this pastoral war,
　And let us like Horace and Lydia agree;
For thou art a girl as much brighter than her
　As he was a poet sublimer than me.

An Ode

THE merchant, to secure his treasure,
  Conveys it in a borrowed name:
Euphelia serves to grace my measure,
  But Chloe is my real flame.

My softest verse, my darling lyre
  Upon Euphelia's toilet lay,
When Chloe noted her desire
  That I should sing, that I should play.

My lyre I tune, my voice I raise;
  But with my numbers mix my sighs;
And whilst I sing Euphelia's praise,
  I fix my soul on Chloe's eyes.

Fair Chloe blushed, Euphelia frowned,
  I sung and gazed, I played and trembled:
And Venus to the Loves around
  Remarked how ill we all dissembled.

JOSEPH ADDISON

1672–1719

Hymn

THE spacious firmament on high,
  With all the blue ethereal sky,
And spangled heavens, a shining frame,
  Their great Original proclaim.
The unwearied Sun from day to day
Does his Creator's power display;
And publishes to every land
The work of an Almighty hand.

Soon as the evening shades prevail,
  The Moon takes up the wondrous tale;
And nightly to the listening Earth
Repeats the story of her birth:

Whilst all the stars that round her burn,
And all the planets in their turn,
Confirm the tidings as they roll,
And spread the truth from pole to pole.

What though in solemn silence all
Move round the dark terrestrial ball;
What though nor real voice nor sound
Amidst their radiant orbs be found ?
In Reason's ear they all rejoice,
And utter forth a glorious voice;
For ever singing, as they shine,
" The Hand that made us is divine."

ALEXANDER POPE

1688–1744

Ode on Solitude

HAPPY the man whose wish and care
A few paternal acres bound,
Content to breathe his native air
In his own ground ;

Whose herds with milk, whose fields with bread,
Whose flocks supply him with attire,
Whose trees in summer yield him shade,
In winter fire.

Bless'd who can unconcern'dly find
Hours, days, and years slide soft away,
In health of body, peace of mind,
Quiet by day;

Sound sleep by night: study and ease
Together mix'd; sweet recreation;
And innocence, which most does please,
With meditation.

Thus let me live, unseen, unknown;
Thus unlamented let me die,
Steal from the world, and not a stone
Tell where I lie.

Characters from the Satires

ATTICUS

PEACE to all such ! but were there one whose fires
True genius kindles, and fair fame inspires;
Blest with each talent, and each art to please,
And born to write, converse, and live with ease,
Should such a man, too fond to rule alone,
Bear, like the Turk, no brother near the throne,
View him with scornful, yet with jealous eyes,
And hate for arts that caused himself to rise;
Damn with faint praise, assent with civil leer,
And, without sneering, teach the rest to sneer;
Willing to wound, and yet afraid to strike,
Just hint a fault, and hesitate dislike;
Alike reserved to blame, or to commend,
A timorous foe, and a suspicious friend;
Dreading e'en fools, by flatterers besieged,
And so obliging, that he ne'er obliged;
Like Cato, give his little senate laws,
And sit attentive to his own applause:
While wits and Templars every sentence raise,
And wonder with a foolish face of praise—
Who but must laugh, if such a man there be ?
Who would not weep, if Atticus were he ?

SPORUS

LET Sporus tremble—— What ? that thing of silk,
Sporus, that mere white curd of ass's milk ?
Satire or sense, alas ! can Sporus feel,
Who breaks a butterfly upon a wheel ?

Yet let me flap this bug with gilded wings,
This painted child of dirt, that stinks and stings;
Whose buzz the witty and the fair annoys,
Yet wit ne'er tastes, and beauty ne'er enjoys:
So well-bred spaniels civilly delight
In mumbling of the game they dare not bite.
Eternal smiles his emptiness betray,
As shallow streams run dimpling all the way.
Whether in florid impotence he speaks,
And, as the prompter breathes, the puppet squeaks;
Or at the ear of Eve, familiar toad!
Half froth, half venom, spits himself abroad,
In puns, or politics, or tales, or lies,
Or spite, or smut, or rhymes, or blasphemies,
His wit all see-saw, between that and this,
Now high, now low, now master up, now miss,
And he himself one vile antithesis.
Amphibious thing! that acting either part,
The trifling head, or the corrupted heart;
Fop at the toilet, flatterer at the board,
Now trips a lady, and now struts a lord.
Eve's tempter thus the Rabbins have express'd,
A cherub's face, a reptile all the rest;
Beauty that shocks you, parts that none will trust,
Wit that can creep, and pride that licks the dust.

WHARTON

WHARTON! the scorn and wonder of our days,
Whose ruling passion was the lust of praise:
Born with whate'er could win it from the wise,
Women and fools must like him, or he dies;
Though wondering senates hung on all he spoke,
The club must hail him master of the joke.
Shall parts so various aim at nothing new?
He'll shine a Tully and a Wilmot too.

Then turns repentant, and his God adores
With the same spirit that he drinks and whores;
Enough if all around him but admire,
And now the punk applaud, and now the friar.
Thus with each gift of Nature and of art,
And wanting nothing but an honest heart;
Grown all to all, from no one vice exempt,
And most contemptible, to shun contempt;
His passion still, to covet general praise,
His life, to forfeit it a thousand ways;
A constant bounty which no friend has made;
An angel tongue, which no man can persuade;
A fool, with more of wit than half mankind,
Too rash for thought, for action too refined;
A tyrant to the wife his heart approves;
A rebel to the very king he loves;
He dies, sad outcast of each Church and State,
And, harder still ! flagitious, yet not great.
Ask you why WHARTON broke through every rule ?
'Twas all for fear the knaves should call him fool.

CHLOE

" YET Chloe sure was form'd without a spot."—
    Nature in her then err'd not, but forgot.
" With every pleasing, every prudent part,
Say, what can Chloe want ? "—She wants a heart.
She speaks, behaves, and acts, just as she ought,
But never, never reached one generous thought.
Virtue she finds too painful an endeavour,
Content to dwell in decencies for ever.
So very reasonable, so unmoved,
As never yet to love, or to be loved.
She, while her lover pants upon her breast,
Can mark the figures on an Indian chest;
And when she sees her friend in deep despair,
Observes how much a chintz exceeds mohair !

Forbid it, Heaven, a favour or a debt
She e'er should cancel—but she may forget.
Safe is your secret still in Chloe's ear;
But none of Chloe's shall you ever hear.
Of all her dears she never slander'd one,
But cares not if a thousand are undone.
Would Chloe know if you're alive or dead ?
She bids her footman put it in her head.
Chloe is prudent—would you too be wise ?
Then never break your heart when Chloe dies.

HENRY CAREY

1693 ?–1743

Sally in Our Alley

OF all the girls that are so smart
  There's none like pretty Sally;
She is the darling of my heart,
  And she lives in our alley.
There is no lady in the land
  Is half so sweet as Sally;
She is the darling of my heart,
  And she lives in our alley.

Her father he makes cabbage-nets
  And through the streets does cry 'em;
Her mother she sells laces long
  To such as please to buy 'em:
But sure such folks could ne'er beget
  So sweet a girl as Sally !
She is the darling of my heart,
  And she lives in our alley.

When she is by, I leave my work,
  I love her so sincerely;
My master comes like any Turk,
  And bangs me most severely:

But let him bang his bellyful,
    I'll bear it all for Sally;
She is the darling of my heart,
    And she lives in our alley.

Of all the days that's in the week
    I dearly love but one day—
And that's the day that comes betwixt
    A Saturday and Monday;
For then I'm drest all in my best
    To walk abroad with Sally;
She is the darling of my heart,
    And she lives in our alley.

My master carries me to church,
    And often am I blamèd,
Because I leave him in the lurch
    As soon as text is namèd;
I leave the church in sermon-time
    And slink away to Sally;
She is the darling of my heart,
    And she lives in our alley.

When Christmas comes about again,
    O then I shall have money;
I'll board it up, and, box and all,
    I'll give it to my honey:
I would it were ten thousand pound,
    I'd give it all to Sally;
She is the darling of my heart,
    And she lives in our alley.

My master and the neighbours all
    Make game of me and Sally,
And, but for her, I'd better be
    A slave and row a galley;

But when my seven long years are out,
   O then I'll marry Sally,—
O then we'll wed, and then we'll bed . . .
   But not in our alley !

WILLIAM SHENSTONE

1714–63

Written at an Inn at Henley

TO thee, fair freedom ! I retire
   From flattery, cards, and dice, and din;
Nor art thou found in mansions higher
   Than the low cot or humble inn.

'Tis here with boundless power I reign;
   And every health which I begin
Converts dull port to bright champagne;
   Such freedom crowns it, at an inn.

I fly from pomp, I fly from plate !
   I fly from falsehood's specious grin !
Freedom I love, and form I hate,
   And choose my lodgings at an inn.

Here, waiter ! take my sordid ore,
   Which lacqueys else might hope to win;
It buys, what courts have not in store,
   It buys me freedom at an inn.

Whoe'er has travelled life's dull round,
   Where'er his stages may have been,
May sigh to think he still has found
   The warmest welcome at an inn.

THOMAS GRAY

1716–71

Elegy

WRITTEN IN A COUNTRY CHURCHYARD

THE Curfew tolls the knell of parting day,
 The lowing herd winds slowly o'er the lea,
The ploughman homeward plods his weary way,
 And leaves the world to darkness and to me.

Now fades the glimmering landscape on the sight,
 And all the air a solemn stillness holds,
Save where the beetle wheels his droning flight,
 And drowsy tinklings lull the distant folds;

Save that from yonder ivy-mantled tower
 The moping owl does to the moon complain
Of such as, wandering near her secret bower,
 Molest her ancient solitary reign.

Beneath those rugged elms, that yew-tree's shade,
 Where heaves the turf in many a mouldering heap,
Each in his narrow cell for ever laid,
 The rude Forefathers of the hamlet sleep.

The breezy call of incense-breathing Morn,
 The swallow twittering from the straw-built shed,
The cock's shrill clarion, or the echoing horn,
 No more shall rouse them from their lowly bed.

For them no more the blazing hearth shall burn,
 Or busy housewife ply her evening care:
No children run to lisp their sire's return,
 Or climb his knees the envied kiss to share.

Oft did the harvest to their sickle yield,
 Their furrow oft the stubborn glebe has broke;
How jocund did they drive their team afield!
 How bowed the woods beneath their sturdy stroke!

Let not Ambition mock their useful toil,
 Their homely joys, and destiny obscure;
Nor Grandeur hear with a disdainful smile
 The short and simple annals of the poor.

The boast of heraldry, the pomp of power,
 And all that beauty, all that wealth e'er gave,
Await alike the inevitable hour:
 The paths of glory lead but to the grave.

Nor you, ye Proud, impute to these the fault,
 If Memory o'er their tomb no trophies raise,
Where through the long-drawn aisle and fretted vault
 The pealing anthem swells the note of praise.

Can storied urn or animated bust
 Back to its mansion call the fleeting breath?
Can Honour's voice provoke the silent dust,
 Or Flattery soothe the dull cold ear of Death?

Perhaps in this neglected spot is laid
 Some heart once pregnant with celestial fire;
Hands, that the rod of empire might have swayed,
 Or waked to ecstasy the living lyre.

But Knowledge to their eyes her ample page
 Rich with the spoils of time did ne'er unroll;
Chill Penury repressed their noble rage,
 And froze the genial current of the soul.

Full many a gem of purest ray serene,
 The dark, unfathomed caves of ocean bear:
Full many a flower is born to blush unseen,
 And waste its sweetness on the desert air.

Some village Hampden, that with dauntless breast
 The little tyrant of his fields withstood,
Some mute inglorious Milton here may rest,
 Some Cromwell guiltless of his country's blood.

The applause of listening senates to command,
  The threats of pain and ruin to despise,
To scatter plenty o'er a smiling land,
  And read their history in a nation's eyes,

Their lot forbade: nor circumscribed alone
  Their growing virtues, but their crimes confined;
Forbade to wade through slaughter to a throne,
  And shut the gates of mercy on mankind,

The struggling pangs of conscious truth to hide,
  To quench the blushes of ingenuous shame,
Or heap the shrine of Luxury and Pride
  With incense kindled at the Muse's flame.

Far from the madding crowd's ignoble strife,
  Their sober wishes never learned to stray;
Along the cool sequestered vale of life
  They kept the noiseless tenor of their way.

Yet even these bones from insult to protect,
  Some frail memorial still erected nigh,
With uncouth rhymes and shapeless sculpture decked,
  Implores the passing tribute of a sigh.

Their name, their years, spelt by the unlettered muse,
  The place of fame and elegy supply;
And many a holy text around she strews,
  That teach the rustic moralist to die.

For who, to dumb Forgetfulness a prey,
  This pleasing anxious being e'er resigned,
Left the warm precincts of the cheerful day,
  Nor cast one longing, lingering look behind?

On some fond breast the parting soul relies,
  Some pious drops the closing eye requires;
Even from the tomb the voice of Nature cries,
  Even in our ashes live their wonted fires.

For thee, who mindful of the unhonoured dead
   Dost in these lines their artless tale relate;
If chance, by lonely contemplation led,
   Some kindred spirit shall inquire thy fate,—

Haply some hoary-headed swain may say,
   " Oft have we seen him at the peep of dawn
Brushing with hasty steps the dews away
   To meet the sun upon the upland lawn.

" There at the foot of yonder nodding beech
   That wreathes its old fantastic roots so high,
His listless length at noontide would he stretch,
   And pore upon the brook that babbles by.

" Hard by yon wood, now smiling as in scorn,
   Muttering his wayward fancies he would rove,
Now drooping, woeful-wan, like one forlorn,
   Or crazed with care, or crossed in hopeless love.

" One morn I missed him on the customed hill,
   Along the heath, and near his favourite tree;
Another came; nor yet beside the rill,
   Nor up the lawn, nor at the wood was he;

" The next, with dirges due in sad array,
   Slow through the church-way path we saw him
     borne.—
Approach and read (for thou canst read) the lay,
   Graved on the stone beneath yon aged thorn."

THE EPITAPH

Here rests his head upon the lap of Earth
   A Youth to Fortune and to Fame unknown.
Fair Science frowned not on his humble birth,
   And Melancholy marked him for her own.

Large was his bounty, and his soul sincere,
  Heaven did a recompense as largely send:
He gave to Misery all he had, a tear,
  He gained from Heaven ('twas all he wished) a friend.

No farther seek his merits to disclose,
  Or draw his frailties from their dread abode
(There they alike in trembling hope repose),
  The bosom of his Father and his God.

WILLIAM COLLINS

1721–59

Ode to Evening

IF aught of oaten stop, or pastoral song,
  May hope, chaste Eve, to soothe thy modest ear,
    Like thy own solemn springs,
    Thy springs and dying gales,

O nymph reserved, while now the bright-haired sun
Sits in yon western tent, whose cloudy skirts,
    With brede ethereal wove,
    O'erhang his wavy bed:

Now air is hushed, save where the weak-eyed bat,
With short shrill shriek, flits by on leathern wing,
    Or where the beetle winds
    His small but sullen horn,

As oft he rises 'midst the twilight path,
Against the pilgrim borne in heedless hum:
    Now teach me, maid composed,
    To breathe some softened strain,

Whose numbers, stealing through thy darkening vale,
May not unseemly with its stillness suit,
    As, musing slow, I hail
    Thy genial loved return !

For when thy folding-star arising shows
His paly circlet, at his warning lamp
    The fragrant Hours, the elves
    Who slept in buds the day,

And many a nymph who wreathes her brows with
    sedge,
And sheds the freshening dew, and, lovelier still
    The pensive Pleasures sweet,
    Prepare thy shadowy ear:

Then lead, calm votaress, where some sheety lake
Cheers the lone heath, or some time-hallowed pile
    Or upland fallows grey
    Reflect its last cool gleam.

Or if chill blustering winds, or driving rain,
Forbid my willing feet, be mine the hut
    That from the mountain's side
    Views wilds, and swelling floods,

And hamlets brown, and dim-discovered spires,
And hears their simple bell, and marks o'er all
    Thy dewy fingers draw
    The gradual dusky veil.

While Spring shall pour his showers, as oft he wont,
And bathe thy breathing tresses, meekest Eve !
    While Summer loves to sport
    Beneath thy lingering light;

While sallow Autumn fills thy lap with leaves;
Or Winter, yelling through the troublous air,
    Affrights thy shrinking train,
    And rudely rends thy robes;

So long, regardful of thy quiet rule,
Shall Fancy, Friendship, Science, rose-lipped Health,
    Thy gentlest influence own,
    And hymn thy favourite name !

Ode

WRITTEN IN THE BEGINNING OF THE YEAR 1746

HOW sleep the brave, who sink to rest
By all their country's wishes blest !
When Spring, with dewy fingers cold,
Returns to deck their hallowed mould,
She there shall dress a sweeter sod
Than Fancy's feet have ever trod.
By fairy hands their knell is rung;
By forms unseen their dirge is sung;
There Honour comes, a pilgrim grey,
To bless the turf that wraps their clay;
And Freedom shall awhile repair,
To dwell, a weeping hermit, there !

OLIVER GOLDSMITH

1728–74

Song

From THE VICAR OF WAKEFIELD

WHEN lovely woman stoops to folly,
And finds too late that men betray,
What charm can soothe her melancholy ? .
What art can wash her guilt away ?

The only art her guilt to cover,
To hide her shame from every eye,
To give repentance to her lover,
And wring his bosom, is—to die.

WILLIAM BLAKE

1757–1827

The Piper

PIPING down the valleys wild,
Piping songs of pleasant glee,
On a cloud I saw a child,
And he laughing said to me:

"Pipe a song about a Lamb !"
  So I piped with merry cheer.
"Piper, pipe that song again;"
  So I piped: he wept to hear.

"Drop thy pipe, thy happy pipe;
  Sing thy songs of happy cheer:"
So I sang the same again,
  While he wept with joy to hear.

"Piper, sit thee down and write
  In a book, that all may read."
So he vanished from my sight,
  And I plucked a hollow reed,

And I made a rural pen,
  And I stained the water clear,
And I wrote my happy songs
  Every child may joy to hear.

The Clod and the Pebble

"LOVE seeketh not itself to please,
  Nor for itself hath any care,
But for another gives its ease,
  And builds a Heaven in Hell's despair."

So sung a little Clod of Clay,
  Trodden with the cattle's feet,
But a Pebble of the brook
  Warbled out these metres meet:

"Love seeketh only Self to please,
  To bind another to Its delight,
Joys in another's loss of ease,
  And builds a Hell in Heaven's despite."

The Sick Rose

O ROSE, thou art sick !
   The invisible worm,
That flies in the night,
   In the howling storm,

Has found out thy bed
   Of crimson joy;
And his dark secret love
   Does thy life destroy.

The Tiger

TIGER, tiger, burning bright
In the forests of the night,
What immortal hand or eye
Could frame thy fearful symmetry ?

In what distant deeps or skies
Burnt the fire of thine eyes ?
On what wings dare he aspire ?
What the hand dare seize the fire ?

And what shoulder, and what art,
Could twist the sinews of thy heart ?
And, when thy heart began to beat,
What dread hand, and what dread feet ?

What the hammer ? what the chain ?
In what furnace was thy brain ?
What the anvil ? what dread grasp
Dare its deadly terrors clasp ?

When the stars threw down their spears,
And watered heaven with their tears,
Did he smile his work to see ?
Did he who made the Lamb make thee ?

Tiger, tiger, burning bright
In the forests of the night,
What immortal hand or eye
Dare frame thy fearful symmetry ?

Ah, Sunflower

AH, Sunflower ! weary of time,
Who countest the steps of the Sun;
Seeking after that sweet golden clime,
Where the traveller's journey is done;

Where the Youth pined away with desire,
And the pale Virgin shrouded in snow,
Arise from their graves, and aspire
Where my Sunflower wishes to go !

The Garden of Love

I WENT to the Garden of Love,
And saw what I never had seen:
A Chapel was built in the midst,
Where I used to play on the green.

And the gates of this chapel were shut,
And " Thou shalt not " writ over the door;
So I turned to the Garden of Love,
That so many sweet flowers bore;

And I saw it was fillèd with graves,
And tombstones where flowers should be;
And priests in black gowns were walking their rounds,
And binding with briers my joys and desires.

A Poison Tree

I WAS angry with my friend:
I told my wrath, my wrath did end.
I was angry with my foe:
I told it not, my wrath did grow.

And I watered it in fears,
Night and morning with my tears;
And I sunnèd it with smiles,
And with soft deceitful wiles.

And it grew both day and night,
Till it bore an apple bright;
And my foe beheld it shine,
And he knew that it was mine,

And into my garden stole
When the night had veiled the pole:
In the morning glad I see
My foe outstretched beneath the tree.

From MILTON

AND did those feet in ancient time
  Walk upon England's mountains green?
And was the holy Lamb of God
  On England's pleasant pastures seen?

And did the Countenance Divine
  Shine forth upon our clouded hills?
And was Jerusalem builded here
  Among these dark Satanic Mills?

Bring me my Bow of burning gold!
  Bring me my Arrows of desire!
Bring me my Spear! O clouds, unfold!
  Bring me my Chariot of fire!

I will not cease from Mental Fight,
  Nor shall my Sword sleep in my hand,
Till we have built Jerusalem
  In England's green and pleasant Land.

ROBERT BURNS

Highland Mary

1759–96

YE banks and braes, and streams around
   The castle o' Montgomery,
Green be your woods and fair your flowers,
   Your waters never drumlie !
There Summer first unfald her robes,
   And there the langest tarry;
For there I took the last fareweel
   O' my sweet Highland Mary.

How sweetly bloomed the gay, green birk,
   How rich the hawthorn's blossom,
As underneath their fragrant shade
   I clasped her to my bosom !
The golden hours on angel wings
   Flew o'er me and my dearie;
For dear to me as light and life
   Was my sweet Highland Mary.

Wi' monie a vow and locked embrace
   Our parting was fu' tender;
And, pledging aft to meet again,
   We tore oursels asunder.
But O, fell Death's untimely frost,
   That nipt my flower sae early !
Now green's the sod, and cauld's the clay,
   That wraps my Highland Mary !

O pale, pale now, those rosy lips,
   I aft hae kissed sae fondly;
And closed for ay, the sparkling glance
   That dwalt on me sae kindly;

And mouldering now in silent dust
That heart that lo'ed me dearly !
But still within my bosom's core
Shall live my Highland Mary.

Song : Mary Morison

O MARY, at thy window be !
It is the wished, the trysted hour.
Those smiles and glances let me see,
That make the miser's treasure poor.
How blythely wad I bide the stoure,
A weary slave frae sun to sun,
Could I the rich reward secure—
The lovely Mary Morison !

Yestreen, when to the trembling string
The dance gaed through the lighted ha',
To thee my fancy took its wing,
I sat, but neither heard nor saw:
Though this was fair, and that was braw,
And yon the toast of a' the town,
I sighed, and said amang them a':
"Ye are na Mary Morison !"

O Mary, canst thou wreck his peace
Wha for thy sake wad gladly die ?
Or canst thou break that heart of his
Whase only faut is loving thee ?
If love for love thou wilt na gie,
At least be pity to me shown:
A thought ungentle canna be
The thought o' Mary Morison.

Ye Flowery Banks

YE flowery banks o' bonnie Doon,
  How can ye blume sae fair ?
How can ye chant, ye little birds,
  And I sae fu' o' care ?

Thou'll break my heart, thou bonnie bird,
  That sings upon the bough:
Thou minds me o' the happy days
  When my fause luve was true !

Thou'll break my heart, thou bonnie bird,
  That sings beside thy mate:
For sae I sat, and sae I sang,
  And wist na o' my fate !

Aft hae I rov'd by bonnie Doon
  To see the woodbine twine,
And ilka bird sang o' its luve,
  And sae did I o' mine.

Wi' lightsome heart I pu'd a rose
  Frae aff its thorny tree,
And my fause luver staw my rose,
  But left the thorn wi' me.

Of a' the Airts

OF a' the airts the wind can blaw
  I dearly like the west,
For there the bonnie lassie lives,
  The lassie I lo'e best.
There wild woods grow, and rivers row,
  And monie a hill between,
But day and night, my fancy's flight
  Is ever wi' my Jean.

I see her in the dewy flowers—
I see her sweet an' fair.
I hear her in the tunefu' birds—
I hear her charm the air.
There's not a bonnie flower that springs
By fountain, shaw, or green;
There's not a bonnie bird that sings,
But minds me o' my Jean.

A Red, Red Rose

O, MY luve is like a red, red rose,
That's newly sprung in June.
O my luve is like the melodie,
That's sweetly played in tune.

As fair art thou, my bonnie lass,
So deep in luve am I,
And I will luve thee still, my dear,
Till a' the seas gang dry.

Till a' the seas gang dry, my dear,
And the rocks melt wi' the sun!
And I will luve thee still, my dear,
While the sands o' life shall run.

And fare thee weel, my only luve,
And fare thee weel awhile!
And I will come again, my luve,
Though it were ten thousand mile!

Flow Gently, Sweet Afton

FLOW gently, sweet Afton, among thy green braes!
Flow gently, I'll sing thee a song in thy praise!
My Mary's asleep by thy murmuring stream—
Flow gently, sweet Afton, disturb not her dream!

Thou stock-dove whose echo resounds through the
    glen,
Ye wild whistling blackbirds in yon thorny den,
Thou green-crested lapwing, thy screaming forbear—
I charge you, disturb not my slumbering fair !

How lofty, sweet Afton, thy neighbouring hills,
Far marked with the courses of clear winding rills !
There daily I wander, as noon rises high,
My flocks and my Mary's sweet cot in my eye.

How pleasant thy banks and green valleys below,
Where wild in the woodlands the primroses blow ;
There oft, as mild Evening weeps over the lea,
The sweet-scented birk shades my Mary and me.

Thy crystal stream, Afton, how lovely it glides,
And winds by the cot where my Mary resides !
How wanton thy waters her snowy feet lave,
As, gathering sweet flowerets, she stems thy clear
    wave !

Flow gently, sweet Afton, among thy green braes !
Flow gently, sweet river, the theme of my lays !
My Mary's asleep by thy murmuring stream—
Flow gently, sweet Afton, disturb not her dream !

My Heart's in the Highlands

FAREWELL to the Highlands, farewell to the North,
The birth-place of valour, the country of worth !
Wherever I wander, wherever I rove,
The hills of the Highlands for ever I love.

    My heart's in the Highlands, my heart is not here ;
    My heart's in the Highlands a-chasing the deer,
    A-chasing the wild deer and following the roe—
    My heart's in the Highlands, wherever I go.

Farewell to the mountains high-covered with snow,
Farewell to the straths and green valleys below,
Farewell to the forests and wild-hanging woods,
Farewell to the torrents and loud-pouring floods !

My heart's in the Highlands, my heart is not here;
My heart's in the Highlands a-chasing the deer,
A-chasing the wild deer and following the roe—
My heart's in the Highlands, wherever I go !

John Anderson my Jo

JOHN ANDERSON my jo, John,
    When we were first acquent,
Your locks were like the raven,
    Your bonnie brow was brent;
But now your brow is beld, John,
    Your locks are like the snaw,
But blessings on your frosty pow,
    John Anderson my jo !

John Anderson my jo, John,
    We clamb the hill thegither,
And monie a cantie day, John,
    We've had wi' ane anither;
Now we maun totter down, John,
    And hand in hand we'll go,
And sleep thegither at the foot,
    John Anderson my jo !

Song : Green Grow the Rashes

GREEN grow the rashes, O;
    Green grow the rashes, O;
The sweetest hours that e'er I spend,
    Are spent amang the lasses, O.

There's naught but care on every han',
  In every hour that passes, O:
What signifies the life o' man,
  An 'twere na for the lasses, O ?

The war'ly race may riches chase,
  An' riches still may fly them, O;
An' though at last they catch them fast,
  Their hearts can ne'er enjoy them, O.

But gie me a cannie hour at e'en,
  My arms about my dearie, O,
An' war'ly cares an' war'ly men
  May a' gae tapsalteerie, O !

For you sae douce, ye sneer at this;
  Ye're naught but senseless asses, O;
The wisest man the warl' e'er saw,
  He dearly loved the lasses, O.

Auld Nature swears, the lovely dears
  Her noblest work she classes, O:
Her prentice han' she tried on man,
  An' then she made the lasses, O.

Tam Glen

MY heart is a-breaking, dear tittie !
  Some counsel unto me come len'.
To anger them a' is a pity,
  But what will I do wi' Tam Glen ?

I'm thinking, wi' sic a braw fellow
  In poortith I might wak a fen'.
What care I in riches to wallow,
  If I mauna marry Tam Glen ?

There's Lowrie, the laird o' Dumeller:
　"Guid-day to you," brute! he comes ben.
He brags and he blaws o' his siller,
　But when will he dance like Tam Glen?

My minnie does constantly deave me,
　And bids me beware o' young men.
They flatter, she says, to deceive me—
　But wha can think sae o' Tam Glen?

My daddie says, gin I'll forsake him,
　He'll gie me guid hunder marks ten.
But if it's ordained I maun tak him,
　O, wha will I get but Tam Glen?

Yestreen at the valentines' dealing,
　My heart to my mou gied a sten,
For thrice I drew ane without failing,
　And thrice it was written, "Tam Glen"!

The last Halloween I was waukin
　My droukit sark-sleeve, as ye ken—
His likeness came up the house staukin,
　And the very grey breeks o' Tam Glen!

Come, counsel, dear tittie, don't tarry!
　I'll gie ye my bonnie black hen,
Gif ye will advise me to marry
　The lad I lo'e dearly, Tam Glen.

Auld Lang Syne

SHOULD auld acquaintance be forgot,
　And never brought to mind?
Should auld acquaintance be forgot,
　And auld lang syne?

> *Chorus.*—For auld lang syne, my dear,
>   For auld lang syne,
> We'll tak a cup o' kindness yet
>   For auld lang syne !

And surely ye'll be your pint-stowp,
  And surely I'll be mine,
And we'll tak a cup o' kindness yet
  For auld lang syne !

We twa hae run about the braes,
  And pou'd the gowans fine,
But we've wandered monie a weary fit
  Sin' auld lang syne.

We two hae paidl'd in the burn
  Frae morning sun till dine,
But seas between us braid hae roared
  Sin' auld lang syne.

And there's a hand, my trusty fiere,
  And gie's a hand o' thine,
And we'll tak a right guid-willie waught
  For auld lang syne !

Willie Brewed a Peck o' Maut

O, WILLIE brew'd a peck o' maut,
  An' Rob an' Allan cam to see.
Three blyther hearts that lee-lang night
Ye wad na found in Christendie.

> *Chorus.*—We are na fou, we're nae that fou,
> But just a drappie in our e'e !
> The cock may craw, the day may daw,
> And ay we'll taste the barley bree !

Here are we met, three merry boys,
Three merry boys, I trow, are we;
An' mony a night we've merry been,
And mony mae we hope to be !

It is the moon, I ken her horn,
That's blinkin' in the lift sae hie:
She shines sae bright to wyle us hame,
But, by my sooth, she'll wait a wee !

Wha first shall rise to gang awa,
A cuckold, coward loun is he !
Wha first beside his chair shall fa',
He is the King amang us three !

WILLIAM WORDSWORTH

1770–1850

Influence of Natural Objects

WISDOM and Spirit of the universe !
Thou Soul, that art the Eternity of thought !
And giv'st to forms and images a breath
And everlasting motion ! not in vain,
By day or star-light, thus from my first dawn
Of childhood didst thou intertwine for me
The passions that build up our human soul;
Not with the mean and vulgar works of Man;
But with high objects, with enduring things,
With life and nature; purifying thus
The elements of feeling and of thought,
And sanctifying by such discipline
Both pain and fear,—until we recognize
A grandeur in the beatings of the heart.
    Nor was this fellowship vouchsafed to me
With stinted kindness.   In November days,
When vapours rolling down the valleys made
A lonely scene more lonesome; among woods

At noon; and 'mid the calm of summer nights,
When, by the margin of the trembling lake,
Beneath the gloomy hills, homeward I went
In solitude, such intercourse was mine:
Mine was it in the fields both day and night,
And by the water, all the summer long.
And in the frosty season, when the sun
Was set, and, visible for many a mile,
The cottage windows through the twilight blazed,
I heeded not the summons: happy time
It was indeed for all of us; for me
It was a time of rapture !   Clear and loud
The village clock tolled six—I wheeled about,
Proud and exulting like an untired horse
That cares not for his home.—All shod with steel
We hissed along the polished ice, in games
Confederate, imitative of the chase
And woodland pleasures,—the resounding horn,
The pack loud chiming, and the hunted hare.
So through the darkness and the cold we flew,
And not a voice was idle: with the din
Smitten, the precipices rang aloud;
The leafless trees and every icy crag
Tinkled like iron; while far distant hills
Into the tumult sent an alien sound
Of melancholy, not unnoticed while the stars,
Eastward, were sparkling clear, and in the west
The orange sky of evening died away.
    Not seldom from the uproar I retired
Into a silent bay, or sportively
Glanced sideway, leaving the tumultuous throng,
To cut across the reflex of a star;
Image that, flying still before me, gleamed
Upon the glassy plain: and oftentimes,
When we had given our bodies to the wind,
And all the shadowy banks on either side

Came sweeping through the darkness, spinning still
The rapid line of motion, then at once
Have I, reclining back upon my heels,
Stopped short; yet still the solitary cliffs
Wheeled by me—even as if the earth had rolled
With visible motion her diurnal round !
Behind me did they stretch in solemn train,
Feebler and feebler, and I stood and watched
Till all was tranquil as a summer sea.

She dwelt among the Untrodden Ways

SHE dwelt among the untrodden ways
 Beside the springs of Dove,
A maid whom there were none to praise
 And very few to love:

A violet by a mossy stone
 Half hidden from the eye !
—Fair as a star, when only one
 Is shining in the sky.

She lived unknown, and few could know
 When Lucy ceased to be;
But she is in her grave, and, oh,
 The difference to me !

I travelled among Unknown Men

I TRAVELLED among unknown men,
 In lands beyond the sea;
Nor, England ! did I know till then
 What love I bore to thee.

'Tis past, that melancholy dream !
 Nor will I quit thy shore
A second time; for still I seem
 To love thee more and more.

Among thy mountains did I feel
    The joy of my desire;
And she I cherished turned her wheel
    Beside an English fire.

Thy mornings showed, thy nights concealed
    The bowers where Lucy played ;
And thine too is the last green field
    That Lucy's eyes surveyed.

A Slumber did my Spirit seal

A SLUMBER did my spirit seal;
    I had no human fears;
She seemed a thing that could not feel
    The touch of earthly years.

No motion has she now, no force;
    She neither hears nor sees;
Rolled round in earth's diurnal course,
    With rocks, and stones, and trees.

The Solitary Reaper

BEHOLD her, single in the field,
    Yon solitary Highland Lass !
Reaping and singing by herself;
Stop here, or gently pass !
Alone she cuts and binds the grain,
And sings a melancholy strain;
O listen ! for the Vale profound
Is overflowing with the sound.

No Nightingale did ever chaunt
More welcome notes to weary bands
Of travellers in some shady haunt,
Among Arabian sands:

A voice so thrilling ne'er was heard
In spring-time from the Cuckoo-bird,
Breaking the silence of the seas
Among the farthest Hebrides.

Will no one tell me what she sings?—
Perhaps the plaintive numbers flow
For old, unhappy, far-off things,
And battles long ago:
Or is it some more humble lay,
Familiar matter of to-day?
Some natural sorrow, loss, or pain,
That has been, and may be again?

Whate'er the theme, the Maiden sang
As if her song could have no ending;
I saw her singing at her work,
And o'er the sickle bending;—
I listened, motionless and still;
And, as I mounted up the hill,
The music in my heart I bore,
Long after it was heard no more.

London, 1802

MILTON! thou shouldst be living at this hour:
England hath need of thee: she is a fen
Of stagnant waters: altar, sword, and pen,
Fireside, the heroic wealth of hall and bower,
Have forfeited their ancient English dower
Of inward happiness. We are selfish men;
Oh! raise us up, return to us again;
And give us manners, virtue, freedom, power.
Thy soul was like a Star, and dwelt apart;
Thou hadst a voice whose sound was like the sea:
Pure as the naked heavens, majestic, free,
So didst thou travel on life's common way,

In cheerful godliness; and yet thy heart
The lowliest duties on herself did lay.

Composed upon Westminster Bridge Sept. 3, 1803

EARTH has not anything to show more fair:
Dull would be he of soul who could pass by
A sight so touching in its majesty:
The city now doth like a garment wear
The beauty of the morning; silent, bare,
Ships, towers, domes, theatres, and temples lie
Open unto the fields, and to the sky;
All bright and glittering in the smokeless air.
Never did sun more beautifully steep
In his first splendour, valley, rock, or hill;
Ne'er saw I, never felt, a calm so deep !
The river glideth at his own sweet will:
Dear God ! the very houses seem asleep;
And all that mighty heart is lying still !

It is a Beauteous Evening, Calm and Free

IT is a beauteous evening, calm and free ;
The holy time is quiet as a Nun
Breathless with adoration: the broad sun
Is sinking down in its tranquillity;
The gentleness of heaven broods o'er the Sea:
Listen ! the mighty Being is awake,
And doth with his eternal motion make
A sound like thunder—everlastingly.
Dear Child ! dear Girl ! that walkest with me herc,
If thou appear untouched by solemn thought,
Thy nature is not therefore less divine:
Thou liest in Abraham's bosom all the year,

And worshipp'st at the Temple's inner shrine,
God being with thee when we know it not.

The World is too much with us

THE world is too much with us: late and soon,
Getting and spending, we lay waste our powers:
Little we see in Nature that is ours;
We have given our hearts away, a sordid boon!
This Sea that bares her bosom to the moon;
The winds that will be howling at all hours,
And are up-gathered now like sleeping flowers;
For this, for everything, we are out of tune;
It moves us not.—Great God! I'd rather be
A Pagan suckled in a creed outworn;
So might I, standing on this pleasant lea,
Have glimpses that would make me less forlorn;
Have sight of Proteus rising from the sea;
Or hear old Triton blow his wreathèd horn.

Ode to Duty

STERN Daughter of the Voice of God!
O Duty! if that name thou love,
Who art a light to guide, a rod
To check the erring, and reprove;
Thou, who art victory and law
When empty terrors overawe;
From vain temptations dost set free;
And calm'st the weary strife of frail humanity!

There are who ask not if thine eye
Be on them; who, in love and truth,
Where no misgiving is, rely
Upon the genial sense of youth:
Glad Hearts! without reproach or blot;
Who do thy work, and know it not:

O if through confidence misplaced
They fail, thy saving arms, dread Power, around them
    cast.

Serene will be our days and bright,
And happy will our nature be,
When love is an unerring light,
And joy its own security.
And they a blissful course may hold
Even now, who, not unwisely bold,
Live in the spirit of this creed;
Yet seek thy firm support, according to their need.

I, loving freedom, and untried;
No sport of every random gust,
Yet being to myself a guide,
Too blindly have reposed my trust:
And oft, when in my heart was heard
Thy timely mandate, I deferred
The task, in smoother walks to stray;
But thee I now would serve more strictly, if I may.

Through no disturbance of my soul,
Or strong compunction in me wrought,
I supplicate for thy control;
But in the quietness of thought:
Me this unchartered freedom tires;
I feel the weight of chance desires:
My hopes no more must change their name,
I long for a repose that ever is the same.

Stern Lawgiver ! yet thou dost wear
The Godhead's most benignant grace;
Nor know we anything so fair
As is the smile upon thy face:
Flowers laugh before thee on their beds,
And fragrance in thy footing treads;

Thou dost preserve the stars from wrong;
And the most ancient heavens, through thee, are
fresh and strong.

To humbler functions, awful Power !
I call thee: I myself commend
Unto thy guidance from this hour;
Oh, let my weakness have an end !
Give unto me, made lowly wise,
The spirit of self-sacrifice;
The confidence of reason give;
And in the light of truth thy Bondman let me live !

Ode

Intimations of Immortality from Recollections of Early Childhood

1

THERE was a time when meadow, grove, and stream,
The earth, and every common sight,
     To me did seem
     Apparelled in celestial light,
The glory and the freshness of a dream.
It is not now as it hath been of yore—
     Turn wheresoe'er I may,
     By night or day,
The things which I have seen I now can see no more.

2

     The Rainbow comes and goes,
     And lovely is the Rose;
     The Moon doth with delight
Look round her when the heavens are bare;
     Waters on a starry night
     Are beautiful and fair;
     The sunshine is a glorious birth;
     But yet I know, where'er I go,
That there hath passed away a glory from the earth.

3

Now, while the birds thus sing a joyous song,
  And while the young lambs bound
    As to the tabor's sound,
To me alone there came a thought of grief:
A timely utterance gave that thought relief,
  And I again am strong.
The cataracts blow their trumpets from the steep;
No more shall grief of mine the season wrong;
I hear the Echoes through the mountains throng,
The Winds come to me from the fields of sleep,
  And all the earth is gay;
    Land and sea
  Give themselves up to jollity,
    And with the heart of May
  Doth every Beast keep holiday;—
    Thou Child of Joy,
Shout round me, let me hear thy shouts, thou happy
    Shepherd-boy!

4

Ye blessèd Creatures, I have heard the call
  Ye to each other make; I see
The heavens laugh with you in your jubilee;
  My heart is at your festival,
  My head hath its coronal,
The fullness of your bliss, I feel—I feel it all.
  Oh evil day! if I were sullen
  While Earth herself is adorning,
    This sweet May-morning,
  And the Children are culling
    On every side,
  In a thousand valleys far and wide,
  Fresh flowers; while the sun shines warm,

And the Babe leaps up on his Mother's arm:—
I hear, I hear, with joy I hear!
—But there's a Tree, of many, one,
A single Field which I have looked upon,
Both of them speak of something that is gone:
The Pansy at my feet
Doth the same tale repeat:
Whither is fled the visionary gleam?
Where is it now, the glory and the dream?

5

Our birth is but a sleep and a forgetting:
The Soul that rises with us, our life's Star,
Hath had elsewhere its setting,
And cometh from afar:
Not in entire forgetfulness,
And not in utter nakedness,
But trailing clouds of glory do we come
From God, who is our home:
Heaven lies about us in our infancy!
Shades of the prison-house begin to close
Upon the growing Boy,
But he beholds the light, and whence it flows,
He sees it in his joy;
The Youth, who daily farther from the east
Must travel, still is Nature's Priest,
And by the vision splendid
Is on his way attended;
At length the Man perceives it die away,
And fade into the light of common day.

6

Earth fills her lap with pleasures of her own;
Yearnings she hath in her own natural kind.

And, even with something of a Mother's mind,
    And no unworthy aim,
    The homely Nurse doth all she can
To make her Foster-child, her Inmate Man,
    Forget the glories he hath known,
And that imperial palace whence he came.

7

Behold the Child among his new-born blisses,
A six years' Darling of a pigmy size !
See, where 'mid work of his own hand he lies,
Fretted by sallies of his mother's kisses,
With light upon him from his father's eyes !
See, at his feet, some little plan or chart,
Some fragment from his dream of human life,
Shaped by himself with newly-learnèd art;
    A wedding or a festival,
    A mourning or a funeral;
    And this hath now his heart,
    And unto this he frames his song:
    Then will he fit his tongue
To dialogues of business, love, or strife;
    But it will not be long
    Ere this be thrown aside,
    And with new joy and pride
The little Actor cons another part;
Filling from time to time his " humorous stage "
With all the Persons, down to palsied Age,
That Life brings with her in her equipage;
    As if his whole vocation
    Were endless imitation.

8

Thou, whose exterior semblance doth belie
    Thy Soul's immensity;
Thou best Philosopher, who yet dost keep

Thy heritage, thou Eye among the blind,
That, deaf and silent, read'st the eternal deep,
Haunted for ever by the eternal mind,—
  Mighty Prophet ! Seer blest !
  On whom those truths do rest,
Which we are toiling all our lives to find,
In darkness lost, the darkness of the grave;
Thou, over whom thy Immortality
Broods like the Day, a Master o'er a Slave,
A Presence which is not to be put by;
Thou little Child, yet glorious in the might
Of heaven-born freedom on thy being's height,
Why with such earnest pains dost thou provoke
The years to bring the inevitable yoke,
Thus blindly with thy blessedness at strife ?
Full soon thy Soul shall have her earthly freight,
And custom lie upon thee with a weight,
Heavy as frost, and deep almost as life !

9

  O joy ! that in our embers
  Is something that doth live,
  That nature yet remembers
  What was so fugitive !
The thought of our past years in me doth breed
Perpetual benediction: not indeed
For that which is most worthy to be blest—
Delight and liberty, the simple creed
Of Childhood, whether busy or at rest,
With new-fledged hope still fluttering in his breast:—
  Not for these I raise
  The song of thanks and praise;
  But for those obstinate questionings
  Of sense and outward things,
  Fallings from us, vanishings;
  Blank misgivings of a Creature

Moving about in worlds not realized,
High instincts before which our mortal nature
Did tremble like a guilty Thing surprised:
    But for those first affections,
    Those shadowy recollections,
  Which, be they what they may,
Are yet the fountain-light of all our day,
Are yet a master-light of all our seeing;
  Uphold us, cherish, and have power to make
Our noisy years seem moments in the being
Of the eternal Silence: truths that wake,
    To perish never:
Which neither listlessness, nor mad endeavour,
    Nor Man nor Boy,
Nor all that is at enmity with joy,
Can utterly abolish or destroy!
    Hence in a season of calm weather
    Though inland far we be,
Our Souls have sight of that immortal sea
    Which brought us hither,
    Can in a moment travel thither,
And see the Children sport upon the shore,
And hear the mighty waters rolling evermore.

          10

Then sing, ye Birds, sing, sing a joyous song!
    And let the young Lambs bound
    As to the tabor's sound!
We in thought will join your throng,
    Ye that pipe and ye that play,
    Ye that through your hearts to-day
    Feel the gladness of the May!
What though the radiance which was once so bright
Be now for ever taken from my sight,
  Though nothing can bring back the hour
Of splendour in the grass, of glory in the flower;

We will grieve not, rather find
Strength in what remains behind;
In the primal sympathy
Which having been must ever be;
In the soothing thoughts that spring
Out of human suffering;
In the faith that looks through death,
In years that bring the philosophic mind.

II

And O, ye Fountains, Meadows, Hills, and Groves,
Forebode not any severing of our loves!
Yet in my heart of hearts I feel your might;
I only have relinquished one delight
To live beneath your more habitual sway.
I love the Brooks which down their channels fret,
Even more than when I tripped lightly as they;
The innocent brightness of a new-born Day
    Is lovely yet;
The Clouds that gather round the setting sun
Do take a sober colouring from an eye
That hath kept watch o'er man's mortality;
Another race hath been, and other palms are won.
Thanks to the human heart by which we live,
Thanks to its tenderness, its joys, and fears,
To me the meanest flower that blows can give
Thoughts that do often lie too deep for tears.

SIR WALTER SCOTT

1771–1832

Soldier, rest! thy Warfare o'er

From THE LADY OF THE LAKE

SOLDIER, rest! thy warfare o'er,
    Sleep the sleep that knows not breaking;
Dream of battled fields no more,
    Days of danger, nights of waking.

In our isle's enchanted hall,
　　Hands unseen thy couch are strewing,
Fairy strains of music fall,
　　Every sense in slumber dewing.
Soldier, rest ! thy warfare o'er,
Dream of fighting fields no more:
Sleep the sleep that knows not breaking,
Morn of toil, nor night of waking.

No rude sound shall reach thine ear,
　　Armour's clang, or war-steed champing,
Trump nor pibroch summon here
　　Mustering clan, or squadron tramping.
Yet the lark's shrill fife may come
　　At the daybreak from the fallow,
And the bittern sound his drum,
　　Booming from the sedgy shallow.
Ruder sounds shall none be near,
Guards nor warders challenge here,
Here's no war-steed's neigh and champing,
Shouting clans or squadrons stamping.

Huntsman, rest ! thy chase is done;
　　While our slumbrous spells assail ye,
Dream not, with the rising sun,
　　Bugles here shall sound reveillé.
Sleep ! the deer is in his den;
　　Sleep ! thy hounds are by thee lying;
Sleep ! nor dream in yonder glen
How thy gallant steed lay dying.
Huntsman, rest ! thy chase is done;
Think not of the rising sun,
For at dawning to assail ye,
Here no bugles sound reveillé.

SAMUEL TAYLOR COLERIDGE

1772–1834

Kubla Khan

IN Xanadu did Kubla Khan
A stately pleasure-dome decree:
Where Alph, the sacred river, ran
Through caverns measureless to man
    Down to a sunless sea.
So twice five miles of fertile ground
With walls and towers were girdled round:
And here were gardens bright with sinuous rills
Where blossomed many an incense-bearing tree;
And here were forests ancient as the hills,
Enfolding sunny spots of greenery.

But oh ! that deep romantic chasm which slanted
Down the green hill athwart a cedarn cover !
A savage place ! as holy and enchanted
As e'er beneath a waning moon was haunted
By woman wailing for her demon-lover !
And from this chasm, with ceaseless turmoil seething,
As if this earth in fast thick pants were breathing,
A mighty fountain momently was forced;
Amid whose swift half-intermitted burst
Huge fragments vaulted like rebounding hail,
Or chaffy grain beneath the thresher's flail:
And 'mid these dancing rocks at once and ever
It flung up momently the sacred river.
Five miles meandering with a mazy motion
Through wood and dale the sacred river ran,
Then reached the caverns measureless to man,
And sank in tumult to a lifeless ocean:
And 'mid this tumult Kubla heard from far
Ancestral voices prophesying war !

The shadow of the dome of pleasure
Floated midway on the waves;
Where was heard the mingled measure
From the fountain and the caves.
It was a miracle of rare device,
A sunny pleasure/dome with caves of ice !

A damsel with a dulcimer
In a vision once I saw:
It was an Abyssinian maid,
And on her dulcimer she played,
Singing of Mount Abora.
Could I revive within me
Her symphony and song,
To such a deep delight 't would win me,
That with music loud and long,
I would build that dome in air,
That sunny dome ! those caves of ice !
And all who heard should see them there,
And all should cry, Beware ! Beware !
His flashing eyes, his floating hair !
Weave a circle round him thrice,
And close your eyes with holy dread,
For he on honey/dew hath fed,
And drunk the milk of Paradise.

CHARLES LAMB

1775–1834

The Old Familiar Faces

I HAVE had playmates, I have had companions,
In my days of childhood, in my joyful school/days;
All, all are gone, the old familiar faces.

I have been laughing, I have been carousing,
Drinking late, sitting late, with my bosom cronies;
All, all are gone, the old familiar faces.

I loved a love once, fairest among women;
Closed are her doors on me, I must not see her—
All, all are gone, the old familiar faces.

I have a friend, a kinder friend has no man;
Like an ingrate, I left my friend abruptly;
Left him, to muse on the old familiar faces.

Ghost-like I paced round the haunts of my childhood.
Earth seemed a desert I was bound to traverse,
Seeking to find the old familiar faces.

Friend of my bosom, thou more than a brother,
Why wert not thou born in my father's dwelling?
So might we talk of the old familiar faces—

How some they have died, and some they have left me,
And some are taken from me; all are departed;
All, all are gone, the old familiar faces.

WALTER SAVAGE LANDOR
1775–1864

Rose Aylmer

AH what avails the sceptred race,
    Ah what the form divine!
What every virtue, every grace!
    Rose Aylmer, all were thine.
Rose Aylmer, whom these wakeful eyes
    May weep, but never see,
A night of memories and of sighs
    I consecrate to thee.

Past Ruined Ilion

PAST ruined Ilion Helen lives,
    Alcestis rises from the shades;
Verse calls them forth; 'tis verse that gives
    Immortal youth to mortal maids.

Soon shall Oblivion's deepening veil
Hide all the peopled hills you see,
The gay, the proud, while lovers hail
These many summers you and me.

On his Seventy-fifth Birthday

I STROVE with none: for none was worth my strife.
Nature I loved, and next to Nature, Art;
I warmed both hands before the fire of life,
It sinks, and I am ready to depart.

Dirce

From PERICLES AND ASPASIA

STAND close around, ye Stygian set,
With Dirce in one boat conveyed,
Or Charon, seeing, may forget
That he is old, and she a shade.

THOMAS LOVE PEACOCK

1785–1866

The War-song of Dinas Vawr

From THE MISFORTUNES OF ELPHIN

THE mountain sheep are sweeter,
But the valley sheep are fatter;
We therefore deemed it meeter
To carry off the latter.
We made an expedition;
We met a host, and quelled it;
We forced a strong position,
And killed the men who held it.

On Dyfed's richest valley,
Where herds of kine were browsing,
We made a mighty sally,
To furnish our carousing.

Fierce warriors rushed to meet us;
We met them, and o'erthrew them;
They struggled hard to beat us;
But we conquered them, and slew them.

As we drove our prize at leisure,
The king marched forth to catch us:
His rage surpassed all measure,
But his people could not match us.
He fled to his hall-pillars;
And, ere our force we led off,
Some sacked his house and cellars,
While others cut his head off.

We there, in strife bewild'ring,
Spilt blood enough to swim in:
We orphaned many children,
And widowed many women.
The eagles and the ravens
We glutted with our foemen;
The heroes and the cravens,
The spearmen and the bowmen.

We brought away from battle,
And much their land bemoaned them,
Two thousand head of cattle,
And the head of him who owned them:
Ednyfed, King of Dyfed,
His head was borne before us;
His wine and beasts supplied our feasts,
And his overthrow, our chorus.

GEORGE GORDON, LORD BYRON
1788–1824

She walks in Beauty

SHE walks in beauty, like the night
    Of cloudless climes and starry skies;
And all that's best of dark and bright
    Meet in her aspect and her eyes:
Thus mellowed to that tender light
    Which heaven to gaudy day denies.

One shade the more, one ray the less,
    Had half impaired the nameless grace
Which waves in every raven tress,
    Or softly lightens o'er her face;
Where thoughts serenely sweet express
    How pure, how dear their dwelling-place.

And on that cheek, and o'er that brow,
    So soft, so calm, yet eloquent,
The smiles that win, the tints that glow,
    But tell of days in goodness spent,
A mind at peace with all below,
    A heart whose love is innocent!

So, we'll go no more a-roving

SO, we'll go no more a-roving
    So late into the night,
Though the heart be still as loving,
    And the moon be still as bright.

For the sword outwears its sheath,
    And the soul wears out the breast,
And the heart must pause to breathe,
    And Love itself have rest.

Though the night was made for loving,
And the day returns too soon,
Yet we'll go no more a-roving
By the light of the moon.

PERCY BYSSHE SHELLEY

1792–1822

To ——

MUSIC, when soft voices die,
Vibrates in the memory—
Odours, when sweet violets sicken,
Live within the sense they quicken.

Rose leaves, when the rose is dead,
Are heaped for the belovèd's bed;
And so thy thoughts, when thou art gone,
Love itself shall slumber on.

The Indian Serenade

I ARISE from dreams of thee
In the first sweet sleep of night,
When the winds are breathing low,
And the stars are shining bright:
I arise from dreams of thee,
And a spirit in my feet
Hath led me—who knows how?
To thy chamber window, Sweet!

The wandering airs they faint
On the dark, the silent stream—
The Champak odours fail
Like sweet thoughts in a dream;
The nightingale's complaint,
It dies upon her heart;—
As I must on thine,
Oh, belovèd as thou art!

Oh lift me from the grass !
I die ! I faint ! I fail !
Let thy love in kisses rain
On my lips and eyelids pale.
My cheek is cold and white, alas !
My heart beats loud and fast;—
Oh ! press it to thine own again,
Where it will break at last.

To Night

SWIFTLY walk over the western wave,
    Spirit of Night !
  Out of the misty eastern cave,
Where, all the long and lone daylight,
Thou wovest dreams of joy and fear,
Which make thee terrible and dear,—
    Swift be thy flight !

Wrap thy form in a mantle grey,
    Star-inwrought !
Blind with thine hair the eyes of Day;
Kiss her until she be wearied out;
Then wander o'er city, and sea, and land,
Touching all with thine opiate wand—
    Come, long-sought !

When I arose and saw the dawn,
    I sighed for thee;
When light rode high, and the dew was gone,
And noon lay heavy on flower and tree,
And the weary Day turned to his rest,
Lingering like an unloved guest,
    I sighed for thee.

Thy brother Death came, and cried,
    Wouldst thou me ?
Thy sweet child Sleep, the filmy-eyed,

Murmured like a noon-tide bee,
Shall I nestle near thy side ?
Wouldst thou me ?—And I replied,
No, not thee !

Death will come when thou art dead,
Soon, too soon—
Sleep will come when thou art fled;
Of neither would I ask the boon
I ask of thee, belovèd Night—
Swift be thine approaching flight,
Come soon, soon !

Chorus from Hellas

THE world's great age begins anew,
The golden years return,
The earth doth like a snake renew
Her winter weeds outworn:
Heaven smiles, and faiths and empires gleam,
Like wrecks of a dissolving dream.

A brighter Hellas rears its mountains
From waves serener far;
A new Peneus rolls his fountains
Against the morning star.
Where fairer Tempes bloom, there sleep
Young Cyclads on a sunnier deep.

A loftier Argo cleaves the main,
Fraught with a later prize;
Another Orpheus sings again,
And loves, and weeps, and dies.
A new Ulysses leaves once more
Calypso for his native shore.

Oh, write no more the tale of Troy,
If earth Death's scroll must be !

Nor mix with Laian rage the joy
   Which dawns upon the free:
Although a subtler Sphinx renew
Riddles of death Thebes never knew.

Another Athens shall arise,
   And to remoter time
Bequeath, like sunset to the skies,
   The splendour of its prime;
And leave, if naught so bright may live,
All earth can take or Heaven can give.

Saturn and Love their long repose
   Shall burst, more bright and good
Than all who fell, than One who rose,
   Than many unsubdued:
Not gold, not blood, their altar dowers,
But votive tears and symbol flowers.

Oh, cease ! must hate and death return ?
   Cease ! must men kill and die ?
Cease ! drain not to its dregs the urn
   Of bitter prophecy.
The world is weary of the past,
Oh, might it die or rest at last !

Ozymandias

I MET a traveller from an antique land
Who said: Two vast and trunkless legs of stone
Stand in the desert.   Near them, on the sand,
Half sunk, a shattered visage lies, whose frown,
And wrinkled lip, and sneer of cold command,
Tell that its sculptor well those passions read
Which yet survive, stamped on these lifeless things,
The hand that mocked them and the heart that fed;
And on the pedestal these words appear:
" My name is Ozymandias, king of kings:

Look on my works, ye Mighty, and despair ! "
Nothing beside remains.   Round the decay
Of that colossal wreck, boundless and bare
The lone and level sands stretch far away.

Ode to the West Wind

I

O WILD West Wind, thou breath of Autumn's being,
Thou, from whose unseen presence the leaves dead
Are driven, like ghosts from an enchanter fleeing,

Yellow, and black, and pale, and hectic red,
Pestilence-stricken multitudes !   O thou,
Who chariotest to their dark wintry bed

The wingèd seeds, where they lie cold and low,
Each like a corpse within its grave, until
Thine azure sister of the Spring shall blow

Her clarion o'er the dreaming earth, and fill
(Driving sweet buds like flocks to feed in air)
With living hues and odours plain and hill:

Wild Spirit, which art moving everywhere;
Destroyer and preserver; hear, oh, hear !

2

Thou on whose stream, 'mid the steep sky's com-
motion,
Loose clouds like earth's decaying leaves are shed,
Shook from the tangled boughs of Heaven and
Ocean,

Angels of rain and lightning: there are spread
On the blue surface of thine airy surge,
Like the bright hair uplifted from the head

Of some fierce Mænad, even from the dim verge
Of the horizon to the zenith's height,
The locks of the approaching storm.   Thou dirge

Of the dying year, to which this closing night
Will be the dome of a vast sepulchre,
Vaulted with all thy congregated might

Of vapours, from whose solid atmosphere
Black rain, and fire, and hail will burst: oh, hear !

3

Thou who didst waken from his summer dreams
The blue Mediterranean, where he lay
Lulled by the coil of his crystàlline streams,

Beside a pumice isle in Baiæ's bay,
And saw in sleep old palaces and towers
Quivering within the wave's intenser day,

All overgrown with azure moss and flowers
So sweet, the sense faints picturing them !   Thou
For whose path the Atlantic's level powers

Cleave themselves into chasms, while far below
The sea-blooms and the oozy woods which wear
The sapless foliage of the ocean, know

Thy voice, and suddenly grow grey with fear,
And tremble and despoil themselves: oh, hear !

4

If I were a dead leaf thou mightest bear;
If I were a swift cloud to fly with thee;
A wave to pant beneath thy power, and share

The impulse of thy strength, only less free
Than thou, O uncontrollable !   If even
I were as in my boyhood, and could be

The comrade of thy wanderings over Heaven,
As then, when to outstrip thy skiey speed
Scarce seemed a vision; I would ne'er have striven

As thus with thee in prayer in my sore need.
Oh, lift me as a wave, a leaf, a cloud !
I fall upon the thorns of life ! I bleed !

A heavy weight of hours has chained and bowed
One too like thee: tameless, and swift, and proud.

5

Make me thy lyre, even as the forest is:
What if my leaves are falling like its own !
The tumult of thy mighty harmonies

Will take from both a deep, autumnal tone,
Sweet though in sadness.   Be thou, Spirit fierce,
My spirit !   Be thou me, impetuous one !

Drive my dead thoughts over the universe
Like withered leaves to quicken a new birth !
And, by the incantation of this verse,

Scatter, as from an unextinguished hearth
Ashes and sparks, my words among mankind !
Be through my lips to unawakened earth

The trumpet of a prophecy !   O wind,
If Winter comes, can Spring be far behind ?

JOHN KEATS

1795–1821

Ode to a Nightingale

MY heart aches, and a drowsy numbness pains
   My sense, as though of hemlock I had drunk,
Or emptied some dull opiate to the drains
   One minute past, and Lethe-wards had sunk:
'Tis not through envy of thy happy lot,
   But being too happy in thine happiness,—

That thou, light-wingèd Dryad of the trees,
  In some melodious plot
Of beechen green, and shadows numberless,
  Singest of summer in full-throated ease.

O for a draught of vintage ! that hath been
  Cooled a long age in the deep-delvèd earth,
Tasting of Flora and the country green,
  Dance, and Provençal song, and sunburnt mirth !
O for a beaker full of the warm South,
  Full of the true, the blushful Hippocrene,
    With beaded bubbles winking at the brim,
      And purple-stainèd mouth;
That I might drink, and leave the world unseen,
  And with thee fade away into the forest dim:

Fade far away, dissolve, and quite forget
  What thou among the leaves hast never known,
The weariness, the fever, and the fret
  Here, where men sit and hear each other groan;
Where palsy shakes a few, sad, last grey hairs,
  Where youth grows pale, and spectre-thin, and dies ;
    Where but to think is to be full of sorrow
      And leaden-eyed despairs,
Where Beauty cannot keep her lustrous eyes,
  Or new Love pine at them beyond to-morrow.

Away ! away ! for I will fly to thee,
  Not charioted by Bacchus and his pards,
But on the viewless wings of Poesy,
  Though the dull brain perplexes and retards:
Already with thee ! tender is the night,
  And haply the Queen-Moon is on her throne,
    Clustered around by all her starry Fays;
      But here there is no light,
Save what from heaven is with the breezes blown
  Through verdurous glooms and winding mossy ways.

I cannot see what flowers are at my feet,
  Nor what soft incense hangs upon the boughs,
But, in embalmèd darkness, guess each sweet
  Wherewith the seasonable month endows
The grass, the thicket, and the fruit-tree wild;
  White hawthorn, and the pastoral eglantine;
    Fast-fading violets covered up in leaves;
      And mid-May's eldest child,
  The coming musk-rose, full of dewy wine,
    The murmurous haunt of flies on summer eves.

Darkling I listen; and for many a time
  I have been half in love with easeful Death,
Called him soft names in many a musèd rhyme,
  To take into the air my quiet breath;
Now more than ever seems it rich to die,
  To cease upon the midnight with no pain,
    While thou art pouring forth thy soul abroad
      In such an ecstasy!
  Still wouldst thou sing, and I have ears in vain—
    To thy high requiem become a sod.

Thou wast not born for death, immortal Bird!
  No hungry generations tread thee down;
The voice I hear this passing night was heard
  In ancient days by emperor and clown:
Perhaps the self-same song that found a path
  Through the sad heart of Ruth, when, sick for home,
    She stood in tears amid the alien corn;
      The same that oft-times hath
  Charmed magic casements, opening on the foam
    Of perilous seas, in faery lands forlorn.

Forlorn! the very word is like a bell
  To toll me back from thee to my sole self!
Adieu! the fancy cannot cheat so well
  As she is famed to do, deceiving elf.

Adieu ! adieu ! thy plaintive anthem fades
　Past the near meadows, over the still stream,
　　Up the hill-side; and now 'tis buried deep
　　In the next valley-glades:
　Was it a vision, or a waking dream ?
　Fled is that music:—Do I wake or sleep ?

Ode on a Grecian Urn

THOU still unravished bride of quietness,
　Thou foster-child of silence and slow time,
Sylvan historian, who canst thus express
　A flowery tale more sweetly than our rhyme:
What leaf-fringed legend haunts about thy shape
　Of deities or mortals, or of both,
　　In Tempe or the dales of Arcady ?
What men or gods are these ?　What maidens loth ?
What mad pursuit ?　What struggle to escape ?
　　What pipes and timbrels ?　What wild ecstasy ?

Heard melodies are sweet, but those unheard
　Are sweeter; therefore, ye soft pipes, play on;
Not to the sensual ear, but, more endeared,
　Pipe to the spirit ditties of no tone:
Fair youth, beneath the trees, thou canst not leave
　Thy song, nor ever can those trees be bare;
　　Bold Lover, never, never canst thou kiss,
Though winning near the goal—yet, do not grieve;
　She cannot fade, though thou hast not thy bliss,
　　For ever wilt thou love, and she be fair !

Ah, happy, happy boughs ! that cannot shed
　Your leaves, nor ever bid the Spring adieu;
And, happy melodist, unwearièd,
　For ever piping songs for ever new;

More happy love ! more happy, happy love !
    For ever warm and still to be enjoyed,
        For ever panting, and for ever young;
All breathing human passion far above,
    That leaves a heart high-sorrowful and cloyed,
        A burning forehead, and a parching tongue.

Who are these coming to the sacrifice ?
    To what green altar, O mysterious priest,
Lead'st thou that heifer lowing at the skies,
    And all her silken flanks with garlands dressed ?
What little town by river or sea-shore,
    Or mountain-built with peaceful citadel,
        Is emptied of its folk, this pious morn ?
And, little town, thy streets for evermore
    Will silent be; and not a soul to tell
        Why thou art desolate, can e'er return.

O Attic shape ! Fair attitude ! with brede
    Of marble men and maidens overwrought,
With forest branches and the trodden weed;
    Thou, silent form, dost tease us out of thought
As doth eternity ! Cold Pastoral !
    When old age shall this generation waste,
        Thou shalt remain, in midst of other woe
Than ours, a friend to man, to whom thou say'st,
    " Beauty is truth, truth beauty,"—that is all
        Ye know on earth, and all ye need to know.

To Autumn

SEASON of mists and mellow fruitfulness,
    Close bosom-friend of the maturing sun:
Conspiring with him how to load and bless
    With fruit the vines that round the thatch-eaves run;
To bend with apples the mossed cottage-trees,
    And fill all fruit with ripeness to the core;
        To swell the gourd, and plump the hazel shells

With a sweet kernel; to set budding more,
  And still more, later flowers for the bees,
  Until they think warm days will never cease,
   ·For Summer has o'er·brimmed their clammy cells

Who hath not seen thee oft amid thy store?
  Sometimes whoever seeks abroad may find
Thee sitting careless on a granary floor,
  Thy hair soft·lifted by the winnowing wind;
Or on a half·reaped furrow sound asleep,
  Drowsed with the fume of poppies, while thy hook
   Spares the next swath and all its twinèd flowers:
And sometimes like a gleaner thou dost keep
  Steady thy laden head across a brook;
  Or by a cider·press, with patient look,
   Thou watchest the last oozings hours by hours.

Where are the songs of Spring? Aye, where are they?
  Think not of them, thou hast thy music too,—
While barrèd clouds bloom the soft·dying day,
  And touch the stubble·plains with rosy hue;
Then in a wailful choir the small gnats mourn
  Among the river sallows, borne aloft
   Or sinking as the light wind lives or dies;
And full·grown lambs loud bleat from hilly bourn;
  Hedge·crickets sing; and now with treble soft
  The redbreast whistles from a garden·croft;
   And gathering swallows twitter in the skies.

When I have Fears that I may cease to be

WHEN I have fears that I may cease to be
  Before my pen has gleaned my teeming brain,
  Before high·pilèd books, in charact'ry,
  Hold like rich garners the full·ripened grain;

When I behold, upon the night's starred face,
Huge cloudy symbols of a high romance,
And think that I may never live to trace
Their shadows, with the magic hand of chance;
And when I feel, fair creature of an hour !
That I shall never look upon thee more,
Never have relish in the faery power
Of unreflecting love;—then on the shore
Of the wide world I stand alone, and think,
Till Love and Fame to nothingness do sink.

La Belle Dame sans Merci

O WHAT can ail thee, knight-at-arms,
   Alone and palely loitering ?
The sedge has withered from the lake,
   And no birds sing.

O what can ail thee, knight-at-arms,
   So haggard and so woe-begone ?
The squirrel's granary is full,
   And the harvest's done.

I see a lily on thy brow
   With anguish moist and fever dew,
And on thy cheek a fading rose
   Fast withereth too.

I met a lady in the meads,
   Full beautiful—a faery's child;
Her hair was long, her foot was light,
   And her eyes were wild.

I made a garland for her head,
   And bracelets too, and fragrant zone;
She looked at me as she did love,
   And made sweet moan.

I set her on my pacing steed,
　And nothing else saw all day long,
For sidelong would she bend, and sing
　A faery's song.

She found me roots of relish sweet,
　And honey wild, and manna dew,
And sure in language strange she said—
　" I love thee true ! "

She took me to her elfin grot,
　And there she wept and sighed full sore,
And there I shut her wild wild eyes
　With kisses four.

And there she lullèd me asleep,
　And there I dreamed—ah ! woe betide !
The latest dream I ever dreamed
　On the cold hill's side.

I saw pale kings and princes too,
　Pale warriors, death-pale were they all;
They cried—" La Belle Dame sans Merci
　Thee hath in thrall ! "

I saw their starved lips in the gloam,
　With horrid warning gapèd wide,
And I awoke and found me here,
　On the cold hill's side.

And this is why I sojourn here,
　Alone and palely loitering,
Though the sedge is withered from the lake
　And no birds sing.

JOHN HENRY, CARDINAL NEWMAN

1801–90

The Pillar of the Cloud

LEAD, Kindly Light, amid the encircling gloom,
　　　Lead Thou me on !
The night is dark, and I am far from home !
　　　Lead Thou me on !
Keep Thou my feet; I do not ask to see
The distant scene—one step enough for me.

I was not ever thus, nor prayed that Thou
　　　Shouldst lead me on.
I loved to choose and see my path, but now
　　　Lead Thou me on !
I loved the garish day, and, spite of fears,
Pride ruled my will: remember not past years.

So long Thy power hath blest me, sure it still
　　　Will lead me on,
O'er moor and fen, o'er crag and torrent, till
　　　The night is gone,
And with the morn those angel faces smile
Which I have loved long since, and lost awhile.

ALFRED, LORD TENNYSON

1809–92

Mariana

WITH blackest moss the flower-plots
　　　Were thickly crusted, one and all:
The rusted nails fell from the knots
　　　That held the pear to the gable-wall.
The broken sheds looked sad and strange:
　　　Unlifted was the clinking latch;
　　　Weeded and worn the ancient thatch

Upon the lonely moated grange.
   She only said, " My life is dreary,
    He cometh not," she said;
   She said, " I am aweary, aweary,
    I would that I were dead ! "

Her tears fell with the dews at even;
   Her tears fell ere the dews were dried;
She could not look on the sweet heaven,
   Either at morn or eventide.
After the flitting of the bats,
   When thickest dark did trance the sky,
   She drew her casement-curtain by,
And glanced athwart the glooming flats.
   She only said, " The night is dreary,
    He cometh not," she said;
   She said, " I am aweary, aweary,
    I would that I were dead ! "

Upon the middle of the night,
   Waking she heard the night-fowl crow:
The cock sung out an hour ere light;
   From the dark fen the oxen's low
Came to her: without hope of change,
   In sleep she seemed to walk forlorn,
   Till cold winds woke the grey-eyed morn
About the lonely moated grange.
   She only said, " The day is dreary,
    He cometh not," she said;
   She said, " I am aweary, aweary,
    I would that I were dead ! "

About a stone-cast from the wall
   A sluice with blackened waters slept,
And o'er it many, round and small,
   The clustered marish-mosses crept.

Hard by a poplar shook alway,
  All silver-green with gnarlèd bark:
For leagues no other tree did mark
The level waste, the rounding grey.
    She only said, " My life is dreary,
      He cometh not," she said;
    She said, " I am aweary, aweary,
      I would that I were dead ! "

And ever when the moon was low,
  And the shrill winds were up and away,
In the white curtain, to and fro,
  She saw the gusty shadow sway.
But when the moon was very low,
  And wild winds bound within their cell,
The shadow of the poplar fell
Upon her bed, across her brow.
    She only said, " The night is dreary,
      He cometh not," she said;
    She said, " I am aweary, aweary,
      I would that I were dead ! "

All day within the dreamy house,
  The doors upon their hinges creaked;
The blue fly sung in the pane; the mouse
  Behind the mouldering wainscot shrieked,
Or from the crevice peered about.
    Old faces glimmered through the doors,
    Old footsteps trod the upper floors,
Old voices called her from without.
    She only said, " My life is dreary,
      He cometh not," she said;
    She said, " I am aweary, aweary,
      I would that I were dead ! "

The sparrow's chirrup on the roof,
  The slow clock ticking, and the sound

Which to the wooing wind aloof
  The poplar made, did all confound
Her sense; but most she loathed the hour
  When the thick-moted sunbeam lay
Athwart the chambers, and the day
Was sloping toward his western bower.
    Then said she, " I am very dreary,
      He will not come," she said;
    She wept, " I am aweary, aweary,
      O God, that I were dead ! "

Song from Maud

COME into the garden, Maud,
  For the black bat, night, has flown,
Come into the garden, Maud,
  I am here at the gate alone;
And the woodbine spices are wafted abroad,
  And the musk of the rose is blown.

For a breeze of morning moves,
  And the planet of love is on high,
Beginning to faint in the light that she loves
  On a bed of daffodil sky,
To faint in the light of the sun she loves,
  To faint in his light, and to die.

All night have the roses heard
  The flute, violin, bassoon;
All night has the casement jessamine stirred
  To the dancers dancing in tune;
Till a silence fell with the waking bird,
  And a hush with the setting moon.

I said to the lily, " There is but one
  With whom she has heart to be gay.
When will the dancers leave her alone ?
  She is weary of dance and play."

Now half to the setting moon are gone,
　And half to the rising day;
Low on the sand and loud on the stone
　The last wheel echoes away.

I said to the rose, " The brief night goes
　In babble and revel and wine.
O young lord-lover, what sighs are those,
　For one that will never be thine ?
But mine, but mine," so I sware to the rose,
　" For ever and ever, mine."

And the soul of the rose went into my blood,
　As the music clashed in the Hall;
And long by the garden lake I stood,
　For I heard your rivulet fall
From the lake to the meadow and on to the wood,
　Our wood, that is dearer than all;

From the meadow your walks have left so sweet
　That whenever a March-wind sighs
He sets the jewel-print of your feet
　In violets blue as your eyes,
To the woody hollows in which we meet
　And the valleys of Paradise.

The slender acacia would not shake
　One long milk-bloom on the tree;
The white lake-blossom fell into the lake
　As the pimpernel dozed on the lea;
But the rose was awake all night for your sake,
　Knowing your promise to me;
The lilies and roses were all awake,
　They sighed for the dawn and thee.

Queen rose of the rosebud garden of girls,
　Come hither, the dances are done,

In gloss of satin and glimmer of pearls,
  Queen lily and rose in one;
Shine out, little head, sunning over with curls,
  To the flowers, and be their sun.

There has fallen a splendid tear
  From the passion-flower at the gate.
She is coming, my dove, my dear;
  She is coming, my life, my fate.
The red rose cries, " She is near, she is near; "
  And the white rose weeps, " She is late; "
The larkspur listens, " I hear, I hear; "
  And the lily whispers, " I wait."

She is coming, my own, my sweet;
  Were it ever so airy a tread,
My heart would hear her and beat,
  Were it earth in an earthy bed;
My dust would hear her and beat,
  Had I lain for a century dead,
Would start and tremble under her feet,
  And blossom in purple and red.

Break, Break, Break

BREAK, break, break,
  On thy cold grey stones, O Sea !
And I would that my tongue could utter
  The thoughts that arise in me.

O well for the fisherman's boy,
  That he shouts with his sister at play !
O well for the sailor lad,
  That he sings in his boat on the bay !

And the stately ships go on
  To their haven under the hill;
But O for the touch of a vanished hand,
  And the sound of a voice that is still !

Break, break, break,
    At the foot of thy crags, O Sea !
But the tender grace of a day that is dead
    Will never come back to me.

Songs from The Princess

I

TEARS, idle tears, I know not what they mean,
Tears from the depth of some divine despair
Rise in the heart, and gather to the eyes,
In looking on the happy autumn-fields,
And thinking of the days that are no more.

    Fresh as the first beam glittering on a sail,
That brings our friends up from the underworld,
Sad as the last which reddens over one
That sinks with all we love below the verge;
So sad, so fresh, the days that are no more.

    Ah, sad and strange as in dark summer dawns
The earliest pipe of half-awakened birds
To dying ears, when unto dying eyes
The casement slowly grows a glimmering square;
So sad, so strange, the days that are no more.

    Dear as remembered kisses after death,
And sweet as those by hopeless fancy feigned
On lips that are for others; deep as love,
Deep as first love, and wild with all regret;
O Death in Life, the days that are no more !

2

The splendour falls on castle walls
    And snowy summits old in story;
The long light shakes across the lakes,
    And the wild cataract leaps in glory.

Blow, bugle, blow, set the wild echoes flying,
Blow, bugle; answer, echoes, dying, dying, dying.

O hark, O, hear ! how thin and clear,
    And thinner, clearer, farther going !
O, sweet and far from cliff and scar
    The horns of Elfland faintly blowing !
Blow, let us hear the purple glens replying,
Blow, bugle; answer, echoes, dying, dying, dying.

O love, they die in yon rich sky,
    They faint on hill or field or river;
Our echoes roll from soul to soul,
    And grow for ever and for ever.
Blow, bugle, blow, set the wild echoes flying,
And answer, echoes, answer, dying, dying, dying.

ROBERT BROWNING

1812–89

Porphyria's Lover

THE rain set early in to-night,
    The sullen wind was soon awake,
It tore the elm-tops down for spite,
    And did its worst to vex the lake:
I listened with heart fit to break;
When glided in Porphyria: straight
    She shut the cold out and the storm,
And kneeled and made the cheerless grate
    Blaze up, and all the cottage warm;
Which done, she rose, and from her form
Withdrew the dripping cloak and shawl,
    And laid her soiled gloves by, untied
Her hat and let the damp hair fall,
    And, last, she sat down by my side
And called me.   When no voice replied,
She put my arm about her waist,
    And made her smooth white shoulder bare

And all her yellow hair displaced,
    And, stooping, made my cheek lie there,
And spread, o'er all, her yellow hair,
Murmuring how she loved me—she
    Too weak, for all her heart's endeavour,
To set its struggling passion free
    From pride, and vainer ties dissever,
And give herself to me for ever.
But passion sometimes would prevail,
    Nor could to-night's gay feast restrain
A sudden thought of one so pale
    For love of her, and all in vain:
So, she was come through wind and rain.
Be sure I looked up at her eyes
    Happy and proud; at last I knew
Porphyria worshipped me; surprise
    Made my heart swell, and still it grew
While I debated what to do.
That moment she was mine, mine, fair,
    Perfectly pure and good: I found
A thing to do, and all her hair
    In one long yellow string I wound
Three times her little throat around,
And strangled her. No pain felt she;
    I am quite sure she felt no pain.
As a shut bud that holds a bee,
    I warily oped her lids: again
Laughed the blue eyes without a stain.
And I untightened next the tress
    About her neck; her cheek once more
Blushed bright beneath my burning kiss:
    I propped her head up as before,
Only, this time my shoulder bore
Her head, which droops upon it still:
    The smiling rosy little head,
So glad it has its utmost will,

That all it scorned at once is fled,
And I, its love, am gained instead !
Porphyria's love: she guessed not how
   Her darling one wish would be heard.
And thus we sit together now,
   And all night long we have not stirred,
And yet God has not said a word !

My Last Duchess

FERRARA

THAT'S my last Duchess painted on the wall,
Looking as if she were alive.   I call
That piece a wonder, now: Frà Pandolf's hands
Worked busily a day, and there she stands.
Will 't please you sit and look at her ?   I said
" Frà Pandolf " by design, for never read
Strangers like you that pictured countenance,
The depth and passion of its earnest glance,
But to myself they turned (since none puts by
The curtain I have drawn for you, but I)
And seemed as they would ask me, if they durst,
How such a glance came there; so, not the first
Are you to turn and ask thus.   Sir, 't was not
Her husband's presence only, called that spot
Of joy into the Duchess' cheek: perhaps
Frà Pandolf chanced to say, " Her mantle laps
Over my lady's wrist too much," or " Paint
Must never hope to reproduce the faint
Half-flush that dies along her throat: " such stuff
Was courtesy, she thought, and cause enough
For calling up that spot of joy.   She had
A heart—how shall I say ?—too soon made glad,
Too easily impressed; she liked whate'er
She looked on, and her looks went everywhere.

Sir, 't was all one ! My favour at her breast,
The dropping of the daylight in the West,
The bough of cherries some officious fool
Broke in the orchard for her, the white mule
She rode with round the terrace—all and each
Would draw from her alike the approving speech,
Or blush, at least. She thanked men,—good ! but
    thanked
Somehow—I know not how—as if she ranked
My gift of a nine-hundred-years-old name
With anybody's gift. Who'd stoop to blame
This sort of trifling ? Even had you skill
In speech—(which I have not)—to make your will
Quite clear to such an one, and say, " Just this
Or that in you disgusts me; here you miss,
Or there exceed the mark "—and if she let
Herself be lessoned so, nor plainly set
Her wits to yours, forsooth, and made excuse,
—E'en then would be some stooping; and I choose
Never to stoop. Oh, sir, she smiled, no doubt,
Whene'er I passed her; but who passed without
Much the same smile ? This grew; I gave commands;
Then all smiles stopped together. There she stands
As if alive. Will 't please you rise ? We'll meet
The company below, then. I repeat,
The Count your master's known munificence
Is ample warrant that no just pretence
Of mine for dowry will be disallowed;
Though his fair daughter's self, as I avowed
At starting, is my object. Nay, we'll go
Together down, sir. Notice Neptune, though,
Taming a sea-horse, thought a rarity,
Which Claus of Innsbruck cast in bronze for me !

Home-thoughts, from Abroad

OH, to be in England
Now that April's there,
And whoever wakes in England
Sees, some morning, unaware,
That the lowest boughs and the brushwood sheaf
Round the elm-tree bole are in tiny leaf,
While the chaffinch sings on the orchard bough
In England—now !

And after April, when May follows,
And the whitethroat builds, and all the swallows ?
Hark, where my blossomed pear-tree in the hedge
Leans to the field and scatters on the clover
Blossoms and dewdrops—at the bent spray's edge—
That's the wise thrush; he sings each song twice over,
Lest you should think he never could recapture
The first fine careless rapture !
And though the fields look rough with hoary dew,
All will be gay when noontide wakes anew
The buttercups, the little children's dower
—Far brighter than this gaudy melon-flower !

Home-thoughts, from the Sea

NOBLY, nobly Cape Saint Vincent to the north-west
    died away;
Sunset ran, one glorious blood-red, reeking into
    Cadiz Bay;
Bluish 'mid the burning water, full in face Trafalgar
    lay;
In the dimmest north-east distance dawned Gibraltar
    grand and grey;
" Here and here did England help me: how can I
    help England ? "—say

Whoso turns as I, this evening, turn to God to praise
    and pray,
While Jove's planet rises yonder, silent over Africa.

Meeting at Night

THE grey sea and the long black land;
    And the yellow half-moon large and low;
And the startled little waves that leap
In fiery ringlets from their sleep,
As I gain the cove with pushing prow,
And quench its speed i' the slushy sand.
Then a mile of warm sea-scented beach;
Three fields to cross till a farm appears;
A tap at the pane, the quick sharp scratch
And blue spurt of a lighted match,
And a voice less loud, through its joys and fears,
Than the two hearts beating each to each!

Parting at Morning

ROUND the cape of a sudden came the sea,
    And the sun looked over the mountain's rim;
And straight was a path of gold for him,
And the need of a world of men for me.

ARTHUR HUGH CLOUGH

1819–61

Where lies the Land?

WHERE lies the land to which the ship would go?
    Far, far ahead, is all her seamen know.
And where the land she travels from? Away,
    Far, far behind, is all that they can say.

On sunny noons upon the deck's smooth face,
Linked arm in arm, how pleasant here to pace;
Or, o'er the stern reclining, watch below
The foaming wake far widening as we go.

On stormy nights when wild north-westers rave,
How proud a thing to fight with wind and wave !
The dripping sailor on the reeling mast
Exults to bear, and scorns to wish it past.

Where lies the land to which the ship would go ?
Far, far ahead, is all her seamen know.
And where the land she travels from ?   Away,
Far, far behind, is all that they can say.

Say not the Struggle Naught Availeth

SAY not the struggle naught availeth,
    The labour and the wounds are vain,
The enemy faints not, nor faileth,
    And as things have been they remain.

If hopes were dupes, fears may be liars;
    It may be, in yon smoke concealed,
Your comrades chase e'en now the fliers,
    And, but for you, possess the field.

For while the tired waves, vainly breaking,
    Seem here no painful inch to gain,
Far back, through creeks and inlets making,
    Comes silent, flooding in, the main.

And not by eastern windows only,
    When daylight comes, comes in the light;
In front the sun climbs slow, how slowly !
    But westward, look, the land is bright !

MATTHEW ARNOLD

1822–88

Requiescat

STREW on her roses, roses,
  And never a spray of yew !
In quiet she reposes;
  Ah, would that I did too !

Her mirth the world required;
  She bathed it in smiles of glee.
But her heart was tired, tired,
  And now they let her be.

Her life was turning, turning,
  In mazes of heat and sound.
But for peace her soul was yearning,
  And now peace laps her round.

Her cabined, ample spirit,
  It fluttered and failed for breath.
To-night it doth inherit
  The vasty hall of death.

Dover Beach

THE sea is calm to-night,
  The tide is full, the moon lies fair
Upon the straits;—on the French coast the light
Gleams and is gone; the cliffs of England stand,
Glimmering and vast, out in the tranquil bay.
Come to the window, sweet is the night-air !
Only, from the long line of spray
Where the sea meets the moon-blanched land,
Listen ! you hear the grating roar
Of pebbles which the waves draw back, and fling,
At their return, up the high strand,
Begin, and cease, and then again begin,

With tremulous cadence slow, and bring
The eternal note of sadness in.

Sophocles long ago
Heard it on the Ægean, and it brought
Into his mind the turbid ebb and flow
Of human misery; we
Find also in the sound a thought,
Hearing it by this distant northern sea.

The sea of faith
Was once, too, at the full, and round earth's shore
Lay like the folds of a bright girdle furled.
But now I only hear
Its melancholy, long, withdrawing roar,
Retreating, to the breath
Of the night-wind, down the vast edges drear
And naked shingles of the world.

Ah, love, let us be true
To one another ! for the world, which seems
To lie before us like a land of dreams,
So various, so beautiful, so new,
Hath really neither joy, nor love, nor light,
Nor certitude, nor peace, nor help for pain;
And we are here as on a darkling plain
Swept with confused alarms of struggle and flight,
Where ignorant armies clash by night.

CHRISTINA ROSSETTI

1830–94

Song

WHEN I am dead, my dearest,
    Sing no sad songs for me;
Plant thou no roses at my head,
    Nor shady cypress-tree:

Be the green grass above me
    With showers and dewdrops wet;
And if thou wilt, remember,
    And if thou wilt, forget.

I shall not see the shadows,
    I shall not feel the rain;
I shall not hear the nightingale
    Sing on, as if in pain;
And dreaming through the twilight
    That doth not rise nor set,
Haply I may remember,
    And haply may forget.

A Birthday

MY heart is like a singing bird
    Whose nest is in a watered shoot;
My heart is like an apple-tree
    Whose boughs are bent with thick-set fruit;
My heart is like a rainbow shell
    That paddles in a halcyon sea;
My heart is gladder than all these,
    Because my love is come to me.

Raise me a dais of silk and down;
    Hang it with vair and purple dyes;
Carve it in doves and pomegranates,
    And peacocks with a hundred eyes;
Work it in gold and silver grapes,
    In leaves and silver fleur-de-lys;
Because the birthday of my life
    Is come, my love is come to me.

Remember

REMEMBER me when I am gone away,
    Gone far away into the silent land;
    When you can no more hold me by the hand,
Nor I half turn to go, yet turning stay.

Remember me when no more, day by day,
You tell me of our future that you planned:
Only remember me; you understand
It will be late to counsel then or pray.
Yet if you should forget me for a while
And afterwards remember, do not grieve:
For if the darkness and corruption leave
A vestige of the thoughts that once I had,
Better by far you should forget and smile
Than that you should remember and be sad.

ALGERNON CHARLES SWINBURNE

1837–1909

The Garden of Proserpine

HERE, where the world is quiet,
   Here, where all trouble seems
Dead winds' and spent waves' riot
   In doubtful dreams of dreams;
I watch the green field growing
For reaping folk and sowing,
For harvest-time and mowing,
   A sleepy world of streams.

I am tired of tears and laughter,
   And men that laugh and weep;
Of what may come hereafter
   For men that sow to reap:
I am weary of days and hours,
Blown buds of barren flowers,
Desires and dreams and powers,
   And everything but sleep.

Here life has death for neighbour,
   And far from eye or ear
Wan waves and wet winds labour,
   Weak ships and spirits steer;

They drive adrift, and whither
They wot not who make thither;
But no such winds blow hither,
   And no such things grow here.

No growth of moor or coppice,
   No heather-flower or vine,
But bloomless buds of poppies,
   Green grapes of Proserpine,
Pale beds of blowing rushes,
Where no leaf blooms or blushes
Save this whereout she crushes
   For dead men deadly wine.

Pale, without name or number,
   In fruitless fields of corn,
They bow themselves and slumber
   All night till light is born;
And like a soul belated,
In hell and heaven unmated,
By cloud and mist abated
   Comes out of darkness morn.

Though one were strong as seven,
   He too with death shall dwell,
Nor wake with wings in heaven,
   Nor weep for pains in hell;
Though one were fair as roses,
His beauty clouds and closes;
And well though love reposes,
   In the end it is not well.

Pale, beyond porch and portal,
   Crowned with calm leaves, she stands
Who gathers all things mortal
   With cold immortal hands;

Her languid lips are sweeter
Than love's who fears to greet her
To men that mix and meet her
From many times and lands.

She waits for each and other,
She waits for all men born;
Forgets the earth her mother,
The life of fruits and corn;
And spring and seed and swallow
Take wing for her and follow
Where summer song rings hollow
And flowers are put to scorn.

There go the loves that wither,
The old loves with wearier wings;
And all dead years draw thither,
And all disastrous things;
Dead dreams of days forsaken,
Blind buds that snows have shaken,
Wild leaves that winds have taken,
Red strays of ruined springs.

We are not sure of sorrow,
And joy was never sure;
To-day will die to-morrow;
Time stoops to no man's lure;
And love, grown faint and fretful,
With lips but half regretful
Sighs, and with eyes forgetful
Weeps that no loves endure.

From too much love of living,
From hope and fear set free,
We thank with brief thanksgiving
Whatever gods may be

That no life lives for ever;
That dead men rise up never;
That even the weariest river
  Winds somewhere safe to sea.

Then star nor sun shall waken,
  Nor any change of light:
Nor sound of waters shaken,
  Nor any sound or sight:
Nor wintry leaves nor vernal,
Nor days nor things diurnal:
Only the sleep eternal
  In an eternal night.

Chorus

From ATALANTA IN CALYDON

WHEN the hounds of spring are on winter's traces,
  The mother of months in meadow or plain
Fills the shadows and windy places
  With lisp of leaves and ripple of rain;
And the brown bright nightingale amorous
Is half assuaged for Itylus,
For the Thracian ships and the foreign faces,
  The tongueless vigil, and all the pain.

Come with bows bent and with emptying of quivers,
  Maiden most perfect, lady of light,
With a noise of winds and many rivers,
  With a clamour of waters, and with might;
Bind on thy sandals, O thou most fleet,
Over the splendour and speed of thy feet;
For the faint east quickens, the wan west shivers,
  Round the feet of the day and the feet of the
    night.

Where shall we find her, how shall we sing to her,
  Fold our hands round her knees, and cling?

O that man's heart were as fire and could spring to her,
  Fire, or the strength of the streams that spring !
For the stars and the winds are unto her
As raiment, as songs of the harp player;
For the risen stars and the fallen cling to her,
  And the south west wind and the west wind sing.

For winter's rains and ruins are over,
  And all the season of snows and sins;
The days dividing lover and lover,
  The light that loses, the night that wins;
And time remembered is grief forgotten,
And frosts are slain and flowers begotten,
And in green underwood and cover
  Blossom by blossom the spring begins.

The full streams feed on flower of rushes,
  Ripe grasses trammel a travelling foot,
The faint fresh flame of the young year flushes
  From leaf to flower and flower to fruit;
And fruit and leaf are as gold and fire,
And the oat is heard above the lyre,
And the hoofèd heel of a satyr crushes
  The chestnut husk at the chestnut root.

And Pan by noon and Bacchus by night,
  Fleeter of foot than the fleet foot kid,
Follows with dancing and fills with delight
  The Mænad and the Bassarid;
And soft as lips that laugh and hide
The laughing leaves of the trees divide,
And screen from seeing and leave in sight
  The god pursuing, the maiden hid.

The ivy falls with the Bacchanal's hair
  Over her eyebrows hiding her eyes;
The wild vine slipping down leaves bare
  Her bright breast shortening into sighs;

The wild vine slips with the weight of its leaves,
But the berried ivy catches and cleaves
To the limbs that glitter, the feet that scare
The wolf that follows, the fawn that flies.

THOMAS HARDY
1840–1928

Drummer Hodge

THEY throw in Drummer Hodge, to rest
    Uncoffined—just as found:
His landmark is a kopje-crest
    That breaks the veldt around;
And foreign constellations west
    Each night above his mound.

Young Hodge the Drummer never knew—
    Fresh from his Wessex home—
The meaning of the broad Karoo,
    The Bush, the dusty loam,
And why uprose to nightly view
    Strange stars amid the gloam.

Yet portion of that unknown plain
    Will Hodge for ever be;
His homely Northern breast and brain
    Grow to some Southern tree,
And strange-eyed constellations reign
    His stars eternally.

Hap

IF but some vengeful god would call to me
From up the sky, and laugh: " Thou suffering thing,
Know that thy sorrow is my ecstasy,
That thy love's loss is my hate's profiting ! "

Then would I bear it, clench myself, and die,
Steeled by the sense of ire unmerited;
Half eased in that a Powerfuller than I
Had willed and meted me the tears I shed.

But not so.   How arrives it joy lies slain,
And why unblooms the best hope ever sown ?
—Crass Casualty obstructs the sun and rain,
And dicing Time for gladness casts a moan. . . .
These purblind Doomsters had as readily strown
Blisses about my pilgrimage as pain.

Let me enjoy

(*Minor Key*)

LET me enjoy the earth no less
Because the all enacting Might
   That fashioned forth its loveliness
   Had other aims than my delight.

About my path there flits a Fair,
Who throws me not a word or sign;
   I'll charm me with her ignoring air,
   And laud the lips not meant for mine.

From manuscripts of moving song
Inspired by scenes and dreams unknown,
   I'll pour out raptures that belong
   To other, as they were my own.

And some day hence, towards Paradise
And all its blest—if such should be—
   I will lift glad, afar off eyes,
   Though it contain no place for me.

ALICE MEYNELL

1850–1923

The Shepherdess

SHE walks—the lady of my delight—
  A shepherdess of sheep.
Her flocks are thoughts.   She keeps them white;
  She guards them from the steep;
She feeds them on the fragrant height,
  And folds them in for sleep.

She roams maternal hills and bright,
  Dark valleys safe and deep.
Into that tender breast at night
  The chastest stars may peep.
She walks—the lady of my delight—
  A shepherdess of sheep.

She holds her little thoughts in sight,
  Though gay they run and leap.
She is so circumspect and right;
  She has her soul to keep.
She walks—the lady of my delight—
  A shepherdess of sheep.

RUDYARD KIPLING

1865–

Recessional

GOD of our fathers, known of old,
  Lord of our far-flung battle-line,
Beneath whose awful Hand we hold
  Dominion over palm and pine—
Lord God of Hosts, be with us yet,
Lest we forget—lest we forget !

The tumult and the shouting dies;
  The captains and the kings depart:
Still stands Thine ancient sacrifice,
  An humble and a contrite heart.
Lord God of Hosts, be with us yet,
Lest we forget—lest we forget !

Far-called, our navies melt away;
  On dune and headland sinks the fire:
Lo, all our pomp of yesterday
  Is one with Nineveh and Tyre !
Judge of the Nations, spare us yet,
Lest we forget—lest we forget !

If, drunk with sight of power, we loose
  Wild tongues that have not Thee in awe,
Such boastings as the Gentiles use,
  Or lesser breeds without the Law—
Lord God of Hosts, be with us yet,
Lest we forget—lest we forget !

For heathen heart that puts her trust
  In reeking tube and iron shard,
All valiant dust that builds on dust,
  And guarding, calls not Thee to guard,
For frantic boast and foolish word—
Thy Mercy on Thy People, Lord !

                              Amen.

ERNEST DOWSON

1867–1900

*" Vitae summa brevis spem nos
    vetat incohare longam"*

THEY are not long, the weeping and the laughter,
  Love and desire and hate:
I think they have no portion in us after
  We pass the gate.

They are not long, the days of wine and roses:
Out of a misty dream
Our path emerges for a while, then closes
Within a dream.

"*Non sum qualis eram bonae sub regno Cynarae*"

LAST night, ah, yesternight, betwixt her lips and mine
There fell thy shadow, Cynara! thy breath was shed
Upon my soul between the kisses and the wine;
And I was desolate and sick of an old passion,
    Yea, I was desolate and bowed my head:
I have been faithful to thee, Cynara! in my fashion.

All night upon mine heart I felt her warm heart beat,
Night-long within mine arms in love and sleep she
    lay;
Surely the kisses of her bought red mouth were
    sweet;
But I was desolate and sick of an old passion,
    When I awoke and found the dawn was grey;
I have been faithful to thee, Cynara! in my fashion.

I have forgot much, Cynara! gone with the wind,
Flung roses, roses riotously with the throng,
Dancing, to put thy pale, lost lilies out of mind;
But I was desolate and sick of an old passion,
    Yea, all the time, because the dance was long:
I have been faithful to thee, Cynara! in my fashion.

I cried for madder music and for stronger wine,
But when the feast is finished and the lamps expire,
Then falls thy shadow, Cynara, the night is thine;
And I am desolate and sick of an old passion,
    Yea, hungry for the lips of my desire:
I have been faithful to thee, Cynara! in my fashion.

WILLIAM HENRY DAVIES

1870–

Leisure

WHAT is this life if, full of care,
We have no time to stand and stare?

No time to stand beneath the boughs
And stare as long as sheep or cows.

No time to see, when woods we pass,
Where squirrels hide their nuts in grass.

No time to see, in broad daylight,
Streams full of stars, like stars at night.

No time to turn at Beauty's glance,
And watch her feet, how they can dance.

No time to wait till her mouth can
Enrich that smile her eyes began.

A poor life this if, full of care,
We have no time to stand and stare.

WALTER DE LA MARE

1873–

Fare Well

WHEN I lie where shades of darkness
Shall no more assail mine eyes,
Nor the rain make lamentation
When the wind sighs;
How will fare the world whose wonder
Was the very proof of me?
Memory fades, must the remembered
Perishing be?

Oh, when this my dust surrenders
Hand, foot, lip, to dust again,
May these loved and loving faces
 Please other men !
May the rusting harvest hedgerow
Still the Traveller's Joy entwine,
And as happy children gather
 Posies once mine.

Look thy last on all things lovely,
Every hour. Let no night
Seal thy sense in deathly slumber
 Till to delight
Thou have paid thy utmost blessing;
Since that all things thou wouldst praise
Beauty took from those who loved them
 In other days.

JOHN MASEFIELD

1878–

Sonnet
From LOLLINGDON DOWNS

HERE in the self is all that man can know
Of Beauty, all the wonder, all the power,
All the unearthly colour, all the glow,
Here in the self which withers like a flower;
Here in the self which fades as hours pass,
And droops and dies and rots and is forgotten
Sooner, by ages, than the mirroring glass
In which it sees its glory still unrotten.
Here in the flesh, within the flesh, behind,
Swift in the blood and throbbing on the bone,
Beauty herself, the universal mind,
Eternal April wandering alone;
The God, the holy Ghost, the atoning Lord,
Here in the flesh, the never yet explored.

ALDOUS HUXLEY

1894–

First Philosopher's Song

A POOR degenerate from the ape
Whose hands are four, whose tail's a limb,
I contemplate my flaccid shape
And know I may not rival him,

Save with my mind—a nimbler beast
Possessing a thousand sinewy tails,
A thousand hands, with which it scales,
Greedy of luscious truth, the greased

Poles and the coco palms of thought,
Thrids easily through the mangrove maze
Of metaphysics, walks the taut
Frail dangerous liana ways

That link across wide gulfs remote
Analogies between tree and tree;
Outruns the hare, outhops the goat;
Mind fabulous, mind sublime and free!

But oh, the sound of simian mirth!
Mind, issued from the monkey's womb,
Is still umbilical to earth,
Earth its home and earth its tomb.

ROBERT GRAVES

1895–

Lost Love

HIS eyes are quickened so with grief,
He can watch a grass or leaf
Every instant grow; he can
Clearly through a flint wall see,

Or watch the startled spirit flee
From the throat of a dead man.
Across two counties he can hear,
And catch your words before you speak.
The woodlouse or the maggot's weak
Clamour rings in his sad ear;
And noise so slight it would surpass
Credence:—drinking sound of grass,
Worm talk, clashing jaws of moth
Chumbling holes in cloth:
The groan of ants who undertake
Gigantic loads for honour's sake,
Their sinews creak, their breath comes thin:
Whir of spiders when they spin,
And minute whispering, mumbling, sighs
Of idle grubs and flies.
This man is quickened so with grief,
He wanders god-like or like thief
Inside and out, below, above,
Without relief seeking lost love.

IRISH

FROM THE GAELIC
COLUM-CILLE

6th century

(Attributed)

Farewell to Ireland

ALAS for the voyage, O High King of Heaven,
  Enjoined upon me,
For that I on the red plain of bloody Cooldrevin
  Was present to see.

How happy the son is of Dima; no sorrow
  For him is designed,
He is having, this hour, round his own hill in Durrow,
  The wish of his mind.

The sounds of the winds in the elms, like strings of
  A harp being played,
The note of a blackbird that claps with the wings of
  Delight in the shade.

With him in Ros-Grencha the cattle are lowing
  At earliest dawn,
On the brink of the summer the pigeons are cooing
  And doves in the lawn.

Three things am I leaving behind me, the very
  Most dear that I know,
Tir-Leedach I'm leaving, and Durrow and Derry;
  Alas, I must go !

Yet my visit and feasting with Comgall have eased me
  At Cainneach's right hand,
And all but thy government, Eiré, have pleased me,
  Thou waterful land.

Douglas Hyde

HUGH O'DONNELL

16th century

(Attributed)

Dark Rosaleen

O MY dark Rosaleen,
   Do not sigh, do not weep!
The priests are on the ocean green,
   They march along the deep.
There's wine from the royal Pope,
   Upon the ocean green;
And Spanish ale shall give you hope,
   My dark Rosaleen!
   My own Rosaleen!
Shall glad your heart, shall give you hope,
Shall give you health, and help, and hope,
   My dark Rosaleen.

Over hills, and through dales,
   Have I roamed for your sake;
All yesterday I sailed with sails
   On river and on lake.
The Erne, at its highest flood,
   I dashed across unseen,
For there was lightning in my blood,
   My dark Rosaleen!
   My own Rosaleen!
Oh! there was lightning in my blood,
'Red lightning lightened through my blood,
   My dark Rosaleen!

All day long in unrest,
   To and fro do I move,
The very soul within my breast
   Is wasted for you, love!
The heart in my bosom faints
   To think of you, my Queen,

My life of life, my saint of saints,
　　My dark Rosaleen !
　　My own Rosaleen !
To hear your sweet and sad complaints,
My life, my love, my saint of saints,
　　My dark Rosaleen !

Woe and pain, pain and woe,
　　Are my lot, night and noon,
To see your bright face clouded so,
　　Like to the mournful moon.
But yet will I rear your throne
　　Again in golden sheen;
'Tis you shall reign, shall reign alone,
　　My dark Rosaleen !
　　My own Rosaleen !
'Tis you shall have the golden throne,
'Tis you shall reign, shall reign alone,
　　My dark Rosaleen !

Over dews, over sands,
　　Will I fly for your weal:
Your holy, delicate white hands
　　Shall girdle me with steel.
At home in your emerald bowers,
　　From morning's dawn till e'en,
You'll pray for me, my flower of flowers,
　　My dark Rosaleen !
　　My fond Rosaleen !
You'll think of me through daylight's hours,
My virgin flower, my flower of flowers,
　　My dark Rosaleen !

I could scale the blue air,
　　I could plough the high hills,
Oh, I could kneel all night in prayer,
　　To heal your many ills !

And one beamy smile from you
  Would float like light between
My toils and me, my own, my true,
  My dark Rosaleen !
  My fond Rosaleen !
Would give me life and soul anew,
A second life, a soul anew,
  My dark Rosaleen !

O ! the Erne shall run red
  With redundance of blood,
The earth shall rock beneath our tread,
  And flames wrap hill and wood,
And gun‑peal and slogan cry
  Wake many a glen serene,
Ere you shall fade, ere you shall die,
  My dark Rosaleen !
  My own Rosaleen !
The Judgment Hour must first be nigh
Ere you can fade, ere you can die,
  My dark Rosaleen !

James Clarence Mangan

O'GNIVE

16th century

The Downfall of the Gael

MY heart is in woe,
  And my soul deep in trouble,—
For the mighty are low,
  And abased are the noble:

The Sons of the Gael
  Are in exile and mourning,
Worn, weary, and pale
  As spent pilgrims returning;

Or men who, in flight
From the field of disaster,
Beseech the black night
On their flight to fall faster;

Or seamen aghast
When their planks gape asunder,
And the waves fierce and fast
Tumble through in hoarse thunder;

Or men whom we see
That have got their death-omen,—
Such wretches are we
In the chains of our foemen!

Our courage is fear,
Our nobility vileness,
Our hope is despair,
And our comeliness foulness.

There is mist on our heads,
And a cloud chill and hoary
Of black sorrow, sheds
An eclipse on our glory.

From Boyne to the Linn
Has the mandate been given,
That the children of Finn
From their country be driven.

That the sons of the king—
Oh, the treason and malice!—
Shall no more ride the ring
In their own native valleys;

No more shall repair
Where the hill foxes tarry,
Nor forth to the air
Fling the hawk at her quarry:

For the plain shall be broke
By the share of the stranger,
And the stone-mason's stroke
Tell the woods of their danger;

The green hills and shore
Be with white keeps disfigured,
And the Mote of Rathmore
Be the Saxon churl's haggard!

The land of the lakes
Shall no more know the prospect
Of valleys and brakes—
So transformed is her aspect!

The Gael cannot tell,
In the uprooted wildwood
And the red ridgy dell,
The old nurse of his childhood:

The nurse of his youth
Is in doubt as she views him,
If the wan wretch, in truth,
Be the child of her bosom.

We starve by the board,
And we thirst amid wassail—
For the guest is the lord,
And the host is the vassal.

Through the woods let us roam,
Through the wastes wild and barren;
We are strangers at home!
We are exiles in Erin!

And Erin's a bark
O'er the wide waters driven!
And the tempest howls dark,
And her side planks are riven!

And in billows of might
Swell the Saxon before her,—
Unite, oh, unite !
Or the billows burst o'er her !

Sir Samuel Ferguson

EGAN O'RAHILLY

18th century

Lament for Banba

O MY land ! O my love !
    What a woe, and how deep,
Is thy death to my long mourning soul !
    God alone, God above,
    Can awake thee from sleep,
Can release thee from bondage and dole !
        Alas, alas, and alas !
            For the once proud people of Banba !

As a tree in its prime,
    Which the axe layeth low,
Didst thou fall, O unfortunate land !
    Not by time, nor thy crime,
    Came the shock and the blow.
They were given by a false felon hand !
        Alas, alas, and alas !
            For the once proud people of Banba !

O, my grief of all griefs
    Is to see how thy throne
Is usurped, whilst thyself art in thrall !
    Other lands have their chiefs,
    Have their kings, thou alone
Art a wife, yet a widow withal !
        Alas, alas, and alas !
            For the once proud people of Banba !

The high house of O'Neill
    Is gone down to the dust,
The O'Brien is clanless and banned;
    And the steel, the red steel
    May no more be the trust
Of the Faithful and Brave in the land !
    Alas, alas, and alas !
        For the once proud people of Banba !

True, alas ! Wrong and Wrath
    Were of old all too rife.
Deeds were done which no good man admires
    And perchance Heaven hath
    Chastened us for the strife
And the blood-shedding ways of our sires !
    Alas, alas, and alas !
        For the once proud people of Banba !

But, no more ! This our doom,
    While our hearts yet are warm,
Let us not over-weakly deplore !
    For the hour soon may loom
    When the Lord's mighty hand
Shall be raised for our rescue once more !
    And all our grief shall be turned into joy
        For the still proud people of Banba !
           James Clarence Mangan

RAFERTY

d. 1835

I am Raferty

I AM Raferty the Poet
    Full of hope and love,
With eyes that have no light,
    With gentleness that has no misery.

Going west upon my pilgrimage
By the light of my heart,
Feeble and tired
To the end of my road.

Behold me now,
And my face to the wall,
A-playing music
Unto empty pockets.

Douglas Hyde

ANONYMOUS

A Poem to be said on hearing the Birds sing

A FRAGRANT prayer upon the air
My child taught me,
Awaken there, the morn is fair,
The birds sing free;
Now dawns the day, awake and pray,
And bend the knee;
The Lamb who lay beneath the clay
Was slain for thee.

Douglas Hyde

THOMAS MOORE

1779–1852

How oft has the Banshee cried!

HOW oft has the Banshee cried!
How oft has death untied
Bright links that Glory wove,
Sweet bonds entwined by Love!
Peace to each manly soul that sleepeth;
Rest to each faithful eye that weepeth;
Long may the fair and brave
Sigh o'er the hero's grave!

We're fallen on evil days !
Star after star decays,
Every bright name that shed
Light o'er the land is fled.
Dark falls the tear of him that mourneth
Lost joy, or hope that ne'er returneth:
But brightly flows the tear
Wept o'er a hero's bier.

Quenched are our beacon lights—
Thou, of the Hundred Fights !
Thou, on whose burning tongue
Truth, peace and freedom hung !
Both mute—but long as valour shineth,
Or mercy's soul at war repineth,
So long shall Erin's pride
Tell how they lived and died.

ANONYMOUS
The Wearin' o' the Green

OH, Paddy dear ! and did ye hear the news that's
goin' round ?
The shamrock is forbid by law to grow on Irish
ground !
No more St. Patrick's day we'll keep; his colour
can't be seen,
For there's a cruel law ag'in' the Wearin' o' the
Green !

I met with Napper Tandy, and he took me by the
hand,
And he said, " How's poor ould Ireland, and how
does she stand ? "
" She's the most distressful country that ever yet
was seen,
For they're hanging men and women there for the
Wearin' o' the Green."

An' if the colour we must wear is England's cruel red,
Let it remind us of the blood that Ireland has shed;
Then pull the shamrock from your hat, and throw it on
the sod,
An' never fear, 'twill take root there, though under foot
'tis trod.

When law can stop the blades of grass from growin' as
they grow,
An' when the leaves in summer‑time their colour dare
not show,
Then I will change the colour, too, I wear in my caubeen;
But till that day, plaise God, I'll stick to the Wearin' o'
the Green.

KATHARINE TYNAN

1861–

The Doves

THE house where I was born,
Where I was young and gay,
Grows old amid its corn,
Amid its scented hay.

Moan of the cushat dove,
In silence rich and deep;
The old head I love
Nods to its quiet sleep.

Where once were nine or ten
Now two keep house together;
The doves moan and complain
All day in the still weather.

What wind, bitter and great,
Has swept the country's face,
Altered, made desolate
The heart‑remembered place?

What wind, bitter and wild,
Has swept the towering trees
Beneath whose shade a child
Long since gathered heartease?

Under the golden eaves
The house is still and sad,
As though it grieves and grieves
For many a lass and lad.

The cushat doves complain
All day in the still weather;
Where once were nine or ten
But two keep house together.

WILLIAM BUTLER YEATS

1865-

To an Isle in the Water

SHY one, shy one,
Shy one of my heart,
She moves in the firelight
Pensively apart.

She carries in the dishes,
And lays them in a row.
To an isle in the water
With her would I go.

She carries in the candles,
And lights the curtained room,
Shy in the doorway
And shy in the gloom;

And shy as a rabbit,
Helpful and shy.
To an isle in the water
With her would I fly.

When You are Old

WHEN you are old and grey and full of sleep,
And nodding by the fire, take down this book,
And slowly read, and dream of the soft look
Your eyes had once, and of their shadows deep;

How many loved your moments of glad grace,
And loved your beauty with love false or true;
But one man loved the pilgrim soul in you,
And loved the sorrows of your changing face.

And bending down beside the glowing bars
Murmur, a little sadly, how love fled
And paced upon the mountains overhead
And hid his face amid a crowd of stars.

The Cold Heaven

SUDDENLY I saw the cold and rook-delighting
    Heaven
That seemed as though ice burned and was but the
    more ice,
And thereupon imagination and heart were driven
So wild that every casual thought of that and this
Vanished, and left but memories, that should be out
    of season
With the hot blood of youth, of love crossed long ago;
And I took all the blame out of all sense and reason,
Until I cried and trembled and rocked to and fro,
Riddled with light. Ah! when the ghost begins to
    quicken,
Confusion of the death-bed over, is it sent
Out naked on the roads, as the books say, and stricken
By the injustice of the skies for punishment?

GEORGE WILLIAM RUSSELL (" A. E.")

1867–

A Mountain Wind

THE cold limbs of the air
Brush by me on the hill,
Climb to the utmost crag,
Leap out, then all is still.

Ah, but what high intent
In the cold will of wind;
What sceptre would it grasp
To leave these dreams behind !

Trail of celestial things:
White centaurs, winged in flight,
Through the fired heart sweep on,
A hurricane of light.

I have no plumes for air:
Earth hugs to it my bones.
Leave me, O sky-born powers,
Brother to grass and stones.

Immortality

WE must pass like smoke or live within the spirit's fire;
For we can no more than smoke unto the flame
. return:
If our thought has changed to dream, our will unto
desire,
As smoke we vanish though the fire may burn.

Lights of infinite pity star the grey dusk of our days:
Surely here is soul: with it we have eternal breath:
In the fire of love we live, or pass by many ways,
By unnumbered ways of dream to death.

JOHN MILLINGTON SYNGE

1871–1909

Prelude

STILL south I went and west and south again,
Through Wicklow from the morning till the night,
And far from cities, and the sights of men,
Lived with the sunshine and the moon's delight.

I knew the stars, the flowers, and the birds,
The grey and wintry sides of many glens,
And did but half remember human words,
In converse with the mountains, moors, and fens.

In Kerry

WE heard the thrushes by the shore and sea,
And saw the golden stars' nativity,
Then round we went the lane by Thomas Flynn,
Across the church where bones lie out and in;
And there I asked beneath a lonely cloud
Of strange delight, with one bird singing loud,
What change you'd wrought in graveyard, rock and
      sea,
This new wild paradise to wake for me. . . .
Yet knew no more than knew those merry sins
Had built this stack of thigh-bones, jaws and shins.

MOIRA O'NEILL

Corrymeela

OVER here in England I'm helpin' wi' the hay,
And I wisht I was in Ireland the livelong day;
Weary on the English hay, an' sorra take the wheat !
Och ! Corrymeela, an' the blue sky over it.

There's a deep dumb river flowin' by beyont the
  heavy trees,
This livin' air is moithered wi' the hummin' o' the
  bees;
I wisht I'd hear the Claddagh burn go runnin'
  through the heat,
Past Corrymeela, wi' the blue sky over it.

The people that's in England is richer nor the Jews,
There's not the smallest young gossoon but thravels
  in his shoes!
I'd give the pipe between me teeth to see a barefut
  child,
Och! Corrymeela, an' the low south wind.

Here's hands so full o' money an' hearts so full o'
  care,
By the luck o' love! I'd still go light for all I did go
  bare.
"God save ye, colleen dhas," I said; the girl she
  thought me wild!
Fair Corrymeela, an' the low south wind.

D'ye mind me now, the song at night is mortal hard to
  raise,
The girls are heavy goin' here, the boys are ill to plase;
When ones't I'm out this workin' hive, 'tis I'll be back
  again—
Aye, Corrymeela, in the same soft rain.

The puff o' smoke from one ould roof before an English
  town!
For a *shaugh* wid Andy Feelan here I'd give a silver
  crown,
For a curl o' hair like Mollie's ye'll ask the like in vain,
Sweet Corrymeela, an' the same soft rain.

THOMAS MAC DONAGH

1878–1916

John-John

I DREAMT last night of you, John-John,
  And thought you called to me;·
And when I woke this morning, John,
  Yourself I hoped to see;
But I was all alone, John-John,
  Though still I heard your call;
I put my boots and bonnet on,
  And took my Sunday shawl,
And went full sure to find you, John,
    At Nenagh fair.

The fair was just the same as then,
  Five years ago to-day,
When first you left the thimble-men
  And came with me away;
For there again were thimble-men
  And shooting galleries,
And card-trick men and maggie-men,
  Of all sorts and degrees;
But not a sight of you, John-John,
    Was anywhere.

I turned my face to home again,
  And called myself a fool
To think you'd leave the thimble-men
  And live again by rule,
To go to mass and keep the fast
  And till the little patch;
My wish to have you home was past
  Before I raised the latch
And pushed the door and saw you, John,
    Sitting down there.

How cool you came in here, begad,
As if you owned the place !
But rest yourself there now, my lad,
'Tis good to see your face;
My dream is out, and now by it
I think I know my mind;
At six o'clock this house you'll quit,
And leave no grief behind;—
But until six o'clock, John-John,
    My bit you'll share.

The neighbours' shame of me began
When first I brought you in;
To wed and keep a tinker man
They thought a kind of sin;
But now this three years since you've gone
'Tis pity me they do,
And that I'd rather have, John-John,
Than that they'd pity you:
Pity for me and you, John-John,
    I could not bear.

Oh, you're my husband right enough,
But what's the good of that ?
You know you never were the stuff
To be the cottage cat,
To watch the fire and hear me lock
The door and put out Shep—
But there, now, it is six o'clock
And time for you to step.
God bless and keep you far, John-John !
    And that's my prayer.

SEUMAS O'SULLIVAN

1878–

The Starling Lake

MY sorrow that I am not by the little dún
By the lake of the starlings at Rosses under the hill,
And the larks there, singing over the fields of dew,
Or evening there and the sedges still.
For plain I see now the length of the yellow sand,
And Lissadell far off and its leafy ways,
And the holy mountain whose mighty heart
Gathers into it all the coloured days.
My sorrow that I am not by the little dún
By the lake of the starlings at evening when all is still,
And still in whispering sedges the herons stand.
'Tis there I would nestle at rest till the quivering
    moon
Uprose in the golden quiet over the hill.

PADRAIC PEARSE

1880–1916

Ideal

NAKED I saw thee,
  O beauty of beauty!
  And I blinded my eyes
  For fear I should flinch.

I heard thy music,
  O sweetness of sweetness!
  And I shut my ears
  For fear I should fail.

I kissed thy lips,
  O sweetness of sweetness!
  And I hardened my heart
  For fear of my ruin.

I blinded my eyes
And my ears I shut,
I hardened my heart
And my love I quenched.

I turned my back
On the dream I had shaped,
And to this road before me
My face I turned.

I set my face
To the road here before me,
To the work that I see,
To the death that I shall meet.

Translated from the Gaelic by Thomas MacDonagh

PADRAIC COLUM

1881–

River mates

I'LL be an otter, and I'll let you swim
A mate beside me; we will venture down
A deep, dark river, when the sky above
Is shut of the sun; spoilers are we,
Thick coated; no dog's tooth can bite at our veins,
With eyes and ears of poachers; deep earthed ones
Turned hunters; let him slip past
The little vole; my teeth are on an edge
For the King fish of the River !

    I hold him up
The glittering salmon that smells of the sea;
I hold him high and whistle !
    Now we go
Back to our earths; we will tear and eat
Sea smelling salmon; you will tell the cubs
I am the Booty bringer, I am the Lord
Of the River; the deep, dark, full and flowing River !

A Drover

TO Meath of the pastures,
From wet hills by the sea,
Through Leitrim and Longford
Go my cattle and me.

I hear in the darkness
Their slipping and breathing.
I name them the bye-ways
They're to pass without heeding.

Then the wet, winding roads,
Brown bogs with black water;
And my thoughts on white ships
And the King o' Spain's daughter.

O ! farmer, strong farmer !
You can spend at the fair,
But your face you must turn
To your crops and your care.

And soldiers—red soldiers !
You've seen many lands;
But you walk two by two,
And by captain's commands.

O ! the smell of the beasts,
The wet wind in the morn;
And the proud and hard earth
Never broken for corn;

And the crowds at the fair,
The herds loosened and blind,
Loud words and dark faces
And the wild blood behind.

(O ! strong men with your best
I would strive breast to breast,
I could quiet your herds
With my words, with my words.)

I will bring you, my kine,
Where there's grass to the knee;
But you'll think of scant croppings
Harsh with salt of the sea.

JOSEPH CAMPBELL

1881–

The Blind Man at the Fair

O TO be blind !
To know the darkness that I know.
The stir I hear is empty wind,
The people idly come and go.

The sun is black, tho' warm and kind,
The horsemen ride, the streamers blow
Vainly in the fluky wind,
For all is darkness where I go.

The cattle bellow to their kind,
The mummers dance, the jugglers throw,
The thimble-rigger speaks his mind—
But all is darkness where I go.

I feel the touch of womankind,
Their dresses flow as white as snow;
But beauty is a withered rind,
For all is darkness where I go.

Last night the moon of Lammas shined,
Rising high and setting low;
But light is nothing to the blind—
All, all is darkness where they go.

White roads I walk with vacant mind,
White cloud-shapes round me drifting slow,
White lilies waving in the wind—
And darkness everywhere I go.

The Old Woman

AS a white candle
    In a holy place,
  So is the beauty
      Of an aged face.

As the spent radiance
    Of the winter sun,
So is a woman
    With her travail done.

Her brood gone from her,
    And her thoughts as still
As the waters
    Under a ruined mill.

JAMES STEPHENS

1882–

Deirdre

DO not let any woman read this verse;
It is for men, and after them their sons
And their sons' sons.

The time comes when our hearts sink utterly;
When we remember Deirdre and her tale,
And that her lips are dust.

Once she did tread the earth; men took her hand;
They looked into her eyes and said their say,
And she replied to them.

More than a thousand years it is since she
Was beautiful: she trod the living grass;
She saw the clouds.

A thousand years !   The grass is still the same,
The clouds as lovely as they were that time
When Deirdre was alive.

But there has never been a woman born
Who was so beautiful, not one so beautiful
Of all the women born.

Let all men go apart and mourn together;
No man can ever love her; not a man
Can ever be her lover.

No man can bend before her; no man say—
What could one say to her ?   There are no words
That one could say to her !

Now she is but a story that is told
Beside the fire !   No man can ever be
The friend of that poor queen.

The Daisies

IN the scented bud of the morning—O,
  When the windy grass went rippling far,
I saw my dear one walking slow,
  In the field where the daisies are.

We did not laugh and we did not speak
  As we wandered happily to and fro;
I kissed my dear on either cheek,
  In the bud of the morning—O.

A lark sang up from the breezy land,
  A lark sang down from a cloud afar,
And she and I went hand in hand
  In the field where the daisies are.

JAMES JOYCE

1882–

I hear an Army

I HEAR an army charging upon the land,
And the thunder of horses plunging, foam about their
  knees:
Arrogant, in black armour, behind them stand,
Disdaining the reins, with fluttering whips, the
  charioteers.

They cry unto the night their battle-name:
I moan in sleep when I hear afar their whirling
  laughter.
They cleave the gloom of dreams, a blinding flame,
Clanging, clanging upon my heart as upon an anvil.

They come shaking in triumph their long, green hair:
They come out of the sea and run shouting by the
  shore.
My heart, have you no wisdom thus to despair?
My love, my love, my love, why have you left me
  alone?

JOSEPH PLUNKETT

1887–1916

The Spark

BECAUSE I used to shun
Death and the mouth of hell
And count my battles won
If I should see the sun
The blood and smoke dispel,

Because I used to pray
That living I might see
The dawning light of day
Set me upon my way
And from my fetters free,

Because I used to seek
Your answer to my prayer
And that your soul should speak
For strengthening of the weak
To struggle with despair,

Now I have seen my shame
That I should thus deny
My soul's divinest flame,
Now shall I shout your name,
Now shall I seek to die

By any hands but these
In battle or in flood,
On any lands or seas,
No more shall I spare ease,
No more shall I spare blood

When I have need to fight
For heaven or for your heart,
Against the powers of light
Or darkness I shall smite
Until their might depart,

Because I know the spark
Of God has no eclipse,
Now Death and I embark
And sail into the dark
With laughter on our lips.

FRANCIS LEDWIDGE
1891–1917

Lament for the Poets: 1916

I HEARD the Poor Old Woman say:
" At break of day the fowler came,
And took my blackbirds from their songs
Who loved me well thro' shame and blame.

"No more from lovely distances
Their songs shall bless me mile by mile,
Nor to white Ashbourne call me down
To wear my crown another while.

"With bended flowers the angels mark
For the skylark the place they lie,
From there its little family
Shall dip their wings first in the sky.

"And when the first surprise of flight
Sweet songs excite, from the far dawn
Shall there come blackbirds loud with love,
Sweet echoes of the singers gone.

"But in the lonely hush of eve
Weeping I grieve the silent bills."
I heard the Poor Old Woman say
In Derry of the little hills.

Ardan Mór

AS I was climbing Ardan Mór
From the shore of Sheelin lake,
I met the herons coming down
Before the water's wake.

And they were talking in their flight
Of dreamy ways the herons go
When all the hills are withered up
Nor any waters flow.

AMERICAN
FROM THE AMERICAN INDIAN
Love-song (Papago)

EARLY I rose
In the blue morning;
My love was up before me,
It came running up to me from the doorways of the
Dawn.

On Papago Mountain
The dying quarry
Looked at me with my love's eyes.

Mary Austin

Neither Spirit nor Bird
(Shoshone)

NEITHER spirit nor bird;
That was my flute you heard
Last night by the river.
When you came with your wicker jar
Where the river drags the willows,
That was my flute you heard,
Wacoba, Wacoba,
Calling, Come to the willows!

Neither the wind nor a bird
Rustled the lupine blooms.
That was my blood you heard
Answer your garment's hem
Whispering through the grasses;
That was my blood you heard
By the wild rose under the willows.

That was no beast that stirred,
That was my heart you heard,
Pacing to and fro
In the ambush of my desire,
To the music my flute let fall.
Wacoba, Wacoba,
That was my heart you heard
Leaping under the willows.

Mary Austin

Come not Near my Songs
(Shoshone)

COME not near my songs,
You who are not my lover,
Lest from out that ambush
Leaps my heart upon you !

When my songs are glowing
As an almond thicket
With the bloom upon it,
Lies my heart in ambush
All amid my singing;
Come not near my songs,
You who are not my lover !

Do not hear my songs,
You who are not my lover !
Over-sweet the heart is,
Where my love has bruised it,
Breathe you not that fragrance,
You who are not my lover.
Do not stoop above my song,
With its languor on you,
Lest from out my singing
Leaps my heart upon you !

Mary Austin

Lament of a Man for his Son
(Paiute)

SON, my son !
   I will go up to the mountain
And there I will light a fire
To the feet of my son's spirit,
And there will I lament him;
Saying,
O my son,
What is my life to me, now you are departed ?

Son, my son,
In the deep earth
We softly laid thee
In a chief's robe,
In a warrior's gear.
Surely there,
In the spirit land
Thy deeds attend thee !
Surely,
The corn comes to the ear again !
But I, here,
I am the stalk that the seed-gatherers
Descrying empty, afar, left standing.
Son, my son !
What is my life to me, now you are departed ?

Mary Austin

The Grass on the Mountain
(Paiute)

OH, long, long
The snow has possessed the mountains.

The deer have come down and the big-horn,
They have followed the Sun to the south

To feed on the mesquite pods and the bunch grass.
Loud are the thunder drums
In the tents of the mountains.
Oh, long, long
Have we eaten chia seeds
And dried deer's flesh of the summer killing.
We are wearied of our huts
And the smoky smell of our garments.

We are sick with desire of the sun
And the grass on the mountain.

Mary Austin

Hunting *song* (*Navaho*)

COMES the deer to my singing,
Comes the deer to my song,
Comes the deer to my singing.

He, the blackbird, he am I,
Bird beloved of the wild deer,
Comes the deer to my singing.

From the Mountain Black,
From the summit,
Down the trail, coming, coming now,
Comes the deer to my singing.

Through the blossoms,
Through the flowers, coming, coming now,
Comes the deer to my singing.

Through the flower dew drops,
Coming, coming now,
Comes the deer to my singing.

Through the pollen, flower pollen,
Coming, coming now,
Comes the deer to my singing.

Starting with his left fore-foot,
Stamping, turns the frightened deer.
    Comes the deer to my singing.

Quarry mine, blessed am I
In the luck of the chase.
    Comes the deer to my singing.

    Comes the deer to my singing,
    Comes the deer to my song,
    Comes the deer to my singing.

Natalie Curtis

Song of the Rain Chant (Navaho)

FAR as man can see,
    Comes the rain,
    Comes the rain with me.

From the Rain-Mount,
Rain-Mount far away,
    Comes the rain,
    Comes the rain with me.

'Mid the lightnings,
'Mid the lightning zigzag,
'Mid the lightning flashing,
    Comes the rain,
    Comes the rain with me.

'Mid the swallows,
'Mid the swallows blue,
Chirping glad together,
    Comes the rain,
    Comes the rain with me.

Through the pollen,
Through the pollen blest,
All in pollen hidden
Comes the rain,
Comes the rain with me.

Far as man can see,
Comes the rain,
Comes the rain with me.

Natalie Curtis

Korosta Katzina Song (Hopi)

1

YELLOW butterflies
Over the blossoming virgin corn,
With pollen-painted faces
Chase one another in brilliant throng.

2

Blue butterflies
Over the blossoming virgin beans,
With pollen-painted faces
Chase one another in brilliant streams.

3

Over the blossoming corn,
Over the virgin corn
Wild bees hum;
Over the blossoming corn,
Over the virgin beans
Wild bees hum.

4

Over your field of growing corn
All day shall hang the thunder-cloud;
Over your field of growing corn
All day shall come the rushing rain.

Natalie Curtis

The Voice that beautifies the Land (Navaho)

1

THE voice that beautifies the land !
The voice above,
The voice of the thunder,
Among the dark clouds
Again and again it sounds,
The voice that beautifies the land.

2

The voice that beautifies the land !
The voice below,
The voice of the grasshopper,
Among the flowers and grasses
Again and again it sounds,
The voice that beautifies the land.

Washington Matthews

Song to the Mountains (Pawnee)

1

MOUNTAINS loom upon the path we take;
Yonder peak now rises sharp and clear;
Behold ! It stands with its head uplifted,
Thither we go, since our way lies there.

2

Mountains loom upon the path we take;
Yonder peak now rises sharp and clear;
Behold ! We climb, drawing near its summit;
Steeper grows the way and slow our steps.

3

Mountains loom upon the path we take;
Yonder peak that rises sharp and clear,
Behold us now on its head uplifted;
Planting there our feet, we stand secure.

4

Mountains loom upon the path we take;
Yonder peak that rose so sharp and clear,
Behold us now on its head uplifted;
Resting there at last we sing our song.

Alice C. Fletcher

A Lover's Lament (Tewa)

MY little breath, under the willows by the waterside
we used to sit,
And there the yellow cottonwood bird came and
sang.
That I remember and therefore I weep.
Under the growing corn we used to sit,
And there the little leaf bird came and sang.
That I remember and therefore I weep.
There on the meadow of yellow flowers we used to
walk.
Alas! how long ago that we two walked in that
pleasant way.
Then everything was happy, but alas! how long
ago.
There on the meadow of crimson flowers we used
to walk.
Oh, my little breath, now I go there alone in sorrow.

H. J. Spinden

The Coyote and the Locust (Zuñi)

LOCUST, locust, playing a flute,
  Locust, locust, playing a flute !
Away up on the pine-tree bough,
  Closely clinging,
    Playing a flute,
    Playing a flute !

Frank Cushing

Ojibwa War-songs

I

HEAR my voice, Birds of War !
I prepare a feast for you to feed on;
I see you cross the enemy's lines;
Like you I shall go.
I wish the swiftness of your wings;
I wish the vengeance of your claws;
I muster my friends;
I follow your flight.
Ho, you young men warriors,
Bear your angers to the place of fighting !

2

From the south they came, Birds of War—
Hark ! to their passing scream.
I wish the body of the fiercest,
As swift, as cruel, as strong.
I cast my body to the chance of fighting.
Happy I shall be to lie in that place,
In that place where the fight was,
Beyond the enemy's line.

3

Here on my breast have I bled !
See—see ! these are fighting-scars !
Mountains tremble at my yell !
I strike for life.

H. H. Schoolcraft

Three Songs from the Haida
(Queen Charlotte's Island, British Columbia)
Love-song

BEAUTIFUL is she, this woman,
As the mountain flower;
But cold, cold, is she,
Like the snowbank
Behind which it blooms.

The Bear's Song

*(Whoever can sing this song is admitted for ever to the
friendship of the bears)*

I HAVE taken the woman of beauty
For my wife;
I have taken her from her friends.
I hope her kinsmen will not come
And take her away from me.
I will be kind to her.
Berries, berries I will give her from the hill
And roots from the ground.
I will do everything to please her.
For her I made this song and for her I sing it.

Song for Fine Weather

O GOOD Sun,
Look thou down upon us:
Shine, shine on us, O Sun,
Gather up the clouds, wet, black, under thy arms—
That the rains may cease to fall.
Because thy friends are all here on the beach
Ready to go fishing—
Ready for the hunt.
Therefore look kindly on us, O Good Sun !
Give us peace within our tribe
And with all our enemies.
Again, again we call—
Hear us, hear us, O Good Sun !

Constance Lindsay Skinner

RALPH WALDO EMERSON

1803–82

The Rhodora

ON BEING ASKED, WHENCE IS THE FLOWER ?

IN May, when sea-winds pierced our solitudes,
I found the fresh Rhodora in the woods,
Spreading its leafless blooms in a damp nook,
To please the desert and the sluggish brook.
The purple petals, fallen in the pool,
Made the black water with their beauty gay;
Here might the red-bird come his plumes to cool,
And court the flower that cheapens his array.
Rhodora ! if the sages ask thee why
This charm is wasted on the earth and sky,
Tell them, dear, that if eyes were made for-seeing,
Then Beauty is its own excuse for being:
Why thou wert there, O rival of the rose !
I never thought to ask, I never knew:

But, in my simple ignorance, suppose
The self-same Power that brought me there brought
you.

Brahma

IF the red slayer think he slays,
  Or if the slain think he is slain,
They know not well the subtle ways
  I keep, and pass, and turn again.

Far or forgot to me is near;
  Shadow and sunlight are the same;
The banished gods to me appear;
  And one to me are shame and fame.

They reckon ill who leave me out;
  When me they fly, I am the wings;
I am the doubter and the doubt,
  And I the hymn the Brahmin sings.

The strong gods pine for my abode,
  And pine in vain the sacred Seven;
But thou, meek lover of the good !
  Find me, and turn thy back on heaven.

Concord Hymn

SUNG AT THE COMPLETION OF THE BATTLE MONUMENT,
JULY 4, 1837

BY the rude bridge that arched the flood,
  Their flag to April's breeze unfurled,
Here once the embattled farmers stood,
  And fired the shot heard round the world.

The foe long since in silence slept;
  Alike the conqueror silent sleeps;
And Time the ruined bridge has swept
  Down the dark stream which seaward creeps.

On this green bank, by this soft stream,
    We set to-day a votive stone;
That memory may their deed redeem,
    When, like our sires, our sons are gone.

Spirit, that made those heroes dare
    To die, and leave their children free,
Bid Time and Nature gently spare
    The shaft we raise to them and thee.

The Problem

I LIKE a church; I like a cowl;
 I love a prophet of the soul;
And on my heart monastic aisles
Fall like sweet strains, or pensive smiles:
Yet not for all his faith can see
Would I that cowlèd churchman be.

Why should the vest on him allure,
Which I could not on me endure?

Not from a vain or shallow thought
His awful Jove young Phidias brought;
Never from lips of cunning fell
The thrilling Delphic oracle;
Out from the heart of Nature rolled
The burdens of the Bible old;
The litanies of nations came,
Like the volcano's tongue of flame,
Up from the burning core below,—
The canticles of love and woe:
The hand that rounded Peter's dome
And groined the aisles of Christian Rome
Wrought in a sad sincerity;
Himself from God he could not free;
He builded better than he knew;—
The conscious stone to beauty grew.

Know'st thou what wove yon woodbird's nest
Of leaves, and feathers from her breast?
Or how the fish outbuilt her shell,
Painting with morn each annual cell?
Or how the sacred pine-tree adds
To her old leaves new myriads?
Such and so grew these holy piles,
Whilst love and terror laid the tiles.
Earth proudly wears the Parthenon,
As the best gem upon her zone,
And Morning opes with haste her lids
To gaze upon the Pyramids;
O'er England's abbeys bends the sky,
As on its friends, with kindred eye;
For out of Thought's interior sphere
These wonders rose to upper air;
And Nature gladly gave them place,
Adopted them into her race,
And granted them an equal date
With Andes and with Ararat.

These temples grew as grows the grass;
Art might obey, but not surpass.
The passive Master lent his hand
To the vast soul that o'er him planned;
And the same power that reared the shrine
Bestrode the tribes that knelt within.
Ever the fiery Pentecost
Girds with one flame the countless host,
Trances the heart through chanting choirs,
And through the priest the mind inspires.
The word unto the prophet spoken
Was writ on tables yet unbroken;
The word by seers or sibyls told,
In groves of oak, or fanes of gold,
Still floats upon the morning wind,
Still whispers to the willing mind.

One accent of the Holy Ghost
The heedless world hath never lost.
I know what say the fathers wise,—
The Book itself before me lies,
Old *Chrysostom*, best Augustine,
And he who blent both in his line,
The younger *Golden Lips* or mines,
Taylor, the Shakespeare of divines.
His words are music in my ear,
I see his cowlèd portrait dear;
And yet, for all his faith could see,
I would not the good bishop be.

Give All to Love

GIVE all to love;
Obey thy heart;
Friends, kindred, days,
Estate, good-fame,
Plans, credit and the Muse,—
Nothing refuse.

'Tis a brave master;
Let it have scope:
Follow it utterly,
Hope beyond hope:
High and more high
It dives into noon,
With wing unspent,
Untold intent;
But it is a god,
Knows its own path
And the outlets of the sky.

It was never for the mean;
It requireth courage stout.
Souls above doubt,
Valour unbending,

It will reward,—
They shall return
More than they were,
And ever ascending.

Leave all for love;
Yet, hear me, yet,
One word more thy heart behoved,
One pulse more of firm endeavour,—
Keep thee to day,
To morrow, for ever,
Free as an Arab
Of thy beloved.

Cling with life to the maid;
But when the surprise,
First vague shadow of surmise
Flits across her bosom young,
Of a joy apart from thee,
Free be she, fancy free;
Nor thou detain her vesture's hem,
Nor the palest rose she flung
From her summer diadem.

Though thou loved her as thyself,
As a self of purer clay,
Though her parting dims the day,
Stealing grace from all alive;
Heartily know,
When half gods go,
The gods arrive.

HENRY WADSWORTH LONGFELLOW
1807–82

My Lost Youth

OFTEN I think of the beautiful town
　　That is seated by the sea;
Often in thought go up and down
The pleasant streets of that dear old town,
　　And my youth comes back to me.
　　　　And a verse of a Lapland song
　　　　Is haunting my memory still:
　　　　" A boy's will is the wind's will,
And the thoughts of youth are long, long thoughts."

I can see the shadowy lines of its trees,
　　And catch, in sudden gleams,
The sheen of the far-surrounding seas,
And islands that were the Hesperides
　　Of all my boyish dreams.
　　　　And the burden of that old song,
　　　　It murmurs and whispers still:
　　　　" A boy's will is the wind's will,
And the thoughts of youth are long, long thoughts."

I remember the black wharves and the slips,
　　And the sea-tides tossing free;
And Spanish sailors with bearded lips,
And the beauty and mystery of the ships,
　　And the magic of the sea.
　　　　And the voice of that wayward song
　　　　Is singing and saying still:
　　　　" A boy's will is the wind's will,
And the thoughts of youth are long, long thoughts."

I remember the bulwarks by the shore,
　　And the fort upon the hill;

The sunrise gun, with its hollow roar,
The drum-beat repeated o'er and o'er,
  And the bugle wild and shrill.
    And the music of that old song
    Throbs in my memory still:
    " A boy's will is the wind's will,
And the thoughts of youth are long, long thoughts."

I remember the sea-fight far away,
  How it thundered o'er the tide !
And the dead captains, as they lay
In their graves, o'erlooking the tranquil bay
  Where they in battle died.
    And the sound of that mournful song
      Goes through me with a thrill:
    " A boy's will is the wind's will,
And the thoughts of youth are long, long thoughts."

I can see the breezy dome of groves,
  The shadows of Deering's Woods;
And the friendships old and the early loves
Come back with a Sabbath sound, as of doves
  In quiet neighbourhoods.
    And the verse of that sweet old song,
      It flutters and murmurs still:
    " A boy's will is the wind's will,
And the thoughts of youth are long, long thoughts."

I remember the gleams and glooms that dart
  Across the school-boy's brain;
The song and the silence in the heart,
That in part are prophecies, and in part
Are longings wild and vain.
    And the voice of that fitful song
    Sings on, and is never still:
    " A boy's will is the wind's will,
And the thoughts of youth are long, long thoughts."

There are things of which I may not speak;
　　There are dreams that cannot die;
There are thoughts that make the strong heart weak,
And bring a pallor into the cheek,
　　And a mist before the eye.
　　　And the words of that fatal song
　　　Come over me like a chill:
　　　" A boy's will is the wind's will,
And the thoughts of youth are long, long thoughts."

Strange to me now are the forms I meet
　　When I visit the dear old town;
But the native air is pure and sweet,
And the trees that o'ershadow each well-known street,
　　As they balance up and down,
　　　Are singing the beautiful song,
　　　Are sighing and whispering still:
　　　" A boy's will is the wind's will,
And the thoughts of youth are long, long thoughts."

And Deering's Woods are fresh and fair,
　　And with joy that is almost pain
My heart goes back to wander there,
And among the dreams of the days that were,
　　I find my lost youth again.
　　　And the strange and beautiful song,
　　　The groves are repeating it still:
　　　" A boy's will is the wind's will,
And the thoughts of youth are long, long thoughts."

Chaucer

AN old man in a lodge within a park;
　The chamber walls depicted all around
　　With portraitures of huntsman, hawk, and hound,
　And the hurt deer. He listeneth to the lark,

Whose song comes with the sunshine through the dark
Of painted glass in leaden lattice bound;
He listeneth and he laugheth at the sound,
Then writeth in a book like any clerk.
He is the poet of the dawn, who wrote
The Canterbury Tales, and his old age
Made beautiful with song; and as I read
I hear the crowing cock, I hear the note
Of lark and linnet, and from every page
Rise odours of ploughed field or flowery mead.

EDGAR ALLAN POE   1809–49

To Helen

HELEN, thy beauty is to me
   Like those Nicæan barks of yore,
That gently, o'er a perfumed sea,
   The weary, wayworn wanderer bore
   To his own native shore.

On desperate seas long wont to roam,
   Thy hyacinth hair, thy classic face,
Thy Naiad airs have brought me home
   To the glory that was Greece
   And the grandeur that was Rome.

Lo ! in yon brilliant window-niche
   How statue-like I see thee stand,
The agate lamp within thy hand !
   Ah, Psyche, from the regions which
   Are Holy Land !

Ulalume

THE skies they were ashen and sober;
   The leaves they were crispèd and sere—
   The leaves they were withering and sere:
It was night, in the lonesome October

Of my most immemorial year;
It was hard by the dim lake of Auber,
  In the misty mid region of Weir—
It was down by the dank tarn of Auber,
  In the ghoul-haunted woodland of Weir.

Here once, through an alley Titanic,
  Of cypress, I roamed with my Soul—
  Of cypress, with Psyche, my Soul.
These were days when my heart was volcanic
  As the scoriac rivers that roll—
  As the lavas that restlessly roll
Their sulphurous currents down Yaanek
  In the ultimate climes of the Pole—
That groan as they roll down Mount Yaanek
  In the realms of the Boreal Pole.

Our talk had been serious and sober,
  But our thoughts they were palsied and sere—
  Our memories were treacherous and sere—
For we knew not the month was October,
  And we marked not the night of the year—
  (Ah, night of all nights in the year!)
We noted not the dim lake of Auber
  (Though once we had journeyed down here),
Remembered not the dank tarn of Auber,
  Nor the ghoul-haunted woodland of Weir.

And now, as the night was senescent
  And star-dials pointed to morn—
  As the star-dials hinted of morn—
At the end of our path a liquescent
  And nebulous lustre was born,
Out of which a miraculous crescent
  Arose with a duplicate horn—
Astarte's bediamonded crescent
  Distinct with its duplicate horn.

And I said—" She is warmer than Dian;
  She rolls through an ether of sighs—
  She revels in a region of sighs:
She has seen that the tears are not dry on
  These cheeks, where the worm never dies,
And has come past the stars of the Lion
  To point us the path to the skies—
  To the Lethean peace of the skies—
Come up, in despite of the Lion,
  To shine on us with her bright eyes—
Come up through the lair of the Lion,
  With love in her luminous eyes."

But Psyche, uplifting her finger,
  Said—" Sadly this star I mistrust—
  Her pallor I strangely mistrust—
Oh, hasten !—oh, let us not linger !
  Oh, fly !—let us fly !—for we must."
In terror she spoke, letting sink her
  Wings till they trailed in the dust—
In agony sobbed, letting sink her
  Plumes till they trailed in the dust—
  Till they sorrowfully trailed in the dust.

I replied—" This is nothing but dreaming:
  Let us on by this tremulous light !
  Let us bathe in this crystalline light !
Its sibyllic splendour is beaming
  With Hope and in Beauty to-night:—
  See ! it flickers up the sky through the night !
Ah, we safely may trust to its gleaming,
  And be sure it will lead us aright:
We safely may trust to a gleaming
  That cannot but guide us aright,
  Since it flickers up to Heaven through the night."

Thus I pacified Psyche and kissed her,
  And tempted her out of her gloom—

And conquered her scruples and gloom;
And we passed to the end of a vista,
  But were stopped by the door of a tomb—
  By the door of a legended tomb;
And I said—"What is written, sweet sister,
  On the door of this legended tomb?"
  She replied—"Ulalume—Ulalume!—
  'Tis the vault of thy lost Ulalume!"

Then my heart it grew ashen and sober
  As the leaves that were crispèd and sere—
  As the leaves that were withering and sere;
And I cried—"It was surely October
  On *this* very night of last year
That I journeyed—I journeyed down here—
  That I brought a dread burden down here!
On this night of all nights in the year,
  Ah, what demon has tempted me here?
Well I know, now, this dim lake of Auber—
  This misty mid region of Weir—
Well I know, now, this dank tarn of Auber—
  This ghoul-haunted woodland of Weir."

Annabel Lee

IT was many and many a year ago,
  In a kingdom by the sea,
That a maiden there lived whom you may know
  By the name of Annabel Lee;—
And this maiden she lived with no other thought
  Than to love and be loved by me.

I was a child and *she* was a child,
  In this kingdom by the sea,
But we loved with a love that was more than love—
  I and my Annabel Lee—
With a love that the wingèd seraphs in Heaven
  Coveted her and me.

And this was the reason that, long ago,
  In this kingdom by the sea,
A wind blew out of a cloud, chilling
  My beautiful Annabel Lee;
So that her high-born kinsmen came
  And bore her away from me,
To shut her up in a sepulchre
  In this kingdom by the sea.

The angels, not half so happy in Heaven,
  Went envying her and me:—
Yes!—that was the reason (as all men know,
  In this kingdom by the sea)
That the wind came out of the cloud, by night,
  Chilling and killing my Annabel Lee.

But our love it was stronger by far than the love
  Of those who were older than we—
  Of many far wiser than we—
And neither the angels in Heaven above,
  Nor the demons down under the sea,
Can ever dissever my soul from the soul
  Of the beautiful Annabel Lee:—

For the moon never beams without bringing me dreams
  Of the beautiful Annabel Lee;
And the stars never rise but I feel the bright eyes
  Of the beautiful Annabel Lee;
And so, all the night-tide, I lie down by the side
Of my darling,—my darling,—my life and my bride,
  In the sepulchre there by the sea—
  In her tomb by the sounding sea.

HENRY DAVID THOREAU
1817-62

Smoke

LIGHT-WINGED Smoke, Icarian bird,
Melting thy pinions in thy upward flight;
Lark without song, and messenger of dawn,
Circling above the hamlets as thy nest;
Or else, departing dream, and shadowy form
Of midnight vision, gathering up thy skirts;
By night star-veiling, and by day
Darkening the light and blotting out the sun;
Go thou, my incense, upward from this hearth,
And ask the gods to pardon this clear flame.

Mist

LOW-ANCHORED cloud,
Newfoundland air,
Fountain-head and source of rivers,
Dew-cloth, dream-drapery,
And napkin spread by fays;
Drifting meadow of the air,
Where bloom the daisied banks and violets,
And in whose fenny labyrinth
The bittern booms and heron wades;
Spirit of lakes and seas and rivers,
Bear only perfumes and the scent
Of healing herbs to just men's fields.

WALT WHITMAN
1819-92

I Saw in Louisiana a Live-oak Growing

I SAW in Louisiana a live-oak growing,
All alone stood it, and the moss hung down from the
branches;

Without any companion it grew there, uttering joyous
    leaves of dark green,
And its look, rude, unbending, lusty, made me think
    of myself;
But I wonder'd how it could utter joyous leaves,
    standing alone there, without its friend, its lover
    near—for I knew I could not;
And I broke off a twig with a certain number of leaves
    upon it, and twined around it a little moss,
And brought it away—and I have placed it in sight
    in my room;
It is not needed to remind me as of my own dear
    friends,
(For I believe lately I think of little else than of them:)
Yet it remains to me a curious token—it makes me
    think of manly love;
For all that, and though the live-oak glistens there in
    Louisiana, solitary, in a wide flat space,
Uttering joyous leaves all its life, without a friend, a
    lover, near,
I know very well I could not.

A Noiseless, Patient Spider

A NOISELESS, patient spider,
  I mark'd, where, on a little promontory, it stood,
    isolated;
  Mark'd how, to explore the vacant, vast surrounding,
  It launch'd forth filament, filament, filament, out
    of itself;
  Ever unreeling them—ever tirelessly speeding them.

  And you, O my Soul, where you stand,
  Surrounded, detached, in measureless oceans of
    space,
  Ceaselessly musing, venturing, throwing,—seeking
    the spheres, to connect them;

Till the bridge you will need be form'd—till the
    ductile anchor hold;
Till the gossamer thread you fling catch somewhere,
    O my Soul.

Out of the Cradle Endlessly
Rocking

OUT of the cradle endlessly rocking,
    Out of the mocking-bird's throat, the musical shuttle,
    Out of the Ninth-month midnight,
    Over the sterile sands and the fields beyond, where
        the child leaving his bed wandered alone,
        bareheaded, barefoot,
Down from the showered halo,
Up from the mystic play of shadows twining and
        twisting as if they were alive,
Out from the patches of briers and blackberries,
From the memories of the bird that chanted to me,
From your memories, sad brother, from the fitful
        risings and fallings I heard,
From under that yellow half-moon late-risen and
        swollen as if with tears,
From those beginning notes of yearning and love
        there in the mist,
From the thousand responses of my heart never to
        cease,
From the myriad thence-aroused words,
From the word stronger and more delicious than any,
From such as now they start the scene revisiting,
As a flock, twittering, rising, or overhead passing,
Borne hither, ere all eludes me, hurriedly,
A man, yet by these tears a little boy again,
Throwing myself on the sand, confronting the waves,
I, chanter of pains and joys, uniter of here and
        hereafter,

Taking all hints to use them, but swiftly leaping
 beyond them,
A reminiscence sing.

Once Paumanok,
When the lilac-scent was in the air and Fifth-month
 grass was growing,
Up this seashore in some briers,
Two feathered guests from Alabama, two together,
And their nest, and four light-green eggs spotted with
 brown,
And every day the he-bird to and fro near at hand,
And every day the she-bird crouched on her nest, silent,
 with bright eyes,
And every day I, a curious boy, never too close, never
 disturbing them,
Cautiously peering, absorbing, translating.

Shine ! shine ! shine !
Pour down your warmth, great sun !
While we bask, we two together.

Two together !
Winds blow south, or winds blow north,
Day come white, or night come black,
Home, or rivers and mountains from home,
Singing all time, minding no time,
While we two keep together.

Till of a sudden,
Maybe killed, unknown to her mate,
One forenoon the she-bird crouched not on the nest,
Nor returned that afternoon, nor the next,
Nor ever appeared again.

And thenceforward all summer in the sound of the sea,
And at night under the full of the moon in calmer
 weather,

Over the hoarse surging of the sea,
Or flitting from brier to brier by day,
I saw, I heard at intervals the remaining one, the he*
bird,
The solitary guest from Alabama.

Blow ! blow ! blow !
*Blow up sea*winds along Paumanok's shore;*
I wait and I wait till you blow my mate to me.

Yes, when the stars glistened,
All night long on the prong of a moss*scalloped stake,
Down almost amid the slapping waves,
Sat the lone singer wonderful causing tears.

He called on his mate,
He poured forth the meanings which I of all men know.
Yes, my brother, I know,—
The rest might not, but I have treasured every note,
For more than once dimly down to the beach gliding,
Silent, avoiding the moonbeams, blending myself with
the shadows,
Recalling now the obscure shapes, the echoes, the sounds
and sights after their sorts,
The white arms out in the breakers tirelessly tossing,
I, with bare feet, a child, the wind wafting my hair,
Listened long and long.
Listened to keep, to sing, now translating the notes,
Following you, my brother.

Soothe ! soothe ! soothe !
Close on its wave soothes the wave behind,
And again another behind embracing and lapping, every
one close,
But my love soothes not me, not me.

Low hangs the moon, it rose late,
It is lagging—O I think it is heavy with love, with love.

O madly the sea pushes upon the land,
With love, with love.

O night ! do I not see my love fluttering out among the
  breakers ?
What is that little black thing I see there in the white ?

Loud ! loud ! loud !
Loud I call to you, my love !

High and clear I shoot my voice over the waves
Surely you must know who is here, is here,
You must know who I am, my love.

Low-hanging moon !
What is that dusky spot in your brown yellow ?
O it is the shape, the shape of my mate !
O moon, do not keep her from me any longer.

Land ! land ! O land !
Whichever way I turn, O I think you could give me my
  mate back again if you only would,
For I am almost sure I see her dimly whichever way I
  look.

O rising stars !
Perhaps the one I want so much will rise, will rise with
  some of you.

O throat ! O trembling throat !
Sound clearer through the atmosphere !
Pierce the woods, the earth,
Somewhere listening to catch you must be the one I want.

Shake out carols !
Solitary here, the night's carols !
Carols of lonesome love ! death's carols !
Carols under that lagging, yellow, waning moon !

*O under that moon where she droops almost down into
the sea !*
O reckless despairing carols !

But soft ! sink low !
Soft ! let me just murmur,
And do you wait a moment, you husky∗noised sea,
For somewhere I believe I heard my mate responding to me,
So faint, I must be still, be still to listen,
*But not altogether still, for then she might not come
immediately to me.*

Hither, my love !
Here I am ! here !
With this just∗sustained note I announce myself to you,
This gentle call is for you, my love, for you.

Do not be decoyed elsewhere :
That is the whistle of the wind, it is not my voice,
That is the fluttering, the fluttering of the spray,
Those are the shadows of leaves.

O darkness ! O in vain !
O I am very sick and sorrowful.

*O brown halo in the sky near the moon, drooping upon
the sea !*
O troubled reflection in the sea !
O throat ! O throbbing heart !
And I singing uselessly, uselessly all the night.

O past ! O happy life ! O songs of joy !
In the air, in the woods, over fields,
Loved ! loved ! loved ! loved ! loved !
But my mate no more, no more with me !
We two together no more.

The aria sinking.
All else continuing, the stars shining,

The winds blowing, the notes of the bird continuous echoing,
With angry moans the fierce old mother incessantly moaning,
On the sands of Paumanok's shore grey and rustling,
The yellow half-moon enlarged, sagging down, drooping, the face of the sea almost touching,
The boy ecstatic, with his bare feet the waves, with his hair the atmosphere dallying,
The love in the heart long pent, now loose, now at last tumultuously bursting,
The aria's meaning, the ears, the soul, swiftly depositing,
The strange tears down the cheeks coursing,
The colloquy there, the trio, each uttering,
The undertone, the savage old mother incessantly crying,
To the boy's soul's questions sullenly timing, some drowned secret hissing,
To the outsetting bard.

Demon or bird ! (said the boy's soul,)
Is it indeed toward your mate you sing ? or is it really to me ?
For I, that was a child, my tongue's use sleeping, now I have heard you,
Now in a moment I know what I am for, I awake,
And already a thousand singers, a thousand songs, clearer, louder and more sorrowful than yours,
A thousand warbling echoes have started to life within me, never to die.

O you singer solitary, singing by yourself, projecting me,
O solitary me listening, never more shall I cease perpetuating you,
Never more shall I escape, never more the reverberations,
Never more the cries of unsatisfied love be absent from me,

Never again leave me to be the peaceful child I was
    before what there in the night,
By the sea under the yellow and sagging moon,
The messenger there aroused, the fire, the sweet hell
    within,
The unknown want, the destiny of me.

O give me the clue! (it lurks in the night here some*
    where,)
O if I am to have so much, let me have more!

A word then, (for I will conquer it,)
The word final, superior to all,
Subtle, sent up—what is it?—I listen;
Are you whispering it, and have been all the time, you
    sea*waves?
Is that it from your liquid rims and wet sands?

Whereto answering, the sea,
Delaying not, hurrying not,
Whispered me through the night, and very plainly be*
    fore daybreak,
Lisped to me the low and delicious word death,
And again death, death, death, death,
Hissing melodious, neither like the bird nor like my
    aroused child's heart,
But edging near as privately for me, rustling at my feet,
Creeping thence steadily up to my ears and laving me
    softly all over,
Death, death, death, death, death.

Which I do not forget,
But fuse the song of my dusky demon and brother,
That he sang to me in the moonlight on Paumanok's
    grey beach,
With the thousand responsive songs at random,
My own songs awaked from that hour,
And with them the key, the word up from the waves,

The word of the sweetest song and all songs,
That strong and delicious word which, creeping to my
feet,
(Or like some old crone rocking the cradle, swathed in
sweet garments, bending aside,)
The sea whispered me.

When Lilacs last in the Dooryard bloomed

From MEMORIES OF PRESIDENT LINCOLN

1

WHEN lilacs last in the dooryard bloomed,
    And the great star early drooped in the western
      sky at night,
    I mourned, and yet shall mourn with ever-returning
      spring.

    Ever-returning spring, trinity sure to me you bring,
    Lilac blooming perennial and drooping star in the
      west,
    And thought of him I love.

2

O powerful western fallen star !
O shades of night—O moody, tearful night !
O great star disappeared—O the black murk that hides
    the star !
O cruel hands that hold me powerless—O helpless soul
    of me !
O harsh surrounding cloud that will not free my soul.

3

In the dooryard fronting an old farmhouse near the
    whitewashed palings,
Stands the lilac-bush tall-growing with heart-shaped
    leaves of rich green,

With many a pointed blossom rising delicate, with the
    perfume strong I love,
With every leaf a miracle—and from this bush in the
    dooryard,
With delicate-coloured blossoms and heart-shaped leaves
    of rich green,
A sprig with its flower I break.

4

In the swamp in secluded recesses,
A shy and hidden bird is warbling a song.
Solitary the thrush,
The hermit withdrawn to himself, avoiding the settle-
    ments,
Sings by himself a song.

Song of the bleeding throat,
Death's outlet song of life (for well, dear brother, I know,
If thou wast not granted to sing thou wouldst surely
    die).

5

Over the breast of the spring, the land, amid cities,
Amid lanes and through old woods, where lately the
    violets peeped from the ground, spotting the grey
    débris,
Amid the grass in the fields each side of the lanes,
    passing the endless grass,
Passing the yellow-speared wheat, every grain from its
    shroud in the dark-brown fields uprisen,
Passing the apple-tree blows of white and pink in the
    orchards,
Carrying a corpse to where it shall rest in the grave,
Night and day journeys a coffin.

6

Coffin that passes through lanes and streets,
Through day and night with the great cloud darkening
  the land,
With the pomp of the inlooped flags, with the cities
  draped in black,
With the show of the States themselves as of crape-
  veiled women standing,
With processions long and winding and the flambeaus
  of the night,
With the countless torches lit, with the silent sea of
  faces and the unbared heads,
With the waiting depot, the arriving coffin, and the
  sombre faces,
With dirges through the night, with the thousand voices
  rising strong and solemn,
With all the mournful voices of the dirges poured
  around the coffin,
The dim-lit churches and the shuddering organs—where
  amid these you journey,
With the tolling tolling bells' perpetual clang,
Here, coffin that slowly passes,
I give you my sprig of lilac.

7

(Nor for you, for one alone,
Blossoms and branches green to coffins all I bring,
For fresh as the morning, thus would I chant a song
  for you, O sane and sacred death.
All over bouquets of roses,
O death, I cover you over with roses and early lilies,
But mostly and now the lilac that blooms the first,
Copious I break, I break the sprigs from the bushes,
With loaded arms I come, pouring for you,
For you, and the coffins all of you, O death.)

8

O western orb sailing the heaven,
Now I know what you must have meant as a month
    since I walked,
As I walked in silence the transparent shadowy night,
As I saw you had something to tell as you bent to me
    night after night,
As you drooped from the sky low down as if to my
    side (while the other stars all looked on),
As we wandered together the solemn night (for some-
    thing, I know not what, kept me from sleep),
As the night advanced, and I saw on the rim of the west
    how full you were of woe,
As I stood on the rising ground in the breeze in the cool
    transparent night,
As I watched where you passed and was lost in the
    netherward black of the night,
As my soul in its trouble dissatisfied sank, as where you,
    sad orb,
Concluded, dropped in the night, and was gone.

9

Sing on, there in the swamp,
O singer bashful and tender ! I hear your notes, I hear
    your call,
I hear, I come presently, I understand you;
But a moment I linger, for the lustrous star has detained
    me,
The star, my departing comrade, holds and detains me.

10

O how shall I warble myself for the dead one there I
    loved ?
And how shall I deck my song for the large sweet soul
    that has gone ?
And what shall my perfume be for the grave of him I
    love ?

Sea-winds blown from east and west,
Blown from the Eastern sea and blown from the Western
    sea, till there on the prairies meeting,
These, and with these, and the breath of my chant,
I'll perfume the grave of him I love.

11

O what shall I hang on the chamber walls?
And what shall the pictures be that I hang on the
    walls
To adorn the burial-house of him I love?

Pictures of growing spring and farms and homes,
With the Fourth-month eve at sundown, and the grey
    smoke lucid and bright,
With floods of the yellow gold of the gorgeous, indolent,
    sinking sun, burning, expanding the air,
With the fresh sweet herbage under foot, and the pale
    green leaves of the trees prolific,
In the distance the flowing glaze, the breast of the river,
    with a wind-dapple here and there,
With ranging hills on the banks, with many a line
    against the sky, and shadows,
And the city at hand with dwellings so dense, and
    stacks of chimneys,
And all the scenes of life and the workshops, and the
    workmen homeward returning.

12

Lo, body and soul—this land,
My own Manhattan with spires, and the sparkling and
    hurrying tides, and the ships,
The varied and ample land, the South and the North in
    the light, Ohio's shores and flashing Missouri,
And ever the far-spreading prairies covered with grass
    and corn.

Lo, the most excellent sun so calm and haughty,
The violet and purple morn with just-felt breezes,
The gentle soft-born measureless light,
The miracle spreading, bathing all, the fulfilled noon,
The coming eve delicious, the welcome night and the
    stars,
Over my cities shining all, enveloping man and land.

13

Sing on, sing on, you grey-brown bird,
Sing from the swamps, the recesses, pour your chant
    from the bushes,
Limitless out of the dusk, out of the cedars and pines.
Sing on, dearest brother, warble your reedy song,
Loud human song, with voice of uttermost woe.

O liquid and free and tender !
O wild and loose to my soul—O wondrous singer !
You only I hear—yet the star holds me (but will soon
    depart),
Yet the lilac with mastering odour holds me.

14

Now while I sat in the day and looked forth,
In the close of the day with its light and the fields
    of spring, and the farmers preparing their crops,
In the large unconscious scenery of my land with its
    lakes and forests,
In the heavenly aerial beauty (after the perturbed winds
    and the storms),
Under the arching heavens of the afternoon swift
    passing, and the voices of children and women,
The many-moving sea-tides, and I saw the ships how
    they sailed,
And the summer approaching with richness, and the
    fields all busy with labour,

And the infinite separate houses, how they all went on,
    each with its meals and minutia of daily usages,
And the streets how their throbbings throbbed, and the
    cities pent—lo, then and there,
Falling upon them all and among them all, enveloping
    me with the rest,
Appeared the cloud, appeared the long black trail,
And I knew death, its thought, and the sacred knowledge
    of death.

Then with the knowledge of death as walking one side
    of me,
And the thought of death close-walking the other side
    of me,
And I in the middle as with companions, and as holding
    the hands of companions,
I fled forth to the hiding, receiving night that talks not,
Down to the shores of the water, the path by the swamp
    in the dimness,
To the solemn shadowy cedars and ghostly pines so still.
And the singer so shy to the rest received me,
The grey-brown bird I know received us comrades three,
And he sang the carol of death, and a verse for him
    I love.

From deep secluded recesses,
From the fragrant cedars and the ghostly pines so still,
Came the carol of the bird.

And the charm of the carol rapt me,
As I held as if by their hands my comrades in the night,
And the voice of my spirit tallied the song of the bird.

Come lovely and soothing death,
Undulate round the world, serenely arriving, arriving,
In the day, in the night, to all, to each,
Sooner or later delicate death.

Praised be the fathomless universe,
For life and joy, and for objects and knowledge curious,
And for love, sweet love—but praise ! praise ! praise !
For the sure-enwinding arms of cool-enfolding death.

Dark mother always gliding near with soft feet,
Have none chanted for thee a chant of fullest welcome ?
Then I chant it for thee, I glorify thee above all,
I bring thee a song that when thou must indeed come,
    come unfalteringly.

Approach, strong deliveress !
When it is so, when thou hast taken them, I joyously
    sing the dead,
Lost in the loving floating ocean of thee,
Laved in the flood of thy bliss, O death.

From me to thee glad serenades,
Dances for thee I propose, saluting thee, adornments and
    feastings for thee,
And the sights of the open landscape and the high-
    spread sky are fitting,
And life and the fields, and the huge and thoughtful
    night.
The night in silence under many a star,
The ocean shore and the husky whispering wave whose
    voice I know,
And the soul turning to thee, O vast and well-veiled
    death,
And the body gratefully nestling close to thee.

Over the tree-tops I float thee a song,
Over the rising and sinking waves, over the myriad
    fields and the prairies wide,
Over the dense-packed cities all and the teeming wharves
    and ways,
I float this carol with joy, with joy to thee, O death.

15

To the tally of my soul,
Loud and strong kept up the grey-brown bird,
With pure deliberate notes, spreading, filling the night.

Loud in the pines and cedars dim,
Clear in the freshness moist and the swamp-perfume,
And I with my comrades there in the night.

While my sight that was bound in my eyes unclosed,
As to long panoramas of visions.

And I saw askant the armies,
I saw as in noiseless dreams hundreds of battle-flags,
Borne through the smoke of the battles and pierced
    with missiles I saw them,
And carried hither and yon through the smoke, and torn
    and bloody,
And at last but a few shreds left on the staffs (and all in
    silence),
And the staffs all splintered and broken.

I saw battle-corpses, myriads of them,
And the white skeletons of young men, I saw them,
I saw the débris and débris of all the slain soldiers of
    the war,
But I saw they were not as was thought,
They themselves were fully at rest, they suffered not,
The living remained and suffered, the mother suffered,
And the wife and the child and the musing comrade
    suffered,
And the armies that remained suffered.

16

Passing the visions, passing the night,
Passing, unloosing the hold of my comrades' hands,
Passing the song of the hermit bird and the tallying song
    of my soul,

Victorious song, death's outlet song, yet varying, ever-
   altering song,
As low and wailing, yet clear the notes, rising and fall-
   ing, flooding the night,
Sadly sinking and fainting, as warning and warning,
   and yet again bursting with joy,
Covering the earth and filling the spread of the heaven,
As that powerful psalm in the night I heard from
   recesses,
Passing, I leave thee lilac with heart-shaped leaves,
I leave thee there in the dooryard, blooming, returning
   with spring.

I cease from my song for thee,
From my gaze on thee in the west, fronting the west,
   communing with thee,
O comrade lustrous with silver face in the night.

Yet each to keep and all, retrievements out of the night,
The song, the wondrous chant of the grey-brown bird,
And the tallying chant, the echo aroused in my soul,
With the lustrous and drooping star with the counte-
   nance full of woe,
With the holders holding my hand nearing the call of
   the bird,
Comrades mine, and I in the midst, and their memory
   ever to keep, for the dead I loved so well,
For the sweetest, wisest soul of all my days and lands—
   and this for his dear sake,
Lilac and star and bird twined with the chant of my
   soul,
There in the fragrant pines and the cedars dusk and
   dim.

EMILY DICKINSON

1830–86

Success

SUCCESS is counted sweetest
By those who ne'er succeed.
To comprehend a nectar
Requires sorest need.

Not one of all the purple host
Who took the flag to-day
Can tell the definition,
So clear, of victory,

As he, defeated, dying,
On whose forbidden ear
The distant strains of triumph
Break, agonized and clear.

A Wounded Deer leaps Highest

A WOUNDED deer leaps highest,
I've heard the hunter tell;
'Tis but the ecstasy of death,
And then the brake is still.

The smitten rock that gushes,
The trampled steel that springs:
A cheek is always redder
Just where the hectic stings!

Mirth is the mail of anguish,
In which it cautious arm,
Lest anybody spy the blood
And " You're hurt " exclaim!

GEORGE SANTAYANA

1863–

I would I might forget that I am I

I WOULD I might forget that I am I,
And break the heavy chain that binds me fast,
Whose links about myself my deeds have cast.
What in the body's tomb doth buried lie
Is boundless; 'tis the spirit of the sky,
Lord of the future, guardian of the past,
And soon must forth, to know his own at last.
In his large life to live, I fain would die.
Happy the dumb beast, hungering for food,
But calling not his suffering his own;
Blessèd the angel, gazing on all good,
But knowing not he sits upon a throne;
Wretched the mortal, pondering his mood,
And doomed to know his aching heart alone.

As in the Midst of Battle there is Room

AS in the midst of battle there is room
For thoughts of love, and in foul sin for mirth;
As gossips whisper of a trinket's worth
Spied by the death-bed's flickering candle-gloom;
As in the crevices of Cæsar's tomb
The sweet herbs flourish on a little earth:
So in this great disaster of our birth
We can be happy, and forget our doom.
For morning, with a ray of tenderest joy
Gilding the iron heaven, hides the truth,
And evening gently woos us to employ

Our grief in idle catches. Such is youth;
Till from that summer's trance we wake, to find
Despair before us, vanity behind.

EDWIN ARLINGTON ROBINSON

1869–

Luke Havergal

GO to the western gate, Luke Havergal,
There where the vines cling crimson on the wall,
And in the twilight wait for what will come.
The leaves will whisper there of her, and some,
Like flying words, will strike you as they fall;
But go, and if you listen she will call.
Go to the western gate, Luke Havergal—
Luke Havergal.

No, there is not a dawn in eastern skies
To rift the fiery night that's in your eyes;
But there, where western glooms are gathering,
The dark will end the dark, if anything:
God slays Himself with every leaf that flies,
And hell is more than half of paradise.
No, there is not a dawn in eastern skies—
In eastern skies.

Out of a grave I come to tell you this,
Out of a grave I come to quench the kiss
That flames upon your forehead with a glow
That blinds you to the way that you must go.
Yes, there is yet one way to where she is,
Bitter, but one that faith may never miss.
Out of a grave I come to tell you this—
To tell you this.

There is the western gate, Luke Havergal,
There are the crimson leaves upon the wall.

Go, for the winds are tearing them away,—
Nor think to riddle the dead words they say,
Nor any more to feel them as they fall;
But go, and if you trust her she will call.
There is the western gate, Luke Havergal—
Luke Havergal.

Mr. Flood's Party

OLD Eben Flood, climbing alone one night
Over the hill between the town below
And the forsaken upland hermitage
That held as much as he should ever know
On earth again of home, paused warily.
The road was his with not a native near;
And Eben, having leisure, said aloud,
For no man else in Tilbury Town to hear:

" Well, Mr. Flood, we have the harvest moon
Again, and we may not have many more;
The bird is on the wing, the poet says,
And you and I have said it here before.
Drink to the bird." He raised up to the light
The jug that he had gone so far to fill,
And answered huskily: " Well, Mr. Flood,
Since you propose it, I believe I will."

Alone, as if enduring to the end
A valiant armour of scarred hopes outworn,
He stood there in the middle of the road
Like Roland's ghost winding a silent horn.
Below him, in the town among the trees,
Where friends of other days had honoured him,
A phantom salutation of the dead
Rang thinly till old Eben's eyes were dim.

Then, as a mother lays her sleeping child
Down tenderly, fearing it may awake,
He set the jug down slowly at his feet
With trembling care, knowing that most things break;
And only when assured that on firm earth
It stood, as the uncertain lives of men
Assuredly did not, he paced away,
And with his hand extended paused again:

" Well, Mr. Flood, we have not met like this
In a long time; and many a change has come
To both of us, I fear, since last it was
We had a drop together.   Welcome home ! "
Convivially returning with himself,
Again he raised the jug up to the light;
And with an acquiescent quaver said:
" Well, Mr. Flood, if you insist, I might.

" Only a very little, Mr. Flood—
For auld lang syne.   No more, sir; that will do."
So, for the time, apparently it did,
And Eben evidently thought so too;
For soon amid the silver loneliness
Of night he lifted up his voice and sang,
Secure, with only two moons listening,
Until the whole harmonious landscape rang—

" For auld lang syne."   The weary throat gave out,
The last word wavered; and the song being done,
He raised again the jug regretfully
And shook his head, and was again alone.
There was not much that was ahead of him,
And there was nothing in the town below—
Where strangers would have shut the many doors
That many friends had opened long ago.

The Sheaves

WHERE long the shadows of the wind had rolled,
Green wheat was yielding to the change assigned;
And as by some vast magic undivined
The world was turning slowly into gold.
Like nothing that was ever bought or sold
It waited there, the body and the mind;
And with a mighty meaning of a kind
That tells the more the more it is not told.
So in a land where all days are not fair,
Fair days went on till on another day
A thousand golden sheaves were lying there,
Shining and still, but not for long to stay—
As if a thousand girls with golden hair
Might rise from where they slept and go away.

AMY LOWELL

1874–1925

Patterns

I WALK down the garden paths,
And all the daffodils
Are blowing, and the bright blue squills.

I walk down the patterned garden paths
In my stiff, brocaded gown.
With my powdered hair and jewelled fan,
I too am a rare
Pattern.   As I wander down
The garden paths.

My dress is richly figured,
And the train
Makes a pink and silver stain
On the gravel, and the thrift
Of the borders.

Just a plate of current fashion,
Tripping by in high-heeled, ribboned shoes.
Not a softness anywhere about me,
Only whale-bone and brocade.
And I sink on a seat in the shade
Of a lime tree.   For my passion
Wars against the stiff brocade.
The daffodils and squills
Flutter in the breeze
As they please.
And I weep;
For the lime tree is in blossom
And one small flower has dropped upon my bosom.

And the plashing of waterdrops
In the marble fountain
Comes down the garden paths.
The dripping never stops.
Underneath my stiffened gown
Is the softness of a woman bathing in a marble basin,
A basin in the midst of hedges grown
So thick, she cannot see her lover hiding,
But she guesses he is near,
And the sliding of the water
Seems the stroking of a dear
Hand upon her.
What is Summer in a fine brocaded gown !
I should like to see it lying in a heap upon the ground,
All the pink and silver crumpled up on the ground.

I would be the pink and silver as I ran along the paths,
And he would stumble after,
Bewildered by my laughter.
I should see the sun flashing from his sword-hilt and
    the buckles on his shoes.
I would choose

To lead him in a maze along the patterned paths,
A bright and laughing maze for my heavy‚booted lover,
Till he caught me in the shade,
And the buttons of his waistcoat bruised my body as he
    clasped me,
Aching, melting, unafraid.
With the shadows of the leaves and the sundrops,
And the plopping of the waterdrops,
All about us in the open afternoon—
I am very like to swoon
With the weight of this brocade,
For the sun sifts through the shade.

Underneath the fallen blossom
In my bosom,
Is a letter I have hid.
It was brought to me this morning by a rider from the
    Duke.
" Madam, we regret to inform you that Lord Hartwell
Died in action Thursday se'n night."
As I read it in the white, morning sunlight,
The letters squirmed like snakes.
" Any answer, Madam," said my footman.
" No," I told him.
" See that the messenger takes some refreshment.
No, no answer."
And I walked into the garden,
Up and down the patterned paths,
In my stiff, correct brocade.
The blue and yellow flowers stood up proudly in the sun,
Each one.
I stood upright too,
Held rigid to the pattern
By the stiffness of my gown.
Up and down I walked,
Up and down.

In a month he would have been my husband.
In a month, here, underneath this lime,
We would have broke the pattern;
He for me, and I for him,
He as Colonel, I as Lady,
On this shady seat.
He had a whim
That sunlight carried blessing.
And I answered, " It shall be as you have said."
Now he is dead.

In Summer and in Winter I shall walk
Up and down
The patterned garden paths
In my stiff, brocaded gown.
The squills and daffodils
Will give place to pillared roses, and to asters, and to
    snow.
I shall go
Up and down,
In my gown,
Gorgeously arrayed,
Boned and stayed.
And the softness of my body will be guarded from
    embrace
By each button, hook, and lace.
For the man who should loose me is dead,
Fighting with the Duke in Flanders,
In a pattern called a war.
Christ ! What are patterns for ?

ROBERT FROST

1875–

The Runaway

ONCE when the snow of the year was beginning to fall,
  We stopped by a mountain pasture to say " Whose
    colt ? "

A little Morgan had one forefoot on the wall,
The other curled at his breast. He dipped his head
And snorted at us. And then he had to bolt.
We heard the miniature thunder where he fled,
And we saw him, or thought we saw him, dim and
      grey,
Like a shadow against the curtain of falling flakes.
" I think the little fellow's afraid of the snow.
He isn't winter-broken. It isn't play
With the little fellow at all. He's running away.
I doubt if even his mother could tell him, ' Sakes,
It's only weather.' He'd think she didn't know !
Where is his mother ? He can't be out alone."
And now he comes again with a clatter of stone
And mounts the wall again with whited eyes
And all his tail that isn't hair up straight.
He shudders his coat as if to throw off flies.
" Whoever it is that leaves him out so late,
When other creatures have gone to stall and bin,
Ought to be told to come and take him in."

An Old Man's Winter Night

ALL out of doors looked darkly in at him
Through the thin frost, almost in separate stars,
That gathers on the pane in empty rooms.
What kept his eyes from giving back the gaze
Was the lamp tilted near them in his hand.
What kept him from remembering what it was
That brought him to that creaking room was age.
He stood with barrels round him—at a loss.
And having scared the cellar under him
In clomping there, he scared it once again
In clomping off;—and scared the outer night,
Which has its sounds, familiar, like the roar
Of trees and crack of branches, common things,

But nothing so like beating on a box.
A light he was to no one but himself
Where now he sat, concerned with he knew what,
A quiet light, and then not even that.
He consigned to the moon, such as she was,
So late-arising, to the broken moon
As better than the sun in any case
For such a charge, his snow upon the roof,
His icicles along the wall to keep;
And slept. The log that shifted with a jolt
Once in the stove, disturbed him and he shifted,
And eased his heavy breathing, but still slept.
One aged man—one man—can't keep a house,
A farm, a countryside, or if he can,
It's thus he does it of a winter night.

The Oven Bird

THERE is a singer everyone has heard,
Loud, a mid-summer and a mid-wood bird,
Who makes the solid tree trunks sound again.
He says that leaves are old and that for flowers
Mid-summer is to spring as one to ten.
He says the early petal-fall is past
When pear and cherry bloom went down in showers
On sunny days a moment overcast;
And comes that other fall we name the fall.
He says the highway dust is over all.
The bird would cease and be as other birds
But that he knows in singing not to sing.
The question that he frames in all but words
Is what to make of a diminished thing.

The Tuft of Flowers

I WENT to turn the grass once after one
Who mowed it in the dew before the sun.

The dew was gone that made his blade so keen
Before I came to view the levelled scene.

I looked for him behind an isle of trees;
I listened for his whetstone on the breeze.

But he had gone his way, the grass all mown,
And I must be, as he had been—alone,

" As all must be," I said within my heart,
" Whether they work together or apart."

But as I said it, swift there passed me by
On noiseless wing a bewildered butterfly,

Seeking with memories grown dim o'er night
Some resting flower of yesterday's delight.

And once I marked his flight go round and round,
As where some flower lay withering on the ground.

And then he flew as far as eye could see,
And then on tremulous wing came back to me.

I thought of questions that have no reply,
And would have turned to toss the grass to dry;

But he turned first, and led my eye to look
At a tall tuft of flowers beside a brook,

A leaping tongue of bloom the scythe had spared
Beside a reedy brook the scythe had bared.

I left my place to know them by their name,
Finding them butterfly weed when I came.

The mower in the dew had loved them thus,
By leaving them to flourish, not for us,

Nor yet to draw one thought of ours to him,
But from sheer morning gladness at the brim.

The butterfly and I had lit upon,
Nevertheless, a message from the dawn,

That made me hear the wakening birds around,
And hear his long scythe whispering to the ground,

And feel a spirit kindred to my own;
So that henceforth I worked no more alone;

But glad with him, I worked as with his aid,
And weary, sought at noon with him the shade;

And dreaming, as it were, held brotherly speech
With one whose thought I had not hoped to reach.

"Men work together," I told him from the heart,
"Whether they work together or apart."

CARL SANDBURG

1878–

Grass

PILE the bodies high at Austerlitz and Waterloo.
  Shovel them under and let me work—
          I am the grass; I cover all.

And pile them high at Gettysburg,
And pile them high at Ypres and Verdun.
Shovel them under and let me work.
Two years, ten years, and passengers ask the conduc‹
    tor:

          What place is this?
          Where are we now?

          I am the grass.
          Let me work.

NICHOLAS VACHEL LINDSAY

1879–

The Eagle that is Forgotten
(JOHN P. ALTGELD)

SLEEP softly . . . eagle forgotten . . . under the stone.
Time has its way with you there, and the clay has its own.

"We have buried him now," thought your foes, and in secret rejoiced.
They made a brave show of their mourning, their hatred unvoiced.
They had snarled at you, barked at you, foamed at you, day after day.
Now you were ended. They praised you . . . and laid you away.

The others, that mourned you in silence and terror and truth,
The widow bereft of her crust, and the boy without youth,
The mocked and the scorned and the wounded, the lame and the poor,
That should have remembered for ever, . . . remember no more.

Where are those lovers of yours, on what name do they call,
The lost, that in armies wept over your funeral pall?
They call on the names of a hundred high-valiant ones,
A hundred white eagles have risen, the sons of your sons.
The zeal in their wings is a zeal that your dreaming began,
The valour that wore out your soul in the service of man.

Sleep softly . . . eagle forgotten . . . under the stone.
Time has its way with you there, and the clay has its
     own.
Sleep on, O brave-hearted, O wise man that kindled the
     flame—
To live in mankind is far more than to live in a name,
To live in mankind, far, far more than . . . to live in
     a name.

EZRA POUND

1885–

The Garden

En robe de parade.

Samain

LIKE a skein of loose silk blown against a wall
     She walks by the railing of a path in Kensington
     Gardens,
And she is dying piece-meal of a sort of emotional
     anæmia.

And round about there is a rabble
Of the filthy, sturdy, unkillable infants of the very
     poor.
They shall inherit the earth.
In her is the end of breeding.
Her boredom is exquisite and excessive.
She would like someone to speak to her,
And is almost afraid that I will commit that indiscre-
     tion.

"H. D."

1886–

Adonis

I

EACH of us like you
has died once,
each of us like you
has passed through drift of wood‑leaves
cracked and bent
and tortured and unbent
in the winter frost—
then burnt into gold points,
lighted afresh,
crisp amber, scales of gold‑leaf,
gold turned and re‑welded
in the sun‑heat.

Each of us like you
has died once,
each of us has crossed an old wood‑path
and found the winter leaves
so golden in the sun‑fire
that even the live wood‑flowers
were dark.

2

Not the gold on the temple‑front
where you stand
is as gold as this,
not the gold that fastens your sandal,
nor the gold reft
through your chiselled locks
is as gold as this last year's leaf,
not all the gold hammered and wrought

and beaten
on your lover's face,
brow and bare breast
is as golden as this.

Each of us like you
has died once,
each of us like you
stands apart, like you
fit to be worshipped.

Oread

WHIRL up, sea—
Whirl your pointed pines,
Splash your great pines
On our rocks,
Hurl your green over us,
Cover us with your pools of fir.

ROBINSON JEFFERS
1887–

Night

THE ebb slips from the rock, the sunken
Tide-rocks lift streaming shoulders
Out of the slack, the slow west
Sombering its torch; a ship's light
Shows faintly, far out,
Over the weight of the prone ocean
On the low cloud.

Over the dark mountain, over the dark pinewood,
Down the long dark valley along the shrunken river,
Returns the splendour without rays, the shining of
    shadow,

Peace-bringer, the matrix of all shining and quieter of
　　shining.
Where the shore widens on the bay she opens dark wings
And the ocean accepts her glory.　O soul worshipful of
　　her,
You like the ocean have grave depths where she dwells
　　always,
And the film of waves above that takes the sun takes also
Her, with more love.　The sun-lovers have a blond
　　favourite,
A father of lights and noises, wars, weeping and laughter,
Hot labour, lust and delight and the other blemishes.
　　Quietness
Flows from her deeper fountain; and he will die; and
　　she is immortal.

Far off from here the slender
Flocks of the mountain forest
Move among stems like towers
Of the old redwoods to the stream,
No twig crackling; dip shy
Wild muzzles into the mountain water
Among the dark ferns.

O passionately at peace, you being secure will pardon
The blasphemies of glowworms, the lamp in my tower,
　　the fretfulness
Of cities, the crescents of the planets, the pride of the
　　stars.
This August night in a rift of cloud Antares reddens,
The great one, the ancient torch, a lord among lost
　　children,
The earth's orbit doubled would not girdle his greatness,
　　one fire
Globed, out of grasp of the mind enormous; but to you,
　　O Night,

What ? Not a spark ? What flicker of a spark in the
    faint far glimmer
Of a lost fire dying in the desert, dim coals of a sand
    pit the Bedouins
Wandered from at dawn. . . . Ah singing prayer to
    what gulfs tempted
Suddenly are you more lost ? To us the near-hand
    mountain
Be a measure of height, the tide-worn cliff at the sea-gate
    a measure of continuance.

The tide, moving the night's
Vastness with lonely voices,
Turns, the deep dark-shining
Pacific leans on the land,
Feeling his cold strength
To the outmost margins: you, Night, will resume
The stars in your time.

O passionately at peace, when will that tide draw shore-
    ward ?
Truly the spouting fountains of light, Antares, Arcturus,
Tire of their flow, they sing one song but they think
    silence.
The striding winter giant Orion shines, and dreams
    darkness.
And life, the flicker of men and moths and wolf on the
    hill,
Though furious for continuance, passionately feeding,
    passionately
Remaking itself upon its mates, remembers deep inward
The calm mother, the quietness of the womb and the
    egg,
The primal and the latter silences: dear Night, it is
    memory
Prophesies, prophecy that remembers, the charm of the
    dark.

And I and my people, we are willing to love the four-
    score years
Heartily; but as a sailor loves the sea, when the helm
    is for harbour.
Have men's minds changed,
Or the rock hidden in the deep of the waters of the soul
Broken the surface? A few centuries
Gone by, was none dared not to people
The darkness beyond the stars with harps and habita-
    tions.
But now, dear is the truth. Life is grown sweeter and
    lonelier,
And death is no evil.

THOMAS STEARNS ELIOT

1888–

The Love-song of J. Alfred Prufrock

S'io credesse che mia risposta fosse
A persona che mai tornasse al mondo,
Questa fiamma staria senza piu scosse.
Ma perciocche giammai di questo fondo
Non torno vivo alcun, s'i'odo il vero,
Senza tema d'infamia ti rispondo.

LET us go then, you and I,
    When the evening is spread out against the sky
Like a patient etherized upon a table;
Let us go, through certain half-deserted streets,
The muttering retreats
Of restless nights in one-night cheap hotels
And sawdust restaurants with oyster-shells:
Streets that follow like a tedious argument
Of insidious intent
To lead you to an overwhelming question. . . .

Oh, do not ask, " What is it ? "
Let us go and make our visit.

In the room the women come and go
Talking of Michelangelo.
The yellow fog that rubs its back upon the window-
    panes,
The yellow smoke that rubs its muzzle on the window-
    panes
Licked its tongue into the corners of the evening,
Lingered upon the pools that stand in drains,
Let fall upon its back the soot that falls from chim-
    neys,
Slipped by the terrace, made a sudden leap,
And seeing that it was a soft October night,
Curled once about the house, and fell asleep.

And indeed there will be time
For the yellow smoke that slides along the street,
Rubbing its back upon the window-panes;
There will be time, there will be time
To prepare a face to meet the faces that you meet;
There will be time to murder and create,
And time for all the works and days of hands
That lift and drop a question on your plate;
Time for you and time for me,
And time yet for a hundred indecisions,
And for a hundred visions and revisions,
Before the taking of a toast and tea.

In the room the women come and go
Talking of Michelangelo.

And indeed there will be time
To wonder, " Do I dare ? " and, " Do I dare ? "
Time to turn back and descend the stair,
With a bald spot in the middle of my hair—
(They will say: " How his hair is growing thin ! ")

My morning coat, my collar mounting firmly to the chin,
My necktie rich and modest, but asserted by a simple
   pin—
(They will say: " But how his arms and legs are thin ! ")
Do I dare
Disturb the universe ?
In a minute there is time
For decisions and revisions which a minute will reverse.
For I have known them all already, known them all:
Have known the evenings, mornings, afternoons,
I have measured out my life with coffee spoons;
I know the voices dying with a dying fall
Beneath the music from a farther room.
      So how should I presume ?

And I have known the eyes already, known them all—
The eyes that fix you in a formulated phrase,
And when I am formulated, sprawling on a pin,
When I am pinned and wriggling on the wall,
Then how should I begin
To spit out all the butt-ends of my days and ways ?
      And how should I presume ?

And I have known the arms already, known them all—
Arms that are braceleted and white and bare
(But in the lamplight, downed with light brown hair !)
Is it perfume from a dress
That makes me so digress ?
Arms that lie along a table, or wrap about a shawl.
      And should I then presume ?
      And how should I begin ?

          .   .   .   .

Shall I say, I have gone at dusk through narrow streets
And watched the smoke that rises from the pipes
Of lonely men in shirt-sleeves, leaning out of win-
   dows ? . . .

I should have been a pair of ragged claws
Scuttling across the floors of silent seas.

And the afternoon, the evening, sleeps so peacefully !
Smoothed by long fingers,
Asleep . . . tired . . . or it malingers,
Stretched on the floor, here beside you and me.
Should I, after tea and cakes and ices,
Have the strength to force the moment to its crisis ?
But though I have wept and fasted, wept and prayed,
Though I have seen my head (grown slightly bald)
    brought in upon a platter,
I am no prophet—and here's no great matter;
I have seen the moment of my greatness flicker,
And I have seen the eternal Footman hold my coat, and
    snicker,
And in short, I was afraid.

And would it have been worth it, after all,
After the cups, the marmalade, the tea,
Among the porcelain, among some talk of you and me,
Would it have been worth while,
To have bitten off the matter with a smile,
To have squeezed the universe into a ball
To roll it toward some overwhelming question,
To say: " I am Lazarus, come from the dead,
Come back to tell you all, I shall tell you all "—
If one, settling a pillow by her head,
    Should say: " That is not what I meant at all;
    That is not it, at all " ?

And would it have been worth it, after all,
Would it have been worth while,
After the sunsets and the dooryards and the sprinkled
    streets,
After the novels, after the teacups, after the skirts that
    trail along the floor—

And this, and so much more?—
It is impossible to say just what I mean!
But as if a magic lantern threw the nerves in patterns
    on a screen:
Would it have been worth while
If one, settling a pillow or throwing off a shawl
And turning toward the window, should say:
  " That is not it at all,
    That is not what I meant, at all "?

No! I am not Prince Hamlet, nor was meant to be;
Am an attendant lord, one that will do
To swell a progress, start a scene or two,
Advise the prince; no doubt, an easy tool,
Deferential, glad to be of use,
Politic, cautious, and meticulous;
Full of high sentence, but a bit obtuse;
At times, indeed, almost ridiculous—
Almost, at times, the Fool.

I grow old . . . I grow old . . .
I shall wear the bottoms of my trousers rolled.

Shall I part my hair behind? Do I dare to eat a peach?
I shall wear white flannel trousers, and walk upon the
    beach.
I have heard the mermaids singing, each to each.

I do not think that they will sing to me.

I have seen them riding seaward on the waves
Combing the white hair of the waves blown back
When the wind blows the water white and black.

We have lingered in the chambers of the sea
By sea-girls wreathed with seaweed red and brown
Till human voices wake us, and we drown.

Morning at the Window

THEY are rattling breakfast plates in basement
    kitchens,
And along the trampled edges of the street
I am aware of the damp souls of housemaids
Sprouting despondently at area gates.

The brown waves of fog toss up to me
Twisted faces from the bottom of the street,
And tear from a passer-by with muddy skirts
An aimless smile that hovers in the air
And vanishes along the level of the roofs.

The Hippopotamus

THE broad-backed hippopotamus
    Rests on his belly in the mud;
    Although he seems so firm to us
He is merely flesh and blood.

Flesh and blood is weak and frail,
    Susceptible to nervous shock;
    While the True Church can never fail,
For it is based upon a rock.

The hippo's feeble steps may err
    In compassing material ends,
    While the True Church need never stir
To gather in its dividends.

The 'potamus can never reach
    The mango on the mango-tree;
    But fruits of pomegranate and peach
Refresh the church from over sea.

At mating time the hippo's voice
    Betrays inflexions hoarse and odd,
    But every week we hear rejoice
The Church, at being one with God.

The hippopotamus's day
Is passed in sleep; at night he hunts;
God works in a mysterious way—
The Church can sleep and feed at once.

I saw the 'potamus take wing
Ascending from the damp savannas,
And choiring angels round him sing
The praise of God, in loud hosannas.

Blood of the Lamb shall wash him clean
And him shall heavenly arms enfold,
Among the saints he shall be seen
Performing on a harp of gold.

He shall be washed as white as snow,
By all the martyr'd virgins kist,
While the True Church remains below
Wrapt in the old miasmal mist.

EDNA ST. VINCENT MILLAY

1892–

Sonnet

EUCLID alone has looked on Beauty bare.
Let all who prate of Beauty hold their peace,
And lay them prone upon the earth and cease
To ponder on themselves, the while they stare
At nothing, intricately drawn nowhere
In shapes of shifting lineage; let geese
Gabble and hiss, but heroes seek release
From dusty bondage into luminous air.
O blinding hour, O holy, terrible day,
When first the shaft into his vision shone
Of light anatomized ! Euclid alone
Has looked on Beauty bare. Fortunate they
Who, though once only and then but far away,
Have heard her massive sandal set on stone.

INDEX TO FIRST LINES

INDEX TO FIRST LINES

INDEX TO FIRST LINES

INDEX TO FIRST LINES

INDEX OF AUTHORS AND TRANSLATORS

INDEX OF TITLES

INDEX OF TITLES

INDEX OF TITLES

INDEX OF TITLES

INDEX OF TITLES